Crusading Peace

The publisher gratefully acknowledges
the generous contribution to this book
provided by the General Endowment
of the University of California Press Associates.

Crusading Peace

*Christendom, the Muslim World,
and Western Political Order*

Tomaž Mastnak

UNIVERSITY OF CALIFORNIA PRESS
Berkeley • Los Angeles • London

University of California Press
Berkeley and Los Angeles, California

University of California Press, Ltd.
London, England

© 2002 by
The Regents of the University of California

Library of Congress Cataloging-in-Publication Data

Mastnak, Tomaž.
Crusading peace : Christendom, the Muslim world,
and Western political order / Tomaž Mastnak.

    p.   cm.
Includes bibliographical references (p.) and index.
ISBN 0-520-22635-6 (alk. paper)
    1. Crusades.   2. Peace—Religious aspects—
Christianity—History of doctrines—Middle Ages,
600–1500.   3. Catholic Church—Doctrines—
History—Middle Ages, 600–1500.   4. Just
war—Doctrine—History—To 1500.   5. Monar-
chy—Europe—History—To 1500.   6. Europe—
Church history—600–1500.   7. Peace—Religious
aspects—Islam.   I. Title.
D157 .M376   2002
909.07—dc21   2001044417

Manufactured in the United States of America

09 08 07 06 05 04 03 02

10 9 8 7 6 5 4 3 2 1

The paper used in this publication is both acid-free
and totally chlorine-free (TCF). It meets the mini-
mum requirements of ANSI/NISO Z39.48-1992
(R 1997) (*Permanence of Paper*). ♾

"... tot et tam magna mala pacem appellant."
(Sap 14.22)

"... they call so many and so great evils peace."
(Wis 14.22)

Contents

Acknowledgments

If one were to study acknowledgments in academic books, thanking wives (much more than husbands) would probably be the most interesting subject. For instance, they most often come last—even if "last but not least." I want to thank my wife, Julia Elyachar Mastnak, first because my first and foremost debt is to her. For long years, working on this book—with all the strain it has put on our daily life, the support it needed, and the sacrifices it required—has been our mutual undertaking. The form and the substance of what is written in these pages would have been weaker, confused, and confusing without her help. Every word in this book carries the trace of her eye, many have been changed by her pen, and the arguments they present were either formed or refined through discussion with her over many versions of this text.

Thanks of a special kind are due to four people. I am grateful to Lynne Jones for her intellectual and moral support at the beginning of this project, and for her commentary on a subsequent version of the first chapter. Throughout my work on this book Igor Kramberger was most generous with his time, his wide-ranging knowledge, and his collection of books. He also helped with formatting and printing out the final manuscript. Dorothea von Moltke's comments on a portion of a previous version encouraged me to rewrite the entire text and bring it close to its current form. My friendship with her and with Cliff Simms sustained me in many ways during the long years of work on this book. Ruth Turner read the manuscript in its different phases and forms. As valuable to me as her improvements of the text was her faith in the worth of this project.

I want to acknowledge the help and support received from other friends and colleagues. Talal Asad's generous praise of an early draft of the manuscript was an important boost. Basheer el Sibaie's belief in the project during a difficult stage was invaluable. Büşra Ersanli gave me the opportunity to present my work to the students at Marmara University in Istanbul and offered stimulating comments over time. Discussion of the project with Cemal Kafadar was very useful. John Keane commented on a version of the first chapter and invited me to talk about my work at the Centre for the Study of Democracy, University of Westminster. He and Kathy O'Neil were wonderful hosts during expeditions to the British Library. For his assistance during my stay in Cairo, I want to thank the Counsellor of the Embassy of the Republic of Slovenia in Egypt, Vladimir Kolmanič. Ervin Hladnik Milharčič and Peter Kovačič Peršin commented on early drafts of the manuscript. Laila Moustafa was a most helpful and supportive friend in Cairo and later in New York. Boris A. Novak and Mara Thomas provided journal articles I would have missed otherwise. Help of a different kind was provided by Miljana Vučičević Salama, M.D., who restored my health during my stay in Cairo.

I am very grateful to Jonathan Riley-Smith for his helpful critique of an early draft of this work. The generous advice and encouragement of István Hont, Arthur Kleinman, María Rosa Menocal, Frank Peters, Emran Qureshi, Michael Sells, and Gabrielle Spiegel after I had completed the manuscript and had begun to explore the unfamiliar terrain of publishing in a foreign country was crucial. My thanks are also due to the anonymous readers of the University of California Press, whose comments and suggestions led to substantial changes in the manuscript. Finally, I am indebted to a number of historians, dead and alive, on whose work I relied when I ventured into areas not my own.

A postdoctoral fellowship awarded by the Social Science Research Council–MacArthur Foundation, Program in International Peace and Security, for the years 1991–93 allowed me to begin this project in the stimulating environments of the Department of History at Johns Hopkins University, Baltimore; the Department of History at the University of Edinburgh; and King's College of the University of Cambridge. During my stay in Baltimore I also had the privilege of participating in the seminar "Empire, Confederation, and Republic: From Atlantic Dominion to American Union" conducted by John Pocock at the Folger Institute Center for the History of British Political Thought in Washington,

D.C. I want to thank all these institutions for their support and help. I am particularly grateful to John and Felicity Pocock, István Hont, Nicholas Phillipson, and Harry Dickinson for stimulating discussions, practical help, and hospitality.

In the academic year 1994–95 I was a visiting scholar at the history unit in the Department of Arabic Studies of the American University in Cairo. My thanks to members of the department and to Enid Hill and Huda Lutfi for their invitations. I also want to thank the Center for Cultural Studies at the Graduate School and University Center of the City University of New York, and its director, Stanley Aronowitz, for providing me with an institutional base in New York in fall 1998. I finalized the manuscript during my stay as a visiting scholar at the Minda de Gunzburg Center for European Studies, Harvard University, in winter and spring 1999. I am grateful to the Center, its director, Charles S. Maier, and associate director, Abby Collins, for the invitation and superb working conditions. Finally, I want to thank the director of the Centre for Scientific Research of the Slovene Academy of Sciences and Arts in Ljubljana, Oto Luthar, and the head of the Centre's Institute of Philosophy, Rado Riha, for their generosity in granting me protracted leaves during my work on this book.

I am also grateful to a number of individuals at the University of California Press. Stanley Holwitz immediately understood and supported my project in a manner few authors are lucky enough to enjoy. Suzanne Knott oversaw the project through to completion in a professional and most helpful fashion. The copyediting of Carolyn Bond was superb. Her thoughtful and challenging interventions made the final text a much better product than it would have been otherwise.

While my debts are many, the responsibility for what is written in this book is mine alone.

ONE

From Holy Peace
to Holy War

In the beginning there was peace: At the close of the tenth century and the commencement of the eleventh, the *pax Dei,* the Peace of God—a peace movement carried out in the name of God—emerged in the territories that today make up central France. The *pax Dei* in turn led to the establishment of the *treuga Dei*—the Truce of God. Yet these peacemaking efforts together resulted in the crusade at the end of the eleventh century. A new kind of holy war grew out of the holy peace.[1]

Peace is a central issue of power, and the holy peace was no different. The eleventh century was a time of great social transformation, involving a redistribution of prerogatives between secular power and ecclesiastical authority. Striving to strengthen their position in a changing world, each party was itself undergoing deep internal change. While secular restructuring was very much visible, ecclesiastical reform germinated behind monastic walls; only gradually did it enter the Church at large and make its way into lay society. The peace movement played a very important role in that process. It was an agent of change that contributed to the articulation—as well as to the eventual resolution—of the competition between secular power and ecclesiastical authority for domination of Christian society. In their endeavors to contain and channel so-

---

1. For the history of this peace movement, see especially Hoffmann 1964; Head and Landes 1992b; *La Paix* 1961–62. On the historiography of the eleventh-century peace movement, see Paxton 1992. Cf. Hoffmann 1964, 7f.; Moore 1992; Bredero 1994, 111.

cial change, both tried to use the movement to their own advantage.[2] It was the Church, however, that kept the initiative in promoting peace. The development of the *pax Dei* movement was the ecclesiastical hierarchy's immediate defense against the violence at the turn of the millennia;[3] but through these peacemaking and peacekeeping efforts, the Church came to direct the social transformation that helped it obtain primacy within Christian society in the long run.

THE PEACE OF GOD AND THE TRUCE OF GOD

Neither the conflict between secular power and ecclesiastical authority nor the Church's striving for peace—nor, for that matter, peace as an issue in conflicts between the two—was new. In the Middle Ages, the most influential view of the duality of power was that of the late-fifth-century pope Gelasius I. His view was succinctly formulated in a famous letter addressed to Emperor Anastasius in 494:

> Two there are, august emperor, by which this world is principally ruled: the consecrated authority of bishops and the royal power. Of these, the responsibility of the priests is more weighty insofar as they will answer for the kings of men themselves at the divine judgment. You know, most clement son, that, although you take precedence over all mankind in dignity, nevertheless you piously bow the neck to those who have charge of divine affairs and seek from them the means of your salvation, and hence you realize that, in the order of religion, in matters concerning the reception and right administration of heavenly sacraments, you ought to submit yourself rather than rule, and that in these matters you should depend on their judgment rather than seek to bend them to your will.[4]

During the Middle Ages, interpretations of Gelasius's statement flourished.[5] The very plurality of interpretations testifies to the statement's importance in medieval debates on power. Thus it is not surprising that the "Gelasian doctrine" was an authoritative point of reference in the conflict between lay and ecclesiastical hierarchies in the eleventh century

---

2. Head and Landes 1992a, 17.
3. Landes 1995, 28.
4. *Epistola* 12,2 (Thiel, *Epp. Rom. pontif.*, 350–51). Cf. trans. in Tierney 1988, 13–14; Canning 1996, 35. (Throughout the notes: Where I cite an English source or a source in an English source, the translation is not my own. In cases where I cite a non-English source and an English translation, I have taken the translation from the English source and may have slightly revised it. Unless otherwise noted, all other quotations are my own translation.)
5. See Knabe 1936; Benson 1982. Cf. Cottrell 1993.

as well. And because the peace movement was both shaped by that conflict and a shaping force in it,[6] the Gelasian doctrine was at the core of the eleventh-century struggles for peace.[7] A basic requisite of peace was what the protagonists of the movement considered the right relationship between temporal power and spiritual authority.[8]

The idea of a duality of powers as the symbolic framework in which secular power and ecclesiastical authority could confront each other was an established tradition by the eleventh century.[9] The vocabulary of the Peace of God movement can be traced back to the Carolingian "imperial peace," or even further back to the sixth century, to the language of the Frankish bishops struggling for *pax ecclesiae,* "peace of the Church." [10] Moreover, the problems confronting the bishops who strove for peace showed a continuity from the sixth century to the eleventh century. The question central to all the debates about, and struggles for, peace was whether it was the Church or the secular authorities who had the right to determine the uses of ecclesiastical property.[11] The aim of the churchmen in all these struggles was to force powerful laymen to renounce the rights they claimed over ecclesiastical property and to reappropriate control of ecclesiastical patrimonies to themselves.[12]

These continuities, however, are not my primary interest here. I want to show what was new about the eleventh-century peace movement. Whereas the early-tenth-century clergy had inveighed against the expropriation of ecclesiastical property, and the Council of Trosly (909) had broadened the concept of sacrilege to include assault upon all goods belonging to the "universal Church," toward the end of the century the clerics began to address and oppose the "blood feud" directly.[13] They began taking practical steps to defend "more than just their own safety and that of church property" [14] and also began allying themselves with

6. Le Goff's general remark that it is "difficult to distinguish cause from effect in the evolution of Christian Europe, since most aspects of this process were both of these aspects at once" (Le Goff 1990, 57), applies to the peace movement as well.

7. Magnou-Nortier 1992, 69.

8. Cf. Magnou-Nortier 1984, 48.

9. For the concept of "tradition" in ecclesiastical history, see Morrison 1969.

10. See Magnou-Nortier 1984, 34–36; 1992, 59 ff. On the Carolingian peace of the Church, cf. Wallace-Hadrill 1983, 258–78.

11. Magnou-Nortier 1992, 61.

12. Ibid., 68–69.

13. Bloch 1977, 108.

14. Bredero 1994, 108–9. On the adoption of laws from Carolingian capitularies by the early Peace of God councils, see also Hoffmann 1964, 13–14; R. Barber 1982, 215; Lauranson-Rosaz 1992, 109–10.

the populace to resist the violence of lay magnates—or at least involving the ordinary people in their peace efforts.[15]

It is difficult to mark the beginning of the Peace of God movement
clearly, not only because decisions by what scholars regard as the first
councils of the *pax Dei* were made on the basis of the authority of earlier Church synods, but also because the term *Peace of God* itself seems
to have appeared after the movement had already been under way.[16]
However, since the mark of the *pax Dei* is the clergy's engagement in opposing violence, it is thus generally accepted that the first wave of Peace
of God councils took place in the last quarter of the tenth century.

One of the first meetings was the Council of Le Puy, convoked by
Guy of Anjou, bishop of Le Puy, about 975.[17] A large meeting held in an
open field outside the city walls, the council was convened to address the
pillaging of ecclesiastical property in the diocese. The bishop threatened the pillagers with excommunication and forced the assembled warriors and peasants to take an oath to keep the peace. It was easy for the
bishop to be persuasive, since his words were backed by the armed force
of neighboring counts, who were his nephews. The success of the meeting—achieved "with the help of God"[18]—inspired and encouraged further action. In the following years, Guy and other bishops organized
new councils, and the movement expanded. The clerics began bringing
relics of saints to the gatherings in order to attract the masses, make an
impression on them, and get their support.[19] The relics assured a tangible
divine presence at the meetings in conformity with the religious attitude of the times, according to which the sacred participated in worldly
affairs.[20]

The earliest council from which canons survive is the Council of Charroux of 989. Its acts state that the legislating bishops—"as well as clerics and monks, not to mention lay people of both sexes"—had gathered
to beseech "the aid of divine justice." The purpose of the gathering was

---

15. See Lauranson-Rosaz 1992, 110.

16. Hoffmann 1964, 3–4, pointed out that the expression *pax Dei* is not to be found
in sources predating 1033. The conclusion has been found "excessive" by Landes 1995,
29 n. 32 (for a milder formulation cf. id. 1992, 201 n. 91), whose evidence to the contrary,
however, is not overwhelming. See Landes 1995, 29 n. 32, 201 n. 91.

17. Hoffmann 1964, 13–16, discusses some earlier peace activities; he adds, however,
that "[v]om Gottesfrieden hören wir zum ersten Mal aus dem . . . Gebiet von Le Puy."

18. From the account of the meeting, quoted in Lauranson-Rosaz 1992, 116–17.

19. Lauranson-Rosaz 1992, 111; Töpfer 1992; Bredero 1994, 5, cf. 122; and documents in Head and Landes 1992b, app. A.

20. Cf. Bredero 1994, 6.

to root out "the criminal activity, which we know has for some time been sprouting up through evil habit in our districts because of our long delay in calling a council," and to implant "more lawful activity." This statement was followed by a declaration:

> Therefore we who are specially gathered together in the name of God decree, as will be made manifestly clear in the following canons, that: (1) If anyone attacks the holy church, or takes anything from it by force, and the compensation is not provided, let him be anathema. (2) If anyone takes as booty sheep, oxen, asses, cows, female goats, male goats, or pigs from peasants [*agricolae*] or from other poor people [*pauperes*]—unless it is due to the fault of the victim—and if that person neglects to make reparation for everything, let him be anathema. (3) If anyone robs, or seizes, or strikes a priest, or a deacon, or any man of the clergy [*ex clero*] who is not bearing arms (that is, a shield, a sword, a breastplate, or a helmet), but who is simply going about his business or remaining at home, and if, after examination by his own bishop, that person is found to be guilty of any crime, then he is guilty of sacrilege, and if he furthermore does not come forward to make satisfaction, let him then be held to be excluded from the holy church of God.[21]

Protection of the church and church property; of church dignitaries, clerics, and monks; and of livestock—though not so much of the peasants and the poor to whom the livestock belonged—was the primary focus of all meetings seeking to establish the Peace of God. Innovations were few, though the emphasis sometimes varied. Protection by peace legislation was extended, for example, to nuns, widows, orphans, women who were traveling and those accompanying them, and merchants. More or less the entire unarmed population came to be protected. The unacceptable behavior was occasionally described in greater detail: Crimes against the Peace of God included not only the theft of farm animals from *agricoles* and *pauperes* but also destroying seeds and burning the harvest, damaging olive trees, assaulting and robbing people who were harvesting, attacking carts bearing wine or harvest goods, gathering grapes on someone else's soil, pillaging mills and granaries, and stealing wax or bees.[22]

These concerns, demands, and prohibitions represent, if not a consistent ideology,[23] at least the basic outlook and direction of the early

---

21. The acts of the Council of Charroux (989); trans. in Head and Landes 1992b, app. A, 327–28.

22. See Bloch 1977, 109; Goetz 1992, 276 ff.

23. Duby 1974, 162–63; questioned by Remensnyder 1992, 281; and Bredero 1994, 121–23.

Peace of God movement.[24] But as the movement spread east, north, and south from Aquitaine, Berry, and Auvergne, and as the movement's first wave was followed between 1019 and 1038 by a second, it underwent important changes, resulting in the succession of the *pax Dei* by the *treuga Dei*. Historians debate this development. Some argue that the Truce of God cannot be considered a sequel to the Peace of God because the custom of observing holy days and holy seasons during hostilities, which lay at the heart of the Truce, was much older.[25] In their opinion, the Truce of God actually began with the Carolingian ban on private warfare on Sundays and was only "revived in 1027 in southern France."[26] The predominant view, however, seems to be that the Truce of God was first announced in the Council of Elne (or Toulouges) in 1027 and that it became the dominant form of the peace movement with the Council of Arles in 1041.[27] And even if, soon after Arles, the Peace of God and the Truce of God became intertwined,[28] the conceptual distinction between the two remains relevant.

Although *truce* is by all standards a weaker term than *peace,* the protection legislated by the Truce of God was actually greater than that of the Peace of God. Whereas the Peace forbade violence against specific social groups, with the aim of keeping their property safe at all times, the Truce banned all violence on certain days and during certain periods.[29] Initially, all acts of violence were forbidden between Saturday evening and Monday morning, so that the faithful could show due respect for the Lord's day. However, the ban on violence was soon extended to begin Thursday evening and end with sunrise on Monday, encompassing the four days associated with Christ's passion. In addition, the use of arms was prohibited on Church holidays. This absolute ban on violence, though intermittent,[30] came to cover approximately three-quarters of the year. The Council of Narbonne in 1054, for example, restricted the lawful use of arms to only 80 days a year.[31]

Earlier historiography tended to see the peace movement as a response to "feudal anarchy" and so placed the emergence of the movement in a

24. Head and Landes 1992a, 4.
25. Bredero 1994, 109–10.
26. R. Barber, 1982, 215. On the Carolingian precepts, see Bonnaud Delamare 1939, 250.
27. Head and Landes 1992a, 7.
28. Flori 1983, 152.
29. See Cowdrey 1970a, 44.
30. Hoffmann 1964, 70.
31. Flori 1983, 152.

historical landscape characterized by the "high incidence of feud and the lack of law and order." [32] The collapse of traditional power structures, it was argued, led to the fragmentation of land and the ascent of local lords, especially castellans. As the Carolingian legal system disintegrated and kingly authority grew weaker, castellans took the exercise of justice into their own hands, engaging in incessant private warfare, encroaching upon ecclesiastical property, and mistreating peasants and the poor. Historian Marc Bloch painted a dramatic picture of those times: People lived "in a state of permanent danger, full of pain," and "the fate of every individual was threatened every day." Violence was the true sign of the age. A call for peace—that most precious of all of God's gifts and the one most difficult to attain—began to resonate in the midst of the lawlessness; and on the margins of the powerless worldly authorities there emerged, on the initiative of the Church, a spontaneous movement to establish the much-desired order and peace. [33]

Recently, however, the "feudal anarchy" thesis has come into disrepute. On the one hand, scholars have developed misgivings about the concept of feudalism, [34] and on the other, they have rejected the idea of anarchy as unwarranted. The decades around the year 1000, when the *pax Dei* movement emerged, might have been violent and disorderly, but they were not anarchic. [35] It logically follows that the peace movement could not have originated in a desire to end anarchy or disorder. [36] This shift of perspective compels us to look differently at the reality described by historians of older generations. The tenth century, which gave birth to the peace movement, *was* violent: "if there is a 'century of violence,' the tenth century was it." [37] Contemporary sources were certainly aware of an increase in conflicts and a loss of control among the ruling elite. [38] One of those sources, for example, noted that the "condition of the realm

---

32. Tellenbach 1993, 136.
33. Bloch 1983, 566–69.
34. See Brown 1974. The author refers to Bisson's study of institutional structures of peace in southern France and Catalonia as "thoroughly enlightening" precisely because this study was freed from the "tyranny" of the concept of "feudalism." See Bisson 1977, presented to a conference in 1973. For the "discovery of feudalism," see Pocock 1987, chap. 4–5, and "Conclusions," especially 249; cf. notes in Cantor 1991, 279f.
35. G. Duby, *La société aux XIe et XIIe siècles dans la région mâconnaise* (Paris, 1953), quoted in Brown 1974, 1082.
36. See especially Magnou-Nortier 1984, 34; 1992, 58–59. Cf. Reynolds 1986, 118–19; Goetz 1992, 260.
37. Lauranson-Rosaz 1992, 106.
38. Landes 1995, 28 n. 24, polemicizing against Magnou-Nortier's thesis. Cf. Bull 1993, 23 ff.

tottered on its foundations" and spoke of the "incompetence of the king and the sins [of men]," which confounded the laws and profaned the customs of the fathers "as well as all manner of justice." [39] Revisionist historians, however, tend to focus on the restructuring of power rather than on anarchy, and on the development of a new order instead of disorder.

The new order was developed against the background of the weakening of kingly authority (*imbecillitas regis*). This crisis of central government affected not only the king but also dukes and counts, and even viscounts. The erosion of their traditional authority, especially of their dispensation of justice, was felt on all levels of society.[40] Securing peace for the Christian people through just rule had been the king's most elementary duty and the primary source of his authority. This, more than any other function he had carried out, had made the king appear as God's deputy on earth.[41] When the castellans' districts became the loci of the effective exercise of power, the castellans became the lords of justice. Their exercise of justice, however, did not bring peace to those under their rule. Because there was no other power able to keep the peace, the Church stepped in, and the men at the top of its hierarchy became the protectors of law and order, the defenders of peace. In short, "God had deputed to anointed kings the task of maintaining peace and justice; kings were no longer capable of so doing; God therefore took back His power of command into His own hands and vested it in those of His servants, the bishops, with the support of local princes." [42] With the emergence of the Peace of God movement, *pax Dei* replaced peace made and defended by the king, *pax regis*.

As defender of peace the Church undoubtedly obtained a decisive say in the ordering of worldly affairs, yet it did not wish to substitute ecclesiastical power for secular power or to suspend secular laws. The legislation passed by peace councils respected secular laws and accepted secular jurisdiction.[43] The ecclesiastics sought the cooperation of powerful lay magnates to help them enforce secular laws. Such a cooperation between religious and secular lords was not surprising, given the "com-

---

39. *Gesta episcoporum Cameracensium* 3.27; trans. in Head and Landes 1992b, app. A, 335–36.
40. Landes 1995, 26.
41. Moore 1992, 309. Cf. Tellenbach 1993, 39. For the Carolingian concept of kingship, see Anton 1968; Nelson 1988, 213 ff.
42. Duby 1974, 163. Cf. Flori 1983, chap. 8.
43. See Head 1992, 219; Goetz 1992, 271. Cf. Bisson 1977, 293–94.

munity of interest" shared by secular and ecclesiastical lordship.[44] More specifically, the high clergy and the higher-ranking lay lords (*optimates*), both disturbed and threatened by the rising power of castellans, joined forces against these new men of power and their soldiers (*milites*).[45] The Church also engaged the populace in its peace activity, which allowed the peace movement to draw on customs at the communal level. Those customs involved "some hazy right of legislation." Among the populace, collective oath taking and some collective responsibility for law and order were taken for granted. Recourse to those customs may partly explain the movement's success.[46]

The peace movement led by the Church—significantly, by the local Church[47]—was thus a stabilizing force in a changing world. Writing in the 1030s, Rodulfus Glaber linked the beginning of the peace movement to stabilization. As a punishment for the sins of men, terrible pestilence had raged "throughout the whole world for three years." It was believed that "the order of the seasons and the elements, which had ruled all past ages from the beginning, had fallen into perpetual chaos, and with it had come the end of mankind." But people raised their heart and hands unto the Lord, and in the year 1033, at the millennium of the Lord's passion, "by divine mercy and goodness the violent rainstorms ended; the happy face of the sky began to shine and to blow with gentle breezes and by gentle serenity to proclaim the magnanimity of the Creator." The earth blossomed again and gave an abundance of fruit, dispelling scarcity. "It was then that the bishops and abbots and other devout of Aquitaine first summoned great councils of the whole people." Many bodies of saints and innumerable caskets of holy relics were brought to the gatherings, which began to be held in other provinces as well. Even in the farthest corners of France "it was decreed that in fixed places the bishops and magnates of the entire country should convene councils for re-establishing peace and consolidating the holy faith."[48]

44. Moore 1992, 315; Bull 1993, 39 and, generally, chap. 2. Cf. Flori 1983, 137; Debord 1992; Bull 1993, 24; Bredero 1994, 121–22.

45. Flori 1983, 153, 155–56, argues that "les institutions de paix furent, à leur origine du moins, antiseigneuriales mais non antiaristocratiques."

46. Reynolds 1986, 34–35.

47. "In the church as in the kingdoms the idea of corporate institutions with public functions had collapsed into bundles of rights owned by individual proprietors. . . . the seigneurial revolution proceeded in parallel in the secular and spiritual spheres." Morris 1991, 27.

48. Rodulfus Glaber *Historiarvm* IV,v,13–14. Cf. ibid., III,iv,13; Morrison 1969, 388.

THE PEACEMAKING CHURCH: FROM PROHIBITING
WAR TO DIRECTING THE USE OF ARMS

Though the peace movement was a stabilizing force in a changing world, it was also an agent of change. As a medium through which the Church came to exercise—or, at the very least, to have a decisive say in exercising—a key function of secular power, the peace movement strengthened the Church's position vis-à-vis secular power. The shifting relationship between ecclesiastical authority and secular power was crucial in the overall restructuring of power within Christian society. Both the Church's authority and secular power underwent transformations that led to the shaping of new power structures and power relations in the Latin West. The resulting social transformation was radical indeed, and its consequences were long-lasting and far-reaching. It has been described as an overturning "both of ideologies and of economic and social infrastructures to a degree even greater than that which occurred during the late Roman Empire or the sixteenth century." [49] In what follows, I examine these momentous changes from the point of view of the transformation of ecclesiastical authority and the Church's position within Christian society.

The Church's assumption of a leading role in peacemaking and peacekeeping, which used to be elementary functions of kingly power, was crucial to its ascension to the preeminent position within Christian society. But what, exactly, did making and keeping peace mean? As canons from the peace councils document, it meant, in the first place, the banning of private wars and other acts of violence by limiting the use of arms. However, the peace councils' prohibitive regulations had a positive aspect as well. By setting rules specifying whom arms-bearers were not allowed to attack, the kinds of property they were not allowed to touch, and days of the week and seasons of the year when they were not allowed to use arms, the peace council regulations also gave the Church the authority to determine who could employ arms, for what purpose, on whose command, against whom, and when. This development suggests that the Church now regarded violence as licit under certain conditions. The circumscription of violence opened the way for the Church not only to assert its control over the use of arms but also to direct violent action.

49. Robert Foisser, "Les mouvements populaires en Occident au XIᵉ siècle," *Académie des Inscriptions et Belles-Lettres: Comptes rendus des séances de l'année 1971;* quoted in Head and Landes 1992a, 9.

THE LICITNESS OF FIGHTING AND KILLING

The peace movement did not ban war altogether. Rather, it limited the sphere of the licit use of arms. Spiritual sanctions were not the only weapon of the peacemaking Church dignitaries; peace regulations could not rest on moral authority of ecclesiastical councils alone, and anathemas and excommunications were often backed by less sublime weapons—the threat, or actual use, of violence against the perpetrators of violence. The ecclesiastical peacemakers labeled the violent as peacebreakers and commanded that armed actions be taken against them. Moreover, in their devotion to peace, the clergy themselves took part in such battles on more than one occasion. Not unconditionally opposed to war, the peace movement rather declared war on war and sometimes even organized its own armies: peace militias.

Rodulfus Glaber reported that whoever broke the truce was "to pay for it with his life or be driven from his own country and the company of his fellow Christians." The Truce of God was to be upheld by "human sanctions" and by "divine vengeance." When "[v]arious madmen in their folly did not fear to break the [peace] pact," Glaber reported, "immediately divine punishment or the avenging sword of men fell upon them."[50] Taking up arms against peace-breakers was not regarded as breaking the peace. Peace oaths administered by bishops would sometimes commit those who entered a "peace pact" to wage war against those who broke the Peace or the Truce, to act together "to the destruction and confusion" of the offenders.[51]

The peace movement that originated in Bourges is perhaps the best-known case in which such oaths were taken and bishops themselves led forces into the battle for peace while the clerics took the "human sword" into their own hands.[52] A contemporary report by Andrew of Fleury tells us that in the year 1038, Aimon, the archbishop of Bourges, "wished to impose peace in his diocese through the swearing of oath." He summoned the bishops of his province to a meeting where he swore to God and His saints over the relics of Stephen, "the first martyr for Christ," that "I will wholeheartedly attack those who steal ecclesiastical property, those who provoke pillage, those who oppress monks, nuns, and

---

50. Rodulfus Glaber *Historiarvm* V,i,15.
    51. Cf. Flori 1983, 156–57; Robinson 1990, 327; Bull 1993, 33–34.
    52. There were other cases of clerics fighting peace wars in the same period. See Erdmann 1935, 39. On peace militias, see Hoffmann 1964, chap. 7, and 175; cf. Delaruelle 1980, 72 f.

clerics, and those who fight against holy mother church, until they repent." He promised not to deviate from this path of righteousness under any circumstances, and "to move with all my troops against those who dare in any manner to transgress the [peace] decrees and not to cease in any way until the purpose of the traitor has been overcome." The bishops had to follow his lead and then make all males fifteen years and over in their separate dioceses subscribe to the peace and take the same oath. Aimon thus bound the male populace "by the following law: that they would come forth with one heart as opponents of any violation of the oath they have sworn, that they would in no way withdraw secretly from the pact," and that, "if necessity should demand it, they would go after those who had repudiated the oath with arms." Clerics were not excepted and "often took banners from the sanctuary of the Lord and attacked the violators of the sworn peace with the rest of the crowd of laypeople [*populus*]."[53]

Once organized, this popular peace army appears to have been quite active. We learn that "they many times routed the faithless and brought their castles down to the ground" and "trampled underfoot" those they labeled rebels, "so that they forced them to return to the laws of the pact which they had ignored." It is also clear that "raging against the multitude of those who ignore God," these armed faithful inspired a lot of terror. However, as Andrew of Fleury points out, they became possessed by blind ambition and fell away from God. Their major success—when they set aflame the castle of Beneciacum, whose lord was accused of violating the peace—ironically also marked the turn of their fortunes. They also killed without pity those who had not been consumed by fire, so that fourteen hundred people of both sexes—mainly the local population, who had sought protection in the castle—perished. Before the blood of the innocents had dried up, the archbishop's peace league—which "no longer had the Lord with them as their leader"—was badly defeated by another peace-breaking noble, and in one valley seven hundred clerics were slain.[54]

For Andrew of Fleury, Aimon had gone too far. The archbishop of Bourges with his peace army had brought up complex questions concerning clerical participation in war and bloodshed, and the place of

53. *Miracula s. Benedicti* V,2; trans. in Head and Landes 1992b, app. A, 339–40.
54. *Miracula s. Benedicti* V,2–4 (ibid., 340–42). Cf. Erdmann 1935, 39, 57; Hoffmann 1964, 105 ff.; Head 1992.

priests and clerics, on the one hand, and armed and unarmed laymen, on the other, within a properly ordered society.

According to traditional ecclesiastical doctrine, clerics and monks were barred from participating in any military activity and were not allowed to bear arms. From early Church councils on, this interdict was "absolute,"[55] and the clerics who transgressed it were threatened with strict disciplinary measures, regardless of whether they took up arms for a just cause or even against the infidels. The rule was loosened a little when the synod of Ratisbone in 743 allowed clerics to accompany a Christian army on campaign. The synod specified the rank and number of the clergy accompanying military campaigns and determined that their task was to celebrate mass, intercede for the protection of saints, confess, and impose penance—nothing else. It did not lift the ban on clerics bearing arms. That ban remained in force during the Carolingian period. The battle among Charlemagne's sons and successors at Fontenoy in 841 gives us an interesting example. Disturbed by the fratricidal war, the Carolingian bishops convened after the battle and concluded that the soldiers of the victorious army fought "for justice and equity alone" and that, for this reason, "every one of them, he who commanded as well as he who obeyed, was to consider himself in this conflict an instrument of God, free from responsibility."[56] However, the clerics who took active part in the battle were punished.[57] The interdict against clerics bearing arms was reaffirmed even when Frankish lands suffered Norman attacks,[58] and it was restated by numerous peace councils held between the Council of Charroux in 989 and the Council of Clermont in 1095.[59]

Though the prohibition against clerics using arms was the Church's normative stance, in practice things looked different. During the Merovingian period (end of the fifth century to the mid-eighth century), bishops took part in wars, even though such behavior was not expected from them;[60] under their Carolingian successors, such a state of affairs was in-

55. Poggiaspalla 1959, 143. Prinz 1971, 5, wrote that "die kirchlichen Canones lassen keinen Zweifel darüber, daß der geistliche Stand mit Waffenhandwerk und Jagd unvereinbar sei."

56. Nithard Histories iii,1.

57. Fliche and Martin, Histoire de l' Eglise, vol. 6 (Paris, 1948), 269; quoted in Poggiaspalla 1959, 143 n. 16.

58. Magnou-Nortier 1992, 65.

59. Delaruelle 1980, 53; Morris 1991, 143; Goetz 1992, 266; Remensnyder 1992, 286–87, 290–91.

60. See Prinz 1971, 65.

stitutionalized.[61] The episcopate became involved in the management of secular affairs, which included military service. Bishops and abbots were responsible not only for equipping but also for personally leading ecclesiastical contingents on imperial military campaigns—indeed, they were bound to take the field—and they never questioned this duty.[62] Moreover, whereas the last important Merovingian council, the Council of St. Jean de Losne in 673/75, explicitly forbade all bishops and clerics to bear arms in the manner of laymen, Carolingian councils did not specify bishops when they reiterated the general prohibition against clerics bearing arms.[63] Thus it is not surprising that in the ninth and tenth centuries bishops occasionally took the initiative to organize defense against foreign peoples invading the lands of Latin Christians.[64] But it is noteworthy that, for example, between 886 and 908, ten German bishops fell in fratricidal wars.[65]

But while many bishops between the eighth and the eleventh centuries engaged in warfare, some Church dignitaries of that period expressed a strongly negative view of clerical military activity, as the following few examples illustrate. At the beginning of the Carolingian rule, St. Boniface denounced Frankish bishops who were "given to hunting and to fighting in the army like soldiers and by their own hands shedding blood." Replying to Boniface's letter, Pope Zacharias called those bishops "false priests" because their hands were "stained with human blood" and repeated that for priests fighting was unlawful.[66] Pope Sergius II, who called proponents of war "sons of the devil," wrote a letter to Transalpine bishops in 844, urging them to "suffer persecution for this will make you blessed." [67] Atto, bishop of Vercelli, sharply criticized the clergy's involvement with war and secular affairs, maintaining that it was not appropriate to priests—it was diabolical.[68] Ratherius of Verona, another tenth-century Italian bishop, reprimanded the clergy for showing con-

---

61. Contamine 1986, 431. Prinz 1971, 91, speaks of the total "'Einstaatung' der Kirche in den karolingischen Verwaltungsaufbau." Cf. Morrison 1969, 205–6, 251; Prinz 1979, 312; Moore 1992, 314.

62. Prinz 1979, 307; Nelson 1983, 20.

63. Prinz 1971, 7, cf. 168 n. 80; 1979, 315 f.

64. See, for example, Blumenthal 1988, 2; Leyser 1994, 198 f.

65. Contamine 1986, 432.

66. Boniface to Pope Zacharias, A.D. 742; Zacharias to Boniface, 1 April 743; Zacharias to the Frankish clergy, Oct. 745 (*Letters of Saint Boniface*, 80, 84, 112).

67. Gilchrist 1988, 183. But as Gilchrist points out, Sergius was a rare exception among belligerent popes.

68. *Epistola* 1 (*Attonis episcopi vercellensis epistolae*, PL 134: 98). Cf. Poggiaspalla 1959, 146; Prinz 1971, 27.

tempt for the canons in their hunting, whoring, and warring.[69] In the late 1020s, Bishop Fulbert of Chartres poured out his indignation at the bishops—he did not even want to call them bishops for fear of injuring the faith—who were more versed in war than lay princes and were not ashamed of disturbing the peace of the Church and shedding Christian blood. Moreover, they dared to enter their churches to celebrate the holy sacraments with bloody hands. The Church had only one sword, he reminded them, the spiritual sword, which does not kill but vivifies.[70]

This and similar criticisms indicate that from the mid-eighth century to the early eleventh century there was tension and conflict between the normative canonical prohibition against clerical participation in war and the actual military duties of the high clergy.[71] Tension between norm and practice can exist only as long as the norm still stands. In the time of Aimon of Bourges, the ecclesiastical norm began to be loosened. Moreover, whereas the military service of the Carolingian episcopate may be seen as imposed on the Church by the imperial power (even though the Church dignitaries did not necessarily experience that imposition as painful), now there was no royal authority to demand that the bishops and abbots act contrary to ecclesiastical precepts regarding clerical participation in warfare. Aimon's military activity was not systemic, as that of the Carolingian and Ottonian bishops had been. He did not organize his peace army at the command of worldly power but on his own initiative, and his effort was directed against the laymen to whom the effective power had devolved. But as problematic as Aimon's military pursuits might have been from the normative point of view, they also influenced the norm, and the bellicose bishop was actually one of those who broke fresh ground on which a new ecclesiastical attitude toward peace and war began to grow.

As long as the Augustinian understanding of peace as "tranquillity of order"[72] prevailed, a cleric bearing arms could be perceived as disturbing the proper order of things. As Fulbert of Chartres warned, such order entailed that the spiritual sword—the word of God—was the only weapon of the Church. The same argument was pressed by Peter Damian in the middle of the eleventh century. The armed clerics, he maintained, represented a reversal of the proper order of things. They were

---

69. *De contemptu canonum* I,17; II,1 (PL 136: 504, 515 f.; quoted in Morrison 1969, 255 n. 6).

70. Fulbert of Chartres to Hildegarius, *Epistola* 112 (*Epistolae*, PL 141: 255–60).

71. Ratherins of Verona, for example, personified this conflict. See Prinz 1971, 27.

72. Augustine *The City of God* XIX, 13.

usurpers of the material sword that God had bestowed on secular power exclusively. The offices of kingship and priesthood were distinct. Citing an example from the Old Testament, Damian pointed out that God had struck King Azariah, who had usurped the spiritual office, with leprosy to the day of his death.[73] A notable Church reformer himself, Damian did not hesitate to disapprove of reform pope Leo IX's armed action against the Normans, regardless of the justice of the cause.[74] Given that the idea of peace was linked to that of order, a cleric who disrupted the order was, *eo ipso,* violating peace. He was a *perturbator pacis,* a *pacis violator.* But Aimon of Bourges and other priests and monks took up arms precisely in the name of peace. Making peace the central purpose of military action affected the ecclesiastical outlook. Not only wars in which priests and monks took part but war in general was beginning to be seen differently.

Traditionally, the Church had been averse to the shedding of blood. *Ecclesia abhorret a sanguine* was a principle ever present in patristic writings and conciliar legislation. Participation in warfare was regarded as an evil; killing transgressed the Fifth Commandment; the stain of blood burdened Christian conscience. Even if a Christian stained his hands with blood in a just war, he still sinned. As Pope Nicholas I (858–67) stated[75]—in an era when Latin Christians had to defend themselves against the inroads of those they regarded as pagans—even killing a pagan was homicide. From the fourth century to the eleventh century, the Church as a rule imposed disciplinary measures on those who killed in war, or at least recommended that they do penance.[76]

In the tenth century a different view began to emerge, emanating from Cluny, a center of monastic reform that played a role in inaugurating the Peace of God (even if only for the Cluniacs' own benefit—to protect their lands from the growing perils of private warfare).[77] Odo, the sec-

---

73. Peter Damian *Epistolarum libri octo* IV,ix (PL 144: 315). Cf. Remensnyder 1992, 291.

74. Peter Damian *Epistolarum libri octo* IV,ix (PL 144: 316). Cf. Erdmann 1935, 131; Poggiaspalla 1959, 146 (referring to Palazzini, *Il diritto strumento di reforma ecclesiastica in S. Pier Damiani* [Rome, 1956]).

75. *Nicolai I. papae epistolae,* ca. A.D. 861 (MGH Epp. 6: 613).

76. A brief survey in Contamine 1986, 428–30. See Leyser 1994, 196.

77. Hoffmann 1964, 47; Blumenthal 1988, 67; Tellenbach 1991, 82. The connection between Cluny and *pax Dei* is a controversial issue among historians. Cf. Erdmann 1935, chap. 2; Rousset 1945, 16; Cowdrey 1973; Delaruelle 1980, 69, 75 ff.; Duby 1985, 232 f.; Becker 1988, 275, 289–93; Blumenthal 1988, 67; Deanesly 1991, 98; Morris 1991, chap. 3, especially 66; Goetz 1992, 274; Mayer 1993, 16.

ond abbot of Cluny (926–44)[78] was one of the first to argue that it was possible to conduct warfare from "proper motives"—and thus to promote a new ethics of war, that is, Christian militarism.[79] In his *Vita Geraldi,* Odo represented the hero, Count Gerald, as a model of the new warrior of Christ—a *miles Christi* who did not lay aside his arms but rather, moved by piety and charity, used arms in a way pleasing to God. His combating evil and malice was the Lord's work, *opus Domini.* Odo called this new kind of combat, in which piety entered the battlefield and became a fact of war, "fighting mingled with piety."[80] A layman carrying a sword in such a spirit was irreproachable. The Old Testament had authorized it, Odo argued, pointing out that "some of the fathers, although they had been the most holy and the most patient, nevertheless used to take up arms manfully in adversities when the cause of justice demanded." With Gerald as an example and the Old Testament to support the idea, the Cluniac abbot felt safe to conclude: "Truly, no one ought to be worried because a just man sometimes makes use of fighting, which seems incompatible with religion."[81]

The idea of "fighting mingled with piety" opened the way to thinking about fighting as a special form of piety, and to the materialization of such thinking in the eleventh century.[82] The peace movement, as we have seen, not only allowed but demanded the employment of arms against the peace-breakers in the interest of peace.[83] It thus supported the notion of permissible violence and helped to establish ecclesiastical control over the use of arms and the determination of the circumstances in which laymen could licitly employ weapons and shed blood.[84] The understanding of warfare as licit was further developed by the Church reformers in the second half of the eleventh century in the idea of warfare as a service to the Church.[85] Pope Gregory VII (1073–85)—after whom

78. Cf. Erdmann 1935, 64; McGinn 1978, 38; Riché 1993, 310.
79. See Erdmann 1935, 62; Delaruelle 1980, 56.
80. "Novo praeliandi genere mista pietate." *Vita Geraldi* I,8 (PL 133: 647). See Rosenwein 1982, 73 ff., whom I follow here; cf. Duby 1968b, 755, 761.
81. *Vita Geraldi* I,8 (PL 133: 647); trans. in Rosenwein 1982, 76–77.
82. McGinn 1978, 39.
83. Delaruelle 1980, 57.
84. Remensnyder 1992, 301.
85. The connection between the peace movement and the eleventh-century Church reform has been a subject of controversy among historians. Immediate links between the two might indeed be difficult to demonstrate. Cf. Tellenbach 1993, 138; Bredero 1994, 124–25. The peace movement, however, developed ideas and practices that fed into the Church reform and were later adopted and brought to fruition by the reformed Church.

this Church reform has been called[86]—is held responsible for the profound changes in the Christian attitude toward bearing arms that this idea implied.[87]

In his uncompromising struggle for liberty and renewal of the Church, Gregory did not shrink from the use of force against those he considered opposed to the true faith and divine justice. Throughout his pontificate he sought to recruit arms-bearers from all over western Christendom—from kings and princes to soldiers—for military service for the papacy, which was now the supreme authority within the Christian Church. He claimed that laymen owed such service to St. Peter, whose vicar on earth was the pope. Those who placed their arms at the disposal of the Apostolic See were thus the army of St. Peter, *militia sancti Petri,* and the individual who provided military service in pursuit of papal ends was his soldier, *miles sancti Petri.*[88] Faithful laymen were vassals to the prince of the apostles, *fideles sancti Petri,* and fighting for St. Peter was an expression of their *fidelitas.*[89] The notions of *fideles sancti Petri* and *milites sancti Petri* became largely synonymous.[90] Gregory's outlook has been summarized, if somewhat harshly, as follows: "The Church is the 'Christian legion,' within which the laity is the 'order of fighters': laymen have no function save that of fighting; they exist solely to suppress the enemies of the Church and all elements which tend to subvert right Christian order. The word of St. Paul, 'No man that warreth for God entangleth himself with the affairs of this world,' has been turned upside down."[91]

War for St. Peter was considered licit. Even though Gregory VII did not formulate a "rounded reassessment of warfare," his pontificate marked a decisive stage in the association of the Church with warfare and bearing arms.[92] The systematization and juridical justification of the new ecclesiastical attitude was the work of Gregorian bishops Anselm of Lucca

86. The term *Gregorian reform* was introduced by Fliche 1924–37. Though it has been criticized for personifying the Church reform (which actually began before Gregory VII's pontificate: on this early phase of the reform, cf. Anton 1987), the term did enter general use. With these reservations it is used in this book.

87. Cowdrey 1997, 34.

88. Cf. Cowdrey 1998, 650; and, generally, Robinson 1973.

89. See Zerbi 1948, 132 ff.

90. Tellenbach 1947, 144; Laarhoven 1959–61, 46–47, 62–63, 92 (for the notion of *fidelitas*). Cf. Gregory to Abbot Hugh of Cluny, 22 January 1075, Gregory VII *Register* II,49 (p. 190).

91. Robinson 1973, 190. Cf. Arquillière 1934; Fliche 1929, 281 f.; Erdmann 1935, chap. 5; Villey 1942, 46 f.; Rousset 1945, 50 ff.; Delaruelle 1980, 79 ff.; Becker 1988, 288 ff.

92. Cowdrey 1998, 658.

and Bonizo of Sutri at the end of the eleventh century.[93] A "canonist of reform," Anselm of Lucca wrote his Collectio canonum as a "book about 'principles,'" postulating "what the reformers desired for the Church and Christian society."[94] In this context he worked to demonstrate that under certain conditions war, as well as the spilling of blood, could be legitimate and just.[95] Citing (and slightly modifying) Augustine as his authority, Anselm stated: "Do not think that one who ministers with warlike arms is unable to please God."[96] One of the two questions Bonizo of Sutri addressed in his polemical work Liber ad amicum, probably written in 1085–86, was whether "a Christian was or is permitted to fight with arms for the [true] doctrine."[97] The answer he provided, based on a set of historical examples, was undoubtedly affirmative. If one might fight for the worldly king, why not for the Heavenly King? If for the republic, why not for righteousness? And if against the barbarians, why not against heretics? "Thus," he drew the lesson from history, "may the glorious soldiers of God fight for truth and righteousness and combat heresy in the truest sense." Indeed, every Christian must fight against "heretical novelties" in the manner corresponding to his social status.[98] In his canonical work Liber de vita christiana, composed between 1090–95, Bonizo laid down a moral code of action for soldiers, making clear that the exercise of their profession was unobjectionable as long as they followed that code. Later in this chapter I outline this postulated military ethic as well as the conditions under which military service was pleasing to God in Anselm's opinion. First, I want to point out a grave consequence of the view that the use of arms was licit and acceptable to Christian religion.

If employment of arms was compatible with religion (in the spirit of Odo's Vita Geraldi), so were the fruits of the use of arms. Bernard of An-

93. Cf. Erdmann 1935, 223 ff.; Laarhoven 1959–61, 63 n. 206; Robinson 1978, 102 f.; Becker 1988, 319 ff.; Morris 1991, 109.
94. Cushing 1998, 142–43. Cf. Pásztor 1987, 377.
95. See Stickler 1947, 245–50; Pásztor 1987; Cushing 1998, chap. 4.
96. "Noli existimare neminem Deo placere posse, qui armis bellicis ministrat." Collectio canonum XIII,4: "Quod militantes etiam possunt esse iusti." Trans. in Cushing 1998, 129–30. Cf. Cushing's abridged edition of bk. XII and XIII of the Collectio canonum, app. II, 194. Cushing pointed out that Anselm changed ministrare for Augustine's militare. Pásztor 1987, 407, in her edition of bk. XIII of the Collectio canonum, has militat. Cf. Anselm Liber contra Wibertum 523–24.
97. Liber ad amicum I (p. 571).
98. Liber ad amicum VIIII (pp. 618–19), II (p. 573). Cf. Erdmann 1935, 229 f.; Berschin 1972, 38 f.

gers, who wrote the first part of the *Liber miraculorum sancte Fidis* in the early eleventh century, unequivocally expressed the view that not only fighting but killing too was pleasing in the eyes of God. He went well beyond representing the death of malefactors—those who wanted to either attack the monks or steal their wine or who slandered the local saint—as due to impersonal celestial vengeance.[99] Bernard told the story of Gimon, prior of the monastery in Conques, who took divine vengeance into his own hands.[100] Although a monk, Gimon had "a cuirass, a helmet, a lance, a sword, and all kinds of instruments of war" always close at hand and was quick to use them "whenever wicked men invaded the monastery with hostile intent." This, Bernard knew, was "an assault on the monastic rule"; but, he suggested, if people considered Gimon's behavior "correctly," they would ascribe it to the monk's moral excellence.[101] "No one could doubt that his bravery was pleasing in the eyes of God." He was an instrument of God, fighting against "men like Antichrist" who "seize the goods of the saints as plunder, laugh at the bishop's interdict, think the legal position of the monks is a pile of shit, and even rail against the army of the living God like insolent Philistines." Gimon's action against such men was pure: "If God's avenging omnipotence should employ the hand of any of His own servants to strike down and slaughter one of these Antichrists, no one could call it a crime."[102] Moreover, "that man will not be regarded as a murderer [*neque iste ut homicida reputabitur*] whom the Lord of Sabaoth and King of Armies and Powers destined to be the sole protection of his own monastic community, as if he were another defender-angel." Such a man should, rather, be rewarded, as David had been rewarded for killing Goliath.[103]

Killing of "false Christians" by the virtuous and zealous servants of God was not to be regarded as homicide. Bernard of Angers singled out as false Christians those who acted violently in disrespect of the bishop's interdict (*interdictum pontificalem deridentes*)—the violators of peace. Peace gatherings, as we saw earlier, would call on "the avenging human sword" and unleash a "raging against the multitude of those who ignore

---

99. See, for example, *Liber miraculorum sancte Fidis* I,5,6,11.

100. Erdmann 1935, 69, remarked that Bernard took special pains to portray this figure.

101. "Sed si quis recte perspiciet, plus hoc ad virtutem quam ad impugnationem monastice regule poterit referre." *Liber miraculorum sancte Fidis* I,26. (I follow the translation in *The Book of Sainte Foy*.)

102. Ibid.

103. Ibid.

God."[104] Effusion of bad Christians' blood was part of the peace package; it was sanctioned by the peacemakers.

A fateful turn in ecclesiastical thinking about licit killing occurred in the pastoral letters of Pope Alexander II. In a letter to Viscount Berenguer of Narbonne, the pope communicated his approval of the viscount's protection of the Jews who lived under his power. "God is not pleased by the spilling of blood, nor does he rejoice in the perdition of the evil ones."[105] In a letter of 1063 addressed to Wifred, archbishop of Narbonne, the pope reiterated the same traditional view: that "all laws, ecclesiastical as well as secular, forbid the shedding of human blood," but he made two exceptions. Bloodshed was allowed as a punishment for crimes and to counter hostile aggression, as in the case of Saracens.[106] Though punishment of criminals was not war, fighting against Saracens was. Consequently, "proceeding against the Saracens,"[107] that is, war against them, could be regarded as licit warfare.

THE SOCIALIZATION OF WARRIORS AND THE FORMULATION OF CHRISTIAN MILITARY ETHICS

The peace movement, in an attempt to bring violence under control, played a key role in defining the conditions under which fighting and killing were permissible. But controlling violence meant establishing authority over the violent. In this section I look at those who lived by the use of arms and at how the Church tried not only to restrain them but to find them a proper place in Christian society by designating a morally acceptable sphere and purpose for their actions.[108]

The perpetrators of violence encountered by the peacemaking bishops and their allies from the higher ranks of lay nobility were the castellans and their military retinue, who came to be called *milites,* soldiers.

---

104. See nn. 50, 54.

105. Alexander II *Epistolae et diplomata* no. 102 (PL 146: 1387). Ewald 1880, 347, suggests 1063 as the year of composition.

106. "Omnes leges tam ecclesiastice quam seculares effusionem humani sanguinis dampnant, nisi forte conmissa crimina aliquem iudicio puniant, vel forte, ut de Sarracenis, hostilis exacerbatio incumbat." Loewenfeld, *Epp. pontif. roman.,* no. 83 (p. 43). A slightly different reading in Jaffé, *Regesta* 4533 (3487). Mansi 19: 980—reproduced in Alexander II *Epistolae et diplomata* no. 103 (PL 146: 1387)—does not have "nisi forte . . . incumbat."

107. Alexander to the bishops of Spain, *Epistolae et diplomata* no. 101 (PL 146: 1386).

108. The discussion of these topics here can only be a simplification, for it is beyond the scope of this study to account for regionally specific and unsynchronous developments. For these differences, see Duby 1968b, 760 f.; Johrendt 1971; Cardini 1981, 314 ff.; Flori 1983 (and, for the later period, id. 1986); and literature cited in these works.

This term (and its singular, *miles*) came into use in this context in the middle of the second half of the tenth century, coinciding with the emergence of the peace movement. The term acquired juridical as well as social meaning, for the soldier became a legal person when he entered the peace pact, subjecting himself to the peace legislation.[109] The term was employed in varying contexts and in shifting sense throughout the eleventh century.[110] Whereas it initially referred to mounted warriors of moderate means and humble social status (unless accompanied by adjectives ascribing excellence for soldiers of higher social rank), at the end of the eleventh century the mounted nobles who carried a sword and shield also began to identify themselves as *milites*. Under the word *milites,* then, the greater nobility and their armed vassals converged as an increasingly coherent group of fighters.[111]

Emerging as it did with the peace movement, the term *milites* had a great future laying ahead. A good century later, with the launching of crusading warfare, the soldiers began to figure as no less than *milites Christi,* soldiers of Christ. But the term *milites* had also had a long past. *Milites Christi* had originally referred to the Christians in general, but from late antiquity onwards the term "soldiers of Christ" became increasingly reserved for the monks—in contrast to "secular soldiers," members of the secular army, the *militia saecularis*.[112] Smaragdus, a Carolingian scholar and the abbot of a monastery in Lorraine, had explained around 820: "There are secular soldiers (*milites seculi*) and there are soldiers of Christ (*milites Christi*); but secular soldiers bear feeble and perilous arms, while those of the soldiers of Christ are most powerful and excellent; the former fight against their enemies in such a way that they lead both themselves and those they kill to everlasting punishment; the latter fight against evil so that after death they may gain the reward of eternal life; the former fight in such a way that they descend to Hell, the latter fight so that they may achieve glory. . . ."[113] Around 861, Pope Nicholas I had declared that soldiers of this world (*milites seculi*) were distinct from the soldiers of the Church (*milites ecclesiae*), so it was not becoming to the soldiers of the Church to fight worldly battles (*saeculo*

---

109. See Duby 1968a, 454; Becker 1988, 281; Paxton 1992, 40.
110. See Duby 1968b, 741 f.; Johrendt 1971, 10–12, 240–45.
111. See Duby 1968a, 455; 1968b, 742–43; Flori 1983, 112 ff., and pt. 3; Keen 1984, 27–28.
112. See a brief survey in Flori 1983, pt. 1, especially 24–28.
113. *Commentaria in regulam sancti Benedicti* (PL 102: 696; quoted in Forey 1992, 10).

militare) in which blood would necessarily be spilled. Just as it was wrong for a layman to interfere with spiritual affairs, so it was ridiculous and inappropriate for a cleric to take up arms and proceed to war.[114] One of the earliest statements of this view is attributed to Martin of Tours, a fourth-century saint, who was quoted as having said: "I am a soldier of Christ, I am not allowed to fight."[115] As soldiers who fought with arms, the *milites saeculi* were undoubtedly inferior to the *milites Christi*. There had been nothing particularly noble about being a "soldier of the world." The prevailing ecclesiastical description of the "soldiers of the world" was, in the words of Burchard of Worms, "those who from greed deliberately slay."[116]

The shift in understanding of who were *milites* was an element in the "revolution in Church thinking about violence" that occurred towards the end of the tenth century and through the eleventh century—described as the most creative period of the High Middle Ages with respect to changes in the concept of war.[117] With the weakening of royal authority and the devolution of effective power to the castellans and their military entourage, the arms-bearers seemed to be free of any control. In the old social order the king had been given the sword to execute justice, to maintain peace, and—as ecclesiastical authorities had never tired of repeating—to defend the Church and protect the poor and the weak.[118] Now those who carried the sword had become the disturbers of peace, violators of ecclesiastical liberty and property, and oppressors of the poor and the weak. Because of their social destructiveness, the *milites* could indeed be characterized as an "as-yet unsocialized class."[119]

The peace movement played a leading role in the socialization of the *milites,* a process that implied circumscribing the place and role of violence in society. For what is peace if not bringing violence under order—an ordered violence? It was largely around the notion of peace that Christian society managed to restore its equilibrium[120] by creating new images of a social order in which *milites* had an honored place.

The image of medieval society that has been made quite popular

---

114. *Nicolai I. papae epistolae* (MGH Epp. 6: 613).

115. Sulpicius Severus *Life of Martin of Tours* IV,3 (*Early Christian Lives,* 139).

116. Burchard of Worms *Decretum* IV,23; quoted in Cushing 1998, 127 n. 17. Burchard is often described as a representative of the traditional anti-war stance of the Church, a view that has been convincingly questioned by Gilchrist 1988, 178–79.

117. Housley 1985, 17; Contamine 1986, 433.

118. See Anton 1968; Flori 1983, 1986.

119. Landes 1995, 28.

120. Contamine 1986, 433, speaking of the "rééquilibrage de la société."

thanks to the research of some French historians is the image of society divided into three orders. Society was imagined as consisting of the order of those who pray (*oratores*), the order of fighters (*milites, bellatores, agonistae, pugnatores*), and the order of workmen (*agricolae, agricoltantes, laboratores*).[121] Each of them had a function to fulfill, but they were interdependent. And in order for society to be well ordered, each person or group had to remain in its own place.

The best known and probably earliest reference to the three orders of society on the continent[122] was made in response to the Peace of God movement. Bishop Adalbero of Laon described the tripartite functional division of society in a few lines of his *Carmen ad Rotbertum regem,* written between 1027 and 1031, if not a decade earlier.[123] "Therefore," he wrote, "triple is the house of God, which is believed to be one. Now, some pray, others fight, and others work. These three are connected and suffer no scission: the workings of two thus stand on the office of one; each one in turn offers support to the others. This threesome is therefore single. As long as this law prevails, the world enjoys peace."[124] The rule of peace thus presupposed that the ministers of God, to whom the whole of humankind, the powerful included, was subordinated, taught the observance of the Christian life; that the king and emperor ruled and commanded the republic and restrained the warriors (whose head they were) so that they would "avoid the crimes" and act as protectors of the Church and the people, *uulgi maiores atque minores;* and that the workmen toiled, with no end to their groans and tears, to feed and clothe the lords.[125]

But Adalbero saw that order collapsing, and in his *Carmen* he pictured the world turned upside down: a peasant crowned king, the nobles living as monks, and the bishops living as peasants. His satire was most biting when he described the monks turned soldiers. He did not hide that he was targeting Cluny. He identified Cluny as the source of the confu-

---

121. See, for example, Duby 1968a; 1968b, 758; and, especially, 1985; Duby 1974, 165 f., where the tripartite division is described as social reality; Le Goff 1985. See also Carozzi 1979, cxx f. (for the origins of the image); Constable 1995, 279–88 (with a brief critical characterization of historians' approaches to social tripartition).

122. Constable 1995, 285; the earliest articulations of the tripartite division of society into the orders of fighters, workmen, and those who pray come from ninth- and tenth-century England (ibid., 279).

123. On the date of composition, see Carozzi 1979, cxv–cxix; Constable 1995, 283 n. 130.

124. I cite Carozzi's edition of the *Carmen:* Adalbero *Poème* (here lines 295–301).

125. Ibid., lines 227–94.

sion of orders and the ensuing disorder, and there was some substance to his criticism. The Cluniacs were involved in the Peace of God movement. Abbot Odilo of Cluny, who was criticized by Adalbero, took part in a peace council of Anse in 994, the first year of his abbacy, and his presence at another council at Le Puy some forty years later is recorded.[126] His large entourage may have had a soldierly bearing,[127] but the evidence for this is debatable.[128] Adalbero's depiction of Odilo and the sacred order of monks hurrying into battle,[129] even though a fiction, is valuable for our understanding of that historical period. In Adalbero's poem a monk whom Adalbero has sent to Cluny returns converted into a soldier. Now, the monk declares, he is a soldier (*Miles nunc!*) fighting for "King Odilo of Cluny" to save the kingdom of Franks from the Saracens.[130] Odilo is "the prince of militia," whom the "warlike order of monks" salute as their lord.[131]

Where one could take over another's social role, the law fell into decay, peace was lost, and morals and order were transformed.[132] Adalbero was a conservative. He wanted the king back as the guarantor of order and peace.[133] He wanted restoration of the *pax regis,* the king's peace. Andrew of Fleury is another who viewed the *pax Dei* as undermining the social order. He disapproved of Aimon of Bourges's peace militia not only because of its cruelty but also because it represented the confusion of orders: under the command of *oratores,* the *laboratores* acted as *bellatores.*[134] To underline the presumptuousness of this idea, Andrew showed them riding into battle on asses—to be routed by the warriors.[135]

In the imagined tripartite society, the order of fighters had a clearly

126. Hoffmann 1964, 41, 45; Rosenwein 1982, 36, 88.
127. Carozzi 1979, xc.
128. For the evidence, cf. Carozzi 1979, lxxxvii–xciii. For scepticism, Hoffmann 1964, 45 n. 2.
129. *Poème* lines 78–79.
130. Ibid., lines 80–128. Carozzi 1979, lxxxviii–lxxxix, interprets these Saracens as a literary artifice. Blumenthal 1988, 67, speaks of the creation of the "legend of the warlike spirit of Cluny."
131. *Poème* lines 155–56.
132. Ibid., lines 170–71, 302–3.
133. Ibid., lines 304–5. Cf. Carozzi 1983, 72; van Caenegem 1988, 180. For a more comprehensive analysis of Adalbero, Carozzi 1979; 1983, 68 ff.; Duby 1985, especially 58 ff.
134. See n. 53. Cf. Flori 1983, 143.
135. *Miracula s. Benedicti* V,4 (Head and Landes 1992b, app. A, 342). Adalbero mounted Odilo's soldiers on asses too: "Ascendant asinum bini, denique camelum! Si non sufficiunt, bubalum conscendite terni!" *Poème* lines 142–43.

defined place. However, the three-orders scheme "remained only one of several ways of ordering society in the Middle Ages, and far from the most important." [136] Adalbero himself, in *Carmen ad Rotbertum regem,* also used a binary division of society into nobles and serfs, who were not bound by the same law.[137] In this scheme, too, warriors had a designated place—in the first division. What was important in the normative ordering of society during the eleventh and twelfth centuries was the recognition of the growing number of professional and occupational groups and the "acceptance of the independence, and rise in status and prestige, of the order of *bellatores* or *milites.*" [138]

Socializing the soldiers, however, took more than fitting them into a well-ordered social scheme. The problem at the beginning of the second millennium lay not so much in defining the professional soldiers as in limiting the violence perpetrated by this group. The key was to incorporate violence into the social order through a code of socially acceptable and, ideally, beneficial behavior for the *milites.* This professional ethic was not so much codified by the soldiers as it was codified for them. In this the peace movement and the Church reformers played the crucial role. Through this process the Church came to recognize the military profession, and the *milites* rose in status and prestige.

The long-prevailing view that the eleventh century saw the formation of Christian knighthood[139] has recently been questioned. Revisionist historians maintain that knighthood—the chivalric class (or rather, caste) with its own self-sustaining value system and rites of passage—only came into existence toward the end of the twelfth century.[140] Thus the term *knight* is inapplicable to the eleventh century.[141] But this does not mean that the development of the Christian military ethic and the rise of Christian militarism[142] did not take place in that period. When the Church became engaged in making and keeping peace in the absence of the king, it began to place itself, step by step, into a direct relation-

---

136. Constable 1995, 288.
137. *Poème* lines 276 ff.
138. Constable 1995, 324.
139. See, for example, Erdmann 1935, 51; Duby 1968b, 759; 1974, 166–68; Delaruelle 1980, 55 ff.; Mayer 1993, 20.
140. The most systematic exposition of this argument is in Flori 1983, 1986; summarized in id. 1992; accepted in Bull 1993, 8. See also Cardini 1981, especially 314 ff.; 1992a, pt. 1; Keen 1984.
141. Bull 1993, 17.
142. McGinn 1978, 38–39; Morris 1991, 143 ff. Erdmann 1935 remains a reference work.

ship with the military order.[143] By prescribing social and moral obligations to all warriors[144] and assigning the right motives and goals for military activity, the Church ennobled the use of arms, pulled the military within its own ethical and religious horizons, and placed war in its own service and progressively sanctified it.[145]

During the tenth and especially the eleventh centuries, Christianization of warfare advanced through liturgical innovations, such as the blessing of banners and consecration of weapons, and the period saw the growth of a warrior-saints cult.[146] But the two points of primary interest here are, first, the Church's taking in its own hands command over the use of arms and, second, its defining the mode and purpose of military action.

The Peace of God and Truce of God movements, as we have already seen, relied on the force of arms. When Bishop Guy of Le Puy convoked one of the first peace councils, the presence of the army summoned by the bishop was enough to convince those present, warriors included, to take the peace oath.[147] The Council of Poitiers (1000–1014) planned military action against recalcitrant peace-breakers.[148] Archbishop Aimon of Bourges sent his peace militia to war.[149] The peace movement created a situation in which Church dignitaries—alone or in collaboration with lay princes—either threatened to command or actually commanded the employment of arms. The type of war now coming into existence was new. First, it was a peace war. The peace movement's *militiae* were not just armies fighting for peace, as armies had often done; they were peace armies, the force of peace. Second, war was ordered by the Church itself.[150] Gregorian reformers justified and elaborated upon this kind of war in doctrinal statements that followed some practical steps of great consequence taken by the reform popes.

Leo IX (1048–54) provided a precedent for "papally conducted war-

143. Anachronistic as it is to speak of the "state" in the given context, Erdmann 1935, 53, has pointed to the crucial issue: "Die Kirche trat also ohne die Vermittlung des Staates in ein direktes Verhältnis zu den eigentlichen Vertretern des Kriegerhandwerk."

144. Forey 1992, 11.

145. Tellenbach 1947, 145; Laarhoven 1959–61, 63.

146. See Erdmann 1935, chap. 1, app. 1; Flori 1983, 97 ff.; 1986, chap. 4, app. 369–82.

147. See n. 18.

148. Hoffmann 1964, 32. Cf. Erdmann 1935, 56, citing an appeal from 1040 by the French clergy to the Italians to join the peace efforts, that celebrated the revenge against peace-breakers as blessed by God.

149. See nn. 53, 54.

150. See Erdmann 1935, 56.

fare" by personally leading the war against the Normans in southern
Italy in 1053.[151] In a letter to the Byzantine emperor, Leo justified his recourse to coercive powers of authority.[152] In a turn of papal policy toward the Normans of southern Italy, Pope Nicholas II (1058–61) succeeded in making Norman princes Robert Guiscard, and probably
Richard of Capua, take an oath of fealty to the Apostolic See, subjecting the Norman army to vassalage to the pope.[153] The pope thus had the
right to demand Norman military support. Alexander II (1061–73) renewed this relationship with Richard on the second day of his
pontificate and renewed it with Robert Guiscard a year later.[154] Pope
Leo IX's letter to the Byzantine emperor was probably written by Cardinal Humbert of Silva Candida, who in the 1050s formulated some
leading ideas of the Church reform.[155] Humbert postulated both a strict
separation between the worldly and spiritual spheres and a relationship
between priesthood and kingship in which priestly power excelled kingship just as the soul excelled the body. As a consequence, secular princes
had to follow churchmen but were not allowed to interfere with ecclesiastical affairs. The function of kings and secular princes and of faithful
laymen in general was to defend the Church. Princes received the sword
from Christ's priests and were anointed by them, Humbert argued, in
order to serve in defense of God's churches and, wherever there was
need, to fight.[156]

Pope Gregory VII also expected the faithful to defend the Church.
Moreover, his notion of *fidelitas* implied the Church's right to demand
that the *fideles* employ arms in its service.[157] Thus he required Count
William of Burgundy to "bring together a military force to protect the
freedom of the Roman Church" and if need be to "come hither with [his]

---

151. Morris 1991, 88. Cf. Erdmann 1935, 109 ff. For Laarhoven 1959–61, 21, Leo's
war marked the emergence of the "military papacy."

152. Leo to Constantine Monomachos, A.D. 1054, *Epistolae et decreta pontifica* no.
103 (PL 143: 778–79). Cf. Erdmann 1935, 110, 133.

153. Cowdrey 1983, 111 f. Cf. Erdmann 1935, 116 ff.; Robinson 1990, 326, 369 ff.;
Morris 1991, 139f. For the reform papacy and the Normans, see Cowdrey 1983, chap. 3;
Blumenthal 1988, 79–84.

154. Cowdrey 1983, 118.

155. For different views on Humbert's role, see Fliche 1924–37, 1: chap. 4; Knabe
1936, 121–22; Blumenthal 1988, 91; Tierney 1988, 36; Tellenbach 1991, 109; Schramm
1970, 143 ff.; 1992, 239 ff.

156. See Humbert of Silva Candida *Adversus simoniacos* III,v,ix,xi,xv,xxi (cols. 1147,
1153, 1157, 1163–64, 1175). Cf. Michel 1947, 85.

157. Cf. n. 89. See Erdmann 1935, chap. 7; Cowdrey 1998, especially 650–58.

army in the service of St. Peter." [158] In a letter to King Sweyn of Denmark, the pope made it clear that he expected "help with soldiers and
material sword [*in militibus et materiali gladio*] against the impious and
the enemies of God"—when the "Holy Roman Mother Church" needed
it. Moreover, he suggested that the king dispatch one of his sons with a
number of trusty warriors to lead a campaign against heretics, probably
in Dalmatia. But the pope left no doubt that it was he who would name
Sweyn's son the "general, prince, and defender of Christendom" and
that the Danish prince would "perform military service for the papal
court." The authority to initiate and direct military action lay in the
pope's hands. [159]

Gregory rested his demand for lay princes' military service on not only
his notion of *fidelitas* but also the idea that the pope could claim authority over the sword *(gladius)*. In the letter to Sweyn, Gregory counted
on the king's "material sword." In another letter, the sword to be wielded
was the pope's. The pope threatened Wezelin, a noble who had rebelled
against King Zvonimir Demetrius of Dalmatia, "whom the apostolic authority has constituted," saying that if he did not repent of his "rash
conduct," "we will unsheath the sword of the blessed Peter against your
audacity." [160] The sword Gregory referred to does not seem to have been
the "spiritual sword" or the "sword of excommunication," [161] but rather,
the material sword. Even if the sword was meant to be unsheathed at the
pope's command rather than literally by the pope himself, Gregory was
expressing the right to authorize armed action. [162]

A third ground on which Gregory VII claimed for the Church the
right to command the use of arms was the sinfulness of the military profession. For remission of their sins soldiers could only turn to the Church.
But the Church could do more than award the appropriate penance;
through ecclesiastical ruling, not only could the individual soldier be absolved of his sins, but the use of arms as such could be freed from sinfulness. If they hoped for eternal life, soldiers could either give up fight-

158. Gregory to Count William of Burgundy, 2 Feb. 1074, *Register* I,46 (p. 70); *Correspondence*, 22.
159. Gregory to King Sweyn of Denmark, 25 Jan. 1075, *Register* II,51 (p. 194). Cf.
Stickler 1948, 99–100; Cowdrey 1998, 650.
160. Gregory to Wezelin, 7 Oct. 1079, *Register* VII,4 (p. 464); *Correspondence*, 144.
161. See Stickler 1948, 94–97.
162. Cf. Stickler 1948, 99–101; Riley-Smith 1997, 51. This was not yet the theory of
two swords: Hauck 1904, 30; Stickler 1948, 102; nor did Gregory "practice" the theory
he had not formulated, as wittily maintained by Arquillière 1947, 508.

ing or employ their arms under the Church's direction. A canon from the Roman synod of November 1078 ranked the military among the professions that could not be exercised without incurring sin and proclaimed that the soldier "cannot perform true penance, through which he can attain eternal life, unless he lays down his arms and bears them no more except on the advice of religious bishops for the defense of righteousness." [163] Arms could thus be justly borne "when men were obedient to the guidance of right-minded clerical mentors." [164]

Anselm of Lucca, Gregory VII's closest collaborator and a foremost theoretician of the ecclesiastical reform, was the first to give a systematic treatment in terms of canonical law to the Church's right to the use of arms (*jus gladii*).[165] In his exposition, the Church had the jurisdictional right of coercive action. It had the right to *persecutio,* that is, to material coercion aiming at impeding evil and compelling toward good (as distinct from *vindicta,* material coercion in general, which meant punishment—including capital punishment—for a crime).[166] The Church's material coercive power was independent of the coercive power of secular princes and could be exercised against them by the Church itself. Ordinarily, however, the Church, while retaining its right of coercive action, would charge a secular power with carrying out the coercion.[167] The king did not bear his sword in vain, Anselm reminded William the Conqueror, but was a servant of God (*minister Dei*) whose duty was to punish the evil.[168] Through the secular prince's armed action the Church could fulfill its mission, yet although he undertook this action at the Church's request, the secular prince had no right whatsoever to meddle in internal ecclesiastical affairs.[169] Secular princes had to fulfil their ap-

163. Protocol of the Autumn Roman Synod, 1078, c. 6, in Gregory VII *Register* VI, 5b (p. 404). Cf. Hefele 1912–13, 5.1: 242. The canon was incorporated into Gratian's *Decretum.*

164. Cowdrey 1997, 24.

165. Stickler 1947, 238, 270, 274.

166. *Collectio canonum* XIII,14: "Quod aecclesia persecutionem possit facere"; XIII,15–17: "De eadem re." Pásztor 1987, 412–13; Cushing 1998, 196. Parallels between *Collectio canonum* XIII,14–17, and *Liber contra Wibertum* are documented in Pásztor 1987, 394–97. The distinction between *vindicta* and *persecutio:* Stickler 1947, 239; followed by Cushing 1998, 131.

167. Stickler 1947, 259–64; Cushing 1998, 132–33. Cf. *Collectio canonum* XII,46: "De scismaticis coercendis a secularibus"; XII,54: "De hereticis per saeculares potestates coercendis"; XII,54: "Ut excommunicati cohibeantur a saecularibus." (Cushing 1998, 188–89).

168. Anselm to William I of England, ca. 1085 (MGH BfdtKz 5: 17). Cf. Hauck 1904, 30.

169. Pásztor 1987, 86, 93.

pointed task—the material defense of the Church—under direct ecclesiastical tutorial guidance or supervision.[170]

For Bonizo of Sutri, the enemy within—heretics and schismatics—had first to be cut down with the "evangelical scythe" and then rooted out with "all our forces and weapons."[171] This was a fight commanded by the Church.[172] Just like Anselm, whom he greatly admired,[173] Bonizo argued that the Church had the right to *persecutio*,[174] aided by secular powers, especially by the higher ranks of the lay order: kings, judges, and soldiers. If this "order of fighters" would not fight to subdue the excommunicated, the heretics, and the schismatics, it would be "superfluous" in the "Christian fellowship" (*legio*).[175] The judges were "given to the Church" as assistants (*in adiutorium*), so that by the fear they inspired they would bring back to the "unity of peace" those who rebelled against the order of the Church and did not honor bishops on grounds of ecclesiastical discipline.[176] Bonizo also outlined a comprehensive code of behavior for soldiers, and for this reason we may regard his *De vita christiana* as the book with which "the Church had finally arrived at a new attitude to war."[177]

It was only logical that the Church that claimed the authority to order the use of arms would simultaneously define the right mode and purpose of military action, that is, would set out to elaborate a new ethic for Christian *milites*. Even though elements of this ethical code may not have been new, their synthesis was. Bonizo's codification of *milites'* behavior shows this well.[178] It included the only commandment known for soldiers in the early Middle Ages:[179] that they should not thirst for booty. Most of the other commandments codified by Bonizo may be seen as ecclesiastical recognition of Roman and Germanic warriors' ethics: soldiers had to be devoted to their lords, willing to risk their lives defending the life of their lords, willing to fight to the death for the well-

---

170. Cushing 1998, 132.
171. *Liber ad amicum* I (p. 572).
172. Cf. Erdmann 1935, 234; Flori 1986, 249–50.
173. Cf. Berschin 1987, 281. On the question of whether Bonizo used Anselm's *Collectio canonum* as a source for his *Vita christiana*, cf. Erdmann 1935, 234; Stickler 1947, 271–72; Berschin 1972, 73–74.
174. *Liber de vita christiana* VII,17: "Quod ecclesia possit facere persecutionem"; VII,18–19: "De eadem re."
175. Ibid., II,43; cf. X,79. On the order of Christian society, see ibid., II,3.
176. Ibid., VII,16. Cf. Berschin 1972, 111.
177. Mayer 1993, 19.
178. *De vita christiana* VII,28; cf. II,43.
179. Cf. the analysis in Erdmann 1935, 235–37; Flori 1986, 250–53.

being of the republic (*pro statu rei publice*), not break their sworn fidelity, and not commit perjury toward their lords. Bonizo's emphasis on the
soldiers' fidelity to their lords, however, may also be seen as insistence
on the cardinal Christian virtue of obedience, which binds Christian society together and without which that society would collapse.[180] The
specifically Christian injunction that soldiers had to defend widows, orphans, and the poor was not new in itself. As a postulated duty of the
king, it was to be found in early medieval "mirrors of princes." The novelty, epoch-making in its importance, was in ascribing these "royal ethics" to *milites*.[181] Also specifically Christian, of course, was the demand
that soldiers wage war against schismatics and heretics.

The fight against schismatics and heretics was an overriding concern
for the Gregorian Church reformers. It was prominent with Gregory VII
and Anselm of Lucca, who, however, took much more care than Bonizo
to define the inner disposition of the soldiers carrying out the fight. For
Gregory, fighting heretics and schismatics meant the employment of
armed laymen in the service of the Church. But fighting for the Church
could only win the soldiers reward in this world and the next if they rose
above sinful human desires and pursued these good works from right
motives. *Proeliandi recta voluntas* meant taking up arms for the love of
one's neighbors, and thus for the love (and fear) of God.[182] Gregory was
"the first to state categorically that taking part in war of a certain kind
could be an act of charity to which merit was attached and to assert in
the end that such an action could indeed be penitential."[183] The supreme
act of love was self-sacrifice, dying as a martyr for Him who had died
for the redemption of mankind, "for if, as some say, it is a noble thing
to die for our country, it is a far nobler and a truly praiseworthy thing
to give our corruptible flesh for Christ, who is life eternal."[184] Dying for
Christ, imitating Christ *usque ad mortem,* was an act of love for one's
neighbors, "for as he laid down his life for us, so ought we to lay down
our life for our brothers."[185] With these ideas Gregory VII assigned a

180. See *De vita christiana* II,2–3.
181. The "Übertragung der kirchlichen Königsaufgaben auf den Ritter" was pointed
out in Erdmann 1935, 236, and has been developed in Flori 1983, 1986, who traced the
descent of the "ethique royale" down to *milites* as the movement that played a key role in
the formation of the knightly ethics and knighthood.
182. For a detailed treatment of this subject, see Cowdrey 1997. Cf. Gregory *Register*
II,37 (p. 137); II,49 (p. 190).
183. Riley-Smith 1997, 49–50.
184. Gregory to Matilda of Tuscany, after 16 Dec. 1074, *Epp. vagantes* no. 5.
185. For this and other examples, see Cowdrey 1997, 34.

distinctive moral quality to fighting and contributed importantly to the moralization of warfare and its association with the Church.[186]

For Anselm of Lucca, the aim of ecclesiastical *persecutio* was to compel the evil ones to turn to good—to correct rather than to kill.[187] Aided by the "force of faithful princes," the shepherds of the Church could fulfill their duty of bringing the errant back into the Church.[188] Advancing an "active policy of incorporation,"[189] Anselm consequently emphasized the benevolent aspects of coercion. Relying heavily on St. Augustine—whose teachings on violence had left no mark on Gregory VII's views of Christian warfare[190]—as his authority, Anselm insisted that wars should be conducted with benevolence and that the punishment (*vindicta*) should be not out of hate but out of love, and with restraint.[191] Charity was the right inner intention, essential for carrying out a good action.[192] As the distinctive feature of just *persecutio,* charity brought military action into accordance with the principles of Christian life.[193] It inspired the effort to reintegrate into the Church, where one could be a member of the Body of Christ, those who had deviated from the right path.[194] The Church's preventing or punishing evil was thus an act of love, not vengeance: an action animated by fraternal desire for salvation; a just endeavor to save all souls, as desired by Christ; an act through which the enemies of the truth were constrained into accepting the truth.[195] Described in these terms of pastoral duty,[196] *persecutio* became an aspect of the pastoral office. Anselm's view of warfare was an aspect of his ecclesiology. Warfare was brought within the Church.

Fighting and killing began to be regarded as not only permissible but also meritorious. Clerics might still more often than not stay away from

186. See Cowdrey 1998, 655, 658.
187. *Collectio canonum* XII,55: "De malis cogendis ad bonum"; XIII,12: "Ut mali non occidantur sed corrigantur"; cf. XII,60: "De schismaticis ad correctionem cogendis" (Cushing 1998, 189–90, 193; Pásztor 1987, 411).
188. *Sermo de caritate*, 103–4. Cf. Pásztor 1965, 88.
189. Cushing 1998, 126. Cf. Stickler 1947, 252.
190. Cowdrey 1997, 27; Cowdrey 1998, 652.
191. *Collectio canonum* XIII,2: "De vindicta non odio sed facienda"; XIII,3: "Quod bella cum benivolentia sunt gerenda"; XIII,10: "Ut temperetur vindicta" (Pásztor 1987, 405–6, 410; Cushing 1998, 193, 195).
192. *Collectio canonum* XIII,27 [Ambrose *Libri de officiis*]: "Non satis est bene velle, sed etiam bene facere. Nec satis est iterum bene facere, nisi id ex bono fonte, hoc est, bona voluntate proficiscatur." Pásztor 1987, 419; Cushing 1998, 199.
193. See *Collectio canonum* XIII,14 (Stickler 1947, 246; Pásztor 1987, 412).
194. Cf. *Sermo de caritate*, 100, 103; Pásztor 1965, 80.
195. *Sermo de caritate*, 104; *Collectio canonum* XII,44: "Quod aecclesia non persequitur sed diligit cum punit vel prohibet malum." Cf. Stickler 1947, 25; Cushing 1998, 130.
196. *Sermo de caritate*, 98. Cf. Pásztor 1965, 50–52.

the battlefield, yet they began to suggest to *milites* that battle against the enemies of the Church, enlivened by charity, was not only free from sin but capable of freeing from sin those who took up arms under ecclesiastical guidance. Such use of arms was penitential. It was commendable and deserving, a special form of piety. The Church came to embrace those who served it in arms, and to recognize their profession. And soldiers were integrated into Christian society.

NO MORE SHEDDING OF CHRISTIAN BLOOD

Gradual recognition of the military metier and finding a place for soldiers in Christian society were aspects of the acceptance of the growing number of diverse professional and occupational groups characteristic of eleventh-century thinking about social order.[197] Simultaneously with this acknowledgment of social differentiation, however, the image of a unitary Christian society developed, grounded in the ideal of the fellowship of Christians united in peace. Both the peace movement and the Church reformers contributed to the articulation of this image. The desire for unity, for example, lay at the heart of Anselm of Lucca's doctrine of coercion.[198] The connection of the image of a peaceful and unitary Christian society with the ecclesiastical rethinking of violence was of crucial importance. The ideal of peace and oneness rested on the imperative that all violence among Christians must cease. Insisting on this led to recommendation that Christian violence be diverted to the non-Christian outside world and to justification for this diversion of Christian violence. In the remainder of this chapter I outline the complex historical process through which the unification of Christian society generated a *fundamental* division between the Christian and non-Christian worlds, while the postulated peace among Christians led to holy war against non-Christians.

TURNING AGAINST THE WORLD OUTSIDE

The peace movement became a prominent force, bringing about Christian unification, because of the movement's religious nature. The peace that the movement strove for was not only a "social pact," a contract between social forces; what its protagonists thought they were bringing

197. Cf. n. 138.
198. Cushing 1998, 137.

about was a "covenant with God." For Rodulfus Glaber, innumerable miracles that happened at peace gatherings were "the sign" of a "perpetual covenant" between those present and God.[199] Christian society living in peace was a society united with God and in God.

The peace movement came into existence at the turn of the millennium, when the millenary of Christ's passion and eschatological, apocalyptic, and chiliastic expectations dominated the mental horizon.[200] This impacted the formation and character of the peace movement. The movement's documents abound with rhetoric either directly or indirectly invoking chiliastic notions of a new age of peace, justice, and harmony in this world below.[201] This mentality was the movement's inner driving force. Violence, famine, natural disasters, epidemics, as well as solar eclipses, comets, and other phenomena in the sky were regarded as having supernatural meaning. Calamities were perceived as the wrath of God, the heavens calling people to mend their ways. People of all social ranks gathered at peace councils and were ready "to obey the commands of the clergy no less than if they had been given by a voice from heaven speaking to men on earth."[202] Those who worked for peace were animated by God. For Glaber, the peace movement came into existence "by divine inspiration."[203] It was accepted that the initiators of *pax Dei* received letters from the heavens.[204]

The peace movement strove to reestablish the peace originally brought to mankind by Christ. The attainment of peace of this nature required moral renovation, religious renewal, and reform and regulation of both clerical and lay behavior. Peace on earth was a *visio Dei*, a prefiguration of and precondition for eternal life.[205] Though peace did not represent or dictate a particular social order, it was nevertheless an order: the right order.[206] Thus the peace movement—at least in the minds of the clergy promoting it, and from the perspective of the movement's goal—stood for the clergy's total view of Christianity. "Upon the basis of the need to provide for physical peace and security was thus erected a superstruc-

---

199. Rodulfus Glaber *Historiarvm* IV,v,16. Cf. Duby 1968a, 457; Cowdrey 1970a, 50; Becker 1988, 277; Landes 1992, 200.
200. See Landes 1995, chap. 2, 14–15. But see nn. 267, 268.
201. Cf. Bredero 1994, 116 f.; Landes 1995, 31.
202. Rodulfus Glaber *Historiarvm* IV,v,14.
203. Ibid., V,i,15.
204. Cf. Hoffmann 1964, 82–83; Goetz 1992, 277; Bredero 1994, 110; generally: Callahan 1992, 170 ff.; Landes 1992, 199 ff.
205. Goetz 1992, 276.
206. Remensnyder 1992, 282, 291.

ture of the preaching and liturgical commemoration of peace in an ideal
sense as the planting upon earth of the order that God willed to prevail."[207] So, for example, the peace gathering at Le Puy in the year 994
declared its intention to establish peace "in the name of God, since without peace no one will see God." Peace was the path to salvation. It was
the message of Christ, for it was peace "which Lord especially loves and
orders to be loved." God himself was asked to give peace. At peace councils, bishops raised their croziers to the heavens, and people "all cried
out in one voice to God, their hands extended: 'Peace! Peace! Peace!'"[208]
Those present at gatherings, swearing to keep peace, made offerings to
Almighty God.[209] And it was God who sanctified peace. This peacemaking was a religious endeavor and the establishment of peace was
seen as a divine act. Consequently, whoever refused to enter the peace
contract (*pactus pacis*) was said to follow the devil.

The peace movement acted under the banner of peace and unity, *pax
et unitas*. To live in peace was the duty of all the faithful. Peace was a
"social bond." Christian society meant living in peace as a unitary body,
corpus christianorum, morally renewed and purified, freed from division
and dissension.[210] Those who gathered at the peace council of Poitiers in
the early years of the new millennium envisioned the peace that Christ
had brought down to earth in order that all Christians would be "one in
one body"—His body.[211] The unitary body of all Christians equaled
corpus Christi, the body of Christ.

On this symbolic basis, the view of Christian society progressed towards a new, higher universality.[212] Although social differentiation (and
the tensions generated by it) increased, all Christians were symbolically
integrated into "one harmonious order, the pure body of Christ."[213] On
certain days as sanctioned by *treuga Dei,* no one was allowed to injure
his fellows—that is, his fellow Christians. That the neighbor, the protected other, was Christian was made explicit.[214] If Christian society
was the body of Christ and individual Christians its members, it was
only logical to see injuring a Christian as injuring Christ Himself. This

---

207. Cowdrey 1970a, 50.
208. Rodulfus Glaber *Historiarvm* IV,v,16.
209. Ibid., IV,v,15. Cf. Goetz 1992, 276; Bredero 1994, 115.
210. Moore 1992, 325; Remensnyder 1992, 281–82.
211. Remensnyder 1992, 295; cf. 296–97.
212. Head 1992, 221.
213. Remensnyder 1992, 306.
214. Hoffmann 1964, 84.

crystal-clear—and one might say ultimate—idea of peace was formulated at the peace council of Narbonne, 1054. The injunction of God as declared in the council's first canon was that "no Christian should kill another Christian, for whoever kills a Christian undoubtedly sheds the blood of Christ." [215]

To understand this founding of the "spirit of peace" on the doctrine of the Mystical Body, rather than on the "natural morality that teaches respect for the human person," [216] we should compare the first canon of Narbonne with several statements that may be regarded as foreshadowing it. In 994, Ademar of Chabannes preached that attacking the "holy men" (the clergy) meant attacking God, for "one who touches you touches the apple of my eye" (Zech 2.8). [217] The peacemakers assembled at the Council of Limoges in 1031, debating the apostolicity of St. Martial, a military saint, maintained that whoever attacks bishops' subjects, attacks bishops (to whom *pauperes* had been entrusted); and he who attacks bishops (Christ's representatives on earth), attacks Christ. [218] Ademar and the Council of Limoges equated harming churchmen with harming God. The 1054 Council of Narbonne extended this equation to all Christians and then to Christ Himself. The prohibition of violent acts against Christians covered any single Christian and, as such, Christian society as a whole.

Comparison of the first canon of the 1054 Narbonne council with an earlier Carolingian, pseudo-Isidorian precept reveals yet another important shift that occurred at the council. The earlier rule prohibited the shedding of human blood. [219] Drawing on Genesis 9.6: "Whoever sheds the blood of a human, by a human shall that person's blood be shed," this Carolingian *capitulum* said a murderer should be punished "blood for blood." [220] With respect to its contents, this rule was certainly not a model for the canon of Narbonne. [221] The Carolingian forger spoke of

215. "Primo ergo omnium institutionum nostrarum. . . monemus, & mandamus secundum praeceptum Dei, & nostrum, ut nullus Christianorum alium quemlibet Christianum occidat: quia qui Christianum occidit, sine dubio Christi sanguinem fundit." *Concilium narbonense* c. 1 (Mansi 19: 827).
216. Delaruelle 1980, 73.
217. *Sermo* III (*Sermones tres Ademari*, PL 141: 120).
218. "Nam quicumque vobis subditos conturbant, vos conturbant: qui autem vos conturbant, Christum conturbant, cuius vice episcopi legatione funguntur." Mansi 19: 509.
219. "Quicumque effuderit humanum sanguinem, fundetur sanguis illius." *Benedicti capitularium collectio* II,1 (PL 97: 753).
220. Hoffmann 1964, 95 n. 15, rejecting Bonnaud Delamare's view (see n. 221). Cf. Sicard 1969, 85 n. 9.
221. As believed by Bonnaud Delamare 1939, 248–49.

the effusion of human blood; the councillors at Narbonne substituted, as it were, the word *Christian* for the word *human*.

Setting the prohibition regarding shedding Christian blood against the advancement of the ideas of the licitness of war and the recognition of the military profession creates a problem whose solution appears almost too obvious to ring true: the licit war was to be fought against non-Christians. Whereas a peaceful Christian society was united with God and was in God, peace need not—and moreover could not—be kept with the ungodly. The letter of 1063 in which Pope Alexander II stated that the laws that forbade the shedding of human blood did not protect either criminals or Saracens[222] supports this seemingly purely logical construction. Whether or not Alexander knew the canons of the 1054 Council of Narbonne, the pope's addressing the letter to the Archbishop of Narbonne becomes meaningful. He could not have chosen a better recipient. This is, of course, an ahistorical statement. But so, in my view, is playing down the importance of Alexander II's pronouncements by interpreting them as no more than an appeal to the doctrine of just war. In this interpretation, Alexander saw warfare against Saracens only as a defense and sanctioned it as an example of just war. Consequently, he did not declare wars against Muslims *ipso facto* just and licit.[223] In my view, he did precisely that (even if only by implication), and I consider the application of the concept of "just war" to this case unwarranted. Observing that the term *justum bellum* only rarely occurred in ecclesiastical statements on war in the eleventh century, it has been suggested that the just war doctrine has become "an enormous red herring drawn across the historian's path."[224] For a better idea of the importance of Alexander II's pronouncements, we should look at them in a broader historical context.

In the early years of the eleventh century, religious dynamics in the Latin West turned from inclusive to exclusive. Some historians have singled out the year 1010 as marking that turn.[225] In 1009, Caliph al-Hakim ordered the destruction of the Church of the Holy Sepulchre in Jerusalem. This was an exceptional case of persecution of the Christians under Muslim rule by a ruler who oppressed his Muslim subjects as well

222. See n. 106.
223. Bull 1993, 78; for the view opposite to his own (and supporting my argument here), Bull cites Pierre David, *Études historiques sur la Galice et le Portugal du VIᵉ au XIIᵉ siècle* (Lisbon, 1947), which has been unavailable to me.
224. Gilchrist 1988, 176, 178.
225. Landes 1992, 210. Cf. Bredero 1994, 124; and, generally, Moore 1987.

and whom medieval historians generally considered mad.[226] William of Tyre insinuated that "the caliph used this extreme measure to prove to the infidels that he was loyal to them. For the name of Christian was used as a reproach against him, because he was born of a Christian mother."[227] When news of the destruction reached the West the following year, making a deep impression upon western Christians, the Jews were made to suffer.[228] In the gathering storm of revengeful feeling they became the first scapegoats, and heretics were very soon to follow.[229] The society that was uniting itself in Christian love and peace was also fostering hatred.

The transition to religious exclusivism overlapped with another shift. The Christian world was entering an era of military expansion. The pagan and infidel inroads into the western Christian world had ended, and with them Latin Christians' defensive wars. The Latin Christians now launched military attacks. They set out to Christianize their pagan neighbors in the northern and eastern parts of the European peninsula and to reconquer the lands in Spain, southern Italy, and Sicily that they thought of as having been unjustly taken from them.[230] Coinciding as it did with the rise of religious exclusivism, Christian military expansion meant the spread of exclusivism—the military march of an exclusivist religion by means of which exclusivism itself became a religion. But this is looking too far ahead, to the time of the Crusades.

Those early military confrontations with the Muslims in the Mediterranean were partly efforts to repel Saracen pirates and partly expeditions in the hope of booty. A prominent role in that warfare was played by Pisans and Genoese, who sometimes joined forces (when they were not at war with each other). In 993, after Saracens had sacked Genoa, Genoese pursued the "sons of the devil" all the way to Sardinia and massacred them.[231] After this, the Latin Christians began to take the initiative. Reggio in Calabria, which had been in Saracen hands since 918, came under Pisan attack in 1005. In 1015 and 1016, Sardinia was set upon by joint Pisan and Genoese forces, with Pope Benedict VIII's sup-

226. See Peters 1985, 254, 258 f.; William of Tyre *History of Deeds* I,iv (1: 66). Al-Hakim's successors allowed the reconstruction of the church, which was completed in 1048. Peters 1985, 266 f. Cf. *History of Deeds* I,vi.

227. *History of Deeds* I,iv (1: 66).

228. Gieysztor 1948–50, 6: 13. But see France 1996, 47, that the West was actually quite ignorant of that event.

229. See Landes 1995, 41 ff.; 1992, 207 ff.; Lobrichon 1992; Moore 1992, 323 f.

230. See Erdmann 1930; 1935, 87 ff., 109 ff., 267 ff.; Rousset 1963, 202; Vismara 1974, 61 ff., 72; Becker 1988, 284, 306, 352; Morris 1991, 134 ff.; Mayer 1993, 17 ff.; generally, Phillips 1988, chap. 3.

231. Balard 1997, 13.

port. In 1034, the Pisans felt strong enough to assault Bône (al-'Anaba) on the North African coast. A Christian flotilla threatened Mahdia, in what is today Tunisia, in 1057. In 1064, the Pisans attacked Palermo. The campaign against Mahdia, in which its suburb Zawila was plundered as well, took place in 1087; and joint Pisan and Genoese attacks on Valencia and Tortosa followed in the early 1090s.[232] Normans, in agreement with the papacy, began the conquest of Sicily and Apulia at the beginning of the 1060s. On the Iberian Peninsula, Christians began to unite against Muslims on the initiative of Fernando I of Castile and León (1037–65), who undertook a series of campaigns in the 1050s and early 1060s. Conquest of Muslim territory continued under his son Alfonso VI (1065–1109).[233]

Pope Alexander II was undoubtedly aware of the campaigns of Fernando I, his contemporary. It is difficult to imagine that Alexander's statement about the licitness of shedding Saracen blood was completely unrelated to what was going on in Spain. Alexander in fact supported— moreover, explicitly advocated[234]—military campaigns against the Muslims in Spain, of which the siege of Barbastro in 1064 is perhaps the best known. More than a few Christian soldiers from north of the Pyrenees were engaged in these campaigns, which could be called defensive only by a stretch of the imagination. He assured the Christians fighting those campaigns that they had the approval of God. The pope promised them remission of their penance and forgiveness of sins.[235] In a letter to the bishops of Spain, in which he expressed his pleasure that they were protecting Jews who lived among them from persecution by those who were "proceeding into Spain against the Saracens," Alexander pointed out that "the cause of the Jews is indisputably different from that of the Saracens." The Jews had been saved by God's mercy to live in eternal penitence and subjugation, scattered all over the world; as such, they should

232. Scalia 1971, 571, 581; Cowdrey 1977, 13–14; Hettinger 1993, chap. 5. Cf. Manselli 1965, 133 ff.
233. Ferreiro 1983, 130.
234. Ibid., 133.
235. See the much discussed letter to the enigmatic "clero Vulturnensi" (Loewenfeld, *Epp. pontif. roman.*, no. 82 [p. 43]). While the letter does not seem to be connected to the Barbastro campaign (Ferreiro 1983, 134–35; Bull 1993, 73–75), there is no evidence either that it was not written for soldiers at all but for pilgrims. Riley-Smith 1997, 49, seems prone to accept this second possibility, referring to Bull, op cit., who, however, has left the question unresolved. Cf. Noth 1966, 119. The nature of Alexander's indulgence is a disputed issue among historians. Cf. Rousset 1945, 49–50; Laarhoven 1959–61, 22; Brundage 1969, 145 f.; 1976, 119; Becker 1988, 285 ff.; Morris 1991, 95; Mayer 1993, 18, 23 f., 293–95; Riley-Smith 1993a, 5.

not be killed. Against the Saracens, however, "who persecute Christians and expel them from their towns and dwelling-places," it was "just to fight." [236]

The Catalan bishops and other leaders from the Iberian peninsula who gathered in a peace council in 1064 in Barcelona appear to have similarly harbored no doubts about the righteousness of war against Saracens. Proclaiming *treuga et pace domini*, they vowed to lay aside any animosity against one another and unite their forces to undertake a campaign.[237] They did not need to specify that the planned offensive was directed against the Muslims. But the writer of a contemporary account of the capture of Barbastro, monk Amatus of Monte Cassino, did name the enemy. Praising the unification of the Christian princes as inspired by God, Amatus described the Christians who had gone to campaign in Spain as fighting for the destruction of the "hateful folly of the Saracens." [238]

In 1073, the year of Alexander II's death, his successor, Gregory VII, referred the case of Peter Raymundi (son of Raymond Berenger I, Count of Barcelona and a leader in the peace council of 1064),[239] who had murdered his stepmother, to "the cardinals of the Roman Church." One provision of the penance imposed on Peter Raymundi was that he "should on no account carry military arms, except in two contingencies: to defend himself against enemies, and to ride to battle against the Saracens." [240] The latter exception does not appear to have been limited to defensive wars.

I see Alexander II's statements on the licitness of fighting against and killing the Saracens as opening up a new perspective on the Christian use of arms, in that his statements laid out the coordinates for thinking about channeling permissible warfare in a specific direction. The novelty of this perspective should not be overestimated. First, the general idea of making war on non-Christians as the alternative to Christians killing each other was not unprecedented. Archbishop Agobard of Lyons, for example, reproached Emperor Louis the Pious in the early 830s for fomenting internal discord and strife instead of waging war "against

---

236. *Epistolae et diplomata* no. 101 (PL 146: 1386–87). Ewald 1880, 347, suggested that the letter was written in 1063; Bull 1993, 74, expressed some reservations.

237. Codex Escurialense Z. j. 4 9 (Fita 1890, 392). Cf. Ferreiro 1983, 132.

238. "Et à ce que la religion de la Foi christiane fust aëmplie, et macast detestable folie de li Sarrazin, par inspiration de Dieu, s'acorderent en una volenté li roy li conte et li prince en uno conseill." *Historia Normannorum* 5 (Smith 1988–89, 1: 84).

239. See Fita 1890.

240. See Cowdrey 1997, 21.

foreign peoples." A Christian emperor should fight and subjugate barbarians "for our perpetual peace" instead of barbarizing his own subjects.[241] Pope Hadrian II (867–72) urged King Louis the German to emulate Emperor Louis II and wage war "not against the sons of holy religion," not against faithful Christians of his own land, but against the "sons of Beliar" and "enemies of Christ's name."[242] Pope John VIII (872–82) categorically prohibited wars among Christians while calling for war against the enemies of Christ.[243] Brun of Querfurt, a Church reformer and a zealous advocate of armed missions against the pagan Slavs, sharply criticized Emperor Henry II for making an alliance in 1003 with the heathen Liutics against Christian King Boleslas Chrobry, who fought for Polish independence from the Saxon emperors. There was no fellowship between light and darkness, no agreement between Christ and Beliar! Instead of fighting Christians, the emperor should make war against the pagans to compel them to embrace Christianity (*compellere entrare*).[244] In the last years of the tenth century another religious reformer, Abbot Abbo of Fleury, while discussing the orders of society, instructed the soldiers (*agonistae*) to be content with their stipend and "not fight against each other in the womb of their mother, but wisely attack the enemies of the holy Church of God."[245] Moreover, the importance of Alexander's view should not be overestimated because during his pontificate Saracens had not yet been instituted as the enemy against whom Christian warfare was to be directed, as was the case later with the launching of the Crusades.

On the other hand, the novelty of the perspective introduced by Alexander and his contemporaries should not be underestimated. For the writers just cited, as well as their contemporaries, the image of the enemy was far from monolithic. For Bernard of Angers, writing his part of the *Liber miraculorum sancte Fidis* half a century before Alexander II was elected pope, false Christians were worse than pagans. Bernard's

241. *Libri duo pro filiis et contra Judith uxorem Ludovici pii* I,3 (MGH SS 15: 275–76; quoted in Morisi 1963, 170).

242. Hadrian to Louis of Germany, 12 Feb. 868 (MGH Epp. 6: 703); repeated in Hadrian to primores of Charles the Bald's kingdom, 5 Sept. 869 (op. cit., 717). Cf. Gilchrist 1988, 182.

243. John to counts of King Louis's realm, A.D. 876, *Epistolae et decreta* no. 23 (col. 674).

244. See Erdmann 1935, 65, 97; Wenskus 1956, 186 ff.; Morisi 1963, 215–23. Cf. Morrison 1969, 378–79. For the "fellowship between light and darkness," etc., see 2 Cor 6.14–15.

245. *Apologeticus ad Hugonem et Rodbertum reges francorum* (PL 139: 464). Cf. Flori 1983, 127 ff.; Constable 1995, 283.

warrior monk Gimon, as we learn, sought to encourage the fearful in his "armored ranks" by telling them that "they had a much greater obligation to vanquish false Christians who had attacked Christian law and willfully abandoned God than to subdue those pagans who had never known God."[246] Here not only are the pagans not presented as the worst of Christians' enemies; they are referred to only generically. Alexander II, on the other hand, specified Saracens as those among the "evil ones" (mali) whom it was permissible to kill. Moreover, unlike the statements of earlier popes and writers, his pronouncement was couched in legal, not moral, terms. With Alexander's declaration that killing the Saracens was licit, the right to kill was brought into the service of the well-being and safety of Christian society.[247] And with the singling out of a specific enemy, Christian violence began to be channeled in a precise direction.

THE BIRTH OF THE CRUSADE OUT OF THE SPIRIT OF PEACE

With the canonical declaration that "no Christian should kill another Christian, for whoever kills a Christian undoubtedly sheds the blood of Christ,"[248] the peace movement reached a critical moment of development: enjoining peace throughout Christian society. At approximately that point the peace movement was adopted by the reform papacy. Leo IX, for example, proclaimed the Peace of God in the synod of Rheims in 1049, and Nicholas II gave a general papal sanction to the Peace and Truce of God in the Lateran synod of 1059.[249] Alexander II was also involved in peacekeeping efforts.[250]

When Christian soldiers were prohibited from fighting within Christian society, an external outlet for Christian militancy was indicated in fairly specific and recognizable terms.[251] Christian milites were allowed to fight outside the body of Christ.[252] At first authorized to "rage against the multitude of those who ignore God" by refusing to enter a peace

246. Liber miraculorum sancte Fidis I,26.
247. "La pensée religieuse de l'Occident intègre le droit de tuer comme une des libertés de son salut." Alphandéry 1954, 27 (commenting on Alexander II's sentence).
248. See n. 215.
249. See Hoffmann 1964, 218–19; Blumenthal 1991, especially 142–44.
250. Blumenthal 1991, 138; for a sceptical view, see Hoffmann 1964, 119–20.
251. Cowdrey 1970a, 53.
252. Duby 1968a, 459–60 (commenting on the council of Narbonne). Cf. Keen 1987, 96 f.; Bredero 1994, 107.

pact,[253] soldiers eventually were directed to fight those seen as ignorant
of God: non-Christians—moreover, specified non-Christians—with
whom no peace pact was possible. What was initially permission was to
become a Christian soldier's mission.

The crusade was the consummation of the peace movement—its accomplishment and the realization of its ideals. It is true that this view,
propounded by a number of historians both before and after World War
II,[254] has recently been questioned. The argument that "the superficially
attractive link between the Peace and the crusade is a chimera,"[255] is
based on a study of the "actual experiences of the lay rank and file," as
opposed to ecclesiastics' theoretical pronouncements.[256] But basing a
general, polemical conclusion on study of a particular aspect of the crusades' history runs the danger of bending the stick too far to the other
side (to use a Leninist metaphor). Analysis of the lay response to the
preaching of the First Crusade surely diversifies our understanding of the
Crusades and may do away with superficial generalizations. Yet accepting that at "the heart of the crusade message lay an appeal to piety," that
crusaders were deeply religious, and that "the piety of nobles and knights
was profoundly influenced by the church," implies that the ideas of ecclesiastics, if not coextensive with those of lay crusaders,[257] must have
influenced them at least indirectly. The intellectual work of ecclesiastics
was after all often aimed at members of the lay aristocracy, and sometimes at broader audiences.[258] But the influence of ideas on social action is rarely direct. Ideas and images, rather, constitute a symbolic and
imaginary framework in which historical agents can conceive of acting
in certain ways to achieve certain goals, feel moved or compelled to act,
and make decisions to actually act (or not to act). Criticism of a "superficial link" between the peace movement and the crusade accepts as in-
contestable that "on the level of practical arrangements the Peace and the
crusade were associated from the beginning."[259] But since "practical
arrangements" are never stripped of ideas, but rather are enclosed in an
imaginary world and rest on specific ideas, I will try to point out not

253. See n. 54.
254. For example, Erdmann 1935, chap. 2; Rousset 1945, 195; Duby 1968a, 460.
255. Bull 1993, 23.
256. Bull 1993, 69. Cf. Riley-Smith 1997.
257. Bull 1993, 10, 14.
258. Cf. Powell 1996, 129, 137, 140 (discussing ecclesiastical historical narratives of
the First Crusade in the second half of the twelfth century and in the thirteenth century).
259. Bull 1993, 57.

only the practical links between the peace movement and the crusade but also imaginary and ideal links between them.

The crusade was embedded in an imagined world largely created by the peace movement. Some aspects of the crusade grew out of and fed on that world, from which it gained meaning and direction. If the peace movement generated imagery and fantasies that were an integral part of historical reality,[260] the crusade helped to materialize them. Of cardinal importance in this regard were the peace movement's messianism and eschatology.[261] And two images intimately connected with the millenarian expectations and apocalyptic concerns behind the *pax* and *treuga Dei* were those of Israel and Jerusalem.

In the language of messianism, the populace involved in the peace movement was identified with the children of Israel.[262] Ademar of Chabannes, for example, compared the people of Aquitaine with the children of Israel,[263] and Andrew of Fleury described the peace army from Bourges as the new people of Israel. "With the help of God they so terrified the rebels," he wrote, "that, as the coming of the faithful was proclaimed far and wide by rumor among the populace, the rebels scattered. Leaving the gates of their towns open, they sought safety in flight, harried by divinely inspired terror. You would have seen [the faithful] raging against the multitude of those who ignore God, as if they were some other people of Israel." [264] In the second half of the eleventh century, a monk from Charroux described the peace council of Limoges held in 994 thus: "It was to see the sons of Israel, after leaving the servitude of Egypt and crossing the Red Sea, wishing to enter the Promised Land with Moses, without any desire to follow the carnal desires of Egypt." [265] The new chosen people were preparing for a new exodus, but the Promised Land remained in the old place.

Pilgrimages to that Promised Land increased considerably in number at the turn of the millennium, and the movement of pilgrims to Palestine in the eleventh century was "widespread, continuous and intensive." [266]

---

260. Cf. Duby 1985, 215.
261. Cf. Becker 1988, 277; Goetz 1992, 277; Landes 1992, 200. See also Alphandéry 1954, 1959. For reservations, cf. Bull 1993, 13.
262. Landes 1992, 199.
263. Landes 1992, 193, 200; 1995, 31, 60.
264. *Miracula s. Benedicti* V,2; trans. in Head and Landes 1992b, app. A, 340. Cf. Hoffmann 1964, 108; Duby 1985, 218; Goetz 1992, 277; Head 1992, 224; Landes 1992, 199.
265. Quoted in Landes 1995, 29–30.
266. Cf. Gieysztor 1948–50, 6: 24; Alphandéry 1954, 10 f.; Brundage 1969, 9; Töpfer 1992, 50; Mayer 1993, 26 f.; France 1996, 48–50; Riley-Smith 1997, chap. 1.

The symbolism of the year 1000 may be a legend created by historians, as was pointed out long ago;[267] Latin Christians may not have approached the millennium of the Incarnation "in fear and trembling and emerged thereafter relieved and reinvigorated," as largely Romantic nineteenth-century historiography used to believe.[268] Nevertheless, the enthusiasm for undertaking the long and dangerous journey to visit Jerusalem and see the Sepulchre of Christ became a mass movement,[269] culminating in the First Crusade as "the largest of the mass pilgrimages of the eleventh century."[270] Jerusalem dominated the eschatological horizon. The mental picture of the Holy City was of special importance in the piety of that age, and for the people of those times, the very sound of the name must have had a "glittering and magical splendour."[271]

The pilgrims to the Promised Land not only carried images of Jerusalem and the holy places with them; as they journeyed to the Orient they moved within the mental world those images formed. When they trod upon the way to Jerusalem they saw themselves following the "path of salvation, the road to a better future." Simple, uneducated people were "filled with dim, vague, and incoherent eschatological dreams, probably pictured in an entirely material fashion."[272] The pilgrimage was a journey through fantasy. Steps followed the imagination. It was fantasy that drew the limits of the world; the boundary between fiction and reality blurred. Just as the peace movement neither distinguished between secular and spiritual peace nor saw a contradiction between temporal and eternal peace,[273] so too, in the imagination of the movement's protagonists the heavenly and earthly Jerusalems merged. This was true for the still-unarmed pilgrims as well as for the crusaders for whom they paved the way.[274] The intimate connection between the two Jerusalems affected

267. "Man hat hier früher mit der angeblichen Bedeutung des Jahres 1000 operirert, die inzwischen längst als Legende verworfen ist." Erdmann 1932, 384.
268. Landes 1995, 16–17. Much more recently, Duby 1985, 238, wrote about "[m]ankind, unified, renovated after the troubles of the millennium, reconciled again with their God, . . . embarking on the journey towards salvation."
269. Landes 1995, 154–58.
270. Riley-Smith 1997, 39.
271. Rousset 1945, 187; McGinn 1978, 40; Riley-Smith 1992, 7; Mayer 1993, 10–11; 1997, 26. For a medieval image of Jerusalem, see Bredero 1994, chap. 3, and references in McGinn 1978, 60 n. 43. For traditional Christian background, Wilken 1992. And, generally, Peters 1985.
272. Mayer 1993, 12.
273. Goetz 1992, 277.
274. McGinn 1978, 48; Cohn 1993, 64–65; Mayer 1993, 11; Bredero 1994, 82 ff.

ways of thinking and acting.[275] What the pilgrims to the Promised Land saw in their minds' eye was the heavenly Jerusalem,[276] the sacred city from the Book of Revelation: "the holy city Jerusalem coming down out of heaven from God" (Rev 21.10).

Symbolic links were forged between the sites associated with the peace movement and Jerusalem, and the paths pilgrims journeyed knitted them together. A "new intimacy" developed between Jerusalem and the Christian West.[277] Glaber's narrative oscillated between Cluny and Jerusalem.[278] A link was forged between Limoges and Jerusalem around the cult of St. Martial. Limoges was interpreted as the New Jerusalem, as was Angoulême, another town in Aquitaine. The vision of a weeping crucifix at Orléans made the people think of this royal city as the New Jerusalem. There were still other New Jerusalems; one may speak of a phenomenon of *translatio Ierosolymae,* the translation of Jerusalem to the West.[279] The discovery of a head (actually, one of the heads) attributed to John the Baptist in an Aquitanian village in 1016 only strengthened this phenomenon.[280] It also added another dimension to the symbolic connection between Jerusalem and the West. From the places to which the apostles had walked westward enthusiastic pilgrims now journeyed eastward, to where the apostles had come from—to Jerusalem, the fountainhead of the Faith. The apostles and the pilgrims walked the same paths.[281] But because the boundary between fantasy and what we commonly call reality was very thin and fluid, because images tended to materialize, and because the world that imagination pictured was a fairly material one, the nets entangling Jerusalem were not merely symbolic. Before the turn of the eleventh century, Jerusalem fell to Christian forces. Those who destroyed it, the army of the new chosen people, had already built an image of the New Jerusalem in their minds' eye.

The peace movement's practical, or institutional, arrangements also enabled the Christian capture and destruction of Jerusalem—the crowning act of the First Crusade. The council of Clermont, where Pope Urban II preached the crusade in 1095, universalized the peace movement's

---

275. See McGinn 1978, 41; Bredero 1994, 89 ff.
276. Mayer 1993, 11.
277. Landes 1992, 204.
278. Duby 1985, 239.
279. Landes 1992, 193, 204; 1995, 60, 164, 167, 213, 304–7.
280. Landes 1992, 193, 198–99; 1995, 47–48; Töpfer 1992, 49.
281. Landes 1992, 204.

legislation. This could not have happened had the Gregorian Church reform not asserted papal supremacy within the Church itself as well as within Christian society—that is, had it not established an authority strong enough to universalize the peace movement's goals and provisions. To understand the importance of the peace movement's institutional arrangements for the crusade, we should thus not lose sight of the reformist popes' peace endeavors. I have already mentioned that these popes supported the Peace and Truce of God. None of the eleventh-century popes, however, was a more prominent peacemaker than Urban II.

As a Frenchman and a Cluniac monk and prior, Odo of Châtillon, the future Pope Urban, must have been acquainted with the peace movement in his home country. As archdeacon of Reims, he must have learned about Pope Leo IX's promulgation of the Peace of God in that diocese in 1049.[282] As Urban II he was an active promoter of peace throughout his pontificate (1088–99). He proclaimed the *treuga Dei* in councils at Melfi (1089) and Troia (1093) in southern Italy, and at Clermont (1095).[283] Reporting on the Council of Clermont, Fulcher of Chartres conveyed how the pope commanded that the Truce of God should be renewed: "I earnestly admonish each of you to strictly enforce it in your own diocese. But if anyone, smitten by greed or pride, willingly infringes this truce, let him be anathema by virtue of the authority of God and by sanction of the decrees of this council."[284]

The Council of Clermont was a peace council. It gave new meaning and new momentum to the peace movement.[285] The *treuga* stipulations of this council, quite conventionally, defined the days of the week and times of year when violence had to cease and protected all the men who did not fight *uuerra*—the clergy, monks, pilgrims, merchants, peasants —and women, as well as animals, except horses used in fighting. Peace was to last for three years.[286] Through the canons of Clermont, *treuga Dei* definitively entered the papal legislation. Whereas until then the peace movement had been carried on predominantly under regional auspices and its regulations had correspondingly been local, the peace legislation was now universalized. The Truce of God proclaimed by the

282. Becker 1964, 33–51; Hoffmann 1964, 220; Bull 1993, 62.
283. Hefele 1912–13, 5.1: 345, 367, 372; Fliche 1929, 311–12; Hoffmann 1964, 220–21; Becker 1988, 277; Cole 1991, 2; Bredero 1994, 126–27.
284. *Historia Iherosolymitana* I,ii,14 (p. 323); *A History of the Expedition*, 65. In 1094, Urban intervened in Beauvais in a case of violation of the Truce. Hoffmann 1964, 221.
285. Hoffmann 1964, 221.
286. See the canons as formulated in different editions, described and reproduced in Somerville 1972, 73–74, 94–95, 108, 113, 124, and the summary, 143.

Council of Clermont was binding on the whole of Christendom.[287] Urban II was the first pope to proclaim a general Peace of God.[288] The Council of Clermont was thus epoch-marking, but only because it was the climax of an epoch of peacemaking.[289]

The Council of Clermont, however, was also epoch-making, for it linked the peace movement with the crusade. The Peace and Truce of God arrangements became institutional elements of the holy war organized by the Church under the guidance of the pope. The Peace promulgated at Clermont protected the crusaders' person, property, and families.[290] The duration of the Peace proclaimed at Clermont was determined by the expected length of the crusade.[291] Peace and stability in the West were crucial for the expedition to Palestine,[292] but exporting war to the East also secured peace in the West. For Latin Christians, the crusade was a kind of Truce of God.[293] And the crusade was itself a struggle for peace: the last war in bringing about the peace of God.[294]

The close connection between the peace movement's endeavors and the crusade was also articulated in the document known as the encyclical of Sergius IV. Sergius was pope between 1009 and 1012, but the document appears to have been forged in the Cluniac abbey of St. Peter in Moissac, in the vicinity of Toulouse, decades later, not long after the Council of Clermont. Pope Urban II stayed at Moissac in May 1096, during the tour of France when he preached the crusade at Clermont, and it is not impossible to imagine that he inspired the composition of this piece of crusading propaganda.[295] The encyclical demanded in the name of God Almighty and all the saints that all churches and provinces, places and people, the great and the small maintain peace among them-

---

287. Hefele 1912–13, 5.1: 400; Rousset 1945, 55; Hoffmann 1964, 225; Vismara 1968, 1193; Cowdrey 1970a, 57; McGinn 1978, 44; Becker 1988, 279; Robinson 1990, 326, 331.

288. Erdmann 1935, 105.

289. Cf. MacKinney 1930, 200.

290. Somerville 1972, 108 (*Codex laurentianus* c. 2). Cf. Hoffmann 1964, 223; Bull 1993, 58. A special aspect of legal protection of the crusader was securing peace within the crusading army: The "pax" or "treuga Dei," or their elements, were taken over and transformed into "leges pacis in exercitu." These developments became prominent at the time of the Second Crusade. See Conrad 1941 (for the "leges pacis in exercitu," 72 n. 4, 79).

291. Somerville 1972, 124 (*Codex Cencii* c. 10).

292. For Bull 1993, 57, here lies the "broad relevance of the Peace to the crusade." Cf. Hoffmann 1964, 223.

293. Rousset 1945, 10, 19, 196.

294. Dupront 1969, 45.

295. See Gieysztor 1948–50, especially 6: 20–28. For Urban's itinerary, see Becker 1988, app., 435 ff. For a recent opinion that the document is genuine, cf. Landes 1995, 41 n. 97.

selves, since without peace no one can serve God. Through the peace
and prayer of all Christians, victory was to be won for the Redeemer's
sepulcher, and eternal life gained.[296] The encyclical's *pax Christi* and
the Council of Clermont's *treuga Dei* were "inseparably interrelated
ideas."[297]

When Urban II preached the crusade, he drew upon what the peace
movement had achieved. The injunctions of the Peace of God had de-
flected the aggressive forces harbored by Christian society away from
Christendom and suggested that against the infidel enemies of God it
was not only permissible but eminently salutary to use arms.[298] Those
injunctions had not been proclaimed in vain. Thanks to the new power
of the papacy, Urban II realized the peace movement's potential by uni-
versalizing its ideals and legislation and—to secure peace within Christendom—turned Christian weapons against the Saracens.[299] He made
the decisive step beyond the first canon of the Council of Narbonne of
1054 (which had prohibited the shedding of Christian blood) and in the
direction imaginatively opened by Pope Alexander II (who had declared
that the shedding of Saracen blood was licit). Under Urban II's pontificate, the idea of diverting war among Christians to war against non-
Christians materialized in an institutional form, or to be precise, in a
form that was to become institutionalized. Moral condemnation of sinful fratricidal wars among Christians was complemented with represen-
tations of wars against the enemies of God as meritorious. The first were
spurred by the devil; the latter were divinely ordered.

Urban's preaching of the crusade at Clermont has survived only in
narratives of chroniclers, most of whom wrote after the fact, with the
knowledge that the First Crusade was a success. The authenticity of the
words ascribed to the pope is therefore questionable. These renderings
of Urban II's sermon, however, authentically express the spirit of the age:
the spirit out of which the crusade had been born, which was, in turn,
invigorated and colored by the successful crusade.[300] Significantly, all
chroniclers agree that in his famous speech the pope exhorted Christians

---

296. The Encyclical of Sergius IV lines 26–27, 30 (Gieysztor 1948–50, 6: 34).

297. Gieysztor 1948–50, 6: 28; "pax Christi": The Encyclical of Sergius IV line 28
(ibid., 34). Cf. Hoffmann 1964, 224.

298. Duby 1974, 164.

299. Cf. Hefele 1912–13, 5.1: 401; Hoffmann 1964, 223; Cowdrey 1970a, 57.

300. Cf. Morris 1983, that these texts illustrate the early history of crusade preaching,
"even if they are not really reminiscences of Clermont."

to stop fighting iniquitous fratricidal wars and to march instead into a just battle against non-Christians.[301]

Fulcher of Chartres reported that the pope, in his "exhortation concerning a pilgrimage to Jerusalem," declared that the military successes of the Turks against the Greeks must be stopped. "They have seized more and more of the lands of the Christians, have already defeated them in seven times as many battles, killed or captured many people, have destroyed churches, and have devastated the kingdom of God." God urged "men of all ranks whatsoever, mounted warriors as well as foot-soldiers, rich and poor," to hasten to action. In the name of Christ, the pope promised the remission of sins for those who would fight the pagans, and—according to Fulcher—he added: "Oh what a disgrace if a race so despicable, degenerate, and enslaved by demons should thus overcome a people endowed with faith in Almighty God and resplendent in the name of Christ! Oh what reproaches will be charged against you by the Lord Himself if you have not helped those who are counted like yourself of the Christian faith!" The climax of his exhortation was the idea of transforming molesters of the faithful into soldiers of Christ, *milites Christi*, of turning fratricidal war into a just war against the infidels. " 'Let those,' he said, 'who are accustomed to wantonly wage private war against the faithful march upon the infidels in a war which should be begun now and be finished in victory. Let those who have long been robbers now be soldiers of Christ. Let those who have once fought against brothers and relatives now rightfully fight against barbarians.' "[302]

The version of Urban's speech reported by Baldric of Bourgueil, Archbishop of Dol, differed from that of Fulcher of Chartres, but the ideas conveyed are very similar. According to Baldric, Urban called upon his listeners to put aside the godless warfare to which they were accustomed and to take up instead the warfare of Christ. They should become Christ's soldiers, whose ordained task had been prefigured in God's plan by the ancient sons of Israel; and like the ancient sons of Israel but now with Jesus as their commander, they should rush to defend the Holy Land and the Church from foreign intruders.[303] "Listen and understand. You have strapped on the belt of soldiery and strut around with pride in your eye. You butcher your brothers and create factions among your-

301. Munro 1905, 239. Cf. Erdmann 1935, chap. 10; Cowdrey 1970b; Robinson 1990, 326–27; Cole 1991, chap. 1; Riley-Smith 1993a, chap. 1, 6.
302. *Historia Iherosolymitana* I,iii,3–7 (p. 324); *A History of the Expedition*, 66–67.
303. Cf. Cole 1991, 18.

selves. This, which scatters the sheepfold of the Redeemer, is not the
army of Christ. The Holy Church keeps for herself an army to come to
the aid of her own people, but you pervert it with knavery." The pope
warned the soldiers that, behaving that way, they were condemning
themselves to damnation. They might hope for the rewards of brigands,
but the path they were following did not lead to life. Oppression of orphans, robbing of widows, blaspheming, plundering, committing homicides—in short, shedding Christian blood—was certainly "the worst
course to follow because it is utterly removed from God." But there was
a solution at hand. Giving counsel for their souls, the pope confronted
Christian warriors with a clear choice: "[Y]ou must either cast off as
quickly as possible the belt of this sort of soldiery or go forward boldly
as soldiers of Christ, hurrying swiftly to defend the eastern Church." Urban then explained that he was saying all this so that "you may restrain
your murderous hands from the destruction of your brothers, and in behalf of your relatives in the faith oppose yourself to the Gentiles." And,
as Baldric tells us, he repeated the same thought for the third time: "You
should shudder, brethren, you should shudder at raising a violent hand
against Christians; it is less wicked to brandish your sword against Saracens. It is the only warfare that is righteous." [304]

Another report in which Urban II appears as having been inspired by
the Old Testament was written by Guibert of Nogent. In Guibert's *Gesta
Dei per Francos,* the pope (among other things) recalled the Maccabees
and then called on the "Christian soldiers" to imitate them. The imitation consisted in changing meritorious "holy battles," *prealia sancta,*[305]
for iniquitous fratricidal wars. "If in olden times the Maccabees attained
to the highest praise of piety because they fought for the ceremonies and
the Temple, it is also justly granted you, Christian soldiers, to defend the
liberty of your country by armed endeavour." The country in question
was the country where Christ had left His footprints on earth, and
defending its liberty meant rescuing "the Cross, the Blood, the Tomb,"
visiting the Holy City, "now polluted by the concourse of the Gentiles."
There was no reason why Christian soldiers should refuse to leave for
those places. "You have thus far," the pope is said to have spoken to
them, "waged unjust wars, at one time and another; you have bran-
dished mad weapons to your mutual destruction, for no other reason

304. Baldric of Dol *Historia Jerosolimitana* I,iv (pp. 14–15); trans. in Peters 1989, 9;
Riley-Smith 1993a, 149.
305. *Gesta Dei per Francos* I,i (p. 124).

than covetousness and pride, as a result of which you have deserved eternal death and sure damnation. We now hold out to you wars which contain the glorious reward of martyrdom, which will retain that title of praise now and forever." What Urban proposed to Christian soldiers was to be "zealous in the practice of holy battles," to repulse the might of the pagans "with the co-operation of God," to "engage in his battles," in short, "to be the soldiery of God." [306]

The opening words of Urban II's crusading speech as related by Robert the Monk in his *Historia Iherosolimitana* are a celebration of the Franks as people chosen and beloved by God, set apart from all nations by their catholic faith and the "honor of the holy church." To them the pope addressed his discourse; for them his exhortation was intended. Because God had conferred on them "remarkable glory in arms," it was upon them to avenge the wrongs afflicted on eastern Christians by the accursed race "from the kingdom of the Persians" and "liberate" the places made illustrious by the Redeemer's life and death on earth. The argument with which Urban hoped to move these valiant people and incite their minds to "manly achievements," was curiously materialistic. In Baldric of Dol's version of Urban II's speech as well, the pope promised material gains to the would-be crusaders: "The possessions of the enemy, too, will be yours, since you will make spoil of their treasures and return victoriously to your own." [307] But whereas in Baldric's report this was a subsidiary point, in Robert's chronicle it was the burden of the argument. The pope first explained that the violence infesting the Frankish lands was due to scarcity of land and wealth. "[T]his land which you inhabit, shut in on all sides by the seas and surrounded by the mountain peaks, is too narrow for your large population; nor does it abound in wealth; and it furnishes scarcely food enough for its cultivators. Hence it is that you murder one another, that you wage war, and that frequently you perish by mutual wounds." Then he posed the conquest of the Promised Land as the means of establishing peace at home. "Let therefore hatred depart from among you," Urban exhorted his Franks, "let your quarrels end, let wars cease, and let all dissensions and controversies slumber. Enter upon the road to the Holy Sepulchre; wrest that land from the wicked race, and subject it to yourselves." If the Franks were the chosen people, that land was rightfully theirs anyway: "That land which as the

---

306. Ibid., II,iv (pp. 138–39); trans. in Peters 1989, 12–15; cf. Guibert of Nogent, *Deeds of God,* 43–44.

307. *Historia Jerosolimitana* I,iv (p. 15); Peters 1989, 9.

Scripture says 'floweth with milk and honey,' was given by God into the possession of the children of Israel." [308]

Robert also reported that when "Pope Urban said these and very many similar things in his urbane discourse, he so influenced to one purpose the desires of all who were present, that they cried out, 'It is the will of God! It is the will of God!'" And when the pontiff heard all present uttering, in one voice, the same cry, he declared that *Deus vult!*—the crusaders' war-cry.[309] A great Enlightenment historian, Edward Gibbon, writing about this event, observed that the "cold philosophy of modern times is incapable of feeling the impression that was made on a sinful and fanatic world. At the voice of their pastor, the robber, the incendiary, the homicide, arose by thousands to redeem their souls, by repeating on the infidels the same deeds which they had exercised against their Christian brethren; and the terms of atonement were eagerly embraced by offenders of every rank and denomination."[310] The crusade, of course, was not as alien to the Enlightenment as these remarks may suggest. Gibbon himself had doubts not about the decision to launch the First Crusade but about the "proportion" of the Christian military offensive.[311] What is important here, however, is to understand that war-cry—*Deus vult!* or the vernacular *Deus le volt!*—as an expression of the piety of the crusaders, as a manifestation of "popular theology" in which God's will was absolute.[312] Just as the peace movement was inspired by God and the peace it brought was ordered by God, so the crusade, for which the peace movement was in many ways the precursor and in which it found its fulfillment, was a war willed by God.

---

308. *Roberti Monachi historia Iherosolimitana* I,i–ii (pp. 727–29); Peters 1989, 2–4.

309. *Roberti Monachi historia* I,ii (p. 729); Peters 1989, 4.

310. *The Decline and Fall*, chap. 58 (3: 567).

311. Partner 1997, 282. (Unfortunately I received this highly relevant book too late to make more than a few passing references to it.)

312. "*Deus le volt!* répondrait à une conception sommaire et globale de Dieu et da sa volonté, sorte de théologie populaire. . . . Cet absolu de la volonté divine, nous le retrouvons chez pluspart des historiens de la époque." Lacroix 1974, 469.

TWO

The Holy Manner of Warfare

In the aftermath of the First Crusade, Guibert of Nogent wrote: "In our own time God has instituted a holy manner of warfare [*instituit nostro tempore praelia sancta Deus*], so that knights [*ordo equestris*] and the common people who, after the ancient manner of paganism, were formerly immersed in internecine slaughter, have found a new way of winning salvation. They no longer need, as formerly they did, entirely to abandon the world by entering a monastery or by some other similar commitment. They can obtain God's grace in their accustomed manner and dress, and by their ordinary way of life." [1]

Guibert was a well-known scholar, and his history of the crusade is said to be the work of a mature and thoughtful man. [2] In the passage just quoted he masterfully depicted in a few lines the change in the Church's attitude toward warfare—a key feature of the great social transformation of the eleventh century that has been termed an "entry into a new world." [3] The reformed Church had recognized the military profession and found for Christian arms-bearers an employment pleasing to God. After "the judgement of Pope Urban granted remission of sins to every Christian setting out to overcome the Gentiles," the mind of a man no longer needed to be "torn two ways, uncertain which path to follow,

---

1. *Gesta Dei per Francos* I,i (p. 124); *The Deeds of God,* 28. (I follow the translation in Cowdrey 1973, 294.)
2. Cole 1991, 27; Riley-Smith 1993a, 136.
3. Rousset 1945, 7.

that of the Gospel, or that of the world."[4] War became a virtue, and "armies were summoned by the trumpet blasts of the Prince of Peace."[5] Deplorable inter-Christian, fratricidal wars were diverted into meritorious, soul-saving combat against non-Christians.

This kind of warfare was new, according to Guibert, and he called it holy. But how right was he to claim that *instituit nostro tempore praelia sancta Deus*—that it was really in his own time that God instituted a holy manner of warfare? How right was he to see this holy war as a historically new phenomenon?

It is a commonplace in our own time to regard the crusade as holy war. But commonplaces most often suspend, rather than enhance, understanding. If I may borrow Bentham's metaphor of nonsense upon stilts, truisms are stilts upon which common sense walks out of what it either cannot or does not want to grasp. I am not saying that the crusade was not holy war. To the contrary, I maintain it was holy war *par excellence,* or rather, that holy war was at the core of the crusade. But there are at least two problems with the common view of the crusade as holy war.

First, though bibliographies of crusade research fill many books, holy war has not been given the attention it deserves.[6] Consequently, it is not surprising that "after nearly a millennium of interest and centuries of academic study, very few people have any clear idea of what crusade was."[7] In fact, it seems that the *idea* of crusade has never been very clear. This is especially true for the beginnings of the crusade itself. What we usually take to be the concept of crusade, or "the crusade idea," appears on closer study to have been something much vaguer: a mentality, a "psychology" or "spirituality of great numbers," a "state of mind," that is, a magma of images, beliefs, fantasies, expectations, feelings, and sentiments.[8]

Of course there were ideas involved in the crusades, even if, as always, a gulf separated the intellectual abstractions elaborated by theologians from the motives that moved ordinary men and women.[9] But the ideas—as different from that "imprecise set of attitudes and habits"[10] just mentioned—followed, rather than directed, the crusade. The "crusade idea" was formed after the fact in the half century following the

4. Ralph of Caen *Gesta Tancredi in expeditione Hierosolymitana* I; quoted in Bull 1993, 4.
5. Morris 1983, 79.
6. Riley-Smith 1977, 16; Johnson 1997, 30, 43.
7. Riley-Smith 1977, 11.
8. Cf. Rousset 1945, 10–11; Alphandéry 1954, 2, 9; Dupront 1969, 19–20.
9. Riley-Smith 1992, xxvii.
10. Tyerman 1988, 21.

First Crusade.[11] In fact, for a long time the crusade had no formal name: the vernacular term *croiserie* appeared in the second half of the thirteenth century, and *crux* at about the same time.[12] A name for crusaders—*crucesignati,* persons signed by the cross—first appeared in the mid-twelfth century but came under more consistent use only with the pontificate of Innocent III at the turn of the twelfth century.[13] For a long period the crusade was without a clear legal status, for a juridical theory of crusade was formulated only in the mid-thirteenth century.[14] Yet though the crusade idea came after the crusade itself, certain elements, including the crucial ideas of penitential and salvatory violence, were involved in the formation of the crusade movement. If most educated clerics had not upheld these ideas, the Church would probably not have dared to encourage laymen to resort to arms.[15] These ideas on violence found clear expression in the phenomenon of holy war.

The second problem with the common understanding of the crusade as holy war is the absence of the concept of holy war among the crusaders themselves. It might be unfair to expect from those mostly illiterate men and also women who joined the armed, and unarmed, Christian bands intent on wrestling the holy places from the hands of the "unclean races" to have conceptualized what they were doing. On their journey to Jerusalem these people lived their holy war, but they did not give it a name.[16] They may have been convinced that they were fulfilling the intentions of God, that they were fighting God's war with God literally on their side;[17] but what has survived of those convictions are "startling images," "very crudely expressed," and "not justified in terms that would have made them acceptable to theologians."[18]

Nor did educated men use the concept of holy war. The term is not to be found in chronicles of the First Crusade.[19] The chroniclers used, instead, descriptive terms such as *bellum spirituale* (spiritual—not carnal—war), *bella Domini* (the Lord's wars), *praelia Domini* (the Lord's battles), *praelium Dei* (God's battle), *opus Domini* (the Lord's work), *prealium in nomine Domini Jesu-Christi* (battle in the name of Lord Je-

---

11. Blake 1970. Cf. chap. 3 n. 338.
12. Villey 1942, 252; Constable 1953, 237 n. 130; Riley-Smith 1977, 12.
13. Markowski 1984.
14. Villey 1942, 256–62; Russell 1975, 206; Gilchrist 1985.
15. Riley-Smith 1992, xxvii. Cf. Alphandéry 1954, 9.
16. Dupront 1969, 32.
17. Riley-Smith 1993a, chap. 4, especially 99, 107, 118. Cf. McGinn 1978, 49 ff.
18. Riley-Smith 1993a, 119.
19. Cf. Dupront 1969, 32; Delaruelle 1980, 125.

sus Christ), and probably more often than any other term, *peregrinatio* (pilgrimage).[20] Moreover, the papal appeals for crusading almost never used the word *war* itself.[21] Gratian's *Decretum*, the authoritative compilation of canon law completed around 1140, only *described* holy war, without using the term. In his discussion of just war, Gratian supplemented the classical doctrine of just war with a significant qualification: Whereas in Isidore of Seville (to whom Gratian referred) a necessary requirement for just war was that it is proclaimed by legitimate worldly authority,[22] Gratian added (citing Augustine) that a war ordered by God is, without any doubt, also just. In such wars, he explained, the commander of the army and the people are not authors of war but servants of God. Such were the wars fought by the sons of Israel.[23] This description may be applied to crusading, though there is no mention of the crusade in the *Decretum*.[24] We can only speculate whether Gratian had crusading in mind when he was justifying the use of violence in the service of the Church and on its command.[25] The *Decretum* could be regarded as a sourcebook for later crusade propagandists, since Gratian, more than any of his predecessors, contributed to the conceptual transformation of war into an ecclesiastical institution.[26] What is telling here is the absence of the holy war concept and the silence on the crusade—characteristic of twelfth-century thought in general.[27]

In view of this, Guibert of Nogent's naming the crusade a "holy manner of warfare" (*praelium sanctum*) in the aftermath of the First Crusade appears exceptional. Thus it can be argued that the abbot of Nogent offered the first specific definition of the crusade.[28] Compared with descriptive terms in use during and well beyond his time, such as *pilgrimage*, *journey*, and *way*, in combination with *Jerusalem*, *Sepulchre*, *Lord*, *God*, and *Jesus Christ*,[29] Guibert's definition indeed presented a concept,

20. See Rousset 1945, 74; Constable 1953, 237.

21. Schwerin 1937, 39, found *bellum* used only in Honorius III's and Innocent III's documents relating to the Crusades.

22. "Iustum est bellum, quod ex edicto geritur" etc. *Decretum* C.XXIII q.1 c.1. In Isidore of Seville: "Iustum bellum est quod ex praedicto geritur" etc. *Etym.* XVIII,i,2.

23. *Decretum* C.XXIII q.ii c.2–3.

24. Villey 1942, 256.

25. Riley-Smith 1992, 93.

26. Brundage 1976, 106; Riley-Smith 1992, 93.

27. Morris 1991, 277.

28. Cardini 1992b, 387.

29. For example, *iter Hierosolimitanum, Dominicum, sepulcri Domini; via Jesu-Christi, Dei, sepulcri Domini, sancta; expeditio Hierosolimitana, Dei.* See Villey 1942, 248 ff.; Rousset 1945, 70; Constable 1953, 237 n. 130. Pope Alexander III spoke of those

even if not yet a clear one.[30] Strictly speaking, Guibert's *praelium sanctum* did not mean holy war, *bellum sacrum*. But the distinction between *praelium* (battle, struggle) and *bellum* (war) is of a later date, apparently formulated by Innocent IV in the context of doctrinal elaboration of the just war and in conformity with Decretalists' aim to systematically limit feudal warfare. Just war, *justum bellum,* was war that a prince with no superior could wage against enemies who, along with their possessions, belonged to the jurisdiction of another, inferior prince. All other military activity—even if it otherwise met the requirements of a just war—did not have the legal status of a war but fell into the category of *justum praelium.*[31] But let us stay in Guibert's time.

All contemporary writers recognized that the crusade was something new,[32] or at least exceptional. Robert the Monk, for example, asked rhetorically: "But apart from the mystery of the healing cross, what more marvelous deed has there been since the creation of the world than that which was done in modern times in this journey of our men of Jerusalem?"[33] Guibert, however, differed from his contemporaries in that he not only was aware of the novelty of the crusade but also conceptualized this new phenomenon, even if only vaguely. If he claimed that holy war in his own time was new, this was not because he did not know of holy wars in past times. At the very least, he would have been well versed in the holy wars of the Maccabees and Israelites.[34] Thus we can understand him as conceiving of the crusade as holy war of a new type. Taking this understanding of the crusade as my departure point, I address the questions of why the crusade was holy war, and why it was holy war of a new type.

JUST WAR, HOLY WAR, THE CRUSADE

Holy war in the broadest sense is war conceived of as a religious action or as a military action directly related to religion.[35] In slightly less abstract terms, holy war is a war waged by spiritual power or fought un-

who "visited" the Lord's Sepulchre. Villey 1942, 213. For further expressions used in the papal crusading letters, see Schwerin 1937, 45.

30. Cardini 1992b, 387.

31. See Russell 1975, 173. Cf. n. 71.

32. Daniel 1989a, 6. Cf. Riley-Smith 1993a, 139 ff.

33. *Historia Iherosolimitana,* preface (p. 723); trans. in Riley-Smith 1993a, 140.

34. See chap. 1 n. 306. Cf. Cole 1991, 27 f.; Riley-Smith 1993a, 141 f.

35. Erdmann 1935, 1. For a more comprehensive characterization of holy war, see Johnson 1997, 37–42.

der the auspices of a spiritual power and for religious interests.[36] It is a war fought for the goals or ideals of the faith and waged by divine authority or on the authority of a religious leader.[37] War in the name of God is war in which God is felt as actively present and in which the warriors—instruments in divine hands—are executing God's will. It is war as divine service, pleasing to God and meritorious in His eyes, in which the deeds of the soldiers are divine work (*opus Dei*).[38] As such, holy war is suprahuman—and correspondingly inhuman. The very spirituality of holy war—the vengeance of God as the motive of war, the execution of divine righteousness by "soldiers of God"—commands, and materializes in, a fight without mercy. A war for the holiest cause, religion, fought under God and with His help by godly soldiers against ungodly enemies "shall be prosecuted unsparingly."[39] Brutality in warfare becomes the expression of religious consistency. Gaining victory means a fight to extermination,[40] and grand victory means a great massacre.[41]

The drive for absolute victory in a war fought for the Absolute is exemplified by the fall of Jerusalem at the crusaders' hands. "No-one has ever seen or heard of such a slaughter of pagans," a chronicler of the crusade noted.[42] Raymond of Aguilers wrote the following vivid account:

> But now that our men had possession of the walls and towers, wonderful sights were to be seen. Some of our men (and this was more merciful) cut off the heads of their enemies; others shot them with arrows, so that they fell from the towers; others tortured them longer by casting them into flames. Piles of heads, hands, and feet were to be seen in the streets of the city. It was necessary to pick one's way over the bodies of men and horses. But these were small matters compared to what happened at the Temple of Solomon, a place where religious services are ordinarily chanted. What happened there? If I tell the truth, it will exceed your powers of belief. So let it suffice to say this much at least, that in the temple and portico of Solomon, men rode in blood up to their knees and the bridle reins.

Raymond did not miss the opportunity to add the moral: "Indeed, it was a just and splendid judgement of God, that this place should be filled

36. Villey 1942, 21–22; Rousset 1945, 142.
37. Russell 1975, 2.
38. See Erdmann 1935, 51, 57; Rousset 1945, 148; Dupront 1969, 32; Becker 1988, 293, 352, 395.
39. Bainton 1960, 148. Cf. Fasoli 1968; Wallace-Hadrill 1975, 20.
40. Cf. Villey 1942, 30; Rousset 1945, 101, 105 ff., 149; Dupront 1969, 33, 38–39.
41. Dupront 1969, 39.
42. *Gesta Francorum* X,xxxix.

with the blood of unbelievers, since it had suffered so long from their blasphemies."[43]

Christianity cannot be credited with originating the holy war tradition; holy war in the broadest sense predates not only the crusades but Christianity as well. Holy war in the Christian tradition had its authoritative base partly in the Old Testament—in the books of Deuteronomy, Numbers, Joshua, Judges, and Maccabees. It found its model in the wars of Yahweh.[44] Those wars in the service of God, carrying out the punishment of God—the collective warlike fury that, in its mystical aspects, was more terrible and impressive than the individual heroism of German and Nordic epics—had significant bearing on the medieval practice of war.[45] The other source of legitimation was the wars of the Romans, which had also had a sacral character.[46] Most inspiring was the Roman tradition and codification of wars against barbarians, robbers, and brigands. *Barbari,* the stereotypical "other" of the Roman imperial imagination,[47] on the one hand, and *latrunculi* and *praedones,* on the other, were of course dissimilar legal categories, but the Romans nevertheless lumped them together. All were seen as the enemies of mankind, and so were excluded from all legal protection. As an anomaly in the perfect political and juridical system of the empire, they had to be eliminated. This approach to the outcasts of humanity was to become a model for Christian hostility toward pagans, infidels, rebels, and heretics.[48]

But holy war was only one current, and at least from the normative point of view not the dominant current, in the tradition of Christian attitudes toward war. When Christianity outgrew the so-called pacifism of the primitive Church (an expression of the early Christians' estrangement from the Roman world, in which war was of central importance),[49] associated itself with institutions of the late Roman Empire, and

43. *Liber,* 150–51; trans. in Peters 1989, 214. Cf. *Gesta francorum* X,xxxviii; and the letter of Godfrey, Raymond, and Daimbert to the pope, Sept. 1099; Hagenmeyer, *Kreuzzugsbriefe,* no. XVIII,10 (p. 171): "[I]n porticu Salomonis et in templo eius nostri equitabant in sanguine Saracenorum usque ad genua equorum." The "Temple of Solomon" was the al-Aqsa Mosque, in which there had never been Christian service. It is said that in that building alone nearly ten thousand Muslims were slaughtered. The Jews were burnt together with the synagogue in which they took refuge.

44. See Bainton 1960, chap. 3; Russell 1975, 8 ff.; Johnson 1997, 34 (summarizing G. von Rad, *Holy War in Ancient Israel* [Grand Rapids, Mich., 1991]).

45. Fasoli 1968, 26; Wallace-Hadrill 1975, 20.

46. Fasoli 1968, 29.

47. Brown 1996, 56.

48. Morisi 1963, 156; Russell 1975, 8.

49. Minucius Felix, a third-century apologist, for example, wrote that the Romans in their origin were "collected" by crime and grew by terror and ferocity, and that what-

began to deal seriously with the problem of war, it took over and elaborated upon the classic doctrine of just war.[50] A just war must not be a
willful exercise of violence but rather should be waged by legitimate civil
authority to recover lost goods (real property or incorporeal rights), that
is, to redress an injury caused by the enemy. As an extraordinary legal
procedure, war ought to be fought within the limits of law. The doctrine
of just war thus sought to regulate warfare and restrain violence. Ever
since its adoption by the Church fathers, the doctrine of just war had a
decisive impact on Christian views of war. Its authoritative Christian
version was worked out by Augustine, who added a few novelties to the
classical doctrine. Besides the exemption of monks and priests from military activity, perhaps most important among these was the idea of the
right disposition of the heart for those exercising violence.

The Christian attitude toward war was characterized by tension between just war and holy war. The code of just war tended to break down
in the fervor of holy war. Whereas just war set limits on warfare and
barred clerics from bearing arms, participating in wars, and shedding
blood, taking up arms for the realization of God's purpose tended to
override all obstacles and do away with all limitations.[51] The authority
of Augustine did not help much to ease the tension, for although Augustine himself had formulated the Christian just war doctrine, in his
tracts against heretics, especially the Donatists, he had provided arguments useful for later advocates of holy war.[52] Many of these arguments
were plucked out of Augustine's discussion of the right inner disposition
of those who resort to violence when he—writing in the context of imperial persecution of pagans and heretics—set out to "vindicate the Old
Testament patriarchs" against the Donatists' calumnies.[53]

Augustine argued that the New Testament precept "resist not evil"
was not a call for passivity in the face of evil and consequently did not
prohibit the use of arms to fight evil. The precept was given "to prevent

---

ever they held, cultivated, and possessed was the spoil of their audacity and violence. *Oc-
tavius* XXV (ANF 6:188). Cf. Morris 1967, chap. 7.

50. For the classic theory of just war, see Bainton 1960, chap. 2; Russell 1975, introduction; Barnes 1988; and critical remarks in Markus 1983.

51. Wallace-Hadrill 1975, 20.

52. For analytical purposes, I discriminate between just war and holy war in Augustine's writings, though this does not do justice to the complexity of his thought. Looking
at his ideas of war from the point of view of later medieval authors is also questionable;
but since I am primarily concerned with this later use, I have adopted here this methodologically problematic approach. On Augustine's views on war and coercion, see especially
Brown 1972; Markus 1983.

53. See Markus 1983, 5 (referring to Augustine *Retractationes* II,xxxiii,1).

us from taking pleasure in revenge, in which the mind is gratified by the sufferings of others, but not to make us neglect the duty of restraining men from sin."[54] In a similar fashion, the commandment to love one's neighbor and one's enemies did not preclude the use of force. Inflicting corporeal punishment might be dictated by charity. It might be a form of maternal correction "inflamed by love"—not "rendering evil for evil" but "applying the benefit of discipline to counteract the evil of sin, not with the hatred which seeks to harm, but with the love which seeks to heal." In sum, the disposition of the heart was of normative importance in judging violence, not the outward deed: "When good and bad do the same action and suffer the same afflictions, they are to be distinguished not by what they do or suffer, but by the causes of each." The use of force was justifiable if its motive was love, "regard to the people's welfare," and not hatred, vengeance, or greed.[55] In accordance with this view, the evil of war lay not in its violence, in the death of some who would soon die anyway; the real evils in war were "love of violence, revengeful cruelty, fierce and implacable enmity, wild resistance, and the lust of power."[56] *Malitia,* evil, was to be opposed, not *militia.*[57]

Along with Augustine, Ambrose of Milan before him and Pope Gregory I later in the sixth century may be credited with doctrinal formulations allowing—or demanding—the use of force against heretics and infidels. Ambrose, for example, eloquently defended Christian violence against the Jews and heretics, representing it as "the judgement of God."[58] Because the believer had nothing to do with the unbeliever, he argued, the "instances of his unbelief ought to be done away with together with the unbeliever himself."[59] Inspired by victories granted to Moses, Joshua, Samuel, and David, he wrote about the "presence of the divine assistance" in battles fought by emperors of his day.[60] They went to war against the barbarians safeguarded "under the shield of faith, and girt with the sword of the Spirit." The Roman army was led to battle by "Thy Name, Lord Jesus, and Thy worship," sure of victory that was given to it by the aid of the Might Supreme as the prize for the Faith. It was "sufficiently plain" that "they, who have broken faith, cannot be

---

54. Augustine to Publicola, A.D. 398, Letter XLVII,5 (*The Letters,* 293).
55. Augustine to Vincentius, A.D. 408, Letter XCIII,ii,6 (*The Letters,* 384).
56. *Contra Faustum Manichaeum* XXII,74 (NPNF, 1st ser., 4: 301).
57. See Bainton 1960, 14, 92; Brown 1967; Morris 1967, 226; Russell 1975, 17; Riley-Smith 1980, 185.
58. Letter XL,8 (*The Letters,* 441).
59. Letter XL,23 (*The Letters,* 444). Cf. 2 Cor 6.14–15 (see chap. 3 n. 135).
60. Letters LXI,3; LXII,4 (*The Letters,* 455, 456).

safe."[61] Gregory I, too, subscribed to coercion in matters of religion. He expected military commanders and civil officials to bring pagans "to the service of Christ." For him force was not only acceptable; it was the normal means for propagation of the faith.[62]

In principle, war was permissible against heretics and pagans, for the protection of the purity of the Church within, and for the spread of the faith without. Until the eleventh century, however, the Church's normative attitude toward warfare and the military profession was dominated by the just war doctrine, even though popes and bishops may have been involved in wars justified as the Lord's war.[63] It was only a small step from a doctrine of war as just and justifiable to representing war as an outright duty.[64] Yet even when—with the Church reform and the launching of the crusade—the idea of holy war grew in prominence and the tension between just war and holy war became acute, that small step had not been taken completely and irreversibly, and certainly not by all of those who had a say in ecclesiastical affairs. Proponents of holy war had to pay homage to the just war tradition and represent holy war as a just war in order to legitimize it in the eyes of their contemporaries.[65]

Against the background of traditional Christian attitudes toward war, and with the general characteristics of holy war in mind, we can now define abstract traits of the crusade. When seen, on the one hand, in relation to traditional holy wars, the Crusades appear as a subset of holy war, as a "special group," "special type," or a "particular form" of holy war.[66] As a "new form of war" with its own ideology and fought by warriors of a new stamp, the Crusades were also a new form of *holy* war (or a new form of "Christian war").[67] They embodied holy war in its most characteristic medieval form and were the most accomplished form of holy war; they were "the holiest of wars."[68]

There has also been a tendency in historiography to discuss the cru-

61. *Of the Christian Faith* II,xvi,136,141–43.

62. Markus 1997, 81–82, 85, referring to Gregory I *Epistolae* I,73; IV,25; XI,12.

63. Erdmann 1935, 8, 10, 27; Gilchrist 1988; 1993, 65–69. Gilchrist is prominent among the scholars who have criticized Erdmann for overemphasizing the role of the eleventh-century reform papacy in the Church's change of attitude toward war, while playing down the ecclesiastical militarism in the two centuries that preceded.

64. Morisi 1963, 155.

65. Cf. Vismara 1974, 62–63.

66. Villey 1942, 9, 263; Dupront 1969, 19; Purcell 1975, 8.

67. Tyerman 1988, 9.

68. Villey 1942, 189, 227; Rousset 1945, 151, 194; Brundage 1976, 105; Leyser 1994, 193.

sade in relation to the Islamic military tradition, as analogous to Islamic "holy war." In this context, the Crusades appear as the western form of holy war.[69] But *jihad* cannot properly be defined as holy war.[70] Because Muslims' wars for religious reasons were not conducted on the "level of the state," they were in a strict sense not "holy wars" but "holy battles."[71] Because the crusade is not a general doctrine of Christian holy war, while *jihad* is a doctrine of spiritual effort of which military action is only one possible manifestation, the crusade and *jihad* are, strictly speaking, not comparable.[72] Some western historians, especially earlier ones, used to represent the Crusades as a response of Latin Christians to *jihad*.[73] But this apologetic view has been convincingly rejected.[74]

Whereas some historians have been reproached for clouding the distinction between holy war and the crusade,[75] others tend to overlook the difference between holy war and just war.[76] Though the Crusades may thus appear to be a subset of just war,[77] this view is questionable. Some argue that the "ideal-type" distinction between just war and holy war is methodologically untenable, sharing the "disadvantage" of all ideal types: "they are not real."[78] Still others simply accept the crusaders' self-perception and self-justification and the crusading propagandists' claim

69. Dupront 1969, 20; Cardini 1992b, 390–91. For Johnson 1997, 80, the First Crusade "provides the archetypal conception of holy war in Western culture."

70. Cardini 1992b, 390.

71. Noth 1966, especially 87, 147. For analogous reasons—the absence of the "state" in religious warfare—one cannot speak of "heilige Kriege" but only of "heilige Kämpfe" in the Christian West in the first period of crusading warfare. Ibid., 93, 139. Cf. n. 31.

72. Partner 1996, 333. Cf. Watt 1976. Johnson 1997, however, has provided a systematic comparison of the idea of holy war in Christian and Islamic culture. Cf. Partner 1997, chap. 5.

73. For example, T. A. Archer and Ch. L. Kingsford, *The Crusades* (New York, 1894); Nys 1894; L. Bréhier, *L'Église et l'Orient au moyen âge: Les croisades* (Paris, 1907); Dérumaux 1953, 74. Relevant passages from Archer and Kingsford and from Bréhier are published in Brundage 1964.

74. Erdmann 1935, 27, questioned this assumption and provided the starting point for Noth 1966. Cf. J. J. Saunders, *Aspects of the Crusades* (Christchurch, N.Z., 1962 [excerpts in Brundage 1964]); Brundage 1976, 103; Becker 1988, 362–63; Daniel 1989a, 35. For a refutation of a subset of the thesis that the Crusades were a response to *jihad*—that the Christian military orders took as their model the Islamic institution of *ribat* (a fortified convent, built in a border area, whose inmates combined a religious way of life with fighting against the enemies of Islam)—see Forey 1992, 8 f.

75. Villey 1942, 15; Rousset 1945, 15 (both criticizing Erdmann 1935).

76. For example, Sicard 1969, 82; but also, occasionally, Russell 1975; Becker 1988; Daniel 1989a.

77. Brundage 1976, 117; Johnson 1997, 43.

78. Johnson 1981, xxv–xxvi (questioning the classification in Bainton 1960, 14). See also Johnson 1997, especially 42 ff.

—that the war they fought was just—as a theoretical statement.[79] But while the advocates of crusading may have felt compelled to represent the Christian military offensive as just war, it never was too difficult to cast the blame for war on the other side. By accusing the Muslims of desecrating the "Christian name" and oppressing and persecuting Christians, and by claiming that the Holy Land was the Lord's "patrimony," which belonged rightfully to Christendom and had to be "defended" or "recovered" and "liberated," the crusaders and their apologists easily construed the crusade as "just," or "the most just," war.[80]

Styling a holy war as just does not, however, invalidate the conceptual distinction between just war and holy war. Categorically speaking, the crusades were not a just war. But taking into account historical intricacies of the relationship between just war and holy war, the crusade can be seen as a "strange hybrid of holy war and just war," or as a "bastard offspring" of just war.[81] As a hybrid or a bastardization the crusade is *also* a just war. On the other hand, as a holy war the crusade evades the formal restrictions of the just war doctrine even when it refers to them. The crusade is a war in which the use of arms is not merely justifiable and condoned but is positively pleasing to and sanctioned by God. Where just war is morally acceptable, the crusade is blessed. Fighting merits God's special favor and is regarded as spiritually beneficial to those engaged in it.[82] Whereas just war refers to human law, holy war appeals to divine justice, "the true justice": to what is just in the imagined eyes of God.[83] Thus, perhaps we should call the Crusades righteous wars, rather than just wars. The doctrine of just war might have sought to tame this righteousness in arms, but the capacity of justice to hold righteousness in check should not be overestimated.[84]

79. For example, Vanderpol 1911, 167 ff.; 1919, 218 ff. Cf. Regout 1934, 49, who points out that the Crusades' legitimacy was never questioned by contemporaries: "Comme causes justes sont invoquées: la défense de la Chrétienté contre l'attaque ou la menace directe du côté des Sarrazins, la protection des croyants contre une agression criminelle lors de leur visite à la Terre Sainte, la reprise des lieux saints qui avaient été injustement ravis aux Chrétiens. Donc ici aussi: defendere, repetere res, ulcisci."

80. Schwinges 1977, 221–30, especially 226; Mayer 1993, 15.

81. Russell 1975, 2, 38–39; Gilchrist 1985, 41.

82. Brundage 1969, 29; 1976, 100, 116; Russell 1975, 2; Cowdrey 1976, 10–11, 27; Riley-Smith 1977, 16.

83. Dérumaux 1953, 68.

84. Bainton 1960, 148, summarized the logic of the Puritan revolutionary saints: "How can the prince determine the justice of a holy war? If it is holy, it is holy no matter what prince, parliament, or people may say to the contrary."

HOLY WARS BEFORE THE CRUSADES

Along with the holy wars of the Old Testament, other holy wars that figured prominently in the crusading imagination were the Carolingian holy wars, associated with the mythical figure of Charlemagne.[85] The crusaders' Charlemagne myth was created at the beginnings of the *reconquista,* a sustained Christian military offensive in Spain that began in the middle of the eleventh century and took root at the time of the First Crusade. It was most potently expressed in the epic poem *Chanson de Roland,* where "Karlemagne" was made a crusader. As the head of Christendom, he waged a never-ending war against the "Sarrazins."[86] But it was not only recollections of Charlemagne and legends that had grown up around his name that inspired the growing enthusiasm for the new holy war;[87] in popular belief, Charlemagne had risen out of his grave and now led the crusaders to the Holy Land.[88] As Robert the Monk tells us, Urban II in his crusading sermon evoked the "glory and greatness of King Charles the Great" and urged the Frankish "valiant soldiers and descendants of invincible ancestors" not to be "degenerate" but to recall the valor of their progenitors.[89] The crusaders believed that on their route to the Promised Land they were following the emperor's footsteps.[90]

But it is only within the framework of the crusading Charlemagne mythology that one can safely speak of Carolingian wars as holy wars. Once emancipated from use by the crusaders, Carolingian history becomes a more nuanced reality. After all, Pippin III had established diplomatic relations with the Islamic empire. In 765, he had sent ambassadors to the "emir Amormuni of the Saracens" (al-Mansur) and three years later received a mission from him "honourably."[91] That his son Charlemagne, far from being a "crusader," cultivated diplomatic relations with the Caliph of Baghdad, his Oriental counterpart, is well known. Einhard, Charlemagne's biographer, recorded that the emperor's relations with Harun ar-Rashid, "King of the Persians, who ruled over almost

---

85. Erdmann 1935, 276.
86. See Rousset 1945, chap. 6. Pirenne fell victim to this mythology "with a complacency alarming in a great historian." Hentsch 1992, 18.
87. Douglas 1969, 92.
88. Erdmann 1932, 413. Cf. Haskins 1967, 267.
89. *Roberti Monachi historia Iherosolimitana* I,i (p. 728); Peters 1989, 3.
90. Rousset 1945, 133.
91. *Fredegarii Chronicorum Continuationes* 51 (pp. 118–19). See Borgolte 1976, chap. 1.

the whole of the East, India excepted, were so friendly that this prince preferred his favor to that of all the kings and potentates of the earth, and considered that to him alone marks of honor and munificence were due."[92] Charlemagne also received ambassadors from Moorish Spain, bearing proposals to establish amicable and peaceful relations.[93] Historians have even speculated that had the Carolingian empire existed longer, the Christian and the Islamic cultures might have been on better terms.[94] But Charlemagne and his successors did wage wars against the pagans, and the question here is whether those wars may be seen as holy wars in a strict sense.

Carolingian wars against the pagans were represented in images associating them with the holy wars of the Hebrews.[95] Contemporary writers described the emperor as the new Moses and the new David, or even as the new Joshua. Charlemagne was a king who was just and clement but who also knew how to lead his army to victory—just like the kings of Israel.[96] In this military role, he was called the helmsman of the Christian people, *rector populi christiani*.[97] But this role was derived from his most exalted function, that of the defender of the Church; and it was this function, built into the foundations of the Carolingian system, that drove the Carolingian empire and the Church toward holy war.[98]

The Church that the emperor had to defend was the mystical body of Christ, imagined as embracing both the empire and the visible, corporate Church.[99] Inhabiting the mystical Church were the "Christian people."[100] This *populus christianus* was an extensive and dynamic category that encompassed both the peoples over whom Charlemagne

---

92. Einhard, *The Life* xvi.

93. On Carolingian relations with Muslim rulers, see Buckler 1931; Borgolte 1976. Cf. Pirenne 1937, 140; Herrin 1987, 299–300; Riché 1993, 115.

94. Kritzeck 1964, 16 (referring to Buckler 1931).

95. Morisi 1963, 164.

96. Morisi 1963, 164; Morrison 1964, 29; Fichtenau 1978, 57; Delaruelle 1980, 3–11; Riché 1993, 303; Brown 1996, 256.

97. Erdmann 1935, 19; Rupp 1939, 29; Delaruelle 1980, 11 ff.

98. Morisi 1963, 158. For the extension of this concept to the *defensio christianitatis*, see Rupp 1939, 38 ff.

99. See *Conc. parisiense VI* I,ii–iii (MGH Conc. 2.2: 610). Cf. Mansi 14: 537–38; Jonas of Orleans *Le métier du roi* I (lines 5–16); *Conc. aquisgranense II*, praefatio (Mansi 14: 673). More sources are cited in Morrison 1964, 45f.; cf. Carlyle and Carlyle 1903–36, 1: 190 ff.; Gierke 1913, 10, 103; Gilson 1963, 205–6; Morrison 1964, 45 n. 30, 50; Ladner 1983, 439–40; Robinson 1988, 288, 298; Tellenbach 1991, 63; Dubreucq 1995, 64–65, 74, 109; Canning 1996, 50.

100. On *populus christianus*, see Rupp 1939, 28–29.

actually ruled and his potential subjects.[101] Defending Christian people thus involved Christianizing the heathen, which was not always a peaceful enterprise. Moreover, defense of the Church was a dynamic notion. It included both protection and propagation of the faith. In his famous letter to Pope Leo III, Charlemagne (actually, Alcuin, his learned scribe) stated: "My task, assisted by the divine piety, is everywhere to defend the Church of Christ—abroad, by arms, against pagan incursions and the devastations of such as break faith; at home, by protecting the Church in the spreading of the Catholic faith." [102] This statement conveys excellently the dynamism of the Carolingian *imperium*. The emperor had to watch over Christianization "at home." [103] If we assume that "home" included recently subjugated Saxony, spreading the Catholic faith at home involved bloody wars against the pagans. Defending the Church against pagan incursions "abroad" makes one think of Christian incursions into the lands where pagans had been "at home." The line between Christian defense and conquest here is not too precise. But whether the wars Charlemagne fought against the pagans are seen as defensive or aggressive, he fought them "assisted by the divine piety"; he was an instrument in God's hands.

The notion that the Frankish kings, defending and exalting the faith, were aided by God and acted as instruments of His justice predated Charlemagne. Clovis was baptized "like some new Constantine" after he had been convinced of the power of Christ by winning a battle through calling His name, and afterwards he fought his wars with God on his side.[104] In 755, Pope Stephen II wrote to Pippin III and his sons that the almighty God was granting victories to the Franks in their fights against the "enemies of the holy Church of God" through the hand of the blessed Peter; it was the sword of God, not a human sword, that was fighting in the Carolingians' battles.[105] The Carolingians made this notion their own, and after the papacy declared them "protectors of the Roman church"

101. Wallace-Hadrill 1983, 187. Cf. McKitterick 1983, 71; Nelson 1988, 230; Brown 1996, 273.

102. Charlemagne to Leo III, A.D. 796 (Alcuin *Epistolae* no. 93 [p. 137]; trans. in Wallace-Hadrill 1983, 186). Cf. Cantor 1963, 145–46. See also Morisi 1963, 166–67; Delaruelle 1980, 17–18; Nelson 1988, 221.

103. For an excellent survey of the historiographic discussion of Christianization, see Van Engen 1986.

104. Gregory of Tours *The History* II,30–31,37.

105. "Non enim gladius hominis, sed gladius Dei est, qui pugnat." MGH Epp. 3: 491. Cf. chap. 3 nn. 65–67.

in the year 754, they "considered themselves, among kings, specially chosen by God." [106] Under the rule of Charlemagne's sons, this notion of the divinely appointed king was joined with the idea of the Franks as the second chosen people, the new Israelites.[107] Charlemagne himself was represented as chosen by divine providence to defend the holy Church and to fight the *extraneas gentes,* peoples who because they were not Christian were "outside." His wars, defensive by definition, though not necessarily so in fact, were willed by God.[108]

But the Carolingian wars were primarily secular. They come across as such in contemporary narratives [109] as well as in the judgment of historians. Their driving force was the struggle for territory and power: they were "massive wars of conquest, a *Machtkampf.*[110] In contemporary moral debates, the justification for war was success in battle and the wealth and aggrandizement of lordship it brought.[111] Alcuin's references to Charlemagne's wars against the Saxons in his letters serve to illustrate this. In a letter to his religious community in York, where he apparently spoke freely, Alcuin simply stated that "the king has gone with his army to lay waste Saxony." [112] When he wrote to Charlemagne himself, Alcuin wanted to bring home to the king that spreading the "kingdom of Christendom" was not the same as imposing "the yoke of tithes upon a simple people who are beginners in the faith, making a full levy from every house." [113] He also exhorted an imperial bishop to be "a preacher of goodness, not an exactor of tithes," and in another letter he postulated that the teachers of the faith (who were involved in Charlemagne's campaigns) should be *praedicatores, non praeditores,* "preachers, not predators." [114] The Carolingian wars against the Normans do not seem to have been any holier than the Saxon wars. The Normans appeared to be less like enemies of Christianity and more like an invading army, and one could say that the Christians themselves fought for pagan

---

106. Fichtenau 1978, 63.

107. See Wallace-Hadrill 1983, chap. 13, especially 245 f.; Riché 1993, 304; Brown 1996, 256.

108. Morisi 1963, 164, 169.

109. Leyser 1994, 191, speaks of "the total secularity" of Einhard's story about the Carolingian wars against the Avars. See Einhard *The Life* vii–viii.

110. Erdmann 1935, 20; Morisi 1963, 170; Leyser 1994, 189.

111. Leyser 1994, 190.

112. Alcuin to the brothers of the holy community of the dearly loved church of York etc., A.D. 795, *Epistolae* no. 43 (p. 89); *Alcuin of York,* 4.

113. Alcuin to King Charles, A.D. 796, *Epistolae* no. 110 (pp. 157–58); *Alcuin of York,* 72–73.

114. Alcuin to Arno; Alcuin to Megenfrid, A.D. 796, *Epistolae* nos. 107, 111 (pp. 154, 161); *Alcuin of York,* 74–75.

ideals: *pro patria, pro vita, pro libertate.*[115] Those wars may indeed be
seen as an extension of the Roman campaigns against the barbarians,[116]
only now the western barbarians thought of themselves as the Romans.[117]
In the summary beheading of 4,500 Saxon prisoners of war by the Franks
one is reminded of Roman virtue rather than of Christian mercy: "Only
Romans had been so self-confidently barbaric in their treatment of un-
reliable neighbours."[118]

Carolingian wars were also absent of religiously based exclusivism.
First of all, even though the Carolingians believed they were assisted by
God in these wars, they did not fight against non-Christians exclusively.
The blood shed by the Carolingians was the blood of "heathens or Christians."[119] Second, it was not uncommon for Christians to fight in infidel
armies, for the unfaithful to serve in Christian forces, and for alliances
to be made across the religious divide. In that era, just as religion was
not the autonomous cause but rather an attribute of temporal power, so
it was no more than an attribute of wars fought by that power.[120] Whereas
most Carolingian military campaigns wore "a decisively religious aspect," they were undertaken for "political reasons."[121] The duty to convert the pagans in defensive wars of conquest might have been strongly
felt by the emperor,[122] but religion was a means of bringing the *exterae
gentes* under his rule: "Charlemagne personally inspired the terrible use
of Frankish religion as an instrument of suppression; but others—bishops, clergy and monks—were his willing lieutenants in the field."[123] The
establishment of episcopal sees in the conquered territories and the nomination of bishops were "instruments of political control."[124] Baptisms
of the vanquished pagans were not primarily affirmations of faith, but
"statements of political realignment."[125]

Taking all this into account, the Carolingian wars against the pagans
can be seen as holy wars in only a limited sense.[126] In an empire that was

---

115. Delaruelle 1980, 26.
116. Villey 1942, 27.
117. Cf. Wallace-Hadrill 1962, 146.
118. Brown 1996, 274.
119. Cf. Boniface to Pope Zacharias, A.D. 742 (*Letters of Saint Boniface*, 80).
120. Cf. Erdmann 1935, 20.
121. Wallace-Hadrill 1983, 181.
122. See Wallace-Hadrill 1983, 418. Cf. Koebner 1961, 24, 27; Folz 1969, 47; Fichtenau 1978, 62–63; Nelson 1988, 218.
123. Wallace-Hadrill 1983, 184.
124. Morrison 1969, 378.
125. McKitterick 1983, 62.
126. Erdmann 1935, 20; Morisi 1963, 169.

not merely "political" but spiritual as well, in a system where temporal and spiritual powers overlapped and temporal power was imbued with religion, everything done by the emperor—a sacred king, an "ecclesiastical person," God's chosen instrument for the establishment of a Christian society—had religious connotations.[127] But whereas holy war is an instrument of religion and is fought, or commanded, by a spiritual power, in the Carolingian wars religion was a means of conquest and oppression, and the initiative for war always rested with the emperor. The pope's role was only to pray. "Your task, holy father," Charlemagne wrote to Leo III, "is to raise your hands to God like Moses to ensure the victory of our arms. Helped thus by your prayers to God, ruler and giver of all, the *populus christianus* may always and everywhere have the victory over the enemies of his holy name, and the name of Our Lord Jesus Christ resound throughout the world." [128]

Though the crusaders may have been inspired by their own image of Charlemagne, the Carolingian imperial wars against the pagans in fact do not seem to have had much in common with the crusades. Neither did the wars fought by lesser temporal powers that came to the fore with the collapse of imperial authority.[129] Were we determined, however, to identify wars that we could say presaged the Crusades,[130] we might settle upon wars that did not figure in the crusaders' imagination: those conducted by the ninth-century and tenth-century popes. In theory, the pope was an *orator:* His task was to pray. He could also exhort Christian soldiers to fight valiantly and send priests to take care of the soldiers' faith and morals. But in no case was he allowed to initiate, direct, or lead a war.[131] In practice, however, things looked rather different. From the late eighth century onward most of the popes were involved through much of their papacy in armed conflicts against their enemies in Italy, and not a few of them fought in person. They justified their armed struggle for

127. For the idea of "Christian empire," cf. Koebner 1961, chap. 2.2; Vereker 1964, 67; Morris 1967, 221 ff.; Folz 1969, chap. 2; Munz 1969, 25; Fichtenau 1978, 64–65; Beumann 1981, 532, 566; Wallace-Hadrill 1983, 187; Nelson 1988, 211; Schramm 1992, 14 ff.; Dubreucq 1995, 64 ff. On the notion of a "theocratized ruler," whose person was sacred *ex officio,* cf. Kern 1968, 44; Ullmann 1973, 271–74; Fichtenau 1978, 56. For a critique of the *rex-sacerdos* (*Priesterkönigtum*) thesis, see Morrison 1964, 27–28; 1969, app. B; Fichtenau 1978, 56–61.
128. Charlemagne to Leo III, A.D. 796 (Alcuin *Epistolae* no. 93 [pp. 137–38]; translated in Wallace-Hadrill 1983, 186).
129. For these types of war, see Villey 1942, 45–48.
130. Riché 1993, 311, wrote that Carolingian wars against the pagans "presaged the notion of holy war that fully emerged . . . in the eleventh century."
131. Villey 1942, 48–49.

personal survival and for power and territory as the Lord's war, drawing heavily on arguments from the Old Testament.[132]

Pope Leo IV, in 849, reputedly led a fleet to victory over pirates who were molesting Rome. Whether this really happened is not absolutely certain, for the event is mentioned in only one source of somewhat questionable reliability.[133] There is no doubt, however, that three years later the same pope asserted the papal initiative and called on Christians to fight against the Saracens. He relied on his own military forces and promised heavenly rewards to those who might lose their lives in the battle for "the truth of the faith and salvation of the soul and defense of the Christian fatherland."[134] John VIII (872–82), after exhorting in vain all Christians to take up arms against Norman and Muslim infidels, also took military initiative into his own papal hands, raised his own fleet, and led his troops both on land and sea against the Saracens.[135] He too gave assurance of eternal life to those who would be killed in the defense of the holy Church of God and the Christian faith and commonwealth.[136] For John VIII, as for Leo IV, war against the infidels was sanctified and sanctifying.[137] In the tenth century, John X (914–28) raised an army against Muslim pirates and took part in hand-to-hand fighting.[138] John XII (955–63) also resorted to war and fought in person. Liudprand of Cremona, listing John's many crimes, recorded that the pope "set houses on fire and appeared in public equipped with sword, helmet and cuirass."[139] Gregory V (996–99) was occupied throughout his pontificate with reconquering his lost territories.[140] And Sylvester II (999–1003), Benedict VIII (1012–24), and Gregory VI (1044–46) also knew how to deal with arms and armies.[141]

---

132. Gilchrist 1988, 179, 181; 1993, 65–68.

133. Morisi 1963, 171.

134. Leo to the Frankish army, A.D. 853 (*Epistola* 28, MGH Epp. 5: 601). Since this became one of the texts most widely cited by the canonist of the later Church reform, the idea of struggle against the pagans as a holy work may be considered a commonplace in the Middle Ages. Cf. Villey 1942, 29; Brundage 1969, 22; Gilchrist 1988, 182 n. 43.

135. Engreen 1945, 323 n. 6; Partner 1972, 67.

136. John to the bishops in Louis's realm, A.D. 879, *Epistolae et decreta* no. 186 (col. 816).

137. See Erdmann 1935, 23; Rupp 1939, 37 f.; Villey 1942, 29; Rousset 1945, 44; Morisi 1963, 172; Brundage 1969, 23; Delaruelle 1980, 24–41, especially 39; Becker 1988, 365–68.

138. Partner 1972, 82; R. Barber 1982, 214; Gilchrist 1988, 183.

139. Liudprand of Cremona *Chronicle* 10 (p. 165). See Partner 1972, 86–89.

140. Morisi 1963, 172; Gilchrist 1988, 184.

141. Erdmann 1935, 101; Cowdrey 1983, 108; Gilchrist 1988, 184.

TRANSFORMATION OF THE CHURCH'S
ATTITUDE TOWARD WAR

Given these historical precedents for divine warfare, what was the novelty in the Christian attitude toward war during the eleventh century, especially at its close, that materialized in the crusade? To answer this question—and before we examine the crusade itself—we need to dwell a little longer on the spiritual change that made the crusade possible: on the transformation of the Christian attitude toward war. The discussion of this transformation in chapter 1 has to be complemented, first, with acknowledgment of the reluctance with which the crusade was received by many canonists and theologians, and second, with a look at Urban II's departure from Gregory VII's understanding of war in the service of the Church.

THE NEW HOLY WAR, CANON LAWYERS, AND THEOLOGIANS

The profound transformation in the Christian doctrine of war that emerged between 1000 and 1300 was not free from conflicts. One aspect of this doctrinal change was the legalization of the ecclesiastical view of war; whereas war had traditionally been considered primarily a moral and theological problem, it now came to be regarded as basically a problem of law. Another aspect of this transformation—one connected with the emergence of the crusade—appeared to have a theological basis.[142] As the crusade emerged, the new ideas about holy war clashed with the legalistic tendencies in ecclesiastical thinking about war. It took about two centuries from the time of the First Crusade's launching for canon lawyers to transform the crusade into something of a legal institution.[143]

In the period immediately preceding the preaching of the First Crusade, collections of canon law were hardly a source of inspiration for crusading. Canon lawyers were not very concerned with the ethics of warfare, and the crusade was primarily an ethical war. Even in the col-

---

142. Brundage 1969, 29; 1976, 99–100.
143. Brundage 1976, 100. Villey 1942, 256, calls Hostiensis "le père de la théorie juridique de la croisade." Gilchrist 1985 consents. Russell 1975 (chap. 4) detects the beginnings of a juridical conceptualization of the crusade in the Decretists' works, especially in Huggucio, but agrees with Villey about Hostiensis (206). But cf. Constable 1953, 248 ff., especially 254, pointing out that Pope Eugenius III's crusading bulls from 1146 to 1147 can be seen as marking the emergence of the crusade "as a Christian institution rather than a mere historical event."

lection of Anselm of Lucca, a pioneer in elaborating on the legitimatization of war in the service of the Church, it is difficult to find "any hint of a justification for the First Crusade."[144] When Urban II organized the crusade, he did not follow the rationale of the canonistic treatment of war. He rather ignored the canonists. They, in turn, were not "converted to his side."[145] Even after the crusade came into being, it seems to have been alien to canon lawyers for quite some time—from Ivo of Chartres at the close of the eleventh century onward.[146] Bishop Ivo is said to have been unmoved by the crusade idea and reserved or even dismissive toward the crusading movement.[147] He refused to support war led by the Church in his collections of canon law (which embraced the Augustinian doctrine of just war).[148] The division between a life devoted to Christian religion and a life devoted to the worldly army was something he wanted to maintain. The Christian's glory was within, not outside.[149]

The legalistic turn in the Church's attitude toward war confirmed the continued relevance of Augustine's doctrine of just war. The Crusades did not render that doctrine irrelevant. Augustine, as we have already seen, was the authority turned to by both the legalistically minded defenders of just war and the advocates of holy war. On the one hand, his teachings shaped the basic attitude of most Christian thinkers toward organized public conflict, and his just war doctrine made a decisive impact on the medieval law of war.[150] On the other hand, though he did not formulate a doctrine of holy war, holy war advocates exploited his approval of the use of force for religious exigency. In this sense, the crusaders' imagination may have been "distantly sired" by Augustine's writings against the Donatists and Manichaeans.[151] Moreover, though holy war propagandists made use of elements of Augustine's just war theory to legitimize their endeavors, they only rarely used the term *bellum justum* and seldom referred to Augustine.[152] The crusade went far beyond the positions set out by the doctrine of just war and thus loosened its re-

144. Morris 1991, 143.
145. Gilchrist 1985, 41.
146. Pacaut 1953; Gilchrist 1985, especially 39, 41; 1988, 177; Brundage 1991.
147. Sprandel 1962, 140, 141 n. 14, 161. Hehl 1980, 11–12, questions Sprandel's interpretation of the evidence but nevertheless concludes that Ivo's attitude toward the crusade was "neutral."
148. See Hehl 1980, 10–12.
149. "Longe est dissimilis haec militia (Christiana) mundanae militiae. . . . Gloria nostra intus non foris est"; quoted in Sprandel 1962, 141 n. 14.
150. Höffner 1972, 64–65; Brundage 1976, 102.
151. Morisi 1963, 223; Russell 1975, 36; Brundage 1976, 103.
152. See Gilchrist 1988, 176–78.

strictive regulations.[153] In fact, by resting on the precepts of just war, the crusade's propagandists distorted the doctrine so much that it was invalidated.[154]

In canon law, however, just war doctrine was not shattered. As a result, a gulf came to separate canon law from the new holy war.[155] From the perspective of canon law, the crusade—in its formative phase—appeared not only extralegal; it also seemed to be a kind of anti-war: a non-war, a phenomenon beyond war.[156] But the crusade was also anti-war in another sense: it was against war, "pacifist," if you will, in that it was a realization of the peace movement. Aimed at realizing God's peace, it was a "work of peace."[157] Most importantly, peace was its precondition. Peace had to be made in order to launch the crusade. In this respect, the crusade was an inversion, or perversion, of the fundamental Augustinian perspective. Augustine wrote that "peace is not sought in order that war may be aroused, but war is waged in order that peace may be obtained."[158] Urban II, however, proclaimed the Truce of God as the first step toward launching the crusade.

The crusade was alien not only to the legalistic approach to war; even though some historians see the crusade as based in theology, it appears to have been repugnant to prominent theologians as well. Theology was certainly partly responsible for the emergence of the crusade (in Pope Urban II's providential view of history, for example). But the main body of what may be called the crusading ideology was an explosive mixture in which piety mingled with eschatological images and millenarian expectations, messianic ideas, and popular beliefs and superstitions. It was shaped by a spirituality that knew no boundary between the relative and the absolute, in which the natural and supernatural merged. That spirituality was fascinated with the marvelous rather than with the divine.[159] As the materialization of such an "ideology," the crusade could not have been easily embraced by theologians. As a case in point I cite St. Anselm of Canterbury.

---

153. Brundage 1969, 29.
154. Erdmann 1935, 87 (who uses the expression *hinweggesetzt*); Cowdrey 1976, 29. Cf. Mayer 1993, 16.
155. Gilchrist 1985, 41.
156. Rousset 1945, 194; Morisi 1963, 170–71; Cardini 1974, 221.
157. Cardini 1974, 221.
158. Augustine to Boniface, A.D. 418, Letter CLXXXIX,6 (*Select Letters,* 331). Cf. *The City of God* XIX,12; Gratian *Decretum* C.XXIII q.i. c.6.
159. Cf. Rousset 1945, 176; Delaruelle 1980, 122; Riley-Smith 1993a, chap. 4; Morris 1984.

In his *Cur deus homo*, Anselm mentioned "infidels" whose objections against Christian doctrine of redemption he wanted to refute.[160] This has led some scholars to believe that Anselm, writing this apologetic work, harbored missionary hopes and even thought of converting the Muslims.[161] It is much more likely, however, that Anselm did not have any actual infidels in mind. It is especially unlikely that he intended to address the Muslims.[162] In all of his writings, he referred to them unambiguously only once, and his whole work betrays "very little interest in any real non-Christians." His apologetics were directed, rather, against "the disbelief of those who were at least nominal Christians."[163] But if these arguments suggest that Anselm was not really a missionary—and much less so a "missionary to the Arabs"[164]—they do not imply that he was an advocate of the seeming opposite, the new holy war. He showed neither much understanding nor much enthusiasm for the crusade. He may have been for some years largely unaware of the labor of "Gregorian" reformers and of the decrees of the Council of Clermont.[165] But this does not explain why his attitude toward the crusade remained "distinctly lukewarm" and why he did "little or nothing" to encourage lay participation in the crusade. There is no doubt that he knew about the crusade during his exile, when he spent some time at the papal court. Anselm's biographer and confidant, Eadmer, appears to have been uninterested in the new holy war as well.[166]

In contrast to the crusaders, who on the march toward Jerusalem blurred the distinction between the heavenly and the earthly cities, Anselm's life was dedicated to the heavenly Jerusalem alone. The earthly Jerusalem, which—as he put it—"is now not the vision of peace," had little attraction for him. The important choice was between the heavenly Jerusalem as the vision of peace and the "carnage of the earthly Jerusalem in this world, which under whatever name was nothing but a vision

---

160. Cf. *Cur deus homo*, Dedicatory letter to Pope Urban II; preface; I,i,iii–iv,vi,viii.
161. See Schwinges 1977, 58 ff., referring to J. Gauss, "Anselm von Canterbury und die Islamfrage," *Theologische Zeitschrift* 19 (1963); id., "Anselm von Canterbury: Zur Begegnung und Auseinandersetzung der Religionen," *Saeculum* 17 (1966). See also "Anselm von Canterburys Weg zur Begegnung mit Judentum und Islam," in Gauss 1967.
162. Southern 1990, 199, 201; Abulafia 1995, 43. But Southern, loc. cit., and Morris 1991, 363, believe that Anselm targeted the Jews. Cf. *Cur deus homo* II,xxii.
163. Abulafia 1995, 43–44.
164. Cf. Gauss 1967, 109.
165. Southern 1990, 255, 265 f., chap. 12
166. Tyerman 1988, 18–19. But see Cowdrey 1995, 727 n. 20, that Anselm rejoiced at the establishment of the Latin kingdom of Jerusalem under Baldwin, with whom he is said to have been in close contact (Gauss 1967, 109).

of destruction."[167] In accord with this view, Anselm was even opposed to monks pilgrimaging to Jerusalem, since monks had opted for the heavenly Jerusalem and should not leave the cloister. "It is not permitted to wander without rule and [for an abbot] to send monks to Jerusalem or to go personally," he argued. "This leads to shame and doom."[168] Not only religious obligations but also political duties took priority over the crusade. Defending one's country came before assisting Christians in other regions.[169] Compared with striving for the peace of the heavenly City, worldly peace—peace in the "political sense"—held little significance in Anselm's view of the world. "In the light of that attitude it is scarcely surprising that he largely ignored the crusade and found little to commend in crusading endeavors."[170]

As a war in the service of the Church, the crusade was a theocratic rather than a theological war.[171] In the epoch-making social transformation of the eleventh century, the Church became the leading power within Christendom and began to dominate the course of temporal affairs. As we saw in the first chapter, an essential moment in the Church's ascendancy to preeminence was the radical change in ecclesiastical attitudes toward war and the military profession. It was this great spiritual turning point[172] that enabled the Church to employ in its service the material force of arms. It was now deemed meritorious to use arms at the Church's command to promote what was believed to be the "right order" in human society.[173] Holy war dispenses with human laws; yet the nature of holy war is such that its protagonists inextricably link a particular temporal order with God's intentions.[174] What they take to be God's intentions they are determined to enforce, by whatever means, as laws governing human lives. In this manner, the new Christian endorsement of warfare as a means to defend or establish the "right order" found its most clear and intense expression in holy war.

Not every holy war, however, is a crusade. The emergence of holy war from the spirit of the Church reform did not simply and automatically

167. *Epistola* 117 (quoted in Hehl 1980, 12); Southern 1990, 169.
168. *Epistola* 195; quoted in Bredero 1994, 101. For a monk of Corbie, dissuading his master from joining the Second Crusade, the "Jerusalem here below may be likened to human intercourse with animals"; quoted ibid., 102.
169. See Hehl 1980, 13.
170. Brundage 1991, 178.
171. Cf. Dupront 1969, 45.
172. "[T]he greatest—from the spiritual point of view perhaps the only—turning point in the history of Catholic Christendom." Tellenbach 1991, 164.
173. Cowdrey 1976, 19.
174. Riley-Smith 1977, 16–17.

mean the birth of the crusade. In substantiating this claim, I contest the widely spread view that Urban II, by organizing the First Crusade, accomplished the reform program that Gregory VII had left unfinished. I argue that the crusade was not the offspring of the Church reform as represented by Gregory VII alone, but that it was a result of the eleventh-century peace movement as adopted and carried through to its logical conclusions by Pope Urban II, himself a Church reformer. Between Gregory VII and Urban II, a crucial shift occurred in the Church's stance toward holy war.

FROM WAR FOR A PURE CHURCH TO WAR AGAINST THE "PAGAN DIRT": GREGORY VII AND URBAN II

Gregory VII played a key role in breaking with the traditional stance of the Church against waging war.[175] In his view, the layman's function was to fight against the enemies of the Church and the subverters of the right Christian order.[176] Gregory interpreted the notion of *fideles*—stretching it from the juridical meaning of vassal to mean one of the faithful—so that it assumed the sense of true soldier of St. Peter. Militarizing thus the traditional idea of the "faithful,"[177] he has been seen as propagating a "theology of armed action."[178] As the creator of the army of St. Peter, as the pope who firmly believed that he had the right—moreover, the duty—to use not only the spiritual but also the material sword if that was what "our Holy Roman Mother Church" needed;[179] this "Monk of a daring and obstinate Spirit," as Gibbon called him, has acquired a reputation as "one of the most energetic and pugnacious men ever to sit on the throne of St. Peter."[180] Because he, "more than anyone before him, overcame the restraints that had in times past hindered the Church from preaching war and waging war," he stands before our eyes as a "man of war" (*Kriegsmann*).[181] Even in his day, hostile contemporaries—for example, imperial polemicist Wido of Ferrara—accused Gregory VII of showing, from his youth, "zeal in secular *militia*."[182]

175. For a survey of historiographical literature on Gregory VII, see Robinson 1985. Cf. Kaufman 1990, 189 ff.

176. See chap. 1 n. 91.

177. Laarhoven 1959–61, 92; Morris 1991, 146. See chap. 1 nn. 90, 157.

178. Douglas 1969, 101.

179. See chap. 1 n. 159.

180. Gibbon, "Outlines of the History of the World" (*The English Essays*, 168); Mayer 1993, 19.

181. Erdmann 1935, 165, cf. 135. For a different view, see Fliche 1920, 28, 35 f., 60.

182. Robinson 1978, 98. Cf. Erdmann 1935, chap. 8.

If Gregory VII passes for a Church militarist, and if Urban II is considered his successor and follower, was Urban a warmonger pope?[183] I suggest that there was a substantial difference between the two popes in this respect.[184] With regard to struggles and wars within the Christian world, Urban was reserved, restrained, and reconciliatory, even pacific. But when it came to wars outside Christendom, against Muslims in particular, his reservations and restraints fell away, in fact turned into their opposite: Urban II became the organizer of the First Crusade.[185] He was not one of those eleventh-century popes of whom it has been said that they "employed armed force against their European enemies before they directed it against the infidels elsewhere."[186] He marked a break with such an attitude.

Mobilizing Christendom for the new holy war, Urban could build on Gregory's Christian militarism.[187] But despite this continuity, Urban is Gregory's inverse, his mirror image. The difference between the two popes lies not so much in their relation to war as in their relation to holy war. Whereas Gregory was an innovator with regard to the Church's official attitude toward war, regarding holy war he was quite a traditionalist. It was Urban II who, in this respect, introduced novelties.

Gregory VII's vindication of the appropriateness of military force when needed by the Church derived from his concept of the Church. All true believers were members of the Church, "the body of true Christ," as opposed to those outside it, "the body of the Devil."[188] Gregory's deep belief in God's active presence on earth was centered on the mystery of the Church,[189] and from this belief sprang his sense of the urgent need for ecclesiastical reform. His greatest concern as pope—as he put it in a late *apologia pro vita sua*—was that the "holy church, the bride of Christ, our mistress and mother, should return to her true glory and stand free, chaste and catholic."[190] Everything was dependent on the

183. Becker 1988, 307 ff.; Capitani 1992, 177, disputes the legitimacy of this question.

184. In opposition to the view prevalent among historians, I am following the interpretation in Becker 1988.

185. Becker 1988, 333. On Urban's dealings with Christian powers, see id. 1964, 113–254.

186. Morris 1991, 146.

187. Brundage 1976, 105.

188. See Gregory to Bishop Hermann of Metz, 15 March 1081, *Register* VIII,21 (p. 557); *Correspondence*, 172. Cf. Laarhoven 1959–61, 38, for further expressions of this dichotomy.

189. Laarhoven 1959–61, 37.

190. Gregory to all the faithful, July-November 1084, *Epp. Vagantes* no. 54.

Church, on its soundness, on its purity and liberty; everything and every-one—that is, all the faithful, whatever their station of life and profes-sion—had to serve her. But because the Church, the bride of Christ, had been entrusted under the Petrine commission to St. Peter as the first Ro-man bishop, it was the popes, as Peter's successors in Rome, who carried the heavy burden of caring for all the faithful by caring for the Church. This was Gregory's leading idea, from which it followed that as the head of the Roman Church, which "has never erred, nor ever, by the witness of the Scripture, shall err to all eternity," the pope could be judged by no one.[191] By the same token, the pope, the vicar of St. Peter, had to judge everyone.

Given the Church's ultimate importance for salvation, which was the purpose of human life on earth, the Church was something one should be willing to fight for. If fighting was deemed necessary, the pope in his supreme position—the highest within the Church and Christian soci-ety—had the right and duty to call on laymen to serve the Church in this manner. Waging war for the Church was intended to purify the Church from within and was directed against those within Christian society who had fallen away from the true faith. For Gregory, only war against the "ungodly" was licit. It could be authorized by the pope alone and was ultimately an internal ecclesiastical affair.

With the newly and vigorously asserted primacy of the Holy See, er-rant Christians were, by definition, adversaries of the pope. For Peter Damian, for example, the pope, the Apostolic See, and the Roman Church were synonymous. "You are the Apostolic See, you are the Ro-man Church," he wrote to the newly elected Gregory VII.[192] Therefore, obedience owed the pontiff was absolute, and Peter declared as a here-tic anyone who did not agree with the Roman Church, since it is the only church founded by Christ Himself.[193] Slightly reformulated, this view became one of the principles announced in Gregory VII's *Dictatus papae:* "That he should not be considered as Catholic who is not in con-formity with the Roman Church."[194] Bernard of Constance, one of the

191. The *Dictatus papae* XXII, XIX [XVIIII], *Register* II,55a (pp. 207, 206).

192. Peter Damian *Opuscula 20* (PL 145: 443). Cf. Morrison 1969, 287; Blumenthal 1988, 72.

193. See *Actus Mediolani, de privilegio Romanae ecclesiae, ad Hildebrandum* (PL 145: 91); Peter Damian to Cadalus, *Epistolarum* I,xx (PL 144: 241): "Praeterea si eos sacri canones haereticos notant, qui cum Romana ecclesia non concordant." Cf. Blumenthal 1988, 72; Tellenbach 1991, 116 n. 1.

194. "Quod catholicus non habeatur, qui non concordat Romanae ecclesiae." *Dictatus papae* XXVI, *Register* II,55a (p. 207).

Gregorian controversialists, declared that the prescriptions of the Holy
See had to be received as if they came from the mouth of St. Peter himself, and all Christians had to consider as enemies those who opposed
the pope.[195] Indeed, Gregory—who saw himself as exercising papal authority jointly with St. Peter—believed that St. Peter spoke through the
pope's mouth.[196] In short, for Gregory VII and his supporters, obedience
to the commands of the Holy See became the test of righteousness and
of catholic belief itself.[197] The pope had the ultimate responsibility to
counter those who had been turning "the Christian religion and the
true faith which the son of God who came down from heaven taught us
through the fathers" into "the evil custom [*prauam consuetudinem*] of
this world." [198] One aspect of that "evil custom" was war for earthly gain
and glory, which Gregory strongly condemned. "And if Holy Church
imposes a heavy penalty upon him who takes a single human life," he
wrote, "what shall be done to those [princes] who send many thousands
to death for the glory of this world?" [199] He contrasted such secular wars
and the readiness for waging them to fighting for God, for which he saw
no enthusiasm among his contemporaries: "Lo! many thousands of secular men go daily to their death for their lords; but for the God of heaven
and our Redeemer they not only do not go to their death but they also
refuse to face the hostility of certain men. And if there are some . . . who
for love of Christ's law are determined to stand firm to the death in the
face of the ungodly, they are not only not helped . . . but they are also
considered to be foolish and of unsound judgement as if they were out
of their minds." [200]

Like the pope himself, the leading Gregorians were preoccupied with
the fight against straying Christians, against heretics and schismatics.[201]
Anselm of Lucca, arguing that the Church had the right to *persecutio,*
mentioned war against the Gentiles only once, without ascribing much
importance to it.[202] *Persecutio* was to be directed against the "enemies

195. *Liber canonum contra Heinricum quartum* 6; quoted in Arquillière 1934, 329.
196. Cf. Gregory to Abbot Hugh of Cluny, 7 May 1078, *Register* V,21 (p. 385); to
Bishop Hermann of Metz, 25 Aug. 1076, *Register* IV,2 (p. 293).
197. Morris 1991, 110.
198. Gregory to all the faithful, July-November 1084, *Epp. vagantes* no. 54.
199. Gregory to Hermann of Metz, 15 March 1081, *Register* VIII,21 (p. 559); *Correspondence,* 173. Cf. Gregory to Henry IV, Sept. 1075, *Register* III,7 (p. 257); Leyser
1965, 58.
200. Gregory to all the faithful, July-November 1084, *Epp. vagantes* no. 54.
201. Cf. Arquillière 1934, 312 ff.
202. *Collectio canonum* XIII,29 (Pásztor 1987, 421). Cf. Erdmann 1935, 228; Stickler 1947, 252.

of the Church" — heretics, schismatics, and excommunicates, and more specifically, unjust and schismatic bishops.[203] According to Bonizo of Sutri, Christian soldiers had to fight heretics and schismatics as well as rebels—those irreverent toward bishops—in order to impose ecclesiastical discipline.[204] Emperor Henry IV and his supporters were especially hated by the Gregorians. Manegold of Lautenbach, it is true, accepted that it was permissible and pleasing to God to kill pagans in defense of the Church.[205] But he argued that Henricians were more detestable than pagans. Thus, he who would defend justice by killing a Henrician would incur less guilt than if he had killed a pagan, because the magnitude of the Henrician's crime would offset the stain of homicide.[206]

For Gregory VII and his supporters, pagans were not necessarily the worst imaginable creatures. When Christians were "bad," they were regarded as worse than pagans. Gregory, for example, described his Italian neighbors—Romans, Lombards, and Normans—as worse than Jews and pagans.[207] This comparison can of course be seen as rhetorical. But as *dissipatores ecclesiae*,[208] those who weaken the Church from within, errant Christians were the Church reformers' first and foremost target.

Though war against pagans was of marginal importance in Gregory VII's outlook and played little part in his pontifical action,[209] in 1074 he planned a military expedition to the east. In a number of letters he claimed that the Christians of Constantinople, "oppressed by frequent attacks of Saracens" and "daily being slain like so many sheep," were urging him "to reach out our hands to them in succor." Thus he made the decision to "cross the sea" and lead an army "against the enemies of God and push forward even to the sepulchre of the Lord."[210] Gregory's plan came to nothing. There seems to be no evidence that it made an impact on his contemporaries, and it cannot really be regarded as a crusading plan.[211]

203. *Collectio canonum* XII,44–46,53,60,68–70 (Cushing 1998, 187–90, 192). Cf. Stickler 1947, 251.
204. *Liber de vita Christiana* II,43; VII,16,28; X,79. See also chap. 1 nn. 98, 171.
205. *Ad Geberhardum liber*, 381, 399. Cf. Erdmann 1935, 218.
206. *Ad Geberhardum liber*, 381.
207. Gregory to Abbot Hugh of Cluny, 22 Jan. 1075, *Register* II,49 (p. 189).
208. Cf. Anselm of Lucca *Collectio canonum* XII,53 (Cushing 1998, 189).
209. Erdmann 1935, 155, 246; Becker 1988, 315. Cf. Villey 1942, 62–63; Daniel 1975, 250.
210. Gregory to Count William of Burgundy, 2 Feb. 1074, *Register* I,46 (pp. 70–71), *Correspondence*, 23; to Henry IV, 7 Dec. 1074, *Register* II,31 (p. 166), *Correspondence*, 57; to Countess Matilda of Tuscany, after 16 Dec. 1074, *Epp. vagantes* no. 5. For a detailed treatment, see especially Cowdrey 1982. Cf. Erdmann 1935, 149 ff., 275; Delaruelle 1980, 90 f.; Becker 1988, 294 ff.
211. Riley-Smith 1977, 75.

It is true that this was the first instance of the idea of a papally directed
military expedition to the Near East.[212] But Gregory VII's "Oriental
project" was actually, in the first instance, directed against Normans in
southern Italy who were threatening both the papacy and the Greek empire. He was trying to bring together a substantial "force of fighting
men" to intimidate his Norman enemies, so they would be "the more
easily won over to the right side." And once the Normans were pacified,
Gregory explained to Count William of Burgundy, "we may cross over
in aid" of the eastern Christians. The "Oriental project" was only "another advantage" that might result from Gregory's confrontation with
the Normans.[213] Although the project contained some elements and motives of the later crusade, it lacked such essential crusade characteristics
as indulgences, taking the vow, and the resulting protection for crusaders.[214] And whereas the notion of the "service of Christ" was pivotal
in Urban II's crusade, Gregory's project rested on the idea of the "service of St. Peter," a leading idea of his Church reform.[215] In sum, the
"Oriental project" of 1074 does not support the view that Gregory VII
was either the originator of the crusade or Urban II's predecessor in this
matter.[216]

In contrast to Urban's thinking, the conflict between Christians and
Muslims was not in the forefront of Gregory's thoughts. From the perspective of what was to come with the Crusades, his attitude toward
Muslims may be described as entailing an "astonishing 'tolerance.'"[217]
Such tolerance, to be sure, is not characteristic of all the views Gregory
expressed about Muslims. Those views were "far from simple or uni-
form;"[218] in fact, their complexity and variety are in themselves significant, for with the launching of the crusade, simplicity and one-
dimensionality were to prevail. On the one hand, Gregory described the
Muslims as *pagani*[219] or lumped them together with *pagani*,[220] a term

212. Brundage 1969, 27; Mayer 1993, 20; Riley-Smith 1993a, 8.
213. See Gregory to Count William of Burgundy, 2 Feb. 1074, *Register* I,46 (pp. 70–
71), *Correspondence*, 23; Fliche 1920, 42; Douglas 1969, 159; Cowdrey 1982, 30–31;
1983, 122 ff.
214. Riley-Smith 1977, 75; Cowdrey 1982, 40; Becker 1988, 300.
215. Mayer 1993, 20; Riley-Smith 1993a, 8.
216. Fliche 1920, 41, 46; Becker 1988, 295 n. 46.
217. Becker 1988, 293.
218. Cowdrey 1988, 489.
219. For example, Gregory to the French barons, 30 Apr. 1073, *Register* I,7 (p. 11);
Gregory's summons to defend Constantinople, 1 March 1074, *Register* I,49 (p. 75); Gregory to Emperor Henry IV, 7 Dec. 1074, *Register* II,31 (p. 166). Cf. Hettinger 1993, 171.
220. Gregory to Countess Beatrice, 16 Oct. 1974, *Register* II,9 (p. 139); to all the
faithful, July-November 1084, *Epp. vagantes* no. 54.

that was, in the Christian language, loaded with distinctively polemical connotations.[221] Occasionally he used conventional expressions like "impious Saracens."[222] But on the other hand, Gregory was "drawn beyond habitual limits of his thinking."[223] The most remarkable case in point is his letter to the Hammadite emir an-Nasir, but also relevant are Gregory's letters to North African Christians and those touching on the affairs of Sicily and Spain.

The complexities of Gregory's correspondence with North Africa are an intriguing subject I cannot broach here,[224] except to note the lack of anything resembling the "crusade idea."[225] In the letter he sent to the clergy and the Christian people of Carthage, Gregory exhorted them to patiently and fearlessly suffer persecution in imitation of Christ. Moreover, he reminded them that St. Paul had taught obedience to worldly powers—if only to impress on the Christians of Carthage that they should be so much more obedient to their bishop, whom they had denounced to the Muslim authorities.[226] In a twin letter to the bishop of Carthage, the pope expressed his compassion for the unfortunate bishop for the suffering caused him by the "pagans" and pseudo-Christians of his church. Praising the bishop's steadfastness in his tribulations, the pope exhorted him to maintain his witness for the faith, implying that death was the most precious confession of Christian religion. Had the Carthagian bishop died at the hands of the Saracens, his death would have demonstrated "their error."[227] These words can be read as indicating that Gregory VII hoped for conversion of the Saracens.[228] Be that as it may, he certainly hoped for better times for Christianity in Africa.[229]

As the pope wrote to the Christian community of Bidjaya (Bougie), had the African Christians ceased to be "false sons of the Church"[230] and ended their factional struggles, they could have induced their Saracen neighbors, by their exemplary lives, to emulate the Christian faith

---

221. Schwinges 1977, 135; on *pagani*, 90 ff., 136. Cf. Kedar 1984, 57.

222. Gregory to Bishop Berengar of Gerona, 2 Jan. 1079, *Register* VI,16 (p. 421).

223. Cowdrey 1998, 494.

224. See Courtois 1945; Hettinger 1993, chap. 4.

225. Becker 1988, 293 (specifically referring to Gregory's letter to Archbishop Cyriacus of Carthage, June 1076, *Register* III,19 [p. 285]).

226. Gregory to the clergy and people of Carthage, 15 Sept. 1073, *Register* I,22 (pp. 37–38).

227. Gregory to Bishop Cyriacus of Carthage, 15 Sept. 1073, *Register* I,23 (p. 39).

228. Kedar 1984, 56.

229. Cf. Gregory to Archbishop Cyriacus of Carthage, June 1076, *Register* III,19 (p. 285).

230. Gregory to Bishop Cyriacus of Carthage, 15 Sept. 1073, *Register* I,23 (p. 39).

rather than hold it in contempt.[231] But Gregory may also have realized that political circumstances in North Africa were favorable to Christianity—both in Africa and Sicily. An-Nasir was in conflict with the Zirids (who ruled in Mahdia), against whom the Normans, under papal auspices, fought for the reconquest of Sicily.[232] An-Nasir made overtures to the pope, releasing a number of Christian captives, sending him gifts, and requesting that the pope ordain a bishop in "the province of Mauretania." In response, Gregory sent to the emir his famous letter: "God, the creator of all, without whom we can do or even think nothing that is good, has inspired your heart; he who enlightens every man who comes into the world [John 1.9] has enlightened your mind in this purpose," Gregory wrote. "For Almighty God, who wills all men be saved and none to perish [cf. 1 Tim 2.4], approves nothing in us more fully than that, after his love for God, a man should love his fellow men and that what he would not have done to himself he should do to no one else [cf. Mt 7.12]. Such charity as this, we and you owe to our own more particularly than to other peoples; for we believe and confess one God, albeit in different way, and we daily praise and revere him as the creator of the ages and the governor of this world. For as the Apostle says, 'He is our peace, who makes both one' [Eph 2.14]." After asking an-Nasir to receive favorably an embassy from Rome, the pope concluded the letter: "For God knows, that we love you sincerely to the honour of God, and that we desire your welfare and prosperity in the present life and in that to come; and we beseech with our heart and lips that, after long continuance in this life, God will bring you into the blessedness of the bosom of the most holy patriarch Abraham." [233]

The question, of course, is what to make of these words. Some see the key to the letter to an-Nasir in the Mahdia campaign and portray Gregory VII as a skillful politician.[234] The letter could also be regarded as a "masterful exercise in ambiguity." [235] But such ambiguity would have been incompatible with the crusade, and if we look at the crusade as the crowning event of the eleventh century, the spirit that animates Greg-

---

231. Gregory to the clergy and people of Buzea (Bougie), May [or June] 1076, *Register* III,20 (pp. 286–87).

232. See Courtois 1945; Cowdrey 1977.

233. Gregory to Anazir, King of Mauretania, [1076], *Register* III,21 (p. 288); trans. in Cowdrey 1998, 493–94.

234. Courtois 1945, 224, 226 (speaking of Gregory's "savant opportunisme"). On the Mahdia campaign, see chap. 1 n. 232.

235. Kedar 1984, 57.

ory's letter is very strange indeed, and his expression of goodwill quite remarkable.[236] If Gregory was insincere, his insincerity was knowledgeable and respectful enough to point out the monotheism of Islam, to speak of "God" (not Christ, whom Islam does not recognize as God), and to mention Abraham, whom Muslims venerate. Favorable assessments of Gregory's letter to an-Nasir expostulate that the pope formulated a possible meeting point between Christianity and Islam (and that he did so as clearly as was possible in the Latin Middle Ages), and represent him as having made "a conscious effort to communicate with Islam," or even to establish peaceful coexistence between Christians and Muslims.[237] Even in the case of Sicily, where Gregory supported war against the "pagans," he admonished the reconquerors to refrain from major offences (*capitalibus criminibus*) and, rather, to think carefully about how to make Christianity (*christiani nominis culturam*) appear as imposing to the "pagans."[238] This would suggest that Gregory wanted the two religions to "quietly coexist" and that Christians should "by their faith and works" win their faith a "good report in Muslim eyes."[239]

With regard to Spain, Gregory was not overly enthusiastic about the *reconquista*.[240] The Saracen possession of Spain, to be sure, he considered a violation of the lawful right of St. Peter—that is, the pope—to that land. As he put it, "the kingdom of Spain has from ancient times appertained to St. Peter."[241] But Gregory considered the wresting of that country from "the hands of pagans" preferable to pagan occupation only if the victorious Christian barons would restore the exercise of the papal right over Spain. For Gregory, Christian power as such was not an unqualified good. It was valuable and acceptable only if it was just, and injustice inflicted by pagans was more bearable than injustice done by Christians. Thus he made it clear to the would-be French *reconquistadores* that "unless you determine to attack that kingdom under a just agreement to uphold the rights of St. Peter, we would rather lay our interdict upon your attempt to go thither than that our holy and universal Mother Church should suffer the same wrongs from her own children

236. Courtois 1945, 103; Cowdrey 1998, 494.
237. Schwinges 1977, 135; Becker 1988, 294; Daniel 1993, 46–47. Cf. Delaruelle 1980, 73–74 n. 91.
238. Gregory to Archbishop Arnald of Acerenza, 14 March 1076, *Register* III,11 (p. 272).
239. Cowdrey 1998, 490.
240. Becker 1988, 288.
241. Gregory to the French barons, 30 Apr. 1073, *Register* I,7 (p. 11); *Correspondence,* 6. Cf. Cowdrey 1998, 468.

as from her enemies."[242] Gregory VII also wrote that the Christian religion in Spain had suffered not only at the hands of the Saracens; it was brought low "after the kingdom of Spain had been long polluted by the madness of the Priscillians, degraded by the treason of the Arians and separated from the Roman ritual, through the invasion first of the Goths and then of the Saracens."[243]

Here Gregory spoke of the Saracens as neither polluting nor mad and treasonable. Elsewhere Gregory conceded that "these men, so far as faith is given them, observe their own laws, even though in this age they are of no avail for the salvation of souls and are not given lustre and confirmation by such miracles as those by which the Eternal King frequently gives his testimony to our law." Again, this may be regarded as a mere rhetorical device to blacken those Christians who had turned the Christian religion into an "evil custom" and reduced it "to a laughing-stock not only of the devil but also of Jews, Saracens, and pagans."[244] But even such rhetoric, not to speak of Gregory's diplomatic "ambiguity," was obliterated by his successors. With the crusade winning the day, a different language prevailed. Gregory's political opportunism— or realism—exemplified by his dealing with an-Nasir, was succeeded by holy war. His attitude toward the Muslims was thus destined to remain "unparalleled almost until modern times."[245]

The reality of "their own inadequate numbers" may indeed have compelled Christians in the "crusader states," such as William of Tyre, to adopt a "broader tolerance toward neighbouring Moslems than was understood in the West."[246] But in the Latin West Gregory VII's position remained exceptional. Moreover, if William of Tyre stands out as a prime example of Christian "tolerance" in the occupied Middle East,[247] Gregory's exceptionalism was not confined to the West. The idea of William's "tolerance" can only be taken with a grain of salt. In his *History of Deeds* William was apparently doing no more than "rehashing, with some material derived at second hand from Christian Arabic sources,

---

242. Gregory to the French barons, pp. 11–12.
243. Gregory to the kings of León and Castile, 19 March 1074, *Register* I,64 (p. 93); *Correspondence*, 29.
244. Gregory to all the faithful, July-November 1084, *Epp. vagantes* no. 54. Cf. n. 198.
245. Rousset de Pina 1952, 178; Daniel 1975, 251; 1993, 136. Gregory VII's formulation about *unum Deum* in his letter to an-Nasir resembles the position taken by the Second Vatican Council. Cf. Hettinger 1993, 167 n. 108.
246. Purcell 1975, 11.
247. As argued in Schwinges 1977.

the accepted western ideas."[248] He seems to have been better informed, rather than more "open-minded," than his contemporaries in the Latin West. The language he used to describe his Muslim neighbors' religion does not strike us as particularly "tolerant." For William of Tyre, Muhammad was the "first born son of Satan" who had "falsely declared that he was a prophet sent from God." The "poisonous seed" Muhammad had sown had "so permeated the provinces that his successors employed sword and violence, instead of preaching and exhortation, to compel the people . . . to embrace the erroneous tenets of the prophet."[249] Such comments about the Muslims support the observation that war against the unbelievers was the one theme that ran through William of Tyre's famous *History*.[250] Tolerant or not, William was a representative of a world whose horizons had been drawn by Urban II, not by Gregory VII.

The crusade was Urban's, not Gregory's, war. Urban II was a lukewarm Gregorian with regard to war inside the Church and within Christendom.[251] When, however, it came to war against external enemies, those outside the Church and Christendom, he was not a Gregorian at all. Whereas Gregory had confined holy war to Christendom and directed it against the Church's internal enemies, Urban conceived of it as war of the whole of Christendom against its external enemies.[252] Gregory was a *Kriegsmann,* a Christian militarist; Urban was a man of peace. Gregory could imagine war as well as peace, that is, normal relations, with the Muslims; the peacemaking Urban was driven to holy war against them.

Urban II's contribution to the invention of the crusade has been discussed elsewhere.[253] Suffice it to say here that his primary contribution was "to bring together a number of accepted and relatively popular ideas in a new form, one that had good fortune to achieve a spectacular and impressive success."[254] He organized those ideas into a theologico-historical scheme and thus gave meaning to actual developments in the Christian world, successfully channeling their further course.[255] Of key

---

248. Morris 1991, 286.
249. *History of Deeds* I,i (1: 60).
250. Edbury and Rowe 1990, 167.
251. Becker 1988, 324.
252. Cf. Erdmann 1935, 284; Vismara 1974, 73.
253. See especially Erdmann 1935, chap. 10; Cowdrey 1970b; Delaruelle 1980, 99 ff.; Becker 1988; Cole 1991, chap. 1; Riley-Smith 1993a, chap. 1.
254. Brundage 1976, 105.
255. Becker 1988, 273, 331, 333 ff., 351–53, 376.

importance here, it bears repeating, is that Urban II was a peacemaking pope.[256] The new holy war is unimaginable without the peace movement. Urban II linked the two inextricably together.[257] He understood, and helped others understand, that peace was a crucial condition of the crusade and that the crusade was the realization of peace: Christian peace—peace in Christendom, by Christendom, and for Christendom.

256. Ibid., 277 ff., 330.
257. Keen 1987, 97.

THREE

Christendom and the Crusade

Christendom, *christianitas,* was the form of Western unity that emerged in the High Middle Ages. Medieval writers spoke of Christendom when they talked about themselves and their civilization.[1] People described themselves as inhabitants of Christendom when they wished to refer to the "limits of a society larger than their village or parish, county or diocese, or kingdom."[2] *Christendom* was the most common term for the lands inhabited by Latin Christians, designating "a community of powers and nations united by their shared religion," or simply, "Christian society."[3] Medieval thinkers invested the idea of Christendom with their hopes for temporal as well as spiritual unity in this world.[4]

The term *christianitas,* however, has a longer history than the self-conscious social body of Latin Christians to which it refers.[5] It was during the pontificate of John VIII, in the second half of the ninth century, that the term began to be used more frequently and to acquire the social meaning of a "temporal Christian society animated and vivified by the spiritual Christian society."[6] For John VIII, however, this unitary society of Christians was fundamentally (if not merely) mystical. His con-

---

1. Van Engen 1986, 539. Cf. Chabod 1991, 29.
2. Hay 1953, 1.
3. Ladner 1983, 490; Housley 1992, 454; Katzir 1992, 4; Bartlett 1993, 252.
4. See Chabod 1991, 33.
5. For the origins of the term, see Rupp 1939, chap. 1.
6. Rupp 1939, 35, 41, 47. Cf. Vismara 1974, 31, 33.

cept of *christianitas* was vague; it was synonymous with the notion of the Church as the mystical body of Christ[7] and did not exceed the meaning of the unity of creed, that is, Christianity, *christianismus*.[8] For almost two centuries after John's death in 882, the word *christianitas* was by and large in eclipse, only to reappear with the eleventh-century reform papacy.[9] In Gregory VII's statements the use of the term increased, but the idea of Christendom was still not clearly articulated.[10] From Gregory VII onward, *christianitas* and related words occurred much more frequently, and it is in that period that the term began to achieve its "true significance."[11] The heyday of *christianitas* coincided with the rise of the papal monarchy, and the idea of Christendom finally "triumphed"[12] under the pontificate of Innocent III, perhaps the mightiest of papal monarchs. This idea lay at the center of Innocent's political outlook and actions.[13]

One finds the full articulation of the notion of *christianitas* in crusading chronicles, where the word was in common use.[14] This is understandable once we realize that the concept of Christendom was the first to take shape among the various preconditions of the crusading movement—as well as the last to vanish.[15] A precondition of the crusade, the concept of Christendom was realized with the crusade.[16] The launching of the crusade can be seen as marking the symbolic point when Christendom became "a living reality," when it was transformed into what could be called a society.[17]

"Christendom (and the idea of Christendom) found its most potent expression in the crusade; the crusade exalted Christendom, carried it to its highest point of fervor."[18] Christendom and the crusade came into existence together: They were "made together, in a reciprocal creation."[19]

---

7. Vismara 1974, 26 ff., especially 29. The same may be said of Jonas of Orleans who, about half a century earlier, used the term *christianitas* a few times as a synonym for the mystical "universal Church." Jonas *Le métier du roi* IX (lines 5, 28); XI (lines 54–55). Cf. chap. 2 n. 99.

8. Rupp 1939, 52; Delaruelle 1980, 32. For the terms *christianitas* and *christianismus*, cf. Rousset 1963, 195 ff.; Hay 1968, 22.

9. Rupp 1939, 53. For Leo IX's use of the term, cf. Morrison 1969, 283.

10. Laarhoven 1959–61, 94; Roscher 1969, 22.

11. Ladner 1983, 490.

12. Rupp 1939, 4; Laarhoven 1959–61, 7, 9.

13. Roscher 1969, 23.

14. Laarhoven 1959–61, 98; Morris 1991, 152.

15. Housley 1992, 454.

16. Rupp 1939, 73; Delaruelle 1980, 108.

17. Fliche 1929, 314; Rupp 1939, 91 n. 1.

18. Rousset 1963, 191. Cf. Laarhoven 1959–61, 76.

19. Dupront 1959, 274.

Christendom had now developed beyond a simple identity with the creed and liturgy of Christianity to become a dynamic social reality, a worldly force. It was a militant community of Christians whose thoughts and will were directed toward the Holy Land and consumed with the struggle against the Muslims, who were now considered the "enemies of God and holy Christendom."[20] *Christianitas* was *populus Christianus*, the Christian people, united under the supreme authority of the pope. The "papal authority over the *populus christianus* constituted the reality we call *christianitas*."[21] The Christian people bound together as Christendom had a common worldly pursuit and a common army and were fighting for the Christian *res publica*, the common weal.[22] Christendom was the Christian world on a military march against paganism.[23]

The creation of holy Christendom, *sainte crestienté*, through holy war and the formation of its identity in holy war should be seen from two complementary perspectives: the unification of Latin Christians and the polarization between them and the outside world. The first was a logical development of the peace movement's striving for Christian unity. The second was the product of the construction of a common enemy, the foundations for which were also laid by the eleventh-century peacemakers.

THE FIRST WESTERN UNION: A COMMON FRONT AGAINST THE PAGANS

Latin Christians found their way to themselves as Christendom through peacemaking. The collective entity that was to become Christendom had begun to show recognizable traits in the Peace of God and, especially, the Truce of God endeavors.[24] Christendom was "an immense *Pax*."[25] As we have seen in chapter 1, the canons of the peace council of Narbonne declared that "no Christian should kill another Christian, for whoever kills a Christian undoubtedly sheds the blood of Christ."[26] Pope Urban II

20. Rousset 1963, 191; "Turci inimici Dei et sanctae christianitatis": *Gesta Francorum* VI,xiii.

21. Kempf 1960, 115 n. 32; cf. 119: "die Christianitas war im Grunde nicht anderes als der lebendige Bezug zwischen dem päpstlichen Führer und der christlichen Gefolgschaft." The language used here is probably a deliberate allusion to the Nazi movement.

22. See especially Delaruelle 1980, 108.

23. Schwinges 1977, 8.

24. Cf. Bredero 1994, 124.

25. Cf. Delaruelle 1969, 59.

26. See chap. 1 n. 215.

built on the achievements of the peace movement and brought the movement to completion. He renewed the precepts of the Council of Narbonne by generalizing them.[27] But in Urban's preaching at the crusading peace council of Clermont, the image of the shedding of Christian blood, which had moved the Church dignitaries at Narbonne to prohibit canonically Christians' killing Christians, took on a broader scope.

Like his peacemaking predecessors, Urban II condemned fratricidal wars in the West. But, as reported by Baldric of Dol, he also pressed hard on the minds of his listeners the "great hurt and dire sufferings" of eastern Christians, calling them "our brothers, members of Christ's body." Oriental Christians were Latin Christians' "blood-brothers," "born from the same womb as you, for you are sons of the same Christ and the same Church." Their suffering at the hands of the Muslims, of which the pope spoke, was as intolerable as inter-Christian violence in the West, because in both cases Christian blood was spilled. *Effunditur sanguis Christianus, Christi sanguine redemptus,* the pope said, referring to Jerusalem, Antioch, and the other cities of the East: "Christian blood, redeemed by the blood of Christ, has been shed." So he believed, or at least wanted his audience to believe. To further impress his audience, Urban added a vivid image: "Christian flesh, akin to Christ's flesh, is delivered up to execrable abuses and appalling servitude."[28] His articulation of this blood brotherhood—the founding of Christian unity in blood[29]— was itself pregnant with the spilling of blood.

The vision of suffering eastern Christians broadened what was expected from western Christians. Ending the shedding of Christian blood now required more than peace among Christians: it called for war against their enemies. Peace and war were intimately linked—not in war for peace but in a war of peace. The peace Urban II was intent to bring to Christians did not mean demilitarization (to use a term from our own times), but an escalation of militarization by redirecting military activity to the world outside. Christendom had been a fortress long before

27. Rousset 1945, 195.
28. Baldric of Dol *Historia Jerosolimitana* I,iv (p. 13); trans. in Peters 1989, 6; Riley-Smith 1993a, 145.
29. Cf. Bartlett 1993, 251–2, speaking of "the 'ethnization' of Christianity," that is, of the Christians' "adopting the terms of race and blood to describe their group identity." This tendency became prominent in the High Middle Ages and triumphed with the expulsion of the Muslims and Jews from Spain after the fall of Granada in 1492 (when "a blood racism of the modern kind" was born, as opposed to the "almost entirely cultural" medieval language of race). Ibid., 197, 241–42.

anxiety about "fortress Europe" was voiced in our own days. [30] Christendom's peace was peace in the Christian citadel, which meant war to those outside the walls: *Intus pax, foris terrores*.[31] Turning the internecine wars among Christians into the new Christian holy war created, out of the internally torn Christians, the unity of Christendom. The crusading army may indeed be called "the first Western union," and the formation of this army actually marked "a spectacular advance toward European peace and unity." [32] The crusade gave peace and unity to Christendom.[33]

This peace and unity were of a dual nature. Interpreted negatively, they called for a kind of passivity: the renunciation of fratricidal wars. Interpreted positively and actively, they found expression in struggle against a common enemy. Peace commended the Christian brotherhood, *fraternité*,[34] to go to war against those who were not of the Christian family. Thus Christian society became conscious of itself through mobilization for holy war. "When Christendom becomes conscious of itself as a political-religious body, there is war. The crusade appears, thus, as Christendom's becoming conscious." [35] War made by "holy Christendom" could only be holy, and that holy undertaking was the common work of western Christians. In its intentions and mythic self-perception, the crusade was an expression of the Christian unity that it was also creating.[36]

Urban II's crusading propaganda was based on the idea of the "community of the whole Christendom" directed against the pagans, and the

30. For a radical-democratic critique of "fortress Europe" in the name of a wished-for "Social or Citizens' Europe," see Delanty 1995, 14. The idea of Christendom as a fortress was not alien to Komensky. Even the meekest of European pacifists could imagine Western unity only as "a common bastion of Christianity against every outward enemy." Comenius *The Angel of Peace,* 49.

31. Delaruelle 1969, 59, 61.

32. Strayer, "The First Western Union," in Strayer 1971, 334. I see no irony in Strayer labeling the crusading warfare the first, peacemaking unification of the West. He admired "the courage of our ancestors and the vision of the great popes of the late eleventh century," who could, in a poor, backward, and disunited "Europe," "dream of attacking the most dangerous of their adversaries, the Mahommedans." Gibbon had seen "the folly and Glory of the first Crusade" as a Great Event which "rouzed Europe from its long and profound Lethargy." "Outlines of the History of the World" (*The English Essays,* 170). For the contribution of the reform papacy to the unification of the West (not "Europe"), see Tellenbach 1947.

33. Rousset 1945, 147, 196.

34. Cf. ibid., 135, 173.

35. Ibid. Cf. Arquillière 1939, 150–51.

36. "Dans son intention et son mythe, la Croisade est réalité de l'unité." Alphandéry 1959, 199. Cf. Rousset 1945, 171; Purcell 1975, 8.

crusade was a massive assault, a common front against the pagans.[37] The battle cry changed. Instead of fighting for the "defense of the Church," Christians now fought for the "liberation of Christendom";[38] *libertas* was substituted for *defensio*.[39] Contemporary sources that discuss the new holy war abound with the words *libertas* and *liberatio,* and *liberatio* was the word most frequently used by Pope Urban when he preached the crusade.[40] It encompassed the liberation of people, that is, the baptized members of the eastern churches, as well as the liberation of territory, the holy places. Where there was blood—the blood of Christ uniting all the Christians—there also had to be soil: the soil sanctified by Christ's blood.

The Christians, equal in Christ, brothers in faith, went to war for liberty. The change of the Phrygian cap for the crown of martyrdom and the *tricolore* for the cross had become a matter of *histoire événementielle.* Fresh ground was broken in the eleventh-century. Central to this shift was the creation of a common enemy: the construction of the Muslims as the normative enemies of Christianity and Christendom.

MAKING THE MUSLIM THE ENEMY

Pagans and barbarians had always inhabited the Christian imaginary world, and waging wars against them had been common in the centuries preceding the Crusades. When, with the Arab expansion in the seventh and eighth centuries, the Muslims reached the European peninsula, they became in the Latin Christians' eyes one among those pagan, or infidel, barbarians. Among the host of Christian enemies they were assigned no privileged place. Western Christians, then, saw neither the Muslims nor their faith as a special threat to the Christian religion. They certainly did not speak of the "military apostleship" of the Muslims,[41] nor of Islam as a religion that "unlike Christianity, which preached a peace that it never achieved, . . . unashamedly came with a sword."[42] Such commonplaces emerged and took root later in Western history and, as the two twentieth-century opinions I have just quoted testify, have not yet been

---

37. Erdmann 1935, 306, 321; Villey 1942, 110, 181; Rousset 1945, 21, 67; Vismara 1974, 76.

38. Erdmann 1935, 306. For Pope Urban II the crusade was "a war of liberation." Riley-Smith 1993a, 17.

39. Cf. Vismara 1974, 64 n. 186.

40. Riley-Smith 1993a, 17–18. Cf. Erdmann 1932, 404–5; Schwinges 1977, 232 ff.

41. Pirenne 1939, 19.

42. Runciman 1991, 1: 15.

uprooted. The Latin Christians' early response to the Muslims, though not friendly, was very moderate in tone, especially in comparison with the language that was to develop with the crusade.[43]

The mild Christian response is well illustrated in the most significant source of information about the Frankish kingdoms between the late sixth and the early eighth centuries, the Merovingian *Chronicle of Fredegar,* probably written in the mid-seventh century.[44] Here, *Sarracleni,* or *Saraceni,* are first mentioned in Biblical genealogies as descendants of Sem: as an oriental people with their own language.[45] Later in this chronicle they appear as the offspring of Ishmael, Abraham's first-born son by his Egyptian maid Hagar. From there came their name: "Ishmaelites, and then Agarens, later still Saracens."[46] From the times of Josephus, this was the conventional genealogy of the Arabs, most often called Saracens by their medieval contemporaries in the Latin West.[47] The convention did not die off with the waning of the Middle Ages. An anonymous author of a pamphlet published in London around 1515, for example, wrote that *Machamet* "was of the kynred of Ismael that was Abrahams sone & he begate hym on Arage [sic] his chamberee. And therfore the sarasyns ben called Ismahelytes and some Agaren and some of Agar."[48] A distant echo of that genealogy was still to be found in Voltaire, who regretted that the Saracens had not been made to be descendants of Sarah, Abraham's lawful wife, which would have made a neater etymology.[49]

When Fredegar moved from sacred history to *histoire événementielle,* he recorded that in the time of Emperor Heraclius (610–41) the "*Agarrini,* who are also called *Saracini,*"[50] had grown "so numerous that at last they took up arms and threw themselves upon the provinces of the Emperor" and defeated the imperial army. Of great interest is the chron-

43. Southern 1962, 16; Kritzeck 1964, 15–16; Daniel 1975, chap. 1; Schwinges 1977, 98; Finucane 1983, 147 f.

44. On "Fredegar" and the chronicle known by this name, see Collins 1996. Cf. Wallace-Hadrill 1960; Rotter 1986, chap. 3.

45. Fredegar *Chronicarum* I,6, 9.

46. Ibid., II,2.

47. Finucane 1983, 148; Rotter 1986, 1. Cf. Josephus *Jewish Antiquities* I,x,5; I,xii,2 ff.

48. Quoted in Beckingham 1976, 608.

49. "J'aurais voulu qu'on eût fait descendre les Sarrasins de Sara, l'étymologie aurait été plus nette." *Dictionnaire philosophique* (*Oeuvres compl.,* 17: 76).

50. *Fredegarii Chronicorum* IV,66. Fredegar falsely attributed this naming to Orosius's *Historiarum adversus paganos,* which has led Sénac 1983, 14, to conclude that Fredegar did not contribute to the advancement of knowledge about the Muslims, for he used "un text déjà vieux de deux siècles."

icler's explanation of the battle of Yarmuk, 636, which opened the way
for the Saracens to take possession of Jerusalem. He reports that the
night before the battle "the army of Heraclius was smitten by the sword
of God [*gladius Dei*]." *Gladius Dei* here may indeed have been a Latin
rendering for *Saif Allah,* the surname of one of the Arab commanders,
Halid b. al-Walid,[51] but it is next to impossible that either the chronicler
himself or his medieval readers would have thought of that. The Saracens, rather, won that battle with God's help as a punishment for Emperor Heraclius's sins. He had embraced a heresy and married his own
niece. The emperor finished his days in agony, tormented with fever,
while the Saracens continued to ravish the empire during the brief reign
of his son, Constantine III.[52] During the rule of Constantine III's successor, Constans II (641–68), the Saracens captured Jerusalem and many
other cities,[53] swept over upper and lower Egypt, took and plundered
Alexandria, and quickly occupied the whole of *Afreca.* The empire had
lost vast territories, and the emperor became a tributary of the Saracens.[54]

The Saracen conquests are represented by the chronicler as secular
wars—no different from the many other wars he recorded—and spoken
of in an objective mode. He did not vilify the Saracens and came nowhere near calling them "dogs," as he did the Slavic Wends.[55] And the
closest he came to talking about the invaders' religion was to mention
circumcision.[56] His lack of curiosity about the Saracens in general, and
about their religion in particular, was also characteristic of the travel-
ogues of pilgrims, whose journeying to the Holy Land had not been prevented by the Arab conquests. Moreover, on the rare occasions when the
pilgrims noted religious differences between Christians and Saracens,
they did not represent them as the basis for condemning the Saracens.
Rather, they left behind a picture of an apparently undisturbed Christian religious life and of coexistence of the two religions, a feature of
which was that Christians and Saracens in some cases shared a church.[57]
Bishop Arculf, for example, who visited the holy places around 680, reported that "the unbelieving Saracens" had built themselves a "church"

51. Rotter 1986, 158.
52. *Fredegarii Chronicorum* IV,66. For an explanation of confusing geographical
names appearing in this narrative, see Rotter 1986, 159–70.
53. In fact, Jerusalem had by then already been in Saracen hands.
54. *Fredegarii Chronicorum* IV,81.
55. Ibid., IV,68. Cf. n. 136.
56. "Gens circumcisa." *Fredegarii Chronicorum* IV,66.
57. See Rotter 1986, chap. 1; cf. Rotter 1979 (republished with some changes as
chap. 4 in id. 1986). On sharing churches, cf. Patzelt 1978, 199.

in Damascus, the royal city of the Saracen "king," and a "praying house" in Jerusalem.[58] He said this in about as many words, and in a neutral tone.

The manner in which early medieval chroniclers spoke of the Saracens became harsher, however, when the Arab expansion reached the Frankish lands. Having taken possession of Spain in 711, they began to make inroads into Gaul in 714. In 719, they conquered Septimania and advanced into Aquitaine and Provence. In 721, they were defeated before Toulouse but scored military successes elsewhere in southern France later in the 720s. In 733, an army led by Emir 'Abdarrahman came as far as Tours but was routed by Charles Martel near Poitiers.[59] Modern historians have constructed a myth presenting this victory as having saved Christian Europe from the Muslims.[60] Edward Gibbon, for example, called Charles Martel the savior of Christendom and the battle near Poitiers an encounter that changed the history of the world. Without Martel's victory, he wrote in a memorable phrase, "[p]erhaps the interpretation of the Koran would now be taught in the schools of Oxford, and her pulpits might demonstrate to a circumcised people the sanctity and truth of the revelation of Mahomet."[61] This myth has survived well into our own times. Haskins, the first professional American medievalist, mentioned that a student of his had written: "we should all be polygamous Mohammedan Turks instead of Christians worshipping the one true God" without Charles Martel's victory.[62] Even today, Poitiers is an indispensable ingredient of European ideology.[63]

Contemporaries of the battle, however, did not overstate its significance. The continuators of Fredegar's chronicle, who probably wrote in the mid-eighth century,[64] pictured the battle as just one of many military encounters between Christians and Saracens—moreover, as only one in a series of wars fought by Frankish princes for booty, power, and ter-

---

58. *Adamnani de locis sanctis libri tres;* quoted in Rotter 1986, 39. Using this source, Bede, *De locis sanctis* xvii, wrote that "the king of the Saracens" "established and consecrated" a "church" in Damascus. In the *Nomina regionum* IX,2, Bede called that building a "basilica."

59. The year usually given for this battle (sometimes called the Battle of Tours) is 732. I follow Roy and Deviosse 1966, 207, and Cardini 1981, 269, who accept the year 733, in agreement with M. Baudot, "Localisation et datation de la première victoire remportée par Charles Martel contre les musulmans," *Recueils des travaux offerts à M. Clovis Brunel* (Paris, 1955).

60. Cf. Cardini 1981, 269.

61. *Decline and Fall,* chap. 52 (3: 336–38).

62. Haskins 1967, 231. On Haskins, cf. Freedman and Spiegel 1999, 560 ff.

63. Cf. Compagnon and Seebacher 1993, 1: 50–55.

64. See Collins 1996, 112–16.

ritory. Charles Martel, it is true, was described as having utterly destroyed the "unbelieving Saracens" with "Christ's help."[65] But that
was not a specific, or exceptional, trait of the fight against the Saracens.
The Franks, as the chronicle relates, enjoyed divine assistance also in
their wars against the Saxons, "detestable pagans,"[66] as well as in their
struggles with Christian princes. Pippin III, for example, fought Waiofar,
Duke of Aquitaine, "with God's help."[67]

One of Fredegar's continuators represented the battle at Poitiers as
what it really was: an episode in the struggle between Christian princes
as the Carolingians strove to bring Aquitaine under their rule. Lumping
together a number of Carolingian campaigns that took place between
728 and 733,[68] Fredegar's continuator blamed Eudo, the Duke of Aquitaine, for provoking the expedition by Charles Martel that involved the
battle at Poitiers. Eudo, who had not fared well in the struggle with the
Carolingians, "summoned to his assistance against Prince Charles and
his Franks the unbelieving Saracen people."[69] Eudo had defeated the
Saracens at Toulouse in 721, of which the chronicle says nothing. But in
the second half of the 720s, the Muslims north of the Pyrenees, seeking
independence from Arab power in Spain, and the Aquitainians, fearing
Carolingian supremacy, seem to have looked for a working agreement
between themselves. Eudo even married his daughter to a Berber chief.[70]
But there is no evidence that he ever fought together with the Saracens
against the Franks.[71] The chronicle, nevertheless, presented Eudo as
having brought the Saracens into the Christian lands, where they burnt
down churches and slew Christians until they were destroyed by Charles
Martel. The chronicler called the Saracens "perfidious," but it was Eudo
who incurred his opprobrium because he had allegedly broken the treaty
with Charles.[72]

---

65. *Chronicarum continuationes* 13 (*Fredegarii Chronicorum*, pp. 90–91).
66. Ibid., 19 (p. 93).
67. Ibid., 44 (p. 113).
68. Collins 1996, 116.
69. *Chronicarum continuationes* 13 (*Fredegarii Chronicorum*, p. 90). Cf. *Chron.
Fontanellensis* (in Roy and Deviosse 1966, 291): "Eudo Dux Aquitanarium cernens se
superatum, et ad defendendam patriam suam contra Carolum se viribus esse destitutum,
gentem perfidam Saracenorum ad auxiliandum sibi invitat." Similarly, the *Chronicle of
Saint-Denis* (Roy and Deviosse 1966, 296); *Ann. mettenses*, 325. Cf. Buckler 1931, 6 n. 5;
Roy and Deviosse 1966, 162.
70. See Rotter 1986, 219. For a broader context, cf. Buckler 1931, 4–7.
71. *Chron. moissiac.*, 291, reported that in 732 Eudo fought against 'Abdarrahman,
was defeated, and sought Charles Martel's help.
72. *Chronicarum continuationes* 13 (*Fredegarii Chronicorum*, p. 90). In fact, Charles
broke the treaty when he twice ravaged Berry in 731. Roy and Deviosse 1966, 150.

In his report of Charles Martel's campaign of 737, the chronicler's hostility was again aimed at a Christian prince, Duke Maurontus of Marseilles (who had handed over Arles, Avignon, and other towns to the Muslim emir of Narbonne). "Once more the mighty race of Ishmael, who are now known by the outlandish name of Saracens, rebelled and burst across the river Rhône. With the base, craven collaboration of the heretical Maurontus and his friends, the Saracens attacked in force the city of Avignon strongly fortified on her rock; and they laid waste the countryside wherever resistance was offered."[73] Charles overpowered his enemies, took Avignon, burnt it to the ground, staged a bloodbath, and then "plunged into Gothic territory as far as the Narbonnaise." Having defeated a Muslim army coming from Spain, Charles's army then laid waste the region, razed a few towns to the ground, and looted their unfortunate fellow Christians.[74] Later on "in the course of this happy year," a Carolingian army marched on Provence, put Maurontus to flight, and Charles "restored the whole country, down to the Mediterranean, to his rule."[75]

It is clear from the chronicle that the Carolingian campaigns against the Saracens were no more than an element in the Carolingians' endeavors to strengthen their rule in what is today southern France.[76] Those wars were not religious wars. Of the infidelity of the "mighty race of Ishmael" we hear nothing. Even Pope Gregory III extolled Charles Martel as the defender of the Church not with mention of Charles's wars against the Saracens but because he hoped that Charles would protect him against the Lombards.[77] In the continuations of Fredegar's chronicle, the language in which the wars against the Saracens are recorded does not differ from reports of other Frankish military pursuits and continues to be as neutral and detached as Fredegar's tone was.

The same is true of the minor chronicles' reports of the Saracen inroads. None of them mentions the Arab conquest of Spain. The first reference to the Saracens, in some of them, is the entry for the year 721, noting Eudo's victory over the invaders.[78] In 725, "the Saracens came,"

---

73. *Chronicarum continuationes* 20 (*Fredegarii Chronicorum*, pp. 93–94).
74. Ibid., 20 (pp. 94–95).
75. Ibid., 21 (pp. 95–96). The chronicler conflated campaigns fought in Provence in 737 and 739 into a single episode. Collins 1996, 116.
76. Cf. Burns 1947, 581–83.
77. Gregory III to Charles Martel, A.D. 739; A.D. 740 (MGH Epp. 3: 476–79).
78. *Ann. Petaviani*, 7; *Ann. Laureshamenses*, 24; *Ann. Alamannici*, 24; *Ann. Nazariani*, 25; *Ann. Sangallenses maiores*, 73.

or "came for the first time." [79] Referring to the battle of Poitiers, the *Annales Tiliani* and *Annales Laubacenses* both simply state that in the year 732, "Charles made war against the Saracens." [80] The *Annales Sancti Amandi* add that the fight took place in the month of October, the *Annales Mosellani, Annales Laureshamenses, Annales Alamanici, Annales Nazariani,* and *Annales Sangallenses* specify that the battle was fought on a Saturday, whereas the *Annales Petaviani* records the day and the month. [81] The most exhaustive reports of Charles Martel's campaign of 737 are those that give Sunday as the day of the battle, [82] whereas the others say the same as they did for the battle of Poitiers (obviously unaware of any unique historical importance): "Charles made war against the Saracens." [83]

Let me turn to Bede the Venerable, the great Northumbrian Biblical exegete of the early Middle Ages. Although contemporary with the Saracens' conquests and a very well-informed scholar reputed for his exceptional sense of history, he knew very little, maybe nothing, of the Arab attacks on southern and western Francia. [84] In his *Greater Chronicle* we read nothing of the Arab conquest of Spain, [85] whereas in the *Ecclesiastical History* he mentioned the Saracens' expansion as one of the misfortunes that had befallen a sinful Christian world. [86] Two comets appeared about the sun in the year 729, he wrote, and presaged terrible destruction to the east as well as the west: "the Saracens, like a very sore plague, wasted France with pitiful destruction, and themselves not long after were justly punished in the same country for their unbelief." [87] That

---

79. *Ann. Petav.*, 9; *Ann. Lauresham.*, 24; *Ann. Alaman.*, 24; *Ann. Nazar.*, 25; *Ann. Sangal. maiores,* 73.

80. *Ann. Til.*, 8; *Ann. Laubac.*, 9.

81. *Ann. St Amandi*, 8; *Ann. Mosel.*, 495; *Ann. Lauresham.*, 24; *Ann. Alaman.*, 24; *Ann. Nazar.*, 25; *Ann. Sangal. maiores,* 73; *Ann. Petav.*, 9.

82. *Ann. Lauresham.*, 26; *Ann. Alaman.*, 26; *Ann. Nazar.*, 27; *Ann. Sangal. maiores,* 74.

83. *Ann. St Amandi*, 8; *Ann. Til.*, 8; *Ann. Laubac.*, 9; *Ann. Petav.*, 9.

84. He "knew nothing." *The Greater Chronicle,* 418, 425 (editors' commentary).

85. Outside Spain, this conquest seems to have been first mentioned in *Chron. moissiac.*, 290.

86. Some fifteen years later, Boniface explained the Saracen conquests as divine punishment: The "peoples of Spain and Provence and Burgundy" turned "away from God and lived in harlotry until the Almighty Judge let the penalties for such crimes fall upon them through . . . the coming of the Saracens." Boniface to King Ethelbald of Mercia, A.D. 746–47 (*Letters of Saint Boniface,* 128).

87. *Eccl. History* V,23 (*Opera hist.*, vol. 2). Since the work was concluded in 731, it is not entirely clear which "punishment" Bede had in mind. The anonymous continuation of Bede's chronology from 731 to 766 does not mention any battle with the Saracens. *Bedae chronologia continuata,* 323–25.

"unbelief" itself, however, "did not stir a flicker of interest in the most comprehensive mind of the time in Latin Europe."[88]

What may account for Bede's indifference to the religion of Saracen invaders is the sense, which Bede shared with many contemporaries, that their presence in the northern Mediterranean was transient.[89] When Abbess Bugga, probably soon after Bede's death but before 738, planned a pilgrimage from England to Rome, she asked St. Boniface for advice. Conscientious man that he was, he made inquiries in Rome with Sister Wiethburga, who had already found at the shrine of St. Peter "the kind of quiet life she had long sought in vain" and was obviously sympathetic with Bugga's wish to come to Rome. The message Boniface sent to Bugga was that she "would do better to wait until the rebellious assaults and threats of the Saracens who have recently appeared about Rome should have subsided." Telling Bugga that Wiethburga was going to send her an invitation, Boniface concluded: "Make ready what you will need for the journey, wait for word from her, and then act as God's grace shall command."[90]

When the Saracens entered his horizons,[91] Bede saw them "as unbelievers of not more than ordinary ferocity."[92] He was slow to see the Arab invasion as a possible threat to the Christian religion (if he ever really saw it as such),[93] though he recorded what he knew about the Arab campaigns. But like his predecessors in the Frankish lands, he wrote about them dispassionately. In the *Greater Chronicle,* for example, he noted under the entry for the year 4639 (according to Bede's calculation of time reckoned since the creation, Christ was born in the year 3952) that the Arabs "invaded Sicily, and returned to Alexandria with an enormous quantity of loot." The entry for the *anno mundi* 4649 states that the Byzantine emperor Justinian II "made a ten-year peace on land and

88. Metlitzki 1977, 14.
89. Daniel 1975, 17.
90. Boniface to Abbess Bugga, before A.D. 738 (*Letters of Saint Boniface,* 56).
91. In his early works, the Saracens did not yet figure as a concept for Bede. Rotter 1986, 73. In the *De arte metrica,* probably his earliest composition, Bede mentioned *Mauri,* "by which he presumably meant Arabs." Wallace-Hadrill 1975, 64. In the *De Temporibus liber* (composed in 703), he wrote that "Abraham annorum C genuit Isaac. Nam primo genuit Ismael, a quo Ismaelitae." He spoke of Ishmaelites and did not use the term *Saracens,* which is not mentioned in Genesis but was employed by Jerome (whom Bede studied) and later by Isidore of Seville in what became a standard exegesis of this Biblical theme. In Jerome's words: "Abraham de ancilla genaret Ismahel, a quo Ismahelitarum genus, qui postea Agareni et ad postremum Saraceni dicti"; cited in Rotter 1986, 71; cf. Isidore, *Etym.* IX,ii,6.
92. Southern 1962, 16.
93. Wallace-Hadrill 1975, 64.

the sea with the Arabs, but the province of Africa that was subject to the Roman empire was assaulted by the Arabs, and Carthage itself was also captured by them and destroyed." But whereas the Christianization of the Frisians is described by Bede as "achieving innumerable daily losses for the devil and gains for the Christian faith," he did not name the Arab conquest a gain for the devil.[94] Rather than religious foes, the Saracens were "barbarians" from whom the Langobard King Liudbrand saved St. Augustine's bones and transported them from Sardinia, depopulated by the Saracens, to Ticino.[95]

Even if in Bede's occasional comments about the Saracens in his later writings moderation seems to have given way to denunciation, this came nowhere near "the hysterical Christian zeal that becomes common enough after 1095." [96] Bede explained that the Saracens, who had worshipped Venus, abandoned themselves to the cult of Lucifer.[97] But because Bede stated this in the past tense (for the pre-Islamic Saracens were believed to have worshipped Venus), and also because "Lucifer" did not self-evidently mean the devil (in Plinius, for example, whom Bede had studied, it was the morning star), that Bede wanted to say that the Saracens in his own time were the devil's followers is not necessarily true.[98] They were, for sure, pagans. Bede's Syrian contemporary, John of Damascus, represented them as praying to Aphrodite/Venus, and supposed that the sacred Black Stone in the Ka'ba in Mecca was a carved head of Aphrodite/Venus.[99] Less ambiguous was Bede's description of the Saracens as "adversaries of the Church" in his exegesis of 1 Sam 25.1: "Then David got up and went down to the wilderness of Paran." [100] As Bede excerpted from Jerome, the desert of Paran was where Ishmael's descendants, the Saracens, lived.[101] Because Ishmael was the bastard son of Abraham, born of his Egyptian maid Hagar, the Saracens were children of a slave. But the Scripture said: "Drive out the slave and her child;

94. Bede Greater Chronicle, 334, 336; Chronicon, 198, 199–200.

95. Bede Chronicon, 204.

96. Finucane 1983, 149–50.

97. Expositio actuum apostolorum VII,43. For this and the two following quotes from Bede, cf. Wallace-Hadrill 1975, 67.

98. See Rotter 1986, 248–49. On the planet Venus, "qui est hesperus, lucifer et vesper," cf. Honorius Augustodunensis De imagine mundi I,lxxi (PL 172: 139). On Lucifer as "foretelling a new day," as the "nuntius celestis aurore," cf. Alain of Lille, "Sermo in die Epiphaniae" (Textes inédits, 242).

99. Beckingham 1976, 607.

100. In primam partem Samuhelis IV,xxv,1.

101. "In deserto autem Faran . . . habitasse Ismahelem unde et Ismahelitae qui nunc Sarraceni." In primam partem Samuhelis, Nomina locorum, 278. Cf. Gen 21.20.

for the child of the slave will not share the inheritance with the child of the free woman." [102] The free woman was Sarah, Abraham's wife and the mother of his son Isaac. And Sarah represented the Church: *Sarra, id est Ecclesia, in libertatem genuit populum Christianum.*[103] Bede's commentary on Samuel was written in 716. Four years later Bede again wrote of the Saracens as unsettled people from the desert who in the past had attacked all other peoples of that desert and had been set upon—and overcome[104]—by all. Now, however, their hand was against all and the hand of all was against them,[105] since they, the hated adversaries, had taken possession of the whole of Africa, a great part of Asia, and some of Europe.[106]

Neither Latin nor Greek sources from that period ever spoke of the "Muslims." Rather than this word, meaning those who trusted in one God, these sources preferred the "ethnic terms" *Saraceni* or *Agareni.*[107] Bede was no exception. No less ignorant of Islam[108] than his contemporaries in the Latin West, Bede was interested in explaining the Saracens' origins in light of Biblical genealogies. For him the problem to be solved was why the descendants of Hagar and Ishmael were called Saracens, as if they had been Sarah's offspring.[109] But Bede offered nothing new in this respect; indeed, Jerome and Sozomen had been more ingenious, explaining that the Saracens had appropriated to themselves the "false name" after Sarah, in order to "conceal the opprobrium of their origin" because their true mother, Hagar, was a slave.[110] Bede's contribution was that he likened Sarah to the Church, recognized the Saracens as *aduersarios ecclesiae,* and related his Scriptural exegesis to the contemporary Saracen conquests. The Biblical story of Ishmael, especially the passages used by exegetes, was not exactly flattering. The Saracens'

---

102. Gal 4.30, cited by Bede, referring to Gen 21.8–10.

103. *Expositio in primum librum Mosis* 21 (PL 91: 242A, quoted in Rotter 1986, 254).

104. In order to convey that the Saracens were defeatable, Bede, transcribing Jerome, changed *expugnantor* for *imugnantor.*

105. Cf. Gen 16.12. Bede made use of the same Biblical reference in the *In cantica canticorum* (PL 91: 1088, quoted in Rotter 1986, 253).

106. *Libri quatuor in principium Genesis* IV,xvi,12.

107. Brown 1996, 181, 187.

108. See n. 84.

109. Cf. Isidore of Seville *Etym.* IX,ii,6: "Ismael filius Abraham, a quo Ismaelitae, qui nunc corrupto nomine Saraceni, quasi a Sara, et Agareni ab Agar." For a more detailed discussion, see Rotter 1986, 68–77. For early Islamic interpretations of this genealogy, see Fowden 1993, 145 ff. Cf. Southern 1962, 16–18; Schwinges 1977, 70, 98–99.

110. Jerome *Comment. in Ezechielem* VIII,25 (col. 233); Sozomen *The Ecclesiastical History* VI,38.

forefather was outside the Covenant: "a wild ass of a man, with his hand against everyone, and everyone's hand against him" (Gen16.12), doomed to "live at odds with all his kin." And so were his offspring, the Saracens, who could not be counted because they were so numerous (Gen 16.10). But the Saracens were nonetheless acknowledged as descendants of Abraham, and as an object of Biblical exegesis, they were given "a niche in Christian history"; the harsh dichotomy between Christian and Muslim worlds characteristic of later times had not yet emerged.[111]

This "lack of rancor" linked with indifference, as found in Fredegar, minor chronicles, and Bede, continued in the Carolingian accounts of the Saracens.[112] The Muslims played a relatively unimportant role in portrayals of the cosmic struggle between good and evil. For Charlemagne and his contemporaries, as for their predecessors, the Saracens were no more than one group of enemies among many, and not the one that worried them the most.[113] The Carolingians waged wars against the Muslims, it is true, but they also maintained diplomatic relations with them. The popular picture of the Carolingian attitude toward the Muslims may be unbalanced because two of the Carolingians' military exploits against the Saracens became legends. I have already mentioned the mythologizing of the battle near Poitiers. The other case in point is the young Charlemagne's expedition to the south of the Pyrenees in 778, when he accepted an invitation to intervene in dynastic struggles in Muslim Spain. The expedition ended in complete disaster but was later sung about in the *Chanson de Roland,* in which the future emperor Charles conquered the proud land as far as the sea.[114] In fact most of the Carolingians' warlike energies were directed at wars against the Lombards, Saxons, Avars, Normans, Danes, and Slavs—these were the "foreign peoples." [115] Frankish, English, and Italian writers at this time did not distinguish too precisely among those who were attacking Christian lands. The Christians fought an amorphous multitude of *pagani, gentiles, infi-*

111. Southern 1962, 17.
112. Southern 1962, 18–19; Metlitzki 1977, 14.
113. Hentsch 1992, 18.
114. "Carles li reis, nostre emperere magnes, / Set anz tuz pleins ad estét en Espagne. / Tresqu'en la mer conquist la tere altaigne." The Muslim "King" of Saragosa, the only town that the *Chanson's* Charlemagne had not conquered, is depicted as one who did not love God but served Muhammad and worshipped Apollo: "Mahumet sert e Apollin recleimet." *The Song of Roland* 1 lines 1–3, 6–8. On the expedition, cf. Metlitzki 1977, 117 ff.; Reilly 1993, 77; Riché 1993, 44, 115–16. Einhard *The Life* ix is a sober ninth-century report.
115. Cf. Morisi 1963, 164 ff.; McKitterick 1983, chap. 3, 5, 9; Wallace-Hadrill 1983, chap. 11, 13, 411–19.

deles and *barbari*.[116] And they fought them without a clean-cut religious motivation.

Christian views of the Muslims began to shift in the mid-ninth century. The episode of the "martyrs of Cordova" aside (where, in the 850s, some Christian fanatics sought martyrdom by publicly insulting Islam and reviling Muhammad),[117] the impetus for this change came not from the imperial court but from Rome.[118] The transformation of Christian views of Islam was intimately linked to new formulations regarding Christian community. One such idea was articulated by Pope Leo IV when he described wars against pagans as the defense of the Christian fatherland.[119] But it was the papal and clerical policy formulated by Pope John VIII—"a stern, able, and profoundly political figure"[120]— that really began to give shape to a new, uncompromisingly hostile attitude toward the Muslims and their religion.[121] Not surprisingly, this was the same pope who injected some social substance into the notion of *christianitas*[122] and who developed the richest vocabulary for the wars against pagans.[123] Yet even here, though the Muslims were the worst *among* Christians' enemies, they were still not *the* enemy.

Pope John, for example, styled the Normans as enemies of Christ's cross and called on Frankish princes to refrain from shedding Christian blood in fratricidal wars and join forces to fight against the Normans for the liberty of the Church of God.[124] As *inimici crucis* themselves, the Saracens did not differ from the Normans in the Church's eyes. But with their military presence in southern Italy, the Saracens began to threaten Rome itself. Their incursions into Christian territory were even more threatening to the pope because Christians, including bishops, of the southern Italian seaports made alliances with the invaders.[125] They acted so either in the hope of averting danger to their homes or for less noble

116. Douglas 1969, 92; Delaruelle 1980, 24.
117. See Southern 1962, 20 ff.; Daniel 1975, chap. 2; Schwinges 1977, 85 ff. (with further references); Smith 1988–89, 1: 42–47; and Colbert 1962; Wolf 1988.
118. Schwinges 1977, 100.
119. See chap. 2 n. 134.
120. Partner 1972, 67.
121. Cf. Daniel 1975, 76.
122. See n. 6.
123. "Heidenskriegterminologie": Becker 1988, 365.
124. See John to the bishops of King Louis's realm, A.D. 876, *Epistolae et decreta* no. 22 (cols. 668–69); to the counts of King Louis's realm, A.D. 876, *Epp. et decr.* no. 23 (col. 673); cf. Becker 1988, 365–66.
125. The first treaty with the Saracens was concluded by Naples in 837. Engreen 1945, 322 n. 1.

motives: the desire to preserve trade with the Saracens and share in what they had plundered in the Roman Campagna.[126] In such a situation, the pope's invocations of Christian unity and his representation of the Christians as a unitary mystical body bound together by the mystery of redemption[127] stood in stark contrast to the actual dismemberment of that imagined body.

As mentioned earlier, Pope John organized and led his own army,[128] but he also repeatedly appealed to secular princes to come to help the Church with "tough fighters."[129] Help was needed for the defense of not only the papal lands but Christendom as a whole (*defensione terre sancti Petri et totius christianitatis*).[130] The impious, wicked Saracens, "hateful to God," were pictured by John VIII as a grave danger to the entire Christian faith and culture (*Christianae religionis cultura*).[131] He compared them to locusts, devastating everything they could reach.[132] But his dramatic announcements and requests for military support, far from arousing religious enthusiasm, were met with indifference.[133] Even those who supported the pope, such as the Salernitans, had their own Christian community, "the Christians of Salerno," rather than "Christendom" before their eyes.[134] And the more unresponsive the Christians were, the more "impious" and "odious to God" the Saracens seemed to become in the pope's pronouncements.

Diabolization of the Saracens was instrumental in disciplining Christians, and the Christians whom John VIII sought to discipline were first and foremost those who had made alliances (*foedera*) with the "impious Saracen people." It was these alliances that the pope attacked the most

126. Partner 1972, 70. For a general view of the problem, see Engreen 1945.

127. "[U]num corpus sumus in capite Christo, et alter alterius membra." John to the bishops in Emperor Charles's realm, March 877, *Epp. et decr.* no. 62 (col. 717). Cf. Delaruelle 1980, 30.

128. See chap. 2 n. 135.

129. John to Archbishop Frotarius, A.D. 877, *Epp. et decr.* no. 64 (col. 718).

130. John to Count Lambert, A.D. 877, *Epp. et decr.* no. 98 (col. 749).

131. See John to Emperor Charles the Bald, A.D. 876, *Epp. et decr.* no. 43 (cols. 696–97). Cf. Becker 1988, 366–67.

132. John to Count Boson, Sept. 876, *Epp. et decr.* no. 30 (col. 684); to Emperor Charles, A.D. 876, *Epp. et decr.* no. 43 (col. 696). On the devastating Saracens, cf. *Epp. et decr.* nos. 58, 62, 79. But Amara, *Storia dei Musulmani di Sicilia* (Catania 1933), pointed out that the pope had only sent such messages "ad uso dei devoti di Francia e Allemagna," whereas to those who had been acquainted with the real situation he "non si potean dir tante bugie." Quoted in Vismara 1974, 49, with a critical commentary; a view similar to Amara's was held by Engreen 1945, 327.

133. Delaruelle 1980, 26–27.

134. Daniel 1975, 77–78.

vigorously. In targeting them, he was not an innovator. Moral condemnation of alliances of the faithful with the unfaithful is Biblical in origin.
Most famous in this regard are the words of the apostle Paul to his brethren in Corinth: "Do not be mismatched with unbelievers. For what part-
nership is there between righteousness and lawlessness? Or what fellowship is there between light and darkness? What agreement does Christ
have with Beliar? Or what does a believer share with an unbeliever?"
(2 Cor 6.14–15). This passage had been frequently cited by Christian writers in different contexts—as when St. Jerome, for example,
argued against marriages between Christians (in particular Christian
women) and heathen.[135] And John VIII, as we shall see, made very specific use of it.

There were instances in Christian history when alliances with the pagans were rejected on principle. "It is impossible for Christians and servants of God to live on terms of friendship [amicicia] with dogs." Such
was the answer King Dagobert's ambassador gave to King Samo, who at
a time when the Franks were in conflict with the Wends, offered his loy-
alty to the Frankish ruler.[136] Up to the time of John VIII, however, the
Church's attitude toward pacts with non-Christians had been markedly
inconsistent. One of John VIII's predecessors, Pope Nicholas I, for instance, had regarded alliances with the infidels as beneficial to the Christian people.[137] John VIII was the first to take a firm doctrinal stance on
the issue.[138] According to John's interpretation of Nolite iugum ducere
cum infidelibus (2 Cor 6), the apostle Paul prohibited any social links
between the faithful and the unfaithful: those who made unclean alliances with the infidels acted not only against the apostolic precept but
against Christ himself.[139] According to John, treaties and alliances with
the infidels went against divine law.[140] But this was not all. In John VIII's

135. Cf. Jerome to Ageruchia, A.D. 409, Letter CXXIII,5 (Principal Works, 231);
Against Jovinianus I,10 (ibid., 353).

136. Fredegar Chronicorum IV,68 (pp. 56–57). The exchange was transcribed in the
Gesta Dagoberti I. Regis Francorum 27 (MGH SS rer. Merov. 2). Amicicia was a term for
alliance. Vismara 1974, 16

137. Vismara 1974, 18 n. 32. Bede was not scandalized by a peace treaty the emperor
made with the Arabs. See n. 94.

138. Vismara 1974, 58; Schwinges 1977, 246.

139. John to Neapolitans, Salernitans, and Amalfitans, A.D. 875, Epp. et decr. no. 9
(col. 655). Cf. Vismara 1974, 19 ff.; Delaruelle 1980, 30–31. This interdict was entered
into the later collections of canons.

140. See John to Amalfitans, A.D. 879, Epp. et decr. no. 269 (col. 889). Cf. Vismara
1974, 25–26.

declarations, the once-abstract "infidel" began to assume specific traits and became the Saracen.

John's prohibition against alliances with the infidel was founded on the idea of the mystical body of Christ, of which all Christians were members. Those who made alliances with Christ's enemies became strangers to his body, tearing apart its members.[141] The pope considered any contact with the infidel as polluting the body of Christian society and any alliance with the impious as contagious. The infidels, and particularly the Saracens, were malign, vicious, and unclean people; they were "sons of fornication," "members of the Devil," "sons of Beliar," the "body of the Devil," and "subject to the diabolical law."[142] A pact with them would bring about the perdition of the soul as well as the destruction of Christendom;[143] the safety of the soul and the security of the Christian community (or at least Christian possessions) were interlinked.[144] An alliance between the body of Christ and the body of the devil was not only unlawful but simply unimaginable. It would be a *pactum cum impiis, pax cum pessimis, foedus cum nefandissimis*—in short, a pact with the enemies of Christ, Christians, and the Christian name. As such, an alliance with the infidel was an *impium foedus*, a *polluta unitas*, and was condemned as an ungodly crime: *crimen, impium scelus*.[145] The obvious means to protect Christian society was to excommunicate anyone making such pacts—to cut off the infested and contaminating limb.

In practice, John VIII was struggling to protect the right Christian order in the face of Christian princes in southern Italy who had either committed the "ungodly crime" of making a treaty with the Saracens or might have been tempted to do so. That those princes may have wanted to negotiate peace to protect themselves and their subjects was, to the pope, no justification. John VIII formulated a clear imperative that left no room for doubt: To keep peace with the "most evil" was a crime. The

---

141. *Epp. et decr.* no. 9 (col. 655). Cf. Balan 1890, 11.

142. John VIII knew how to synthesize such characterizations: "Christiani nominis viri paganorum foedera fugiant et solum in Deum, qui eos creavit, et non in diaboli membra, quae sunt filii fornicationis et vasa irae, spem suam ponere discant." *Epp. et decr.* no. 68 (col. 722). "Agareni" as "filii fornicationis": *Epp. et decr.* no. 62 (col. 716); "falsi filii Sarae": *Epp. et decr.* no. 60 (col. 714); "iniqui et ancillae filii": *Epp. et decr.* no. 273 (col. 893). Cf. Vismara 1974, 40–42.

143. "Pro salute animae tuae ac pro defensione totius Christianitatis," Pope John VIII, in 879, pressured the prefect Pulcaris to break "cum paganis pactum." *Epp. et decr.* no. 253 (col. 878).

144. Cf. John to Amalfitans, A.D. 879 or 880, *Epp. et decr.* no. 288 (col. 901).

145. For these and many other descriptive terms, see Vismara 1974, 42–47. Cf. Rupp 1939, 38; Daniel 1975, 77; Schwinges 1977, 246.

faithful had to desist from making peace with the enemies of God.[146] The only peace that was acceptable and commanded was peace among Christians, peace among members of the mystical body of Christ. This peace was threatened by any violation of the Biblical precept: *exiens exibis de medio ipsorum et pollutum non tanges.*[147]

Peace treaties with the Saracens were ruinous for the Christian peace. Pope John thus worked doggedly to persuade the Christian rulers to abandon them. Where his diplomacy and bribes[148] failed, he did not hesitate much to use the ultimate means at his disposal, excommunication. A case in point was his dealing with Athanasius, the duke and bishop of Naples. Because the bishop had made alliances with the "Agareni," the "enemies of the Christian name," and refused to be persuaded by the pope to renounce them,[149] John VIII declared: "We anathemize him until such time as he separates himself wholly from these same Saracens, as the enemy of the whole of Christendom."[150] Because the pact with the Saracens was injurious to Christians and the whole of Christendom,[151] the bishop who had made it became the enemy of the whole of Christendom (*totius Christianitatis inimicum*). There was no middle ground: either cut off all social ties with the sons of Ishmael—totally withdraw from "the fellowship of pagans"[152]—or suffer excommunication. If *christianitas* was to be whole—and a threat to *christianitas* was a threat to its wholeness—it had to be wholly separated from the infi-

---

146. Quoting Ps 138 [139].21–22, John VIII demonstrated "[q]uantum praetera sit Deo delectabile ab inimicorum Dei pace desistere"; and also "quanto crimine cum pessimis pax tenetur." *Epp. et decr.* no. 9 (col. 656).

147. "Depart, depart, go out from there! Touch no unclean thing." Isa 52.11.

148. See Partner 1972, 70–71.

149. John to Athanasius, March 881, *Epp. et decr.* no. 318 (cols. 927–28). Threatening excommunication, the pope hoped to compel the Amalfitans, too, to renounce their treaties with the Saracens. In a letter from October 879 he ordered them—"ex auctoritate Dei et sanctorum apostolorum Petri ac Pauli"—"ut nullum cum impia Saracenorum gente pactum haberetis, habitumque omnimodo rumperetis, in tali scelere, et in consortio inimicorum Dei manere non formidatis." *Epp. et decr.* no. 269 (col. 889). Cf. *Epp. et decr.* nos. 253, 273, 287, 288.

150. "[E]t quosque se ab ipsis Saracenis penitus separaverit, velut totius Christianitatis inimicum anathematizamus." John to different bishops, *Epp. et decr.* no. 321 (col. 931). When the pope later lifted the anathema, he reminded Athanasius how he had "abjecto Christi levi jugo, cum infidelibus jugum obscena cupiditate ducere," and warned him to never again in any way make any alliance with the Saracens. John to Athanasius, A.D. 881–82, *Epp. et decr.* no. 352 (cols. 945–46). For a detailed description of John VIII's practical endeavors against "impious alliances," see Vismara 1974, 50 ff. Cf. Balan 1890, 74 ff., 81, 103 ff.

151. "[A]d perditionem Christianorum" and "ad perditionem totius Christianitatis." *Epp. et decr.* no. 321 (cols. 930–31).

152. "[A]b eorum societate separaturum." *Epp. et decr.* no. 321 (col. 931). See also no. 288 (col. 901): "relicta nunc penitus Saracenorum societate." Cf. Daniel 1975, 78.

dels. This idea implied the disciplining of Christians: If they wanted to live within the Christian community, they had to keep themselves clean by suspending any contact with the infidels, the unclean ones *(pollutum non tanges)*. Prohibition of social contacts between the faithful and the infidels generated the idea of territorial separation as well, which entailed the cleansing of Christian territory. John VIII "demanded," "prayed," and "earnestly besought" that "the impious race may be driven out of our territories." [153] Such calls set forth conceptually the splitting of the world into two irreconcilable parts.[154]

In an era long since passed, early Christians had separated themselves from the infidel world by proclaiming that their true city was "Jerusalem, the city above." [155] Now, according to John VIII, Christians should set out to separate the infidels from their own, Christian world. Whereas in the old times the separation was from infidel culture,[156] now a culture of separation from the infidels had apparently begun to take root. An ominous feature of these developments was that religiously motivated territorial separation became ethnically based. Those to be driven out were a *gens,* a race, a people of a single origin.

Here, however, we are only at the beginning of the story that was to unfold with the Crusades. Practice lagged behind the ideal world of Pope John VIII. His exhortations were not universally heeded, and his efforts to break the "impious alliances" were in vain.[157] In fact, the reality was so unfavorable to the endeavors of Pope John (who was finally poisoned and hammered to death by his fellow Christians) that he himself had to resort to bribing the Saracens.[158] The Christians in Italy and Spain continued to make pacts and alliances with the Muslims not only through the turn of the millennium[159] but into the late eleventh century, when the Norman conquest of Sicily was achieved as much by peace treaties with

153. "[G]ens impia nostris eliminetur e finibus: hoc est quod exigimus, hoc est quod ante speciali voto deposcimus." John to Bishop Wigbod of Parma, April 877, *Epp. et decr.* no. 67 (col. 721). Cf. Daniel 1975, 78.

154. Delaruelle 1980, 29.

155. See Tertullian *The Chaplet, or De corona* xiii (ANF 3: 101).

156. When Jerome, for example, cited 2 Cor 6.14–15—for "what fellowship is there between light and darkness? What agreement does Christ have with Beliar?"—he continued: "How can Horace go with the psalter, Virgil with the gospels, Cicero with the apostle?" Jerome to Eustochium, A.D. 384, Letter XXII,29 (*Principal Works,* 35). Examples could be multiplied.

157. Vismara 1974, 58.

158. See John to King Carloman, A.D. 787, *Epp. et decr.* no. 117 (col. 771). Cf. Engreen 1945, 322, 328; Partner 1972, 71, 74.

159. Erdmann 1935, 90, 98–99; Vismara 1974, 65 ff.; Schwinges 1977, 85 ff.; Ferreiro 1983, 130.

the Muslims as by arms.[160] The destruction of the *convivencia* in Spain, whatever that really was,[161] seems to have begun only with outside help. French—especially Cluniac—monks, driven by religious zeal kindled by the monastic reform at the turn of the millennium, crossed the Pyrenees in order to take possession of mosques or simply "to kill a Moor."[162] A notorious case of the exported Gallic religious intolerance was the seizure in 1085 of the chief mosque of Toledo, continued use of which had been guaranteed to the Muslims under terms of the town's capitulation to King Alfonso IV. When the king was away, a monk from Cluny, Bernard de Sédirac, in agreement with Alfonso's French wife, entered the mosque with the support of Christian troops "and having purged it of the filth of Muhammad [*spurcitia Mahometi*], set up an altar of the Christian faith, and placed bells in the main tower so that the Christians could be called to worship."[163] Under this new religious militancy the *reconquista* wars—fought initially for secular purposes—gradually assumed the character of holy war.[164] In this context, the cult of St. James, who had earlier, it seems, been venerated as a man of peace, was fully established as the cult of *Santiago Matamoros,* the slayer of the Moors.[165]

Such hardening of religious exclusivism and militancy, however, took place only in the late eleventh century. Before we get there, we must dwell a bit longer in a world not eager to follow John VIII's lead. In chronicles from the last century before the First Crusade, which report on clashes between the Christians and the Saracens, for example, nothing distinguishes the Saracens *qua* Saracens from other enemies.[166] The chroniclers did rejoice in Christian victories over the Saracens, but their reports of wars and descriptions of the Muslim enemies were written in a language that was dull, flat, dry, and detached.[167] The sole exception

160. Abulafia 1992, 26. Cf. Douglas 1969, 107, on Roger I of Sicily's treaty with the sultan of Mahdia in 1075, and on the employment of Saracen mercenaries in the Norman forces (also in the Norman army that, under Robert Guiscard, sacked Rome in 1084).

161. For a realistic view of that "coexistence," see Nirenberg 1996.

162. Haskins 1967, 42–43; Schwinges 1977, 97; Rosenwein 1982, 13, 22; Ferreiro 1983, 131; Becker 1988, 289–90; Le Goff 1990, 64; Bull 1993, chap. 2. For reservations, see Blumenthal 1988, 67.

163. *De rebus Hispaniae* VI,24 (Smith 1988–89, 1: 88–89). Cf. Metlitzki 1977, 11, 19.

164. On the secular character of these wars, see Daniel 1975, 79; Schwinges 1977, 9; Ferreiro 1983, 130; Reilly 1993, 90 ff. On the imposition of the crusading concept from without, see Becker 1988, 290; Phillips 1994, 57. On the twelfth-century popes' concern for the reconquest, see Constable 1953, 258–60.

165. Douglas 1969, 96.

166. Daniel 1975, 73.

167. France 1996, 44 (speaking of Thietmar of Merseburg and Ademar of Chabannes).

appears to be Rodulfus Glaber, whose depictions of Christian struggles with the Muslims are reminiscent of crusading appeals and chronicles.[168] But even in the case of Glaber, his clear-cut dislike of Muslims is paralleled with a "vindictive dislike" of the Jews, who were also seen as "strangers to God's revelation," as well as animosity toward the pagan Liutics of Pomerania and Mecklenburg, and the recently converted Hungarians.[169] The Saracens were no more than an element of the "ravages of the pagans," and not the one that attracted most of Glaber's attention.[170] Moreover, his account of the capture of Abbot Mayol by the Saracens displayed very little of that "fierce hatred of Islam" characteristic of other passages of his chronicle. Here, Glaber mentioned a Saracen "moved by compassion," as well as other "less ferocious Saracens."[171]

Lack of focus on the Saracens as the worst among Christians' enemies seems to have prevailed even in the middle of the eleventh century. Pope Leo IX considered the Normans more impious than the pagans.[172] For Gregory VII and his polemicists, as we have seen, the worst enemies were bad Christians—more detestable than Jews and pagans, among whom the Saracens were hardly ever named. Nor were Muslims seen as the enemy by imperial writers of the mid-eleventh century. Under the reign of Henry III and during the minority of Henry IV, the Saracens still figured as only one of numerous peoples whom imperial propagandists considered potential subjects of the emperor.[173] In the writings of Benzo of Alba, perhaps the most articulate imperial ideologist in that period, the Saracens appear to have been almost beyond the imperial gaze. They bordered on the world of marvels, for Benzo talked about the Saracens in connection with the Amazonians.[174]

It took time for the growing militant animosity toward non-Christians to become focused on the Muslims. Until the end of the eleventh century, it was diffused. The Muslims were not yet the chosen enemy people. Latin Christians were, in general, indifferent to the Muslim culture and religion, about which before 1100 even the educated among them knew

168. See France 1988; 1996, 45 f.
169. France 1988, 113, 115.
170. Rodulfus Glaber *Historiarvm* I,v: "De paganorum plagis."
171. Ibid., I,iv,9.
172. See Housley 1985, 18.
173. See Schramm 1992, 257, who cites Anselm of Besate's *Rhetorimachia* and the *Exhortatio ad proceres regni* by an anonymous imperial writer. The *Exhortatio* is published in Dümmler 1876 ("Sarracenos," line 7). Cf. Robinson 1978, 73–74.
174. Schramm 1992, 260 n. 3.

virtually nothing.[175] They regarded the Muslims as "only one of a large number of enemies threatening Christendom from every direction, and they had no interest in distinguishing the primitive idolatries of Northmen, Slavs, and Magyars from the monotheism of Islam, or the Manichaean heresy from that of Mahomet." Moreover, there appears to be no evidence that, before the launching of the First Crusade, "anyone in northern Europe had even heard the name of Mahomet."[176]

The success of Urban II's propaganda for the crusade may partly (but only partly) be explained by his contemporaries' lack of knowledge about the people they were called on to fight.[177] In practical life, ignorance is often a powerful argument. The fact that Latin Christians knew nothing (or next to nothing) about Islam did not prevent them from making Muslims *the* enemy of Christianity and Christendom. The ambiguities characteristic of Gregory VII's attitude toward the Muslims (discussed in chapter 2) had been eliminated. Urban II raised to new heights the hostility toward the Muslims that had hitherto been dormant in the Latin West.[178] Without the elaboration of this enemy image, the new holy war, the crusade, was unimaginable. Whereas from the Carolingian times onward, holy wars had been fought against infidels in general, the crusade was at its inception the war of Christendom against the Muslims,[179] animated by a "generalized hatred of Islam."[180] Whereas the enemy is by definition the "other," in the crusade and through the crusade a concrete, particular "other" was instituted as the universal— "normative"[181]—enemy. The Christian attitude toward the Muslims came to differ from the Christian attitudes toward other known peoples, other eastern peoples included, due to its fundamentally antagonistic nature.[182] The crusade was of a different quality than the sporadic pre-

175. Cf. Munro 1931; Southern 1962; Kritzeck 1964; d'Alverny 1965a; Davis 1973, 71; Daniel 1975, 73; 1993; Metlitzki 1977; Schwinges 1977, 95–98; Prawer 1986, 34; Becker 1988, 334, 361; Morris 1991, 153, 286; Pavlović 1992, 96. An overly optimistic view: Rodinson 1991, 12 f., 23 f.; followed by Hentsch 1992, chap. 2.

176. Southern 1962, 14–15, 28 (mentioning Rodulfus Glaber *Historiarvm* I,iv,9 as the only exception). In southern Europe, outside of Spain, Muhammad was mentioned in the *Carmen in victoriam Pisanorum* 32 (*Agareni invocant Machumata*), 52. For a brief discussion of Latin accounts of the origin of Islam from the twelfth century to the fifteenth century, see Vandecasteele 1996.

177. Cf. Menache 1990, 107.
178. France 1996, 56.
179. See Rousset 1945, 17, 20–21, 151, 175.
180. France 1996, 44.
181. Purcell 1975, 14–15.
182. Phillips 1994, 54–55.

crusade wars against the Muslims in Spain and Sicily,[183] it was based on a different "conceptual panorama" than holy wars *contra christianos*,[184] and it stood apart from more or less simultaneous wars against the pagans on the northern and eastern borders of Latin Christendom. There, the enemy image was hazy;[185] here, it was sharply defined and fixed.

We may get an impression of the degree to which the Muslims were made *the* enemy of Christendom if we consider that *Saracen* gradually became the generic term for Christians' enemies altogether.[186] In the second half of the eleventh century, the Normans were often called *Agareni*.[187] If this naming policy was the papacy's attempt to deproblematize its struggle against Christians by relating it to warfare against pagans,[188] this only proves my point. With the twelfth century, *Saracen* came to be used more frequently in this manner. In the mid-twelfth century, for example, about the time when St. Bernard of Clairvaux was preaching the Crusade against the Slavs, Vincent of Prague used the term *Saracens* for undefined enemies of Christianity in Eastern Europe.[189] Pope Eugenius III, too, called the East-European Slavs *Saracens*.[190] A monk writing in twelfth-century England had the Saxons worshipping "maumets."[191] The *Sarazins* in the *King Horn* (a very early, mid-thirteenth-century Middle English romance) may, after all, not be Vikings, as has been generally assumed.[192] But in some other, not much older, English sources the Danes (together with Scots and Irishmen) and Saxons are named *Sarrazins* or *Saracens*.[193] In the *chansons de geste*, Vandals, Vikings, Arabs,

---

183. "[M]ieux que les guerres des Normands en Sicilie et les guerres de la *reconquista* elle [la croisade] opposa de manière durable chrétiens et musulmans en un lieu sacré pour l'une et l'autre religion." Rousset 1983, 39.

184. Cardini 1992b, 396; cf. Höfner 1972, 62.

185. "Die Verschärfung des Feindbildes für einen Heiligen Krieg war hier unpopulär." Schwinges 1977, 10. During the Wendish Crusade, for example, the Saxon knights objected to the more enthusiastic crusaders who wanted to lay the countryside waste to force a surrender: "Is not the land we are devastating our land, and the people we are fighting our people?" Christiansen 1980, 52.

186. A "general name for heathen of any sort." *King Horn*, 96 (n. to line 38).

187. Erdmann 1932, 407; 1935, 110.

188. Housley 1985, 19.

189. *Vincentii Pragensis Annales* (MGH SS 17: 664; quoted in Purcell 1975, 15–16 n. 19).

190. "L. dux Poloniae, collecta Saracenorum multitudine, quod nostris temporibus inauditum et inhumanum est, terram Christianorum invasit," etc. Eugenius to Moravian Bishop Henry, 3 March 1149, *Epistolae et privilegia* no. 351 (PL 180: 1385).

191. Metlitzki 1977, 119.

192. See Speed 1990, 565 for older views, 595 for her own conclusions.

193. The *Gloucester Chronicle* and *Of Arthour and Merlin*; quoted, along with some other references, in *King Horn*, 96–97, n. to line 38; cf. Speed 1990, 566–67.

and other "unbelievers" appear under the generic heading of *Saracens*,[194] and in the French romances, Saracens are associated with places where the historical Saracens had never set foot.[195]

Earlier in this chapter I argued that the launching of the First Crusade was the historical moment in which the *respublica christiana* became conscious of its unity. An essential moment in the articulation of the self-awareness of the Christian commonwealth was the construction of the Muslim enemy. The antagonistic difference between themselves and the Muslims was a constitutive element of the Latin Christians' collective identity. The work of this collective identity or, rather, this collective identity at work was the new holy war against this fundamental enemy; for the Muslims represented infidelity as such.[196] They were regarded as precisely the fundamental enemy of Christendom: the personification of the very religion of the Antichrist.[197] The Muslim world became no less than "the antithetical system, the social Antichrist." This determined the nature of Christian war against the Muslims, which was harsher and more ferocious than wars against any other adversary.[198]

THE CHRISTIAN OFFENSIVE: *ESSALCIER SAINTE CRESTIENTÉ*

In the eleventh century, Latin Christians entered a military offensive that kicked off a state of permanent warfare against the Muslims in the Mediterranean.[199] This warfare enjoyed the Church's support, as is well illustrated by the Norman conquest of Apulia and Sicily in the second half of the century. The Normans' campaign to wrest southern Italy from Muslim hands cannot be called holy war (and was represented as such only in forged charters of later date), but it was an extension of the frontiers of Latin Christendom under papal encouragement. Some contemporary sources suggest that the wars of conquest were fought on God's behalf and that Roger I, for example, saw himself as a "conqueror with a Christian mission."[200] Seen and represented as a struggle against the

---

194. Bennett 1986, 102; see 118 n. 25 (for further references).
195. Metlitzki 1977, 126.
196. Manselli 1965, 136.
197. Cf. Cardini 1992b, 396.
198. Vismara 1974, 13.
199. Morris 1991, 147. Cf. Abulafia 1992, 24. See chap. 1 n. 232 ff.
200. Haskins 1967, 265; Morris 1991, 142; Abulafia 1992, 24.

enemies of the Roman Church, the Christian military offensive went "beyond a simple response to the exigencies of the situation." [201]

With the shift from military defensive to military offensive, the nature of holy war began to change.[202] The change culminated with the launching of the First Crusade. But there are substantial differences between the crusade and the eleventh-century Christian wars against the Muslims that preceded them. It is true that Urban II, at the close of the eleventh century, holding a holistic view of the Christian military confrontation with the Muslims, had linked the crusade with the *reconquista*. As he saw it, in his own lifetime through Christian forces God had battled down the Turks in Asia and the Moors in Europe.[203] But the wars on these two fronts can be seen as connected only insofar as the *reconquista* was assimilated into and subordinated to the crusade. Spain had not been the "breeding-ground for a holy war ethos which only needed fine tuning to became crusade enthusiasm." [204] On the contrary, the wars of reconquest were to borrow from crusading ideas and images to define their meaning, and from crusading institutional provisions to improve their own organization. The *reconquista* came to be seen as a second march to Jerusalem, and in 1125 archbishop Diego Gelmírez had a vision of the defeat of Christ's "wicked enemies the Muslims" in the Iberian peninsula opening the way to the Sepulchre of the Lord "through Spain, which is shorter and much less laborious." [205]

As opposed to the earlier *reconquista,* the crusade was not a war against the enemies of the Church on the frontiers of western Christendom; it was a war against enemies of Christendom who neither bordered on the territories populated by Latin Christians [206] nor threatened Christian possessions, and who gave no pretext for war. Not only did Muslims, at least in the later eleventh century, not attack Christians in the West; there is also no evidence that the Christians in the East were actually oppressed by their Muslim rulers, whatever Urban II may have said at Clermont. They continued to live as a subject minority population, protected by Islamic law, paying taxes, and having a measure of

201. Morris 1991, 145.

202. Cf. Vismara 1974, 62.

203. Urban to Bishop Peter of Huesca, 11 May 1098 (PL 151: 504). Cf. Becker 1988, 348–49.

204. Bull 1993, 12, chap. 2.

205. Villey 1942, 193 ff.; Riley-Smith 1992, 92. Cf. Vismara 1974, 78. See also Constable 1953, 222, on crusading in Portugal in the 1140s as a stop on the way to the Lord's Sepulchre.

206. Villey 1942, 82.

freedom of worship. Apart from the persecution under al-Hakim, "there is no evidence of anti-Christian pogroms in the eleventh century."[207] The launching of the First Crusade had little to do with the circumstances in the Near East, or more specifically, with anything happening in Jerusalem, and was sought neither by the local Christians nor by the Latin visitors to the city.[208] There was "no real identity of interest" between the oriental Christians and Latin Christians, and the eastern Christians had never appealed for help to their western "blood-brothers" (as the latter conveniently began to call themselves).[209] The oriental Christians did not necessarily experience the crusade as a deliverance from the so-called Turkish yoke, and may well be counted among the victims of the crusade.[210]

The specific "crime" of the Muslims against whom the First Crusade was directed consisted solely in their "unlawful possession" of the holy places (which were, of course, holy not only to the Christians).[211] The crusade was an unprovoked military offensive far beyond western Christian borders. It was Christendom's war for the Holy Land.[212] But the "Holy Land" itself was a crusading invention. It was with the crusade that Palestine had ceased to be the Promised Land (*terra repromissionis*) of the Old Testament and became the Holy Land, *terra sancta*.[213] It was called holy because Jesus Christ had sanctified it with his physical presence (*loca sancta quae salvator noster corporali praesentia illustravit*), with his birth (*loca in quibus redemptor humani generis pro nobis nasci*

---

207. Mayer 1993, 5–6. On al-Hakim, see chap. 1 nn. 226–27.
208. Peters 1985, 251, 253.
209. Morris 1991, 282–83; Mayer 1993, 6.
210. See Runciman 1986, 22. But Runciman's phrasing ("it was the Christians of the East who were the most unwilling and most unhappy victims" of the Crusades) may be read as implying that the Muslims were the "willing" or "happy" victims, or were not "victims" at all. Moreover, only the Fourth Crusade—called the "betrayal of Christendom," because the Christian army sacked Christian Constantinople—is considered by this author to be a "crime against humanity." Runciman 1991, 3: 130.
211. Purcell 1975, 14.
212. E.g., Villey 1942, 190, 195; Rousset 1945, 194; Becker 1988, 404, 407. These authors may be called "traditional" crusade historians, defining the crusades by their destination and seeing the recovery of the Holy Land as their defining characteristic—an approach that has been questioned as "*simpliste*" (Purcell 1975, 7) by the "pluralist" crusade historians. The latter define the crusades by their origin and stress the papal *auctoritas principalis* as the distinctive feature of crusading warfare, making it a more inclusive concept and a longer-lasting historical phenomenon. Cf. Housley 1992, introduction; Riley-Smith 1993b, 9–10. In my view, the crusade as papal war was initially a holy war to the Holy Land; an idea that had a lasting impact on the crusade idea and imagination, and also influenced military operations that were not directed toward Palestine. For a recent discussion, see Tyerman 1998.
213. Erdmann 1935, 279; Schwerin 1937, 51; Schein 1996, 126.

voluit), with his life among men (*terra in qua pedes Christi steterunt*), and with his death and resurrection (*terra aspersione vivificae sanguinis consecrata*). As such, it was styled *patria Christi* and *haereditas Domini*.[214] It followed logically that the Muslims living in Palestine were not only guilty of sacrilege but also invaders and usurpers. By the same token, the crusaders were pious Christian patriots, liberating their own fatherland (the "heritage" of God the Father), recovering their lawful possession.[215] The Holy Land was the condensation of what today we may call the crusading "ideology." Endeavors to attain the object of that ideology unfolded as a long march through the ruins of the earthly Jerusalem to the heavenly City—through the ruins that were the result of the march. But *terra sancta* was a sublime object of this war. As such it was unattainable. Winning even the entirety of this world could not have quenched the holy desire that animated the crusade. The crusade, once launched, was destined to become permanent. The crusading ideal was indeed a "state of permanent war against the heathen."[216]

The Carolingian holy war, in contrast to the crusade, was never directed toward the Orient. Charlemagne may have thought about the Holy Land, but he never planned a military expedition there. He held his power firmly within the horizon of the Latin West.[217] Emperor Otto III only thought of going to Jerusalem in the last year of his reign (1001), after his project of the "renovation of the Roman empire" had collapsed. But he would travel to Palestine to become a monk.[218] The idea of Palestine as the aim of Christian military expedition first appeared in Gregory VII's plan of 1074. Some ten years later, Bishop Benzo of Alba thought of a military march to the Holy Sepulchre.[219] Urban II finally made the idea materialize by sending a united Christian army to the Middle East.[220] This pope's attention, as we have seen, was focused on the conflict between Christendom and the Muslim world, and he placed the confrontation between them on the broadest basis thus far.[221] The march to Jerusalem was not solely a "liberation" of the capital of the

---

214. See Schwerin 1937, 52–53.
215. Cf. Purcell 1975, 4. For the concept of "recovery," *recuperatio*, see Regout 1934, 31, 99, 140 ff.
216. Cf. R. Barber 1982, 222.
217. Delaruelle 1980, 23.
218. Schramm 1992, 180.
219. Erdmann 1932, 405.
220. Rousset 1945, 17.
221. Schwinges 1977, 97; Becker 1988, 294.

Christian world;[222] it was also a conscious attack on the enemies of Christ, a "thrust into the heart of the Mohammedan world."[223] This war was not fought for the Church, as Gregory VII's wars had been; it was fought for Christendom and by Christendom, by the "community of the whole Christendom against the pagans."[224] It was a war willed by God, Christ's war, fought by an elect, that is, godly and holy, people in arms against the nefarious, foreign pagan nations, blasphemous persecutors of the faith, the enemies of Christ's cross, sons of the slave (Hagar), and instruments of the devil. It was a totalizing religious war, a "horrifying totality of religious struggle."[225]

The Christian offensive, however, was not simply a military operation but a broad social movement as well. The new holy war was more than *reconquista;* it was an expansion of Christendom. Being a recent creation, there was nothing for Christendom to reconquer; what lay open to it was conquest. But this was a specific kind of conquest, determined by the nature of Christendom. As a religiously based collective entity, Christendom was conquering not simply territory but Scriptural landscapes. Those were to be reclaimed for the Eternal King. But because the foundation of Christendom was a universal religion, what was to be conquered was the whole world (which was, it is true, much smaller than the world we know today).[226] The crusade was a drive into the outside world—*Drang nach außen,* as Erdmann wrote in the 1930s, in the shadow of the *Drang nach Osten,* the "eastward expansion," of his own time.[227] It was an expansionist holy war waged by a formless society[228] that was unified within, exclusivist without, and—perceiving itself as universal—knew no borders or limits.

The drive to expansion was a corollary to the ideal of Christian unity, and both were the constitutive elements of the notion of Christendom.[229]

---

222. Rousset 1945, 73, 136; on the place of Jerusalem in Urban's preaching of the crusade, see Cowdrey 1970b; 1995; Becker 1988, 383, 388, 397. But see Schein 1996 (arguing that the goal of the First Crusade was the Holy Sepulchre rather than the city of Jerusalem). Cf. Beasley 1897–1906, 2: 556 n. 3, noting that Jerusalem was fixed as the center of the earth only on the maps from the crusading period.

223. Erdmann 1935, 295.

224. Erdmann 1935, 306; Becker 1988, 354.

225. Schwinges 1977, 11.

226. See Wright 1925. Cf. Phillips 1994.

227. Erdmann 1935, 249. Cantor 1991, 402–3, considers Erdmann's *Die Entstehung des Kreuzzugsgedankens* a coded critique of Nazism. (There are a few unnecessary inaccuracies in his portrait of Erdmann.)

228. See Dupront 1969, 44.

229. Rousset 1963, 203.

Christendom was a closed society. Its unification was predicated, first of all, on cleansing the Christian social body from within. As already mentioned, the wars among Christians that were polluting and lacerating Christendom were regarded as sinful, and those engaged in them were described as serving the devil. All Christians everywhere had to live in peace, "since without peace no one can serve God."[230] Peace meant unity of the right order. The other aspect of the unification of Christians in Christendom was exclusion of the non-Christian. Through constructing a radical difference between themselves and others, and through separating themselves from foreign peoples on a principled basis, Christians placed themselves in opposition to the outer world. The unity of Christendom rested upon and at the same time generated a fundamental (and fundamentalist) division in the world.[231] That division could easily assume apocalyptic traits, as with Hugh of St. Victor, who divided mankind into the damned, bearing the sign of the Beast on their forehead, and the just, marked by the cross of Christ; or St. Bernard, for whom the world was split into the uncompromisingly exclusive kingdoms of light and darkness, and who identified the Saracens with Satan.[232]

Serving God (for which unity was required) was easily envisioned as Christian vassals fulfilling the duty they owed to their Lord God by avenging injuries inflicted on Him by the infidels. Serving God was thus going to war for Him.[233] The most offensive among those imagined injuries was the infidels' possession of the Holy Land, which was the Lord's land. Serving God with arms entailed driving out non-Christians from the land the Christians called their own and holy.

The expansion of Christendom was not the spreading of Christianity. Papal crusading documents did not discuss conversion of the Muslims. Since at least as far back as the time of Rodulfus Glaber, the Muslims had been deemed inconvertible.[234] The very logic of the crusade made the popes call for the expulsion of the enemy from the *terra sancta* and not for conversion.[235] If the expansion of Christendom was the opening of Christendom to the outer world, it was a strange kind of opening in-

---

230. See chap. 1 n. 296.
231. See Rousset 1945, 187; Dupront 1969, 29.
232. See Dérumaux 1953, 68–69, 73.
233. This imagery—and conceiving the crusade in terms of "vindicare iniuriam crucifixi, ulcisci iniuriam crucis"—was elaborated especially by Innocent III. See Schwerin 1937, 43; Roscher 1969, 281 ff. For the same images employed by Bishop Henry of Strassburg when preaching the crusade at Frederick I's court in 1187, see Munz 1969, 385–86.
234. Rodulfus Glaber *Historiarvm* I,v,24.
235. Schwerin 1937, 41.

deed. Christendom, a closed society, could open only by confronting and fighting—and only in order to confront and combat—its enemies,[236] that is, those whom the Christians had made their enemies and nothing but their enemies. The opening of Christendom was an extension of its closedness; it remained a closed society, but on a larger scale than before.

The Crusades were God's wars for the expansion of Christendom (*bella Domini . . . ad dilatationem Christianitatis*), wars intended to *essalcier sainte crestienté*.[237] The ultimate praise of a Christian hero in holy war poetry of that period was that he had extended Christendom: *Moult essaucia sainte Crestienté; eshalcier sainte crestiënté*.[238] But the expansion of Christendom cannot be understood as a simple redrawing of frontiers. At that time, frontiers were hardly drawn at all; they meant little and were certainly not what the term denotes in our day.[239] Christendom was actually frontierless. It was a mobile, moving space.[240] A consideration of medieval maps is telling. They rank among the "most expressive and ideological of all cultural objects" and as such represent "cultural conflicts" of the medieval world.[241] On these maps, Christendom was apparently never indicated. The word *Christianitas* did not appear on maps of the world, and the frontiers of Christian territory were nowhere drawn.[242] It is true that Gregory VII, for example, used the term "boundaries of Christendom" (*fines Christianitatis*).[243] But it would be wrong to imagine that this stood for an elaborated territorial notion of Christendom. Rather, Christendom was wherever the Roman Church was obeyed, and the limits of Christendom lay where kings had fewer persons to instruct them in the Christian religion and a lesser share in religious services.[244]

This geographical indeterminacy was accidental. But because Christianity was universalist, Christendom by nature knew no frontier and so extended potentially over the whole earth.[245] Christendom was all-embracing not in geographical reality but "virtually"—in relation to an

236. See Rousset 1963, 203.
237. See Rousset 1945, 100–1; 1963, 199.
238. See Rousset 1945, 126–27.
239. Cf. Haskins 1967, 21.
240. Sénac 1983, 9.
241. Friedman 1994, 65.
242. Hay 1968, 55.
243. Gregory to Archbishop Udo of Trier, 30 Sept. 1077, *Register* V,7 (p. 358); to King Olaf of Norway, 15 Dec. 1078, *Register* VI,13 (p. 417).
244. Gregory to King Olaf of Norway, 15 Dec. 1078, *Register* VI,13 (p. 416). King Olaf was placed "in extremo orbe terrarum."
245. Hay 1968, 27 ff., 55.

"ideal of unity and expansion."[246] Crusaders were consistent in wanting to expand Christendom "from sea to sea." The crusading leaders
Godfrey, Raymond, and Daimbert, in a letter they wrote to the pope in
September 1099, described how the crusaders, upon their knees, invoked the aid of the Lord, "that He who in our other adversities had
strengthened the Christian faith, might in the present battle break the
strength of the Saracens and of the devil and extend the kingdom of the
church of Christ from sea to sea, over the whole world."[247] These holy
warriors wanted to reach the outer limits of the earth, the Biblical "ends
of the world."[248] They were true cosmopolitans.

However, a frontier for Christendom did exist: the infidels. The Christian frontiers were where Christians met non-Christians and clashed
with them; more precisely, they were where the cross had been brought.
Expansion of the frontiers of Christendom—especially to the east and
south, where peoples lived who were regarded as inconvertible—meant
driving out (or exterminating) the infidels.[249] It seems as if the infidels
existed only to make Christendom feel its own expansionist vitality.[250]
Like Hegelians *avant la lettre,* Latin Christians knew that the frontier
(*Grenze*) existed only to be crossed—moreover, it existed only if crossed
over. Because that frontier was the infidels, the Middle Ages were a long
struggle between Christendom and the Muslim world.[251] In its ideal formulation, Christendom was an endless holy war. If the frontiers of
Christendom were marked with the cross,[252] it was only logical that the
inevitable expansion of Christendom's frontiers meant taking the cross
and carrying it to the infidel world; that is, it meant the crusade.

But the arm of the cross pointing toward Heaven is the shortest.
The crosspiece of the cross symbolizes the horizontal expansion, and the
longest arm points downward. The extension of Christian territorial
conquests appears to be less significant than the depth to which the
Christians' holy war against the Muslims cut into the world. For the
Christians, there was only one right, one faith, and one law (*un droit,
une foi, une loi*). Needless to say, it was the Christians who were right,
and in the right, as declared, for example, by "Charlemagne" of the

246. Rousset 1963, 198.
247. Hagenmeyer, *Kreuzzugsbriefe,* no. XVIII,12 (pp. 171–72); trans. in Peters 1989,
236.
248. Rousset 1945, 149. Cf. Ps 18.5 [19.4]; Rom 10.18.
249. Rousset 1945, 150.
250. Cf. Dupront 1969, 40.
251. Rousset 1945, 172.
252. Delaruelle 1969, 61.

Chanson de Roland: "You well know that I am in the right against the pagans." Roland himself asserted: "We are right, but these wretches are wrong"; or "The pagans are wrong and the Christians are right."[253] The crusaders' world was simple and brutal. The infidels were regarded as outside the law and without rights because they did not have faith (that is, because they were not of the Christian faith).[254] Because Christians were prohibited from making contracts with infidels, it was also impossible to make truce or peace with them.[255] Unable to make peace, the infidels were finally denied the right to wage war. This logical step was taken a century after the First Crusade, when Alanus Anglicus formulated the legal principle that the right to make war pertained only to the Christians.[256] A great historian of the Crusades suggested that the 1099 massacre in Jerusalem occurred because the crusaders were enraged that the inhabitants had defended themselves.[257]

The Muslims, *the* infidels, did not have freedom of choice; they could not choose between conversion and death because (as already mentioned) they were seen as inconvertible.[258] Mission, if it was thought of at all, would only have been possible after the "preaching with iron tongues," that is, after war.[259] But the war was a war of extermination.[260] The extermination (*excidium*) of the "pagans" was preached by the popes[261] and also by St. Bernard. This holy man showed more than a good sense of word-formation when he declared that to kill an infidel was not homicide but "malicide," annihilation of evil, and that a pagan's death was a Christian's glory because, in it, Christ was glorified.[262]

---

253. *The Song of Roland* 252 line 3413; 93 line 1212; 79 line 1015. In the original: "Ja savez vos cuntre paiens ai dreit"; "Nos avum dreit, mais cist glutun unt tort"; "Paien unt tort e chrestïens unt dreit." For the same idea as expressed by the crusading chroniclers, see Schwinges 1977, 220, 224.

254. Villey 1942, 30–32; Rousset 1945, 175. Before the Crusades "standen die Ungläbigen keineswegs außerhalb der Rechts- und Weltordnung." Schwinges 1977, 228–29.

255. See Villey 1942, 204–5; Rousset 1945, 172; Delaruelle 1980, 73. Fraternities of knights for waging war against the Moors, created by Alfonso I of Aragon, were explicitly committed "never to make peace with the pagans." Barber 1995, 26–27.

256. See Russell 1975, 198.

257. Michaud 1838, 1: 442. Cf. Cowdrey 1985, 52; Partner 1997, 81.

258. Villey 1942, 230; Rousset 1945, 150; Dérumaux 1953, 73; Delaruelle 1980, 73.

259. Becker 1988, 359.

260. Cf. Schwinges 1977, 247.

261. Cf. Schwerin 1937, 41.

262. "Sane cum occidit malefactorem, non homicida, sed, ut ita dixerim, malicida, et plane Christi *vindex in* his *qui male agunt,* et defensor christianorum reputator. . . . In morte pagani christianus gloriatur, quia Christus glorificatur. . . ." Bernard *Éloge* III,4. Cf. Erdmann 1935, 218; Villey 1942, 32; Rousset 1945, 161; Delaruelle 1980, 69, 94; Becker 1988, 286–87. I discuss St. Bernard in chap. 4.

Augustine had taught that charity was the right inward motive justifying the use of force.[263] That view was now obliterated.[264] Augustinian love for one's enemies might have tempered the violence. But in its
place came the "one-dimensional notion of fraternal love for fellow-
Christians."[265] The declaration of fraternal love for the eastern Christians was a pretext for launching the First Crusade; Urban II had laid
much emphasis on this love when he preached the crusade at Clermont.[266] The substance of that brotherhood was blood, consanguinity
in faith.[267] And once faith was filled with blood, it was just a short step
to the letting of blood of the unfaithful. Or rather, if faith was in blood,
with the shedding of unfaithful blood, unbelief was drained. Crusaders
responded to Urban II's preaching of the crusade "fired with the ardour
of love."[268] But ironically, the crusaders' love was neither asked for nor
gladly accepted by the eastern Christians. And no love was shown, nor
was it required to be shown, to non-Christians. The new exclusivity of
Christian love—love that inspired the use of violence—opened the gate
for the crusaders' shocking brutality toward the Muslims. Canon law was
not a factor in the treatment of the infidels, neither in battle nor in the
settled areas.[269] A disciplinary force within the Christian family, love
turned into the annihilation of those outside the family. The power of that
love was expressed in the fullness of hatred. That hatred was taught by
those who, in the opening decades of the twelfth century, formulated new
ideas about love, like Bernard of Clairvaux.[270] But this hatred was not the
exclusive possession of an educated elite. It was democratic: the crusading spirit most deeply affected the lowest classes, and "blind, uncom-
prehending hatred of the infidel" was rampant in illiterate lay society.[271]

When God was used for military purposes, victory could only be absolute. The destruction of paganism, the eradication of infidel peoples,[272]
became logical and necessary. Ideally, Christian holy war was genocidal,

263. See chap. 2 n. 54 ff.
264. Cf. Schwerin 1937, 42.
265. Riley-Smith 1980, 189; Gilchrist 1985, 39.
266. On the prominence of charity and fraternity in the crusading "ideology," see
Erdmann 1935, 295; Villey 1942, 117; Rousset 1945, 52, 56, 59–61, 135, 173; Delaruelle 1980, 31, 77, 83, 95; Riley-Smith 1980; 1993, especially chap. 4 and 6; Becker 1988,
405.
267. Cf. Rupp 1939, 76; n. 28.
268. Pope Eugenius III's crusading bull *Quantum praedecessores* (Riley-Smith and
Riley-Smith 1981, 57).
269. See Gilchrist 1985, 39.
270. See Morris 1991, 368 ff.
271. Riley-Smith 1980, 190; Le Goff 1990, 69.
272. See chap. 4 nn. 108–9.

the ultimate victory in that war was genocide, and the peace achieved was the peace of the cemetery: perpetual peace (*pax perpetua*)—"for the dead do not fight any longer."[273] Integration of the infidel into Christian society, which perceived itself as a manifestation of the absolute, was inconceivable: "In Christendom, there is no place for non-Christians."[274] In the Latin West, where non-Christians were minorities, legislation aimed at isolating Muslims and Jews from the Christian community, as a preparatory step to expulsion.[275] In the occupied Middle Eastern lands, however, where the "colonizers" were a tiny minority among the local population, crusaders established two societies in the frame of their rule, a system reminiscent of apartheid.[276]

The eleventh-century Church reform that had created the basis for the formation of Christendom and Christendom's holy war had been driven by the idea of purity. Its goal was to purify the whole of Christian society. This purification was understood as a moral and religious reformation: since with the ordering of clerical and lay life in accordance with the precepts and rules of the Christian doctrine, the peace announced by Christ would finally begin to reign among Christians. With the launching of the First Crusade, this perspective shifted. Whereas the initiators of Church reform had focused on the purity of the Church, Urban II, while preaching the crusade, pointed toward the Holy Land. Pollution was now seen as existing outside the Church, and outside Christendom.

Now it was the pagans who became the "dirt." The Holy Sepulchre had fallen into their dirty hands and was "polluted by the concourse of the Gentiles"; the Holy Land had been occupied by "unclean races"; the holy places were "polluted with their filthiness" and defiled with "their uncleanness"; Holy Jerusalem had been "reduced to the pollution of paganism."[277] The conclusion was obvious: the places of Christ's birth, life, death, and resurrection had to be cleansed. The crusade was fashioned as a big cleansing operation,[278] and cleansing the holy places was posited as the Christians' *point d'honneur*. According to Guibert of No-

273. Cf. Leibniz to Grimarset (*Political Writings*, 183); Kant, *Zum ewigen Frieden*.
274. Rousset 1945, 150.
275. See Erdmann 1935, 88; Dupront 1969, 42; Prawer 1986; Powell 1990.
276. Prawer 1986, 27, 34.
277. Robert the Monk *Historia Iherosolimitana* I,i (p. 727–28); Baldric of Dol *Historia Jerosolimitana* I,iv (p. 13); Guibert of Nogent *Gesta Dei per Francos* II,iv (p. 138), *Deeds*, 43; Fulcher of Chartres *Historia Iherosolymitana* I,iii,3–7 (p. 324). For a detailed treatment of this theme, see Cole 1993.
278. Cf. Cole 1991, 24–25; 1993; Riley-Smith 1993a, 108, 147.

gent, Pope Urban urged his armed brethren—with God leading them, with God fighting on their behalf—to strive with "utmost efforts to cleanse the Holy City and the glory of the Sepulchre" and to "apply a new cleansing to this place." [279] An example of how the cleansing was understood is given by Fulcher of Chartres. He praised Urban II for his "vigorous effort to drive out the pagans from the lands of the Christians [terris Christianorum]," while in his report of the pope's crusading speech at Clermont he wrote that Urban had exhorted Christian knights and footmen "to hasten to exterminate this vile race from our lands." [280] In Baldric of Dol's view, God himself had decreed that the polluters be "eliminated." [281]

The idea of cleansing was not limited to the First Crusade, as a few examples demonstrate.[282] In his bull *Quantum preadecessores,* with which he initiated the Second Crusade, Pope Eugenius III described the First Crusade as freeing "from the filth of the pagans that city in which it was Our Saviour's will to suffer for us and where he left us his glorious Sepulchre as a memorial of his passion." [283] Mobilizing for the same crusade in 1147, Peter the Venerable preached about Christ's Sepulchre and highly praised the protagonists of the First Crusade as men who had "with pious swords . . . cleansed this place and habitation of heavenly purity from the defilements of the impious." [284] Bernard of Clairvaux, arousing the Germans for the crusade, also glorified "the swords of our fathers" by which "the filthiness of the heathen was eradicated." [285] Images of the Holy Land as suffering at the dirty hands of the infidels persisted in the calls to the crusades by Urban II's successors. This imagery logically supported the imperative that pagan dirt had to be eliminated from the Holy Land (*a Terra Sancta eliminare spurcitias paganorum*).[286] Similarly, in the Spanish *reconquista,* the Christians looked down at the Moors as "pagan dirt." One of the chronicles reported that a town to the south of León had been cleansed of all the *spurcitia pagano-*

---

279. *Gesta Dei per Francos* II,iv (p. 138); *Deeds,* 43.

280. "[I]d genus nequam de regionibus nostrorum exterminandum." *Historia Iherosolymitana* I,iv,6; I,iii,4 (pp. 324–5); *A History,* 68, 66.

281. *Historia Jerosolimitana* I,ii (p. 12).

282. For a more comprehensive treatment, see Cole 1993, 86–88, 100 ff.

283. Riley-Smith and Riley-Smith 1981, 57.

284. *Sermo . . . de laude Domini sepulchri,* 247. I discuss Peter the Venerable in chap. 4.

285. "[P]atrum gladiis eliminata est spurcitia paganorum!" Bernard, *Briefe* no. 363,2 (p. 652).

286. See Schwerin 1937, 40–41, 55.

rum: mosques—"Satan's synagogues"—were destroyed, the Qur'an was burnt, and the Muslim "priests" were killed.[287]

Before the eleventh century drew to its close, the Church that at the beginning of the ecclesiastical reform had been working so hard for its own purity became obsessed with the cleansing of Christendom, and it was that cleansed Christendom that set out to cleanse the Holy Land of "pagan dirt." The Church that, not so long before, had considered bloodshed as a source of pollution now encouraged the shedding of blood— non-Christian blood—as a means to purification. When the reformed Church established its domination over Christendom, Christendom launched a military offensive to establish its domination over the world. The Church that had preached peace of the Gospel became an institution of conquest.[288] Christian conquest—the extension of Christendom— was holy war. And by commanding this holy war, the Church effectively established and secured its supreme position within Christian society.

The First Crusade was a war invented, willed, and organized by the pope. It was his own work, his war: *bellum, quod tuum proprium est,* as the crusaders wrote to the pope after the capture of Antioch, inviting him to join them on the march to Jerusalem, the Christian capital.[289] It was a march of the Christian people itself, without their secular princes, unfettered by what we would today call political ties;[290] this was its essential characteristic.[291] Their leader (*dux*) was Jesus;[292] the march was led by God Himself: *Sine domino, sine principe, solo videlicet Deo impulsore.*[293] Indeed, as long as an emperor was regarded as the one to fight God's wars, there could be no proper crusade.[294] Whatever divine leadership might be attributed to the military expedition of the Christian people to Jerusalem, it was the call of the pope that prompted these people to take up arms. Through organizing the crusade the pope established a direct relation with and primatial power over the Christian people.[295] In this most important, most holy, effort for Christendom, the papally led Church pushed aside the prominent secular rulers and took

---

287. See Schwinges 1977, 95. On "spurcitia Mahometi," cf. n. 163.
288. Delaruelle 1980, 109.
289. Hagenmeyer, *Kreuzzugsbriefe,* no. 16 (p. 164).
290. Cf. Barber 1993, 14.
291. Erdmann 1932, 413; 1935, 309–10; Rousset 1945, 135, 145, 173; Dupront 1969, 44; Becker 1988, 407–8.
292. Cf. Becker 1988, 403, 407–8.
293. Guibert of Nogent *Gesta Dei per Francos* I,i (pp. 123–24); *Deeds,* 28.
294. Christiansen 1980, 48.
295. Kempf 1960, 116, 119.

affairs into its own hands. With the holy war, the pope effectively became the supreme leader of Christendom. Christendom was the papal monarchy.

THE PAPAL MONARCHY AND THE CRUSADE

Papal monarchy could be described as a universal Christian society under the supreme rule of the papacy. The papacy attained supremacy within Christian society through successfully carrying out the eleventh-century Church reform. That reform revolved around restoring purity to the Church. One of its primary targets was the practice of simony: the purchase or sale of ecclesiastical offices, estates, and sacraments, even if money changed hands disguised as fees or gifts; the acquisition of ecclesiastical goods through service or favors or intercession.[296] The other primary target was nicolaitism: priests' nonobservance of the rule of celibacy through concubinage or marriage. Both evils represented lay influence within the Church, and the struggle to uproot them meant excluding that influence.[297] Obvious targets of Church reform, then, were clerics who had succumbed to such vices. Peter Damian, for one, attacked bishops who "hotter than the breath of Etna in their pursuit of ecclesiastical honors, give themselves over to the service of the rulers [*in clientelam potentium*] with disgusting subservience like captive slaves." In their greed for churches, he charged, they deserted "the things of the church."[298] But not only clerics were party to the vices the Church reformers were unwilling to tolerate; also guilty were those who gave clerics churches and conferred on them other benefices: lay princes performing investiture.

Purification of the Church meant liberating it from the lay dominance that had been progressively established through the successive rule of the Carolingian, Ottonian, and Salian emperors.[299] Inevitably, the Church

296. Blumenthal 1988, 75. Cf. Tellenbach 1991, 128.

297. Cf. Blumenthal 1988, 87.

298. "Ecclesiastica quippe deserunt, dum Ecclesias concupiscunt." Peter Damian *Contra clericos aulicos, ut ad dignitates provehantur* (PL 145: 463); partly trans. in Tierney 1988, 37.

299. On the king's (or emperor's) involvement in church affairs, cf. Morrison 1964, 30–34; Fichtenau 1978, 58–59; Wallace-Hadrill 1983, chap. 14; Blumenthal 1988, 34; Luscombe 1988, 166; Robinson 1988, 294 ff.; Lynch 1992, 119. On the mobilization of ecclesiastical personnel and resources in the running of the kingdom, cf. Morrison 1964, 16–17, 29–30; Leyser 1965, 43; Wallace-Hadrill 1983, 258 ff.; Nelson 1988, 220; Robinson 1988, 291; Lynch 1992, 71; Riché 1993, 290. On *Eigenkirchentum*, cf. Blumenthal 1988, 4–7, with further references; Tellenbach 1991, 70, 90 ff. On imperial nomination of bishops and popes, and control over the Church, cf. Morrison 1969, 382–87; Carozzi 1983, 75; Blumenthal 1988, 35, 43 ff., 55 ff.; Luscombe 1988, 166–67; Robin-

reform led to a bitter conflict between the ecclesiastical reformers and lay rulers, culminating in the so-called investiture contest about who had the right, the pope or the lay ruler, to invest bishops with their office. [300] The main protagonists of that conflict were Pope Gregory VII and Emperor Henry IV.

The investiture struggle ended early in the twelfth century with a practical compromise. Nevertheless, a newly empowered papacy began to assert a firm boundary around the sacred as its own sphere, from which temporal power was barred. This involved desacralization of temporal power and clericalization of the Church.[301] What did this mean? As opposed to the Church—which was of divine origin, having been founded by God and commissioned by Christ to St. Peter and his successors, the popes—temporal power was a human invention. "Who does not know," Gregory VII wrote, "that kings and princes derive their origin from men ignorant of God who raised themselves above their fellows by pride, plunder, treachery, murder—in short, by every kind of crime—at the instigation of the Devil, the prince of this world, men blind with greed and intolerable in their audacity?"[302] As such—allowed but not willed by God, as Cardinal Deusdedit put it at the close of the eleventh century[303]— temporal power was strictly forbidden to interfere with "ecclesiastical business."[304] This "ecclesiastical business" could only be administered by a separate social order, the clerical order (*ordo clericalis*), to whom God had entrusted the *sacra* and *sacramenta* as its exclusive possession. Through the clerical order, set apart from the lay populace by the mys-

---

son 1988, 296–97; Leyser 1989, 79; Tellenbach 1991, 59, 87f., 97 ff., 169 ff.; Schramm 1992, 90, 115, 229, 236; Riché 1993, 271; Canning 1996, 75.

300. The contest over the investiture of bishops was preceded by the establishment of "canonical election" of the pope, free of imperial interference. See the decree on papal election, published in the Lateran synod of April, 1059, in Mirbt and Aland, *Quellen*, no. 540; trans. in Tierney 1988, 42–43. Cf. the encyclical *Vigilantia universalis* 1, announcing the decisions of the Lateran synod of 1059 (Mirbt and Aland, *Quellen*, no. 541). For Gregory VII's assertion that the pope had to be recognized as the only authority that could create, depose, transfer, or reinstate bishops, see *Dictatus papae* III, XIII, XXV (*Register* II,55a [pp. 202, 204, 207]). For recent research on the investiture struggle, see Schieffer 1981; Engelberger 1996.

301. See, especially, Ladner, "The Concepts of 'ecclesia' and 'christianitas' and their Relation to the Idea of Papal 'plenitudo potestatis' from Gregory VII to Boniface VIII" (in Ladner 1983); Carozzi 1983. Cf. Heer 1949, 1: 93; Leyser 1965, 60; Munz 1969, 26; Morrall 1971, 39–40; Blumenthal 1988, 124; Tellenbach 1991, 125; Canning 1996, 104.

302. Gregory to Bishop Hermann of Metz, 15 March 1081, *Register* VIII,21 (p. 552). On Gregory's view of the origin of worldly power, see Stürner 1991. For the opposite, imperial view, cf. Wenrich of Trier *Epistola* 4 (p. 86).

303. *Libellus contra invasores;* quoted in Carlyle and Carlyle 1903–36, 3: 99; cf. Leyser 1965, 57, 64.

304. Cf. Humbert of Silva Candida *Adversus simoniacos* III,ix (col. 1153).

tery of ordination, worked the divine grace that brings salvation to men.[305] The creation of clerics—the distribution of "ecclesiastical sacraments and episcopal or pastoral grace"[306]—passed exclusively into the hands of the clerics. The Church became essentially a clerical corporation, hierarchically constituted, in which clerics were subordinated to Rome and to the pope; and lay Christians, whatever their station of life, were subordinated to the Church—as its "subjects rather than members."[307]

The clericalization of the Church and desacralization of kingship was an achievement with far-reaching consequences. On the one hand, the papacy began to exercise the fullness of jurisdictional power within the Church. On the other hand, the internally consolidated Church was able to claim for itself jurisdictional authority in Christian society at large (*in foro exteriori*). Under vigorously asserted papal leadership, the Church ascended to the position of the supreme power in Christendom. The pope alone now possessed the fullness of power in Christendom and with this power began to exercise his right to supervise the secular princes, who had to rule the Christian people in the service of the Church.[308]

THE THRONE OF PEACE

The Christian prince's primary duty, as we have seen, was to make and keep peace. The ability to maintain peace, in today's terms, was central to the legitimation of power. He who could make peace was entitled to rule. Any struggle for power therefore necessarily involved a struggle over who had the authority to make peace. This struggle was an important aspect of the conflict between the Gregorian reformers and lay rulers in the second half of the eleventh century. Two conceptions of peace—and two powers claiming the authority to make peace—clashed.

Conflict over the authority to make peace was couched in the prevailing understanding of power. One of the basic principles of power

---

305. Tellenbach 1991, 134. Cf. Southern 1967, 127, that between clergy and laity there was "a great gulf fixed."

306. See Humbert of Silva Candida *Adversus simoniacos* III,vi (col. 1149); trans. in Tierney 1988, 40.

307. Ladner 1983, 444–45, 491–92. For the "clerical concept" of the Church, see ibid., 444, 491; Lewis 1954, 2: 515–16; Roscher 1969, 21; Carozzi 1981, 83; Southern 1990, 232–33.

308. Cf. Morris 1991, 2; Oakley 1991, 52.

was that of monarchical rule. Rule by one (*monarchia*) was considered the best form of government, since it was best suited to bring about and maintain "unity, or peace" (*unitas sive pax*)—or "the unity of peace" (*pacis unitatem*)—which was the very purpose of government. This is a thirteenth-century authoritative formulation by Aquinas,[309] but the idea was familiar long before. The supreme peacemaker had to be a monarch. Because there could not be two monarchs—for a body with two heads was a monster—the struggle over who was going to be the supreme peacemaker was the most intense between the two supreme powers within Christian society: the papacy and the (German) empire. It is extraordinary to realize that the term *papacy* (*papatus*) did not even exist before 1047,[310] for within a few decades, the pope had become the virtual monarch of the Church. As head of the *monarchia ecclesiae,* he could now claim for himself universal rule over Christian society, over and above the emperor, head of the *monarchia imperii.*[311]

Another principle of power shared by emperors and popes alike was the Gelasian doctrine of the dualism of powers.[312] This doctrine had to be reconciled with the idea of monarchical rule as the guarantee of unity.[313] Dualism of powers was interpreted in a way that rendered one power supreme. Representing spiritual and temporal power as autonomous and coequal was simply not a viable solution. Adherence to the principle of monarchical rule, rather, dictated a unitary interpretation of the two powers, spiritual and temporal.[314] In this spirit, the Church reformers argued for supremacy of the papacy over any existing temporal power. This argument is well exemplified in Gregory VII's letter to Hermann of Metz, in which the pope cited the doctrine of the dualism of powers only to raise—and answer—the question of which of the two powers was

---

309. *Summa theologica* I, Q.103, Art.3; cf. *De regno* I,2. For the basic definition of monarchy, cf. Isidore of Seville *Etym.* IX,iii,23.

310. Morris 1991, 107; Canning 1996, 85.

311. Cf. Bosbach 1988, 19.

312. For the degree to which the dualism of powers was common doctrinal ground for advocates and opponents of papal monarchy alike, cf. Emperor Henry IV's statement that "the pious ordinance of God, which especially commanded these two [powers]—namely, the kingship and the priesthood—should remain, not as one entity, but as two" (Henry to the German bishops, A.D. 1076, *Briefe Heinrichs* no. 13 [p. 19]; trans. in Tierney 1988, 62); and Pope Boniface VIII's assertion that "we know very well that there are two powers ordained by God" (*Address to the ambassadors of the French Estates,* June 1302; Tierney 1988, 187).

313. Unity, in turn, was understood as the constitutive principle of the universe and of social order. Cf. Gierke 1913, 9.

314. Cf. Watt 1988, 368.

preeminent. Having cited Gelasius I's statement on the "sacred authority of priesthood and the power of kings," Gregory then referred to Ambrose of Milan. The pope construed "that blessed Ambrose" as an important predecessor of the view he himself promoted. Ambrose, Gregory wrote, had not only excommunicated the emperor but also demonstrated that "the priestly office is as much superior to royal power as gold is more precious than lead."[315] Gregory VII's assertion of the superiority of priestly authority over royal power was cited in Gratian's *Decretum* and became established opinion among canonists and theologians.[316]

Imperial propagandists, needless to say, did not accept the view that royal power had to be subordinated to priestly authority as the supreme power. They wanted to see *regnum* and *sacerdotium* bound together with ties of peace and concord,[317] and they promoted the ideal of an "intimate co-operation of *regnum* and *sacerdotium*," in which "in charity the province of one extends into the other."[318] But when it came to making peace in a universal Christian society, the apologists of the empire maintained the emperor's exclusive right to the title of peacemaker.

Throughout the investiture struggle, imperialist propagandists portrayed the emperor as the divinely ordained defender of peace, concord, and unity in both Church and *regnum*.[319] The emperor's mission as the "lord of peace" was to "pacify the *regnum* and equally bring back the Church of Christ to unity."[320] If the emperor was the ideal "prince of peace" and his power the only guarantee of peace and concord, the pope logically enough became the "enemy of peace."[321] Imperialists accused the pope of "shattering the holy Church of God and the peace of the whole world."[322] Emperor Henry IV made the following charge: "By the sword you have come to the throne of peace, and from the throne

315. Gregory to Hermann of Metz, 15 March 1081, *Register* VIII,21 (p. 554); *Correspondence,* 170. Cf. *Register* IV,2; IX,37 (pp. 294, 631). On Ambrose's dealings with Emperor Theodosius, see McLynn 1994, chap. 7.

316. *Decretum* D.XCVI c.10. Cf. Watt 1965, 12 ff.; Blumenthal 1988, 118; Pennington 1993a, 3. For a famous medieval treatment of this theme, see Hugh of St. Victor *De sacramentis christianae fidei* II,ii,4 (PL 176: 417).

317. Wido of Osnabrück *De controversia,* 242.

318. Henry IV to the German bishops, A.D. 1076, *Briefe Heinrichs* no. 13 (p. 19); trans. in Tierney 1988, 62. Cf. Robinson 1978, 92.

319. See Robinson 1978, 89, 92.

320. *De unitate ecclesiae* I,6 (p. 298).

321. Petrus Crassus *Defensio Heinrici* 6 (p. 210).

322. Ibid., 3 (p. 184). In an imperial document from June 1083 (MGH Diplomata regum et imperatorum germaniae 6.2: 464), Gregory VII was called the *perturbator orbis*.

of peace you have destroyed the peace." [323] Usurper of the "throne of peace," the pope had allegedly dissolved "the bond of the one catholic peace." [324]

The Church reformers actually upheld the same ideals of peace, concord, and unity as the imperial propagandists. But in their view, those ideals could only be realized in the *right* Christian order, which was, of course, the one they fought for. Gregory VII's idea of peace was traditional: peace coincided with order. [325] This idea, backed by Augustine's authority, [326] could hardly be contested, but exactly what constituted "order" was a contested issue. Though Gregory's understanding of peace was conventional, his idea of order—the right order of Christian society—ran contrary to the order established during centuries of imperial domination over the Church. Gregory wanted to have the "peace which is in Christ" with not only the emperor but with "all men" as well. He wanted to "give every one his right." [327] But he would not allow the emperor to make peace and order, even though God had placed the emperor "at the summit of human affairs." [328] The establishment and maintenance of the *right* order required that the pope retain for himself the right to give every one his right. Right order was the papal monarchy.

The papal monarchy implied the obliteration of the king's peace, *pax regis*. As I argued in chapter 1, the eleventh-century peace movement substituted *pax Dei* for *pax regis*. But imperial apologists naturally clung to the *pax regis,* insisting that the emperor was the "protector of peace." [329] They even wanted to appropriate *pax Dei* for the emperor. Ironic as it might appear, in 1085, the Council of Mainz, an imperialist gathering engineered by Henry IV, declared the "peace of God." [330] The council was an assertion of the emperor's power. Its aim was to "recuperate peace for the Church and for the commonwealth." And because it dealt with such important matters as "the catholic faith, peace, and unity of the Church," the imperial apologists argued, the council's decisions had

---

323. Henry IV to Gregory VII, A.D. 1076, *Briefe Heinrichs* no. 12 (p. 16); trans. in Tierney 1988, 60.
324. Henry IV to the German bishops, A.D. 1076, *Briefe Heinrichs* no. 13 (pp. 18–19); trans. in Tierney 1988, 61.
325. Cf. Tellenbach 1991, 138 n. 1.
326. Cf. chap. 1 n. 72.
327. Gregory to Henry IV, Sept. 1075, *Register* III,7 (p. 257); *Correspondence,* 83.
328. Ibid.
329. Petrus Crassus *Defensio Heinrici* 3 (p. 182).
330. Robinson 1978, 91.

to be given authority by the emperor: "for nothing can be secure and permanent in such matters, unless the royal authority defends and approves it by virtue of supreme power of the empire."[331] After all, this imperial "peace of God" was actually the king's peace. But it was precisely this kind of peace that was unacceptable to the reform papacy, for whom the king's peace was an expression of a perverse order characterized by lay domination over the Church. As an aspect of the *pax regis,* the Frankish *pax ecclesiae* had been a peace made by the king for the visible Church within the mystical universal Church.[332] Now things were to be radically different. By asserting itself as the peacemaker through the eleventh-century peace movement and ecclesiastical reform, the Church began to make peace in the world outside its clerical—and increasingly clericalized—body.

It was largely by establishing themselves as peacemakers and defenders of peace that the popes had acquired supremacy in the Christian world.[333] But the decisive factor in the papal ascendancy as supreme peacemaker within Christian society was not—or not solely—the merits of the papal conception of peace, but the papal leadership of the new holy war. The papacy ascended to the throne of peace essentially by launching the crusade: peacemaker is he who is master of war. Commanding both peace and war, the Church effectively became the supreme power in Christian society, leading it in spiritual matters and directing it in temporal affairs.

THE POWER OF THE CRUSADE

Having played a crucial role in the creation of Christendom, the crusade was later linked to attempts to reform Christendom and the Church. From the Third Crusade onward, Christians were called on to amend their ways at the same time as they were called on to join a crusade. The convocation of general councils to reform Christendom coincided with proclamation of crusades.[334] The aim of the Fourth Lateran Council

---

331. *De unitate ecclesiae* II,19 (pp. 446, 448); II,22 (p. 456); trans. in Robinson 1978, 92.

332. The apologists of the empire actually insisted on the Carolingian idea of the unitary Church as the body of Christ. Cf., for example, *De unitate ecclesiae* I,1 (p. 272). Wido of Osnabrück spoke of *sacerdotium* and *regnum* as the "two heads of the Church." *De controversia,* 268.

333. Cf. Landry 1929, 6.

334. Riley-Smith 1992, 110.

(1215), for example, was not only the bodily journey to recover Jerusalem, but also the spiritual journey from corruption to reform that would lead to the eternal journey from earth to heaven. Summoning the council, Pope Innocent III wrote: "Two things are especially near our heart: the deliverance of the Holy Land and reform of the Church." The council was to "extirpate vices and make virtues flourish, redress wrongs and reform customs, annihilate heresies and strengthen faith, put an end to discords and establish peace, restrain oppressions and protect liberty, gain Christian princes and peoples for the cause of the Holy Land and, finally, lay wise regulations for the high and low clergy." [335] The Second Council of Lyons (1274–76) likewise aimed at reforming Christendom and promoting the crusade, as did the Council of Vienne in 1311–12. [336]

As Innocent III's words make clear in the sentences just cited, the reform of Christendom bore on important issues of power. So did the crusade. As a vehicle for achieving Christendom's ideal aims, it had a formative impact on the development of public authority in the West, [337] and played an important role as well in the formation of relations among public authorities—that is, in shaping Western political order. I have already argued that the crusade played a key role in the constitution of the papal monarchy. Through launching the crusade, the papacy effectively established control over peace and war in Christendom, thus winning the monarchy of the world. Not surprisingly, the two centuries following the "Gregorian reform," the great age of the papal monarchy, was also the heyday of crusading. But we should keep in mind that the papal monarchy and the crusade were coming of age together. They were mutually dependent and reinforced each other; the elaboration of the very idea of papal monarchy was intimately linked to the formation of the crusade idea. By the time of the Second Crusade (launched by Pope Eugenius III in 1145), a historical image of the First Crusade was "beginning to take shape," and by the time of the Second Crusade's failure (in 1149), a "coherently-formed 'crusade idea'" had emerged that was to have, from that point onward, a "continuous life." [338] The idea of papal

335. Hefele 1912–13, 5.2: 1316–17.
336. See Roscher 1969, 261; Setton 1976, 112; Morris 1991, 285, 433, 447; Housley 1992, 28.
337. Of great interest in this regard are Jordan 1979; Tyerman 1988. Cf. Munz 1969 on how the crusade, as the ultimate end of his rule, determined Frederick I's approach to the business of government.
338. Blake 1970, 28; Powell 1996, 131. Cf. Delaruelle 1953, 53, 55 (who called the digesting of the experience of the First Crusade un travail des esprits); Tyerman 1988, 30; Riley-Smith 1993a, chap. 6 (who spoke of the theological refinement of the experience of

monarchy was advanced at the same time, and some of those who played a key role in organizing the Second Crusade were also central to the formulation of the idea of papal monarchy.

Bernard of Clairvaux, spiritual counselor to Eugenius III, is a good example. He argued that the pope, as the sole supreme Shepherd of a single flock, was called to the fullness of power and had received "the whole world" to govern—for whereas the "power of the others is bound by definite limits," the pope's power "extends even over those who have received power over others." [339] To bring home this argument Bernard applied the allegory of two swords.[340] Both swords, the spiritual and the material, belonged to the Church; "however, the latter is to be drawn for the Church and the former by the Church. The spiritual sword should be drawn by the hand of the priest, the material by the hand of the knight, but clearly at the bidding of the priest and at the command of the emperor." [341] Bernard first formulated this view of the supremacy of papal power in a letter addressed to Pope Eugenius in 1150, when the Second Crusade had already failed but influential men in the Latin West still harbored the hope that a new military offensive would be possible.[342] He urged the pope to send crusaders to the Holy Land: "The time has now come when the swords spoken of in the Lord's passion must be drawn, for Christ is suffering anew where he suffered formerly. But by whom, if not by you? Both swords are Peter's: one is unsheathed at his sign, the other by his own hand, as often is necessary. Peter was told concerning the sword which seemed less his: 'Put up thy sword into the scabbard' [Jn 18.11]. Thus that sword was undoubtedly his, but it was not to be drawn by him." [343]

---

the First Crusade). But see Constable 1953, 238 n. 130, that at the time of the Second Crusade there was as yet little consciousness of it being a successor to the first.

339. *On Consideration* II,viii,15–16. On Bernard's use of the term *plenitudo potestatis,* see Bredero 1996, 153 ff.

340. The allegory had been used before Bernard. See Lecler 1931. Moreover, "ce ne sont pas les théologiens pontificaux qui ont commencé à raffiner le symbolisme des deux glaives." Ibid., 307. See, for example, Henry IV to the German bishops, A.D. 1076 (*Briefe Heinrichs* no. 13 [p. 19]; trans. in Tierney 1988, 62), written by imperial chaplain Gottschalk of Aachen. What was believed to have been an earlier use, in Peter Damian's *Sermo* 69 (cf. Mirbt and Aland, *Quellen,* no. 546), is now accepted as a twelfth-century work, written perhaps by Bernard's secretary Nicholas of Clairvaux (Canning 1996, 99). Among Bernard's contemporaries, the allegory of the sword was used by Peter the Venerable (Peter to Pope Eugenius III, *Letters* no. 174, p. 415; cf. Kritzeck 1964, 22).

341. *On Consideration* IV,iii,7.

342. See Constable 1997. Cf. Bredero 1996, 149–50.

343. *Epistolae* no. 256 (PL 182: 463–64); trans. in Watt 1988, 372–73.

Bernard's articulation of papal supremacy was not limited to the two swords allegory. He "could find no language too exalted to describe the pope's eminent dignity."[344] The point important for the argument here is that Bernard "expressly applied his two swords doctrine to the crusade,"[345] thus conceptually linking the two together and building the power of the crusade into the supreme papal power. The material crusading sword was to be drawn "at the bidding" of the pope. It was to be wielded by the hand of the knight at the command of the emperor, it is true, but even the emperor himself had to listen to the pope. The chain of command was clearly defined. As commander of the crusade, the papal monarch was in position to animate, and to an important degree determine, the life of Christian society.

Within Christian society of the high and late Middle Ages, the crusade played a central role in what today we would call political life. It was "deliberately refracted into areas of the greatest political sensitivity and importance."[346] Popes used the crusade as an "occasion, and justification, for wide-ranging papal intervention in temporal matters,"[347] and secular rulers deliberately brought it into play in the pursuit of their own interests. Crusading involved "internal political ordering and military preparations, the external peace-making and search for allies."[348] Claims of promoting—and charges of obstructing—a crusade were weighty arguments in diplomatic relations among the papacy, the empire, and various kingdoms. The standing of a prince at home and abroad depended largely on his participation or nonparticipation in the crusade.[349] Preparations for the crusades involved huge flows of money within Latin West that brought massive financial gains to the crusade's promoters and contributed to the rise and fall of commercial centers in the northern Mediterranean.[350] Last but not least, the formation of a regular taxation system in the West was closely linked with papal efforts to efficiently collect funds for crusading warfare.[351]

---

344. Tierney 1988, 88. Cf. Watt 1988, 373–74; Bernard, *Briefe*, 3: 1118. See, e.g., *On Consideration* II,viii,15–16; *Briefe* no. 131,2; 238,6.
345. Roscher 1969, 33. Cf. Katzir 1992, 6–7.
346. Tyerman 1984, 171.
347. Housley 1992, 12
348. Ibid., 421.
349. Cf. Tyerman 1984, 173; Housley 1992, 449.
350. See Tyerman 1984; Le Goff 1990, 66; Housley 1992, 30.
351. Cf. Jordan 1979, chap. 4; Tyerman 1984; Siberry 1985, chap. 4; Schein 1991; Sayers 1994, 73–74, 188. Cf. chap. 5 nn. 31, 32.

CONTROLLING THE CRUSADE AS AN INSTRUMENT OF POWER

As the pope's own war,[352] the crusade was the pope's instrument of power: the greatest at the disposal of the papal monarch.[353] But just because the crusade was by definition a war organized, or at any rate authorized, by the papacy, the pope did not automatically control it. The importance of the crusade was such that the struggle for command of it was a constant feature of crusading history.

Before the turn of the thirteenth and fourteenth centuries, when territorial powers, or "national kingdoms," entered the struggle for control over the crusade, it was the two universal powers of the Latin Middle Ages, the papacy and the empire,[354] who were prominently engaged in that contest. In retrospect, the conflict between the papacy and the empire can be seen as "tragic," because the two parties pushed for extreme and mutually exclusive solutions that ultimately undermined them both. Yet the two parties shared a desire for unity and peace. It was seemingly their common "sense of the need of unity" of the Christian commonwealth, rather than ill will or diplomatic inflexibility, that pushed the papacy and the empire into conflict.[355] Each of them strove for supremacy within Christendom because monarchical rule was the best conceivable foundation for unity.

Because the crusade was linked with the ideals of peace and unity, both the pope and the emperor were desirous of crusading: To decide who had the right to make peace in unitary Christendom, Christian monarchs were ready to go to war. They struggled with each other, as well, for control over the crusade as a war that would bring peace and unity. To the leader of the crusade belonged leadership in Christendom;[356] he who controlled the crusade was Christendom's head, the lord of peace and war.

The failure of the Second Crusade led to depression and pessimism among western Christians. This mood was overcome by the intense crusading activity in the Latin West in response to the military disaster of Christians at Hattin and Saladin's liberation of Jerusalem forty years

---

352. See n. 289.
353. Riley-Smith 1992, 145.
354. In terms of "Realpolitik," the empire was becoming a territorially defined dominion, but in theory it retained the aura of universal rule. Holtzmann 1939, 251; Folz 1969, 145, 171 ff.; Appelt 1983, 37. Cf. Munz 1969, 373.
355. Figgis 1922, chap. 3, especially 45, 49; Ladner 1983, 478–79.
356. Cf. Mayer 1993, 217.

later, in 1187. The Third Crusade (1187–92), called the Emperor's Crusade, was led by Emperor Frederick I. After his army had been on the march for a year and had reached Christian territory beyond Turkish Asia Minor, the emperor drowned and most of his soldiers returned home. Frederick began a second life, as it were, in legend in the sixteenth century, and his legend in turn became a source of historical knowledge.[357] The Emperor's Crusade itself has also not remained legend-free. Two sixteenth-century German writers believed that Frederick I had been the greatest of all emperors after Charlemagne because of his crusade.[358] Modern historians, influenced by Frederick's story, have tended to see the crusade as issuing from the fullness of Frederick's power, as the "crowning glory to a successful political career." It seems, however, that Frederick did not go on the crusade because he was a successful emperor, but rather because he had "allowed feudalism to grow and flourish so that he would be freed from attending to his daily tasks as a ruler and administrator." The emperor's decision to undertake the crusade thus appears as the "antithesis to a political career" and a consequence of the "ultimately transcendental direction" of his reign. The crusade had been the telos of Frederick I's rule from the beginning: the task "for the sake of which he had become emperor and for the sake of which he had undertaken all his political experiments."[359]

Imperial and crusading "ideologies" blended. Frederick was *miles Christi*—soldier of Christ and head of Christian knighthood—and the protector of the Church. And he who had the right and ability to protect, it was believed, was the master or lord. Imperial propaganda drew on the belief that the emperor's entitlement and power to protect the Church raised him to an office of excellency over which the pope had no say: the emperor was the pope's master. Logically enough, the "protector of the successor of Peter perceived himself as the lord of the world and of the eternal city," Rome. As the defender of the Church and the faith, the emperor was the head of the whole of Christendom.[360] When Frederick I appeared as a crusading leader, these ideas seemed to materialize. In this light, the crusade was the emperor's apogee, and he was "indeed recognized in the West as the supreme lord of Christendom."[361] But even in this idealist perspective, it was at the moment of his greatest

357. See Munz 1969, chap. 1.
358. Ibid., 17 n. 3.
359. Ibid., 21, 372, 385.
360. Appelt 1983, 31, 37.
361. Mayer 1993, 137.

strength that Frederick I disclosed his weakness. In preparation for the crusade, for Pentecost 1188, he summoned a diet known as the Curia Christi, or Curia Iesu Christi. But meaning to display his power, the emperor decided that not he, but Christ, was to preside over the event.[362] As a democrat before his time, he left the place of supreme power empty.[363]

Research has shown that Frederick I's preparations for the crusade marked the nadir, not the peak, of his power as emperor. Pope Clement III, it seems, was de facto the supreme authority in the West at the time and the organizer of the crusade, which further strengthened his power.[364] And yet, contemporaries saw the Third Crusade as the "Emperor's Crusade." The papacy had to reclaim the crusade for itself—and through regaining control over the crusade assert its superiority over the empire. That task was successfully accomplished by Innocent III. A great papal monarch,[365] he was perhaps the "greatest apostle" of the crusading movement.[366] He preached "more crusades than any other pope and contributed more to the crusading movement than anyone since Pope Urban II."[367] He introduced a number of technical innovations in organizing the crusades—particularly regarding raising funds, preaching the cross, and exploiting redemptions—and "extended the use of crusading within a traditional framework of thought which few expressed as lucidly and beautifully as he, or his draftsmen, did."[368] Since the First Crusade, "there had been no pope who had fought more keenly to make the crusade an ecclesiastical and specifically a papal enterprise."[369] Innocent III's crusading bulls "emphatically reclaimed the direction of the crusade for the papacy."[370] The pope assumed control over all aspects of the crusade. Under Innocent, the Church for the first time led the crusade movement in "all its breadth."[371]

Innocent III's crusading activity can best be understood as the duty of a papal monarch. His "high sense of moral and historical purpose" and

362. For the Curia (Iesu) Christi, also called Concilium Christianitatis, see *Historia de expeditione* 12, 14. Cf. Zerbi 1955, 34–35; Munz 1969, 386; Roscher 1969, 45–46, 282; Riley-Smith 1992, 111.

363. For the democratic concept of power as an empty space, see Lefort 1981, 1986.

364. See Zerbi 1955, 42–50; Munz 1969.

365. Cf. Watt 1965, 34 f.; 1988, 381; Roscher 1969, 261; Morris 1991, 205–7, 431 ff.; Pennington 1993a; Sayers 1994.

366. Cole 1991, 141.

367. Sayers 1994, 166.

368. Riley-Smith 1992, 145.

369. Mayer 1993, 217.

370. Robinson 1990, 523.

371. Roscher 1969, 262.

feeling of responsibility for the maintenance of good government (rather than personal ambition, as older historiography used to argue)[372] led him to build up the papal monarchy. Innocent and his supporters regarded the papal monarchy as the best form of government for shaping worldly affairs in such a fashion that "the ordered peace of a universal society would reflect the immanent harmony and justice of God's universe."[373] In this sense, the special duty of the pope—of which Innocent often wrote in his correspondence—was to defend and make peace.[374] Innocent wrote, for example, to the French king: "We who are, however unworthily, the vicar of Christ on earth, following his example and imitating the custom of our predecessors' wish and are obliged to attend the restoration of true peace and concord between those who are in dispute."[375]

Maintenance of peace implies judgment in temporal affairs. The pope claimed the right to judge in cases concerning sin (ratione peccati).[376] And because peace and war—as either the maintenance or the disruption of the stability and harmony of Christian order—were moral issues par excellence, this eminently applied to them. Innocent was explicit that papal intervention in temporal affairs was especially urgent when it was peace that was being sinned against. As a pope, Innocent felt "empowered" to "rebuke any Christian for any mortal sin and to coerce him with ecclesiastical penalties if he spurns our correction." He had to "proceed in this fashion against any criminal sin in order to recall the sinner from error to truth and from vice to virtue," but "this is especially so when it is a sin against peace, peace which is the bond of love."[377]

Disparate within Christian society, peace and war were linked together when the faithful faced those with whom they were not united in "the bond of love." When Innocent tied peacemaking to crusading, he was very much a man of his age. Peace as the necessary precondition for a crusade was "a leading political concept of the twelfth century."[378] More specifically, he "stood firmly in the tradition of ecclesiastical activity since the Peace of God movement,"[379] and followed the steps of his predecessors on the papal throne for whom peacemaking was an im-

372. Tierney 1988, 127–28; Morris 1991, 426; Pennington 1993a, 25.
373. Tierney 1988, 131. Cf. Arquillière 1934, 522–23.
374. Morris 1991, 423.
375. Innocent to Philip Augustus, A.D. 1198 (quoted in Morris 1991, 426–27).
376. For the pope's right to judge ratione peccati, see Innocent's decretal Novit (1204), in Tierney 1988, 135.
377. Ibid.
378. Munz 1969, 384 n. 2.
379. Morris 1991, 427.

portant part of preparations for the crusades.[380] The Fourth Lateran Council, summoned by Innocent III in 1215, for example, published a crusading decree stating that it was "of the greatest necessity" for the fulfillment of the crusade that "the princes of Christian people keep peace with one another." Therefore the pope, in the name of the council, decreed "that peace should be generally observed throughout the whole Christian world for at least four years." The prelates of the Church were ordered to resolve discords "into unbroken peace or into the inviolable observance of steadfast truces," and to "most firmly" compel those who might "treat this order with scorn" to acquiesce by the "excommunication of their persons and the laying of interdicts on their lands."[381]

If Innocent was "haunted by the crusading idea,"[382] it was because the crusade was a manifestation of peace and a moral imperative. Peace in Christendom sums up Innocent's vision of what Christendom needed, and he devoted his life's work to fulfilling that need. It was the common denominator of the three programmatic goals of his pontificate: the crusade, the reform of the Church, and the "correction" of heresy. The crusade, peace, and Christendom converged in Innocent's thinking. Because peace was at the heart of the pope's idea of the right order in Christendom, and because the crusade idea was firmly embedded in his very notion of Christendom,[383] the crusade expressed and helped to bring about sound Christian order, peace, and unity.

The notion of Christendom lay at the foundation of Innocent III's doctrine of papal power and was the "key to his view of the world and his political concepts."[384] He conceived of the crusade as the work of the whole of Christendom, united under the leadership of the supreme pontiff.[385] This conception was not new. Pope Alexander III, for example, had envisaged the crusade as an enterprise of Christendom; Clement III's negotiations with the Armenians about Western military help had expressed a clear consciousness of Christendom; and at the time of the Third

380. See Alphandéry 1959, 162–63; Roscher 1969, 24, 84 f., 148 f., 167, 275; Morris 1991, 426; Sayers 1994, 86. Specifically on the crusading peacemaking of Innocent's predecessors and successors (Alexander III, Gregory VIII, Clement III, Gregory IX, and Honorius III), see Roscher 1969, 37, 43; Morris 1991, 563.

381. *Ad liberandam* (Hefele 1912–13, 5.2: 1394; trans. in Riley-Smith and Riley-Smith 1981, 128–29). The relationship between Innocent III's peace program and the crusade is traced in Powell 1986.

382. Sayers 1994, 166.

383. See Roscher 1969.

384. Ibid., 23–24.

385. The crusade concerned "die ganze Christenheit" (ibid., 27; cf. 262, 266, 295 f.); it was "l'oeuvre essentiel de la Chrétienté une" (Alphandéry 1959, 149).

Crusade, the crusade had been spoken of as *servitium christianitatis* and *negotium christianum*.[386] Innocent's "great genius was as an innovative executor of a broadly conceived vision of the crusade."[387] In particular, he built on the growing prominence of the notion of Christendom to articulate the idea of the crusade as service to Christendom, and as Christendom's struggle against all foreign, unfaithful peoples. What was new was the consistency with which he linked Christendom and the crusade.

Innocent III was not led astray by the "democratic" deviations that had led Frederick I to leave the place of highest power empty. He believed in the pope's fullness of power and presided uncompromisingly over his own Church councils. As the vicar of Christ,[388] he sat in Christ's place over the whole of Christendom. But the consistency with which he linked Christendom and the crusade brought about a populist shift in the meaning of Christendom and introduced a "democratic" element into Innocent's crusade. This is especially true of his preparations for the Fifth Crusade.

Because the execution of the Fourth Crusade (in 1204) had slipped out of Innocent's hands, ecclesiastical leadership of the crusade had to be reasserted.[389] The Fifth Crusade (the preparation for which started in 1213) was to be the first "truly pontifical" crusade.[390] No previous pope had marshaled the resources of his office and of the whole Church as vigorously on behalf of the crusade as did Innocent.[391] While preaching the Fifth Crusade, he repeatedly addressed himself to the "Christian people." He referred to the difficult situation of the whole Christian people (*necessitas totius populi christiani*) and called on princes and Christian people (*principes et populus christianus*) to bring help to the Holy Land. The term *populus christianus* became, "to a degree unknown before, a notion interchangeable with 'christianitas.'"[392] More clearly and consis-

---

386. See Zerbi 1955, 30 f., 44, 152 f.; Roscher 1969, 36–37, 43–44; Rowe 1993, 128.
387. Powell 1986, 4.
388. The title *vicarius Christi* was first applied to the pope by Peter Damian. But it was Bernard of Clairvaux who first applied it to the pope alone, thus breaking with an ancient tradition by which the title was used for other bishops as well, and even for lay princes. Paraviana-Bagliani 2000, 58. See Bernard of Clairvaux *On Consideration* II,viii,16; IV,vii,23. Innocent III was the first pope who publicly called himself the vicar of Christ. Sayers 1994, 16. Compared with *vicar of St. Peter,* as the Gregorian reformers called the pope, the term *vicar of Christ* introduced a new theological perspective. See Maccarrone 1974, especially 115; Katzir 1992, 5.
389. Libertini 1996, 291.
390. Alphandéry 1959, 199.
391. Powell 1986, 4.
392. Roscher 1969, 24, 265.

tently than ever before, the crusade was now an enterprise of the entirety of Christendom, while Christendom meant the whole of the Christian people, for whom crusading was a moral obligation and a quasi-feudal service to God.[393] It followed logically that any Christian should be allowed to take the cross. Innocent drew exactly this conclusion and "democratized" recruitment for the crusade.

We may see Innocent's approach to recruitment for the crusade against the background of the "early poverty movement" and the widely spread belief that the poor were the "true chosen ones" who would achieve victory in the crusade through divine favor (as Fulk of Neuilly, a Parisian parish priest and the most famous preacher of that crusade, put it).[394] As the so-called Children's Crusade of 1212 had shown,[395] the potential for a mass response was great. Innocent obviously knew how to read the signs of the time and took the initiative. He fused the "ideology of the crusade" with the beliefs animating the movements of lay piety into an impressive "theology of the crusade," embedding the crusade in the religious currents of the age.[396]

Innocent initiated preparations for the Fifth Crusade with the publication of his bull *Quia maior* in April, 1213. He addressed all the people of Christendom and clearly stated that "anyone who wishes, except persons bound by religious profession, may take the cross in such a way that this vow may be commuted, redeemed or deferred by apostolic mandate when urgent or evident expediency demands it."[397] Before this call, the crusading vow had normally been taken only by men able to fight and to finance their journey to the east. All others had been considered a burden and an impediment to the military efficiency of the cru-

393. See Innocent III *Quia maior* (Riley-Smith and Riley-Smith 1981, 120). Cf. Powell 1986, 17; Riley-Smith 1992, 143; Gilchrist 1993, 73–74. On the influence of feudal imagery of vassalage on the crusade idea, see Roscher 1969, 281 ff., especially 284: "Solange die Kreuznahme in Analogie zum Mönchgelübde gesehen wurde, war sie ein freiwilliger Akt. Wenn die Kreuznahme dagegen eine rechtlich faßbare Vasallenpflicht jedes Christen gegen seinen Herrn war, war es prinzipiell möglich, die gesamte Christenheit zum Kreuzzug aufzubieten."

394. Powell 1986, 7.

395. For a brief traditional account, see Mayer 1993, 215 f. Revisionist interpretations have questioned the assumption that most of the participants were children, arguing that the term *pueri* referred to the class of dependents rather than children and that the crusade was linked to the apostolic poverty movement. Powell 1986, 8 (referring to G. Miccoli, "La crociata dei fanciulli," *Studi medievali*, 3rd. ser, 2 [1961]; Raedts, "The Children's Crusade of 1212," *Journal of Medieval History* 3 [1971]).

396. Powell 1986, 16–17. On Innocent III's profoundly theological understanding of the crusade, see Gilchrist 1993, 68 ff.

397. *Quia maior* (Riley-Smith and Riley-Smith 1981, 122).

sading army. The change introduced by Innocent III was theologically based but did not ignore military considerations. Innocent retained the right for the Church to "commute, redeem, or defer" the vow. Regulations concerning commutation, redemption, and deferring of crusading vows have often been seen as a device for extracting money from fickle would-be crusaders. But Innocent's vow-taking policy was much more than a new source of money. The pope's ruling that "anyone, except a religious, may take the sign of the cross at will," [398] gave all Christians the chance to express their will. Recruitment for the crusade became a popular vote. Democratic elections, of course, do not give voters a share in the exercise of power. Nor did this crusading vote qualify all electors to become effective crusaders. But the electors could nonetheless feel elect: they were the elect people. Even the poorest and weakest was now given a chance to enjoy the spiritual benefits of the crusade and to play a part in the "war against Islam." [399] The crusade was open to all Christians. The whole of the people of God now became the Lord's army.[400] More than a test of faith "for all men," [401] the crusade was the very practice of faith. Following Christ, Innocent explained, meant following Him "to the battle." [402]

Anna Comnena, daughter of the Byzantine Emperor Alexius I, in her account of her father's reign, left a vivid picture of Latin Christians who had followed Christ "to the battle" in the First Crusade. She noted a marked difference between Latin and Greek customs "with regard to priests." She was struck to see that a "Latin barbarian will at the same time handle sacred objects, fasten a shield to his left arm and grasp a spear in his right. He will communicate the Body and Blood of the Deity and meanwhile gaze on bloodshed and become himself 'a man of blood.'" This led her to conclude that the Latins were "no less devoted to religion than to war." [403] From another perspective, by launching the First Crusade, Pope Urban II had brought together religion and war.[404]

---

398. Innocent to Conrad, Dean of Speyer, 9 Sept. 1213 (Riley-Smith and Riley-Smith 1981, 131).

399. Powell 1986, 20; Mayer 1993, 217.

400. "The *militia dei* thus received its final, revolutionary meaning." Gilchrist 1993, 79.

401. *Qiua maior* (Riley-Smith and Riley-Smith 1981, 119). Innocent, however, did not exclude half of the human race from crusading. When he stated that "anyone may take the sign of the cross," he was also thinking of women. Innocent to Conrad, Dean of Speyer, 9 Sept. 1213 (ibid., 131).

402. See *Qiua maior* (ibid., 119).

403. *The Alexiad* X,viii (p. 317).

404. Cf. Libertini 1996, 281.

But it was only under Innocent III's reign that the historical process of removing all barriers between religion and war was completed. "Religion as war and war as religion were now one."[405]

The struggle between papacy and empire for control over the crusade is highlighted when we look at the conflict that broke out about Emperor Frederick II's crusading. The origins of this conflict reach back to the coronation of Frederick (who, as a minor, had been under Innocent III's wardship) as the king of the Romans, in 1215. Frederick II was deeply influenced by the myth of Charlemagne as a model crusader and was proud of his family's crusading record. The crusade was one of his central concerns. He took the cross as soon as he was crowned king. But that was on his own initiative, without papal approval, and, as such, was an infringement on papal control over the crusading movement.[406] By the time Frederick's imperial coronation was staged in Rome in 1220, the curia had become fully reconciled to Frederick's self-imposed crusading mission and saw the crusade as Frederick's first major act as emperor.[407] In response to the disastrous end of the Fifth Crusade at Damietta in 1221, Frederick and Pope Honorius III began to plan a new crusade.[408] But Frederick had been postponing the fulfillment of his crusading vow, and did so for so long that Pope Gregory IX used Frederick's failure to leave for the crusade by the negotiated deadline as a pretext for excommunicating him. Fearing the amassing of power in Frederick II's hands and hoping to weaken his position, the pope wanted Frederick's crusade to fail.[409] But excommunication did not dampen Frederick's crusading zeal. He finally parted for the Holy Land in 1228, as an excommunicate. Instead of giving up on the crusade, he made it an imperial enterprise. Confrontation between the emperor and the pope became sharp. A crusade unblessed by the pope was a "threat to the political standing of the papacy, as organizer of holy war and mediator, through the offer of remission of sins, between God and man."[410] Moreover, Frederick II threatened to corrupt the very principle of Christendom's holy war when he translated his crusade into diplomatic action. In the course of his expedition, the emperor eventually negotiated a peace treaty with the Egyptian sultan al-Malik al-Kamil, signed at Jaffa in February, 1229. Ac-

405. Gilchrist 1993, 83.
406. See Abulafia 1992, 120–22.
407. Ibid., 138; Powell 1986, 180 f.
408. Abulafia 1992, 148 ff.
409. Ibid., 164–70. Cf. Powell 1986, 198–99.
410. Abulafia 1992, 170.

cording to the terms of the treaty, the sultan restored Jerusalem and a number of other places to Christian rule.[411] But far from being greeted favorably by ecclesiastical authorities, this *pacis concordia*, as Frederick called the treaty, was thoroughly condemned.

The disapproval of Frederick II's mode of regaining Jerusalem was not without a preface. Misgivings had been expressed about his way of life in the Christian West long before he fulfilled his crusading vow. He was called a "disciple of Muhammad," a "baptized Sultan of Sicily," and an Antichrist.[412] The key factor in the reaction to Frederick's recovery of Jerusalem, however, was that he had been excommunicated even before he and his army had set sail for the East. An impenitent, excommunicated crusader, from the pope's point of view, was a contradiction in terms. Frederick's crusade was a false holy war.[413] Moreover, even though the Church held making alliances or treaties with the infidels illicit, Frederick had signed a treaty with the "Sultan of Babylon." From the ecclesiastical perspective, this treaty was impious, an *impium foedus*.[414] The first to condemn it was the patriarch of Jerusalem, Gerold, "a fanatical Saracen-hater."[415] In his eyes, the treaty was fraudulent and malicious, an insane crime lacking any foundation in truth. It was to the great detriment of the cause of Jesus Christ and did great injury to the Christian faith and the Holy See's rights in the Holy Land. Moreover, Sultan al-Kamil, Gerold pointed out, was in no position to negotiate the fate of Jerusalem, since the legitimate lord over that territory was his uncle, the Damascene sultan Dawud. The treaty was consequently invalid. Moreover, and equally egregious, Frederick had recognized the right of the infidels to retain possession of the "Temple of Solomon," which they had transformed into a mosque,[416] and to con-

---

411. For the background of Frederick's negotiations with al-Kamil, see Abulafia 1992, 170 ff. For a detailed analysis of the negotiations and their success, see Vismara 1974, 96 ff.; cf. Abulafia 1992, 182 ff. For al-Kamil's interest in concluding a treaty with Frederick, see Powell 1986, 199–200; Aziz 1996, especially 375 f. See also Frederick's own report in his letter to Henry III of England, A.D. 1229 (Peters 1991, 163 f.).

412. Metlitzki 1977, 7–8; Pavlović 1992, 123; Abulafia 1992, 171. When the conflict between the emperor and the papacy lingered on, in 1245 Pope Innocent IV still found it expedient to accuse Frederick II of practicing the Muslim rite and having a harem. Vismara 1974, 134.

413. Abulafia 1992, 173, 174.

414. Cf. n. 145; Gatto 1959, 67. Innocent III kept secret his attempt to negotiate a settlement with the "Sultan of Damascus and Babylon." See Potthast, *Regesta*, no. 4719 (26 Apr. 1213); cf. Powell 1986, 28, 32 n. 54.

415. Mayer 1993, 236.

416. See chap. 2 n. 43.

tinue to profane that holy site. Echoing 2 Corinthians 6.14–15,[417] Gerold declared the treaty impious: *hec est conventio Christi ad Belial.* [418]

Gregory IX followed Gerold's lead. The papacy "made more fuss about the disadvantages of Frederick's treaty with al-Kamil than about the obvious fact that the holiest city of Christendom had been recovered by Frederick II." [419] In a letter to the archbishop of Milan, the pope expressed his outrage over the treaty agreed to by this "spurious emperor" (*dictus imperator*). The treaty was legally null and void because its terms obstructed the "cause of Christ and his people." [420] Gregory sent a circular letter to Duke Leopold of Austria and to princes and bishops of Christendom a month later, in July 1229, that contained accusations against Frederick II on four grounds.[421] First, the emperor had misused the crusade. As a crusading leader, he should have used his sword against the enemies of the faith. But instead, refusing to fight the infidels, he made an abominable pact with them, thus abusing his imperial power and dignity as well. Second, he had abandoned the "Temple of Solomon" to the infidels, as a result of which Muslim law was being proclaimed where the truth of the Gospel should be heard.[422] Third, because he had not included them in the treaty, Frederick had exposed Christian dominions in Syria (including Tripoli and Antioch) to the danger of occupation by the enemies of the faith. Even worse, the terms of the treaty forbade the emperor from assisting the Christian dominions in case of necessity, and even committed him to preventing others from delivering help. Fourth, because of his contractual obligation to protect the sultan against any eventual Christian attack—in case the Christian army wanted to avenge the injuries suffered by the Redeemer and to cleanse the Temple of God and the Holy Land from pagan dirt (*spurcitias paganorum*)—the emperor's treaty with the pagans was in fact directed against the entire Christian people (*contra totum populum Christianum*).

Frederick was found guilty because he had liberated Jerusalem via a treaty with the heathen, rather than via a crusade.[423] He had not fought

417. See n. 135.
418. See Vismara 1974, 120–21; Peters 1991, 166–67 (a selection from Gerold's letter to all the faithful).
419. Abulafia 1992, 194.
420. Cf. Vismara 1974, 121 n. 335.
421. For the following summary, see ibid., 123–25.
422. The accusation was also made in Gregory's letter to the archbishop of Milan. See ibid., 124 n. 352.
423. Roscher 1969, 287. In contrast to this, King Louis IX of France was later praised because, unlike Frederick II, he departed for the East "pour combattre, et non pour traiter." Berger 1893, 317. Rebellious German peasants in the early sixteenth century,

the enemies of the faith with his sword (*cum executionem gladii contra hostes fidei*)[424] and had thus abused the crusade. His expedition was an "anti-crusade."[425] An emperor who concluded an alliance with the infidel was a traitor to the *respublica Christiana*.[426] To "celebrate" Frederick II's recovery of Jerusalem from Muslim rule, the patriarch of Jerusalem placed the city under interdict.[427] The pope confirmed Frederick's excommunication and absolved the emperor's subjects from their oath of fidelity,[428] while the papal army invaded Frederick II's Sicilian kingdom.

Meanwhile, in the Holy City, the emperor visited the Church of the Holy Sepulchre and performed the ceremonial act of crown-wearing to celebrate the accomplishment of his holy work and devoted service to Jesus Christ. After worshipping at the Holy Sepulchre, as Frederick himself wrote to the English king, "we, as being a catholic emperor, . . . wore the crown, which Almighty God provided for us from the throne of His majesty, when of His especial grace, He exalted us on high amongst the princes of the world."[429] The grand master of the Teutonic Knights delivered a speech on the emperor's behalf to mark the occasion. In this imperial manifesto, addressed to all the peoples of the world, Frederick II was represented as God's vicar on earth. As the Christ-king, Frederick stood "between God and mankind," chosen to rule over the earth from end to end.[430] No longer was it only the pope who was to be "lower than God but higher than man" (as Innocent III had put it).[431] The crown-wearing ceremony was a jubilation of the emperor's immediate relationship with God.[432] Under attack by the Roman curia, Frederick II struck back. Willing to compromise no longer, he stated outright that his imperial monarchy had been bestowed upon him directly by God.[433] "He

---

however, believed that the emperor had laid siege to Jerusalem and that the first over the walls of the city, after a ten-day assault, had been the son of a Bavarian miller carrying the flag of the *Bundschuh* (the banner of German peasant revolts). Munz 1969, 10.

424. Gregory IX to the Duke of Austria; quoted in Vismara 1974, 123.
425. Purcell 1975, 20; Abulafia 1992, 170.
426. Vismara 1974, 125.
427. Gerold to all the faithful (Peters 1991, 169).
428. Vismara 1974, 126.
429. Frederick to Henry III (Peters 1991, 162, 164). Cf. Abulafia 1992, 186–87.
430. Abulafia 1992, 197–98; Mayer 1993, 237.
431. In Innocent III's words, the pope was set "between God and man, lower than God but higher than man, who judges all and is judged by no one." *Sermon on the Consecration of a Pope* (Tierney 1988, 132).
432. Kantorowicz 1993, 182–88, who describes the episode with much pathos, speaks of "Gottunmittelbarkeit," pointing out that Frederick achieved this triumph (in which he became "united with God") "ohne Mittler der Kirche": not through the Church but alongside and outside the Church. Cf. Abulafia 1977, especially 198.
433. Cf. Abulafia 1992, 188.

is great, greater, and greatest: great since he is king of Sicily, greater since he is king of Jerusalem, greatest since he is Roman emperor," an eulogist wrote. "He it is whom the Lord crowned with glory and honor, and set over the work of his hands."[434] In Jerusalem, however, it was the patriarch's propaganda that held sway. When Frederick, the "new David" appointed to bring deliverance to his people, hurried from the Holy Land to deliver his Sicilian kingdom from the armed forces of the supreme spiritual power of Christendom, the butchers of Acre pelted him with entrails.[435]

The story of Frederick II's crusade is as telling as it is curious. It shows how little the Latin Christians, the pope included, actually cared about Jerusalem and Palestine—except for the Holy City and the Holy Land they had constructed in their own heads. The "liberation" of the earthly Jerusalem, this story seems to say, was less important to them than armed struggle against the infidels. By the end of the twelfth century, crusading had ceased to be a movement for the "liberation of the Holy Land" and had become instead a movement for the extermination of the infidels[436]— for the "elimination of pagan dirt."[437] The story of Frederick II also illustrates the extent to which the crusade was actually an internal affair of western Christendom: what really mattered were the effects that crusading produced within Christendom. I would venture to add that the story also shows how genuinely western Christians cared about peace. Because the crusade had begun—and had to begin—in peace, every new crusade brought more "peacemaking." If the crusade had in fact ended in peace, the whole project would have failed. Frederick II mistakenly thought that with his treaty of peace with al-Kamil "that business has been brought to a conclusion."[438] But perpetual peace required a perpetual crusade. For there was nothing more precious than peace.

434. Nicholas of Bari *Eulogy of Frederick II* (Cantor 1963, 295).

435. Philip of Novara *History* (Peters 1991, 160). Cf. Riley-Smith 1992, 151; Abulafia 1992, 191.

436. "[L]a Croissade dépasse la libération de le Terre Sainte pour devenir, au sens plein, extermination de l'Infidèle." Alphandéry 1954, 220.

437. "[E]liminare spurcitias paganorum." Gregory IX to the Duke of Austria (quoted in Vismara 1974, 125).

438. Frederick to Henry III (Peters 1991, 162).

FOUR

Monks, Philosophers, and Warrior Monks

In chapter 3, I examined the role that the crusade idea and crusading movement played in the articulation of structures of public authority and the formation of political order in the Latin West. To round out the picture of those developments, I now turn to some leading intellectual and spiritual figures of the twelfth and thirteenth centuries and the ways they thought about the relation of Christendom to the Muslims. I show how these different ideas blended into an overall hostile view of the non-Christian world. With regard to the Muslim world, this hostile outlook was organized along two main axes: the crusade and the mission. The era of the papal monarchy was the golden age of the former, but it also saw the birth and advancement of the latter. The crusade and mission are often seen as opposites: one is war, the other peace; one is carried out by the soldier, the other by the cleric; one is accomplished by the sword, the other by reasoning. But the aim of both mission and crusade was the same: the expansion of Christendom. Nor were the means they employed in pursuing that aim as contradictory in practice as one might suppose. Christian arms and Christianized reason worked closely together, mutually supporting each other, even though reason seems to have sought the support of arms more often than Christian soldiers solicited the arguments of reasoning clerics.[1]

---

1. The authoritative account of the crusade *and* mission is Kedar 1984. See also Siberry 1983. For the "Christianization of reason," see Abulafia 1995.

Rather than playing crusading and missionary ideas against each other, I try to show how strains of thought frequently characterized as peaceable, conciliatory, and preferring reason to violence ultimately demanded the complete submission of those called infidels. Should the infidels turn out to be "obstinate"—that is to say, not susceptible to the "compelling reasons" of the propagandists of the "true faith" and unwilling to renounce their own faith and identity—they would have to suffer physical violence. Just as the crusade was ever anew bringing about peace, missionary peace was pregnant with the crusade. Christianized reason, in the last instance, spoke the "iron tongue" of war, and in the Christian mental universe, war against the infidel was not unreasonable.

SANCTIFICATION OF CRIME: ST. BERNARD OF CLAIRVAUX

In both the crusade and the mission new religious orders played a central role. The time span under consideration here is bound by the emergence (most probably in 1119) and suppression (about two centuries later) of the first and most famous of the military orders, the Templars. The formation of the Order of the Temple was an important moment in the institutionalization of the First Crusade. The order was a materialization par excellence of the crusade spirit.[2] But what is of interest here is not the history of the Templars per se,[3] but rather the spirit engendered by the First Crusade that found its ideal embodiment in the Knights of the Temple.

In both its self-representation and the view of a great majority of its contemporaries, the Order of the Temple was founded for defensive purposes. Like other military orders, however, the Templars were also encouraged to slaughter the infidel.[4] As John of Salisbury stated straightforwardly, the "normal occupation" of the Knights of the Temple was "to shed human blood."[5] It is a nicety of history that in Jerusalem they were given their quarters in, and derived their name from, the Temple of Solomon—the place that upon the capture of the city by the crusaders was washed with the "blood of unbelievers."[6] As an organization spe-

2. Cf. Blake 1970, 27.
3. For the history of the order, see R. Barber 1982, chap. 14–15; Forey 1985, 1992; Barber 1993, 1995.
4. Cf. Forey 1992, 184–86.
5. *Policraticus* VII,21 (p. 173).
6. Cf. chap. 2 n. 43.

cialized in fighting the infidels, the Templars became an inspiration for subsequent Christian military orders.[7] But warfare against infidels was neither a novelty nor a contested issue in those times; to the contrary, by the time the first Templars took their vows, "holy violence" had achieved "a high level of general acceptance."[8] Even John of Salisbury, not their great friend, maintained that the Templars, "almost alone among men," waged "legitimate war."[9] What was new, and unsettling to some, was that these knights were monks fighting infidels with secular arms.

A wide gap had been thought to exist between warriors and monks, though the latter had been called the soldiers of Christ.[10] The Templar, however, combined the figures of soldier and monk in one person; he was a monk who took up arms. For Isaac of L'Etoile, the abbot of a Cistercian House in Poitou, this was a deformity, the "Fifth Gospel," and he labeled "the new knighthood" a *novum monstrum*.[11] Henry, archdeacon of Huntingdon, also wrote (around 1145) of a "certain new monster composed from purity and corruption, namely a monk and a knight."[12] But such critical views, even though voicing a legitimate concern, were rare. In general, the military orders were greeted with "enormous enthusiasm by lay people and clergy."[13] The critical minority, moreover, consisted mostly of "notable individualists" from Christendom's remote corners, whose writings had only a small circulation.[14] The Templar Founding Brothers, on the other hand, were close to the great and wealthy Cistercian abbeys. The greatest of the Cistercian abbots, Bernard of Clairvaux, wrote a highly influential defense of the *milites templi*. Soon the Templars were officially recognized by the papacy. Papal bulls "underwrote the new order so unequivocally that henceforth doubts about the validity of the concept no longer found a place in the mainstream of thought in the western Church."[15] As the very embodiment of the new Christian militarism, the Templars and other military orders following in their footsteps came to be highly esteemed in crusading Christendom. Late in the eighth century, Alcuin, with Christ's pas-

---

7. Valous 1953, 32.
8. Barber 1995, 40.
9. *Policraticus* VII,21 (p. 173).
10. See chap. 1 nn. 113–15.
11. Kedar 1984, 105; Zerbi 1992, 294; Barber 1995, 61.
12. Barber 1995, 41.
13. Nicholson 1995, 3.
14. Ibid., 38.
15. Barber 1995, 56.

sion in front of his eyes, had spoken of "soldiers by the cross." [16] Now, true soldiers *of* the cross had come into being.

Bernard of Clairvaux was perhaps the most famous monk of his time and one of the most influential men in all of Latin Christendom. He was "looked upon by all the peoples of France and Germany as a prophet and apostle." [17] Although not marked by great originality, his contribution to the crusade was crucial. He interpreted the commonly shared ideas and practices that came to prominence with the First Crusade in a way that set into motion the spiritualization of the crusade. [18] His most important contribution to crusading ideology was his laudation of the Templars, *De laude novae militiae (In Praise of the New Knighthood)*.

As the first military order, the Templars were an institution of a new kind. They were warriors under monastic vows, permanent crusaders subject to monastic discipline. They went far beyond what Guibert of Nogent had represented as a "new way of winning salvation." Guibert had had in mind laymen whose "ordinary way of life" was using arms and who could hope for salvation once the crusade had given them the opportunity to slaughter the infidels instead of their fellow Christians. [19] But the Templars were monks, not laymen. They were holy warriors of a new type. As such, as already mentioned, they faced misgivings, suspicions, and even outright criticism, marginal as that criticism may have been. [20] Moreover, their dual nature as monks and soldiers appears to have created "uncertainty and doubt among the Templars themselves." [21] The outside criticism and the internal doubts together apparently plunged them into a "serious crisis." [22] To boost their morale, a certain Hugh the Sinner sent them a written sermon, the *Sermo ad milites templi*. [23] But in need of further reassurance and an authoritative justification of their mission, the Templars sought help from Bernard. [24]

16. Alcuin to the brothers of the church of York, A.D. 795, *Epistolae* no. 43 (p. 89); *Alcuin of York*, 4.

17. Otto of Freising *The Deeds* I,xxxv.

18. Rousset 1945, 163, 167; Blake 1970, 29; Cardini 1974 (on Bernard, 210 ff.), 1993a.

19. See chap. 2 n. 1.

20. Cf. nn. 11, 12, 14. See Morris 1991, 280–81; Barber 1995, 41 ff., 59 ff.; Nicholson 1995. For the later period, Forey 1992, 204–20.

21. Bulst-Thiele 1992, 58; Selwood 1996, 225, speaks of "self-doubt."

22. Graboïs 1992, 50.

23. Some historians hold that this *Hugo peccator* was Hugh of St. Victor; others opt for Hugh of Payns, the first master of the Temple (who was on a mission in the Latin West); and still others see the problem of authorship as unresolved. For a brief survey of these positions, see Selwood 1996, 223 n. 9.

24. See Emery 1990, 20; Forey 1992, 15; Barber 1995, 44.

Some maintain that Bernard helped the Templars formulate the Rule of the order.[25] Be that as it may, there is no doubt about his authorship of the *Liber ad milites Templi,* better known as *De laude novae militiae.*[26] The Templars found his help so important that they regarded Bernard as their founder.[27]

In his *Liber,* St. Bernard created a positive image of the "new knighthood." A clever demagogue, he exploited "the currents of opinion which had been a precondition of the calling of the crusade and which in turn had made the establishment of the Templars possible."[28] Bernard's pamphlet was marked with "clear brutality,"[29] and may well be "the most aggressive statement of militant Christianity."[30] But the saint who wrote it was a proponent of peace who devoted "a good portion of his time and all the weight of his personal influence" to endeavors to restore peace in Christendom.[31]

De laude novae militiae includes sections sharply critical of knighthood. Bernard censured the lack of discipline, the luxury, and the effeminacy of knights. Regarding the ostentatious vestments, the horses covered with silk, and the arms painted and embellished with gold and precious stones, Bernard asked bitingly: "Are these military insignia or rather womanish ornaments?" Gold and jewels were unlikely to strike the enemy with awe, and silk was easy to pierce.[32] The holy man who praised the merging of soldier with monk was clearly upset because knights in their apparel looked feminine. The fusing of social orders implied in blending of monk and soldier was less disturbing to him than a blurring of gender differences. It was hard for him, he wrote, to see knights growing their hair just like women. With their hair falling over

25. The view that he did (held, e.g., by Cousin 1953; Valous 1953; Bulst-Thiele 1992, 61 f.) is questioned in Selwood 1996, 221. For an exposition of the Rule, see Barber 1995, 15 f.

26. The date usually given for the composition of Bernard's treatise is the early 1130s. Selwood 1996, however, argues that the text was written prior to the Council of Troyes in 1129, which promulgated the Rule and promoted the Templars.

27. Bulst-Thiele 1992, 60.

28. Forey 1992, 15; Barber 1995, 44–45, cf. 38–39.

29. In his imagery Bernard "thirsts for blood." Daniel 1989b, 46.

30. Morris 1991, 281.

31. Emery 1990, 23.

32. Bernard *Éloge de la nouvelle chevalerie* II,3. The Rule of the order demanded that the Templars wear simple clothing and refrain from embellishing their weapons and horses. At the time of the Second Crusade these rules were transferred to crusaders. See Conrad 1941, 92–97. Cf. Eugenius III's crusading bull, *Quantum praedecessores:* "those who fight for the Lord ought not to care for precious clothes or elegant appearance . . . or other things that are signs of lasciviousness." Riley-Smith and Riley-Smith, 1981, 58–59. See also Gregory VIII's bull *Audita tremendi* (ibid., 67).

their eyes so they could not see, their feet entrapped in their long and
extravagant tunics, and their gentle hands hidden in flowing sleeves,
knights were obviously of little use as soldiers. [33]

But Bernard's critique did not stop there. Armed with Augustinian
"right intention" and "just cause," he made a more substantial criticism
of war. "Is there, O knights, a more stupendous error, a more insuffer-
able madness, than spending so much money and so much labor for a
war that brings nothing but death and crime?" [34] Wars and strife among
Christians "are only caused by impulse of irrational anger, or desire for
vain glory, or else by greed for terrestrial possessions of whatever kind."
And, Bernard added, if these were the causes for war, it was safe neither
to kill nor to be killed.[35] For the safety Bernard was principally concerned with was safety of the soul. Death of the body was the lesser
evil—if it was evil at all. He who waged war for the wrong reasons lived
as a murderer (*vivis homicida*) [36]—that is, in sin. Victory in such a battle
would not save one from perdition. "Unfortunate is the victory if, van-
quishing a man, you succumb to vice." [37] In this sense, waging war was
evil, *militia* was *malitia*. If "he who kills sins mortally while he who is
killed is lost for eternity," no one could gain.[38]

Bernard's criticism, to be sure, was a criticism of secular warfare and
secular knighthood, *militia saecularis*. The Templars were something
different, a new type of militia, *novum militiae genus,* unknown in previous centuries.[39] Their war was of a double nature. It was waged with
bodily strength against the corporal enemy and with the force of the soul
against vices and demons. Their armor was double as well: the body was
protected with iron, and the soul with faith. As such, they feared neither
man nor demon.[40] Bernard rejoiced at the sight of these warriors: they
filled the world with monks! But how to praise them, as monks or as
knights? [41]

Rhetorician that he was, Bernard knew his answer before he asked the

33. *Éloge* II,3.
34. *Éloge* II,3; cf. *Briefe* no. 363,5 (p. 656).
35. *Éloge* II,3.
36. Ibid., I,2.
37. Ibid.
38. Ibid., II,3. For the context of Bernard's opposition of *militia* and *malitia*, see Graboïs 1992.
39. *Éloge* I,1.
40. Ibid., I,1; IV,8.
41. Ibid.

question. By calling the Templars monks, he had already made up his mind. He did not reduce the monk to soldier, but rather elevated the soldier to monk.[42] But the figure of the warrior monk was disturbing to a number of his contemporaries. Though the Templars' doubters were few and relatively powerless, their doubts stemmed from traditional Christian doctrine and had to be taken seriously. Combining monasticism and war was a "departure from scriptural teaching."[43] As followers of a "new kind of religion," mixing "religion with military service" (as they stated in the Rule of the order),[44] the Templars represented a confusion of values to Christian traditionalists and caused unease. Being a cleric deeply involved in secular business, Bernard seems to have had doubts about his own composite nature.[45] But he set out to clear the Templars of any suspicion by defending and praising precisely their dubious dual nature. A great master of eloquence, Bernard was able to turn the Templars' weak point into a virtue.

Bernard boldly called the Templars *milites Christi*, soldiers of Christ— the conventional term for monks. To Bernard, abbot of Clairvaux, the ideal Christian life was monastic, and lauding the Knights of the Temple as monks was the highest possible praise. The first crusaders had occasionally been styled *milites Christi*, it is true. But they had been soldiers of Christ only metaphorically—as secular soldiers who thought they were waging war for Christ. Now the Templars were proclaimed soldiers of Christ in a literal sense: They were simultaneously monks and professional killers. This new reality was full of implications that Bernard did not fail to draw out.

The Templars were an alternative to the secular army. They supplied Christendom with professional holy warriors, the perfect soldiers for its holy war. Secular knights waged war "not for God, but for the devil." The Templars, in contrast, were "the knights of Christ," "God's militia."[46] Assured that it was the Lord they were fighting for,[47] they did not

42. Cardini 1974, 213.
43. R. Barber 1982, 227.
44. Cf. Bulst-Thiele 1992, 61.
45. See Bernard to Prior of Portes, A.D. 1147–50, *Briefe* no. 250,4 (p. 334): "Clamat ad vos mea monstruosa vita, mea aerumnosa conscientia. Ego enim quaedam Chimaera mei saeculi, nec clericum gero nec laicum. Nam monachi iamdudum exui conversationem, non habitum."
46. *Éloge* IV,7. In this sense, the Rule of the Order of Santiago described the founders of the order as having ceased to be the *equites diaboli*. Forey 1985, 184.
47. *Éloge* III,4.

need to worry either about committing a sin if they killed or about being killed themselves. For "death for Christ, either suffered or caused,
does not incur any guilt and merits the greatest glory."[48] The crucial
shift Bernard made here from the traditional ecclesiastical doctrine was
not the assurance that the Templars would have eternal life. Heavenly rewards had been promised to soldiers fighting for a holy cause long before Bernard.[49] Bernard's daring novelty lay in assuring the Knights of
the Temple that there was nothing wrong in killing. Convinced that the
Templars were waging war for Christ, Bernard gave them *carte blanche*
to kill. They were safe to violate the cardinal commandment *non occi-
des*.[50] "The soldier of Christ," Bernard was to repeat, "is safe when he
kills, even safer when he is killed. If he is killed, it is for his own good;
if he kills, he does it for Christ."[51]

Bernard's earlier criticism of war soon evaporated and gave way to
praise. The peace-loving saint incited Christians to war he considered
holy. He spiritualized and sacralized war to the extent that the theological and juridical considerations of the just war doctrine became irrelevant.[52] Killing for Christ, in his eyes, was not homicide. Killing for
Christ was killing *His* enemies, "the enemies of the cross of Christ" and,
as such, should be done without hesitation, with an intrepid heart.[53] As
a knight, the Templar killed a corporeal enemy; as a monk, he killed vice
incarnated. In Bernard's celebration of the new Christian knighthood, the
"pagans" do not appear as human.[54] Their very being is blasphemous.
They are the embodiment of evil: "malefactors,"[55] a force of darkness
Bernard identified with Satan.[56] If the "detestation of Saracens" was characteristic of those times and needed an authoritative sanction, Bernard
provided it.[57] The conclusion to be drawn was obvious. With the psalmist's voice behind him Bernard declared that killing the pagan gave cause

48. Ibid.
49. Cf. chap. 2 nn. 134, 136.
50. Selwood 1996, 230.
51. *Éloge* III,4.
52. Cardini 1974, 212–13. On how Bernard otherwise respected canon law, see Brundage 1992, 28.
53. *Éloge* I,1.
54. Ullmann 1975, 287, praised Bernard's "perennial wisdom and enduring humanity" as foreshadowing the "true Humanism" and represented him as "an inspiring force
in the making of modern international law," aimed at humanizing the "atrocious manner
of waging war." This argument is only defensible on the premise that those whom the
Christians were fighting were not human.
55. *Éloge* III,4. Cf. Delaruelle 1953, 58.
56. See Delaruelle 1953, 62; Dérumaux 1953, 69.
57. Cf. Christiansen 1980, 73.

for joy: "In the pagan's death, 'the righteous will rejoice when they see vengeance done.'"[58]

Bernard's doctrine of *malicidium*—that the killing of non-Christians is a praiseworthy annihilation of evil and not the crime of homicide—is much more than a clever play on words. "Truly, he who kills a malefactor is not a homicide but, if I may say so, a malicide [*malicida*] and is clearly held to be the avenger of Christ in regard to those who do evil [*qui male agunt*], and the defender of Christians." Taking away a pagan's life was a gain for Christ and a cause of glory for the killer. "In the death of the pagan the Christian glories because in it, Christ is glorified."[59] A few lines later Bernard remarked that "[c]ertainly, the pagans should not be killed if there would be some other means of restraining them from their excessive harassment and oppression of the faithful." But the conditional of this sentence seems to indicate that Bernard did not believe that "other means" existed. In any case, his conclusion to this brief aside left no doubt about how the pagans were to be treated: "Now, however, it is better that they be killed than to let the scepter of wickedness remain resting on the land allotted to the righteous, so that the righteous might not stretch out their hands to do wrong."[60]

The psalmist's "scepter of wickedness" resting on the "land allotted to the righteous" was here the pagans' existence itself. The very existence of non-Christians demanded that Christians take up arms. But while Bernard's stance most often placed holy war beyond the law, at moments he wanted to accommodate his warmongering to the doctrine of just war. It was the pagans, he claimed, who wanted war. He again cited the Psalms to call on the holy Christian warriors to fearlessly scatter those "peoples who want war" (*gentes quae bella volunt*). He found other Biblical references to support his case. Warriors of the "righteous nation that keeps faith" were encouraged to "scatter" all who did not obey the

---

58. *Éloge* III,4. Bernard stopped short of citing the other half of Ps 57.11 (58.10): "they will bathe their feet in the blood of the wicked"—probably because he lauded the Templars for washing themselves rarely (*Éloge* IV,7). Not washing was a sign of saintliness. Athanasius relates that St. Anthony "never washed his body, and never wiped the dirt from his feet except when necessity compelled him to cross through water." *Life of Anthony* 47 (*Early Christian Lives*, 38).

59. *Éloge* III,4. Cf. chap. 3 n. 262. Similarly, *Hugo peccator* argued that the Templars, killing infidels, hated not the man but the iniquity. *Hugo* justified the Templars' taking the spoils, pointing out that the infidels, on account of their sins, deserved to lose what was taken from them. Forey 1992, 16; Barber 1995, 42–43. But Isaac of L'Etoile commented that the order "despoils licitly and murders religiously" *(licenter expoliet et religiose trucidet).* Kedar 1984, 105.

60. *Éloge* III,4 (quoting Ps 124.3 [125.3]).

law of God, to "cut off" those who derange the faithful, and to rid "the city of the Lord" of "all evildoers," for "they are eager to take away the inestimable riches of Christian people deposited in Jerusalem, to pollute the holy places, and to take to themselves the heritage of the sanctuary of God. So draw both swords of the faithful and slit the skull of the enemies in order to cast down every proud obstacle raised up against the knowledge of God, that is, against the faith of the Christians." [61] For, "[d]o not I hate those who hate you, O Lord? And do I not loathe those who rise up against you?" [62]

As they confronted the pollution of the holy places by the infidel, the Templars—"keeping the unity of the spirit in the bond of peace"— marched to battle peacefully, like true Israelites (*procedunt ad bella pacifici*).[63] They also killed with peace in their hearts.[64] The Templar's life was a "veritable peaceful sacrifice."[65] In Bernard's praise, these monastic warriors appear as a "peace corps."[66] Characterizations of the *De laude novae militiae* as a peacemaker's manifesto aimed at limiting violence[67] should be taken seriously. But the reason is not Bernard's use of the just war doctrine to present Christian military activity in Palestine as a defensive war fought in the spirit of love. Rather, it is his rejoicing approval of the transportation of violence from Latin Christendom to the Holy Land that makes *De laude novae militiae* a peace-promoting pamphlet.

Bernard was clear that "in all this multitude of men streaming to Jerusalem, there are relatively few who have not been criminals and impious ones, robbers and sacrilegious men, homicides, perjurers, and adulterers." Their departure for the Holy Land brought double benefit and

61. *Éloge* III,5. Cf. Isa 26.2; Ps 67.31 (68.30); Ps 82.13 (83.12); Ps 100.8 (101.8); 2 Cor 10.5.

62. *Éloge* IV,8; Ps 138.21 (139.21).

63. *Éloge* V,9; IV,7 (Eph 4.3); IV,8.

64. *Hugo peccator* admonished the Templars to go about their ordained function in a tranquil frame of mind, like true servants of God: "If you feel thus, most dear brothers, and you serve your society in peace, the God of peace will be with you." One may get a clearer sense of what was meant by "serving one's own society in peace" from Bishop Anselm of Havelberg's description of the Templars: "they have sworn to defend the glorious tomb of the Saviour against the Saracens; peaceful at home, outside they are valiant fighters." Quoted in Barber 1995, 43, 50.

65. *Éloge* V,9.

66. Cf. Zerbi 1992, 283 (referring to Leclercq). *Hugo peccator* pictured the Templars as carrying arms for the defense of Christians "against the enemies of the faith and peace." Quoted in Barber 1995, 42.

67. Zerbi 1992, 279 (quoting Leclercq, *Bernard de Clairvaux* [Paris, 1989]).

was cause for double joy: "Their neighbors are happy because they see them leaving, and happy are those who see them coming to their aid. They are therefore useful in two ways: not only by protecting the latter but also in renouncing oppression of the former." Their voluntary departure freed western Christendom from its most cruel devastators, and the Holy Land received them with joy as its most faithful defenders. "What good fortune and what success," exclaimed Bernard, empathizing with Christ, "to see how those whom He has long suffered as oppressors begin to transform themselves into defenders! An enemy He makes His knight, just as He made the former persecutor Saul the preacher Paul." [68]

Bernard's words seem to have been echoed in the historian Gibbon's comment on the robber, the incendiary, and the homicide arising by thousands to redeem their souls by "repeating on the infidels the same deeds which they had exercised against their Christian brethren." [69] But in Bernard's eyes this repetition was not a repetition. The transportation of violence was rather a transsubstantiation: the criminal perpetrators of violence within Christendom turned holy as soon as they stepped foot in the Holy Land and directed their arms against "the enemies of the cross." What in the Latin West was "madness" [70] became, when transferred to Palestine, Christian spirituality.

Bernard's praise of warrior monks was complemented with a description of the sacred geography of the Holy Land in the second, longer part of *De laude novae militiae*. This spiritual exegesis of Palestine was built around Bernard's interpretation of the mystery of Christ's life and redemptive death. But why should Christocentric spirituality become the inspiration for and foundation of the justification of holy war? Why should those who were anxious to enter the celestial Jerusalem tread the physical land designated as holy? Bernard never visited Palestine. He opposed the desire of monks to leave their monastic *iter Hierosolymitanum* (the journey to the heavenly City they began when they took monastic vows) and depart for the earthly Jerusalem. [71] Yet he supported the crusade that some contemporaries had called *iter Hierosolymitanum* (the journey to Jerusalem). [72] This suggests that Bernard considered the

---

68. *Éloge* V,10.
69. See chap. 1 n. 310.
70. See n. 34.
71. Cf. *Briefe* nos. 65, 399; Cardini 1993a, 253.
72. See chap. 2 n. 29.

bodily journey to the terrestrial Jerusalem (as a detour to the celestial City) appropriate only for those who lacked the spiritual strength for monastic life. But such an answer prompts further questions. What did Bernard's spiritualized Holy Land have to do with geographical Palestine? Why did the spiritual quest require territorial conquest? And what about the Templars, the monastic soldiers? To my mind, the spiritual landscape was the raster on which medieval Christians composed for themselves a picture of a geographical space. Palestine existed for them as the places marked by Christ's life, death, and resurrection. As such, Palestine was deemed Christian. It was precisely the spiritual geography that demanded territorial conquest and rendered the "recovery of the Holy Land" an eminently religious enterprise. In the Templars the monastic and crusading "journeys to Jerusalem" overlapped in an ideal form. Their use of arms was a work of Christian piety par excellence. Thus the second part of the *De laude novae militiae* was essential to Bernard's praise of the new Christian knighthood.[73]

The only place in *De laude novae militiae* where Bernard brings his spiritual Holy Land down to earth is where he says that "it is of no small advantage to see with corporeal eyes the place where the Lord's body was laid to rest." Even if empty now, for the Christian that place is nevertheless filled with joyful mysteries.[74] This passage sheds light on Bernard's sanctification of the crime of killing and his agitation for holy war. The gaze that needs to see what cannot be seen, cannot see what needs to be seen. As such, it is a gaze of annihilation. Bernard drew on a host of prophets to picture Palestine as desolate and forsaken since it was not in the hands of God's people. His vision of populating that land—*et terra tua inhabitatur*—contained the imperative that Christians (meaning Latin Christians) take possession of it.[75] The Holy Land was populated only when it was populated by the people of God. They alone counted, and not only for Bernard. In those times, "uncultivated and inhabitable places" seem to have generally connoted places "unconquered" by the Christians.[76] In Bernard's pamphlet, the non-Christians living in Palestine are not seen. They only become visible when it comes

73. The importance of this part of the *De laude* is pointed out in Barber 1995, 45 ff. Cf. Cardini 1993a, 252–53.

74. *Éloge* XI,29.

75. Ibid., III,6. Cf. Isa 62.1–5.

76. See Barber 1995, 27 (citing an Aragonese source from the *Cartulaire général de l'Ordre du Temple*).

to "driving them out," "scattering them," "cutting them off," "slitting their skulls." These children of darkness step out of the shadow when Christian society is set against them.[77] The gaze that does not see them, and does not want to see them, renders them invisible. It demands their elimination. Populating the Holy Land was a license for depopulation.

Bernard's contemporaries were making the same point. In a letter to Hugh of Payns, Guigo, fifth prior of La Grande Chartreuse, suggested: "Let us first purge our souls of vices, then the lands from the barbarians." Ulger, bishop of Angers, commended the Templars who "fight against the enemies of God" and do not hesitate "to give their souls and to shed their blood, until they have destroyed and exterminated the impious pagans from the most holy places." And Pope Celestine II, in the bull *Milites Templi,* portrayed the Templars as carrying out the divine work of liberating the "eastern church from the filth of the pagans."[78]

With the Templars, the act of "assuming the cross was taken to its logical conclusion."[79] Consequently, when Bernard "girded himself with the sword of the Word of God" to arouse "the hearts of many for the expedition overseas"[80] in preparations for the Second Crusade, his preaching—"the most powerful crusade propaganda of all time"[81]—was led by the logic he had developed earlier in his laudation of the Templars. The obvious difference was that when preaching the crusade, Bernard called on the whole of Christendom to take the cross under papal leadership, whereas in the praise of the Templars he addressed a single military order.[82] The Christocentric spirituality found in the *De laude novae militiae* inspired Bernard's practical crusading work.[83] He portrayed the crusade as a jubilee, a great opportunity for salvation offered by a merciful God to his sinful people.[84] At the heart of the crusade was the deliverance of the souls of western Christians. A grand picture of the heavenly Jerusalem that would receive those who took the cross rose

77. And not, as Dérumaux 1953, 73, wrote: "Ainsi le païen ne sort de l'ombre que dans l'acte même où il se dresse contre la société chrétienne."

78. Quoted in Barber 1995, 49, 51, 58.

79. Blake 1970, 27.

80. Otto of Freising *The Deeds* I,xxxvii. Odo of Deuil *De profectione* I (p. 9) portrayed Bernard the preacher as "heaven's instrument" pouring forth "the dew of the divine word."

81. See *On Consideration* II,i,1–3; Riley-Smith 1992, 95.

82. See Delaruelle 1953, 53–54; Leclercq 1974; Cole 1991, 42 ff.; Riley-Smith 1992, 94 ff.; Zerbi 1992, 285 ff.; Mayer 1993, 93 ff.

83. Leclercq 1974, 482, 484; Cole 1991, 59.

84. *Briefe* no. 363,4 (p. 654).

above the earthly Jerusalem.[85] The crusade was a living communion with Christ. Taking the cross meant reexperiencing Christ's passion in thought and deed.[86] But Bernard also presented the crusade more profanely: as a good deal for the remission of sins. In an often-cited passage he addressed the would-be crusader: "Or are you a shrewd businessman, a man quickly to see the profits of this world? If you are, I can offer you a splendid bargain. Do not miss the opportunity. Take the sign of the cross. At once you will have indulgence for all the sins which you confess with a contrite heart. It does not cost you much to buy and if you wear it with humility you will find that it is the kingdom of heaven."[87] The crusade was literally the "business of Christ," *negotium Christi*.[88]

A spiritualized vision of the crusade unencumbered by political and military considerations made for poor strategy,[89] and Bernard was eventually forced to reflect on the failure of the Second Crusade.[90] But though his crusading activity came to an inglorious end, Bernard's thinking about the crusade's role in the cosmic struggle between good and evil was glorious indeed.[91] Like the "new knighthood," the crusade was a miraculous device for turning criminals into God's servants: "What is it but a unique opportunity for salvation, such as only God could think of, that the Almighty treats murderers, robbers, adulterers, perjurers, and criminals of all kinds as worthy to be summoned to his service as if they were men of righteousness."[92] In response to Bernard's preaching, as Otto of Freising reports, "so great a throng of highwaymen and robbers (strange to say) came hurrying forward that no man in his senses could fail to comprehend that this so sudden and so unusual a transformation came from the hand of the Most High."[93]

As the Second Crusade got underway, peace began to reign in Christendom. "And so, as countless peoples and nations . . . were moved to take the cross, suddenly almost the entire West became so still that not only the waging of war but even the carrying of arms in public was con-

---

85. Alphandéry 1954, 183; Katzir 1992, 9; Cardini 1993a, 256.
86. Delaruelle 1953, 60; Alphandéry 1954, 176 ff.; Leclercq 1974, 483; Riley-Smith 1992, 95. Cf. Roscher 1969, 268 ff.
87. *Briefe* no. 363,5 (p. 656); trans. in Mayer 1993, 97.
88. *Briefe* no. 363,1 (p. 648). Cf. Delaruelle 1953, 62.
89. Delaruelle 1953, 60; Tyerman 1988, 32; Cardini 1993a, 257.
90. See the *De consideratione* II. Quillet 1989, 257, has interpreted this work as an invitation of the pope "à un itinéraire spirituel."
91. Alphandéry 1954, 172; Zerbi 1992, 281.
92. *Briefe* no. 363,4 (p. 654).
93. *The Deeds* I,xlii.

sidered wrong." [94] Bernard was, indeed, "announcing peace." [95] His concept of the crusade revolved around the idea of peace. [96] But the peace he preached was peace among Christians that could only be attained if Christians ceased fighting each other and turned their arms against their common enemy instead. "With the plowshare of preaching," [97] Bernard exhorted his fellow Christian: "O mighty soldier, O man of war, you now have a cause for which you can fight without endangering your soul; a cause in which to win is glorious and for which to die is but gain." [98] Allowing the Land of the Lord, His "inheritance," [99] to remain in Saracen hands amounted to giving to dogs that which was holy and casting pearls before swine. [100] The right of the Christians to the Holy Land could only be supported by the argument of might, even if not all might was right. Bernard opposed the anti-Jewish violence aroused by the preaching of the Second Crusade because God had reserved for Himself the settling of accounts with the Jews. [101] But when it came to the Saracens, he left no doubt that divine judgment was to be executed by God's people themselves.

The Second Crusade was pictured as "the whole human race" set in motion "against the Saracens." [102] Those seen as standing in its path were allotted the same fate as the Saracens. Perhaps fearing that the devil might incite some northern heathens to attack the crusading army from the rear, [103] Bernard also preached a crusade against the Slavic Wends in what today is eastern Germany. [104] He even took the liberty to begin preaching this Wendish Crusade without papal authorization. [105] The pope followed in Bernard's footsteps when he issued a bull that endorsed

94. Ibid., I,xliv.

95. In the bitter moments after the failure of the Second Crusade, looking back at his preaching of that campaign, Bernard wrote: "We said, 'Peace,' and there is no peace." *On Consideration* II,i,1. Cf. Leclercq 1974, 483.

96. Cf. Cardini 1993a, 252, 256.

97. Otto of Freising *The Deeds* I,xl.

98. *Briefe* no. 363,5 (p. 656); trans. in Mayer 1993, 96–97.

99. *Éloge* III,6; *Briefe* no. 363,3 (p. 652).

100. *Briefe* no. 363,2 (p. 652).

101. *Briefe* no. 363,6 (p. 658). Cf. Otto of Freising *The Deeds* I,xxxix,xliii. See Cole 1991, 43 f.

102. Cole 1991, 54 (quoting *Annales Herbipolenses*).

103. Kahl 1992, 37; Zerbi 1992, 290 ff. Christiansen 1980, 55, speaks of a "global strategy against the army of darkness."

104. Cf. Constable 1953, 224–26; on the Wendish Crusade, see Christiansen 1980, chap. 2.

105. In his "apologia on the plight of Jerusalem," however, Bernard maintained that he had preached the crusade at the pope's command. *On Consideration* II,i,1. Cf. Otto of Freising *The Deeds* I,xxxvii; Brundage 1992, 29.

this extension of holy war to "subjugate to the Christian religion" the "heathens of the North." [106] This was the first official papal sanction of the use of force against heathens in order to convert them. [107] But conversion was only an option. The alternative was death. While preaching the Wendish Crusade, Bernard formulated a guideline that Christian arms were to be used to either exterminate or convert the infidel nations: *ad delendas penitus aut certe convertendas nationes illas.* [108] He exhorted the crusaders to carry out their work with vigor. Forbidden to make any treaty with the Wends, the "servants of God" had to fight until such a time that "with God's help" either the rite of the Wends or the Wends themselves were annihilated: *aut ritus ipse, aut natio deleatur.* [109] In this way, Bernard's main goal—to extirpate from the face of the earth the enemies of the Christian name—would be achieved. [110]

THE INFIDELS ARE UNREASONABLE AND THEREFORE NOT HUMAN: PETER THE VENERABLE

In the middle of the twelfth century conversion began to figure prominently in crusade thinking. [111] In *On Consideration,* Bernard addressed the pope as a "debtor to the wise and to the foolish" (Rom 1.14) and pressed him to "consider most vigilantly how those who are foolish may become wise, and how those who are wise may not become foolish, and how those who have lost wisdom may recover it." But because, in Bernard's opinion, "no foolishness is more foolish than lack of faith," the pope was "a debtor to the infidel, whether Jew, Greek, or Gentile." Therefore it was important for the pope to do all he could "so that unbelievers may be converted to the faith, that converts may not turn away, that those who have turned away may return." Heretics and schismatics are not my main concern here. As to the Jews and Gentiles, Bernard argued that the Jews had their time (Rom 9.28), which excused the pope from dealing with them. Thus, the "full number of the Gentiles must come in first." The pope had to set to work: "Are we waiting for faith to fall

---

106. *Divina dispensatione* (Kahl 1992, app. B, 44); Constable 1953, 255.
107. Kahl 1992, 40.
108. *Briefe* no. 457 (p. 892); Kahl 1992, app. A, 42. For different interpretations of this formulation, see Kedar 1984, 70–71; Zerbi 1992, 289–93; Cardini 1993a, 258.
109. *Briefe* no. 457 (p. 892). Cf. Christiansen 1980, 51.
110. "[E]xtirpandos de terra christiani nominis inimicos." *Briefe* no. 457 (p. 890).
111. Burns 1971; Kedar 1984, 71.

upon them? To whom has belief come by chance? How shall they believe without preaching?"[112] But these afterthoughts on the failure of the Second Crusade aside, Bernard's preoccupation was the conversion of the Christian sinner: *peccatoris et maligni . . . conversio.*[113]

It was Peter the Venerable, abbot of Cluny, who seriously contemplated the conversion of Muslims. Peter is famous for having commissioned a translation of a collection of Arabic books—including the Qur'an—into Latin.[114] These translations have been seen as marking the birth of "Islamic," or "Oriental," studies.[115] Given the "abysmal state of knowledge about Islam" in the Latin West, Peter's efforts to make Islamic doctrine available to the Christian world appear as the labor of an enlightened man. He believed that the false doctrine would be more easily refuted if it were known to Christians. Against the background of the crusading West, Peter's emphasis on conversion of the Muslims makes him look tolerant and charitable—a man who preferred reason to violence. In comparison with most of his contemporaries, including his fellow prelates, he stands out as a man of peace. In fact, he has been singled out "as the most peaceful man of his age."[116]

This idealized portrayal of Peter the Venerable, it seems to me, may be the product of pervasive assumptions about his times. Historiography on the twelfth century in general, and on Peter the Venerable in particular, seems characterized by more than the usual number of anachronisms inescapable while writing history. From the early twentieth century onward, historians have found in the twelfth century, as a period of great cultural revival, a wealth of material for deconstructing the image of the "dark Middle Ages" and for substantiating the thesis that the contrast between medieval and (early) modern culture was "not nearly so sharp as it seemed to the humanists and their modern followers."[117] These historians' politics of the "making of the Middle Ages" have rested on faith in progress, which in turn, relies on faith in knowledge. Peter the Venerable appears, from this perspective, a "worthy

---

112. *On consideration* III,i,2–4.

113. *Éloge* V,10.

114. See Kritzeck 1964; d'Alverny 1965a, 599 ff.; Pavlović 1992, 92 ff.; Mayer 1993, 230. On translators, see Gantar 1965; Metlitzki 1977, 30 ff. Setton 1992, 48, has called Ketton's translation of the Qur'an a "paraphrase."

115. Rousset de Pina 1952, 181; Kritzeck 1964, 15; Schwinges 1977, 106; Pavlović 1992, 97.

116. Kritzeck 1964, 6; Schwinges 1977, 107; Morris 1991, 286; Mayer 1993, 230.

117. Haskins 1967, 6.

type." [118] Because he not only contributed to the advancement of learning but was also an exemplar of tolerance, the temptation to project
back onto him the Enlightenment mentality is sometimes overwhelming.
Though progressionism has in the meantime been discredited, it continues to color dominant views of Peter the Venerable in our own days. Peter at times stands for a "politically correct" Western attitude toward
the Muslims. Such backward-looking benevolence relies, as a rule, on the
achievements of progressionist historiography. One of the meeting points
for historiographic progressionism and historicized "political correct-
ness" is the minimizing of the role of the crusade in Western history. For
the former, the crusade had "in itself no decisive importance in intellectual history." [119] For the latter, the hostile attitude toward the Muslims,
characteristic of the crusade, began to change for the better as early as
the twelfth century, as exemplified in particular by Peter the Venerable.

Christian attitudes toward the Muslims, as benevolent historians
maintain, became more favorable, objective, and rational—even "tolerant"—thanks to a better knowledge of Islam in the twelfth-century
Latin West. [120] Peter the Venerable is regarded as a key agent of that
change, and his work as its expression. His inquiry into Islamic doctrine
appears as "disinterested curiosity." He is believed to have provided
"authentic information about Islam" to satisfy "both the growing European intellectual interest in the sciences cultivated by the Muslims and
popular curiosity about Islam." [121] But the idea of "popular curiosity
about Islam" seems to rest on an admirable belief in the "people" rather
than on historical evidence. Western Christians in Peter the Venerable's
times were still extremely ignorant about peoples living outside their
closed, though expanding, world. [122] They displayed a lack of curiosity
about and indifference to the nearby "barbarians," and those living further away existed for them only in fables and legends. [123] Some believed
that the Near Eastern peoples were cannibals. [124] The more general view
was that they were not only infidels but "heathen devils about whom no

118. Ibid., 43. On Haskin's progressivism, see Spiegel 1997, 63 f.

119. Haskins 1967, 9.

120. Cf. Rousset de Pina 1952, 174 ff.; Kritzeck 1964; Southern 1962, 36; Watt 1972,
60 ff., 73 f.; Rodinson 1991, 13 f.

121. Rodinson 1991, 13–14.

122. On the crusading chroniclers' view of the Muslim peoples, see Loutchitskaja
1996.

123. Hodgen 1964, 33–35, 51, 67.

124. In fact, it was the "Tafurs"—bands of the poor accompanying the First Crusade—who fed on the roasted corpses of their Muslim enemies. Cohn 1993, 65.

invention was too far-fetched to be believed." As the "followers of Mohamet," they were "crudely and systematically libeled." [125]

"Intellectual interest in the sciences cultivated by the Muslims" is also to be taken with a grain of salt. The interest in science, it seems, was dissociated from interest in Islam and the Muslims. Latin Christians were interested not so much in "Arabian learning" (or "Oriental lore"), but rather in gaining access to the Greek sciences and philosophy that had been preserved (and often developed) by the Arabs. That corpus of knowledge that has for centuries now been called "Western intellectual tradition" was available only via the Arabic language. Arabic (along with Syriac, Hebrew, and other oriental languages through which much of the Greek learning had passed into Arabic) was "the chief vehicle for the transmission of Greek science and philosophy to Latin Europe." [126] But mastering the medium—and a "refracting medium" at that [127]—was, for Latin Christians, no more than the *faux frais* of the production of knowledge. In 1370, after the transmission of Greek knowledge to the West had been largely accomplished, Petrarch could freely vent to his aversion to Arab science: "I will not be persuaded that any good can come from Arabia." [128] But even "at the very time when the superiority of Arabian learning was taken for granted" and the *Arabum studia* were practiced in the Latin West, "the crude caricature of the medieval Saracen flourished in the popular imagination." [129]

Other factors—the Levantine trade, pilgrims, freed captives, the Crusades, the new courtly culture—are commonly regarded as contributing to the change in Christian attitudes toward the Muslims. But a closer look casts doubt on these assumptions also. Christian commercial activity in the eastern Mediterranean repeatedly clashed with crusading enterprises. The uninhibited pursuit of financial gains on the part of Christians provoked accusations and papal legislative regulations that banned trade with the enemies of Christendom. [130] But traders' practical knowledge and the information they gathered through trade did not seriously affect, or contradict, the outlook that engendered the prolonged

---

125. Hodgen 1964, 86, 88.

126. Haskins 1967, 281. For the "Graeco-Arabic translation movement," see Gutas 1998.

127. Haskins 1967, 299. Roger Bacon maintained that Jews and Arabs—the enemies of Christians—had mutilated Greek manuscripts. *Opus tertium* VIII (p. 472).

128. *Epp. seniles* XII,2 (Cassirer, Kristeller, and Randall 1948, 142).

129. Metlitzki 1977, 167.

130. See, e.g., the Fourth Lateran Council's decree *Expeditio pro recuperanda Terra Sancta*. Hefele 1912–13, 5.2: 1394.

struggle against the Saracens. It would be a mistake to suppose that the "exchange of goods implied the exchange of culture." [131] Pilgrims, often pictured as agents of cultural exchange, "expressed little or no curiosity about their fellows, little interest in alien ways, little reaction to cultural diversities." [132] Moreover, after the Latin kingdom of Jerusalem had fallen to its doom at the close of the twelfth century, several popes forbade not only trade but also pilgrimages beyond Cyprus, to "prevent the Saracens from enriching themselves by the tax which they had instituted for Christians and other non-Muslims." [133] Christians who had lived in Muslim captivity, moreover, did not leave behind (at least not before the mid-thirteenth century) any written material testifying to intellectual acquaintance with the Muslim world.[134] The Crusades and the Latin Christian dominions founded by the crusaders were not transmitters of medieval Muslim knowledge to the West, as used to be believed. Crusading warfare did little to further understanding of the Muslim world and certainly did not contribute to a more favorable Christian attitude toward Muslims.[135] The Frankish colonies' intellectual activity, on the other hand, was "almost inexistent." [136] The Holy Land was "a battle front, not the centre of cultural borrowing." [137] Finally, reception of the crusade by the new courtly culture generated exoticism.[138] The creation of the "noble heathen" by protagonists of this culture,[139] or even courtly dames wearing Saracen robes,[140] may have "humanized" the image of the Saracen,[141] but whether such inventions and new conventions amounted to a new attitude toward Muslims remains doubtful.[142]

131. See Olschki 1943, 3; Hodgen 1964, 33, 51, 105. Of different opinion was Haskins 1967, 64 (that "ever since the Greek and Phoenician traders it has been impossible to separate the interchange of wares from the interchange of knowledge and ideas").

132. Hodgen 1964, 86. Such an attitude goes back to the sixth to eighth centuries. See Rotter 1986, chap. 1. And it was not until the later seventeenth century that narratives of Western travelers to the Levant became "precise and reliable." Chew 1965, 543.

133. Cardini 1974, 229; Metlitzki 1977, 134.

134. Hiestand 1986, 201.

135. Cf. Gilchrist 1993, 81; Kedar 1996, 355; Loutchitskaja 1996, 107.

136. Sivan 1985, 29–30.

137. Le Goff 1990, 66.

138. "Les imaginations se sont enchantées de ces pays fabuleux et les vieilles chansons de geste se sont enrichies de nouveaux décors et d'épisodes dont la couleur locale en faits des *Orientales*." Delaruelle 1953, 65.

139. Mayer 1993, 230.

140. Cf. Guillaume de Lorris and Jean de Meun *The Romance of the Rose* 1155 (p. 46), where the allegorical figure of Generosity wore "a completely new robe of Saracen purple."

141. Burns 1971, 1386; Schwinges 1977, 13 f., 105 ff.; 142 ff.; Kedar 1984, 134.

142. "It would be too much to speak of tolerance in this context but there was certainly a genuine humanity springing from a courtly culture." Mayer 1993, 230.

The main misconception about the changing Christian attitude toward the Muslims is that knowledge played a role—even a central role—in the assumed change. Actually, knowledge was not of decisive importance. The dominant value of that age was life in harmony with Christian belief. In pursuit of the good Christian life the master faculty was will rather than intellect. In such a worldview, if "virtue" was frustrated, it was sin, not ignorance, that stood in the way. And for sin there was only divine remedy.[143] Knowledge was subordinated to faith and good only insofar as it served faith and helped effect what God willed. There are no grounds for assuming that, in such a context, new information would change belief. A hostile attitude toward Muslims had been integrated into Christian belief and become almost an article of faith. Given the centrality of the Muslim "enemy" to the constitution of the Christian world of that age, there was little possibility of seeing the Muslim world in any "objective" way. Since the hostile image of the Muslim world was not based on knowledge about the Muslims, it was unaffected by increases in knowledge.

Let me now turn to Peter the Venerable himself and his efforts to provide information about Islam. Peter was no exception among his contemporaries concerning the lack of curiosity about the Muslim world. He showed interest only in those aspects of Muslim culture that he considered of importance for his apology of Christianity. After he had read the translations he had commissioned, he admitted that he was a stranger to the Muslims' customs and life. He gave no impression that he perceived that ignorance as a disadvantage. He dwelt on what Western imagination painted as Muslim sexual licentiousness,[144] for that was a handy argument against Islam. But since he wanted to refute Muslim religious doctrine, he needed to know something about that which he wished to refute. With some knowledge at hand, his aim could be achieved more effectively. Indeed, because Peter could read the translations he paid for, his views of Islam were more accurate than those commonly held in western Christendom.[145] Ignorance of Islam was such that "any even moderately informed statement of fact" was a gain.[146] But advanced as Peter's views of Islam may have been, Islam remained for him the hostile religion.

143. See Vereker 1964, 59, 65.
144. See, on this topic, Daniel 1993, 164 ff., 351–53.
145. Cf. d'Alverny 1965a, 598 ff.; Daniel 1993.
146. Kritzeck 1964, 150.

Often cited as a departure from Latin Christian hostility toward Islam are Peter the Venerable's introductory words to book I of his *Liber contra sectam sive haeresim Saracenorum,* a polemical treatise addressed to a Muslim reader. "A certain Peter, by nationality a Frenchman, by faith a Christian, by profession an abbot of those who are called monks, to the Arabs, the sons of Ishmael, who observe the law of that one who is called *Mahumeth.* It seems strange, and perhaps it really is, that I, a man so very distant from you in place, speaking a different language, having a state of life separate from yours, a stranger to your customs and life, write from the far parts of the West to men who inhabit the lands of the East and South, and that I attack, by my utterance, those whom I have never seen, whom I shall perhaps never see. But I do not attack you, as some of us often do, by arms, but by words; not by force, but by reason; not in hatred, but in love." [147] Both Christian faith and human reason, Peter explained, commanded his love for the Muslims. Obedient to divine instruction and to human nature endowed with reason that is "known to love what is like himself," he loved them, and "loving, I write to you; writing, I invite you to salvation." [148]

What stood in the way of salvation for the Muslims was that they were Muslims. The "obstinacy of superstition" (that is, their religion), Peter argued, led the Muslims to refuse to hear anything against their laws and customs. But such refusal was contrary to rational human nature, which does not want "to be deceived in temporal things," or to "take certain things for uncertain or uncertain things for certain." [149] And this requirement cast doubt on Muhammad: If he had been confident about the truth of his law, why did he prohibit his followers from debating it? And if he had not that confidence, why did he write things his followers could not defend? [150] The rational disputation between Christians and Muslims, of which Peter the Venerable's is a prime example, set out from the beginning to prove that Islam was not reasonable. [151] Because God endowed men with reason, a faith that could not stand the test of reason could not be the true faith. And because they upheld beliefs they could not reasonably defend, Muslims were unreasonable. For Peter the Venerable and other Christian thinkers of that period, to be

147. *Liber contra sectam,* 231. Where possible, I cite Kritzeck's translations from the study preceding his edition of Peter's writings. Kritzeck 1964.
148. *Liber contra sectam,* 232.
149. Ibid., 234–35.
150. Ibid., 240. Cf. Daniel 1993, 146 f.
151. For Peter the Venerable's argument, see Kritzeck 1964, 155 ff.; Daniel 1993.

sure, reason did not represent "anything secular in the modern atheistic sense of the word." Reason only "opened their eyes to an alternative route to the divine than the tried and tested route of faith." Properly used, reason could only serve faith.[152] And this reason, which led—and had to lead—the Christian to where faith had already taken him, should also bring the infidel (who here appears as *insipiens*, the fool)[153] to the true faith. That is, if he wanted to be reasonable.

Peter accused the Muslims of resorting to violence because they did not have reason on their side: Muhammad relied not on reason but on arms, and instead of giving an answer to those who asked him questions, he turned *furiosorum more* to stones, sticks, and swords.[154] True to his law, Muslims had been stifling discussion with stones, swords, and other murderous instruments ever since.[155] Considering the importance of the crusade—armed Christian offensive against the Muslims—in Peter's own time, this was a curious accusation indeed. But Peter was unperturbed. He proudly announced to his expected Muslim audience that he had chosen to attack those who observe the law of "Mahumeth" with words, not arms. As a polemical statement, his declared reliance on reason alone calls for admiration. But the idea of Christian polemics against Islam as put forward by Peter the Venerable—and by others who came later—is problematic at the core.

Peter's dialogue between Christians and Muslims was illusionary, marked by a "certain unreality."[156] That he wrote in Latin and did not arrange for his refutation of Islam to be translated in hope of reaching Muslim readers is telling but circumstantial. More important is that, like most medieval polemicists, he failed to conceive of the possibility that Muslims might be unimpressed by his arguments. Typical of Christian anti-Islamic—as well as anti-Jewish—polemics, Peter was talking to a Muslim of his own imagination who never raised substantial objections to what was asserted against him and his religion. "The mediaeval Latins seem always to be defending a public dissertation before favourable judges, judges whose approval has been assured in advance. It is a nightmare reversed: it is the opponent who cannot answer, except in words set in his mouth."[157] In this rational disputation, the opponent

152. Abulafia 1995, 6, 25, 46.
153. Cf. ibid., 41.
154. *Liber contra sectam*, 241.
155. Ibid., 235.
156. Daniel 1993, 140.
157. Ibid., 287.

was absent. But it is hard to believe that Peter the Venerable actually intended to reach a Muslim audience; it seems much more likely that he was, in fact, convincing the convinced. As I argue, his anti-Islamic polemics were addressed to his fellow Christians.

It is worth noting that Peter's idea of using word instead of sword against the Muslims was not completely free of violence. His words were used as swords and his mental picture of a peaceful approach to the Muslims was rather militant. Peter the Venerable had wished that Islamic doctrine be refuted, and holy Christianity defended, "with zeal." He had been waiting "a long time" for that to happen, but no one had opened his mouth. Thus Peter decided to speak out himself.[158] Peter of Poitiers, his notary, lauded the abbot as the only man in his times who "slaughters by the sword of the divine Word the three greatest enemies of holy Christianity": the Jews, heretics, and Saracens.[159] These words of praise reflected Peter the Venerable's idea of interconfessional dialogue. In a letter announcing the translations from Arabic, Peter urged Bernard of Clairvaux to write against the Muslim doctrine: "to combat, destroy, and trample underfoot by every study, through word and writing, 'all knowledge that exalts itself against the height of God.'"[160] The words that were the alternative to arms in Peter's address to the fictional Muslim reader of the *Liber contra sectam*[161] figured—when Peter wrote to Bernard—as "Christian armory" and "weapons."[162] Peter's *armarium*—his "library" of books translated from Arabic—was indeed an *armamentarium*.

What was to be attacked with those weapons apparently deserved destruction. When Peter spoke directly to the Christians—freed from the laudable, and rare, restraint from invective shown in the *Liber contra sectam*—he passed harsh judgment on Islam. If his writing had greater doctrinal accuracy than most, and if he was the first Christian polemicist to cite Qur'anic (and Talmudic) sources,[163] he departed from the common Latin opinion on Muslim religion in neither tone nor intention. His attitude toward the Muslims in works that were not addressed to

158. *Summa totius haeresis*, 211.
159. *Epistola . . . ad domnvm Petrvm abbatem*. Kritzeck 1964, 216. On Peter the Venerable's anti-Jewish polemics, see Abulafia 1995, 87–88, 116, 128.
160. *Epistola ad Bernardum*, 213. Kritzeck 1964, 43, pointed out the inversion of "altitudo" and "scientia" in the citation of 2 Cor 10.5.
161. See n. 147.
162. *Epistola ad Bernardum*, 213. But see *Liber contra sectam*, Prologus, 230.
163. Kritzeck 1964, 25.

them was "surprisingly conventional." [164] Like his less peace-minded contemporaries, Peter the Venerable subscribed to the Latin Christian *ceterum censeo*. Just as Roman censor Cato had repeatedly ended his speeches with the call that Carthage had to be destroyed (*Ceterum censeo Carthaginem esse delendam*), orators of the Christian republic, whatever else they may have said, ended up demanding the destruction of the Muslims. From Peter's point of view, such a demand was understandable enough. If (to cite a few characterizations) Islam was "the unholy sectarian doctrine," a plague, a diabolical plan, maddest absurdities; if the Qur'an was a "diabolical scripture," woven together in "barbarous fashion" by Muhammad; if Muhammad was "the nefarious man," a beastly man, possessed by the devil, a man through whom Satan spoke, a liar who poisoned "with a deadly poison" the Arab people who had not known God; [165] then Muslim religion could indeed not be tolerated.

Here and there, Peter described the Muslim people as victims of a diabolical scheme executed through their false prophet. The "very wretched and wicked *Mahumet* has taught them who, by denying all the mysteries of the Christian religion [*pietatis*] whereby particularly men are saved, has condemned almost a third of the human race by some unknown judgement of God and by unheard-of, raving-mad tales, to the devil and eternal death." [166] This humanist tenderheartedness was echoed by Robert of Ketton, the translator of the Qur'an, for whom Islam was "a foul and poisonous thing" that was beneficial and appropriate only to "touch rather than to hold onto." But Robert distanced himself from those Christian priests who were so overcome with hatred that they declared that the conversion of the Muslims was not even desirable. He deplored that the Muslims, God's "beautiful portion of the human race," be left "held fast in the chains of darkness." [167]

The humanists' sympathies found their limits, however, when confronted with something understood as manifestly inhuman, such as an "obstinate" refusal to follow reason, the faculty that made men human. For the reasoning Christian, to "follow reason" meant to accept Christianity. Failing to accept the Christian disputant's reasons for the

---

164. Berry 1956, 146.
165. Quotes from *Summa totius haeresis, Epistola ad Bernardum, Liber contra sectam*.
166. *Summa totius haeresis*, 205; cf. 206–7. Later in the same text, Peter estimated that the race that Muhammad plunged along with himself into everlasting flames constituted "almost one half of the world." Ibid., 210.
167. Dedicatory letter to Ketton's translation of the *Fabulae Saracenorum*; quoted in Kritzeck 1964, 63–64.

truthfulness of Christianity never meant that those reasons might be un-
convincing. The fault always lay with the unbeliever. In light of the arguments presented to him, he could believe if he wished to—if he were
rational.[168] His failing to be convinced was his failing as a rational being and therefore as a human being. Christianized reason was an exclu-
sionary mechanism: those unwilling to accept Christian doctrine were
seen as rejecting reason and thus denying their own humanity. As such,
"twelfth-century perceptions of what was reasonable and what was not
had a lasting influence on European perceptions of what it was to be
properly human." [169]

Peter the Venerable's final judgment on the Muslims abandoned his
humanitarian representation of them as victims of Muhammad's trickery. Because they did not obey the dictates of reason and refused to embrace the true, Christian religion, they were not only "the barbaric
people" but also the "most wicked race." [170] They had to be fought, and
fighting these "enemies of Christ's cross" was identical with waging war
against the devil, the prince of this world.[171] But why they should be
fought with "words" as well is not so obvious.

For Peter, Islam was the summation of Christian heresies. In a letter
to Bernard of Clairvaux, the Cluniac abbot called the Muslim doctrine
the "foremost error of errors," the "dregs of all the heresies into which
all the remnants of the diabolical doctrine have flown together, which
came into existence since the very coming of the Saviour." [172] This view
was shared by at least one of the translators he hired. For Robert of Ketton, Islam was "the greatest heresy of all." [173] Peter spoke also of the
spread of Islam. He described how "the Mohammedan fury" first cor-
rupted almost all of Asia, then by violent invasion—*non miti ratione,
sed uiolenta incursione*—subjugated Egypt, Libya, and "all of Africa,"
and finally broke into Spain, thus not leaving even Europe wholly to
Christians.[174] But the expansion of Muslim temporal power was not Peter the Venerable's main concern. It was Islam as heresy that he saw as a

168. Cf. Abulafia 1995, 86.
169. Ibid., 6; cf. 123, 133.
170. *Liber contra sectam*, 229; *Summa totius haeresis*, 210.
171. *Letters* no. 172. Cf. Dérumaux 1953, 73; Kritzeck 1964, 21.
172. *Epistola ad Bernardum*, 213.
173. Quoted in Kritzeck 1964, 64. These translators were not enthusiastic about sac-
rificing their scientific pursuits for Peter the Venerable's polemicist project and were "fanatical only on request." But in their fanaticism on request, they "out-Petered Peter in pro-
fessing the contempt for Islam and its ways." Kritzeck 1964, 139 f.; Metlitzki 1977, 31–32.
174. *Liber contra sectam*, 226. But in his anti-Jewish *Adversus Iudeorum inveteratam
duritiem*, Peter wrote that the Christians were spread all over the world: "there is not any

threat to Christianity and consequently wanted to attack with the sword of the Spirit: "What heresy yet, O reader, has so injured the Church of God? Which error yet has so vexed the Christian republic? What has broken down its boundaries by so much? What has increased the number of the damned by such a mass of lost ones?"[175]

Peter was shocked by the absence of anti-Islamic polemics. Will the Christian tongue, he asked rhetorically, "which passed by no (or even little) heresy intact, being sluggish, greatly overlook this greatest error of all errors?"[176] It was imperative for the faithful to fight each and every heresy: to refute every "error," to seize upon (and if possible, correct) "everything wicked and against the mind [intellectus] of faith."[177] But Peter observed among his fellow Christians only ignorance and lack of zeal: "Because the Latin-speaking peoples, and most particularly those of recent times, losing their ancient zeal, . . . have not known the various languages of the former wonderful Apostles, but only their own language into which they were born, in that condition they could not know what such an error [Islam] was or, consequently, put up any resistance to it," he wrote, referring to Psalms 38.4 (39.3), and continued: "I was indignant that the Latins did not know the cause of such perdition and, by that ignorance, could not be moved to put up any resistance; for there was no one who replied [to Islam] because there was simply no one who knew [about it]."[178]

Peter wanted to know and wanted his fellow Christians to know. But was it really the hope of "correcting" the Muslims that motivated him to gather information about Islam? He does not seem to have believed that newly acquired knowledge would help convert Muslims. He voiced his doubts when he set about to answer imagined objections to his enterprise. A refutation in Latin of the Muslims' "deplorable error" appeared indeed a waste of time. Even if it were "put into Arabic letters," into that "strange language," it could at best help only "some" of the Muslims whom God might wish to save. Peter certainly believed in the superiority of the Christian religion, but his thoughts on the possibility of converting the Muslims were not triumphalistic. His apologia pro domo sua essentially explained that a compelling reason for his polemics

part, or a significant part, of the land, not of the remotest island of the Mediterranean or the ocean itself," where there were no Christians. Quoted in Abulafia 1995, 128.

175. Liber contra sectam, 225.
176. Ibid., 226.
177. Ibid., 225.
178. Ibid., 228–29.

against Islam was to serve Christians. His refutation of the Islamic doctrine, he said, might "counteract the secret thoughts of some of us, by which they may be led into scandal, who think that there is some piety among those impious and believe that there is some truth among the servants of falsehood."[179] Robert of Ketton agreed. To his mind, it was "manifestly a pernicious thing that the flower of that perverse sectarian doctrine, covering up a scorpion, fails to draw the attention of, and destroys by trickery, ministers of the law of the Christian faith, to whom alone the law can be afforded truly and absolutely—which, alas, we have very often seen already."[180]

This explanation of—if not justification for—the need to study Islam rings the most true. The long-range purpose of Peter's *Liber contra sectam* seems indeed to have been to strengthen Christian resistance to Moslem doctrine rather than to organize a missionary program.[181] But in view of the historical reality, the need to defend Christians against Muslim doctrine was not very pressing indeed. If we assume for a moment that Islam was a heresy—although Peter the Venerable himself sometimes wavered about whether the Muslims were heretics or pagans[182]— it was a heresy that had "never made the slightest appeal in Europe."[183] In Peter's own time, conversions in areas where Christendom bordered on Muslim dominions were never numerous enough to inspire a sense of danger to the orthodoxy of Latin Christianity. But still one cannot simply dismiss Peter's feeling that a refutation of Islam might be of help in looking after and providing for "the weak ones in the Church [*infirmis ecclesiae*], who are inclined to be tempted to evil."[184]

In Peter the Venerable's musings about counteracting secret heretical inclinations of Christians, and in Robert of Ketton's anxiety that Islam might seduce "ministers of the law of the Christian faith," the Christian dialogue with the Muslims is laid bare as a Christian monologue. The utopia of converting the Muslims turns out to be the dystopia of preventing Christians from falling into heresy. On the one hand, the idea of defeating Islam by rational argument can be seen as an expression of Latin Christians' new confidence in reason—Christianized reason—

179. Ibid., 230.
180. Quoted in Kritzeck 1964, 64.
181. Berry 1956, 145.
182. *Liber contra sectam*, 227.
183. Southern 1962, 39.
184. *Epistola ad Bernardum*, 213–14. Cf. Southern 1962, 39.

that followed in the footsteps of the successful First Crusade. On the other hand, the Muslim adversary of the anti-Islamic polemics was so fictitious that we can hardly avoid guessing that the real addressee of Christian polemicists was the insecure Christian self. The potential enemy was not so much without as within. The Muslim was used—or abused—so that the Christian could talk to himself.

When it came to dealing with real Muslims—as opposed to the imaginary Muslim of his internal dialogue—Peter the Venerable approved of the use of the material sword. His declaration that he had chosen to fight the sons of Ishmael with words and not with arms should not be understood as a dissociation from the crusaders. His study of Islam neither estranged him from the crusade nor caused him to give "mere lip service to it." To the contrary, throughout his life he was "consistently sympathetic to the crusade." [185] He wished the Saracens destroyed. He praised Christian princes devoted to the crusade, like King Sigurd of Norway and Roger of Sicily, through whose valor the Church of God had gained a lot from "the lands of the enemies of God, that is, of the Saracens." He urged Roger to make peace with Conrad III of Germany so he could make war on the Greeks (to punish them for the "most wicked, unheard of and lamentable treachery done . . . to our pilgrims," that is, the participants of the Second Crusade) and to extend the Church of God by fighting the Saracens. [186] He expressed his respect for the Templars— "virtuous monks, active soldiers"—lauding their incessant and assiduous fight against the Saracen "infernal armies." [187] He longed to accompany the crusading "army of the Eternal King" and join the king of Jerusalem, sword in hand. Since the monastic vow prevented him from doing that, his aid to the crusader king was limited to prayer and advice. He wished that the king "may rule with a rod of iron the enemies of the Cross of Christ and of the Christian name, the Turks, . . . and the Saracens, the Persians and the Arabs, and whatever barbarians there are who oppose themselves to their own salvation, and . . . destroy them with a powerful right hand, like a vessel of clay." [188]

Besides corresponding and praying, Peter the Venerable participated in the preparations for the Second Crusade, and after its disastrous end,

185. Berry 1956, 141, 145; Siberry 1983, 104.

186. Peter to King Sigurd of Norway, *Letters* no. 44 (p. 141); to Roger of Sicily, *Letters* no. 162 (pp. 394–95). Cf. Constable 1953, 236; Berry 1956, 156.

187. *Letters* no. 172 (p. 408).

188. *Letters* no. 82 (p. 219). Cf. *Letters* no. 83. See Berry 1956, 148; Kedar 1984, 100.

supported the efforts to launch a new expedition.[189] The crusade, quite
simply, was the order of the day. "Whom would it not move," the Cluniac abbot wrote to Bernard of Clairvaux, "if by chance that holy land,
snatched forth from the yoke of the wicked by the exertions of our fathers, by the shedding of so much Christian blood not long ago, should
be subdued again to the wicked and blasphemous?"[190] While preaching
the cross he urged that the Holy Sepulchre be cleansed of the defilements
of the infidel with pious swords.[191] There was nothing greater than the
crusade: the crusade was *omnium maxima*. "For isn't it the greatest of
all matters to provide and to see that the Holy Land should not be given
to dogs? lest the places where stood the feet of Him Who brought salvation into the midst of the earth should again be trampled by the feet of the
wicked? lest royal Jerusalem, consecrated by the prophets, the apostles,
the very Saviour of all, lest Antioch, that noble metropolis of all Syria,
should be subjected again to blasphemous and wicked men?"[192]

For Peter the Venerable—as for Bernard of Clairvaux—the crusade
was something sublime and spiritual. And Peter's crusading spirituality,
like Bernard's, was centered on the Holy Sepulchre.[193] Peter's call for the
cleansing of the holy places was an expression of this spirituality. In his
view, joining the "army of the living God"[194] offered to Christians an
excellent opportunity for spiritual purification: the cleansing of the Holy
Land was a cleansing away of their sins. The crusade was "above all a
gift from God, an opportunity for men to restore something of the image of God within them."[195] It was a gift, in particular, for those who
had committed crimes against their fellow Christians: "so salutary a
journey for penitent sinners, which, as is fitting to believe, now for fifty
years has saved innumerable thousands of pilgrims from Hell and restored them to Heaven."[196]

Peter the Venerable does not seem to have given much thought to the

189. See Berry 1956, 144, 148; Kritzeck 1964, 21–23; Kedar 1984, 100; Cole 1991,
49 ff.; Mayer 1993, 104; Constable 1997, 69 f.
190. *Letters* no. 164 (p. 397); trans. in Berry 1956, 160.
191. *Sermo . . . de laude Domini sepulchri*, 247. Cf. chap. 3 n. 284.
192. Peter to Suger of St. Denis, *Letters* no. 166 (pp. 399–400); trans. in Berry 1956,
160. Suger was among the most active in efforts to organize a new crusade after the failure of the second. Berry 1956, 159; Constable 1997.
193. See *Sermo . . . de laude Domini sepulchri*; Berry 1956, 153–54. Cf. Peter to Suger
of St. Denis, *Letters* no. 166 (p. 400): "sepulcrum Domini, qoud hactenus, juxta
prophetam, gloriosum toto in orbe fuerat [Isa 11]."
194. Peter to Roger of Sicily, *Letters* no. 162 (p. 395).
195. Cole 1991, 59.
196. Peter to Bernard of Clairvaux, *Letters* no. 164 (p. 397).

material effects of this spiritual war. On one occasion he warned that "God does not will cold-blooded murder or outright slaughter." But that was in reference to the persecution of Jews, not to the crusade.[197] Peter's views, like Bernard's, conformed with Pope Eugenius's instructions to the crusaders (as recorded by Odo of Deuil): "to visit the Holy Sepulchre and to wipe out our sins with the blood or the conversion of the infidels."[198] Whatever one may think of Peter's study of Islam, he was a conventional crusading propagandist.

But his study had great potential. Though Peter did not develop the juridical implications of his Muslim heresy thesis, his description of Muslims as heretics placed them under Christian jurisdiction and provided legitimation for war against them. His thoughts about conversion of the Muslims were a mixture of triumphalism and resignation. They were sidetracked because the prospects of anti-Islamic polemics winning over a substantial portion of the Muslims appeared so dim to Peter. But had they been brought to their logical conclusion and put into practice, they would have provided the crusade with a goal it lacked, remedying its main deficiency.[199] The military struggle for material annihilation of the "enemies of the Cross" would have been complemented with a spiritual fight against their false religion. The result would have been a perfect crusade, a total war, conquering not only the earthly but also the otherworldly possessions of Muslims, subjugating their souls as well as their bodies.

ORDEAL BY FIRE: ST. FRANCIS OF ASSISI

Peter the Venerable's views—the first systematic refutation of Islamic doctrine in Latin—had only a slight direct influence on anti-Islamic polemics that followed.[200] The *Liber contra sectam sive haeresim Saracenorum* and *Summa totius haeresis Saracenorum* were probably drawn upon by Aquinas in his *Summa contra gentiles*,[201] and by Nicholas of Cusa even later.[202] But generally speaking, Peter's early study of Islam "yielded little more than a closet literature for parochial Christian intellectuals."[203] Nevertheless, this early anti-Islamic polemics gives us an

---

197. Quoted in Kritzeck 1964, 21.
198. Odo of Deuil *De profectione* IV (p. 70).
199. See Kritzeck 1964, 23, 42 ff.
200. Ibid., 195, 198. Cf. Daniel 1993, 260.
201. Pavlović 1992, 119 ff. But see Hagemann 1988, 471.
202. Setton 1992, 49.
203. Burns 1971, 1387.

insight into the articulation of the logic supporting totalized struggle against Islam. Once the polemicists' idea of conversion materialized in missionary activity, the crusade and the mission—often espoused by one and the same person—came to complement one another. The "praise of peace"[204] by Peter the Venerable and by missionaries later was more than compatible with crusading warfare. The opposition between the two is artificial, and the work of missionaries could be supplemented smoothly by the labor of armies.[205]

The view that the rise to prominence of the mission corresponded to the decline in crusading enthusiasm is now seen as one of the major errors of earlier historians of the late Middle Ages.[206] St. Francis of Assisi fit well into this erroneous view of history. The life of the saint long ago became legend. Because Francis's writings are scanty, his personality gained the more in fascination. He was a peacemaker in the manner of the Gospel of Matthew, with which he identified himself. "*Blessed are the peacemakers, for they shall be called the children of God* (Mt 5.9). They are truly peacemakers who are able to preserve their peace of mind and heart for love of our Lord Jesus Christ, despite all that they suffer in this world," wrote Francis.[207] He has been described as a "practitioner of peace" in whom the idea of peace appeared in its most touching and captivating form.[208] The Franciscan order has been represented as the "greatest peace action ever undertaken," and what the Franciscans, his followers, strove for as "the most elevated peace ideal ever proclaimed."[209] In fact, St. Francis's life and work are typical of the symbiosis of crusade and mission and, as such, reveal the intricacies of Christian peacemaking.

St. Francis's attitude toward the crusade is not very clear. He has been called a "pacific crusader"[210]—not a very meaningful description once we realize that the crusaders were all warriors of peace and the crusade was an *opus pacis*.[211] His enrollment as a young man in Innocent III's

204. Kritzeck 1964, 22.
205. Siberry 1983; Paciocco 1992, 715; Daniel 1993, 140.
206. Housley 1992, 381.
207. *The Admonitions* 15 (p. 83). (Francis's texts as well as some other source material I cite are quoted from *St. Francis of Assisi: Writings and Early Biographies*, hereafter referred to as WEB.)
208. Constantinescu-Bagdat 1924, 100–101.
209. H. Felder, *Die Ideale des hl. Franziskus von Assisi* (Paderborn, 1923); quoted in Berg 1985, 181.
210. Basetti-Sani 1959, 36.
211. Cardini 1974, 221.

anti-imperial "crusade" against Markward of Anweiler[212] is of marginal importance for understanding Francis's relation to the crusade. The important thing is that none of the sources recording the saint's life attribute to Francis a single remark that may be interpreted as critical of the crusade, and nothing of the kind can be found in his own writings.[213] To the contrary, there are grounds for arguing that St. Francis embraced the knightly ideal of the crusading age and never dissociated himself from the Crusades.[214] St. Bonaventure, the seventh minister-general of the Franciscans, called him "the soldier of Christ," as did Marino Sanudo, an early-fourteenth-century crusade propagandist.[215] Thomas of Celano spoke of St. Francis as "the very strong soldier of the Lord."[216]

Unreserved support for the crusade was normative in the Franciscan order as well.[217] That support was not limited to words. From the 1220s onward, the burden of preaching the crusade and collecting crusading taxes fell on the Franciscans and Dominicans,[218] while the Tertiaries, the Franciscans' lay brethren, obtained papal permission to carry arms in defense of the Roman Church, the Christian faith, and Christian lands. But the Franciscans themselves also knew how to take up arms. Jacques of Vitry, a contemporary of Francis, reported that the Friars Minor "do not withhold their sword from blood: they fight, they travel through the city in all directions, they know how to bear up under hunger, like wandering dogs."[219] Four centuries later, Father Joseph, a Capuchin of great political influence and an "apostle of the crusade," wrote that Francis was a name that brought doom to the "Turks."[220] And a biographer of Joseph praised the "sons of St. Francis of Assisi" for having been "always ready to either preach holy war or themselves take up arms against the infidels."[221]

If a story told by St. Bonaventure and related by an anonymous Friar Minor is reliable, St. Francis explicitly approved of the crusade. The

212. See Abulafia 1992, 98; Riley-Smith 1992, 133.
213. Cardini 1974, 234; Kedar 1988, 130.
214. Cardini 1974, 219 f., 233; Siberry 1983, 105–6; Paciocco 1992, 712–13.
215. Bonaventure *Legenda* IX,7 (p. 100); Rousset 1983, 134–35.
216. Thomas of Celano *First Life* II,ii,93.
217. Kedar 1984, 158.
218. Sayers 1994, 195.
219. *History of the Orient* 32 (WEB, 1613).
220. "Francia, Franciscus, fatalia nomina Turcis." *Turciados* IV,568; quoted in Dedouvres 1894, 35.
221. Dedouvres 1932, 1: 35–37. To an advocate of the Reformed Church, the "multitude of Fryers ready to be put in Arms" became an article of accusation against the Roman Church. Sandys, *Europae speculum*, 74 ff.

story is about Francis's dispute with the sultan of Egypt. The sultan reputedly argued that if Christians had been true to the Gospel (he allegedly referred to Mt 5.40), they "should not invade our land." " 'It seems,' Blessed Francis answered, 'that you have not read the gospel of our Lord Jesus Christ completely. In another place we read: if your eye causes you sin, tear it out and throw it away [cf. Mt 5.29]. Here he wanted to teach us that every man, however dear and close he is to us, and even if he is as precious to us as the apple of our eye, must be repulsed, pulled out, expelled if he seeks to turn us aside from the faith and love of our God. That is why it is just that Christians invade the land you inhabit, for you blaspheme the name of Christ and alienate everyone you can from his worship.' " [222]

Regardless of how spurious this story may be, St. Francis did meet the Egyptian Sultan al-Kamil at Damietta in 1219, during the Fifth Crusade. Francis's preaching of the true faith to the sultan was recorded by Francis's early biographers and has been cited ever since. [223] The encounter between the Christian saint and the Muslim ruler has become Francis's most celebrated effort at peacemaking [224] and has recently been represented as a "peaceful oasis in the story of the holy war." [225] But to my mind, the extraordinary part of this story is that the sultan received Francis, an unauthorized messenger of the invading army, "very honorably" [226] and "willingly listened to him and earnestly invited him to stay longer with him." [227] Al-Kamil's parting words to Francis—"Pray to me that God may reveal to me that law and that faith which is to Him most pleasing" [228]—have been seen as an expression of high Islamic spirituality. [229]

With regard to Francis's encounter with the sultan, one should not lose sight of the fact that it took place "at a time when great and severe battles were raging daily between the Christians and the pagans," when there was a "fierce war between the Christians and the Saracens." [230]

222. Anonymous in *Verba fr. Illuminati* (WEB, 1614–15).
223. Dante, among many others, sang about the event: "ne la presenza del Soldan superba predicò Cristo." *Paradiso* XI,100–101. Cf. remarks on the episode in Cardini 1974, 225 ff.
224. It is less known that Francis worked—as a virtuous republican, one might say—for the resolution of factional struggles in Italian city republics. Berg 1985, 190.
225. Armstrong 1992, 406–7.
226. Thomas of Celano *First Life* I,xx,57.
227. Bonaventure *The Life* IX,8.
228. Jacques of Vitry *History;* incorporated in the *New Fioretti* no. 54 (WEB, 1879).
229. Cardini 1974, 228.
230. Thomas of Celano *First Life* I,xx,57; Bonaventure *The Life* IX,7.

Francis was in Egypt with the crusading army, and his peaceful preaching took place in the middle of the crusade. He apparently preached peace to the sultan; he did not go to Damietta to speak of peace to the crusaders.[231] Staying with the Christian army, St. Francis did not voice opposition to the crusade. He is reported to have "forbid[den] the war, denouncing the reason for it," only once—when he saw in a vision that if the battle took place on a certain day, it would "not go well with the Christians."[232] He objected to a single battle, not to war. He did not denounce the crusade but rather wished to avert defeat of the crusaders.

Seen as a whole, Francis's endeavors contributed to the spiritualization of the crusade and may be regarded as an attempt to make it more sublime.[233] Telling in this regard is the language used by Francis and the Franciscans. The notion of *militia Christi* (central to the conventional crusade idea of the time) was set aside, while terms denoting service, such as *servire* and *servus,* took its place.[234] St. Francis and his followers called themselves God's servants, *servi Dei,* not soldiers of Christ, *milites Christi,* and the mission to the Saracens was presented by Francis in terms of serving God. The mission was integral to the Franciscan ideal of apostolic life. Living in absolute poverty and humility, giving themselves up unreservedly to God, the Franciscans devoted their lives to announcing the word of God to all men for the salvation of their souls, because—as Francis is quoted as saying—"it was for souls that the only-begotten Son of God deigned to hang on the cross."[235]

At the core of the Christian redemptive mission was peace. In all his preaching, Francis first prayed for peace for those who had gathered to listen to him. "He always most devoutly announced peace to men and women, to all he met and overtook."[236] "At the beginning and end of every sermon he announced peace; in every greeting he wished for peace; in every contemplation he sighed for ecstatic peace."[237] Peace was the gift of God that Christ had brought to earth: "This is the peace proclaimed and given to us by our Lord Jesus Christ and preached again and again by our father Francis," wrote Bonaventure. And this was the peace in the way of which Francis "guide[d] our feet."[238] To announce

231. Cf. Cardini 1974, 234.
232. Thomas of Celano *Second Life* II,iv,30.
233. See Cardini 1974; Paciocco 1992, 713.
234. Paciocco 1992, 705.
235. Bonaventure *The Life* IX,4.
236. Thomas of Celano *First Life* I,x,23.
237. Bonaventure *The Soul's Journey* prol. 1 (p. 53).
238. Ibid. Cf. Berg 1985, 182–84.

peace through word and through the example of one's own life[239] was
to follow Christ. Living as a peacemaker meant imitating Christ (*imita-*
tio Christi). This is why the Franciscan movement was seen as a mission
of peace (*pacis legatio*). But for the Franciscans, speaking "a peaceable
tongue"[240] was not talking of peace in the abstract: it was preaching
Christianity. If they "strove for *peace* and gentleness *with all men*,"[241] it
was because they were dedicated to spreading the true faith and wished
all men to be Christians so that they would be saved.

Bonaventure left behind an insider's description of Francis's missionary activity: "By his zeal for the Faith, St. Francis became God's chosen
instrument. He went all over the world to spread the Faith."[242] But apparently there was also a more subjective, less selfless motive for preaching Christianity to the infidels. Thomas of Celano, Francis's first biographer, wrote that "[g]lowing with the love for God, . . . burning
intensely with the desire for holy martyrdom," Francis "wanted to take
ship for the regions of Syria to preach the Christian faith and penance
to the Saracens and infidels."[243] Francis thought about the Saracens a
lot, and before he reached Egypt he had unsuccessfully tried twice to go
among them.[244] He "longed to offer to the Lord *his own life* as a *living*
sacrifice [Rom 12.1] in the flames of martyrdom." The "fruit of martyrdom had so attracted his heart that he desired a precious death for the
sake of Christ more intensely than all the merits from the virtues."[245]
When he proclaimed the Christian faith to the sultan, Francis hoped
that he "would be torn limb for limb for it."[246] This "sublime purpose
of attaining martyrdom and the ardent desire for it," that made the saint
"drunk, as it were, in spirit,"[247] may be understood as striving for spiritual perfection, pushing the imitation of Christ to the point of no return, to a Christ-like death. But, as we will see shortly, what such an attraction to death brought about in practice was not always blameless.

---

239. On the preaching with the example of one's own life, see, e.g., the "Fragments of
the Worcester Cathedral Manuscript" (*Spisi*, 161): "All brothers should preach with their
lives."

240. Thomas of Celano *First Life* I,xv,38.

241. Ibid., I,xv,41.

242. *Sermon II on St. Francis* (WEB, 838).

243. *First Life* I,xx,55.

244. Cardini 1974, 218; Bonaventure *The Life* IX,6.

245. Bonaventure *The Life* IX,5–6.

246. Bonaventure *Sermon II* (WEB, 838). Cf. *Little Flowers of St. Francis* I,24 (WEB,
1354), on "fervent longing for martyrdom."

247. Thomas of Celano *First Life* I,xx,56.

First, however, we have to turn to the regulative idea of the Franciscan mission.

The leading idea of the Franciscan mission is clearly worded in the first version of the Rule of the order. This Rule is believed to have been formulated by Francis in 1221 after his return from Egypt and is generally considered an authentic expression of his views.[248] Because it failed to get the papal approval, it is called the *Regula non bullata,* as opposed to the edited version of the Rule, which was authorized by the pope two years later (the *Regula bullata*). In the *Regula non bullata* Francis stated that the friars who felt themselves "inspired by God to work as missionaries among the Saracens and other unbelievers," and who were given permission by the minister of the order to go to the infidel lands (after having been found suitable for the mission), "can conduct themselves among them [the Saracens] spiritually in two ways."[249] "One way is to avoid quarrels or disputes and *submit to every ordinance of man for the Lord's sake,*[250] so bearing witness to the fact that they are Christians. Another way is to proclaim the word of God openly, when they see that is God's will, calling on their hearers to believe in God almighty, Father, Son and Holy Spirit, the Creator of all, and in the Son, the Redeemer and Saviour, that they may be baptized and become Christians, because *unless a man be born again of water, and the Spirit, he cannot enter into the kingdom of God* [Jn 3.5]."[251]

New themes pertaining to the crusade movement appear here: the departure of unarmed mendicant friars to Muslim lands, bearing witness to God silently by the way the friars lived, and especially, the recommendation that they submit to Muslim law (which was based on apostolic commandment [1 Pet 2.13] but contradicted the canons of the Third and Fourth Lateran Councils).[252] These new themes, however,

---

248. Cf. Basetti-Sani 1959, 182.

249. *Regula non bullata* 16. The phrasing in the fragments of the *First Rule* from the Worcester Cathedral: the brothers who go among the infidels "can spiritually communicate with them in two ways." *Spisi,* 161. The fragments of the *Regula* preserved by Hugo Digne speak of the brothers' "acting spiritually." Ibid., 167.

250. 1 Pet 2.13–14: "subiecti estote omni humanae creaturae propter Dominum sive regi quasi praecellenti/sive ducibus tamquam ab eo missis ab vindictam malefactorum laudem vero bonorum."

251. *Regula non bullata* 16. Basetti-Sani 1959, 42 ff., interpreted these two *modi* as two phases, making the point that the first period might last for centuries, because for God "a thousand years is as one day" (2 Pet 3.8).

252. Cf. Hefele 1912–13, 5.2: 1105–6 (Third Lateran, canon 26), 1387–88 (Fourth Lateran, canon 69); Basetti-Sani 1959, 43, 223–24.

were added to the old crusading ideas, supplementing rather than substituting for them.[253] And much of what was new seems to have been undone by friars on missionary journeys. For example, the rules for the behavior of the friars "when they travel about the world" demanded that they should "not be quarrelsome or take part in disputes with words," but should be "gentle, peaceful, and unassuming, courteous and humble, speaking respectfully to everyone"; that they "should not offer resistance to injury"; and that, *whatever house* they *enter,* they should *first say, 'Peace to this house'* [Lk 10.5]."[254] Another regulation prescribed that in their preaching the friars should always use words that are "examined and chaste" and "do their best to humble themselves at every opportunity."[255] Yet judging by the Franciscan missionaries' behavior, these general regulations were not rigidly observed when they traveled about infidel lands and preached to the Saracens. Specific regulations for "missionaries among the Saracens and other unbelievers" were no more likely to be heeded. And not many of those regulations entered into the papally approved Rule of the order.[256]

As the bishop of Acre (appointed in 1216), Jacques of Vitry was well acquainted with the situation in the Holy Land. In his view, the Franciscan order "constitutes a danger because it sends out not only formed religious, two by two, throughout the world, but also imperfectly formed young men who should better be tried and subjected to strict conventual discipline for a period of time."[257] It seems that, for many a Franciscan, the desire to die a martyr's death was stronger than the need to spread Christianity. In his *Historia Orientalis* Jacques first told his reader that "even the Saracens" admired the Franciscans' humility and virtue: "they receive them very gladly and give them all they need." Moreover, the "Saracens gladly listened to the Friars Minor preach as long as they explained faith in Christ and the doctrine of the gospel." But, Jacques also informs us, "as soon as their preaching attacked Mohammed and openly condemned him as a liar and traitor, then these ungodly men heaped

253. Cf. Daniel 1993, 140; Kedar 1984, 131.
254. *Regula bullata* 3; *Regula non bullata* 14; Fragments from the Worcester Cathedral (*Spisi,* 161).
255. *Regula bullata* 9; *Regula non bullata* 17.
256. In the *Regula bullata* 12, the instructions about the missionary work were omitted.
257. Letter from Jacques of Vitry, Spring 1220 (WEB, 1609). A revised version of the letter, without the quoted critique, was incorporated in the *New Fioretti* no. 53 (WEB, 1878.) On Jacques, see Kedar 1984, 116–20, 124–29; Cole 1991, 114–15, 132 ff.

blows upon them and chased them from their cities; they would have killed them if God had not miraculously protected his sons." [258]

The founder of the order went to Muslim lands desirous of shedding his blood "for the spread of the faith in the Trinity," [259] but his desire was not fulfilled. Some of his brethren were more successful in their search for martyrdom, abusing Muslim law and religion in order to achieve that goal. These preachers of the Gospel perceived themselves as instruments of God: as instrumental in bringing about the salvation of the Muslims. But in practice, a less noble instrumentalism seems to have prevailed. The seeker of martyrdom used the mission as the shortest path to heaven; he used the Muslims he was supposed to bring to salvation as instruments to obtain his own salvation. Following the logic of the mission, such holy selfishness sealed the perdition of the Muslims: they remained infidels and became murderers. This approach was St. Bernard's teachings turned upside down. Bernard advocated killing the infidels as a way to salvation; here, the path to salvation was being killed. Either way, the conceptualizing of Christian relations with the Muslims involved violent death.

By the end of the thirteenth century, violence provoked by missionary zealots had strengthened the conviction that an alleged Muslim prohibition against Christian preaching made peaceful evangelization in Muslim lands impossible. At the same time, an older conviction that the Muslims were inconvertible was reinforced. Early Franciscan sources, it is true, are not unanimous on this issue. Bonaventure described Francis's mission at Damietta as unsuccessful: true piety had not "taken root in the Soldan's soul," and Francis "saw that he was making no progress in converting these people." [260] But another story claimed that Francis actually converted the sultan, who "generously granted permission to him and his companions to go anywhere and freely preach whatever they wished in all his empire." [261]

As a matter of fact, the mission to the Saracens experienced problems that arose from the mission's driving force: the Christian claim to universality. The will to spread Christianity throughout the world had been reinvigorated by new religious fervor in the Latin West, of which the

---

258. *History* 32 (WEB, 1612–13). Cf. Kedar 1984, 143, 156.
259. Bonaventure *The Life* IX,7. An exception among the Franciscans was Giles of Assisi, who did not wish "for a martyr's death." See *Vita beati fratris Egidii* 18.
260. *The Life* IX,8–9.
261. *Little Flowers* I,24 (WEB, 1354).

Franciscan movement was a prime example. A key expression of that new religiosity was the preaching of the Gospel. The Franciscan desire to proclaim the word of God to the Saracens was part of a deeper urge to convert all human beings to the true faith.[262] But though that urge was clearly felt, how to bring about conversion of the infidels was sometimes less clear in practice. The problem first emerged in the context of preaching the crusade and was partly due to inefficient preaching. As a remedy, Paris theologians in the late twelfth century set about to define a new orientation to preaching the cross and to provide instruction to the laity both by preaching and by training preachers.[263]

Early-thirteenth-century missionaries could have benefited from these developments in the art of preaching. Francis of Assisi, however, appears to have relied on his talents alone. He claimed that no one but the Most High Himself had told him what to do. This is probably what prompted Jacques of Vitry, who had been one of the Parisian moral theologians working on the reform of preaching, to characterize Francis as "a simple unlettered man, loved by God and men."[264] Coming from an educated cleric, this does not seem to have been entirely an encomium. But the image of Francis that attracts the popular imagination comes very close to Jacques of Vitry's portrayal. It is the image of a simple holy man living according to the tenets of the Gospel, moved to proclaim the joyful news to the whole world and to see and love all men as his friends and brothers. But such a view calls for qualifications.

When Francis talked about "the whole world," he meant the Christian world. This is clear from the prayer that closes the *Regula non bullata*. Here Francis beseeches "the whole world, . . . all those who serve our Lord and God within the holy, catholic and apostolic Church, together with the whole hierarchy, . . . and all clerics and religious, male or female, . . . all lay folk, men and women, infants and adolescents, young and old, the healthy and the sick, the little and the great, all peoples, tribes, families and languages, all nations and all men everywhere, present and to come; . . . to persevere in the true faith and in a life of penance."[265]

262. Cf. Kedar 1984, 119.
263. See Cole 1991, 113 ff.
264. *History* 32 (WEB, 1612). In the *New Fioretti* no. 54 (WEB, 1879), the same text reads: "a simple and ignorant man." The papacy, for its part, took care to subject Franciscan missionary work to its own supervision. But Francis's thinking about universal evangelization conformed to the thinking prevalent in the ecclesiastical hierarchy and intellectual centers.
265. *Regula non bullata* 23.

Francis of course wanted to enlarge this "whole world." He wanted to preach to the unbelievers. He called them friends, declared his love for them, and commended his brethren to love them. Had the infidels heard Francis talking of his love for them, they would probably have found it a strange kind of love indeed. But even from the Christian point of view, that love was not as pure as appears at first sight. It was not without reservations; even worse, it was calculating and self-interested. Love for the unbelievers was commended because it was the Lord's commandment to love one's enemies. "Love your enemies" is perhaps the most frequently cited Scriptural reference in Francis's *Opuscula*. It is as enemies that the infidels are loved, and they are loved for the love of Him.[266] However, loving God is unconditional; loving unbelievers is not. For they will only be truly loved if they cease to be who they are: infidels. "But if you were to recognize, confess, and adore the Creator and Redeemer, Christians would love you as themselves," Francis is reported to have said to the sultan.[267] Talking about the infidels as friends also had a very specific meaning for Francis. The infidels were friends because through suffering the misdeeds of the infidels, Christians were able to enter heaven. "Our Lord Jesus Christ himself," Francis explained, "called the man who betrayed him his friend, and gave himself up of his own accord to his executioners. Therefore, our friends are those who for no reason cause us trouble and suffering, shame or injury, pain or torture, even martyrdom and death. It is these we must love, and love very much, because for all they do to us we are given eternal life."[268]

However one judges their motives, the Franciscans strove to win the unbelievers over to eternal life in Christ. But that was not an easy task. At the turn of the thirteenth and fourteenth centuries the incompetence of Christian preachers was blamed for the failure to convince the infidels—that is, the Muslims—that Christianity was the true faith. Christian propagandists were able to negate Islam but did not know how to affirm Christianity. This view was vividly put forward by Ramon Lull early in the fourteenth century:

> It is said that a certain Christian religious learned in Arabic was in Tunis disputing with the king. This religious proved by an attack on Moslem morality that the law of Mahomet was erroneous and false. The king, who knew something of logic and of natural philosophy, was convinced and said to the

266. Cf. ibid., 16.
267. Anonymous in *Verba fr. Illuminati* (WEB, 1615).
268. *Regula non bullata* 22.

Christian, "From now on I refuse to be a Moslem; prove to me that your Faith is true and I will embrace it and see that it is adopted in my whole kingdom under pain of death." The religious replied: "The Christian faith cannot be proved, but here is the creed in Arabic, accept it." . . . The king replied: "I refuse simply to abandon one belief for another without proof and without understanding the new faith. You have done ill, for you have taken from me the belief I had and gave me nothing in return." [269]

The Franciscans did their share of abusing Islam, but they also reflected on the difficulty of convincing unbelievers about the truth of the Christian faith. This was most clearly expressed by Bonaventure (who also worked for the crusading movement)[270] when he described Francis's meeting with Sultan al-Kamil. The core of the problem was the incapacity of human reason to prove religious truth. In his second sermon on St. Francis, Bonaventure related that after Francis had reached the sultan and proclaimed the Christian faith, the sultan replied: "We will call our philosophers and discuss our faith and yours." The saint, however, refused the invitation to discussion: "Our faith is beyond reason, and reason is of use only to him who believes." [271] Furthermore, in religious disputation with unbelievers, reason could not be supported with Christian authorities: "I cannot argue from Sacred Scripture either," Francis said, "because they [the Muslim philosophers] do not believe in it." [272] In a slightly different version of this story, Bonaventure has the sultan suggest to Francis that he hold a disputation with his "priests," which Francis declined because "the Christian Faith could never be discussed from the standpoint of reason, because it transcends reason, and it could not be discussed on the basis of the Holy Scripture, because they did not accept it." [273] Bonaventure added a moral: "We should therefore not mix so much water of philosophy with the wine of the Holy Scripture that wine becomes water; that would be a very bad miracle; for we read that Christ changed water into wine, not the other way around." [274]

Though he refused to enter into dispute, St. Francis did not waver in his determination to prove the truth of Christianity. He asked the sultan to "make a big fire with wood, and I will go into it with your philoso-

---

269. *Liber de acquisitione terrae sanctae;* quoted in Hillgarth 1971, 22. Cf. Lull *Blanquerna* 84 (p. 356); *Felix* I,7 (pp. 693–94).
270. Cardini 1974, 245–46.
271. *Sermon II on St. Francis* (WEB, 838). Cf. Basetti-Sani 1959, 267.
272. *Sermon II on St. Francis* (WEB, 838). Cf. Basetti-Sani 1959, 176, 267.
273. *Collationes* XIX,14 (p. 352).
274. Ibid.

phers. When we see who is burned, we shall know whose religion is wrong."[275] But because the sultan feared that he could not find anyone "willing to expose himself to the fire to defend his faith or to undergo any kind of torment,"[276] Francis insisted that he be allowed to go into the flames on his own: "If I am burned, it is because of my sins. If not, then you should welcome our Christian Faith." The story has the sultan replying that he could never do that because "my people would stone me."[277] Unfortunately for St. Francis, Islamic jurisdiction did not recognize trial by ordeal. And as Francis must have known, a few years earlier Pope Innocent III had prohibited clergy from participating in trial by ordeal.

The problem of how to make unbelievers accept the universalist claims of Christianity had predated St. Francis and continued to engage the minds of Christian dignitaries and intellectuals after Francis's death. Part of the problem in disputation with unbelievers, as we have seen, was the impossibility (or limited possibility) of using Scriptural arguments. Before the mission to the Muslims, St. Anselm's pupil Gilbert Crispin, for example, had pointed out in his *Disputatio Judei et Christiani,* a seminal work of the last decade of the eleventh century, that Christian apologists reasoning with the Jews must accept that the Jew would recognize only the authority of the Old Testament and limit their arguments accordingly.[278] A century later, in the *De articulis catholicae fidei,* Nicholas of Amiens bemoaned the sway of the "ridiculous teaching of Mahomet" in the East and the corruption of the West with heresies. How, he asked, were all those infidels to be convinced when there was no text they all accepted as authoritative, so that all they had in common with the Christians were their rational minds?[279]

However logical the idea that reason provides common grounds for religious discussion, not all Christian apologists were as confident in reason as was Peter the Venerable. The possibility of rational argument caused quite a bit of unease in some quarters because reason unbridled by the authority of the Bible and the Christian Fathers could lead to unsafe conclusions. According to Alain of Lille, writing at the end of the twelfth century, monsters had been the outcome of the heretics' philosophical speculations. His own solution was to marshal against them

275. *Sermon II on St. Francis* (WEB, 838).
276. *The Life* IX,8.
277. *Sermon II on St. Francis* (WEB, 839). Cf. *The Life* IX,8.
278. Evans 1983, 129.
279. Ibid., 129–30.

first reasons and then authorities.[280] Theoretically, at least, this was an easier task with the Cathars and Waldensians than with the Muslims, since the heretics challenged only priestly authority, not the authority of the Scripture. But the final argument in both cases was the crusade.

The unreliability of reason unsupported by sacred authorities was only one aspect of what Christian propagandists experienced as the difficulty in persuading the infidels to embrace Christianity. The core of the problem (as expressed by St. Bonaventure in his reminiscences of St. Francis) was the incapacity of human reason to grasp divine truth. In this light, representing the unfaithful as irrational, as Peter the Venerable had done, was not a compelling argument; for at least some Christians themselves doubted the powers of reason. St. Francis's attempt to resort to trial by ordeal demonstrates how weak was the case for rational discussion between Christians and Muslims. Another Franciscan, Roger Bacon, tried to restore faith in reason as the guiding light to the establishment of a universal Christian republic.

THE SCIENTIFIC CRUSADE: ROGER BACON

Like Francis of Assisi half a century earlier, Roger Bacon is a fascinating figure. "It is impossible to read him without loving him—yet we have to ask ourselves whether we love him so much, now that he is dead, because he was not loved when he was alive."[281] His troubled life, however, is not my subject. At issue here are his troubling thoughts. Few historians who have studied Bacon have found his ideas disquieting. He is often praised as a critic of the crusade and, therefore, as a pacifist.[282] Since Bacon argued for conversion of the Muslims, many commentators think that he rejected the Crusade.[283] But Bacon's criticism of the crusade was qualified.[284] Neither his advocacy of preaching to the Muslims nor his desire for the establishment of "universal peace" can be disputed. But the universal peace he sought was the peace of the universal rule of the Roman Church: the Greeks would rejoin the Roman Church, the Tartars would be converted, the Saracens exterminated, and there

280. Ibid., 129–32.
281. Gilson 1952, 75.
282. E.g., Throop 1940, 132–33.
283. Cf. Southern 1962, 59.
284. Cf. Siberry 1983, 108; Housley 1992, 377.

would be only one shepherd and one sheepfold (Jn 10.16).[285] Bacon had a noble dream: the idea of one universal people encompassing all men of good will united by their common profession of the Christian faith.[286] But he realized that the establishment of such a Christian cosmopolis might require more than preaching to the Muslims and other infidels, and he suggested turning the crusade into scientific warfare.

Bacon's starting point was pessimistic. The Christians were few. "We also know that the majority of human race has always erred both in philosophy and with regard to divine wisdom," he stated. "And when the apostolic church was gathered together through preaching, few remained in the true faith, and up to this time they are few when counted against the multitude of the world, namely, those who are subject to the Roman Church. All the remaining multitude is in error, like the pagans, idolators, Jews, Saracens, Tartars, heretics, [and] schismatics, in comparison with whom the supporters of the true Christian faith are very few."[287] Moreover, among this Christian minority, the state of their faith was shaky. For the greater number of Christians, as he saw it, faith was dead.[288] The imminent coming of the Antichrist was always on his mind, and the end of the world, he thought, was nigh.[289]

Against this gloomy historical landscape, Bacon worked tirelessly to reorganize the entirety of Christian learning. His program was not aimed at knowledge for knowledge's sake. Bacon strongly believed in the usefulness of sciences (as branches of knowledge), for knowledge was the only reliable guide through this world. In Bacon's view, "the welfare [utilitas] of the whole world depends on the study of wisdom,"[290] for one cannot do good if one does not know what good is. Bacon was concerned for the well-being and prosperity of all the people. But life in the world below had one supreme purpose: the life thereafter. The knowledge that was to guide men in temporal affairs was thus, ultimately, Christian knowledge leading to eternal life. The highest wisdom and truth had been revealed to the Christians. Bacon did not doubt that "there is only one perfect wisdom, given by the one God to one human

285. Opus tertium 24 (p. 86). Cf. Carton 1924, 87, 96; Landry 1929, 82; Gilson 1952, 90. On the destruction of the Saracens, cf. Part of the Opus tertium, 19; Opus minus, 321. For the conversion of the Tartars, cf. chap. 5 n. 239.
286. Gilson 1952, 76.
287. Compendium . . . Theology I,2.
288. Ibid. Cf. Compendium . . . philosophiae, 398 f.; Part of Opus tertium, 62.
289. Cf. Carton 1924, 108 ff.
290. Opus tertium 1 (p. 11).

race for the one purpose, that is, the eternal life, [and that wisdom is] contained in its entirety in the Holy Scripture."[291] Under the guidance of this true knowledge, Christian society had to be morally renovated and reordered,[292] and the infidels converted. The welfare of the world must be based on religious unity, for only on this basis could all matters be directed "in the proper way."[293] In other words, developing the sciences was a necessary means of saving and consolidating Christianity and the Christian commonwealth. But because the Christian republic could only be perfect if it were universal, the inner reform of Christendom had to be complemented with spreading the true faith.

The methodical application of knowledge to all aspects of life as envisioned by Bacon had to follow four main objectives. Sciences were to be used for the governance of the Church of God, for the regulation of the commonwealth of the faithful (*respublica fidelium*), for securing the conversion of unbelievers, and for the suppression of those "who persist in their malice."[294] Knowledge was an instrument of domination, both useful and necessary for governing the world. And for Bacon, how the world was to be governed was not open for discussion. He was an ardent papal monarchist. The pope, he believed, was the mediator between God and mankind, "the vicar of God on earth, to whom the whole human race is subject, and who must be believed without contradiction." As such, the Holy Father was "the lawgiver and the high priest who in things temporal and spiritual has full power, as it were, a human God, . . . whom it is lawful to adore after God."[295]

Bacon placed his highest hopes in Clement IV, who was elected pope in 1265 and whom he knew personally and esteemed.[296] But that personal acquaintance was circumstantial. Bacon subscribed as a matter of principle to the idea that the pope, as head of the Church of God, should rule the world.[297] Foremost among men, it was the pope who above all others needed knowledge. Bacon therefore wanted to provide the pope with all the knowledge he had recovered from ancient sources and de-

291. Ibid., 23 (p. 73).
292. Cf. Maloney 1988, 1–5.
293. Cf. Bacon *Opus majus*, 3.
294. Ibid.; *Compendium . . . philosophiae,* 395. The last point, although an aspect of Bacon's thought of capital importance, "a été peu étudié jusqu'à présent." Gilson 1952, 77 n. 1.
295. *Opus majus,* 639.
296. Cf. Gilson 1952, 89.
297. "Habetis ecclesiam Dei in potestate vestra, et mundum totum habetis dirigere," was Bacon's message to Pope Clement. *Opus tertium* 24 (p. 87).

veloped through his lifelong studies. The studious Franciscan monk compared himself to Aristotle. Because Aristotle had initiated Alexander the Great into the secret paths of knowledge, Alexander had been able to conquer the world.[298] So too, possessing the knowledge gathered by Bacon, the pope would be able to sway the world.[299] Sciences when employed by papal authority would drive out evil, promote blessings of all kinds, and hinder what ailed Christianity.[300] Bacon was convinced that the Antichrist "will employ the potency of science and will convert all things into evil." He believed that the Antichrist and his followers were going to make full use of scientific knowledge for evil ends.[301] It was thus of vital importance that the Church also be armed with knowledge. The Church had to meet the doings of the Antichrist "by similar means"—that is, by utilizing sciences—in order to hinder and destroy his work.[302]

In sum, the Roman Church under the supreme authority of the pope was to make use of sciences to attain one overarching goal: the welfare of a triumphant Christian republic. This Christian triumphalism entailed conversion of the infidels and suppression of the obdurate—those whom it would be "impossible to convert"—with "warlike labor."[303] Bacon never forgot to back conversion of the unbelievers with force: should words fail to effect the adoption of Christianity, violence was always in stock. When his dedication to conversion is taken out of context, Bacon looks like a critic of the crusade who believed that preaching was the only path to the expansion of Christendom. But Bacon was aware that not every infidel was "the assiduous man who is amenable to the force of reason."[304] If "persuasion" failed, Bacon had other methods for "reprobation" of the "obstinate." But first let us examine in more detail Bacon's ideas about "persuasion" of the infidels.

"Persuasion in regard to the faith," the aim of which was conversion of the infidels, could be accomplished either by miracles "which are above believers and unbelievers," or by philosophy, "the road common

298. *Opus majus*, 634.
299. But Bacon also hoped for the pope's help in promoting Christian learning by attacking violently "weak authorities and the multitude itself" as two of the causes of error. *Opus majus*, 35. On the general causes of human errors, cf. *Compendium . . . Theology* I,2.
300. *Opus majus*, 417.
301. Ibid., 415; *Part of Opus tertium*, 17.
302. *Opus majus*, 417.
303. *Opus tertium* 1 (p. 4); *Opus minus*, 395.
304. *Opus majus*, 797.

to believers and unbelievers."[305] Bacon planned a prominent role for philosophy in conversion endeavors. The primary target of conversion was the Muslims, and thirteenth-century developments in philosophy in the Latin West were indebted to Muslim philosophy. Bacon conceded that the unbelievers were "more studious than Christians" when it came to philosophy.[306] He also knew that arguing on the basis of Christian authorities was compelling only to Christians. In accordance with the rules of disputation, he wrote, the unbelievers "can deny all things in the law of Christ, just as Christians deny what is contained in other laws. And since they deny Christ, it is not strange if they deny the authorities of the Christians." Therefore, he argued, the Christian faith had to be proved with philosophical methods.[307] But therein lay a problem.

For Bacon, philosophy was "merely the unfolding of the divine wisdom by learning and art."[308] The power of philosophy, he argued, was not alien to the wisdom of God because "all wisdom is from the Lord God" and "the truth wherever found is thought to belong to Christ."[309] Before we see these phrases as nothing more than Bacon's platform for Christian missionary activity, we need to pause for a moment. His thoughts here appear to have a personal ring as well. To the Christian authorities, Bacon was suspect. It seems therefore likely that Bacon, while expressing his ideas about conversion of the infidels, was also defending the usefulness of the study of "pagan" philosophy for Christianity and justifying his own eclectic method of "plucking out" of non-Christian philosophy whatever he could make use of.[310] But even if Bacon's phrases cited here are an *apologia pro domo sua* at least as much as they are an attempt to pave the way to engaging with learned potential converts, I dwell here only on the latter, his ideas about religious "persuasion."

Bacon's statement that "the whole aim of philosophy is that the Creator may be known through the knowledge of the creature" was acceptable to any Muslim or Jewish philosopher of his day. For Bacon,

305. Ibid., 71. Cf. 703.
306. Ibid., 73.
307. Ibid., 71. Restated in ibid., 793.
308. Ibid., 65.
309. Ibid., 39, 43, 48.
310. This attitude is reminiscent of Augustine: "If those who are called philosophers, especially the Platonists, have said things which are indeed true and are well accommodated to our faith, they should not be feared; rather, what they have said should be taken from them as from unjust possessors and converted to our use." Augustine drew a parallel between the spoils that the Israelites took from the Egyptians and the things of value that Christians could derive from pagan learning. Augustine *On Christian Doctrine* II,xl,60.

however, there was only one God, one world, and one human race. And thus, it followed, "God's wisdom cannot be plural." [311] When Bacon wrote that "all that which is contrary, or alien, to the wisdom of God is false and vain, and can be of no service to the human race," [312] he meant his own, Christian, God. There could be only one true philosophy, one unfolding of the one divine wisdom serving the one divine truth. Bacon, it is true, did not deny a certain degree of rationality to the religion of the Saracens: like the religion of the Jews and the Christians, it was "more rational" than the religions of the pagans and idolaters. [313] And yet philosophy was in perfect conformity only with the Christian religion. [314] And only the philosophy that conformed to Christianity was true and useful. Philosophy on its own, unconnected to divine wisdom, was of "no utility." Worse than that, such philosophy led "to the blindness of hell" and therefore must have been in itself "darkness and mist." [315]

What, we might ask, would the imagined dialogue between Christians and infidels gain by its translation into philosophy? In Bacon's scheme, philosophy dissolved into Christianity and was subordinated to the Christian faith. It was Christian law that made philosophy true by adding "to the law of philosophers the formulated articles of faith, by which it completes the law of moral philosophy, so that there may be one complete law." Only Christian philosophy could do what philosophy was supposed to do: "enter into the proofs of the principles of theology," the principles of which were the articles of faith. [316] A non-Christian philosopher could not enter the path of conversion through philosophical disputation because he first needed to be converted, lest his philosophizing lead him to hell. For Bacon it was "obvious" that "man should not attempt to inquire regarding these divine verities before he is taught and believes." [317] Christian belief was thus not only the goal to which philosophical argument should lead; it was also the starting point of sane philosophical inquiry. The circle was closed. The true faith was the key to philosophy, rather than philosophy being the key to conversion.

Bacon nonetheless believed in conversion, argued for it, and cited

311. *Opus majus*, 49, 805.
312. *Opus tertium* 23 (p. 73).
313. Pagans lived according to custom, not according to laws based on reason. *Opus majus*, 789.
314. Ibid., 807.
315. Ibid., 66, 74.
316. Ibid., 72, 71.
317. Ibid., 804.

practical reasons for his position. When Christians confer with pagans, he wrote, the pagans "are easily convinced and perceive that they are in error." The proof of this is found in reports from the northern crusading front stating that the pagans "would become Christians very gladly if the Church were willing to permit them to retain their liberty and enjoy their possessions in peace. But the Christian princes who labor for their conversion, and especially the brothers of the Teutonic order, desire to reduce them to slavery, as the Dominicans and Franciscans and other good men throughout all Germany and Poland are aware. For this reason they offer opposition: hence they are resisting oppression, not the arguments of a superior religion."[318] Bacon's choice of this case is significant. The Northern Crusades, as they are called, were more open to criticism than the Eastern Crusades. Crusades to the Holy Land might be criticized for their failures and abuses; but it is difficult to imagine anyone in Latin Christendom arguing for permitting the Muslims "to retain their liberty and enjoy their possessions in peace." Bacon certainly did not. His criticism of the crusade was limited to the Northern Crusades, the Children's Crusade, and the Crusade of Shepherds. The Children's Crusade, Bacon wrote, took children from their fathers, mothers, and friends and led to a loss for Christendom because the children were in the end sold to the Saracens. The Crusade of Shepherds he blamed for its "contempt of the clergy" and for stirring up disorder in Germany and confusion in the Church. Whereas the originator of the former was "an evil man," the originators of the latter were doubtlessly "emissaries of the Tartars and Saracens."[319] There was nothing exceptional about Bacon's selective criticism of the crusades. His contemporary Humbert of Romans, the fifth master of the Dominican order, for example, also regarded the "idolaters in northern parts" as benign but insisted that the war against Muslims be continued.[320] "Liberty" of Palestine, in Bacon's conceptualization, meant its occupation by Latin Christians. Be the fortunes of other Christian conquests as they may, the Holy Land and Jerusalem had to remain securely in Christian possession.[321]

To bring home to his fellow Christians the need for conversion of the infidels, however, Bacon could not rest with his sympathetic portrayal of the pagans on Christendom's northeastern borders and his criticism of

318. Ibid., 797. Cf. 111. For the historical context of this criticism, cf. Christiansen 1980, 145 ff.; Nicholson 1995, 39.
319. *Opus majus*, 416–17.
320. Christiansen 1980, 146. Cf. Siberry 1983, 108.
321. *Opus majus*, 112.

the Teutonic Knights. He put forward a very pragmatic and realistic argument: war alone could not secure Christian domination. The Fifth Crusade, as "all the world knows," he pointed out, had been a failure.[322] But even if Christian armies could conquer the infidel countries, there would be "no one to defend the lands occupied." After making a foreign expedition, Christian victors "return to their own lands," while "the natives remain and multiply."[323] In war, unbelievers are not converted but "slain and sent to hell," while those who survive become an intractable problem: "The survivors of the wars and their sons are angered more and more against the Christian faith because of those wars, and are infinitely removed from the faith of the Christ, and are inflamed to do Christians all possible evils."[324] Oppression bred resistance. Reliance on force of arms alone frustrated the work of conversion, which was a better way to obtain and secure the Christian dominion.

The success of conversion efforts required that "we may be skillful preachers to all who are in need of preaching, and so also in regard to the other forms of persuasion useful for salvation."[325] Moreover, "the knowledge of languages is necessary to the Latins for the conversion of unbelievers."[326] Neglecting the study of tongues—argued Bacon, who himself did not learn Arabic[327]—was synonymous with irresponsible failure on the part of Christians to fulfill their duty to God. "For the Christians are few, and the whole broad world is occupied by unbelievers; and there is no one to show them the truth."[328] Astronomy and geography were also needed to convert the infidels—astronomy because celestial causes determine the course of terrestrial affairs, and "terrestrial things will not be known without a knowledge of the celestial." Because astronomy "regulates all things," "every splendid work ought to be done at times selected." Geography was needed because "whether one sets forth to convert unbelievers or on other matters of the Church, he should know the rites and conditions of all nations, in order that with definite aim he may seek the proper place."[329]

Bacon delighted in words[330] and believed that there was "a very great

322. Ibid., 111; *Part of Opus tertium,* 19.
323. *Opus majus,* 111–12.
324. Ibid., 111.
325. Ibid., 81.
326. Ibid., 110.
327. See Metlitzki 1977, 41, 257 n. 75 (with further references).
328. *Opus majus,* 112.
329. Ibid., 129, 405, 321. Cf. *Part of Opus tertium,* 10–12
330. Man "delights" in word, he said. *Opus majus,* 414.

potency in words." Word, he wrote, "is the most ready instrument of the
rational soul, therefore it has greater efficacy than any other thing man
does, especially when uttered with definite intention, great desire, and
strong confidence." [331] But he thought of other means of bringing about
conversion as well. He expected great service from experimental science,
especially because the Antichrist was going to accomplish his designs
scientifically, so that "men will obey him just as beasts." [332] Thus it was
urgent to employ experimental science in the service of Christ—even before the time of meeting the Antichrist. The "works" that the Antichrist
was going to use against the Church "could now be employed against
the Tartars, Saracens, idolaters, and other infidels," for it was certain
that these could not otherwise be properly overcome. [333]

A plea for the faith could be made effectively through experimental
science—"not by arguments but by works, which is the more effective
way." [334] For example, people could be influenced indirectly through
transforming the human environment: "changing the character of a region" would change "the habits of its people." Science could also be
used to affect humans directly: "The body . . . can be changed by the influence of things, and the minds of people are then aroused and influenced to desire voluntarily that to which they are directed; just as we see
in the book of Medicine that through potions and many medicines
people can be changed in body and in the passions of the soul and in the
inclination of the will." [335]

Performing miracles was another way of using experimental science
to spread the faith. "For to the man who denies the truth of the faith because he cannot understand it," explained Bacon, "I shall state the mutual attraction of things in nature. . . . Likewise I shall tell him that a jar
may be broken without human force, and the wine contained in it remain motionless and without flow for three days; and that gold and sil-
ver in a pouch, and a sword in its scabbard may be consumed without
injury to their containers. . . . For these facts and similar ones ought to
influence a man and urge him to accept the divine verities. Since if in the
vilest creatures verities are found by which the pride of the human intellect ought to be subdued so that it may believe them although it does
not understand them, conviction should follow, or injury will be done

331. Ibid.
332. Ibid., 415.
333. *Part of Opus tertium,* 19.
334. *Opus majus,* 632.
335. Ibid., 628; *Part of Opus tertium,* 52.

to infallible truth, since a man ought rather to humble his mind to the glorious truths of God." [336] These examples may appear fantastic to today's reader, but the underlying consideration is certainly not naive. The function of experimental science was "the formation of judgement." By performing this function, sciences could—and should—be used for "the direction of the whole world." [337] Their usefulness for the conversion of unbelievers was obvious.

Where neither speculative nor experimental sciences—neither "words" nor "works"—succeeded in bringing the infidels over to Christianity, Bacon suggested applying scientific knowledge for their suppression. He was the first orthodox Latin Christian to renounce the use of the sword against the unfaithful—in favor of more effective means of destruction. "On behalf of the Church of God," experimental sciences could be used with great advantage "against the enemies of the faith . . . who should be destroyed rather by the discoveries of science than by the warlike arms of combatants." [338] The crusaders appeared from Bacon's perspective as ignorant laymen fighting battles at random. Such nescience had to be overcome. The future expansion of the Christian republic should principally depend on scientifically conducted war.[339]

Bacon argued that by dealing with conflict in a scientific manner the prohibition against shedding Christian blood could be observed. His dislike of conflict and war within Christendom was conventional: he said they were sown by the enemies of Christians. Less conventional was his conviction that wars among Christians could be averted with the proper use of knowledge. Had astronomy been consulted in recent history, he argued, peace could have been promoted among Christians and "so great a slaughter of Christians would not have occurred nor would so many souls have been sent below." [340] Truly original were his proposals for sparing Christian blood in wars against the infidels. He envisaged how inconvertible unbelievers "who persist in their malice" could be "held in check by the excellence of knowledge, so that they may be driven off from the borders of the Church in a better way than by the shedding of Christian blood." [341]

However, driving the infidels away from the borders of the Church

336. *Opus majus*, 632.
337. Ibid., 632, 587.
338. Ibid., 633.
339. Gilson 1952, 82.
340. *Opus majus*, 401, cf. 416.
341. Ibid., 3.

could never be realized. Even if those borders were determined, driving
infidels away would only move back the borders. Infidels would always
be there, representing borders and thus posing a threat to the Church.
They would have to be driven away endlessly. Bacon's idea was a recipe
for permanent war until the terrestrial Church became universal and
thus borderless and the last of the unfaithful was annihilated. But Bacon
did not see this as a problem. His mind was absorbed with solving another problem: the invention of technical means to a bloodless struggle
against the enemies of the faith. If, as the Christians thought, wisdom
given by God ordained them to destroy His enemies; the wisdom of the
Church should lead them to consider using science against unbelievers
and rebels "in order that it may spare Christian blood." [342]

Bacon thought so highly of his idea of scientific warfare that he preferred not to call it war. Instead, he called it "the way of wisdom" as opposed to "the labour of war." [343] The two could be combined. An assemblage of learned men should be sent with any military expedition so
that the infidels could be subjugated more permanently and completely.
In this synthesis of material and spiritual coercion "the power of languages and of the different letters must not be despised." [344] Bacon's program thus reiterated the link between crusade and mission. [345] The true
"way of wisdom," however, meant more than having men of learning
assist Christian soldiers. Those who had knowledge should, rather, lead
war against the unbelievers.

The unbelievers to be fought with science were the Saracens. Bacon
was convinced that war against them could be greatly enhanced by the
use of optics. In perhaps the first argument for psychological warfare,
Bacon suggested that with a proper arrangement of mirrors, for example, "a single object will appear in as many images as we wish." "Images of this kind might profitably be produced" to the advantage of the
Christian republic. Such images "might also be used against unbelievers
to inspire terror. Moreover, if one knew that the air is dense, so that reflection could be obtained from it, he might produce many unusual ap-
pearances of this kind. In this way we believe that demons show camps
and armies and many wonders to men; and by reflected vision all things
hidden in secret places in cities, armies, and the like can be brought to

342. Ibid., 287, 643. Cf. Carton 1924, 95.
343. Opus majus, 112; cf. 415.
344. Ibid., 112.
345. See Kedar 1984, chap. 5.

light. . . . Similarly mirrors might be erected on an elevation opposite hostile cities and armies, so that all that was being done by the enemy might be visible." But the "wonders of refracted vision are still greater." With the proper use of mirrors, "a child might appear a giant, and a man a mountain. He might appear of any size whatever, . . . and close as we wish. Thus a small army might appear very large, and situated at a distance might appear close at hand, and the reverse. So also we might cause the sun, moon, and stars in appearance to descend here below, and similarly to appear above the heads of our enemies, and we might cause many similar phenomena, so that the mind of a man ignorant of the truth could not endure them." [346]

Other inventions of experimental science could "disturb the hearing to such a degree that, if they are set off suddenly at night with sufficient skill, neither city nor army can endure them. No clap of thunder can compare with such noises. Certain of these strike such terror to the sight that coruscations of the clouds disturb it incomparably less." [347] Still other wonders could be effected with explosives. [348] Important arts had been discovered, "so that without a sword or any weapon requiring physical contact they could destroy all who offer resistance." For example, a consuming fire could be produced by yellow petroleum "which can be extinguished with difficulty; for water cannot put it out." [349]

This brings us to Bacon's most famous idea of bloodless holy war: the burning mirrors. "This is the ultimate which the power of geometry can do. For this mirror would burn fiercely everything on which it could be focused. We are to believe that Antichrist will use these mirrors to burn up cities and camps and armies." [350] Once again, the Church had to meet the Antichrist on his own terms. As Bacon wrote to the pope (probably advertising his own work), the "most skilful of the Latins is busily engaged on the construction of this [burning] mirror, and the glory of your Magnificence will be able to order him to complete it when he is known to you." [351] Bacon regretted that "Christians beyond the sea" had not had such mirrors. Had "the men of Acre" had twelve such mirrors, "they would have chased the Saracens from their borders without bloodshed."

---

346. *Opus majus,* 581–82; *Part of Opus tertium,* 41.
347. *Opus majus,* 629.
348. *Part of Opus tertium,* 51.
349. *Opus majus,* 629.
350. Ibid., 135. For Bacon's "basic research," see *De speculis comburentibus.* Cf. *Epistola . . . de Secretis* V (p. 535); *Part of Opus tertium,* 51–52.
351. *Opus majus,* 644, 135.

And if the king of France had had mirrors "that burn up every opposing object," he "would not have had to cross the sea to conquer that
land" but could have burnt Saracen armies from afar. Any future crusade should therefore count on a master of burning mirrors who, with
his two assistants, would be more helpful than most, if not all, the soldiers.[352] Wishing to spare Christian blood, Bacon ended up sparing
Muslim blood—but not, however, their lives.

THE INFIDEL'S CONSCIENCE IS INVIOLABLE
BUT NOT HIS LIFE: ST. THOMAS AQUINAS

Bacon took special pride in having classified all the religions of the
world in his *Opus majus*.[353] He thought this part of his "moral or civil
science," as he wrote to the pope, superior to the rest of philosophy.[354]
Indeed, Bacon is regarded today as one of the first to make a comparative study of religion.[355] He explained the differences among religions
with the help of theories of climate and the influences of planets, and
classified religions according to the ends they pursued (pleasure, riches,
honor, power, fame, or future felicity).[356] The "law of the Saracens," for
example, was the law of Venus, in which "a delight in sin abounds."
Very conventionally, Bacon wrote of the Saracens as "wholly volup-
tuous and lascivious." Their concerns were confined to the present life.
Because they abused temporal blessings and yielded to the allurements
of pleasures, they lost the chance for future felicity. In accordance with
their law, Bacon added, they took "as many wives as they wish." Muhammad himself had been even worse, for "every beautiful woman he
took forcibly from her husband and violated her." Astronomy and astrology were also a source of consolation: they predicted the imminent
destruction of Mohammedan law.[357]

The aim of Bacon's study of religions was to prove that Christianity
was the only perfect religion.[358] The outcome of his study was thus "a

---

352. *Opus tertium* 36 (p. 116–17); *Opus majus*, 633.
353. *Opus minus*, 320.
354. *Part of Opus tertium*, 61–62.
355. See especially Heck 1957.
356. See *Opus majus*, 272 ff.; 788 ff., 804 ff.; *Part of Opus tertium*, 65–67. Cf. Heck
1957, pt. 2, chap. 2–4.
357. *Opus majus*, 287, 289, 294, 278, 788, 811.
358. "Nam quid est pulchrius," Bacon wrote of his own work, "quam per vias as-
tronomiae distinguere omnes sectas et eligere sectam Christianam?" *Opus minus*, 320. Cf.
Part of Opus tertium, 62.

general survey of all the possible enemies of Christendom," [359] and in his scheme non-Christian religions appear as different forms of unbelief. In his opinion, "there can only be one perfect sect of the faithful." Consequently, "the law of Christ should be preferred to the others." There must be "no other law than that one, the establishment of which, since it is the best, must then be extended throughout the whole world." [360] One of the objects of Bacon's "comparative study of religion" was to "reduce the whole world to the law of truth in which alone is the salvation of the humankind." [361]

But as long as Christianity was not universally accepted, Bacon saw the world as divided into two opposing blocs. This view was common enough to western Christendom. In his *De fide catholica* (written at the end of the twelfth century), for example, Alain of Lille had synthesized dissenting Christians (Cathars and Waldensians), Jews, and Muslims into "one general heresy," as opposed to the "faithful people" living under Christian law. For Alain, people (*populus*) was a technical term denoting a company of men living in one place under a single law. Heretics, on the other hand, were not a *populus*. They were *gentes*: undistinguished by any character, they were merely begotten (*geniti*) and united simply by birth. [362]

Like Bacon and others, Thomas Aquinas thought of the infidels as a single enemy. He called them *gentiles*—those who had not yet found their way to the Christian faith. [363] He wrote the *Summa contra gentiles* against this sum total of all who did not belong to the faithful people. Composed on the initiative of Raymond of Peñafort, a leading figure in the Dominican order, the *Summa* appears to have been intended as a handbook for the education of Dominican missionaries. [364] Aquinas also wrote a small treatise against the Saracens, *De rationibus fidei*, which

359. Southern 1962, 59. Cf. Daniel 1993, 216.
360. *Opus majus*, 662, 805, 814.
361. *Part of Opus tertium*, 63.
362. Evans 1983, 128–29. Alain's definition of "people" echoes Cicero *De re publica* I,xxv,39 ("populus autem non omnis hominum coetus quoquo modo congregatus, sed coetus multitudinis iuris consensu et utilitatis communione sociatus") discussed in Augustine *The City of God* II,21; XIX,21. Cf. Isidore of Seville *Etym.* VIII,x,12. On Alain's life and work, see d'Alverny 1965b. Alain preached the Third Crusade. See his *Sermo de cruce Domini* (*Textes inédits*, 279 f.). Alain's construction of "one general heresy" is characteristic of the blurring of the difference between heretics, on the one hand, and Jews, pagans, and Muslims, on the other, that became predominant among Christian writers in the thirteenth century. Jensen 1996, 186–87.
363. Cf. Isidore *Etym.* VIII,x–xi; Schwinges 1977, 91; Evans 1983, 128.
364. Hagemann 1988, 465–66. Cf. Burns 1971, 1408 (on Peñafort, ibid., 1401); Pavlović 1992, 105.

was meant to be of help to Christians conversing with Muslims while living in Muslim lands. A reply to questions by a cantor from Antioch, it provided arguments with which Christians could answer Muslim criticism of their faith. It was a "missionary handbook." [365]

In contrast to the Franciscans, whose "forte was a mission of heart more than of head," [366] the Dominicans are known for a more intellectual approach to missionary work.[367] Thomas Aquinas was a luminary of the Dominican order. His writings against the infidels are seen even today as inspiration for dialogue with the Muslims and other non-Christians.[368] It is beyond the scope of the present volume to discuss the theological arguments made by Aquinas to support Christian polemics against Islam, and the Christian reception and critique of Muslim philosophy (in which Aquinas played a major role).[369] In what follows, I outline Aquinas's approach to debate with the Muslims alone.

Aquinas's starting point in the *De rationibus fidei* was the apostle Peter's sentence: "Always be ready to give an answer to anyone who asks you a reason of the hope *and faith* that is in you." [370] Aquinas's basic premise was that Christian controversialists should not try to prove their faith, because faith cannot be proved. "In this regard I want to admonish you," Aquinas wrote to the cantor of Antioch, "that in disputations with the infidels about the articles of faith you should not try to prove the faith by necessary reasons, because this would detract from the sublimity of the faith, the truth of which exceeds not only the human mind but that of the angels as well." [371] Christians believe in the truths of the faith because they were revealed to them by God. "Therefore, because what proceeds from the supreme truth cannot be false and because what is not false cannot be attacked by necessary reason, so our faith, which is beyond the human mind, cannot be proved by necessary reasons, nor, because of its truth, can it be proved false by necessary reasons." [372]

This was a programmatic statement. Attacks on Christian faith could

365. Burns 1971, 1397. Cf. Dondaine 1968, B6.

366. Burns 1971, 1401.

367. Cf. Hagemann 1988, 462.

368. Pavlović 1992, 135–40.

369. Cf. el-Khodeiry 1988; Nader 1988; Pavlović 1992, 107 ff. (with further references).

370. 1 Pet 3.15; "and faith" is Aquinas's insert. Anselm of Canterbury had quoted the same Biblical verse in his *Cur deus homo* I,i.

371. *De rationibus fidei* 2.

372. Ibid.

not prove wrong the reason of the faith, just as Christians themselves could not prove it true. The reason of faith was not, and could not be, the subject of the dispute between Christians and Muslims. What was at issue and had to be demonstrated was, rather, the reasonableness of Christian faith.[373] Since faith cannot be grasped by the human mind, the Christian disputant's intention, according to Aquinas, should be not to prove but to defend the faith. This, Aquinas assured the cantor, was in full accord with the apostolic precept that Christians should always be ready "to give an answer" regarding their faith.[374] The Christians' task in responding to attacks on Christianity should be "to rationally show that that which the Catholic faith confesses is not false."[375]

Aquinas's program was negative and critical. Since divine truth was beyond the reach of reason and the ultimate cognizance about God was that God was incognizable,[376] he aimed rather at using natural reason to refute objections and insults against the Christian faith. Citing Christian authorities whom unbelievers did not accept would be fruitless[377] and would take the dispute into a sphere beyond human reasoning. Natural reason, by contrast, was shared by Christians and Muslims alike. Muslims and pagans, Aquinas explained, were those among the unbelievers who "do not agree with us regarding the authority of the Scriptures, on the basis of which we could convince them, whereas against the Jews we can dispute with the help of the Old Testament, and against the heretics with the help of the New. They [*Mahumetistae* and *pagani*] certainly do not accept either [of the Testaments]. Therefore it is necessary to recur to natural reason, to which all have to assent."[378]

Defense of the Christian faith and its mysteries should aim not at convincing adversaries by reasons but rather at removing the reasons raised against Christian truth. It should aim, that is, at "confuting errors."[379] Christians could be confident that they were able to refute attacks against

---

373. Hagemann 1988, 469.

374. *De rationibus fidei* 2. In the Greek text, Peter encouraged Christians to be ready to defend the faith (*pròs apologían*). Aquinas, *O razlozima vjere*, 227 n. 16. Cf. Anselm of Canterbury *Cur deus homo* I,i (p. 47 n. b).

375. *De rationibus fidei* 2.

376. See Hoye 1988.

377. *De rationibus fidei* 1. This position was not as self-evident as it might appear: "Immer wieder ist nämlich in der Geschichte der Auseinandersetzung zwischen Christentum und Islam versucht worden, den Koran biblisch und die Bibel koranisch zu interpretieren. Dieser Weg führt allerdings in eine Sackgasse." Hagemann 1988, 469. Cf. Daniel 1993, 75.

378. *Summa contra gentiles* I,ii,11.

379. *Summa theologica* II-II, Q.10, Art.7. Cf. *Summa contra gentiles* I,ix,52.

their faith with natural reason, because natural reason could not contradict the truth of their faith.[380] Defending the mysteries of the faith meant showing that those mysteries were not opposed to natural reason (*rationi naturali non sunt opposita*).[381] One would expect that the obverse of Aquinas's strictly rational argument[382] in defense of the faith would be the denial of rationality to arguments against Christianity or to those who argued against it. But some dismissive remarks aside (for example, that the Saracens were sensual people, in contrast to "every wise man," and could not think about anything but that which belonged to flesh),[383] Aquinas did not rest his argument on insulting the Saracens. He rather looked for moral and philosophical reasons that he thought would be acceptable to them.[384] Both the *Summa contra gentiles* and the *De rationibus fidei* were remarkably unpolemical works.[385] They were, rather, works of Christian apologetics.

Aquinas's knowledge of Islam was rudimentary.[386] But since his approach to religious dispute was limited to the defense of the Christian position and did not require considerations of the Muslim creed, that was not a serious deficiency. Aquinas's arguments were so convincing that his fellow Christians believed, in the words of Dominican Ricoldo da Monte Croce, that "all objections (*rationes*) brought against the Catholic faith are soluble."[387] It is difficult to imagine that Muslims would share this assessment, but their views were not of grave importance. The paradox of both the *Summa contra gentiles* and the *De rationibus fidei* was that they were intended for non-Christians but addressed to Christians.[388] They never reached their intended readers, while their readers did not need to be convinced. Aquinas's apologetics moved firmly within the framework of Christian thinking and stayed safely at home. Aquinas was holding a monologue: "Taken away by the stream of his own theology, he cannot reach the shore on which he actually wants to land. The intended translation, or 'handing over' [*Über-setzung*], of the Christian faith to the Muslims thus failed. His apology is an *apologia ad intra*, not

380. *Summa contra gentiles* I,ix,52.
381. Ibid., IV,i,3348.
382. Hagemann 1988, 481.
383. *De rationibus fidei* 3. (On this topic, cf. Daniel 1993, 169.) A less academic language is also characteristic of *Summa contra gentiles* I,vi,41.
384. *De rationibus fidei* 1.
385. Cf. Pavlović 1992, 106; Hagemann 1988, 480.
386. Hagemann 1988, 470–71.
387. Quoted in Daniel 1993, 209.
388. Albert Patfoort, *Thomas d'Aquin* (Paris, 1983), quoted in Pavlović 1992, 104.

an *apologia ad extra.*"[389] But this failure, this implosion of mission, could have become a great achievement—had Aquinas only left things at that.

But Aquinas did not opt for leaving the non-Christians alone. The relevant passage is found in the *Summa theologica,* in answer to the question of whether the unbelievers ought to be compelled to embrace the faith. Aquinas's position was as liberal as any true liberal might wish, but his answer was qualified. In accordance with his categorization of the "sin of unbelief"—in which he distinguished between those who resisted the faith before they had accepted it (like pagans) and those who resisted after they had received it (either "in figure," like the Jews, or "in the very manifestation of truth," like heretics and apostates)[390]— he argued that only heretics and apostates "should be submitted even to bodily compulsion, that they may fulfil what they have promised, and to hold what they, at one time, received."[391] For "[j]ust as taking a vow is a matter of will and keeping a vow is a matter of obligation, so acceptance of the faith is a matter of will, whereas keeping the faith, once one has received it, is a matter of obligation."[392] Among unbelievers,

> there are some who have never received the faith, such as Gentiles and the Jews;[393] and these are by no means to be compelled to the faith, in order that they may believe, because to believe depends on the will; nevertheless, they should be compelled by the faithful, if it be possible to do so, so that they do not hinder the faith either by blasphemies, or by evil persuasions, or even by open persecution. It is for this reason that Christ's faithful often wage war against the unbelievers, not indeed for the purpose of forcing them to believe (for even if they were to conquer them and take them prisoners, they should still leave them free to believe, if they will), but in order to prevent them from hindering Christ's faith.[394]

The categorical rejection of violence in spreading the faith did not exclude waging war against the infidels. The principles Aquinas formulated for conducting religious disputes and waging religious wars are

389. Hagemann 1988, 482–83. But see Burns 1971, 1409–12, for different views on Aquinas's "missionary motives."

390. *Summa theologica* II-II, Q.X, Art.5.

391. Ibid., II-II, Q.X, Art.8, adding that those Jews who had received the faith "ought to be compelled to keep it" as well. Cf. II-II, Q.XII, Art.2, for the specific case of an apostatic prince.

392. Ibid., II-II, Q.X, Art.8.

393. The contradiction between this statement regarding the Jews and *Summa theologica* II-II, Q.X, Art.5 (cf. n. 390) may be resolved with reference to *Summa theologica* II-II, Q.X, Art.6, that the Jews "have never accepted the Gospel faith."

394. Ibid., II-II, Q.X, Art.8.

homologous. Faith could be neither proved by reason nor installed by the force of arms. Christian action in either case was construed as defensive. The Christian controversialist was not to prove the reason of faith and the Christian soldier was not to compel the infidel to embrace the faith. Rather, the controversialist was to refute objections against the Christian faith, and the soldier was to prevent the unfaithful from impeding it. Because the Church had no jurisdiction over infidels who had never received the faith,[395] neither conversion nor punishment of these unfaithful could justify waging war against them. Both religious controversy and religious war were dissociated by Aquinas from the reason of faith, and both had to defend the faith against attack. As a purely defensive war, religious war was not directed against infidelity as such, but rather against its possible influence on the true faith.[396]

To fully appreciate Aquinas's position, it is crucial to understand what he meant when he said that "hindering Christ's faith" by the unfaithful had to be prevented by force. He defined "hindering Christ's faith" so broadly that the defense of Christianity went on a warpath against the very existence of unbelievers. The clearest case of hindering the faith was the persecution of the faithful. In the doctrine of just war (to which Aquinas gave a new authoritative interpretation),[397] "open persecution" of Christians by unbelievers was legitimate grounds for Christians to wage war. From a legal point of view, that case was definite. But the same can hardly be said about the other two categories of hindering the faith, which Aquinas introduced as justification for war with unbelievers: "blasphemies" and "evil persuasions." Those categories were so extensive as to justify practically any act of war against non-Christians. Such vagueness was not inconsistent with Aquinas's views on war. For when it came to waging war against unbelievers, he a priori accepted the lawfulness of war, rather than examining the basic premises on which war could be considered just.[398] When it came to infidels, at any event, the Church had the authority to annul human law. Infidels' dominion or authority over the faithful, even where sanctioned by human law, could be "justly done away with by the sentence or ordination of the Church that has the authority of God: since unbelievers in virtue of their unbe-

395. Ibid., II-II, Q.XII, Art.2.
396. Cf. Gmür 1933, 24.
397. See, especially, *Summa theologica* II-II, Q.40, Art.1. For a general treatment, see Russell 1975, chap. 7.
398. Gmür 1933, 60, 75.

lief deserve to forfeit their power over the faithful who are converted into children of God." [399]

We now need to look more closely at the "blasphemies" and "evil persuasion" that justified war with unbelievers. To medieval Christians, the very profession of "unbelief" could easily be blasphemy. Both unbelief and blasphemy were sins. [400] Because unbelief consisted in "resisting the faith," [401] and blasphemy was "opposed to confession of faith," [402] unbelief was inherently blasphemous. Specific aspects of the Muslim creed, like denying the Holy Trinity, the divinity of Christ, or the redemptive act of Christ's death (which Aquinas discussed in the *De rationibus fidei*), could only be seen as blasphemous in Christian eyes. Cardinal Cajetan, in his authoritative commentary on *Summa theologica* II-II, Q. X, Art. 8, described blasphemy as "saying bad things about Jesus Christ, or his saints, or his Church" and, as such, regarded it as an impediment to the faith and thus a just cause for war. [403] In a world constructed this way, "Islam's very existence, hindering as it did the spread of Christianity, could be construed as a legitimate cause for Christian warfare." [404] Similarly, non-Christian rites could be seen as "evil persuasions." The Jewish rite, even if evil, was an exception because it "prefigured the truth of the faith which we hold." The good that followed from this was "that our very enemies bear witness to our faith," and for this reason the Jews were to be tolerated in the observance of their rites. [405] But the rites of non-Christians other than Jews were "neither truthful nor profitable" and were "by no means to be tolerated." If the Church had at times tolerated them, this was only because of circumstances— for example, "when unbelievers were very numerous." In such cases, the Church wanted "to avoid an evil, e.g., the scandal or disturbance that might ensue, or some hindrance to the salvation of those who if they were unmolested might gradually be converted to the faith." [406]

Aquinas did not explicitly see mere infidelity as a sufficient justification for Christian war against unbelievers. But by accepting his contemporaries' view of the infidels' "intention to do evil" and by representing

399. *Summa theologica* II-II, Q.X, Art.10.
400. Ibid., II-II, Q.X, Arts.1, 3–4; Q.XIII, Arts.2–3.
401. Ibid., II-II, Q.X, Art.5.
402. Ibid., II-II, Q.XIII, Art.1.
403. In Kedar 1984, app. 4, 218.
404. Ibid., 183–84.
405. *Summa theologica* II-II, Q.X, Art.11.
406. Ibid.

infidels' "evil persuasions" and "blasphemies" as just cause for war, Aquinas gave "almost unlimited permission to fight infidels" and provided "justification for Christian crusade of conquest."[407] His ruling was elegant. Not reasons of unbelief but rather the very existence of unbelief justified war. Unbelievers represented an obstacle to the Christian faith, a hindrance that had to be removed, just as the missionary had to remove the reasons raised by infidels against Christian truth. While unbelievers' consciences were not to be violated, the unbelievers themselves could be annihilated.

ONE LANGUAGE, ONE CREED, ONE FAITH: RAMON LULL

Ramon Lull[408] was a self-taught man who after a conversion experience in his early thirties, felt called to spend the rest of his long life teaching others. His plan was ambitious. He wanted to teach the Saracens and other unbelievers the true faith and convert them to Christ's service. He traveled to North Africa to preach to the Muslims, not fearing but rather desiring a martyr's death for Christ. (That he died a martyr in Tunisia in 1316 is a legend originating in the mid-sixteenth century.)[409] Lull also wanted to convince his fellow Christians of the urgency of converting the unbelievers. He occasionally called himself a fantast, but he knew well where power lay: he found his way to kingly courts, established connections with Italian maritime republics, and ran after popes with his different plans and projects. One plan was to establish convents where future missionaries would learn infidel languages. This project bore fruit when Lull, with King James II's support, founded a monastery in Miramar, in his native Majorca, where a small community of Franciscans began to learn Arabic. On Lull's initiative, moreover, the Council of Vienne in 1312 ordered that Arabic, Hebrew, and Chaldaic should be taught at the universities of Paris, Oxford, Bologna, and Salamanca, and at the papal court.[410] Some action seems to have been taken at the curial university and at Oxford, but nothing much appeared to have come of this order; and what did begin did not last long.[411]

---

407. Russell 1975, 286; Jensen 1996, 187.

408. I use this common form of the name, although in today's Catalonian the name is spelled Llull. Cf. Pindl 1996, 37 n. 6.

409. Ibid., 42. For Lull's life, see Hillgarth 1971, chap. 1; and Bonner 1985a (both with numerous references).

410. See *Petitio Raymundi* Prima ordinatio (p. 165); Hillgarth 1971, 128.

411. Burns 1971, 1408; Hay 1977, 89 n. 2; Abulafia 1997, 98.

Lull himself learned Arabic. He wanted to study Islamic doctrine and philosophy in order to dispute with the Saracens and convert them to Christianity. His "reasonably sound" knowledge of Arabic literature and thought[412] has won him much praise by some modern historians, who consider him a candidate for the title of the father of "Oriental studies."[413] But Lull had more practical concerns. Bacon had considered the study of tongues mainly a maidservant of theology; for Lull, learning oriental languages, Arabic in particular, was directly related to efforts to "recover the Holy Land."

The story of how Lull learned and mastered Arabic is not without a moral. Lull bought himself a Moorish slave for the express purpose of learning Arabic. This master-slave relationship lasted for nine years, after which, we are told, the slave apparently blasphemed the name of Christ while Lull was away travelling. "Upon returning and finding out about it from those who heard the blasphemy, Ramon, impelled by a great zeal for the faith, hit the Saracen on the mouth, on the forehead, and on the face." After some time had passed, the embittered slave attacked Lull with a sword and wounded him, upon which Lull knocked him down and had him put in jail, where the Saracen hanged himself. Upon learning the news, Lull "joyfully gave thanks to God" for freeing him from making a decision about his slave's fate and "for keeping his hands innocent of the death of this Saracen."[414]

This story is intriguing in itself. But no less intriguing is its retelling by a nineteenth-century French historian, who argued that when the slave and teacher of Arabic came to understand "the designs of the missionary" (Lull, that is), "religious fanaticism roused in him and he attempted to assassinate his pupil."[415] The supposed moral of the story is that Lull's "design" of peaceful persuasion represented an unbearable threat to Muslim religious fanaticism, and the slave died for trying to prevent Lull from becoming a missionary. In another interpretation a century later, the slave's death inspires Lull to become a missionary. In this retelling, the episode with the slave opens Lull's eyes to the fact that nothing could be gained by violence and that only through rational dia-

412. Bonner 1985a, 20. See, e. g., Lull *Book of the Gentile* IV.

413. Atiya 1938, 86. Cf. Alphandéry 1959, 250: "Lentement l' 'orientalisme' naît en Occident." On earlier Dominicans' promoting the study of Arabic, see Burns 1971, 1402 ff.; Smith 1988–89, 2: 60 ff.; Abulafia 1997, 93–94; Bonner, introduction to the *Book of the Gentile*, 95–96.

414. *Contemporary Life* 11–13. Cf. Thomas le Myésier *Breviculum seu parvum Electorium*, plate III (Hillgarth 1971, 450–51; app.).

415. Delaville le Roulx 1886, 28–29.

logue, based on respect and friendliness, could the infidels be won over to Christianity.[416] The story of Lull's Arabic lessons is open to other interpretations as well. We can only guess what was the "blasphemy" that cost Lull's slave-teacher his life. Lull himself heard it only secondhand. For all we know, it might have been "no more than an expression of Islamic piety toward Jesus as Prophet."[417] But the Moor's death may suggest that the study of Arabic in the Latin West was pregnant with the annihilation of those whose language it was. The aim of western Christians in learning Arabic appears to have been to render silent those who spoke it, to reduce them to listeners. "The unsympathetic story represents a general attitude; Islam could be tolerated only in silent subjection, the only final solution was its destruction."[418]

As a matter of principle, however, Lull loved the Saracens. It was because of that love that he worked obsessively to bring them to the path of salvation.[419] Much of that work was writing, and he wrote so profusely that today there is an academic discipline, Lullian studies, dedicated to his opus.[420] From those quarters we hear that no serious reader of Lull has not become his apologist.[421] These scholars uphold the image of a man who "violently" rejected the violent Christian approach to the Muslims and who, as a resolute opponent of the crusade,[422] opted for peaceful conversion of the unbelievers by way of rational argument. As such, Lull appears as "the first theorist and publicist of missions"— the "doctor of missions"[423]—whose life and writings were dedicated to the peaceful union of all men.

Actually, Lull did not reject the crusade because of pacifist aims. He had "a genuine and earnest desire to promote an armed crusade against the Saracens."[424] This juxtaposition of crusade and mission used to perplex historians,[425] but it did not trouble Lull's contemporaries. Thomas

---

416. Pindl 1996, 39.
417. Daniel 1975, 311. In support of this guess, see Lull *Felix* VIII,79 (p. 944): "Observe how Saracens believe strange things about God, . . . and how they say vile words about Christ and our Lady, dishonoring them and falsely blaspheming them without our doing anything about it."
418. Daniel 1993, 141.
419. Sugranyes de Franch 1986, 17. Cf. Hillgarth 1971, 13.
420. Bonner lists 263 titles. Lull, *Selected Works*, 2: 1257–1304.
421. Sugranyes de Franch 1986, 9. Cf. Delaville le Roulx 1886, 28.
422. Cf. Sugranyes de Franch 1986, 10–11.
423. Hillgarth 1971, 24. The "docteur des missions" is the title of Sugranyes de Franch's renowned book on Lull.
424. Atiya 1938, 76. Cf. Gottron 1912; Wieruszowski, "Ramon Lull et l'idée de la Cité de Dieu," *Estudis Franciscans* (1935); reprint in Wieruszowski 1971.
425. Cf. Gottron 1912, 11.

le Myésier, for example, a disciple of Lull, saw "no contradiction in Lull's thought on missions and crusades."[426] Today, Lull is seen as an exceptional man "who ran almost the entire gamut of positions, from rejecting the crusade as essentially unchristian and extolling peaceful persuasion, through simultaneously supporting mission and crusade, to advocating the launching of a crusade against infidels who had refused to convert."[427]

Lull's confidence in the possibility of converting the Saracens stemmed, it seems, from his own abundant self-confidence. He believed that, illuminated by God, he had written a "book, the best in the world, against the errors of unbelievers"[428] and had discovered a way of proving the Christian faith to the unfaithful, not by means of authorities, about which there could be no agreement, but "by means of demonstrative and necessary reasons."[429] Lull believed that the human intellect could and should understand God, "which it was created to understand." He also believed that the truth about Christian articles of faith could be demonstrated to people in this world.[430] This appears to be a polemical statement against the Dominican approach to mission by a man who thought highly of St. Dominic but, late in his life, entered the Franciscan Third Order.[431]

While still a young man, Lull had invented a demonstrative method of proving the truth of the Christian religion and the falsity of all others. He called this method *Ars* (the usual scholastic translation for *téhne*). He developed it in a number of versions and applied it in numerous writings.[432] The *Ars* was based on a conception of creation as a similitude of the divine dignities. Because of the presupposed conformity of the *modus intelligendi* with the *modus essendi*, Lull's "Art of thinking" was "infallible in all spheres because it was based on the actual structure of reality, a logic which followed the true patterns of the universe." The Christian mysteries were part of the very structure of the universe and could therefore be "demonstrated" by "necessary reasons."[433] Lull's

426. Hillgarth 1971, 246.
427. Kedar 1984, 189.
428. *Contemporary Life* 6.
429. *Book of the Gentile* Prologue (p. 116).
430. *Felix* VIII,79 (pp. 944–45). Cf. *Felix* I,12 (p. 717).
431. See text for n. 269, which is taken to be an attack on Dominican missionary Ramon Martí. Bonner 1985b, 58; id., introduction to the *Book of the Gentile*, 96. For Lull's appraisal of Dominic, see *Felix* X,121 (p. 1099).
432. See Bonner 1985b, 56 f.
433. See ibid., 59 f. The citation is from Frances Yates, *The Art of Memory* (London, 1966); quoted in Bonner 1985b, 61. On Lull's Neoplatonic view of the universe, see also

closed system of thought was perfect in itself, and worked with the precision of a computer.[434] Lull knew the truth and he knew how to organize it mechanically so that any nontruth would be rejected.[435]

Lull, a master of his own Art, always had "compelling arguments" for the Christian faith. Unfortunately, however, non-Christians might not find them convincing.[436] Lull himself reported that although he had conversed widely with eminent and scholarly Saracens, he had never met one who grasped Christian belief rightly.[437] But if his non-Christian interlocutors, real or imagined, did not find his arguments as compelling as Lull himself found them, he had in reserve another method, where "mechanization" entered religious persuasion in the form of repetition of a "mechanically" proven truth. In one of the countless stories Lull wrote about a Christian disputing with a Saracen, the Saracen was not convinced by the Christian's exposition of his articles of faith, and "wondered" about their truth. But "after the Christian had gone over these things many times he no longer experienced any wonder, for these explanations had accustomed his ears to hearing, his mind to understanding, and his will to loving them."[438] Lull explained that "everything a person can feel with the five bodily senses is a wonder, but because he is continually experiencing these bodily feelings, they no longer constitute a sense of wonder. The same thing happens with all the spiritual things he can remember and understand."[439]

Lull thought that "a few days"[440] of his intense intellectual treatment would suffice to gain a convert. His plan for converting Muslim captives was of the same mold. He wanted to send learned clerics to dispute with captives and make them memorize books proving that Muhammad was not a true prophet.[441] Lull had a remedy for non-captive unbelievers as well. He envisioned that for the "Jews and Saracens who are in the lands of the Christians there be assigned certain persons to teach them Latin and to expound the Scriptures, and that within a certain time they shall learn these, and if they have not done so, that there shall follow punish-

---

Hillgarth 1971, 13 ff.; Pindl 1996, 42 f. For a brief presentation of Lull's "Art," see Abulafia 1997, 96 ff.

434. Lull is actually seen as a remote forerunner of modern computer science and information theory. See Bonner 1985b, 63 f.; Sugranyes de Franch 1986, 9.

435. Cf. Alphandéry 1959, 250.

436. See *Felix* VIII,81 (p. 952).

437. Burns 1971, 1398.

438. *Felix* VIII,115 (pp. 1076–77).

439. Ibid., VIII,115 (p. 1078).

440. *Contemporary Life* 27.

441. *Liber de fine* II,6 (p. 88).

ment." [442] This was Lull's fantasy. But with regard to the compulsory disputations and conversionist sermons delivered by friars in the mosques and synagogues of thirteenth-century Spain,[443] Lull's ideas on this subject were far from fantastic. He suggested that the Council of Vienne order the preaching of Christianity to Jewish subjects in Spain on Saturdays and to Muslim subjects on Fridays.[444] In view of this religious coercion, practiced and wished for, one is struck by Lull's categorical statement that "free will is such a noble and lofty creation that no man can constrain another man to desire or to love by force." [445]

Only in the *Book of the Gentile,* an early work by Lull, is religious dispute depicted as polite. The beliefs of the three great monotheistic religions are presented to a Gentile, who at the end refrains from declaring which he has chosen to accept as the most true. Lull later amended that surprising open-endedness [446] and claimed that the Christian succeeded in proving his religion true.[447] The *Book of the Gentile* was Lull's utopia of "communicative action," a utopia Lull himself could not let be. But even in that utopia, Lull talked of "filth" in the Muslim Paradise. He pointed out, rather graphically, that "from a man who eats and drinks and lies with women there must come forth filth and corruption, which filth is an ugly thing to see and touch and smell, and to talk about." [448]

For Lull, the contemplative life was the source of fulfillment, but the active life was a necessity.[449] Much as the purpose of man's life in this world was to remember, understand, and love God so that he might live in the next world in everlasting glory,[450] the reality was that Christians were few—and good Christians even fewer—and infidels many: "observe how many unbelievers there are, and how few Catholics; and even

---

442. *Blanquerna* 80 (p. 326); *Libre de Blanquerna* (p. 298).

443. Cf. Pindl 1996, 35; Abulafia 1997, 92 ff.

444. *Petitio Raymundi* De octava ordinatione (p. 168).

445. *Felix* VIII,84 (p. 962).

446. "[A]n ending most surprising in a piece of medieval polemical literature." Bonner, introduction to the *Book of the Gentile,* 98.

447. *Felix* VIII,79 (p. 942).

448. *Book of the Gentile* IV,12 (p. 291). The filth that seems to have often come to Lull's mind was that coming from beautiful women. Just as Bacon feared menstrual blood, so was Lull disturbed by beautiful women's excrement. For example: "There was once a woman who was very beautiful and who, because of this great beauty, was proud. One day, after looking at herself in the mirror and admiring her own beauty, she went off, still thinking about her beauty, to the toilet, where she saw all the ugliness that had come out of her body; then she wondered why she had ever been proud of her beauty, with such ugliness coming out of her body." *Felix* VIII,93 (p. 998–99).

449. Ibid., VIII,62 (p. 880).

450. Ibid., VIII,47 (p. 840).

among Catholics see how few there are who love to honor and exalt the faith that has been entrusted to their care."[451] Such a situation called for urgent action, since infidels were multiplying, taking possession of Christian lands, and blaspheming the Holy Trinity and Christ's incarnation.[452] Their possession of the Holy Land was a disgrace to heaven and a defacement to the Holy Land.[453] The infidels' very existence was a "dishonor to God," for it showed that men could live who did not know Him and, worshiping their strange gods, felt no gratitude to Him for having had created them and kept them alive.[454]

Lull's response to the existence of so many who did not praise God is surprising in a man believed to have dedicated his life to conversion of the unbelievers. He reacted to the perceived "dishonor to God" not with desire to convert the unbelievers but with a zealous determination to praise God. His zeal seems to have been spurred by a lack of fervor among his fellow Christians. Felix, the protagonist in Lull's *Felix,* for example, "wondered greatly at how the Christian faith was not preached among the infidels by people praising and honoring it so nobly that they would not hesitate to honor it in spite of hardships, danger, death, or anything else; since for the sake of great honor there should be little hesitation in such things."[455] This comment introduced a story about a minstrel who wished to go overseas to "honor the faith," but whose prelate was unwilling to grant him permission to leave because he feared the minstrel would die fruitlessly. "The minstrel replied, saying that the fruit consisted more in praising and honoring God than in saving and converting men, for praising and honoring God and the faith is nobler than converting men."[456] This thought was repeated later in the same book, where we read that "man was created for the purpose of praising God, and therefore I cannot shrink from going to praise God out of fear of death, or because it might not bring something useful to man."[457] And in another book, the *Blanquerna,* the hero wanted to comfort Lady Faith, who was sad in her soul because among the Saracens God was not loved, honored, or believed. She wanted to convert the infidels. Lull's hero comforted her, saying that desiring the conversion of unbelievers is

451. Ibid., VIII,63 (p. 886).
452. Cf. *Liber de fine* Prologue (p. 65).
453. Cf. ibid.; *Felix* VIII,63 (p. 886).
454. Ibid., VIII,102 (p. 1033).
455. Ibid., VIII,63 (p. 885).
456. Ibid., VIII,63 (p. 886).
457. Ibid., VIII,86 (p. 970).

a merit as great as their actual conversion.[458] Not by their fruits, but by their desires, are true Christians known.

That zeal for praising God prompted Lull to sail to Bidjaya (in today's Tunisia) on what is mistakenly called a mission (if a mission aims to convert the infidel). Upon landing, his biography tells us, he went to the main square and "standing up and shouting in a loud voice, burst out with the following words: 'The Christian religion is true, holy, and acceptable to God; the Saracen religion, however, is false and full of error, and this I am prepared to prove.'"[459] This kind of "fanatic confrontation" has been called a typical Franciscan technique of spreading the faith.[460] (It is recorded, for example, that in the mid-fourteenth century a Franciscan provoked his own death by crying out against Islam—in French—during the sultan's Friday prayer in a Cairo mosque.)[461] If "invasions" like this pass for defense of the Christian faith,[462] then military aggression like the Crusades can also be called a defensive war. Lull himself suggested that "barking" was a more fitting description of this kind of "mission."

Lull compared a Christian protecting the faith to a good shepherd dog. Again in *Felix*, the protagonist came to a field where a wolf had entered a sheepfold and was killing and devouring the sheep. The shepherd lay in his hut nearby, not wanting to get up because it was rainy and cold. Not far away, his dog was fighting another wolf and was barking loudly for the shepherd to come and help him. Felix wondered at this scene and told the shepherd some hard things: "Christ entrusted the care of the world to the pope, the cardinals, and to the prelates of the holy Church. Christians who are near infidels bark so that the pope and holy men may come running to destroy all errors against the holy Christian faith. I feel sorrow and pity for the sheep I see killed by the wolf, as well as for the dog fighting with no one to help him. What a wonder it is that the dog, who lacks the use of reason, understands and carries out the task entrusted to him, whereas you, who are shepherd, do not carry out the task entrusted to you."[463]

Lull was not a Dominican, but he was a *Domini canis*, a hound of the

458. "Deus sab que vos, Fe, havets fet vostre poder en voler convertir los infeels . . ., e es aytàn gran vostre mérit com si vos havíets convertits los infeel que tant desirats convertir." *Libre de Blanquerna* 43 (p. 141).
459. *Contemporary Life* 36.
460. Burns 1971, 1395.
461. Luttrell 1965, 125.
462. Daniel 1993, 141.
463. *Felix* VIII, prologue (pp. 826–27).

Lord, barking loud and indefatigably. And he had a clearer idea than the Christian authorities themselves about the task they and the faithful should be carrying out. Because God had placed the faith for safekeeping in the hands of the pope, cardinals, prelates, and other churchmen, they should "keep it and defend it against the disbelief of Jews, Saracens, heretics, and unbelievers, who are continually trying to destroy the Roman faith." For Lull, there was no question about what was to be done: "Christian laymen should guard and maintain the faith by force of arms, and churchmen should maintain it by force of reason and Scriptures, of prayers and of holy life." Shedding tears that never dried, Felix sighed: "Ah, Lord God, in what a state of dishonor lies the holy Christian faith, for the defense and exaltation of which You willed to be man and to deliver that man unto death! And the Saracens, who are sons of disbelief, hold and possess that Holy Land beyond the sea where the faith was founded and given in charge of the holy Church! Ah, Lord God, when will the day come that combatants, lovers, and praisers will set out, using physical and spiritual arms, to bring honor to the faith and destroy the error by which faith is put to such shame in this world?"[464]

Lull sometimes argued that "intellectual war" carried out by "the arms of devotion and desire of martyrdom" might be more efficient than "sensual war" waged by "arms of iron."[465] He said that peaceful discussions were "a much more effective war."[466] But this does not mean that he advocated the mission in one phase of his life to advocate the crusade in another, as some historians have maintained. He knew that the Church had two swords.[467] Peaceful persuasion and war were not alternatives. He knew how to tailor his arguments for particular projects according to his audience. But his grand project was one and unchangeable. Mission was not, as has been argued, the end to which crusade served as the means.[468] Both crusade and mission were means to the same end. War by peace or war by war were to be used according to expedience. Most often it seemed most expedient to use them both to attain the desired end.[469]

464. Ibid., VIII,63 (p. 884).

465. *Liber contra Antichristum;* quoted in Hillgarth 1971, 245.

466. *Contemplationes in Deum;* summarized in Gottron 1912, 20.

467. *Liber de fine* De divisione huius libri (p. 69); *Disputatio clerici et Raymundi phantastici;* quoted in Wieruszowski 1971, 151.

468. Hillgarth 1971, 50.

469. Cf. Gottron 1912; Atiya 1938, chap. 4; Wieruszowski, "Ramon Lulle" (in id. 1971); Hillgarth 1971, chap. 1–2; Bonner 1985a; Kedar 1988, 189–99.

The end toward which both Lull's contemplative life and his active life were directed was peace in this world. Not surprisingly, this ideal appears in Lull's "most important" crusading treatise, the *Liber de fine*.[470] The ideal of peace rested on the idea of unity, and unity was seen as a state in which "difference" and "contrariety" were eliminated and "concordance" reigned. Such an order would reflect divine unity. The dissimilarities and disagreements that caused peoples to be "enemies with one another and to be at war, killing one another and falling captive to one another," were "difference or contrariety of faith or custom." From this followed the ideal solution: "For just as we have one God, one Creator, one Lord, we should also have one faith, one religion, one sect, one manner of loving and honoring God."[471] In a later work, Lull depicted the diversity of tongues as another cause for war among men. He wanted to "destroy the diversity of languages"[472] and reduce all existing languages to one.[473] Consequently, he had to figure out by means of which language all men "might be brought together, that they might have understanding, and love one another, and agree in the service of God."[474] Because the linguistic question was linked to the service of God, Lull's choice was not difficult. He chose Latin, because "Latin is the most general tongue . . . and in Latin are all our books."[475] And because God had given to the papacy the power "for the ordering of the world,"[476] the pope as the ruler of Lull's ideal one and indivisible world had to ensure that all men learn Latin. This would bring to pass a world in which there was but one language, one belief, and one faith.[477] For Lull there was no doubt that the one God to be loved and known by the whole world was the Christian God,[478] and that the whole world should be given over to Christianity.[479] This would bring about "the greatest good possible in the world" and would be the work of the greatest wisdom, for "the greatest wisdom consists in trying to get the entire world

---

470. *Liber de fine* III (p. 93); Hillgarth 1971, 65.
471. *Book of the Gentile* epilogue (pp. 301–2).
472. *Libre de Blanquerna* 94 (p. 364).
473. Ibid., 94 (p. 365).
474. Ibid., 94 (p. 364); *Blanquerna* (p. 396).
475. *Libre de Blanquerna* 94 (p. 364); *Blanquerna* (p. 396).
476. *Blanquerna* 78 (p. 314). For Lull's utopian papal world order, see ibid., 80, 88 (pp. 325, 373 ff.).
477. "[C]om en tot lo mon no sia mas un lenguatge, una creença, una fe." *Libre de Blanquerna* 94 (p. 364).
478. *Felix* VIII,44 (p. 836)
479. Ibid., VIII,89 (p. 982). Cf. Gibert 1962, 146: "el fin era reducir el mundo a la paz en la unidad de la fe romana con el poder de las dos espadas."

beneath a single faith, believing what the Christians believe." [480] Lull's basic conviction was that the Christians were "in the way of truth." [481]

A plurality of gods and religions was generally at odds with the structure of the universe. But when Lull spoke more concretely, it was the existence of Muslims that appeared as the greatest obstacle to peaceful unity. [482] It was the Saracens who impeded the universe (*ipsi sunt qui impediunt universum*). [483] Their existence was a defect in its structure. Since order meant understanding and loving God, the Saracens were an element of disorder. [484] Their "disbelief" was disobedience to God. [485] They were the embodiment of falsehood against truth. [486] They were injustice materialized, since they contradicted God's justice. [487] Last but not least, they were an offence to the beauty that is in God, for "it is a very ugly thing that the Saracens hold and possess the Holy Land where Jesus Christ was born and died." [488]

Given Lull's mental constellation, nothing important would change even if the Muslims were at peace with the Christians. The Christians could not be at peace with those who, simply by their existence, were disturbing the unity of universe in God which is peace. We should take Lull seriously when he writes about making peace between Christian kings so they can go on a crusade. [489] But we cannot take him at his word when he speaks about peace between the Christians and Saracens. [490] In his universe, peace is only imaginable among Christians, and universal peace presupposes universal Christian rule. Peace between the Christians and the Saracens could only be genuine if the Saracens ceased to be Muslims and became Christians. This same principle applied to all infidels. The logic of Lull's peace was spelled out very clearly in the *Blanquerna*. The hero, Blanquerna, was a bishop who desired to act as peacemaker (*volc haver lufici de pacificar*). The Jews once complained to him because the Christians, on the eve of the Passover, had stoned and

480. *Felix* VIII,67 (p. 900). On *bonum publicum et communem*, cf. *Liber de fine* III (pp. 92–93); Wieruszowski 1971, 157.
481. *Blanquerna* 77 (p. 307).
482. Cf. Hillgarth 1971, 12.
483. *De loqutione angelorum* (quoted in Gottron 1912, 50 n. 5).
484. See *Felix* VIII,82 (p. 956).
485. See ibid., VIII,81 (p. 954).
486. See ibid., VIII,79 (p. 941).
487. See ibid., VIII,66 (p. 894).
488. Ibid., VIII,93 (p. 999). This statement immediately followed Lull's reflections on the ugliness of a beautiful woman's excrement. See n. 448.
489. *Blanquerna* 81 (p. 334).
490. Cf. *De participatione Christianorum et Saracenorum*, 171.

wounded two of their number. "Long did the Bishop think upon the complaints which the Jews had made concerning the Christians, and he reflected that if Christians and Jews held one belief, the ill-will and strife that was among them would cease; wherefore the Bishop went every Sabbath to the Synagogue to preach and hold discussion with the Jews, to the end that they might become Christians, and praise and bless Jesus Christ, and be at peace with the Christians."[491]

Because the Saracens were the worst among the non-Christians, only if there were peace between Christians and Saracens would there be peace in the world.[492] The precondition stood: the Saracens must renounce their disbelief and embrace Christianity. Lull's peace was Christian peace, a peace that implied waging and winning war—spiritual or material (but most likely spiritual and material) war—against the Muslims and other unbelievers, including heretic and schismatic Christians.[493] It was *pax Christiana,* described in the *Blanquerna* as "a society of nations presided over by the papacy."[494] Peace was to be obtained by bringing the world back to the divine order by whatever means necessary: peace was the transformation of the world into the City of God.[495]

Lull longed for the presence of people like St. Bernard in his own time.[496] One Lullian scholar, however, has seen St. Bernard risen from the dead in Lull. When Lull preached the crusade in Pisa in 1308—proposing the founding of a new order, the Order of Christian Religious Knights that would devote itself to "doing continual battle against the treacherous Saracens for the recovery of the Holy Land"[497]—he was so successful that, to this scholar, he appears "almost a St. Bernard *redivivus.*"[498] But the age of St. Bernard had passed. Bernard had praised the Templars, the model Christian knighthood. But the Templars were destroyed during Lull's lifetime—not by the enemies of the cross, but by the most Christian king, King Philip IV of France. Even as Lull preached in Pisa, the Templars had been accused of heresy, and members of the order had

491. *Blanquerna* 75 (p. 296).
492. *De participatione,* 171.
493. In the *Liber de acquisitione terrae sanctae,* Lull advocated Latin conquest of Constantinople. Gottron 1912, 40; Hillgarth 1971, 84.
494. Thus characterized by Hillgarth 1971, 41. Cf. Gottron 1912, 9 f. See also Pindl 1996, 40, for whom some aspects of Lull's utopian world peace are reminiscent of the United Nations General Assembly.
495. See Wieruszowski 1971, 152, 159.
496. *Felix* X,121 (p. 1099).
497. *Contemporary Life* 42.
498. Hillgarth 1971, 100.

been arrested by Philip's agents. In the year 1310, fifty-four Templars, accused of being relapsed heretics, were burned at the stake near Paris. At the Council of Vienne (1311–12), the pope gave in to the pressure from the French monarch and abolished the Order of the Temple. In 1314, James of Molay, the last Master General of Bernard's *milites Christi*, was executed.[499]

Lull did not defend the Templars, even though he was personally indebted to their leader. During his travels to Cyprus, Lull had fallen ill and been "cheerfully received" by James of Molay, who took Lull into his house until he recovered.[500] What exactly Lull thought of the accusations against his former host and his knights is difficult to know. He may have "allowed himself to be convinced of the Templars' guilt."[501] What is known, however, is that precisely in the years when the Templars came under attack, Lull accepted the "Oriental policy" of the French.[502] An element of that policy, advocated by Philip IV, was the unification of the Christian military orders. That policy had been one of Lull's ideas even before he placed his hopes in the French king.[503] But we do not need to place too much weight on ideas. Lull may have called himself a fantast, but he was realist enough to know that *Realpolitik* was the politics that shaped reality. He wanted to shape reality himself and was convinced that "what I say is possible, it has to happen, and will bring abundant fruit."[504] But for that he needed support. Lull may have lived in his own world, but he saw that in the outer world the future lay in the type of power successfully asserted first by the French kingdom.

For two centuries the Templars had "appeared to be an integral part of the body politic of Latin Christendom, indispensable in the fight against the infidel, in the servicing of the Crusades, and in financing popes and monarchs."[505] The Templars' destruction indicates a significant change in the Christian "body politic." War against the infidel continued to be of central importance. But it was to be carried out differently.

499. See Barber 1993; 1995, chap. 8.
500. *Contemporary Life* 35.
501. Barber 1995, 309.
502. See Hillgarth 1971, 85–86.
503. See, e.g., *Blanquerna* 88 (p. 327). Cf. Hillgarth 1971, 71; Barber 1995, 284–85; Pindl 1996, 40–41. Some twenty years after he had first conceived the idea, Lull pressed for its acceptance at the Council of Vienne: "that of all the Christian military religious orders a single order be made, one that would maintain continual warfare overseas against the Saracens until the Holy Land had been reconquered." *Contemporary Life* 44; *Petitio Raymundi* De secunda ordinatione (pp. 165–66).
504. *Disputatio clerici et Raymundi phantastici* prologue; trans. in Gottron 1912, 96.
505. Barber 1995, 280.

FIVE

The Fall of the Papal Monarchy and the Rise of Territorial Power

The papal monarchy sank with its banners flying high. Pope Boniface VIII's opening words in his famous bull of 1302, the *Unam sanctam*, do not lack confidence: "That there is one holy, Catholic and apostolic church we are bound to believe and to hold, our faith urging us, and this we do firmly believe and simply confess; and that outside this church there is no salvation or remission of sins." The bull was a clear statement of papal monarchism. Firstly, the one and unitary church was monarchical in structure: "there is one body and one head of this one and only church, not two heads as though it were a monster." And secondly, because there was, according to the Gospel of John, one shepherd and one sheepfold, the one head of the one Church held supreme power in this world. Temporal power was subordinated to the pope. "We are taught by the words of the Gospel that in this church and in her power there are two swords, a spiritual and a temporal one," wrote Boniface. "Certainly anyone who denies that the temporal sword is in the power of Peter has not paid heed to the words of the Lord when he said, 'Put up thy sword into its sheath' (Jn 18.11; cf. Mt 26.52). Both then are in the power of the church, the material sword and the spiritual. But the one is exercised for the church, the other by the church, the one by the hand of the priest, the other by the hand of kings and soldiers, though at the will and suffrance of the priest. One sword ought to be under the other and the temporal authority subject to the spiritual power."[1]

1. Mirbt and Aland, *Quellen*, no. 748; trans. in Tierney 1988, 188–89.

Boniface was resolute when he proclaimed that there was no one on earth who could judge the pope. "Therefore, if the earthly power errs, it shall be judged by the spiritual power, if a lesser spiritual power errs it shall be judged by its superior, but if the supreme spiritual power errs it can be judged only by God not by man." The power given to the apostle Peter, whose successors were the popes, was divine. Those opposing the papal doctrine of power were accused of heresy. The accusation must have sounded ominous to those for whom Innocent III's anti-Manichaean crusades had set a model for dealing with the heretics. "Whoever therefore resists this power so ordained by God resists the ordinance of God unless, like Manichaeans, he imagines that there are two beginnings, which we judge to be false and heretical, as Moses witnesses, for not 'in the beginnings' but 'in the beginning' God created heaven and earth (Gen 1.1). Therefore we declare, state, define, and pronounce that it is altogether necessary to salvation for every human creature to be subject to the Roman Pontiff." [2]

This final, dogmatic statement was most probably inspired by Aquinas.[3] But Boniface changed the context, for Aquinas had not written those words when discussing the relation between spiritual and temporal powers,[4] while the *Unam sanctam* was concerned precisely with this relationship. The bull was a declaration of fundamental principles regarding what the papal monarchists considered the right relationship between the two powers. It summed up arguments in favor of papal supremacy that had been articulated over the preceding two centuries.[5] In this respect, the bull contained nothing new.[6] Moreover, Boniface's language in the bull, as well as the claims he made, was guarded and moderate in comparison to the writings of contemporary curial polemicists.[7]

Boniface, whose views of the Church's authority did not go beyond the earlier views of Innocent III and Innocent IV,[8] did not explicitly claim direct power in temporal affairs. Moreover, he categorically denied that he could ever have entertained "such a fatuous and foolish

2. *Unam sanctam* (Tierney 1988, 189).
3. Ullmann 1965, 115, 185; Tierney 1988, 182; Canning 1996, 139. See Aquinas *Contra errores Graec.* II,38.
4. Aquinas *Contra errores Graec.* II,32–38.
5. Cf. Rivière 1926, 405–23; Ullmann 1965, 114; Watt 1988, 374, 401; Canning 1996, 139.
6. McIlwain 1932, 246; Canning 1996, 139.
7. Carlyle and Carlyle 1903–36, 5: 393; McIlwain 1932, 247; Morrall 1971, 86.
8. Cf. McIlwain 1932, 247; Dyson 1995, vi, xiv.

opinion" and that he had ever wished "to usurp the jurisdiction of the king in any way."[9] He was trained in canon law and presumably knew what he was talking about. But canonists had made arguments for papal power much stronger than the one he proposed in the *Unam sanctam*,[10] as had publicists directly supporting him. An anonymous writer commenting on one of Boniface's earlier bulls (the *Clericis laicos*) asserted that the laymen who said that the pope had no power over temporal matters were on the brink of slipping into heresy, and that disputing papal judgments or regulations was sacrilegious.[11] Henry of Cremona, in his *De potestate papae*, set out to refute the opinion of those who said the pope did not have universal jurisdiction in temporal matters[12] and to prove the opposite. Because Christ was the Lord in temporal things and had transferred his dominion to Peter, the pope as Peter's successor was lord in all things (*in omnibus dominatur*).[13] For Arnald of Villanova, the Roman pontiff was Christ on earth (*Christum in terris*), whereas those seeking to belittle the authority of the Apostolic See were the Antichrist's precursors.[14]

The two most impressive statements of the fullness of papal power were Giles of Rome's *On Ecclesiastical Power* and James of Viterbo's *On Christian Government*. The former, completed in 1302, has been considered a source for the construction of the *Unam sanctam*.[15] *On Christian Government* may also have been written before the publication of that bull, and James's considerations on the one, catholic, holy, and apostolic Church may have been either a commentary on or an inspiration for the opening words of the *Unam sanctam*.[16] Both treatises, composed by eminent theologians and dedicated to Boniface VIII, argued that the pope had supreme jurisdiction in spiritual and temporal matters alike, and that secular princes were in all respects subject to his judgment.[17]

Giles of Rome is best known for his theory of lordship. He argued that

---

9. *Address to the ambassadors of the French Estates,* June 1302 (Tierney 1988, 187).
10. McIlwain 1932, 246.
11. The fragment published in Scholz 1903, 479.
12. Ibid., 459.
13. Ibid., 462.
14. Mirbt and Aland, *Quellen,* no. 747.
15. Ozment 1980, 147 (calling Giles the ghost writer of the *Unam sanctam*); Canning 1996, 142.
16. See *On Christian Government* I,iii–vi; Dyson 1995, xvi–xvii.
17. For summaries of and judgments on these two works, cf. Scholz 1903; Carlyle and Carlyle 1903–36, 5: 402 ff.; McIlwain 1932, 248 ff.; Dyson 1986, 1995; Canning 1996, 142 ff.

no earthly power could be justly held unless it was appointed through ecclesiastical power and served spiritual power as its superior.[18] He also argued that there could be no lordship with justice (*dominium cum iustitia*) over either temporal things or lay persons "except under the Church and as instituted through the Church." For he who is carnally generated of a father could not be "lord of anything or . . . possess anything with justice unless he is spiritually regenerated through the Church.[19] Since true justice was from God while sin was estrangement from God, a sinner could not have lordship with justice; and since all men were sinners, and the Church alone could reconcile them to God, just lordship could only be derived through the Church. As such, the Church was more the lord of laymen's possessions than they were themselves.[20] It was "mother and mistress of all possessions and of all temporal goods," and had such lordship "universally and in a superior manner, whereas that of the faithful is particular and inferior."[21] Giles identified the Church with the pope, who had absolute jurisdiction in temporal matters and was "without bridle and without halter," even though—as the one who establishes the law—he was expected to observe the law.[22]

For James of Viterbo, as for Giles of Rome, papal power was "without number, weight and measure."[23] And "while the power of the Vicar of Christ is itself without number, weight and measure, he establishes and determines the number, weight and measure of the other powers."[24] The pope's fullness of power originated in the power Christ had communicated to the apostle Peter and by succession to the popes. Christ had both priestly and royal power and was the king "not only of the heavenly and eternal, but also of a temporal and earthly kingdom."[25] In short, the pope had fullness of power "because the whole of the power of government [*potentia gubernativa*] which has been communicated to the Church by Christ—priestly and royal, spiritual and temporal—is in the Supreme Pontiff, the Vicar of Christ."[26]

We may see better now just how guarded were Boniface's statements.

---

18. Cf. *On Ecclesiastical Power* I,iv–v; II,v–vi.
19. Ibid., III,vii,2.
20. Ibid., II,vii,11.
21. Ibid., II,vii,13.
22. Ibid., III,vii,7.
23. *On Christian Government* II,ix (p. 132). Cf. Giles of Rome *On Ecclesiastical Power* III,xii.
24. *On Christian Government* II,ix (p. 132).
25. Ibid., II,i (pp. 46, 53).
26. Ibid., II,ix (p. 131).

But even though the *Unam sanctam* was relatively moderate and contained no new claims, it was nevertheless one of the most important documents of the Middle Ages.[27] One reason for its importance is its status as a formal papal announcement—the fact that "the pope had chosen to make an official pronouncement of this kind."[28] The other reason is circumstantial: the bull was published during a dramatic conflict between the papal monarchy and the French kingdom. The pope's statement was a moment in a bitter struggle that modern historians see as both a watershed between the high and late medieval papacies and as a great turning point in Western history in general.[29] As such, it is not surprising that the real fame of the *Unam sanctam* grew after the Middle Ages had already waned, especially in modern historiography.[30]

POPE BONIFACE VIII AND KING PHILIP IV OF FRANCE

Boniface issued the *Unam sanctam* in November 1302, in a late stage of his conflict with King Philip IV of France. The conflict had begun in 1296, and concerned the king's right to tax the clergy in his realm. According to ecclesiastical law, the issue had been settled at the beginning of the thirteenth century, when the Fourth Lateran Council decreed that taxation of the clergy by the king required papal authorization. This, of course, presupposed the existence of supreme ecclesiastical jurisdiction, set above the laws of particular kingdoms, and it exempted the clergy from the direct jurisdiction of lay princes. More specifically, this rule secured the curia's upper hand in collecting money for Christendom's war against the infidels. It was precisely in the context of the crusading movement that Innocent III had laid the foundations for a papal system of taxation, "securing agreement to the notion that all benefices should be expected to contribute a percentage of their revenues to the support of the crusade."[31] Papal efforts to effectively collect crusading taxes led to attempts to create administrative order in the West. When, for example, under the pontificate of Gregory X (1271–76), the first truly universal tithe was levied, Christendom was divided into twenty-six collectorates.[32]

---

27. McIlwain 1932, 245.
28. Canning 1996, 139.
29. Ibid., 137.
30. Cf. ibid., 140.
31. Oakley 1991, 47–48. Cf. Powell 1986, chap. 5.
32. Gatto 1959, 87–88. Cf. Riley-Smith 1992, 171, 176.

But in 1296, with their countries at war against each other, the kings of England and France, Edward I and Philip IV, bypassed ecclesiastical jurisdiction and taxed their respective churches without papal permission in order to finance their military campaigns, which were against fellow Christians. Moreover, they used the pretext of preparing for the crusade as the grounds for this tax.[33] In the eyes of many a contemporary, their war must have seemed a sinful waste of resources that could have been used for the recovery of the Holy Land.[34] The pope in particular must have considered the war a scandal. The pontiff had to care for the safety and well-being of the Christian people, and most prominent among his offices was the role of arbiter and pacificator. He was the prince of peace, and anything connected with peace came within the compass of his authority.[35] True to his role as peacemaker, Boniface VIII set out to make peace between France and England. His duty to do so was compounded by his responsibility for the Holy Land. He urged the Christian princes to come to peace so they would be able to undertake the crusade.[36]

King Philip IV, however, saw the pope's peacemaking efforts as interference in his royal prerogatives. The legate sent by Boniface to the French court to negotiate a truce between France and England reported back that Philip had lodged a protest even before the papal letter had been read. In Philip's name, and in his presence, the legate was told that temporal rule in Philip's kingdom belonged solely to himself and to none other, that Philip neither recognized nor had any superior to himself in his kingdom, and that he would not submit to anyone in matters pertaining to temporal rule of his kingdom.[37] Boniface conceded to Philip and offered to arbitrate between Philip and Edward not as the pope but as a private person.[38] But Boniface soon had to take a firm, principled position.

The Anglo-French war appeared especially scandalous to the pope because of the kings' decisions to levy taxes from the clergy within their realms without his permission. Boniface may have used this issue to try to achieve peace by cutting off one of the major sources for financing the war.[39] But the importance of unauthorized taxation of the clergy tran-

33. Ozment 1980, 145.
34. Cf. Canning 1988, 346.
35. Wilks 1964, 445–46.
36. See Heidelberger 1911, 10, cf. 14; McNamara 1973, 40; Schein 1991, 149.
37. Carlyle and Carlyle 1903–36, 5: 375; McNamara 1973, 55.
38. Carlyle and Carlyle 1903–36, 5: 376; Smalley 1965, 40.
39. Tierney 1988, 173.

scended such instrumentalist considerations. At stake was the very authority of ecclesiastical jurisdiction. Well aware of the graveness of the
problem, Boniface made his case against Philip and Edward in unam-
biguous doctrinal language. In the bull *Clericis laicos*, published early in
1296, the pope accused the two Christian kings of "a terrible abuse of
secular powers" because they collected taxes from their churches without papal authorization. He furthermore threatened French and English
prelates and ecclesiastical persons with excommunication if they paid
anything to the kings under the pretext of any obligation "without the
express leave of the said [Apostolic] see."[40]

With the publication of the *Clericis laicos* the conflict between the
pope and the lay princes burst into the open. The bull cannot be regarded
as a great diplomatic maneuver. Boniface may not have realized the "nature of the threat posed by the new national monarchies."[41] He may
indeed have conducted his dispute with Philip IV with "incautious tru-
culence" and scorned the possibility of negotiation, and by commanding the clergy of England and France to disobey their kings he may have
"caused the quarrel to turn from the start upon the unadorned question
of whether a king is or is not sovereign within his own realm."[42] But
such judgments are easier for modern historians to make than they were
for the historical actors themselves. Boniface and his partisans appear to
have been moved to act as they did by a deep sense of ultimate reality,
in the light of which factual reality was of much less significance: "True
reality, the basis for procedure, is what is known to be right, not the inadequacy of the existing situation."[43] Inspired by righteousness, Boniface appears not to have been aware that his legate to France, instead
of working for peace, was involved in efforts to secure French aid for
deposing Boniface, and that he worked consistently to undermine the
pope's reputation in France and to induce quarrel between the pope and
the king.[44]

Be that as it may, both kings reacted vigorously against the pope's
command to the clergy to disobey royal authority. And both kings eventually had their way. Edward I's outlawing of most of the clergy of England seems to have struck the pope less painfully than did Philip IV's

40. *Clericis laicos* (Tierney 1988, 176).
41. Oakley 1991, 37.
42. Dyson 1995, vii. On Boniface, cf. Morghen 1975.
43. Wilks 1964, 418–19.
44. McNamara 1973, 42–43.

return blow. Philip sequestered funds collected for the crusade,[45] and he deprived the papal government of essential revenue when he forbade the export of precious metals and stones and of all forms of negotiable currency. Pressured by his rivals, the powerful Colonna family of Rome, the Spiritual Franciscans (to whom he was "a new Lucifer on the papal throne, poisoning the world with his blasphemies"),[46] and the worsening financial situation, Boniface felt compelled to withdraw the provisions of the *Clericis laicos*.[47] In a new bull, *Etsi de statu* (issued in July 1297), he conceded to the French king the right to levy taxes without papal authorization "if some dangerous emergency should threaten the aforesaid king [Philip] or his successors in connection with the general or particular defence of the realm." Moreover, the decision to declare such a state of necessity was left to the "consciences of the aforesaid king and his successors."[48]

Thus ended the first phase of the conflict between Philip IV and Boniface VIII. Philip provoked a new crisis, however, when in the summer of 1301 he ordered that a French bishop be arrested on charges of treason, blasphemy and heresy; put on trial; and imprisoned.[49] Such blatant violation of the canonical principle that a delinquent bishop should be tried by the pope alone may have been a deliberate provocation, "calculated to bring about a further and decisive contest for supremacy between the French crown and the papacy."[50] The pope, of course, replied. In a new bull, *Ausculta fili,* he declared that "although our merits are insufficient, God has set us over kings and kingdoms, and has imposed on us the yoke of apostolic service to root up and to pull down, to waste and to destroy, to build and to plant in his name and according to his teaching." Having thus cited Jeremiah 1.10, Boniface warned the king in a fatherly tone: "let no one persuade you, dearest son, that you have no superior or that you are not subject to the head of the ecclesiastical hierarchy." The warning turned into a threat: "For he is a fool who so thinks, and whoever affirms it pertinaciously is convicted as an unbeliever and is outside the

45. Ibid., 46.
46. Jacopone da Todi *The Lauds* 58.
47. McNamara 1973, 58, has questioned the thesis that Boniface had surrendered: the pope may have in fact been making "every effort to clarify a genuine misunderstanding." But on the other hand, in 1298, Boniface reissued the bull in the *Liber sextus,* a new official collection of canon law. Izbicki 1989, 180.
48. *Etsi de statu* (Tierney 1988, 178–79). For the bulls leading to the *Etsi de statu,* see McNamara 1973, 58–59.
49. See ibid., 98–111.
50. Dyson 1995, x.

fold of the good shepherd." Boniface listed a number of Philip's alleged transgressions and asserted the principle that "no power over clerics or ecclesiastical persons is conceded to laymen."[51]

This papal letter, it is said, was burnt by the king. Whether the story is true or not, the bull was suppressed and a forgery, *Deum time,* drafted and circulated in its place by royal agents. In the forged document—a "disrespectful parody," a "grossly misleading simplification"[52]—Boniface was made to say to the king: "We want you to know that you are subject to us in spiritualities and temporalities."[53] The royalist propagandists did not have to work hard to respond to the Boniface they had themselves created: the claim to absolute sovereignty in temporal matters could be supported by no law or custom.[54] In a spurious letter to the pope, Philip replied: "Let your great fatuity know that in temporalities we are subject to no-one." This undiplomatic opening to the letter was matched by the ending: "All who think otherwise we hold for fools and madmen."[55]

The letter's argument is less impressive than its tone. But Philip IV seems not to have relied primarily on arguments. It is true that he commissioned the University of Paris to comment on the fabricated assertion from the *Deum time* that the king was subject to the pope *tam in spiritualibus quam in temporalibus.*[56] The university may indeed have "commanded the sovereign's utmost respect," but it is also true that it was integrated into the king's power apparatus, loyal to the crown, and mindful of the royal favors it received.[57] We may wonder whether the king—even though reputed a "highly educated" man by his contemporaries[58]—was really interested in hearing learned opinion on the issue or simply wanted to demonstrate to the pope that the university was under royal sway. For he did not leave matters to intellectuals or waste time arguing. His maneuvering against the pope was firmly grounded in power politics.

In the *Ausculta fili,* Boniface VIII had informed the king that he was convoking a council to be held in Rome in November 1302. He sum-

---

51. *Ausculta fili* (Tierney 1988, 185–86). Cf. McNamara 1973, 112–13; Dyson 1995, x–xi.
52. McNamara 1973, 113; Waley 1985, 53.
53. *Deum time* (Tierney 1988, 187).
54. McNamara 1973, 114.
55. *Sciat tua maxima fatuitas* (Tierney 1988, 187).
56. "Assavoir se le pape est seigneur de tous tant es choses espirituelles que temporelles." Saenger 1981, 45 (citing *Miroir historial abrégé de France* from a manuscript in the Bodleian Library).
57. Cf. Fawtier 1960, 219–21.
58. Spiegel 1978, 114.

moned the senior ecclesiastics of France to attend, "that we may consider the more carefully and ordain the more profitably what shall seem fitting for the reform of the above mentioned matters [that is, what to the pope's mind was Philip's misconduct, infringing upon the Church's liberty] and for your guidance and peace and health and for the good government and prosperity of that realm." [59] But Philip did not feel he needed the pope's guidance. He forbade French ecclesiastics to attend Boniface's council and summoned his own assembly, so that—as he claimed—his "prelates, barons and other faithful subjects" might advise him. He decided to fight the papal monarch not with arguments but with democracy: the assembly he organized was the first convocation of the Estates General of France.[60] In this *parlement,* which convened half a year earlier than Boniface's council, the king mobilized his subjects for his antipapal policy more than he consulted them about its wisdom. The argument against Boniface—that is, against the claim attributed to the pope by the royalist propaganda—was presented by Pierre Flotte, Philip's keeper of the seal. Flotte simply restated the imputation that the pope had pretended to be the lord of France in temporal matters and to hold the French kingdom as a fief.[61] That sufficed. Newly aware of the usefulness of "public opinion" as a basis for legitimation of power,[62] the king and his ministers generated nationwide support, both lay and clerical, for Philip's action against Boniface.

Boniface was indignant, and understandably so. He protested to the ambassadors of the Estates of France that he could never have claimed jurisdiction in French temporal affairs.[63] The College of Cardinals, to whom Philip's nobles had sent a letter castigating Boniface and refusing to acknowledge him as pope, also wrote in response that "our lord Pope has never written to the king that he is subject to him in temporal things and that he holds the kingdom as a fief." [64] Boniface insisted, however, that "the king cannot deny that, like all the faithful, he is subject to us by reason of sin." As such, he could be deposed, like the three other kings of France who were deposed by Boniface's predecessors. If Philip "committed the same crimes as they committed or greater ones we would de-

---

59. *Ausculta fili* (Tierney 1988, 186).
60. Cf. Fawtier 1960, 224.
61. Cf. McNamara 1973, 117 f.; Dyson 1995, xii.
62. Menache 1982, 140; 1990, 165, 177. On the formation of "public opinion," *Öffentlichkeit,* under Philip IV, see Wieruszowski 1933, 116 ff. Cf. Fawtier 1960, 224.
63. See n. 9.
64. Cf. McNamara 1973, 119; Dyson 1995, xii.

pose him like a servant with great grief and greater sorrow." [65] But these arguments and threats counted for little in France. The grip of Philip's power was firm. Less than half the French bishops attended Boniface's council in November 1302, and it was a fiasco. The *Unam sanctam* he published in its wake was no less ineffective. In reply, Philip sent his minister Guillame de Nogaret to Italy with a band of mercenaries to arrest the pope and bring him to Paris to be judged for usurpation of power, heresy, and other crimes,[66] and to be deposed. Nogaret indeed arrested Boniface at Anagni but had to flee the hostile territory to save his life after holding the pope in custody for a few days. Boniface died from the shock soon after.[67]

Events moved quickly in the aftermath. The papal court moved to French-controlled Avignon during the pontificate of Clement V. The first of a line of French popes, Clement was often described as a weak and pliable Francophile. Some contemporaries saw him as a traitor to the church and called him the Pilate of Philip the Herod.[68] Clement soon acceded to Philip IV's demands. He repealed the *Clericis laicos* and denounced the *Unam sanctam*. In his bull *Meruit* he wrote that "we do not wish or intend that anything prejudicial to that king or kingdom [Philip IV and France] should arise from the declaration of our predecessor of happy memory Pope Boniface VIII, which began with the words 'Unam sanctam'; nor that the aforementioned king, kingdom and people should be any more subject to the Roman church on account of it than they were before. But everything is understood to be in the same state as it was before the said definition, both as regards the church and as regards the aforementioned king, kingdom and people." [69] But this annulment of

---

65. *Address to the ambassadors of the French Estates,* June 1302 (Tierney 1988, 187–88).

66. Boniface's alleged crimes were catalogued by Nogaret, who was Flotte's successor, in March 1303 and further elaborated by Guillame of Plaisans in June 1303. Tierney 1988, 184, 190. Cf. McNamara 1973, 132. Hillgarth 1971, 123, speculates that one reason for the charge of heresy was that Boniface prevented the Inquisition from proceeding against "heretics," probably Averroists, at the University of Paris, the purge of whom was one of Lull's obsessions in his later years. During his last stay in Paris, Lull "repeatedly invoked royal authority against heresies rife in the university." Hillgarth 1971, 49. Boniface incurred the opprobrium of idolatry because he ordered portraits and statues in the new naturalistic style of art. Ullmann 1977, 87.

67. Cf. an eyewitness report in Tierney 1988, 191; Dyson 1995, xv (with further references).

68. Hillgarth 1971, 62.

69. *Meruit* (Tierney 1988, 192). The *Clericis laicos* was repealed in Clement's constitution *Pastoralis* (1306). But Clement's predecessor, Benedict XI, had already loosened the provisions of *Clericis laicos*. See Izbicki 1989, 183–84.

the *Unam sanctam* did not satisfy Philip. He wanted more, and he got it. Clement released Nogaret from the sentence of excommunication imposed by Boniface VIII's immediate successor, Benedict XI, for his actions at Anagni. Clement also assented to the suppression of the Templars, the confiscation of their property,[70] and the burning of a number of them at the stake. Finally, in April 1311, he commended Philip IV for his dealings with Boniface. He pronounced with apostolic authority that the king and his men "were and are guiltless of malicious accusation and that they acted out of an estimable, just and sincere zeal and from the fervor of their Catholic faith."[71] Four months later, the bull *Rex gloriae virtutum* ordered the deletion from the registers of the papal chancery all matter that could be injurious to the king of France. Philip's action against Boniface was once more declared "good, sincere and just," and the king "absolutely innocent and without fault."[72]

The French king had triumphed. Even after Clement V had gradually recovered a degree of papal power,[73] Philip presided with him over a solemn session of the Council of Vienne (1311–12). This ostentatious joint appearance at the last great medieval church council was meant to symbolize the healing of the rift between the French kingdom and the papacy. It certainly showed that the two powers needed each other. The maintenance of harmonious relations with the French crown had been the cornerstone of papal diplomacy throughout the thirteenth century, until the clash between Boniface VIII and Philip IV.[74] Two major objectives the Roman curia shared with the French court were the suppression of heresy and the promotion of crusade.[75] Not surprisingly, both objectives were on the agenda at the Council of Vienne: the ceremonial dissolution of the "heretical" Order of the Temple and the promulgation of a new crusade. But many contemporaries remained unconvinced of the Templars' guilt. Some believed that Philip had forced the new pope to destroy the Templars "in hope of extracting great sums of money from them."[76] As a matter of fact, the Templars' wealth passed into the hands of the papacy. But money was needed for the crusade, and on this account, Philip succeeded in securing for himself more finances. This was easy, since the

---

70. *Vox in excelso* (Mirbt and Aland, *Quellen,* no. 749). Cf. Barber 1993, 228–29.
71. In Tierney 1988, 192.
72. Fawtier 1960, 95.
73. See Fasolt 1991, especially 287 ff. Cf. Hillgarth 1971, 62.
74. See Oakley 1991, 32 f.
75. Watt 1988, 399.
76. Giovanni Villani *Cronica;* quoted in Barber 1993, 230.

bull of suppression of the Templars, *Vox in excelso,* declared that "goods of this order" were to be used "for the honour of God and the exaltation of the Christian faith and the prospering state of the Holy Land." [77] In accord with this declaration, as an eyewitness reported, "a tenth from the universal Church was granted for six years to the King of the French; so that at the end of six years he could go personally to the Holy Land." But, if we are to believe this report, the Church fathers at Vienne were not enthusiastic about this, for "the holy council neither consent[ed] nor expressly contradict[ed]" the grant.[78]

The collaboration of the French king and the pope at Vienne may be seen as the founding moment of the "Church of Avignon." [79] Even in his old age, Ramon Lull was quick to realize what was taking place. He was happy to dedicate his *Reprobatio aliquorum errorum Averrois* to Philip and Clement jointly, flattering them as "the *doctors of the Christian faith,*" and encouraged them to use his book "to root out utterly errors against the Catholic faith." [80] He must have enjoyed the show that took place at Vienne. But harmony and unity between the papacy and the French kingdom—based on a common dedication to crusading and combating heresy, and displayed in the joint chairing of the council by the pope and the king—did not signal a comeback of the good old days. It rather signaled a new chapter in Western history. The old Christian order was becoming a thing of the past.

RESACRALIZATION OF KINGSHIP
AND THE LAW OF NECESSITY

Historians often regard the confrontation between Philip IV and Boniface VIII as a decisive turning point, marking "the end of the Middle Ages" or "the dawn of the modern era." [81] That confrontation appears less dramatic and the suggested break between two eras less abrupt when we trace the beginning of the deterioration of the papal monarchy back to the later thirteenth century. Without those preceding developments, "the humiliation of Boniface VIII would have been inconceivable." [82]

77. *Vox in excelso;* quoted in Barber 1993, 229.
78. *Chronicon Domini Walteri de Hemingburgh;* quoted in Barber 1993, 229.
79. Fasolt 1991, 289.
80. Hillgarth 1971, 114.
81. For these dramatic characterizations, see Arquillière 1934, 489; 1939, 163. Cf. Rivière 1926, 371, on "l'avènement des temps modernes"; Lagarde 1956, 189, on "l'introduction aux temps modernes."
82. Cf. Oakley 1991, 27, 32.

The same applies to the triumph of Philip IV: it is to be seen against the gradual strengthening of territorial—or national—kingdoms, against the rise of *reges provinciarum* (as Frederick I's chancellor called them).[83] But the conflict between Philip and Boniface still stands out as a critical moment. Its special significance, a number of historians agree, lies in the sphere of the relationship between Church and "state." The prevalent view continues to be that this was "the first medieval conflict of church and state which can properly be described as a dispute over national sovereignty."[84] According to this interpretation, in the course of the conflict the advocates of royal power successfully advanced "the fundamental claims of the modern state confronting religious society: sovereignty over property and persons, exclusive exercise of justice, absolute autonomy of legislation, even . . . control over the spiritual life of the nation."[85] Occasional reservations notwithstanding—such as, for example, that France at the time was "indeed still far from being a centralized nation state in the modern sense"[86]—historiography has been inclined to mark this conflict as the moment where "national sovereignty" and the "modern state" (or, at least, the modern concept of state) emerged.[87]

But only a modern historian could write that "by 1300 it was evident that the dominant political form in western Europe was going to be the sovereign state."[88] That was not evident at all to Boniface VIII, Philip IV, and their contemporaries—even the most radical among them. They knew nothing of the "sovereign state." The concept did not exist in the political language of the period, and "no political writer before the middle of the sixteenth century used the word 'State' in anything closely resembling our modern sense."[89] Arguing that "sovereignty existed in fact long before it could be described in theory" and on this basis be-

83. Morghen 1975, 21.
84. Tierney 1988, 172.
85. Lagarde 1956, 210.
86. Tierney 1988, 172.
87. E.g., Scholz 1903, 445; Rivière 1926, 370; McIlwain 1932, 270; Wieruszowski 1933, 155; Arquillière 1934, 491; Lagarde 1956, 191, 198 ff.; Ullmann 1965, 199; 1977, 131 f.; Strayer 1970; 1971, 319; Canning 1988, 346. For a less-than-flattering post–World War II characterization of Philip IV as "the earliest forerunner of modern totalitarian nationalism," see Ladner 1983, 514. A cursory survey of different historians' positions can be found in Fell 1991, chap. 11, and especially 340 ff.
88. Strayer 1970, 57. Strayer, it seems, was true to "Wilsonian progressivism," whose prominent representative in historiography he was. Cantor 1991, 245 ff. Cf. Spiegel 1997, 67.
89. Quaritsch 1970; Shennan 1974; Skinner 1978, 1: xxiii; 1989; Fell 1991, especially chap. 3.

moaning "the inadequacy of the European political vocabulary of early periods"[90] is a strange way of acknowledging that the conflict between the pope and the French king at the turn of the thirteenth and fourteenth centuries was, after all, not a struggle for or against the sovereign state. The "inadequacy" lies not in the political vocabulary of the period, but rather, in describing that conflict in terms imported from the modern era. To style the apologists of royal power who flourished around Philip IV as harbingers of modern ideas of sovereignty and the state is anachronistic.[91] And defending the use of anachronisms through fear of the "great explanatory problems" and "ugly jargon" that "terminological purism" (that is, insisting that one cannot adequately describe past institutions with modern terminology) is expected to create[92] fails to convince. We need to address precisely the "explanatory problems" hidden behind these anachronisms, which were first fashioned by nineteenth-century historiography, were restated in standard works on the Philip-Boniface dispute from the beginning of the twentieth century, and have passed more or less unchallenged into more recent histories of political thought.[93]

Historians have "often exaggerated the importance of church-state conflicts in French political theory, 1260–1303."[94] Moreover, their description of those conflicts as conflicts between Church and "state" is a misnomer. The confrontation between Philip IV and Boniface VIII in particular is better understood as a conflict due to the characteristic medieval overlapping of secular and spiritual jurisdictions.[95] One has to be careful not to regard the kingdom as standing for pure secular jurisdiction or to consider the royal victory over the pope as resulting in a "secular state." Philip IV's successful confrontation with the pope has sometimes been presented as triumphant secularism, based on what historians advancing such an interpretation call the "statism" of "worldly tracts" written in support of the king and arguing for lay "sovereignty" in the "national kingdom."[96] But the outcome of the confrontation between

90. Strayer 1970, 9. On page 22, however, Strayer speaks of the "invention of the concept of the state" in precisely this historical context. Cf. Post 1964, 449, who also writes that "fact preceded the theory."
91. Cf. Fell 1991, 120.
92. See Pennington 1993a, 2 n. 5; 1993b, 284.
93. See Renna 1973, 677, 678 n. 27; "standard works" from the beginning of the twentieth century are, especially, Scholz 1903, and Rivière 1926.
94. Renna 1978, 310.
95. Cf. Erickson 1967, 288.
96. See, e.g., Scholz 1903, 351–52. Cf. Renna 1973, 676.

Philip IV and Boniface VIII was actually a devolution of the secular nature of temporal power, a resacralization of royal power.

The pope's humiliation enabled the French kingdom to appropriate for itself "the glamour of the papacy at its height."[97] Granted, the French king had traditionally been praised as the "most Christian" (*rex christianissimus*),[98] yet never had the religious character of the French monarchy been "so stressed as it was now."[99] It was only in the early years of Philip IV's reign that the royal house began using the term "most Christian" for propaganda purposes. Philip was the first king of France to require his subjects to address him regularly as the "most Christian king."[100] That was in line with the "political theology of royal bloodline" that made its appearance during Philip's reign.[101] According to this new political theology, Philip's royal blood gave him supernatural healing powers. But he was not only a "thaumaturgical king" whose touch cured scrofula. He was also believed to be in charge of *cura animarum*, which had traditionally been within the ecclesiastical domain.[102] He was a "theocratic ruler" par excellence. Hostile contemporaries suspected him of striving to ascend to the throne of St. Peter.[103] His flatterers called him an "elect champion of Jesus Christ," "semi-divine" if not "wholly divine," *rex et sacerdos,* and *quasi semideus.*[104] Praised as "the insuperable shield and support of the faith, the strong arm of the Holy Church and the firmest foundation of the whole of Christendom," or as the *murus Jerusalem,* the wall of Jerusalem, Philip assumed the role of protector and tutor of both pope and Church.[105]

Not only the king, however, was venerated as sacred. The people and territory over which he ruled were beneficiaries of the resacraliza-

97. Hillgarth 1971, 107.
98. On this title, see Beaune 1991, 173 ff. Cf. Kämpf 1935, 27 ff.; Hillgarth 1971, 111.
99. Hillgarth 1971, 109. For the sanctification of French kingship as linked to the cult of St. Denis, see Spiegel 1997, chap. 8, especially 160–62.
100. Beaune 1991, 174–75.
101. Ibid., 181.
102. Ibid., 176, 331; Kämpf 1935, 33 ff.
103. Hillgarth 1971, 125.
104. Ibid., 110–11.
105. Ibid., 109–10; Wieruszowski 1933, 146; Kämpf 1935, 45. Cf. Renna 1973, 677. Portraying the French king as the protector of Christendom, the Church, and the faith survived Philip IV. In a work written in 1387 and enormously popular "among laymen and among writers whom we may term non-academic" (Coopland 1949, 21), Honoré Bonet, for example, wrote that the kingdom of France "has always protected and still protects all Christendom, and maintains the Holy Church and the Faith in their estate. Hence the King of France is, par excellence, named, among all Catholic kings, the Very Christian King, and with good reason, for he has never left the right way." Bonet *The Tree of Battles* IV,lxxxiii.

tion process as well. Clement V's bull *Rex gloriae virtutum* depicted the French kingdom as the new Israel and the French as the chosen people.[106] France was *Francia Deo sacra*.[107] It was the land in which the "religion of the Christian priesthood" flourished best.[108] The French became the most Christian of nations—Nogaret spoke of the *natio Gallicana, natio notorie christianissima*.[109] Not surprisingly, it was believed that the French kingdom, "chosen and blessed by the Lord before the other kingdoms of the world,"[110] had been given a special place in God's providential plan.[111]

The outcome of the conflict between Philip and Boniface was sanctification of kingship rather than creation of a "secular state." The royalist propagandists were not fighting the pope's efforts to subject the king to himself in temporal matters—much as it was expedient for them to impute such pretensions to the pope. The struggle was about establishing the king's direct relationship with and access to God. It did not cross the minds of those alleged "secularists" to question, let alone do away with, the divine sanction of kingship. What they wanted to remove was the mediating role of the Church in conferring divine grace on the king. Their task was to "keep kingship sanctified while circumventing the intermediary of the clerical church."[112] The special relationship of the French king and the French people with God, it was argued, excluded on principle the need for any mediator.[113] Royalist apologists cast the French king as a *typus Dei*. They identified him with the priest-kings of the Old Testament, who had safeguarded the chosen people and castigated the priests. These apologists likened the king to God rather than to Christ (in order to undermine the possible claim of the Church, the bride of Christ, to dispensing grace). The ideal king they constructed was "less a king by grace than a king by his similarity to God and prophets of the Old Testament."[114]

As a *rex-sacerdos*, Philip IV was not only head of the realm; he became

106. "[R]egnum Francie in peculiarem populum electum a Domino." Quoted in Hillgarth 1971, 120. Cf. Kantorowicz 1957, 237–38 (on *Francia* as the home of a new chosen people); Wilks 1964, 430; Strayer, "France: The Holy Land, the Chosen People, and the Most Christian King," in Strayer 1971, especially 309 (on France as a "holy land").

107. Kantorowicz 1951, 480.

108. John of Paris *On Royal and Papal Power* V (p. 95).

109. Hillgarth 1971, 110.

110. M. Barber 1982, 22 (citing the royal minister de Plaisians).

111. Wieruszowski 1933, 146.

112. Renna 1973, 680 n. 42.

113. Wieruszowski 1933, 149–50.

114. Renna 1973, 683.

head of the church within his realm as well. Moreover, the realm itself was transformed into the church, to which belonged laymen as well as clergy.[115] Royal polemicists played with the double meaning of *church*, understood "narrowly" as "the clerical community" and "in the general sense" as "the community of the faithful."[116] They benefited from exploiting this distinction while at the same time obscuring it. The Church as a clerical body was not to judge things "outside her"; but because "people are part of the Church," the spiritual sphere was open to temporal jurisdiction. Clerical property, for example, could most justly be spent "where the people's safety is concerned."[117] The resort to the "general" (pre-Gregorian) meaning of *church* made it possible to immerse the Church as a clerical corporation into the people and incorporate it as the community of all the faithful into the realm. The Church was thus subjected to the king, who assumed omnicompetence in the religious sphere as well the temporal.

The right to tax the clergy (over which Philip and Boniface had clashed) was, at least by implication, a fundamental question of Christian order and the argument with which the king had had his way became the founding logic of the territorial kingdom. Philip, as we have seen, taxed the clergy within his kingdom because he needed money to finance his war against England. When that caused conflict with the pope and gave rise to a lively literary production, the argument for the king's right to tax the clergy without papal authorization was grounded in the twin concepts of *necessitas* and *utilitas*.[118] Both these concepts allowed the king to suspend existing laws and resort to the exercise of extraordinary jurisdiction. *Casus necessitatis* customarily referred to emergencies arising from dangers from without, such as defense of the fatherland against hostile invasion, war against political or religious enemies, and suppression of rebels and heretics. A special case of emergency was conflict with the spiritual powers,[119] a case that became prominent in the paper war accompanying the confrontation between Philip IV and Boni-

---

115. See ibid., 685–86; for references to *regnum* equaling *ecclesia* in the contemporary literature, see Scholz 1903, 140, 266, 363, 373.

116. See John of Paris *On Royal and Papal Power* XVI.

117. See *A Dispute between a Priest and a Knight* 297/305, 299/307. (The first number refers to Erickson's critical Latin edition and the second to her translation.)

118. In "Ordonanzen des Königs erscheinen utilitas rei publicae, commun profit, bon estat neben oder in gleichem Sinne wie necessitas." Wieruszowski 1933, 173–74. Cf. ibid., 168 ff., 187; Post, "*Ratio publicae utilitatis, Ratio status,* and 'Reason of State,' 1100–1300," in Post 1964.

119. Kantorowicz 1957, 286.

face VIII. Royal polemicists did their best to represent the abuses, alleged or actual, with which they charged the spiritual authorities as threats to the common good. Once the premise was accepted that the proper functioning of spiritual power was essential for the common good, it must not have been too hard to make this argument stick.

Both *necessitas* and *utilitas* were cited in polemics against Boniface and in support of Philip. That the clergy would use its revenues for "selfish purposes" instead of contributing toward the defense of the realm was considered detrimental to the public welfare. "In any major necessity of faith and morals," John of Paris wrote, "all the possessions of the faithful are common property and must be shared, even the chalices of churches." [120] The anonymous author of the *Dispute between a Priest and a Knight* argued to the same effect: "Nor should the material temple, nor the things consecrated in it, be spared to restore peace and safety to the Christian people." [121] *Necessitas* bound everyone to aid in defense of the realm, and in case of necessity the king was allowed to act in any way expedient for the realm's defense. Public welfare and defense of the realm entitled the king to give, take, and use any property, movable or unmovable, in the realm.[122]

Whereas the notion of *necessitas* was not new, the idea of *necessitas perpetua* was. This innovation occurred around 1300 and implied the indeterminate prolongation of what was by definition a momentary deviation from the rule.[123] Philip IV's France was the model for the new type of power based on this notion, and the old adage *necessitas non habet legem*—necessity knows no law—became its fundamental law. At the turn of the thirteenth and fourteenth centuries, the logic of "necessity," linked with the "defense of the realm," justified actions carrying royal power far beyond its old limits.[124] In the France of Philip IV, the king was freed from law, since defending the realm overrode all law. Pierre Dubois, for example, approvingly quoted Siger of Brabant's com-

---

120. *On Royal and Papal Power* VII (p. 104).

121. *A Dispute between a Priest and a Knight*, 299/307.

122. Strayer, "Defense of the Realm and Royal Power in France," in Strayer 1971 (here 298). Cf. Renna 1973, 681. Ironically, one of the first to link public welfare with the emergency powers of the king was Giles of Rome in his *De regimine principum*. He had written this work for the instruction of the future Philip IV some fifteen years before he composed *On Ecclesiastical Power* in support of Boniface VIII and papal supremacy. The two works, however, represent two conceptual levels of pro-papalist thought. Cf. McCready 1973, 665. Giles also gave the future king instruction on the love of one's country (*amor patriae*). Cf. Beaune 1991, 301–2.

123. See Kantorowicz 1957, 286.

124. Strayer 1971, 297.

mentary on Aristotle about the value of good laws for the government of the city.[125] But in the same work he argued that "in the case of necessity of defense of the realm, that knows no law," the king was allowed to transgress the laws that protected ecclesiastical property.[126] Indeed, what "reason of state" was to be to the late sixteenth century, "defense of the realm" was to the late thirteenth century.[127] There is, however, an important difference between these concepts. In the "reason of state" debates, the transgression of law by the prince was conceived of in moral terms,[128] whereas the limits transgressed by the king in "defense of the realm" were formulated in juridical language. It was thus hard to see the king's extralegal action in "defense of the realm" as an offence against Christian morality. As a result, it was precisely the religious, and not the "secular," character of the new kingship that was affirmed and condensed in this apparently "Machiavellian" moment. With Philip IV, the logic of necessity was permeated with the logic of holy war.

War in defense of the realm became religious war.[129] The crown of martyrdom passed from crusading holy warriors to the victims of wars for territorial kingdom.[130] These developments cannot be explained only by the pronounced religious character of the French kingship and kingdom. They were not limited to France. The "religion" of kingship, it is true, was most notably developed by Philip IV, his ministers, and his propagandists in the early fourteenth century, but a "roughly similar process" of the "fusion of the religious and secular, centered on the figure of the ruler and the perception of nationality," occurred in England.[131] There too, royal and national identity merged, the king's battles were characterized in terms of the welfare of his subjects, the image of the king's war as holy and just was consolidated, patriotism was sanctified, and the soldier of the king was assimilated to the soldier of Christ.[132] Christ himself was nationalized and the English became the new Israelites. "Now the pope has become French and Jesus has become English," was a popular contemporary verse about the battle at Poitiers in 1356,

---

125. "[L]onge melius est civitatem regi legibus rectis quam probis viris." *De recuperatione terre sancte* 132. The reference is to Aristotle *Politics* 3.16.1287b.20. Contemporary answers to the question "Is it better to be ruled by the best man or by the best laws?" are discussed in Renna 1978 (a reference to Pierre Dubois, 318).

126. *De recuperatione* (p. 115; cited in Strayer 1971, 298 n. 30).

127. Strayer 1971, 296.

128. See Fernández-Santamaria 1983.

129. Cf. Renna 1973, 681, 686.

130. Kantorowicz 1957, 244, 256 (speaking of "secular state").

131. Tyerman 1988, 324–25.

132. See ibid., chap. 12, cf. chap. 5–6 (for earlier developments).

where the English defeated the French.[133] And in his opening address to the parliament of 1376–77 the chancellor said that "Israel is naturally the heritage of God as is England. For I truly think that God would never have honoured this land in the same way as he did Israel through great victories over their enemies, if it were not that he had chosen it as his heritage."[134]

The representation of war in defense of the realm as religious war was facilitated by identification of the realm with *patria*. The Christian *corpus mysticum* took new shape in the French fatherland,[135] and the territory of the kingdom was "super-christianized."[136] The sacred soil of France[137] was assimilated to the Holy Land. A distinctively religious character was thus imprinted on "defense of the realm."[138] In a war so religiously colored, the king acted as an instrument of God's will, as a repository of divine justice. He acted in accordance with what was "lawful for him by divine law,"[139] destroying the enemies of the realm and reprimanding the clergy. Sacred in his office, he had a sacred task to accomplish. What was actually at stake in the defense of the realm was the "safety of the Christian people": *salus populi Christianae, salus*—or *pax—genti Christianae*. Nothing was more sacred: "And in fact, what could be more holy than the Christian people's welfare, and what more precious to the Lord than to keep enemies and ravenous murderers away from the Christian people and to win peace for His faithful subjects?"[140] God's interests were at stake.[141]

Defense of the realm—that is, defense of the most Christian kingdom and its most Christian people by the most Christian king—was synonymous with defense of the faith and the Church. Should he fail to perform his duty of defending the faith and the Church, the king would have God's wrath to fear.[142] However, defense of the Church, traditionally a

133. *Chronicon Henrici Knighton* (quoted in Barnie 1974, 12). Cf. Tyerman 1988, 333.
134. Quoted in Barnie 1974, 102–3.
135. Hillgarth 1971, 107. Cf. Kantorowicz 1957, 258. On the concept of *patria*, see id. 1951; 1957, 232 ff.; Post 1964, chap. 10.
136. Cf. Beaune 1991, 175.
137. Cf. Wilks 1964, 430.
138. See Kantorowicz 1957, 232 ff., especially 236–38; 1951, 479.
139. Cf. the shift in *A Dispute between a Priest and a Knight*, 296, 299/303, 307 from secular laws, according to which justice and injustice concerning temporal matters should be determined in normal circumstances, to divine law, which takes precedence in extraordinary circumstances.
140. Ibid.
141. Cf. Renna 1973, 681–86.
142. Wieruszowski 1933, 188.

primary function of the Christian prince, now became secondary. Defense of the realm took precedence. Because the Church was considered an integral part of the realm, defense of the Church became derivative of defense of the realm. And the role of the Church was henceforth auxiliary: to contribute toward defense, not to initiate or direct it. Defense of the Church within the realm made the Church's supremacy untenable. *Necessitas* allowed the king to override separate spiritual jurisdiction originating outside his realm that had exempted the clergy within the realm from his jurisdiction.

The consequences were profound and far-reaching. The king's use of extraordinary jurisdiction eroded the distinction between the temporal and spiritual spheres. With defense of the realm represented as war in the interest of religion, the separation of the two spheres became meaningless.[143] The dualism of clergy and laity was transcended "not by the *corpus mysticum* of the Church, but by the mystical *corpus politicum* of the French *patria*."[144] As the highest temporal ruler, the king appropriated to himself jurisdiction in the spiritual sphere. Deriving his authority directly from God and using his powers without limitation (and, not least importantly, beyond the limits of temporal sphere), the emergency king was high priest *in regno suo*.

These developments were not the creation of royal "absolutism" or "sovereignty" any more than they were the emergence of the "secular state." In particular, we should be careful not to apply the modern concept of sovereignty to conflicts concerning the overlapping jurisdictions of medieval powers.[145] In Philip IV's France, kingly prerogatives remained highly restricted even in the royalist pamphlets, and the king had to consult his "feudal magnates."[146] The thirteenth-century French lawyers in a few instances used the vernacular term *sovraineté*. The term more often employed by Philip IV's polemicist, however, was *summa superioritas,* a common term in the political language of the age.[147] The term used in the *Dispute between a Priest and a Knight* is supremacy.[148]

---

143. Renna 1973, 691.
144. Kantorowicz 1957, 258; for the *corpus mysticum,* 194–232.
145. Cf. Canning 1989, 17–18, 30, 44, 59, 64, 66. For an older, opposing view, see Kämpf 1935, 12.
146. See Renna 1973, 679, 690.
147. See Watt 1971, 18.
148. See *A Dispute between a Priest and a Knight,* 300: By definition, the king is supreme (*rex . . . est summus*) and has no superior above him (*nullus est superior*); by his royal power the king is supreme over the laws, customs, privileges, and liberties (*regia potestate preesse*).

The king was supreme and, as such, *souverain* "over all." He lawfully had "his whole kingdom in his general care," as Philippe de Beaumanoir put it. But this writer also observed that "each baron is sovereign in his barony." What belonged to the king was precisely "some sovereignty." [149] Philip IV did not ignore the customs that supported the "sovereignty" of his barons. And only in case of necessity did he place himself—and himself alone—above the laws concerning clerical liberties. His achievement in the conflict with Boniface was annulling the autonomy and extraterritoriality of spiritual jurisdiction. Spiritual jurisdiction passed into the hands of the lay territorial ruler, with the clergy subjected to the power he exercised in his *regnum-ecclesia* founded on the logic of *necessitas*.

Out of the conflict between the French and papal monarchs emerged a territorial kingdom cutting across and undermining the universality of papal jurisdiction. On the one hand, the king exempted his kingship and kingdom from the jurisdiction of the pope. On the other, the Church became territorially circumscribed, and within this territory, as the "Gallican church," subordinated to royal jurisdiction. But radical as this conflict between the French and papal monarchs may have been, and much as it might mark a historical turning point, it was nevertheless fought within the framework of well-established and conventional ideas and power relationships. In neither theory nor practice was the "papal view" completely overthrown, and the king showed himself reluctant to make "a clean break with past convention." [150] Even though the papal monarchy had been dealt a blow from which it never recovered, the conflict was contained within the "basic constitutional law of Christendom." That constitution was based on the assumption that both the pope and the emperor possessed "universal sovereignty," either de facto or de jure, and that all other forms of power fit into this basic structure to form a typically medieval "hierarchy of sovereignty." [151] The consolidation of territorial powers, be they kingdoms or Italian city republics, took place and was conceptualized in this context.

It is thus not surprising that Philip IV, having defeated Boniface VIII, sought to reestablish cooperation with the papacy. The papacy was not something the king could dispense with. In the Templars affair, for example, "the king was reluctant unequivocally to override the papacy's

---

149. *Coutumes de Beauvaisis* ch. 34,1043. Cf. ch. 59 and especially ch. 60, discussing the "sovereign" powers in war and in making peace and truces.
150. M. Barber 1982, 18–19, 26.
151. See Canning 1989.

well-established jurisdiction over the heretics."[152] He needed the pope
to suppress the order.[153] Generally, he sought to use the papacy as an instrument of French politics at home and abroad.[154] For its part, the papacy played a vanguard role in legitimizing the formation of territorial
powers, especially in promoting the French kingdom. Innocent III's bull
Per venerabilem and Clement V's *Pastoralis cura* were prime examples
of such a policy.[155] That policy, it seems obvious, was part of the papal
struggle against the German (Holy Roman) empire, although when it
supported territorial power against imperial universal jurisdiction, the
papacy was actually undermining its own universal authority. But what
matters here, to reiterate, is that the papacy was not adverse to the formation of territorial power. In fact, the papacy itself had become a territorial power, with the pope exercising temporal power like any lay ruler
in what had traditionally been called the lands of St. Peter.[156]

The emergence of territorial power as such was not contradictory to
the "basic constitutional law of Christendom," which rested on the universal jurisdiction of papacy and empire. Rather, it was the universalist
claims made by the model territorial kingdom, France, that led to the
dissolution of Christendom. In the French case, at least, the claim that
territorial kingdoms or "national monarchies" were antithetical "to the
very ideal of universalism itself"[157] is unwarranted. Philip IV was only
opposed to "all forms of universal domination other than his own."[158]

To say that when "Roman Christendom" had "defined its unifying
structure, Christendom was already no more,"[159] may be an exagger-
ation. But Christendom had begun to decline as the new constellation
of powers took shape with the conflict between Philip IV and Boniface VIII. The decline of Christendom is not, of course, synonymous
with the decline of Christianity and cannot be understood as an advancement of "secularization." It was, rather, the dissolution of an order
unified and maintained by the papal monarchy as the seat of universal

152. M. Barber 1982, 23.
153. Cf. Menache 1982.
154. Hillgarth 1971, 62.
155. For the *Per venerabilem,* see Tierney 1988, 136 ff. The role of the *Pastoralis cura*
(1313) in furthering the case of "territorial conception" of kingdom is stressed in Ullmann
1965, 198. But see Pennington 1993b, 187 ff. Cf. Setton 1976, 171; Canning 1989, 22.
156. A landmark in these developments was the pontificate of Innocent III. For this
reason, some historians portray him as the creator of the papal state. Cf. Morris 1991,
421; Sayers 1994, 66 ff. For the later period, see Prodi 1982.
157. Cf. Oakley 1991, 24.
158. Wilks 1964, 421.
159. Alphandéry 1959, 254.

authority, backed by the universal (even if only de jure universal) temporal power of the empire. And, once again, it was the universalist pretensions of the French monarchy, rather than the affirmation of the territorial power per se, that shook the universalist premises of the "constitution of Christendom."

THE UNIVERSALISM OF TERRITORIAL POWER: FRENCH DOMINION OF THE WORLD

The universalist ambitions of the French kingdom were neatly captured by a contemporary who, in 1308, wrote that Philip IV *es rey et papa et emperador.*[160] Indeed, royal polemicists argued for French lordship over the whole world. John of Jandun, a master of arts at the University of Paris, for example, declared that "monarchical dominion over the whole world should belong to the most illustrious and preeminent kings of France, at least because of their innate proneness to perfection."[161] For Pierre Dubois, writing two years earlier, the king should be more than *imperator in regno suo.* This view seems to have become the official view at the French court as early as 1300.[162] Dubois wished to make Philip IV emperor not only in his own realm but outside the realm as well.[163] For the well-being of the world, he wanted to subject the whole world to the French kingdom.[164]

This desire for world domination was characteristic of fourteenth-century French "national royalism." But claiming world dominion meant striving for empire. Indeed, French royalist pamphleteers in that period exhibit "an almost total adoption of the imperial ideology."[165] This led to confrontation with the empire, even though that confrontation remained more or less limited to a paper war. Claiming the imperial title for France[166] was only one aspect of the confrontation. The other, more prominent, aspect was undermining the universality of the emperor's jurisdiction by exempting France from its sway. Philip IV said all that needed to be said in this regard when he stated that France had never,

160. Hillgarth 1971, 63 (with further examples of the French king's image in the eyes of unsympathetic contemporaries).
161. *Tractatus de laudibus Parisius* (quoted in Hillgarth 1971, 107). Cf. Landry 1929, 158; Zeller 1934, 300.
162. Fawtier 1960, 88.
163. Cf. Post 1964, 448.
164. *Summaria brevis,* 11. See Kern 1910, 32.
165. See Wilks 1964, 428–29.
166. See Kern 1910, 298 ff.; Zeller 1934; Kämpf 1935, 97–105; Wilks 1964, 428 ff.

since the time of Christ, recognized a temporal superior.[167] Many of his
literate subjects said the same time and again.[168] Bishop William Durant
the Elder, for example, explained that the emperor was *dominus mundi*,
whose lordship extended over all the provinces, nations, and princes,
"except the king of France."[169] The anonymous writer of the *Rex pacificus*—perhaps John of Paris[170]—argued that "there are and have been
from time immemorial definite boundaries by which the kingdom and
the empire are divided."[171] Another unidentified author was more specific and explained that France had separated from the empire when
Charlemagne's empire had been divided among his sons. Because France
had been separated from the empire by "an equal division," it was
"equal in dignity and authority" with the empire.[172]

Such denial of universal jurisdiction, even if that jurisdiction existed
only de jure, was the source for the universalist aspirations of the French
territorial kingdom. France confronted both the papacy and the empire
even as empire and papacy were themselves in conflict.[173] I noted earlier
that the papacy, in its protracted conflict with the empire, had supported
the emergent territorial kingdoms' claims for independence from the
empire. But at the time of Philip IV, the papacy appears to have become
more mindful of how much its own fate was connected with the condition and destiny of the empire. The papacy began to realize that French
denial of imperial authority was an oblique attack on papal supremacy.[174] This connection was clearly expressed in the pro-royal pamphlet
Rex pacificus. The pope, the pamphleteer argued, "is not supreme lord
in temporals in regard to those kingdoms that are not under the Roman
empire. Now the kingdom of France is not under the Roman empire. . . .
Therefore the pope is not lord in the kingdom of France, nor supreme in
temporals."[175]

Royalist writers exploited both Innocent III's bull *Per venerabilem* to
support the supremacy of their king in his realm and Innocent IV's rejection of the idea that the king of France could be subordinate to the

167. See Pennington 1993b, 168.
168. Cf. Post 1964, 471 ff.
169. *Speculum judiciale* (quoted in Zeller 1934, 292). On Durant, see Fasolt 1991,
64 ff.
170. Cf. Saenger 1981.
171. *Rex pacificus* (Lewis 1954, 2: 469). Cf. John of Paris *On Royal and Papal Power*
XXI (pp. 220–25).
172. *A Dispute between a Priest and a Knight*, 300/308–9.
173. Cf. Rivière 1926, 371.
174. Cf. Wilks 1964, 426, 428.
175. *Rex pacificus* (Lewis 1954, 2: 469).

emperor.[176] Boniface VIII took a different stance. He attacked the "Gallic arrogance" he saw in the French refusal to recognize the empire. He declared that the French lie when they proclaim that they are independent from the empire, for by right, the French are and should be under the rule of the "King of the Romans and Emperor"—lest the rights of the papal monarchy be infringed.[177] Augustinus Triumphus, a leading curialist writer, compared the "modern kings" of France to Nebuchadnezzar because they, too, refused to recognize any superior.[178] The territorial kingdom's refusal to acknowledge temporal superiors, which eroded both universal powers (empire and papacy), was paving the way to territorial power's own universalism.

The universalist ambitions of the French kingdom rested on the conviction that the sacred kingdom and its most Christian king had a religious mission to fulfill. Philip IV's victory over Boniface reinforced that conviction.[179] The welfare of the French kingdom was identified with the well-being of the Christian faith. At the beginning of the fourteenth century, a Dominican royalist preacher went so far as to liken the French kingdom to the kingdom of Christ. He proclaimed that "properly speaking, no kingdom should be called *regnum Franciae* except the Kingdom of Christ and the blessed."[180] This can be read as establishing intimacy between the holy realm of this world and the heavenly kingdom—or even projecting the this-worldly *regnum Franciae* as the model for *regnum coelorum*.[181] But ascension of the French kingdom to heaven is only part of the story. At the same time, the idea of political society as *corpus Christi* was shifting from a universal to a territorial—"national"—level.[182] Once territorialized, however, this *corpus Christi* could not rest there. As Christ's body, the territorial kingdom was charged with universalist potential and drive. The Dominican's proclamation can thus be read as suggesting that the French king should establish his kingdom in such a way that it could properly be called the kingdom of Christ.[183] Parisian masters of theology designated the French king "the principal

176. See Fawtier 1960, 86.

177. Wilks 1964, 426 n. 2.

178. *Tractatus contra articulos* (quoted in Wilks 1964, 426 n. 2).

179. See Schein 1985, 125 (referring to Fawtier, *L'Europe Occidentale de 1270 à 1380* [Paris, 1940]).

180. William of Sauqueville, quoted in Kantorowicz 1957, 255; cf. 238 n. 138 (with further references); Kämpf 1935, 109–11.

181. See Kantorowicz 1957, 255.

182. Wilks 1964, 431.

183. For France as the "doux royaume de Jésu Christ," see Kämpf 1935, 111.

fighter and defender" of the faith.[184] Others agreed, and saw him and his most Christian people as the vanguard, if not the shock troops, of the *ecclesia militans,* called on to realize the reign of Christ throughout the world.[185]

Once established, the equation of the welfare of the French kingdom with the welfare of the Christian faith was bound to be read in reverse as well. Another French cleric, preaching at the time of the French-Flemish war, declared that he who "carries war against the king [of France], works against the whole Church, against the Catholic doctrine, against holiness and justice, and against the Holy Land." [186] This was a daring proclamation.[187] Not only the Church, as *ecclesia militans,* but *fides,* the faith itself, was now defined territorially or, one may say, understood and determined "nationally." [188] The "national" became the bearer of the universal. This was precisely the logic that eventually destroyed Christendom even as it preserved the spirit of holy war that had been born with Christendom as its *spiritus movens.*

THE KING'S PEACE AND THE RECOVERY OF THE HOLY LAND

The appropriation of the overseeing of the Christian faith by the newly consolidated territorial powers (best represented by France under Philip IV), triggered a reordering of the Christian world. Of key importance for that reordering was a rearticulation of the relation between holy war and peace. At the heart of holy war, as we have seen, was peace. Because peace is a central issue of power, conceptions of peace were bound to transform with the redistribution of power within Christendom, while ideas of holy war remained basically the same. In the changing relationships among the papacy, the empire, and territorial powers, there were competing claims to the authority to make and maintain peace in the Christian commonwealth. In the forefront of these power struggles was, once again, the question of who would control the crusade.

The crusade had not waned with the fall of Acre in 1291. As a movement and as an idea, it continued to be relevant for a long time to come.[189]

---

184. M. Barber 1982, 22.
185. Kämpf 1935, 109.
186. *Sermo cum rex Franciae est processurus ad bellum,* 170. Kantorowicz 1957, 255, saw such statements foreshadowing Joan of Arc's "Tous ceulx qui guerroient au dit saint royaume de France guerroient contre le roy Jhesus."
187. See Schein 1985, 122.
188. Kämpf 1935, 108, 111.
189. Cf. Housley 1992, 1, 427; Rousset 1983, 7.

However, temporal government's role in organizing and implementing the crusade was expanding.[190] This important shift has led some historians to speak of "national crusading." By that they mean that the crusades became more "secular" in nature and began to serve "worldly ambition" and "national interests." This, they maintain, signaled the "failure of crusades."[191] In contrast to this view, recent research has pointed out that the crusade was revitalized by "nationalization."[192] Crucial to the crusade's revitalization was its "cross-fertilization" with a new phenomenon, "national war."[193] Crusading ideology and emotions "infected other sorts of warfare in a process from which emerged the sanctified patriotism distinctive of late medieval and early modern Europe." In fact, according to this view, it was precisely through its "nationalization" that the crusade had "a formative influence on the development of the modern world."[194]

Territorial powers fighting wars for "national" or dynastic interests appropriated for themselves the aura of crusading warfare. The violence committed in the name of the fatherland[195] was sanctified through association with crusading ideas and ideals. Philip IV and his men boasted (as did Pierre Flotte in an exchange with Boniface VIII) that they held "real" power, as opposed to the pope's "verbal" power.[196] But the power they were amassing had to be "verbalized" to become effective. It needed to be connected to Christendom's revered ideals, whose keeper was the papacy. Much of the territorial kingdoms' struggle with both the empire and the papacy revolved around claims to Christendom's common ideals and the institutions in which those ideals materialized. In other words, they often revolved around the crusade, an ideal institution.

Appropriation of the defense of the Holy Land for the defense of the realm[197] has led some historians to mistake sacralization of secular warfare for secularization of holy war. Thus we read, for example, that "the crusader idea of a holy war was all but completely secularized, and its place was taken by a quasi-holy war for the defense of the realm or of

---

190. Cf. Housley 1992, chap. 14.

191. E.g., Throop 1940, vii–viii, 285 ff.

192. Housley 1992, 453 (and 499 for further references).

193. Tyerman 1988, 4.

194. See ibid., 324–25, 327.

195. See Post 1964, 435 ff. For use of the concept of *pugna pro patria* by a prominent crusading theoretician, see Humbert of Romans *Treatise* LXXXV,7.

196. Flotte is quoted as having responded to Boniface's claim that "Nos habemus utramque potestatem" with: "Utique, Domine, sed vostra est verbalis, nostra autem realis." Fasolt 1991, 81.

197. Cf. Kantorowicz 1951, 480; Menache 1990, chap. 8.

the nation symbolized by the 'crown' of France." [198] I find this view questionable. Unqualified use of the term *secular* to describe the transfer of crusading activities from the papacy to territorial temporal rulers is misleading. [199] Speaking of secularization when interpreting historical processes that actually led to a resacralization of kingship seems curious. When territorial powers began to take over the crusade, holy war, it is true, came under control of the secular ruler. But this involved neither a decrease in the holiness of war nor a reduced role for religion in matters of power in the Christian West. The crusade became no more "secular" when it began to pass from the hands of the pope to the hands of the most Christian king. Rather, territorial power acquired a holy nimbus.

There are other problems with the thesis of "secularization" of the crusade. "Defense of the Holy Land" was not replaced by "defense of the realm"; rather, the two were explicitly linked together by patriotic propagandists. In their view, what was good "for the *regnum Christi regis,* Jerusalem and the Holy Land, was good for the *regnum regis Siciliae* or *Franciae.*" Conversely, what was good for France was good for the crusade.[200] The crusade as such (that is, not translated into patriotic warfare) was still held in the highest esteem. In France, the whole ethos of kingship was "inextricably bound up with the rhetoric of crusading." [201] Crusading had become "part of the essence of French kingship," [202] a pronounced element of the "royal ideal of the French monarchy." [203] The pamphlet *Rex pacificus* referred to French kings who had lost their lives on crusades. "Louis, great-grandfather of the lord king who now reigns, died on his way to fight the Albigensians for the defence of the church. His father Philip passed to God while pressing the cause of the church in Aragon. The blessed Louis, Philip's grandfather, paid the debt of all flesh at Carthage for the extension of the Christian faith." [204] It was, in particular, the image of Louis IX (St. Louis, who passed away in Tunisia and was canonized by Boniface VIII) that Philip IV's publicists invoked when they wanted to call the French the chosen people and

198. Kantorowicz 1951, 482.
199. Cf. Tyerman 1988, 340; Housley 1992, 14, 427 (speaking of the increasing importance of "secular leadership," or the "sphere of secular government," in crusading matters).
200. Kantorowicz 1951, 478. Cf. n. 186; Tyerman 1985b, 49 (for the same argument as put forward by Philip VI); Housley 1986, 89; Schein 1991, 161.
201. Edbury 1991, 134.
202. Tyreman 1985b, 51. Philip IV's taking of the cross in 1313 "became one of the greatest ceremonies of the French monarchy." Schein 1985, 124.
203. Schein 1985, 124.
204. *Rex pacificus* (Lewis 1954, 2: 470).

their king the most Christian king: "France was a Holy Land largely because an Ideal Crusader, Louis IX, had sanctified it by his sojourn upon earth and because his blood coursed through the veins of his royal descendants." [205] When royal publicists propounded the idea that the *negotium Terrae Sanctae* was France's particular responsibility and concern, they invoked St. Louis's crusading achievements.[206]

In royalist propaganda, the crusade was an often-deployed and "potent reference point," [207] used, for instance, during the conflict between Philip IV and Boniface VIII and in its aftermath. Boniface, for example, reproached the king of France for caring less about the Holy Land than the pagan Mongols. He accused Philip of injuring "public welfare, augmentation of the Catholic faith, preservation of ecclesiastical liberties," and aid to the Holy Land (*subsidium Terre Sancte*).[208] Royalist propaganda paid Boniface back in kind and branded the pope (after his death) "a devious anti-Christian monster who persecuted the king of France more than the sultan of Egypt and the French more than the Saracens," the one who "cared nothing for the Holy Land and spent the money collected for its aid on persecuting the faithful." He was blamed for the loss of the Holy Land.[209]

Furthermore, neither the popularity of the Crusades nor the enthusiasm for them abated. Western Christendom's ties to the Holy Land were still "very much alive." [210] The Holy Land and Jerusalem remained linked with Christian physical, moral, and spiritual renewal. "Throughout the thirteenth and fourteenth centuries men wrote, read, heard and talked about the Holy Land incessantly." The appeal of the Holy Land and the lure of Jerusalem—the "acme of Christian respectability and resolve"—were "a fixed point in a changing world." [211]

Finally, it is misleading to see the crusade to the Holy Land as "becoming increasingly nationalised." [212] In fact, if we accept the language of "nationalism," it is only the rise of "national" power interests that al-

205. Jordan 1979, 218. Philip IV allegedly suffered emotionally from constant comparison with Louis IX. On St. Louis the Crusader, see Beaune 1991, 97 ff.

206. Housley 1986, 18.

207. Ibid., 89.

208. Schein 1985, 123.

209. Ibid., 122–23. On suspicions that the pope was not genuinely interested in the affairs of the Holy Land, cf. Heidelberger 1911, 11, 23; Hillgarth 1971, 75; Housley 1992, 24.

210. Stickel 1975, 98.

211. Tyerman 1985a, 108, 110. Cf. Housley 1992, 45–48.

212. Tyerman 1985a, 108.

lows us to speak of the "internationalization" of the crusade.[213] When it was decided, during the preparations for the Third Crusade, that the crusaders of each "nation" would wear crosses of different colors,[214] that was still within the unquestioned framework of a unitary Christian West. The colors reflected "feudal, rather than national divisions" (though national divisions had began to emerge),[215] and the crusaders in question should be seen as members of what Thomas More was later to call "the common corps of Christendom," rather than as members of "national" armies. Things changed in the fourteenth century, when the consolidation of territorial powers enhanced the territorial prince's responsibility for, and control over, military organization and warfare.[216] The lay ruler, increasingly able to control his subjects' movements and actions, could now prevent his fighting men and administrators from joining the crusade. Lay rulers' consent began to be an "essential prerequisite to the declaration of any crusade which would affect them."[217] But these changes did not affect either the sanctity or the universal Christian character of the crusading.

What had changed, however, was the composition of Christian universality. The organization of the crusade as an universal Christian enterprise became territorially centered. France is a good example. A new crusading Franco-centrism meant that the "most Christian king" had successfully asserted himself as guardian of the faith and leader of the holy war. And although the pope retained the right of final authorization of the crusade, he conceded to a weakening of his power in this matter. Clement V released Philip IV and his successors from their crusading commitments—in the event of *necessitas*.[218] Because it was left to the king's conscience to decide if his royal person or his realm were in danger—that is, if an emergency situation had occurred—he now had full freedom in dealing with the crusade. The pope's concession to Philip was indeed "a *carte blanche* for inaction on the slenderest of excuses."[219] Much had changed from the times when Innocent III had commanded

213. Morris 1991, 581, cites the crusading endeavor as perhaps the most dramatic aspect of the "growing internationalism" under the late papal monarchy.

214. A precedent had been set by the Second Crusade. Riley-Smith 1992, 110.

215. Cf. Tyerman 1988, 329.

216. Cf. Housley 1992, 430. Powell 1986, 203, sees this shift as occurring with Frederick II's crusade and argues that Frederick's crusading army was a royal army.

217. Housley 1986, 84–85.

218. "[D]urantibus periculo vel impedimento regis vel regni ad transfretandum vel mittendum subsidium non teneatur et super huiusimodi periculis vel impedimentis voluit papa, quod staretur conscientie regis vel successorum." Heidelberger 1911, 25.

219. Housley 1986, 13–14.

the kings of England and France to head the military expedition to the Holy Land.[220]

With the king recognized as the guardian of the faith and the leader of holy war,[221] peace became, once again, the king's peace, *pax regis.* "The king's peace is the peace of the kingdom," it was declared.[222] And the peace of the realm, guaranteeing the safety and well-being of the Christian people, had as its consequence the peace of the Church. This was the message given by the royal advocate to his clerical opponent in the *Dispute between a Priest and a Knight:* the king's power is your bulwark, his peace is your (that is, the Church's) peace, his welfare is your welfare.[223]

Even though he was a territorial prince, the king of France believed he had a universal mission—a belief certainly nurtured by a host of literary pretenders for his favors. The peace of the king was, it is true, in the first place the "peace of the realm," but only in the first place. Such an understanding was implicit in the statement already cited by a preacher from the time of the 1302 French war against the Flemings, who declared that waging war against the king of France meant working against the whole Church, against the Catholic doctrine, against holiness and justice, and against the Holy Land.[224] He did not shy away from stating the consequences of his thoughts: "[P]eace of the realm is peace of the Church, learning, virtue, and justice, and means the acquisition of the Holy Land." [225]

Equating the king's peace with the peace of the Church and with the crusade to the Holy Land was not confined to political fiction writing. The crusade continued to be a vehicle for peacemaking among Western powers. Given the French king's preeminence in crusade planning, Clement V justified his residence in Avignon with his desire to achieve peace between France and England as a necessary precondition for the crusade.[226] French kings undertook peace initiatives in the name of the imminent crusade, and the French presented their candidacy for the impe-

---

220. "La lettre *Mediator Dei* ne propose pas, mais impose aux deux rois la guerre sacrée." Alphandéry 1959, 43.

221. Schein 1991, 147, cf. 145.

222. *Sermo cum rex Franciae,* 170.

223. "Regia manus est murus vestra, pax regis, pax vestra; salus regis, salus vestra." *A Dispute between a Priest and a Knight,* 298/306.

224. See n. 186.

225. *Sermo cum rex Franciae,* 170.

226. Heidelberger 1911, 24, 61. On the Avignonese papacy and the crusade generally, see Setton 1976, chap. 9–13; Housley 1986.

rial title in the West in terms of its benefits for the Holy Land.[227] The failure of Philip VI's crusade to materialize, on the other hand, played a role
in the outbreak of the Hundred Years' War.[228] I anticipate these developments because they shed light on the logic that shaped power relations in the Christian West. But let us stay with Philip IV and his reign
a bit longer.

Philip IV emphasized that the very honor of the French nation was at
stake in the crusade. The popes, it seems, more than agreed. Clement V
continually exhorted Philip IV to take the cross and reminded him (retaining the place of honor for his own papal majesty) that to the king of
France "above all other men after the Roman Pontiff appertains the matter of the Holy Land."[229] John XXII went a step further when he spoke
of "French power, whose aid is second only to that of God in the needs
and expectations of the Holy Land."[230] It would be simplistic to explain
French commitment to the crusade in purely instrumentalist terms and
to see the crusade as a pretext for developing a full program for French
conquest of the world.[231] There is no need to doubt French ambitions
for world dominion, and the French monarch's championing of the crusade was certainly "politically expedient." But the age of "instrumental
reason" had still to come. Even as Christendom was waning, the crusade
was not a choice but was the solemn obligation of a Christian ruler. The
crusading zeal of the French kings from Philip IV to Philip VI was not
mere show.[232] The crusade was "less an instrument of policy than an inescapable part of the burden of Catholic rule." It was "a unique com-
pound of personal commitment to Christ, dynastic honour, prestige,
and political benefit."[233]

If the most Christian king was to live up to his ideal image, he simply

227. Heidelberger 1911, 59.
228. See Tyerman 1985b, 49; cf. 45. Edward III of England (whom English propagandists "without exception presented as the man of peace") also wanted to avoid the outbreak of that war when he suggested to Philip VI a joint crusade against the Saracens. Barnie 1974, 5. At the heart of the Church's efforts, first to prevent the war and then to stop
it, was the intention of furthering the crusades "to divert the attention of Christian princes
from their secular wars." Jenkins 1933, 79; Haines 1983, 153.
229. Hillgarth 1971, 75–77.
230. Housley 1986, 18.
231. Cf. Kantorowicz 1957, 254 n. 188.
232. See Tyerman 1984, 1985a. On the question of whether Philip IV was sincerely
concerned with the crusade as "une fausse question," see Schein 1985.
233. Housley 1992, 449. But Menache 1990, 176, speaks of the "manipulative use of
the Crusade theme by royal communicators."

had to be the leader of the crusade.[234] Philip IV actually asserted himself as such, and in the early fourteenth century the crusade "came near to becoming the preserve of the French." [235] Contemporaries expected that all aid to the Holy Land would come from the French king and took it for granted that any major military campaign to the east would be led by the French royal family.[236] A missionary of the time claimed that "the king of France alone could conquer the whole world for himself and the Christian Faith, without anybody helping him." [237] With this in mind, it is not surprising that most of the crusading tracts of that time (especially after 1305, when the importance of the crusade in Philip IV's policy increased) [238] were addressed to the French court.

However much the writers of those tracts may have been anxious to attract royal attention, please the king's eye, and gain his support for their projects, their crusading literature was not particularly original in either substance or form. From the turn of the thirteenth and fourteenth centuries onwards, these authors generally followed crusading policy as redefined by the Second Council of Lyons (1274–76), summoned by Gregory X. The main features of that policy were a preference for small-scale expeditions over large-scale military operations; professionalization of the crusading army with a permanent, disciplined, and dependable mercenary force; the stationing of permanent garrisons in the Levant; the new prominence of commercial warfare (especially the blockade of Egypt); reform of military orders; innovations in financing the crusade; and hopes for a military alliance with the Mongols, who were perceived, when their invasion reached the Muslim lands, as the glorious champions of Christianity against Islam.[239]

Untouched by the Council of Lyons, however, was the spirit of crusade: the love of peace. Gregory X proclaimed a six-year truce in Christendom as a first step toward recovering the Holy Land, and the Coun-

---

234. Cf. Schein 1985, 124.
235. Housley 1992, 26.
236. Heidelberger 1911, 12; Edbury 1991, 134.
237. See Housley 1986, 17–18.
238. Schein 1985, 123.
239. Boniface VIII praised them as "viri magnifici gentis Tartaricae." On the new crusading policy, see Gatto 1959, 82 ff.; Setton 1976, 111 ff.; Muldoon 1979, 59 ff.; Schein 1991, chap. 1, 167, 169; Housley 1992, 5, 11 ff. For the Mongol invasion, see Schein 1973; 1991, 43f., 87 f.; Edbury 1991, 104 ff.; Housley 1992, 9 f., 21 f., 179 f. On missions to the Tartars and on the Roman curia's hope to win the Tartars over to Christianity (based on a misunderstanding of the Mongols' religion as monotheistic), see Lupprian 1981. Cf. Olschki 1943, 26 f.

cil of Lyons ordered spiritual punishment for those who broke the peace.[240] For authors of the memoirs submitted to the council,[241] peace in the Christian world was the necessary condition of a successful crusade. Gregory X's successors to the See of St. Peter worked for the same goal. Among them, Nicholas IV (1288–92) stands out for his efforts to unite all the forces of Latin Christianity for the crusade.[242] In 1313, Clement V renewed Innocent III's and Innocent IV's ban on tournaments to ensure that the nobility "preserved their energy for the Holy War, as well as to keep them from illegal warfare."[243] This unwavering commitment to peace was echoed by crusading propaganda outside the curia. Mobilizing for war meant a series of calls for peace.

Also influencing the crusading literature of the time was the Muslims' retaking of Acre and the ensuing loss of Latin territorial possessions in the Levant.[244] The fall of Acre prompted an outpouring of tracts discussing events in the Holy Land and looking for an explanation of the "catastrophe." "Never before had there been so many projects for a new military enterprise written and presented from so different quarters as after the events of 1291."[245] While the loss of the Holy Land neither "fundamentally transformed the concept of the crusade"[246] nor brought about military action, it inspired the creation of a new literary genre. In the years 1291–92, treatises on the recovery of the Holy Land appeared: a "new branch of literature which, in volume and importance, occupied a notable place in the literature of the age."[247]

By the time the French king became the main addressee of that literature—which was bristling with solutions to the great issues of world history, the total defeat of Islam, the re-ordering of Christendom, the reformation of the Church, and the apotheosis of the line of St. Louis[248]—the authors had little new to say. The crusading plans composed between

---

240. Cf. Gatto 1959, 80.

241. On these crusade memoranda, see Schein 1991, 22–35; Humbert of Romans's *Opus tripartitum* is discussed in detail in Throop 1940, chap. 6–7. Cf. Daniel 1989b, 49 ff.

242. Heidelberger 1911, 2; Atiya 1938, 34; Siberry 1985, 220; Schein 1991, 41, 46, 51, 75, 135, 149.

243. Heidelberger 1911, 60; Schein 1991, 41.

244. For different views on Western reactions to the fall of Acre, see Stevenson 1968 (1st ed. 1907), 355; Stickel 1975, 95.

245. Stickel 1975, 97.

246. For different views on this question, cf. Luttrell 1965, 127; Stickel 1975, ii, 243, 252; Schein 1991, 73, 139.

247. Heidelberger 1911, 66; Atiya 1938, 45; Schein 1991, 91 ff., 269–70 (a list of these treatises).

248. Tyerman 1984, 170.

1305 and 1312 were "far less original than it is commonly accepted, or than they appear when individual plans are discussed in isolation from the contemporary treatises on the same subject."[249] The question of originality seems not to have been too pressing in that period, when the first anthologies of crusading plans were being compiled.[250] An example of that literature, Pierre Dubois's *De recuperatione Terre Sancte,* probably written in 1306, is interesting precisely because of its lack of originality,[251] which verges on plagiarism.[252] Dubois, a provincial lawyer, has been called a typical representative of the views of the "hundreds of officials who worked for the king throughout France."[253] His *De recuperatione Terre Sancte* knit together various ideas and plans referring to the Holy Land that were in circulation in the late thirteenth and early fourteenth centuries.

ONCE THE WORLD WERE MADE CATHOLIC: PIERRE DUBOIS

Dubois has confused more than one modern reader. Many have passed one-sided judgments on him by concentrating on only a particular aspect of his project. Typical in this regard are those who style Dubois a pacifist. Dubois has been considered "one of the most remarkable men in the history of the peace movement,"[254] and he is standard fare in histories of peace thought and international organizations.[255] At the beginning of the twentieth century, Dubois's ideas were read into articles of the Hague Convention,[256] and the view that Dubois was an ideologist of the *Völkerbund* was accepted in Nazi Germany (where the League of Nations, which had grown out of the Hague gathering, was in disrepute).[257] But the Middle Ages were an era of the "ecumenical idea of *Res publica christiana*" rather than a time of pacifist projects properly speaking, and

249. Schein 1991, 200.
250. Tyerman 1984, 174, 180.
251. Cf. Delaville le Roulx 1886, 49; Scholz 1903, 376, 385; Heidelberger 1911, 70. McIlwain 1932, 269, on the contrary, presents Dubois as "disproof of the prevailing belief in medieval uniformity." For a detailed review of opinions on Dubois, see delle Piane 1959, chap. 1; cf. Heater 1992, 11–12.
252. Schein 1991, 208.
253. See Strayer 1971, 310.
254. Souleyman 1972, 2.
255. For better examples of this literature, cf. ter Meulen 1917; Lange 1927; Hemleben 1943. In Wynner and Lloyd 1944, pt. 2, Dubois appears as the first author in the history of "theoretical" peace plans to "unite nations."
256. References in Zeck 1911, 205.
257. Schmid 1938.

Dubois cannot really pass as the "first ideologist of universal peace." Neither was he an early "modern spirit." But as a discovery of nineteenth-century historians[258] who projected onto him their own intellectual agendas, Dubois has ever since been represented as a secularist modernizer. In a more qualified assessment, he is shown to be "the last voice of the medieval outlook," who occasionally sounded a new note.[259]

The strong religious bent of this French pamphleteer's ideas has not gone completely unnoticed. Dubois has thus been portrayed not only as a practical-minded "secular" reformer but also as a "mouthpiece of the most extreme tendencies of 'religious cesarism.'"[260] Whereas some traits make his work look like "a treatise of modern politics," Dubois shared the "unconscious Manichaeism that runs through the whole of the Middle Ages" and moved within the "occult" and "eschatological" horizons of his own time.[261] The foundations of his thought were those characteristic of medieval political conceptions: the unity of Christian society and the distinction within it of two powers, both ordained by God and both necessary for the *unum regnum, ecclesia catolica,* or *respublica christiana,* outside of which there was neither salvation nor ordered life.[262] And even though some of his reform ideas called into question the basis of that scheme, Dubois was "certainly not a 'modern' mind."[263]

When Dubois is seen as a pacifist or an early advocate of secularist and modernizing ideas, his advocacy of the crusade appears as a disturbing element to be explained away as a mere "pretext" for his reform proposals.[264] But once Dubois is understood as a more or less typical medieval writer, the centrality of the crusade idea in his work ceases to be surprising.[265] In *De recuperatione Terre Sancte,* the crusade became "part of a general reform in all branches of society as well as its vehicle."[266] Dubois's reform proposals were "inscribed within a more general doctrine to which the necessity of the crusade gave the full meaning."[267] Because in Dubois's Christian West there was no contradiction between

258. McIlwain 1932, 269.
259. Saitta 1948, 11.
260. Delle Piane 1959, 55.
261. Alphandéry 1959, 214–15, 221.
262. Delle Piane 1959, 57.
263. Ibid.; Scholz 1903, 376.
264. Kern 1910, 33; Rivière 1926, 343.
265. Zeck 1911, chap. 4.
266. Schein 1991, 217.
267. Rousset 1983, 131.

advocating holy war and arguing for peace, it seems appropriate to approach the work of this "crusade theorist" [268] through his ideas of peace.

Dubois's renown as a pacifist rests largely on his proposal to establish an arbitration mechanism for the elimination of wars.[269] But he left no doubt that his interest was in the prevention of wars between Christian powers alone. His peacemaking device, moreover, should be seen in a broader framework. Perpetual and universal peace within Christendom (Dubois spoke of *pax universalis, generalis,* and *perpetua*) was a precondition for the recovery of the Holy Land. Dubois's reasons for establishing peace among Christians were, first of all, pragmatic: "In order that a sufficient number of people may be induced to journey thither and remain there [in the Holy Land], it will be necessary for Christian princes to live in harmony and avoid war with one another." Otherwise these armed journeyers, upon hearing that their countries were at war, would rush home to defend their possessions. "It is therefore necessary to establish peace among all Christians—at least those obedient to the Roman Church—on such a firm basis that they will form in effect a single commonwealth so strongly united that it cannot be divided, because 'every kingdom divided against itself shall be made desolate,' as the Saviour says."[270]

Dubois was not, however, a cynical pragmatist; his desire for peace had a clearly normative dimension. "Internecine wars among Catholics," he wrote, "are greatly to be deplored, since in such wars many meet death under circumstances which make their status in the world to come very uncertain."[271] Dubois was anxious to avert the Christian from "bodily and spiritual death by making war upon his brethren in faith."[272] As someone who had studied Aristotle at the University of Paris, Dubois quoted approvingly from the *Nichomachean Ethics,* where the Philosopher had stated that to seek war for its own sake was the extreme of wickedness.[273] On the other hand, as a religious Frenchman of his time, he had no objections to righteous war. War fought by the righteous was no threat to their future life and made their life in this world more virtuous. "[W]hen it is impossible to secure peace except by means of war,"

---

268. Housley 1992, 54.

269. *De recuperatione* 12. For Dubois's arbitration plan, see Sherwood 1955.

270. *De recuperatione* 2 (quoting Mt 12.25). (I quote Langlois's edition of Dubois's *De recuperatione* and English translation in Dubois, *The Recovery.* References are to paragraphs of Dubois's work.)

271. Ibid., 2.

272. Ibid., 3.

273. *Nichomachean Ethics* X.7.1177b 8–10.

Dubois explained, "it is permissible for righteous men to seek and even to urge war in order that men may have leisure for acquiring virtue and knowledge after war is over and lasting peace has been established." [274] Such wars were "a means of betterment." [275]

Since war among Catholics was inadmissible, Dubois suggested diverting war elsewhere: killing unbelievers was not only permissible but meritorious. [276] To Dubois and his contemporaries, this solution was a commonplace. When universal peace and harmony among all Roman Catholics had been established, Dubois enthused, "Catholics will be more virtuous, learned, rich and long-lived than hitherto, and more able to subjugate barbaric nations. They would no longer make war upon one another," and "Catholic princes, mutually zealous, would at once join together against the infidels, or at all events send innumerable armies of warriors from all directions to remain as a permanent garrison in the lands to be acquired." [277] Dubois did not tire of repeating the argument: "The whole commonwealth of Christian believers [*tota respublica christicolarum*] owing allegiance to the Roman Church must be joined together in the bonds of peace. United in this way, all Catholics will refrain from making war upon one another." That was the imperative. "Let no Catholic rush to arms against Catholics; let none shed baptized blood. If anyone wishes to make war let him be zealous to make war upon the enemies of the Catholic faith, of the Holy Land, and of the places made sacred by the Lord." [278]

Dubois thus espoused conventional ideas of *pax et unitas* in Christendom. For him, just as for the founding fathers of the crusading movement more than two centuries earlier, peace was both a necessary condition of holy war and its expected result. Springing forth from peace and bringing peace, the proposed "aid for the Holy Land" was, for Dubois, a "new alternative for military force," bringing an end to wars between Catholics. [279] As such, Dubois's planned crusade aimed at nothing

274. *De recuperatione* 2. Cf. *Summaria brevis,* 5.
275. *De recuperatione* 2.
276. Cf. Scholz 1903, 420.
277. *De recuperatione* 70. Heater 1992, 12, has characterized Dubois as a "true herald of a modern style of thinking about European unity"; and Sherwood 1955, 149, described his peace proposal as "an early and important step on the road we are still travelling."
278. *De recuperatione* 3 (the image of the Holy Land as sanctified by the precious blood of our Lord reappears on page 99). Faced with this matrix of European peace thought, Lange 1927, 209, had to admit that, here, "le principe de la paix est . . . la paix entre chrétiens et la guerre contre les infidèles, considéré comme un devoir suprême. La paix n'est qu'un moyen pour faire la guerre."
279. *De recuperatione* 109.

less than Catholic lordship over the world. If Latin Christians would make peace among themselves and successfully carry out the crusade, "the commonwealth of Catholics [*republica catholicorum*] obedient to the Roman Church would be greatly increased in a short time." If the Catholics, Dubois continued, would form a single republic in all kingdoms and places (*si secta catholicorum unam in omnibus regnis et locis faciat respublicam*), "this commonwealth would in the course of time obtain dominion over the whole world [*republica mundi monarchiam*], waxing greater with the passage of the years." [280]

With this grand vision in mind, Dubois was not willing to leave to individual discretion the decisions whether to join the "league of peace" and whether to comply with the regulations of the "league of universal peace." [281] Those petty Christian lords who would not conform to the new spirit of peace were to be punished. The peace-breaker who aggressed against his fellow Christians would be starved into surrender by economic blockade. He and all who helped him in any way would have their property confiscated, and they would be exiled to the Holy Land. Populating the Holy Land and serving as a wall of defense for other Christian settlers, such offenders would, moreover, lead the attack on the enemy into hostile—that is, not yet Christian—territory. They would become the vanguard of Christian expansion. Spiritual excommunication was thus replaced by geographical excommunication. Compared to eternal damnation, argued Dubois, who wanted to reduce the number of the damned, [282] such temporal punishment "will be feared more and will be of more advantage to the Holy Land." [283]

Dubois thought out a number of reform projects prerequisite to a successful crusade. Law and court procedures should be simplified and made more efficient. [284] Military service was to be fulfilled under strict obligations (though in case of emergency Dubois would resort to *levée en masse*). Warfare should be made more efficient and wars shorter—if necessary, by means that approach total war, like devastation of the land, destruction of crops, and starving of populations. In cases of *necessitas*, the king would be allowed to "levy upon and seize the property of

280. Ibid., 70. Dubois added that "it is hoped . . . that this will come to pass in the realm of spiritual, not temporal, obedience." (I argue later in this chapter that this spiritual obedience was not to the pope.)

281. See *De recuperatione* 101, 104.

282. See Alphandéry 1959, 218.

283. *De recuperatione* 4–8.

284. Ibid., 91 ff.

churches and ecclesiastics" to finance wars.[285] Reform of the Church was vital because the Holy Land could not be recovered and peopled by sinners,[286] and prayers necessary to recover the Holy Land could only be obtained from a reformed Church.[287] A thorough moral reform, purification, and unification of the Church would lead to the identification of the Church with the people. That would give birth to one spiritual body politic,[288] in which the Church would be under the most Christian king's jurisdiction. Finally, Dubois envisaged a plan for educational reform. Here, he looked beyond military success in the Holy Land to the future of the conquered territory.

Dubois's new educational system would train Western youth of both sexes for service in the East: for colonization and administration of conquered distant lands. The instruction of students in military arts, of course, was not to be neglected, and students were also to be taught mechanical arts useful in warfare.[289] But central to the reformed curriculum was the study of oriental languages. For, as Dubois asked his reader, how could the natives of the occupied lands be governed by Christians "who understand them no better than they understand the twittering birds of the air, the roaring beasts, and the hissing serpents?"[290] Linguistic skills, here, had ceased to be imagined as a means of converting non-Christians and became instead an instrument of administration and domination.

But Dubois did not forget about conversion. In fact, his discussion of conversion contributed to ideas about the education of women.[291] He wanted to establish schools for Christian boys and girls in every province at the priories of the Templars and Hospitalers.[292] He would have "some wise philosopher" choose children who were to be educated, and the chosen ones would never return to their families unless the parents would refund all the expenses incurred in their training.[293] In an age less

285. Ibid., 121 ff. Cf. *Summaria brevis*, 38 ff.; Scholz 1903, 420; Kern 1910, 31; for Dubois's support for the unification of military orders, cf. *Oppinio* 3.
286. *De recuperatione* 108. This point may be seen as contradicting the idea of populating the Holy Land with those who sinned against inter-Christian peace. See n. 283.
287. *De recuperatione* 3.
288. See ibid., 27.
289. Ibid., 84.
290. Ibid., 57, 117.
291. Brandt 1956, 59. For Brandt, the professional training for women and the plan for international arbitration are Dubois's "truly original ideas." Ibid., 61.
292. Dubois wholeheartedly supported Philip IV's attack on the Templars and confiscation of their property.
293. *De recuperatione* 60.

sentimental about childhood than our own, Dubois was not alone in contemplating taking children away from their parents, although his idea had some specific traits. Duns Scotus, the *doctor subtilis* and regent master in the Parisian theology faculty in 1305, argued that a Christian ruler not only might but should take children by force from their Jewish and infidel parents and have them baptized. He advised the ruler to do this with proper caution, lest the parents be forewarned and kill the children to prevent their baptism.[294] The Dominican Burchard of Strasbourg, writing at approximately the same time, concurred: "It is asked whether Jews and Saracens may be coerced into being baptized by the carrying off of their sons or property. I answer yes, because they are slaves and have no right to property or sons." [295] Dubois, however, would take Christian children away from their parents, using them as a means of establishing Christian domination over the infidels.

Their education accomplished, the boys would be sent from their native country to the Holy Land: some as priests, others to practice medicine and human and veterinary surgery and so help the army and the whole populace. The girls, too, would be instructed in surgery and medicine. "With such training and a knowledge of writing, these girls— namely, those of noble birth and others of exceptional skill who are attractive in face and figure—will be adopted as daughters and granddaughters by the greater princes of their own countries, of the Holy Land, and of other lands adjacent thereto. They will be so adorned at the expense of the said foundation that they will be taken for daughters of princes, and may then conveniently be married off to the greater princes, clergy, and other wealthy easterners." [296]

Once married off, these young ladies were expected to convert their husbands—last but not least to monogamy[297]—and presumably, to have Christian offspring. The theme, again, was not new. Marriage between a Christian (a Christian lady, as a rule) and a Saracen was a popular topic of medieval romance literature. The offspring of the Christian woman and heathen prince is often pictured as a formless lump of flesh that becomes a handsome boy as soon as the infant is baptized, as a shaggy masculine creature whose hairiness disappears upon baptism, or as a child who is white on his right side and black on his left and is

---

294. *Quaestiones in Quartum Librum Sententiarium;* quoted in Kedar 1984, 187.
295. *Summula iuris;* quoted in Kedar 1984, 187.
296. *De recuperatione* 61; cf. 69, 85 f.
297. Ibid., 69.

turned "cler withoute blame" or "fair and lovely" when he receives the sacrament of baptism. It is the mother who convinces the father to have the child baptized—and thus humanized. And when the father sees the baby monster turned white and human, he too adopts the Christian faith and sometimes changes himself in the baptismal water from black to white.[298] But Dubois was not a romancer. He was a political pamphleteer. His educated women's "love of their native land" was thought of as instrumental to the "most Christian" domination in the East—as was their very education.

Dubois's idea of conversion through procurement must have rested on the image of the Saracens—who had seized "that country, which by Saviour's testimony is richer than all others"—as men who "follow such a sensual mode of life, all being at liberty to beget and rear as many children as they can, that not even the many kingdoms and provinces lying to the east, west, and south of the Holy Land were adequate for their needs."[299] Dubois thought of cleverly exploiting their imagined weakness. Yet Dubois's disdainful image of the Saracens contrasted with his opinion regarding the French king on the same subject: he advised the king that he should not leave his kingdom for military campaigns but stay safely at home and beget children.[300] That advice was, indeed, at variance with the medieval ideal figure of the Christian king.[301] The king of France as envisioned by Dubois came close to the image of the Oriental prince.[302] Yet Dubois had good reasons for his advice. Obviously, he did not want his king to die on a military expedition, as had some of Philip's predecessors. But Dubois was thinking of new life rather than death. A believer in astrology, which was popular in his time, Dubois was anxious to ensure that the king of France, lord of the world, be conceived and born under the most auspicious constellation of stars—that is, in France.[303] More specifically, the king's second-born son would be needed as the French lord of the Orient. That dominion was one of Dubois's main preoccupations.[304] He systematically thought of its establishment and maintenance.

Dubois was aware that the patriotic devotion of educated Christian

---

298. See Metlitzki 1977, 136 ff.
299. *De recuperatione* 2.
300. Ibid., 139.
301. Stickel 1975, 248.
302. Scholz 1903, 412.
303. Cf. Alphandéry 1959, 216; Tooley 1953, 67, 81–82.
304. See *Oppinio*.

women was alone insufficient for securing possession of the Holy Land. Nor was killing all the local population a practical solution. A good prince, Dubois wrote, ought not to aim at the destruction of the whole subject people. But sparing even a proportion of the conquered people presented a new problem. Dubois now had to consider how the Christian conqueror should "attempt to gain the love [*dilectio*] of the survivors." Raising this question gave Dubois a place in history as one of the first to elaborate on methods of Christian expansion[305] and to think systematically about the "administration of colonies." In response to his own question, Dubois argued for both exemplary punishment of the "recalcitrants" in order to "strike terror in the hearts of many and all men would be made good," and rewards for the "well-disposed."[306] But that was not all. Dubois also envisaged that "the names of these districts should be changed" and that the lands should be acculturated (as one would say today), so that the newcomers from the Latin West would find there "the joy and pleasure of familiar surroundings."[307]

In one brief tract, Dubois suggested that the king of France invade Egypt and make his second-born son the ruler of the kingdom of Jerusalem and Cyprus. Certainly, Egypt was attractive for its "very fertile" land, but by invading Egypt the French king would also liberate the Egyptian people. As Dubois saw things, the "whole Egyptian people will easily be converted to the Catholic faith and be raised from slavery to freedom."[308] He was, however, realistic enough to note that numerous "warriors" would be needed to convince the Egyptians to submit to their own liberation. In his mind's eye he saw a multitude of warriors streaming to Egypt to acquire wealth—which he judged preferable to their lying idle in their native land.[309] Combined traffic in goods and soldiers would take place in other parts of the "liberated" eastern Mediterranean as well. Probably thinking of the cedars of Lebanon, he wrote: "In those places along the coast where excellent timber may be had for next to nothing they [the new kings of the East] will provide for the building of galleys and cargo boats by which iron and other products abundant in the north, but rare and expensive in the south, may be brought thither, as well as weapons not readily and easily procured there, and other things

305. Kern 1910, 30.
306. *De recuperatione* 117–18.
307. Ibid., 20. Cf. Rousset 1983, 132: "la guerre et la conquête ne suffisent pas, il faut imaginer une politique d'assimilation."
308. *Oppinio* 10.
309. Ibid.

conducive to living and fighting efficiently. Those vessels will carry warriors; in the time of peace, lest they remain idle, they will carry back aromatic spices and other commodities useful to us." [310]

The economic advantages—or, in his words, "temporal benefits"—resulting from the occupation of the Levant were reasonably clear to Dubois. Referring to the system of education he proposed, Dubois explained that "[o]ne result of establishing schools of this sort and sending learned persons of both sexes to the Orient would be that valuable commodities [*res preciosas*], abundant in those regions but rare and highly prized among us, would be transported to us Occidentals in adequate amounts at a reasonable price, once the world were made Catholic." [311] As a special inducement to the benefactors of his proposed schools—the pope, the cardinals and greater clergy, and kings and princes—Dubois declared that for their generosity they would be furnished with spices and any other rare and precious thing they desired "for next to nothing." [312] But to secure such advantages and privileges, commerce, according to Dubois, would be neither excessively pacific nor entirely free. His idea of commerce was far from the Enlightenment idealization of "pacific commerce." On the one hand, traffic in soldiers and traffic in goods would go hand in hand. On the other hand, the Catholic ruler of the "recovered" lands was to control trade and regulate prices in order to curb the "greed of the merchants." Those merchants whose greed Dubois wanted to curb, however, were not French merchants, but rather the Italians, and the Arab and other "oriental" merchants. Those merchants would be forced to embrace free trade. Once "these projects have, by the grace of God, been accomplished" and "Catholics of the same mind" were in possession of the whole Mediterranean coast, Dubois wrote, the Arabs will be "unable to prosper materially unless they share with the Catholics the commerce in their products. This will also be true in the case of Oriental peoples and their products." [313]

There are good reasons to argue that, for Dubois, the recovery of the Holy Land was "a consciously imperialistic colonial policy more than a holy concern of Christendom." [314] His work, it has been maintained, marks a historical shift away from the "imperial" idea to "imperialistic"

310. Ibid., 6.
311. *De recuperatione* 13, 63; cf. 67.
312. Ibid., 68.
313. Ibid., 67, 105.
314. Schmid 1938, 20.

power politics,[315] and in his writings the "first outlines of *colonial politics*" have been detected.[316] Because he portrayed the recovery of the Holy Land no longer as "the accomplishment of a religious goal but already as a conquest of land," Dubois has been characterized as a "colonizer" before his time.[317] In his work, it is said, the notion of one universal Christian society is outweighed by the expression of a national consciousness in which a particular Christian people is believed to be superior and to bear the universal mission of Christianity.[318] And yet, such views of Dubois are riddled with anachronisms.

Dubois's projects aimed at securing for western Christians an ever bigger share of the "temporal benefits" of this world that should "long since have accrued to us." [319] He argued that to accomplish this the Holy Land should be jointly occupied and divided among the western Christian powers.[320] But these powers would not be equal partners in their domination over the known world (which was still Mediterranean-centered).[321] Dubois's fundamental concern was to ensure French supremacy in the Christian West and in the newly conquered territories. The geographical expansion he proposed—the conquest of the Holy Land and also of "Egypt and Babilonia," Tunis,[322] and "Oriental peoples"—was part of establishing French hegemony within the Christian West. The planned recovery of the Holy Land—"the progress [*profectum*] of the Holy Land," [323] as Dubois called it—would be a unifying force within Christendom only to the degree to which Christian powers were willing to submit to French ambitions. Similarly, the idyllic peace to be accomplished through holy war—the entirety of mankind living in peace and harmony[324]—would be universal only through universal submission to France.[325] If French leadership were not universally accepted, the crusade that had been the vehicle for attaining Christian unity and peace would become the rationale for a policy of exclusion and coercion within Christendom, undermining Christendom's very foundation.

315. Kämpf 1935, 102.
316. Scholz 1903, 425.
317. Alphandéry 1959, 220, 222.
318. See Kämpf 1935, 86, 97–105.
319. *De recuperatione* 13.
320. Ibid., 20.
321. Cf. Kämpf 1935, 74.
322. See *Oppinio* 7, 11.
323. *De recuperatione* 141.
324. Ibid., 9.
325. Zeck 1911, 208.

Dubois made this clear when he discussed coercive measures against Italian cities. Should the Lombards, Genoese, and Venetians refuse to render obedience to the French king and pay him the tribute and dues they had formerly owed the emperor, "they will at once be shut off from the intercourse [*tota communio*] with all Catholics obedient to the lord pope and who observed the new plan and statute of peace. Trade in all commodities would also be forbidden them." Once these "recalcitrants" had been brought to their knees and "thoroughly subdued," they would be "sent into perpetual exile." [326] Accusations that Italian maritime republics had hindered the recovery of the Holy Land because of their quarrelsome spirit and selfish commercial interests in the Levantine trade [327] had long been common. But when Dubois unreservedly lent his voice to the new ethos of the French kingdom, he was saying something new.

There were simply no juridical grounds for France to demand that Italian cities render to the French crown the obedience they had owed to the emperor. The demand was based on and fueled by French aspirations to imperial dignity. Dubois's unconditional support for "French imperialism" bordered on chauvinism.[328] He simply declared that the whole world should agree to submit to the French.[329] In the face of the two universal Christian powers, the empire and the papacy, Dubois eagerly argued for French universal lordship [330]—indeed empire—in both Occident and Orient.[331] When he wrote that Catholic powers owed "obedience to the lord pope," he presupposed the pope's obedience to the French king. Dubois wanted to see French kings made "Roman senators" served by the pope and his curia,[332] and the Church subordinated to the French kingdom. He "dreamed of a world in which the Holy See would be in the service of French nationalism." [333] His proposals for Church reform were based on "purely political French plans for dominion of the world," in which the king of France appeared as the future

326. *De recuperatione* 116.
327. Ibid., 10.
328. Kern 1910, 30, called him "der erste Dogmatiker des Chauvinismus."
329. *De recuperatione* 141; *Summaria brevis*, 11.
330. Scholz 1903, 251; Zeck 1911, 8.
331. Cf. *De recuperatione* 116, 117; *Summaria brevis*, 10–20; *Oppinio*. Whereas in the *Pro facto Terrae Sanctae* (1308) Dubois wanted the pope to crown the French king emperor (see Scholz 1903, 436; Alphandéry 1959, 221–22), the crusade was also "intended to create an eastern empire for France" (Daniel 1989b, 89). Cf. Scholz 1903, 411, 436; Zeck 1911, 28–29; Brandt 1956, 37; Alphandéry 1959, 215–16.
332. See *Summaria brevis*, 12.
333. Rivière 1926, 349.

head of the ecclesiastical organization.[334] Dubois also suggested that the French should be elected popes and cardinals and the papal court moved to France.[335]

Dubois has been described as an "enemy of the Holy See" whose work was permeated with ardent love for France and its grandeur and defiance to the papal court at Rome.[336] Yet he did not relinquish the idea of the pope as the maker and promoter of world peace (*totius pacis actor et promotor*), whose duty was to ensure not only that all Catholics would live in lasting peace and justice, but also that they would "honestly strive to recover and protect the patrimony of the crucified Lord."[337] This demonstrates how profoundly medieval was Dubois's idea of peace.[338] It was within the conventional medieval framework of ideas that Dubois advocated a displacement of power. The pope whom he called the author of peace was a pope made obedient to the French, speaking on behalf of the king of France.[339] In a peacemaking project aiming at bringing about French universal lordship,[340] Dubois attributed only a minor role to the papacy.[341]

And yet while clearly arguing for French universal rule, Dubois rejected the idea of a single monarch who would make "the whole world a unit" (*totum mundum unum facere*). He doubted that "there is any man of sound mind who thinks that in this day and age there can be a single temporal monarch for the whole world, who would rule all things and whom all would obey as their superior. If there were a tendency in this direction there would be wars, rebellions, and dissensions without end."[342] "But it is plausible," he added, "that in spiritual matters there can and ought to be a single prince and monarch who might in a spiritual sense wield coercive authority in the east, the west, the south, and the north."[343] True to the categorical imperative of unity, Dubois did, after all, propose a single world ruler (*monarcha mundi*). But this prin-

334. "Inhaber des Kirchenstaats." Scholz 1903, 401.

335. For the "Französirung der Kurie," see Scholz 1903, 415; Kern 1910, 34. As a matter of fact, 112 out of 134 cardinals elected by the Avignonese popes were French. See Setton 1976, 169; Oakley 1991, 38, 42.

336. Delaville le Roulx 1886, 49, 51.

337. *De recuperatione* 40.

338. Scholz 1903, 394; Zeck 1911, 205. For a different view, see Kämpf 1935, 106–7.

339. Alphandéry 1959, 217.

340. Zeck 1911, 64.

341. Daniel 1989b, 89.

342. *De recuperatione* 63.

343. Ibid.

ceps unicus et monarcha was not to be the pope. For Dubois, firmly entrenched in the framework of the "Capetian messianism," it was the French king in whom the two powers would now merge.[344] Sanctification of the French kingship had born fruit. After the king of France had been made a spiritual ruler *in regno suo,* he could be envisaged, through the prism of coercive spirituality, as the monarch of a world dominated by western Christians.

344. Alphandéry 1959, 217.

SIX

Imperialists, Separatists, and Crusaders

The decline of Christendom involved the weakening of the two competing forms of medieval universal power—the papal monarchy and the empire. At the same time, the ascending territorial kingdoms attempted to appropriate Christendom's universalism. During this long and uneven process both defense and questioning of the idea of universal rule played a part. In this chapter, I first discuss the work of three late medieval writers who defended the empire as the legitimate world monarchy, necessary for the establishment and maintenance of universal peace and the defense and spread of Christianity. I then present the ideas of three of their contemporaries whose advocacy of territorial powers called into question the legitimacy of universal rule as such. Neither the proponents nor the opponents of universal rule had overcome the Latin Christian animosity toward non-Christians (the Muslims in particular) or rejected the idea of the crusade, even though the crusading spirit was much less prominent among the advocates of the particularism of power. The crusade idea survived the decline of Christendom, which the crusade had helped to create. In fact, in the second half of the fourteenth century, as the work of the two authors presented in the concluding section of this chapter shows, the crusade idea was actually rejuvenated.

VINDICATIONS OF THE EMPIRE

When a polemicist denies reason in his adversary's ideas, it is often the reasonableness of his own argument that is the problem. The discussions of Peter the Venerable and Pierre Dubois in earlier chapters contain examples of this point. There is, however, a difference between denying the reasonableness of one's adversary, as Peter the Venerable and other Christian disputants did at the turn of the eleventh and twelfth centuries, and the polemical devices of Pierre Dubois in the early fourteenth century. Peter and his contemporaries had critiqued those unwilling to embrace the Christian faith. Pierre, on the other hand, called of unsound mind those who might disagree with his proposal for reordering of the world in favor of the French kingdom.

Whatever this French apologist may have thought, men of perfectly "sound mind" among his contemporaries were convinced that it was not only possible but desirable to have "a single temporal monarch for the whole world, who would rule all things and whom all would obey as their superior." In their view, such a *princeps unicus et monarcha* would not be the cause of "wars, rebellions and dissensions without end," as Dubois contended,[1] but rather would bring about peace.

THE IMPERIAL "SUN OF PEACE" AND THE
INFIDEL "GENTE TURPA": DANTE ALIGHIERI

The most famous fourteenth-century argument for universal rule was penned by Dante Alighieri. Had Dante known Dubois, it would be easy to read the opening paragraphs of his *Monarchia* as a polemic against the Frenchman. But Dante developed his conceptions of secular government, and especially of the empire, independently of the "church-state pamphlet war" of the late thirteenth and early fourteenth centuries.[2] Based on his study of Aristotle, Virgil, and Augustine, Dante wanted to "draw out of the shadows into the light" the "truth about temporal monarchy."[3] To him, temporal monarchy was synonymous with empire. It

---

1. See chap. 5 n. 342.
2. Davis 1993, 72.
3. *Monarchia* I,i,5. (Dante's writings are cited from *Opere*, ed. by Chiappelli. I quote, with minor changes, Nicholl's translation of the *Monarchia* and Hardie's translation of *Epistolae* V–VII.)

meant "a single Command exercised over all persons in time, or at least in those matters which are subject to time."[4] He set himself the task of proving that temporal monarchy was necessary for the well-being of the world, that it rightly belonged to the Roman people, and that the monarch's authority was derived directly from God.

Whatever the time, circumstances, and motives connected with the formulation of his ideas on empire,[5] and however abstract his discussion in the *Monarchia*,[6] Dante certainly had in mind the lamentable situation in his own country when he wrote that work.[7] Once envied throughout the globe, Italy was now "pitied even by Saracens."[8] Since for Dante (as for so many others) *Saracen* was a term of abuse,[9] using it shows how desperate he must have been to see "the Sun of peace" rise again.[10] That rising sun of peace was Henry VII, who in October 1310 set off from Germany for Rome with the pope's approbation to be crowned Roman emperor and restore peace in Italy.[11] The prospect of that event led Dante to write of Italy greening again and bearing "the fruit of true peace." As an exile who desired peace, he kissed the ground before the feet of him who was bringing to his country "the inheritance of peace" that God in His immeasurable love had bequeathed to mankind.[12]

Dante's language in a letter of vicious criticism addressed to Florence, the city from which he had been banished, was less poetic and more conceptual. "The merciful providence of the everlasting King, who does not abandon in contempt our world below while maintaining the heavens above by His goodness, has entrusted to the sacrosanct Roman Empire the governance of human affairs so that mankind might have peace under the cloudless sky that such a protection affords, and that everywhere, in accord with the dictates of nature, the organized life of society may be upheld."[13] For "when the throne of Augustus is vacant, the whole world

---

4. *Monarchia* I,ii,2. Cf. *Convivio* IV,iv,6–7.

5. According to d'Entrèves 1952, 31–32, whom I follow here, there is no definite answer to these questions. D' Entrèves dates the *Monarchia* as c. 1312. Mazzotta 1993, 10, thinks it was written in 1316. Cf. references in Vasoli 1975, 39 n. 2.

6. See Lewis 1954, 2: 443; Wieruszowski, "Der Reichsgedanke bei Dante" (originally published in 1932), in id. 1971, 575.

7. Carlyle and Carlyle 1903–36, 6: 123. Cf. Skinner 1978, 1: 18.

8. *Epistola* V,2.

9. See Southern 1973, 136, commenting on *Purgatorio* XXIII,103.

10. *Epistola* V,1.

11. Cf. Kaufman 1990, 42 ff.

12. *Epistolae* V,5; VII,1.

13. *Epistola* VI,1.

loses its way, the pilot and oarsmen in the ship of St. Peter fall asleep, and Italy, unhappy and forsaken, abandoned to private caprice and deprived of all public direction, drifts in such a battering from wind and wave as words could not express." [14]

These citations give the impression that Dante desired imperial rule in order to see peace restored in Italy.[15] But in the philosophical underpinnings of Dante's argument for empire, peace was a means to a higher end. Temporal power was to serve the end of the universal civil order of mankind (*universalis civilitatis humani generis*).[16] *Humana civilitas*— or *la umana civilitade*[17]—was a notion "embodying political jargon new in Dante's day." [18] It was "the keystone in demonstrating the function and necessity of the universal Empire" in the *Monarchia*, and the one and only point in this treatise where Dante appears to have broken away from "any known tradition of political thought in the Middle Ages." [19] The ultimate end of the "civil order of mankind" was the fulfillment of that particular function for which the human species in its multitudinous variety was created. That function—"beyond the capacity of any one man or household or village, or even of any one city or kingdom"— was mankind's "intellectual capacity or potentiality." Because that potentiality "cannot wholly and at once be translated into action by one man, or by any one of the particular communities listed above, mankind has to be composed of a multitude through which this entire potentiality can be actualized." [20]

Laying the basis for his subsequent argument, Dante declared that "the task proper to mankind considered as a whole is to fulfil the total capacity of the possible intellect [*totam potentiam intellectus possibilis*] all the time, primarily by speculation and secondarily, as a function and extension of speculation, by action." [21] The best conditions for accomplishing this were in the "quietude or tranquillity of peace." Hence, "universal peace," *pax universalis,* was "the most excellent means of securing

14. Ibid.
15. Davis 1993, 69.
16. *Monarchia* I,ii,8. I follow the translation in d'Entrèves 1952, 47.
17. *Convivio* IV,iv,1.
18. Davis 1993, 68. In early translations of the *Nicomachean Ethics,* civilitas was used to render the Greek *politeía,* later translated as *politia.* Ibid.; d'Entrèves 1952, 48. For *politia,* cf. Gewirth 1980, lxxix. In his notes to *Opere,* 981, Chiappelli renders *umana civilitade* as "società civile." Lewis 1954, 2: 486, translates *humana civilitas* as "civil society."
19. D'Entrèves 1952, 47.
20. *Monarchia* I,iii.
21. Ibid., I,iv,1.

our happiness," "the very best means available to mankind for fulfilling its proper rôle."[22] From this point on it was relatively easy to demonstrate that temporal monarchy or empire was the best suited to securing peace and was therefore necessary for human happiness and well-being.

The world monarch's function—which only a single world ruler, guiding the multitude of men toward their single end, could perform—was to keep the whole in order: to create and maintain harmony and unity by reproducing (so far as human nature allowed) the perfection of the heavens, which are governed and directed in every movement by a single mover.[23] Because the world is best ordered when justice is at its strongest, and because the stronger the just man, the greater will be his justice, the emperor as the most powerful and just ruler was necessary to settle disputes, dispense justice, and guarantee freedom.[24] The emperor was the supreme lawgiver. Because imperial law, regulating things common to all men, would be issued from one source, confusion about universal principles would be eliminated. Like Moses, the emperor would leave minor judgments to inferior princes while reserving to himself the major decisions that affected everyone.[25] The empire was thus "that jurisdiction which comprehends every temporal jurisdiction within its scope."[26]

Dante believed that "the Monarch has nothing to desire, since the ocean alone is the limit of his jurisdiction."[27] Freeing the emperor from the *libido dominandi,* Dante envisioned him dominating, in the fullness of justice, the wills of all others,[28] holding them in concord and unity, "for the wills of mortals, influenced by their adolescent and seductive delights, are in need of a director."[29] Thus the image of the emperor as the "rider of the human will—which had appeared earlier in the *Convivio,* where Dante first presented his idea of the empire[30]—reappeared in the *Monarchia.* In the later work he remained true to the basic proposition of the earlier one: that empire is necessary for establishing the "civil

---

22. Ibid., I,iv,2–3,5.
23. Ibid., I,v–ix.
24. Ibid., I,x–xii.
25. Ibid., I,xiv.
26. Ibid., III,x,10.
27. Ibid., I,xi,12.
28. In the *Convivio* IV,iv,4, Dante speaks of the single "prencipe" who "tutto possedendo e più desiderare non possendo, li regi tegna contenti ne li termini de li regni, sì che pace intra loro sia. . . ."
29. *Monarchia* I,xv,8–9.
30. *Convivio* IV,ix,10. Cf. Holmes 1988, 29, 39–40.

order of mankind" to accomplish the happy life.[31] In the *Monarchia* the demonstration of this need led to the conclusion that "at no time do we see universal peace throughout the world except during the perfect monarchy of the immortal Augustus."[32]

Dante pictured the human species without the "Monarch or Emperor"[33] to curb men's wills as a "many-headed beast lusting after a multiplicity of things."[34] Therefore, Dante argued, not only "those parts below the level of a kingdom," but also "kingdoms themselves, must be subordinate to one ruler or rule, that is, to the Monarch or to Monarchy."[35] This view implied that small communities—like city republics (*civitates*)—were not self-sufficient. Self-sufficiency was an Aristotelian-Thomistic requirement for a perfect community, but *civitates* were not perfect communities, since they "could not guarantee the peace without which the good life was impossible."[36] Dante's Monarchy was the world monarchy (*imperium mundi*), which could not suffer any divisions. The Emperor, the sole supreme ruler of the world (*mundi Monarcha*), stood "in immediate relationship to the prince of the world, who is God," elected and confirmed by God alone, receiving his authority "directly, and without intermediary, from the Source of all authority."[37]

Henry VII's Italian campaign ended disastrously, and afterwards Dante's political preferences seem to have shifted. Since Dante remains an enigmatic figure,[38] historians' interpretations of his life and work are sometimes speculative. One such speculation is that the Dante of the *Monarchia* was carried away by his enthusiasm for empire and temporarily forgot "the fundamental Christian idea, that from within and not from without, must mankind be redeemed and saved." Once the imperial cause appeared to have been lost, his passion and interest turned back to the holy Church.[39] From this perspective, his advocacy of world monarchy could seem to have been a "doctrinal error."[40] He was, indeed,

31. "Lo fondamento radicale de la imperiale maiestade . . . è la necessità de la umana civilitade, che a uno fine è ordinata, cioè a vita felice." *Convivio* IV,iv,1.

32. *Monarchia* I,xvi,1.

33. Ibid., I,x,5.

34. Ibid., I,xvi,4.

35. Ibid., I,vi,4.

36. Lewis 1954, 2: 442. Speaking of "the overarching importance of the value of the *civitas* in Dante's political thought" (Viroli 1992, 48) does not seem to be the most fortunate characterization of Dante's political thought.

37. *Monarchia* II,viii,1; III,x; III,xvi,2–3,13,15.

38. Mazzotta 1993.

39. D'Entrèves 1952, 51, 60–61. This interpretation has been questioned in Davis 1993.

40. D'Entrèves 1952, 109.

accused of heterodoxy. The charge was brought against the *Monarchia*
by its first resolute critic, the Dominican Guido Vernani, in 1327, who
accused Dante of Averroism. The accusation was effective,[41] even if not
fitting. It seems safe to conclude that Dante was "more interested in a
universal monarchy than in the philosophy of Averroes."[42] It is unlikely
that Guido would have seen Dante's insistence on the need for a supreme
power to conduct mankind to salvation as a "doctrinal error." The Dominican himself believed that such a power was necessary, but he maintained that that power was vested in the pope and that mankind needed
"no other power" than that of the pope.[43] Therein lay Dante's "error."

The relations among the world monarchy, the papacy, and the kingdoms (as well as smaller units than kingdoms) were clear in Dante's vision. Because the emperor received his authority directly from God, he
was not subordinated to the pope. Kings and princes, in turn, were under the emperor's command. This notion informed Dante's judgment of
contemporary politics. In his letter to the Florentines he represented the
"Roman Prince," that is, the emperor, as the king of the world (*mundi
regis*) and the minister of God. Emperor Henry VII, in particular, was
portrayed as "our Elect, our triumphant Henry," who "carries the burden of the Roman Commonwealth, thirsting not for his own personal
interest, but for the general good of the world."[44] Consequently, the Florentines, who led the opposition to the emperor in northern Italy, Dante
saw as following "monstrous designs"—as subverting the right world
order. He likened his ex-compatriots to builders of a second tower of Ba-
bel who had abandoned the Holy Empire to institute new kingdoms
(*nova regna*). They acted as if the Florentine polity (*Florentina civilitas*)
were separate from that of Rome, that is, outside the empire. They seemed
to be attempting to "duplicate" the empire. To drive home to them the
absurdity of their political designs, Dante asked why did they not feel
the same envy of the "apostolic monarchy" as they did of the empire.[45]
This rhetorical question, however, should not be read as Dante's wish to
see the papacy undermined as well.

The papacy and the pope in his official capacity were untouchable.
Dante, it is true, disliked Boniface VIII; he was the pope's declared en-

41. In 1329, the *Monarchia* was condemned by the Church. On the charge of Averroism, see D'Entrèves 1952, 107–9; Gilson 1963, 212 f.; 298–307.
42. Gilson 1989, 524.
43. Baethgen 1964, 196; Wilks 1964, 32.
44. *Epistola* VI,2, 6.
45. *Epistola* VI,2.

emy.[46] But he nevertheless compared the arrest of Boniface by Nogaret in Anagni to the laying of murderous hands on Christ himself.[47] The French monarchy's support of the attempt on the pope's life was, in Dante's famous verses, *la mala pianta / che la terra cristiana tutta aduggia*.[48] These statements, it is true, derive from Dante's post-*Monarchia* phase. But even in the *Monarchia*, where Dante refuted the papal monarchy, his position on the Church and papacy was orthodox enough. Church and empire were the two guides appointed by God to lead mankind to the twofold goal: happiness in this life and eternal happiness in the life hereafter.[49] But while Dante strictly separated papacy and empire, he did succumb to sacralizing empire.[50] He pictured the emperor as a new Messiah,[51] with spiritual traits and a divine mission.[52] This tendency to sacralize imperial power could easily be seen as diminishing the pope's authority. But it could also be interpreted as a reaction to the advent of national kingdoms, as "an early and premature attempt to nip the incipient concept of national sovereignty in the bud."[53] The "evil plant" (*mala pianta*) of the French monarchy was not only rising against the pope; it was also casting a shadow over "the truth about temporal monarchy" that Dante had wanted to "draw into the light." In his opposition to the French kingdom Dante was close to Boniface.[54] And while Dante rejected the papal claim to "supreme jurisdiction," his own concept of empire was a "vindication of the necessity of some such jurisdiction if the world was to be saved from anarchy, and the blessings of civic life to be assured."[55]

46. Morghen 1975, 41. Cf. n. 63. The *Monarchia* has been seen as a direct response to the *Unam sanctam*. Vasoli 1975, 39. Cf. Mazzotta 1993, 7–8.

47. See *Purgatorio* XX,86 ff.:

> "veggio in Alagna intrar lo fiordaliso,
>   e nel vicario suo Cristo esser catto.
>   Veggiolo un'altra volta esser deriso;
>   veggio rinovellar l'aceto e 'l fele,
>   e tra vivi ladroni esser anciso."

Cf. Kantorowicz 1957, 454.

48. *Purgatorio* XX,43–44.

49. *Monarchia* III,xvi. Cf. Wieruszowski 1971, 568 (stressing that Dante saw the separation of powers as essential for peace), 578 f.

50. Davis 1993, 78.

51. Cf. d'Entrèves 1952, 51; Kaufman 1990, 51.

52. Cf. Wieruszowski 1971, 572.

53. D'Entrèves 1952, 21; Ullmann 1965, 191.

54. Cf. chap. 5 n. 177. Schmid 1938 played Dante against Dubois with good reason.

55. D'Entrèves 1952, 25.

Dante's argument for world monarchy was impressive. On its own terms, it was irrefutable. But I still see it as problematic. One looks in vain for any reflection, on Dante's part, concerning the implications of world monarchy for the world outside his own, or what universal peace might mean for those outside his world to whom it was brought. Of course, it might be demanding too much to expect such reflections from Dante. Like most of his contemporaries, he did not transcend the horizons of his world when it came to seeing and understanding the world outside his own.[56] He was a cosmopolitan, it is true, but myopia is all too often a friend of the cosmopolitan vision. His understanding of the little he saw beyond the limits of Latin Christendom was circumscribed by his own world's normative structure—one from which he did not deviate. But precisely because I am interested in Dante's world more than in Dante himself, or to put it differently, because I am primarily interested in Dante as a point of access to the normative structure of the world in which he lived, both his silence on the implications of world monarchy for the outside world and his few references to the infidels are important for my argument.

Dante may have exchanged Christendom for a "world state,"[57] but the new entity was Christian, and as such, it inherited the problem of Christendom's relations to those considered pagan and infidel. Dante's ignorance of the wider world and its inhabitants is evident in his writings. In the *Divine Comedy,* the crown of his opus, discussion of even contemporary affairs outside Italy lacks clarity of detail. Beyond the narrowest limits of western Christendom, "all is dark." But Dante was not "specially hostile" to the rest of the world that lay in darkness.[58]

Dante's attitude toward Islam, in particular, even if not *specially* hostile, was a blend of indifference, ignorance, and animosity. What has appeared to some historians as sympathy came from Dante's disillusionment with Christendom.[59] He shared the view, popular among contemporary critics of the Church, that the corrupt Christian clergy was to be blamed for the rise of Islam.[60] But this did not mean he said anything good about Islam. The crusade holds an honorable place in the *Divine Comedy,* conveying the poet's animosity toward the enemies of Chris-

---

56. Cf. Southern 1973, 138–39.
57. Morrall 1971, 102.
58. Southern 1973, 138–39.
59. Ibid., 137. Reference is to Miguel Asin Palacios, *Escatología musulmana en la Divina Commedia* (Madrid, 1919 [a number of subsequent ed.]).
60. *Paradiso* XV,142–44; Southern 1973, 136.

tendom as well as his ignorance of what he could only see as "the large indefinite mass of the *gente turpa* who were outside the fold." [61] The Jews, Saracens, and Gentiles personified impiety. Dante pictured them as laughing at "us" and asking "where is your God?" (bringing to mind St. Bernard's meditations on the crusade).[62] It is worth remembering that Dante sent Boniface VIII to hell—that is, the *Inferno* of the *Divine Comedy*—because Boniface had waged war against Christians at home instead of fighting the Saracens and Jews.[63]

The textual evidence provides no direct answer to the question of what Dante's universal peace would have brought to the Saracens, Jews, and Gentiles, but there are ample grounds for speculation. The examples in the previous paragraph are telling enough. Other statements and images of his call for reflection as well. The empire that would yield universal peace was, by Dante's pen, earthly paradise.[64] In the *Paradiso* of the *Divine Comedy,* one would look in vain for a *Saracin.* But one can find Muhammad and Ali in hell. There, in the *Inferno,* the body of the Prophet is perpetually cleft in two from his chin to his bowels, and that of his son-in-law and successor is cleft from forehead to chin. Muhammad has thus the honor of demonstrating that man's body is a wretched sack that produces filth (*'l tristo sacco che merda fa*).[65] This eternal punishment was incurred for sowing discord. Muhammad's and Ali's equals in hell are other sowers of scandal and schism—all secular figures, mostly from Italian factional struggles. It may not be too far-fetched to imagine that in Dante's "earthly paradise," not belonging to Christianity would be punished as a political crime.

---

61. Southern 1973, 139. "Gente turpa" (abject, vile, despicable folk): *Paradiso* XV,145.
62. *Epistola* XI,3. Cf. Bernard, *On Consideration* II,i,1.
63. *Inferno* XXVII,85–90:

> "Lo principe de' nuovi Farisei,
>   avendo guerra presso a Laterano,
>   e non con Saracin né con Guidei,
>   ché ciascun suo nimico era Cristiano,
>   e nessun era stato a vincer Acri
>   né mercatante in terra di Soldano."

For a more comprehensive discussion of the reasons for Dante's condemnation of Boniface, see Grundmann 1977.
64. *Monarchia* III,xvi,7. In the *Divine Comedy,* "God's government in paradise resembles imperial court life"; in Dante's vision, "imperial government and undivided sovereignty reflected God's reign in heaven." Kaufman 1990, 51.
65. *Inferno* XXVIII,26 ff. Cf. Southern 1973, 137–38.

WAR BETWEEN ALL CHRISTENDOM AND
THE PAGAN WORLD: ENGELBERT OF ADMONT

Dante's vision of the empire was a "philosophical ideal,"[66] and his imperialism was correspondingly uncritical. The defense of the empire elaborated by Engelbert, who in 1297 became the abbot of the Benedictine monastery of Admont in Styria, was of a different quality. Engelbert, reputed to be a man of broad learning, was acutely aware of the existing empire's weakness. In his *De ortu et fine Romani imperii,* he tackled both the contemporary crisis and the contemporary critique of the empire. Like Dante, Engelbert relied on Aristotelian philosophical arguments. In *De ortu et fine* he buttressed the conviction that the empire was essential to the safety of Christendom with "the principles of Augustine and Aristotle, the technicalities of the lawyers, and the questions of practical men."[67] Because he composed this work a few years earlier than Dante wrote the *Monarchia,*[68] Engelbert may be credited as "the first to ground the argument for empire on the new range of political concepts and arguments available from Aristotle."[69]

Working within the Aristotelian conceptual framework, Engelbert first dealt with the general history of "kingdom." *Regnum,* for him, was the generic term for government, of which the Roman empire was a species. He began his discussion with the principle that felicity (*felicitas*) is the general aim of all kingdoms and with the classification of human communities according to their size. With these standards he set out to examine the question of which form of human community was the most conducive to achieving felicity: that is, which was the most likely to be self-sufficient (lacking nothing), tranquil (suffering nothing), and secure (fearing nothing).[70]

66. Nardi 1944, 202.
67. Lewis 1954, 2: 444. Cf. Woolf 1913, 280, 296 ff.; Menzel 1941, 401. Black 1992, 93, has rightly added Cicero to the list. On Engelbert's life and intellectual pursuits, see Riezler 1874, 159 ff.; Fowler 1947 (with further references); on the reception and influence of the *De ortu et fine,* see Menzel 1941, 403 ff.
68. That is, if the *Monarchia* was indeed written around 1316, and *De ortu* between 1308 and 1313. Posch 1920; Mazzotta 1993, 10.
69. Black 1992, 93. Cf. Woolf 1913, especially 289. Engelbert's reliance on Aristotle— so much so that "der christliche Einschlag fehlt"—is stressed by Posch 1920, 33, 35. Cf. Menzel 1941, 401–2.
70. *De ortu* IX, XIV. (Whenever possible, I cite the translation in Lewis 1954, 2: 473– 84. If not otherwise indicated, page references are to this edition.) Cf. Woolf 1913, 280– 82; Lewis 1954, 2: 444–46; Black 1992, 93–95.

Because felicity thus defined would be concurrent with peace, peace could be seen as the aim toward which all human communities and societies strove.[71] Engelbert's initial question—Which human community is most conducive to achieving felicity?—was thus translated into: Which community best promotes peace? In answer, Engelbert advanced the argument that by the dictates of art and reason (both of which imitate nature) and by the ordination of divine providence, it was better, and also more just, that all kingdoms be under one king or emperor as monarch of the whole world,[72] this being the order most likely to advance peace and the most favorable for the defense and propagation of Christianity.

To substantiate this argument, Engelbert discussed the merits of communities smaller than empire. The willingness to consider merits of smaller communities shows that his imperialism—in contrast to Dante's—was marked by a cautious relativism. This may be partly due to Engelbert's respect for Augustine, who had been critical of the Roman Empire of his own time, and partly a result of his living under imperial power. For Engelbert, "the great monarchy was an experience and not a prayer."[73]

Engelbert rested his argument for the necessity of the empire on his understanding of the diversity of the human condition. In his outlook, the "whole constitution of this world" was "made up of things diverse, unlike, and contrary." Kingdoms of this world were "diverse from one another, according to the diversity of fatherland and tongue, and of customs and laws," as well as of "inherited rites."[74] But the world made of "things diverse, unlike, and contrary" could not endure "except through the concord of the diverse, the unlike, and the contrary." Concord lacking, superiors would destroy inferiors, the active would by their power conquer and destroy the passive, and the greater would consume the lesser. But agreement and peace do not come about automatically; they have to be made. An omnipotent power, distinct from all these elements, was needed "to harmonize all things with one another, and to preserve their peace."[75] It was against the background of discord generated by the diversity of nations and kingdoms that Engelbert asserted that "there

71. *De ortu* XIV; Woolf 1913, 282 n. 7.
72. *De ortu* XV. In the title he himself gave to his treatise (*De ortu, progressu et fine regnorum et praecipue regni seu imperii Romani*), the preface, and elsewhere, Engelbert speaks of "Roman empire or kingdom" and "Roman kingdom or empire." For an interpretation of this use of categories, see Woolf 1913, 280 ff.
73. Lewis 1954, 2: 446.
74. *De ortu* XV (p. 475); XVI (p. 479).
75. Ibid., XV (p. 475).

will necessarily be some one power and dignity which is supreme and universal in the world, to which all kingdoms and nations of the world should by right be subject in order to make and preserve the concord of nations and kingdoms throughout the world."[76]

Speaking of the diversity of kingdoms of this world according to "fatherland and tongue," "customs and laws," and "inherited rites" amounted to saying that all of mankind was not one people, for a people was understood to be a multitude associated together by a common and harmonious consent to divine and human law.[77] But this very definition of the people as the basis of the notion of *respublica* (implying the understanding of *respublica* as *res populi*) was used by Engelbert to argue that there was one people after all—the Christian people—and to promote his ideal of one Christian republic. The empire was precisely a unitary Christian republic; a non-Christian imperial commonwealth was inconceivable.[78] Arguing in favor of the empire, Engelbert stated that there was but one true divine law: the one true cult of the one true God; one human law: the canons and laws consonant to the divine law; one consent of the people to that one divine and human law: the Christian faith; one people: the Christian people; and therefore there was but one commonwealth: that of the whole Christian people.[79]

Engelbert presented the main objections against empire,[80] and after refuting them point by point, asserted his final conclusion:

[S]o long as the course marked out by God for the things of the world shall please Him, it is and always will be better and more just that all kingdoms and all kings be under one empire and Christian emperor, so far as is proper and suitable for each kingdom by right or by rational and established custom, than the single kingdoms and kings should stand apart without any subjection and obedience to the empire, like many heads in the one body of the Christian commonweal, which is one commonweal of one Christian people and therefore has one head of all, unless someone should wish to make a many-headed monster of that commonweal, of that one Christian people.[81]

Engelbert's understanding of world monarchy as a unitary Christian

---

76. Ibid., 476.

77. Ibid., XVI (p. 479). See chap. 4 n. 362.

78. Cf. Menzel 1941, 401, that Engelbert "sich kein außerchristliches Kaisertum denken konnte."

79. *De ortu* XV (pp. 474–75); cf. Woolf 1913, 285. Rather than arguing that "Engelbert is one of the first medieval writers to develop accurately the conception that mankind is one people with only one true law," Fowler 1947, 173, should have seen Engelbert as reviving the traditional notion of the Christian republic.

80. *De ortu* XVI.

81. Ibid., XVIII (p. 480); cf. XV (p. 475).

republic was directed toward securing the spread of Christianity and preventing the coming of the Antichrist. In his firm conviction, kingdoms should be brought under one empire in order that "the world may be at peace and Christianity protected and extended." [82] In this sense, it is not unfair to call Engelbert's world monarchy "the crusading empire." [83] World peace went hand in hand with the defense and extension of Christianity. Indeed, the idea of universal peace was pregnant with war. As Engelbert made clear, "if there should be war today, as there has often been in the past, between all Christendom and the pagan world, or between greater parts of both, it would be more just and more noble that all Christians should be united under the one head of the empire, the emperor (since such a war could not prosper unless all were united under one head), than that someone else should be elected captain, leader, or king for that particular period." [84] A peacemaking empire was necessary for a successful war of united Christians against the sum total of the pagans.

The subjection of kingdoms to the empire, Engelbert argued, "is just and useful and necessary especially for this purpose: that the church and the faith may be defended by all its members when they are brought to concord and unity under their own proper head against those who are outside the church, and outside the faith, and against the church, and against the faith, and that it may extend its boundaries to enlarge the place of its tabernacle. And for this reason we believe that no Christian kingdom is free or exempt from subjection and obedience to the empire." [85] At this point, Engelbert turned his argument against the emergent territorial kingdoms. "The privileges of a few do not make a common law," he asserted against the French and the Aragonese, who in the past had been granted liberty by Roman emperors. Engelbert spoke with precisely chosen words of the "tribe of the Franks" and the "tribe of the Goths"—not of their kingdoms—to stress that it was not the French and Aragonese kingdoms that had been granted imperial privileges. But the weightier point was that such privileges were null and void anyway, because as a matter of principle, it had been disallowed for the emperors to limit and restrict the boundaries of the Roman Empire.[86]

Should kingdoms seek to exempt themselves from imperial rule, they

82. Ibid., XVIII.
83. Lewis 1954, 2: 447.
84. *De ortu* XVIII (p. 481).
85. Ibid., 482–83.
86. Ibid., 483–84.

would destroy the empire and thus clear the way for the coming of the Antichrist. Invoking the prophecy of the apostle Paul (2 Thes 2.3), Engelbert wrote that "in the approaching time of the coming of Antichrist there will come first the falling away of all kingdoms from the empire, then of churches from their obedience to the apostolic see, and finally of the faithful from their faith." Consequently, "those who apply their zeal and ingenuity to weakening and shattering the empire seem to be hastening directly toward the preparation of room and opportunity for the tyranny of Antichrist." [87] This conclusion shows that it is inaccurate to interpret the *De ortu et fine* as a treatise advocating the restoration of the empire that was necessary for defense against the Antichrist.[88] Rather than arguing for a restoration of the empire, Engelbert furnished a justification for its continuing existence. The empire was needed to defend and extend the Christian faith. Obversely, kingdoms seeking to free themselves from the imperial rule served the Antichrist.

Engelbert's notion of the empire, however, was riddled with conceptual problems. As the unitary republic of the Christian people, the empire would encompass "the greater part of the world." [89] Yet Engelbert did not want to accept that the Christian empire would be less than the entire world. But if the empire was to hold sway throughout the world, and assuming that the spread of Christianity would not do away with all non-Christians at one go, a basis had to be found for the coexistence of Christian and non-Christian peoples. For Engelbert, that basis was natural law and the law of peoples (*jus gentium*). Following the dictates of necessity and usefulness, diverse peoples, each governed according to their own laws, would also be ruled in accordance with "natural law, which is common to all peoples and kingdoms, or in accordance with those parts of the Roman law which can justly and usefully be suitable to all peoples and kingdoms, and which all peoples and kingdoms are bound to observe within themselves and with their neighbors and with foreigners." [90] Nevertheless, the emperor whom all should obey was to be a Roman, that is, a Christian, prince, for the lasting benefit of Christians:

> either in order that the peace and quiet of each kingdom and people within itself and with outsiders should be preserved, as in the case of Christian kingdoms, or at least in order that those Christian kingdoms themselves should

87. Ibid., 483.
88. Cf. Ullmann 1965, 186–87; Burns, 1988, 667.
89. Cf. *De ortu* XV (p. 476).
90. Ibid., XVIII (pp. 483–84).

not be invaded nor disturbed by others, as by kingdoms of infidels and pagans, which are considered to be under Roman empire to this extent; for to assign to each his own and not to injure another unjustly are not only principles of Christian law but also of the law of peoples and of all men as such; and in order that this may be preserved for the Christian kingdoms infidels and pagans themselves can and should be legally subject to the coercion of the empire.[91]

The introduction of natural law and the law of peoples broadened the discussion of empire conceptually without solving the problem of the rightful basis for legally subjecting "infidels and pagans" to the coercive power of the Christian monarch. The resort to natural law only served to veil, rather than exclude or eliminate, divine law, for natural law was only conceivable with reference to divine law. And "there is only one true divine law in the whole world," asserted Engelbert—the one codified in Christian canons.[92] Given the principle that there "never was, nor could be, nor can be a true empire outside the church" ("although there were emperors of a sort, in a relative, not absolute sense, outside the Christian faith and church"),[93] the subjection of the infidels and pagans to the emperor's coercive jurisdiction would either annul the principle that "to each should be assigned and maintained what is his own, and that none should be unjustly injured by others,"[94] or would leave open to interpretation what was "one's own" or "just"—at least for those who did not accept the one true divine law as the ultimate basis for all law and for discerning the just from unjust. Moreover, the argument for Christian lordship over the whole world on the basis of natural law and the law of peoples did not do away with the issue of war between Christians and non-Christians, addressed earlier in Engelbert's treatise.

Engelbert recognized that eternal peace could truly be enjoyed only in the perfect felicity of the heavenly kingdom. As for earthly kingdoms, the best they could do was to strive with zeal and joy toward a peace they could never fully attain.[95] This, of course, did not mean that Engelbert renounced the vision of universal peace. To the contrary. The empire as he imagined it was synonymous with a permanent struggle for peace. But with universal peace inextricably coupled with war between Chris-

---

91. Ibid., 484. It is not clear to me on what basis Fowler 1947, 178, came to the conclusion that Engelbert advocated "a world federation of states."
92. *De ortu* XV (p. 475). Cf. n. 79.
93. *De ortu* XV (p. 475), referring to Augustine *De civitate Dei* XIX.
94. *De ortu* XVIII (p. 484).
95. Ibid., 481–82.

tendom and the infidel and pagan world,[96] one cannot brush aside the impression that world peace was a recipe for perpetual world war.

ANTIPAPAL FUNDAMENTALISM AND CIVIL CRUSADE: MARSIGLIO OF PADUA

Neither Dante nor Engelbert of Admont were ultimately hostile to the papacy. Their vindication of empire rested on the assumptions that between the two universal powers instituted by God there was a division of labor, and that these two ought to cooperate.[97] Marsiglio of Padua was an imperialist of a different stamp: a fundamentalist enemy of papal power. Whereas Giles of Rome formulated the idea of papal "total" power, Marsiglio elaborated the idea of its total destruction. Giles of Rome's *De Potestate Ecclesiastica* and Marsiglio of Padua's *Defensor pacis* have thus been seen as "the two really epoch-making political books appearing between 1300 and 1500."[98]

Marsiglio's fame rests almost exclusively on his authorship of the *Defensor pacis,* one of the most remarkable political treatises of the Middle Ages. He completed this virulent antipapal polemics in 1324. Marsiglio had taught at the University of Paris; in 1313, he had been its rector. When he was identified as the author of the *Defensor pacis,* he fled Paris to the court of Lewis of Bavaria. Lewis was himself engaged in a protracted conflict with the papacy and offered hospitality to the learned exile.[99] When Lewis had himself crowned Roman emperor in Rome in January of 1328, he appointed Marsiglio (who had accompanied him on his Italian expedition) as the "spiritual vicar of Rome." Because Lewis's imperial coronation is considered inspired by Marsiglio's ideas, the *Defensor pacis* is regarded as a theoretical work that had "the fortunate privilege of being immediately put into practice in the historical and political reality of its day, albeit for a short time."[100] Not all historians, however, think Marsiglio's influence on Lewis a fortunate thing. The application of the *Defensor pacis*'s theories, they maintain, ushered in a politics of violence against the papacy, including a military campaign in

---

96. Regarding Jews, Engelbert wrote that they are persecuted now and will forever be persecuted by the blood of Christ, which they brought on themselves. Fowler 1947, 174.

97. See n. 49; McIlwain 1932, 274.

98. Ibid., 313 (McIlwain still considered John of Jandun the coauthor of the *Defensor Pacis*).

99. Cf. Pennington 1993b, 193–94; Lewis 1954, 2: 456–59.

100. Black 1992, 58 (referring to J. Quillet, *La philosophie politique de Marsile de Padoue* [Paris, 1970]).

Italy aimed at putting the pope on trial and deposing him.[101] The coronation of Lewis was a "charade" that ended with the emperor's retreat.[102] But Marsiglio had had his brief moment of power. As imperial vicar in Rome, he persecuted those clergy who remained loyal to the pope, and he acquired a reputation for cruelty. He may have indeed "enjoyed himself enormously at Rome." [103]

A few months before Marsiglio assumed his vicariate in the eternal city, Pope John XXII had condemned him for teaching heresies in the *Defensor pacis*.[104] Soon after Marsiglio's death in 1343, Pope Clement VI also condemned the book, in which he detected 240 heretical opinions, as the most heretical work he had ever read. But whereas the Roman curia was unanimous in condemning the *Defensor pacis*, this cannot be said of the book's reception in later centuries. Marsiglio has been claimed by Protestants, liberals, democrats, and National Socialists alike as their predecessor.[105] He has been praised as a pioneer of popular sovereignty and originator of a concept of the state that embodies genuine democratic elements.[106] He has also been given bad press as an early inspirer of the modern totalitarian state.[107]

Marsiglio's political philosophy has attracted great interest for its allegedly "modern character," [108] and he has been admired as "in advance of its time." It is easy to agree that such a characterization is "foolish." [109] But Marsiglio has been tendentiously modernized and actualized.[110] Because "so many writers on Marsiglian thought have all too often taken the opportunity to interpret it in the dubious light of their own convictions for or against the Catholic Church, the lay State, democracy, liberalism, totalitarianism and whatever not," studies of Marsiglio are notable for their frequent imposition of anachronisms.[111]

101. Lagarde 1932, 468–69.
102. Morrall 1971, 105.
103. Allen 1923, 191.
104. *Licet iuxta doctrinam* (Mirbt and Aland, *Quellen*, no. 755; trans. in Ozment 1980, 154).
105. See Segall 1959, 14; Ozment 1980, 155.
106. Cf. Gierke 1913, 46; Ullmann 1965, 204 ff.; Skinner 1978, 1: 65; Black 1992, 71. This view has been questioned, for example, in Lewis 1954, 1: 30, 256.
107. Cf. Gewirth 1956; Lagarde, *Marsile de Padoue*, vol. 2 of *La naissance de l'esprit laïque au déclin de moyen âge* (St. Paul-trois-Chateaux, 1934–46), as summarized in Morrall 1971, 142.
108. Figgis 1922, 60–61.
109. "[W]hen someone says that the thought of a book was far ahead of its time he really means that the view it expresses is nearer his own than the views of most people at that time were." Allen 1923, 172.
110. See Segall 1959.
111. Morrall 1971, 106.

Typical of such anachronisms are claims that with Marsiglio, "secularization attained the status of political ideology" and "the State" came of age.[112] The *Defensor pacis* has been represented as the "*compendium* of the rights of lay societies facing the Church," and Marsiglio has been credited with formulating "something like the idea of the modern state."[113] Marsiglio, however, never used the term *state*.[114] What is commonly taken to be Marsiglio's theory of the "secular state" in the first of the three discourses of the *Defensor pacis* is in fact a generic account of the origins and nature of political community, developed with extensive use of quotations from Aristotle. Marsiglio's use of Aristotle is another source of oversimplification and misunderstanding. Some believe that through "close reading of Aristotle, Marsilius made available the image of politics as the art of instituting and preserving a community of free and equal people under the rule of law."[115] It seems to me, however, that those scholars who question Marsiglio's dedication to Aristotelianism have the stronger argument. In their view, Marsiglio only cloaked the doctrines of the first discourse of the *Defensor pacis* in Aristotelian garb "in order to attract fellow schoolmen by demonstrating that opposition to the papacy was an inescapable consequence of Aristotle's teaching." He colonized Aristotelian scholasticism in the name of antipapalism, and as a "pope adversary who firmly relied on the Bible," "forcibly adapted" Aristotle for his own purposes.[116]

The *Defensor pacis* is a thoroughly medieval book.[117] Its "main purpose" was the "annihilation of the papacy"[118] and refutation of any possible claim by the Church to have a say in ordering the civil community. Marsiglio's anticlericalism (about which there was "nothing really peculiar")[119] should not be mistaken for secularism. He was not an anti-Christian writer. There is no reason to doubt the sincerity of his adherence to the Holy Scriptures.[120] He was a self-styled herald of the Chris-

---

112. Le Goff 1990, 97; Morrall 1971, chap. 7.
113. Lagarde 1932, 464; Black 1992, 67.
114. Cf. Morrall 1971, 106. For problems concerning the translation of Marsiglian terms into English and German, see Segall 1959, 64 (who suggested that "das Wort 'Staat' . . . durch die Ausdrücke 'Gesamtheit' oder 'Gemeinschaft der Bürger' ersetzt [werden sollte]"); Gewirth 1980, lxxvi ff. In my citations of Gewirth's translation, checked against Scholz's ed., I render *regnum* as "kingdom" and *civitas* as "city."
115. Viroli 1992, 52.
116. Segall 1959, 46–47, 50; Nederman 1993, xxi.
117. Carlyle and Carlyle 1903–36, 6: 9–10; Allen 1923, 172.
118. Setton 1976, 171.
119. Allen 1923, 172–73; Segall 1959, 38–39, 41.
120. Cf. *Defensor pacis* II,v,8; II,xix,2. (I cite Gewirth's translation, with changes mentioned in n. 114.) Marsiglio "believed that all the valid claims of Christianity would

tian truth,[121] who regarded the papacy's claims to temporal power as the work of the devil [122] and his own negation of those claims as godly work. He opposed the papal monarchy in the name of peace. He called his famous work the *Defender of Peace* because, in his words, "it discusses and explains the principal causes whereby civil peace or tranquillity exists and is preserved, and whereby the opposed strife arises and is checked and destroyed." [123] His principal aim was to demonstrate that "tranquillity or peace" is the benefit and fruit of a well-ordered civil community.[124] The peace he defended was thus "civil peace" (*civilis pax sive tranquillitas*).[125] But this civil peace he understood as *pax Christi* and his use of the notion of *pax et tranquillitas* placed him firmly within medieval conventions.[126] The intonation of Marsiglio's exploration of peace with Jesus's words, citing all four evangelists,[127] was not dissimulation.

Marsiglio's defense of peace was intimately linked to his fundamentalist antipapalism and anticlericalism because he considered the Church as *corpus juridicum* and its striving for temporal power as the main threat to civil order and, therefore, the worst enemy of peace.[128] His leading

---

be satisfied by his solution." Lewis 1954, 2: 544. The *Defensor Pacis* "[will] die Grundfesten des Glaubens weder verrücken noch erschüttern." Segall 1959, 27; cf. 28, 43 ff.

121. *Defensor Pacis* II,xxv,18.

122. Ibid., II,xxv,7. Pope John XXII, too, called Marsiglio and John of Jandun (who had long been considered the coauthor) "filii Belial." *Licet iuxta doctrinam* (Mirbt and Aland, *Quellen*, no. 755).

123. *Defensor pacis* III,iii.

124. Seeing *pax et concordia* as "the most desirable effects of just government" was typical of the early trecento political thought. N. Rubinstein, "Political Ideas in Sienese Art: The Frescoes by Ambrogio Lorenzetti and Taddeo di Bartolo in the Palazzo Pubblico," *Journal of the Warburg and Courtauld Institutes* 21 (1958), criticized in Skinner 1978, 1: 57. Skinner understands Marsiglio as saying that "just government is the effect of which *pax* is taken to be the precondition." Cf. Gewirth 1956, 95 ff. (maintaining that Marsiglio departed from the notion of peace as "concord"); Rubinstein 1965, 55 ff.

125. *Defensor pacis* III,iii. For A. Dempf, *Sacrum imperium* (Munich and Berlin, 1929), 450, Marsiglio's peace was "Ruhe als Bürgerpflicht." Cited in Segall 1959, 20.

126. Segall 1959, 19, 23 (polemicizing with Gewirth 1956, 95–98). For a discussion of peace in contemporary Italian republican tracts, see Gewirth 1956, 55 ff.; Davis 1959; Skinner 1978, 1: 56 ff.; 1986;

127. Lk 2.14; Jn 20.19; 14, 27; Mk 9.50; Mt 10.12. See *Defensor pacis* I,i,1.

128. It appears unwarranted to regard "the specific problems of the Italian City Republics," especially the "prevalence of faction," as the context in which Marsiglio's work is to be analyzed. Skinner 1978, 1: 57–65. Cf. id. 1986, 1; Rubinstein 1965. Rather than with the "factious disturbances" of Italian cities, Marsiglio was occupied with the so-called church-state conflicts. The whole thrust of his argument was directed against the plurality of overlapping jurisdictions, and his "practical interests" were completely absorbed with the need to eliminate the coercive jurisdiction of the Church. See Ozment 1980, 150; Morrall 1971, 104. For the conflict between Philip IV and Boniface VIII as an important inspiration for Marsiglio, cf. Riezler 1874, 227; Lagarde 1932; Segall 1959, 31;

thought, expressed time and time again, was that "it is necessary for the peace of the city or polity [*necessarium est ad civilitatis seu policie quietem*] that every bishop, priest, and clergyman be subject to the coercive judgement of the rulers in accordance with human law." [129]

Marsiglio defined the priesthood as one of the offices, or parts, of the political community. [130] By incorporating the priesthood into the civil order, Marsiglio, right at the beginning of the *Defensor pacis*, stepped out of the conventional discussion of power, which was focused on the relation between the temporal/secular and the spiritual/sacerdotal powers. [131] This alone distinguished him from other fourteenth-century opponents of the pope, who "continued to assert some variant of Gelasian theory." [132] Marsiglio's concept of civil power was all-inclusive: spiritual power ceased to exist as a power and the notion of secular power was obliterated as well. Next, he subordinated the priesthood to the government, or the ruling part of civil community, as civil community's first and most important part. This subordination was unquestionable, unless the very civil order were threatened, since the existence of the civil order depended on the government's establishing and differentiating the other, subordinate parts of civil community so that each could perform its proper function without disruptive interference from the rest. Within this scheme, the government exercised coercive jurisdiction in accordance with the law made by the "human legislator": by the people, or the whole body of citizens (*universitas civium*), or its "weightier part" (*valencior pars*). [133]

Marsiglio's definition of the human legislator as the primary and proper efficient cause of civil community, and more specifically, as the body with the efficient power to establish or elect government, [134] simply and elegantly erased any role for the Church in instituting civil power. Once defined as an office within civil community, the priesthood was not

---

Rubinstein 1965, 44; Oakley 1991, 45–46. See also *Defensor pacis* I,xix,10; II,v,5; II,xviii,18; II,xx,8–9; II,xxi,9, 14.

129. Ibid., II,xxx,5.

130. Ibid., I,v.

131. Cf. Gewirth 1956, 92–93.

132. Lewis 1954, 2: 540.

133. *Defensor pacis,* I,xi,1; xii,3; cf. I,xii,5. Elusive as the concept of *valencior pars* is (see Segall 1959, 65–67; Gewirth 1956, 182 ff.), the "human legislator" is "highly inclusive," at least by medieval standards, with regard to its social composition (Nederman 1993, xxi–xxii). It encompasses all free male adults regardless of social or economic status, and excludes "children, slaves, aliens, and women." *Defensor minor* II,7; *Defensor pacis* I,xii,4.

134. Ibid., I,vii,3; I,xv,2; II,xv,1.

only prevented from rising above the civil community but was subordinated to its laws. Because coercive jurisdiction belonged to the government—and the supreme government "must necessarily be one in number, not many, if the kingdom or city is to be rightly ordered" [135]—all ecclesiastical persons were excluded from exercising temporal jurisdiction and subjected to the coercive power of civil government.[136] Any attempt by the priesthood to exercise coercive judgment itself would amount to interference with government and impediment to its proper functioning, leading to disturbances of civil government and finally to the worst of all evils, civil death.[137]

Complementary to Marsiglio's definition of civil community was his concept of the Church. The Church was the *universitas fidelium:* "the whole body of the faithful who believe in and invoke the name of Christ, and all the parts of this whole body in any community, even the household." Should the priests appropriate for themselves the name Church, they would be "abusing the word in order to advance fraudulently their own temporal well-being to the detriment of others." Since it was not the "ministers of the temple" alone who were the Church, "all the Christian faithful, both priests and non-priests, are and should be called churchmen." [138] With any Christian believer set equal with priests and with all the faithful regarded as churchmen of the Marsiglian Church, the Church as a clerical institution ceased to exist. Once the Church as *corpus juridicum* was dissolved into the *universitas fidelium,* what distinguished the priests from lay believers and made them a separate civil body, the priesthood, was purely their priestly office in the civil community. They were priests because they dutifully had to perform a specific civil service.

Both Marsiglio's definition of political community and his concept of the Church were informed by the desire to thwart any attempt by the Church to play a role in ordering civil affairs. His account of the nature of civil community in the first discourse of the *Defensor pacis,* it is true, was abstract and applicable to any "assemblage of men," [139] to any form of polity, be it city, province, kingdom, and empire, or at least to "every species of temperate regime." [140] But at the close of the first discourse,

135. Ibid., I,xvii,2.
136. Ibid., I,xix,12; II,iv, v.
137. Ibid., II,xxiv,15; xxv,14; xxiii,11; xxvi,12.
138. Ibid., II,ii,3.
139. Ibid., I,xvii,9.
140. Ibid., I,ii,2. It seems to me that there is little basis in the *Defensor pacis* itself to justify its interpretation as a vindication of the city republics, much as Marsiglio's argument may have been influenced by their experience. Cf. n. 128; Gewirth 1956; Segall

his argument switched from the generic to the highly specific: the papacy was expressly made the main target of Marsiglio's writing. He considered the papacy's desire for temporal power and wealth the "singular cause of wars" and the principal menace to civil order. That "pestilence" was "the common enemy of the human race,"[141] endangering all kingdoms and cities. Marsiglio most frequently mentioned Italian kingdoms and cities as suffering from the interference of papal politics.[142] He also dedicated a whole chapter to papal meddling with the affairs of the empire[143] and referred to the French king's valiant struggle against the pope.[144] He pictured the pope as stealthily worming his way "through all the kingdoms in the world," stating that if the pope's insatiable desire for power went unchallenged, this would allow "the root of all governments to be cut up, and the bond and nexus of every city [*civilitas*] and kingdom to be destroyed."[145] Marsiglio was convinced that it was his own Christian duty to unravel this "hidden malignity" and "pernicious pestilence," so "completely opposed to all the peace and happiness of man,"[146] and called for "the coercive power of rulers" to "enter upon the final rout of the shameful patrons and stubborn defenders of this evil."[147] His generic definition of civil community served as the basis for marshalling the support of all civil powers for the struggle against the papacy.

The struggle to exclude ecclesiastical persons from exercising temporal jurisdiction was in the vital interest of any civil authority, and following from Marsiglio's definition of civil community, it was an imperative. But he did not want to rest his argument there. Drawing on Christian authorities,[148] he demolished both the concept of papal fullness of power, which legitimized the pope's appetite for power, and the notion of the

---

1959, 51 ff.; Rubinstein 1965; Morrall 1971, 104 ff.; Black 1992, 59; Canning 1996, 157. Rubinstein 1965, 69, himself noted that Marsiglio was reluctant "to commit himself to an opinion on the best constitution."

141. *Defensor pacis* I,i,3–5.

142. Ibid., I,i,2; I,xix,4,11–12; II,xxiii,11; II,xxv,14–5; II,xxvi,19.

143. Ibid., II,xxvi; cf. I,xix,8,11–12; II,xxv,10–16.

144. For Marsiglio, Philip IV was "of bright memory." Ibid., I,xix,10; II,xvii,17; II,xx,8–9; II,xxi,9.

145. Ibid., II,xxvi,13,15; cf. I,xix,12.

146. Ibid., I,xix,4,13. "Following the example of Christ," he wrote, "we must strive to teach the truth whereby the aforesaid pestilence of civil regimes may be warded off from the human race, especially the worshipers of Christ—the truth which leads to the salvation of civil life, and which also is of no little help for eternal salvation." Ibid., I,i,5

147. Ibid., I,i,5; cf. I,xix,13.

148. Cf. ibid., lxii–lxiv. In these anti-papal polemics, Aristotle appeared rarely, and when he did, it was as "the wise Gentile." Ibid., II,xxiv,15; cf. Scholz 1932, lxi–lxii.

Petrine commission, upon which rested the idea of papal *plenitudo po-testatis*.[149] Having done away with that "sophistic opinion, wearing the guise of the honourable and beneficial," upon which the papal claims for temporal power were based,[150] Marsiglio could more effectively assert that "the office of coercive rulership" over any individual, community, or group "does not belong to the Roman or any other bishop, priest or spiritual minister," and that all ecclesiastical persons should be subject to the coercive power of secular rulers.[151] For ecclesiastical persons only had the power to administer sacraments, which is uncoercive.[152]

More important still for buttressing his antipapal argument was Marsiglio's concept of the Church. He uncompromisingly drew out the consequences of his concept of the priesthood as civil service and of his conceptual dissolution of the Church as a clerical corporation into the community of all the faithful. All the priests, the pope included, were to be elected and appointed to their office — one of the "offices of the city" — by the human legislator.[153] This was a view subversive of the entire ecclesiastical hierarchical structure.[154] In the face of the ultimate authority of the human legislator, all priests were equal; they were all subjects of the government. But priests were equal in their "essential" or "inseparable" authority as priests as well; that authority was "the same in kind among all priests," and the "Roman or any other bishop" had no more of it than had "any simple priest."[155] Having thus made the pope "essentially" equal to any other priest, Marsiglio still wanted to do away with the pope's privileged position among bishops. Because bishops as the successors of the apostles were equal among themselves just as the apostles had been, the pope as the bishop of Rome had no coercive power over them. In their own "priestly household," no particular bishop had coercive juridical authority or power over his fellow bishops or priests.[156] Marsiglio, in his thoughts, annihilated the papal monarch, allowing him

149. *Defensor pacis* I,xix,12; II,iii, xvi, xxiii; cf. II,xxiv–xxvi; *Defensor minor* XI.
150. *Defensor pacis* I,i,3–5.
151. Ibid., I,xix,12; II,iv–v.
152. Ibid., II,vi–x.
153. Ibid., I,xix,6; II,xvi,1; II,xvii,8 ff. This involved the prerogative to determine the number of clergymen, "lest by their undue increase they be able to resist the ruler's coercive power, or otherwise disturb the polity, or deprive the city or kingdom of its welfare by their insolence and their freedom from necessary tasks." Ibid., II,viii,9. For the election of the pope, the "head bishop," see ibid., II,xxii,11.
154. Gewirth 1956, 262.
155. *Defensor pacis* II,xv,4.
156. Ibid., II,xvi,1,8.

and other bishops to survive as managers or stewards (*oeconomi*)[157] of the sacerdotal department of the political community.

Once elected to their posts, priests would not have a free hand in exercising their office. The human legislator, or the government instituted by the legislator, had the final say in a number of sacerdotal matters affecting civil life, such as excommunications,[158] the persecution of heretics,[159] the canonization and veneration of saints,[160] the dissolution of marriage or the removal of impediments to a marriage within a certain degree of consanguinity,[161] the determination of the meaning of doubtful sentences of the Holy Scripture, and the definition of the articles of faith.[162] This last task was assigned to a general council of the faithful, composed of priests and laymen elected and summoned by the human legislator, who also was to enforce the council's decision.[163] Finally, no ecclesiastical person was to be allowed to bestow teaching licenses, since this prerogative had enabled bishops to "subject to themselves colleges of learned men, taking them away from the secular rulers, and use them as no slight but rather powerful instruments for perpetrating and defending their usurpations against the secular rulers." Teaching appointments were to be a domain of the human legislator, so that the learned and the wise would serve the civil government and become a prime aid for "stabilizing and defending governments and constitutions."[164]

When Marsiglio began to discuss these matters—that is, when he moved from the realm of generic politico-theoretical discourse to his specific attack on the papacy—an essential transition occurred in his argument. The "human legislator" metamorphosed into the "faithful (human) legislator," *legislator humanus fidelis,* and the whole body of citizens, *universitas civium,* became faithful: *universitas civium fidelium.* The relation between the two categories may be seen as "largely" coex-

---

157. See *Defensor minor* IV, 3; cf. *Defensor pacis* II, xxii, 6.
158. Ibid., II,vi,11 ff.; *Defensor minor* X. Marsiglio's particular concern in this context was to dogmatically preclude the possibility of the papal excommunication of Christian rulers and of absolving the subjects from the oath binding them to their ruler. Cf. ibid., VIII–IX.
159. *Defensor pacis* II,x.
160. Ibid., II,xxi,15.
161. *De matrimonio* and *Forma dispensationis super affinitatem consanguinitatis,* incorporated as the last four chapters into the *Defensor minor.* (The "secular" background for writing these two treatises was Emperor Lewis's engineering of such a legally delicate marriage for his son.) See especially *Defensor minor* XV–XVI.
162. *Defensor pacis* II,xviii,8; II,xix,3; II,xx.
163. Ibid., II,xx–xxi.
164. Ibid., II,xxi,15.

tensive[165] and as having a common *fundamentum in re*.[166] It is unclear whether they corresponded "entirely" and whether all their members were "the same."[167] For inclusive as the concept of human legislator may have been,[168] the "faithful (human) legislator" was clearly broader yet. But Marsiglio did not elaborate upon the problematic relationship between the human legislator and the faithful human legislator, or between the whole body of the citizens and the whole body of the faithful. He simply used the concept of faithful legislator analogously with the concept of human legislator.[169] This analogy allowed him to employ the logic by means of which he had constructed polity in the first, more generic, discourse of the *Defensor pacis* to take apart the Church in the more practical and political second discourse. This conceptual demolition of the Church had been, it seems, the aim of Marsiglio's enterprise. But because the faithful legislator had the *fundamentum in re* in common with the human legislator, Marsiglio's discussion of the faithful legislator, specific as it may have been, rebounded on his generic theory of polity. With the demolition of the ecclesiastical hierarchy in the second discourse of the *Defensor pacis,* the political community *qua* political community of the first discourse acquired the distinctive traits of Christian polity.

Marsiglio conceptualized a polity with differentiated offices in which the Church ceased to exist while religion permeated the political community as a whole. The dissolution of the Church as a clerical corporation (which the denial of temporal, coercive jurisdiction to the Church, based on the postulate that the supreme government must be one in number, did not logically necessitate) resulted in a transformation of the civil community into a church. Developing his argument in conscious opposition to Boniface's *Unam sanctam,* Marsiglio constructed a new "one and holy" Church, a popular and healthy "mystical body of Christ,"[170] into which transmigrated the fullness of power (once the papal monarchy had conceptually been eliminated).[171] This structureless

---

165. Gewirth 1956, 291.
166. Segall 1959, 70.
167. Gewirth 1956, 291; Lewis 1954, 2: 545.
168. See n. 133.
169. Black 1992, 67–68, sees the faithful legislator as "doubling" the human legislator.
170. In Marsiglio's view, the Church's claim to coercive jurisdiction made the mystical body of Christ ill. *Defensor pacis* II,xxiv,2,11,15.
171. Watt 1988, 421; Lewis 1954, 2: 545. Cf. Hay 1977, 17. For Marsiglio's slandering of the *Unam sanctam,* see *Defensor pacis* II,xx,8; II,xxv,15. (Against Boniface,

"lay church"[172] became the effective cause of the polity. The people as the human legislator, the ultimate source of political community, were the faithful, Christian people. Marsiglio's theory had set out to explain the origin of political community as natural. But as it unfolded, it incorporated the true faith into the very foundations of polity.

Just how much the generic polity was transfigured into Christian polity, and just how much the generic principles on which was organized the political community as political community were transmuted into principles of Christian political communities called "perfect," becomes very clear when Marsiglio addresses the question of infidel rulers. One of his absolute principles of political community, postulating unquestioned subjection of civil community's members to the ruler, was not necessarily binding for the faithful living under infidel rulers. Significant in this context is Marsiglio's formulation of the imperative that "the church and all the Christian faithful must be subject to secular rulers, especially faithful ones."[173] The word "especially" specified that the Church and the faithful must be subject to Christian secular princes and thus relativized the imperative and permitted its suspension under certain conditions. For example, "in a place where the legislator and the ruler by its authority were infidel," the priest alone or together with the "sounder part of the faithful multitude" would be allowed to appoint prelates or curates "without any consent or knowledge on the part of the ruler," especially if doing so might lead to the "spreading of Christ's faith and salutary doctrine among the people."[174] (To act this way was, to be sure, "in default of the legislator,"[175] not in default of Marsiglio's doctrine.)

Consistent with his generic theory of political community, Marsiglio wrote that even infidel rulers ought to be obeyed.[176] But since Christian polity was the perfect political community, the imperative was, once again, relativized. It applied, Marsiglio argued, only in "those cases where obedience is not contrary to divine law in word or deed."[177] In principle, divine law and human law should be consistent and reinforce each other. In this sense, "divine law commands obedience to human rulers and laws"—but only to those "which are not contrary to divine

---

Marsiglio even praised a papal statement, namely Clement V's denunciation of the *Unam sanctam*.)

172. Cf. Morrison 1969, 357.
173. *Defensor pacis* II,v,7.
174. Ibid., II,xvii,15.
175. Ibid.
176. Ibid., II,v,5, 8; II,xxviii,17.
177. Ibid., II,xxvi,13.

law." [178] If prescriptions of human and divine laws conflict, "then one ought to observe the precepts of divine law, condemning or dismissing human law or its contrary precept or permission since the precepts of divine law contain infallible truth, whereas human law does not encompass this." [179] But because there is only one true divine law, Christian law [180]—with other religions at best containing certain elements of the (Christian) truth [181]—it is only in a Christian political community that divine and human laws can be in concord and that the legislator can be not "in default."

The implication that, ultimately, it is only Christians who can form and maintain perfect political communities may help explain Marsiglio's vagueness as to the form of government. His polity falls short of being a genus and fails to appear as a species: it is a family, the family of Christian political communities. One can imagine any Christian political community conforming to his definition of the nature and purpose of the political community. But it is impossible, in the end, to characterize Marsiglio's doctrine as a departure from either medieval tendency: particularism or universalism. [182] True enough, his insistence on the numerical unity of government abolished the plurality of jurisdictions within political communities. But he still left the door open to a plurality of political communities, without saying anything about how relations among them should be organized. At one point Marsiglio mentioned that "some rulers perhaps claim exemption from the authority of the ruler of the Romans," but he did not give his own opinion on the matter, [183] and on the whole, the relations of the empire to *regna* and *civitates* in his writings "remained indefinite." [184] His concern with order within the Christian family did not go beyond an ardent desire to suppress papal ambitions for rulership. As a fighter against the papal monarchy, Marsiglio departed from one form of medieval universalism. But the same cannot be said with respect to the other form of medieval universalist rule: the empire.

---

178. *Defensor minor* VIII,3.

179. Ibid., XIII,6.

180. *Defensor pacis* I,x,3.

181. At one point, the Qur'an is said to contain "certain elements common to the law of Moses and the Gospel." *De translatione imperii* III. (From this conciliatory view it followed that Muhammad was an apostate. Ibid., IV.) *Defensor pacis* I,x,3 denies that religions (*sectae*) "of Mohammed or of the Persians" contain the truth. *Defensor minor* XII,4 argues that the Greeks "ought not to be judged schismatics," but *De translatione* III presents them as having knowingly fallen into diverse errors.

182. Cf. Gewirth 1956, 126.

183. *Defensor pacis* II,xxv,17.

184. Lewis 1954, 2: 459.

On the desirability of one supreme government in the world, Marsiglio gave answers that were sometimes negative, sometimes affirmative, and sometimes—by avoiding discussion of the problem—neutral.[185] In his negative bent, he argued that it was neither expedient nor necessary to have a numerically single head of the entire world. "For in order that men may live together in peace, it is sufficient that there be a numerically single government in each province. . . . But that it is necessary for eternal salvation that there be one coercive judge over all men does not yet seem to have been demonstrated, although this seems more necessary for the believers than that there be one universal bishop, because a universal ruler can better preserve the believers in unity than can a universal bishop."[186] Moreover, because a single world government would establish peaceful coexistence of men and abolish wars, Marsiglio feared that it might cause excessive procreation of men. In his view, wars were a means (in addition to epidemics) by which nature "moderated the procreation of men and the other animals in order that the earth may suffice for their nurture."[187]

Even in his rejection of world monarchy, Marsiglio expressed a preference for the empire over the papal monarchy. A clearly affirmative view of world government is to be found in Marsiglio's writings subsequent to the *Defensor pacis*. In the *De translatione imperii*—a treatise which is, "to all intents and purposes, a copy of Landulfus Collona's *De statu et mutatione Romani imperii,* with Landulfus's papalist arguments reversed"[188]—Marsiglio described the transfer of the empire, meaning "a universal or general monarchy over the whole world,"[189] from Rome to Greece to the Franks to the Germans. Here he did not question the imperial idea. To the contrary, he accepted the ideal of the *pax romana:* the image of all the "kings, princes and tyrants of the age with all their people," subject to the Roman rule, living in ease and enjoying "the blessings of peace."[190] That "peaceful lordship" was broken when the peoples of the East seceded from Latin rule, breaking not only with the imperial government but also with Christianity.

The secession of the eastern peoples from the empire was caused by

---

185. E.g., *Defensor pacis* I,xvii,10.
186. Ibid., II,xxviii,15.
187. Ibid., I,xvii,10.
188. Rubinstein 1965, 44 n. 2.
189. *De translatione* I.
190. Ibid. The enjoyment of "sweet fruits of peace" enabled the "inhabitants of Italy" to bring "the entire habitable world under their sway." *Defensor pacis* I,i,2.

the prophet Muhammad: "But so as to set aside their obedience to the
Roman Empire irrevocably, following the advice of Mahomet, who at
that time was allied with rich and powerful Persians, they adopted a different religion, so that on account of different beliefs and faiths or sects
they would not return to this first lordship from the other one." [191] For
a moment, "this Mahomet" appeared as prudent, but Marsiglio immediately fell back into the familiar pattern of portraying him as an im-
postor who, by "trickeries, by his own power, by a loosening of the laws
concerning matters of sexual desire, and by promising much for the future, . . . seduced many nations and by the power of arms compelled
them to follow him in his apostasy." Muhammad's followers were the
peoples "who had taken up arms against the Empire," spread with violence from Arabia through Egypt to Africa and Spain, compelled "whatever territories they occupied to follow the law of Mahomet," and "multiplied beyond number." [192] They were the anti-empire.

In the *Defensor minor,* Marsiglio's last word on the matter, his pro-
imperial stance is even clearer. Here Marsiglio argued that the supreme
human legislator, especially from the time of Christ up to the present,
"was and is and ought to be the community [*universitas*] of human beings who ought to be subject to the precepts of coercive laws, or their
greater part, in each region and province. And since this power or authority was transferred by the communities of the provinces, or their
greater part, to the Roman people in accordance with their exceeding
virtue, the Roman people have and had the authority to legislate over all
of the world's provinces." The empire—universal legislation by the Roman people and its rulers—was thus to endure until it might be revoked
from the Romans by the communities of the provinces that had once
transferred their own legislative authority to the Romans, or by the Roman people itself from its ruler. [193] That, of course, had not yet happened. In this late work Marsiglio even claimed that he had given evidence—in the *Defensor pacis*—supporting the view that the Roman
people and ruler "exercised a just monarchy over the whole of the world's
provinces." [194] Moreover, in contrast to his earlier view that the Romans
"sent their armies all over the world with such courage and might and
crushed all the kingdoms of the world by their strength," [195] he now felt

191. *De translatione* III. The Greeks followed the same pattern.
192. Ibid., IV.
193. *Defensor minor* XII,1.
194. *Ibid.,* XII,2 (referring to *Defensor pacis* II,iv–v).

he had to strengthen his pro-imperial argument by refuting the objection raised by "some people"[196] that "the lordship [*dominium*] of the Roman people as well as their rulers had been violent and had originated out of violence. For although the Roman people sometimes coerced certain wicked peoples who willed to live unjustly and barbarously, still it did not subject the whole of the provinces or their greater parts by means of violence."[197]

Also driving Marsiglio's "politics" toward universalist rule was his concept of the Church.[198] With the people as legislator coeval with the Church, the one and universal Christian faith was built into the foundations of the political community itself. The oneness of the faith was not threatened by Marsiglio's conceptual deposition of the pope. He viewed as invalid the analogy between the necessity for the numerical unity of coercive jurisdiction in political community on the one hand and, on the other, the need for such a unity within the Church.[199] But with the papal monarchy ruled out, the question of the "universal church," that is, the question of the unity of Christianity, remained unsolved. Marsiglio had to suggest how the affairs of "all the church offices in the world" could be managed. Thoroughly medieval in his views,[200] he argued that decisions concerning the "universal church"—for example, defining the articles of universal faith or excommunicating Christian rulers or provinces—could only be made by the "supreme faithful legislator" (who was also described as "universal" or "primary") or the "general council of Christians."[201] But to summon a general council lay within the authority of the faithful human legislator who had no superior (*superiore carentis*), or those to whom this legislator had granted such authority.[202]

The unity of Christianity as the true and universal faith required a unitary universal human legislative authority, a preeminent civil, even if religious, power: the supreme faithful legislator. Once Marsiglio introduced the primacy of the supreme faithful legislator, the possibility was

195. *De translatione* I.
196. One of them was John of Paris. Cf. n. 241. Lagarde 1932, 478–79, thinks that Marsiglio did not know John's work.
197. *Defensor minor* XII,3.
198. Cf. Gewirth 1956, 129 ff.
199. *Defensor pacis* II,xxviii,13–14.
200. Lewis 1954, 2: 457.
201. *Defensor pacis* II,xxi,9; *Defensor minor* XI. On *supremus,* or *universalis,* or *primus* "*humanus fidelis legislator,*" see *Defensor pacis* II,xviii,8; II,xxi,8.
202. Ibid., II,xviii,8.

open for the traditional figure of the emperor (who was juristically equiv-
alent to the legislator)[203] to assume this newly defined universal rule. It
is true that Marsiglio, whose position on the question of the empire (especially in the *Defensor pacis*) was "far from clear or consistent,"[204] recognized the necessity of a universal legislator rather obliquely. There are
only indications that his *supremus legislator fidelis* referred to the universal authority of the Holy Roman Empire.[205] He never spelled out relations between the supreme faithful legislator and territorially based (if
territorially unspecified) faithful legislators, nor did he specify the relationship between the "universal church" and *universitas fidelium*. But
even if obliquely, Marsiglio brought the emperor back in.[206]

When Marsiglio discussed the crusade, however, the emperor came
directly and clearly to the fore as the rightful ruler not only of the Christian political family or the universal church, but also of the world outside. Even if Marsiglio did not deal with the crusade systematically, the
crusade was integrated into his doctrinal system. Since he rejected the papal monarchy, Marsiglio placed the crusade under the authority of the
human and faithful legislator. He denied the pope the right to remit sins,
for the total or partial forgiveness of sins was reserved for no one but
God, "who alone knows the inner condition of sinners and the hearts of
penitents as well as the quality or quantity of the penance to be offered
by those who are deserving or blameworthy."[207] He also disallowed the
pope the power to grant "certain immunities from public or civil bur-
dens,"[208] to confer indulgence of punishment in the future world upon
those "who travel across the ocean in order to subdue or otherwise constrain the infidels,"[209] and to absolve the faithful from a vow.[210] Denying these rights to the pope meant negating the papal authority to organize the crusade. "[I]f a foreign journey is made or will be made in order
to subdue or restrain infidels for the sake of the Christian faith, then

203. Lewis 1954, 1: 28.
204. Gewirth 1956, 131; Lewis 1954, 2: 457; cf. 459.
205. *Defensor pacis*, 272 n. 21. He did, however, refer to the *supremus Imperii Romani humanus legislator*. Ibid., II,xxx,8. Cf. Gewirth 1956, 131.
206. The logic of Marsiglio's argument is well depicted in Lewis 1954, 2: 543. Cf.
Landry 1929, 156 (seeing the *Defensor pacis* as opposing "un monisme impérial" to "monisme papal"); Watt 1988, 387 (speaking of a reasoned exposition of the imperial ideology); Black 1992, 68; Canning 1996, 157–58.
207. *Defensor minor* VII,4.
208. *Defensor pacis* II,ix,9.
209. *Defensor minor* V,3.
210. Ibid., IV,3; V,3–4; VII,1,4; VIII,1.

such a foreign journey would in no way seem to be meritorious," Marsiglio argued. "But if such a foreign journey is to be made in order to obey the Roman ruler and people in civil precepts and in order that the tribute owed to them may be surrendered, as is their right, then I think that such a trip should be considered meritorious for the sake of the peace and tranquillity of all who live civilly."[211]

Defining the purpose of the crusade as "the aiding of the republic," Marsiglio repudiated the crusade as an instrument of priestly power, but he did not renounce its religious merit. The "overseas crossing" retained a "pious purpose";[212] and because the crusade was an eminently pious deed, Marsiglio could use it as a weapon against the pope (whom he saw as impious). He denounced bishops, especially those in Rome, for neglecting "almost entirely the defense of the true bride, that is, the faith, . . . taking no measures to prevent her from being destroyed through vicious practices or acts, or through attack by infidels."[213] Marsiglio leveled the same words of criticism specifically against Pope John XXII, invoking as his witnesses the king and kingdom of Armenia.[214] With reference to his crusading policy, John was also accused of bringing about the eternal confusion and destruction of the Christians. Marsiglio singled out as "the most vicious and most gravely harmful of all the acts of this present Roman bishop" his use of the crusade against the emperor and his supporters: "[H]e has issued oral and written pronouncements 'absolving from all guilt and punishment' every soldier, in cavalry or in infantry, that has waged war at a certain time against those Christian believers who maintain steadfast and resolute subjection and obedience to the Roman ruler." And "what is horrible to hear, this bishop declares that such action is just as pleasing in God's sight as fighting the heathen overseas."[215] Moreover, the pope also unjustly laid claim to and tried to make "vicious use" of the temporal funds that had been bequeathed for "the cause of religion, such as for crossing overseas."[216] All temporal goods set aside for religious purposes, "such as legacies bequeathed for overseas crossing to resist the infidels," were to be "dis-

211. Ibid., VII,3.
212. *Defensor pacis* II,xxiv,16.
213. Ibid., II,xxix,11.
214. Ibid., II,xxviii,18. On Armenian pleas for help and on plans for a crusade to help them, cf. Housley 1986, 21 ff., 30–31; 1992, chap. 6; Edbury 1991, chap. 6.
215. *Defensor pacis* II,xxvi,16. Popes fomented wars among the Christians (spending wealth on mercenary soldiers) in order that they may in the end be able to subject the faithful to their own tyrannical power. Ibid., II,xxiv,11.
216. Ibid., II,xxiv,16; II,xxvi,16.

tributed only by the ruler in accordance with the designation of the legislator and the intention of the donor." [217]

Marsiglio's charge that the pope had neglected the crusade overseas is, of course, at odds with the principles of his doctrine, which precluded the pope from organizing the crusade. The charge also contradicted Marsiglio's insistence on the traditional ban on the use of arms by clerics, including the illicitness of priests and bishops ordering others to take up arms on their behalf.[218] But such charges were a powerful propaganda weapon not to be left unused for the sake of theoretical consistency. And in any event, for Marsiglio the crusade was more than an idea to be used for propagandistic purposes. His remarks on the crusade succinctly summarize the crusade idea and show that he was well acquainted with the crusading movement. Incorporated into his doctrine, the crusade became a pious and meritorious war fought for civil purposes, "for the sake of the peace and tranquillity of all who live civilly," to exact the tribute owed to the universal faithful ruler,[219] and to bring about civil peace worldwide.

Only with Marsiglio can one speak of "political crusades" in the strict sense of the word.[220] Understood politically, as a civil mission, the crusade was to be directed against the peoples who appeared to Marsiglio as "hateful foreign nations," "wicked," and "stupid in an absolute sense"—that is, because they did not know the true God.[221] But most importantly, these non-Christian peoples lacked civility. They were used to living under despots because of their "barbaric and slavish nature and the influence of custom." They were willing "to live unjustly and barbarously,"[222] while peace and tranquillity were only to be enjoyed by those "who live civilly." With Marsiglio, the infidels became civil enemies of the Christian polity.

REFUTATION OF UNIVERSAL RULE

The world order was being reshaped at the turn of the thirteenth and fourteenth centuries. But established ideas of "the right order in the world"

217. Ibid., III,ii,28.
218. Ibid., II,xxv,5.
219. See n. 211. As such, the crusade was not affected by Marsiglio's rejection of the compulsion to faith (*Defensor pacis* II,v,6–7; II,ix,2,5,7; *Defensor minor* III,2).
220. The term *political Crusades* was made popular by Strayer 1992 (1st ed. 1971).
221. The deicidal Jews he called malicious and insane. *Defensor pacis* I,i,2; I,xiii,4; I,xix,4; *Defensor minor* XII,3.
222. *Defensor pacis* I,ix,4; *Defensor minor* XII,3.

were not discarded overnight. As we have seen, the old universalism retained "a quite remarkable degree of currency" in fourteenth-century
political thought.[223] This century, however, also witnessed the first serious questioning of universal power as such.

The advocates and defenders of empire believed world monarchy was
necessary for the reign of peace. In support of their belief, they often referred to the *pax romana*. Their idealized image of the Roman Empire
as a pacifying force bringing peace to the whole world had been cultivated by imperial apologists since the reestablishment of the western empire under the Carolingians. Dante, as we have seen, was a devotee of
the idea of "Roman peace." Under Emperor Augustus, he maintained,
mankind had been "resting happily in universal peace."[224] Marsiglio of
Padua wrote, in a similar vein, that under Roman imperial rule all had
enjoyed "the blessings of peace."[225] Engelbert of Admont, however,
under the influence of Augustine's concept of the *civitas terrena* and his
critical judgment of the Roman Empire in particular, relativized the *pax
romana* ideal. Augustinian "pessimism" about the earthly city colored
Engelbert's reflections on empire as well. If empire was the most perfect
regnum, as a terrestrial *regnum* it could only be imperfect. Peace was
thus something it could ever strive for but never fully achieve.

The idealized image of "Roman peace" fared much worse at the hands
of French royalist propagandists from the beginning of the fourteenth
century—not because they disagreed with the idea of universal peace,
but because that universal peace had been Roman and not French. Obsessed as they were with the mystique of French kingship and kingdom,
and driven by the idée fixe of the universal mission of their "most Christian" king and people, they could not feel at rest until *pax romana* had
been replaced by *pax gallica*. Universal peace remained the ideal, but
now this peace was to be made and kept by the king—by the French king,
that is, since the ideal peace could only be realized by the ideal king.

Refutation of the "Roman peace" went hand in hand with rejection of
empire. By the time the idea of empire came to be contested by the king's
asserting himself as the supreme authority within the territory of his
rule, the western "Holy Roman" empire had reclaimed its Roman line-
age. As such, the empire in the West was supposed to be the realization
of a lofty ideal. Rejection of the existing late-medieval empire could not

223. Wilks 1964, 422.
224. *Monarchia* I,xvi,2. Cf. n. 32.
225. See n. 190.

hope to be really effective unless it involved renunciation of the empire's ideal image and ideal claims.

IT IS BETTER THAT MANY SHOULD RULE
IN MANY KINGDOMS: JOHN OF PARIS

Historians concur that among the polemical treatises written in support of Philip IV, John of Paris's work was "much the ablest" in its "comprehensiveness of treatment and in its overall intellectual force." [226] John's most famous treatise, *On Royal and Papal Power (De potestate regia e papali)*, was written in the first years of the fourteenth century.[227] Together with Giles of Rome's *On Ecclesiastical Power* and James of Viterbo's *On Christian Government,* it is one of the key theoretical tracts in the conflict between Philip IV and Boniface VIII.[228]

John directed his argument against the papal claim to jurisdiction in temporal affairs. His opposition to papal temporal power rested on the affirmation of kingdom as "the government of a perfect or self-sufficient community by one man for the sake of the common good" and the form of government most suited to providing unity and peace.[229] But John's justification of kingdom was a polemical device. To undermine the basis on which the pope could claim temporal authority over the king, John had to demonstrate that "neither in principle nor practice does the royal power . . . come from the pope but from God and the people who choose a king either as an individual or as a member of a dynasty." [230] Given kingdom's nature, origin, and goal, there were no grounds for the priesthood to claim superiority over royal power in temporal matters.[231] But John's antipapal argument was simultaneously anti-imperial. By declaring that kingly power rested on the choice of God and the people, John was asserting the independence of royal power from imperial authority as well.

John's central thesis was that universal power in temporal affairs could be founded on neither divine nor natural law. His first "systemic" argu-

---

226. See Watt 1971, 11.
227. On John of Paris and his *De potestate,* see Bleienstein 1969; Watt 1971. Cf. Scholz 1903, 275 ff.; Carlyle and Carlyle 1903–36, 5: 422 ff.; Rivière 1926, 148 ff., 281 ff.; McIlwain 1932, 263 ff.; Lewis 1954, 1: 115 ff.; Tierney 1988, 195 ff.; Canning 1996, 145 ff.
228. Canning 1996, 142.
229. *On Royal and Papal Power* I (pp. 76, 78).
230. Ibid., X (p. 124).
231. Cf. ibid., XVIII (p. 190).

ment to substantiate his thesis went as follows: While the "ordering of all to one supreme head" was valid for the Church, this principle of order did not apply to secular rule. It did not follow from the monarchical structure of the Church that "the ordinary faithful are commanded by divine law to be subject in temporalities to any single supreme monarch." Their natural instinct, implanted by God, taught them to live as citizens in ordered communities. But "[n]either man's natural tendencies nor divine law commands a single supreme temporal monarchy for everyone."[232] John rested this conclusion on four premises. First, temporal power is characterized by diversity of climate and differences in physical constitution. Second, "one man cannot rule the world in temporal affairs as can one alone in spiritual affairs," because it is far easier to extend the verbal authority by which spiritual power governs than to establish physical authority over space. The length of the arm that wields the sword is limited. Third, "the temporalities of laymen are not communal" and there is therefore no need for one "to administer temporalities in common."[233] And fourth, from the fact that all the faithful are united in the one universal faith without which there is no salvation, it does not follow that "all the faithful should be united in one political community." Against such a view John asserted that "there are different ways of life and constitutions adapted to the different climates, languages and conditions of people."[234] To support his final conclusion—that "the temporal rulership of the world does not demand the rule of a single man as does spiritual rulership"—John mustered the authority of Aristotle and Augustine. Aristotle, John pointed out, had shown in his *Politics* that individual political communities "are natural but not that of an empire or one-man rule." And in book IV of the *City of God* Augustine had said that "a society is better and more peacefully ruled when the authority of each realm was confined within its own frontiers."[235] John also referred to Augustine's denunciation of the expansion of the Roman Empire, which he said was driven by Rome's ambition to dominate and by injurious provocation of others.[236] Augustine indeed had portrayed the expansion of the Roman Empire as an unhappy story. "Is it wise or

232. Ibid., III (p. 85).

233. For the discussion by twelfth-century and thirteenth-century lawyers on whether the emperor had the right over his subjects' private property, see Pennington 1993b, 13 ff.

234. *On Royal and Papal Power* III (pp. 85–86). On the medieval theory of climate and its implications for the moral teaching of the Church, see Tooley 1953.

235. *On Royal and Papal Power* III (p. 87).

236. Ibid.

prudent to wish to glory in the breadth and magnitude of an empire when you cannot show that the men whose empire it is are happy?" Augustine asked. And he continued: "For the Romans always lived in dark fear and cruel lust, surrounded by the disasters of war and the shedding of blood which, whether that of fellow citizens or enemies, was human nonetheless. The joy of such men may be compared to the fragile splendour of glass: they are horribly afraid lest it be suddenly shattered."[237] Augustine also wrote that had the wars that aided the growth of the Roman Empire not taken place, human affairs would have been happier and all kingdoms would have been small, rejoicing in concord with their neighbors. "There would be as many kingdoms among the nations of the world as there are now houses of the citizens of a city."[238]

John further demystified the Roman imperial peace in his discussion of the *Donation of Constantine*. This famous eighth-century forgery claimed that Emperor Constantine the Great had exalted "the most sacred seat of St. Peter" above the "empire and earthly throne"; given it "imperial power, the dignity of glory, strength, and honor"; and "translated" the western empire to Pope Sylvester I and to his successors at the Papal See.[239] As such, the document bolstered the pope's position vis-à-vis the emperor. The aim of John's critique of the alleged translation of the western empire was to prove that the pope had no power over the king of France. Even if the *Donation of Constantine* were valid, that would be of no consequence for the Franks. The Franks, John argued, had never been subject to the Roman emperor. Therefore the emperor could not transfer power over them to the pope, since the emperor had not possessed that power.[240] Once again, a polemical blow directed against the pope struck the empire as well. Another blow was dealt by John directly to the empire. "The world was never as peaceful in the time of the emperors," he stated, "as it was beforehand and afterwards." Under the rule of the emperors, "[b]rother would murder brother and mother her son and *vice versa,* while dreadful crimes and great strife ran riot throughout the world."[241]

If the Romans had usurped the empire from the Greeks and estab-

---

237. *The City of God* IV,3 (Dyson's translation).
238. Ibid., IV,15 (Dyson's translation).
239. *Constitutum Constantini* 11, 17; trans. in Cantor 1963, 130, 132. Cf. Morrison 1969, 155 ff.; Herrin 1987, 304; Canning 1996, 73 f.
240. *On Royal and Papal Power* XXI (pp. 224–25). Cf. Carlyle and Carlyle 1903–36, 5: 147, 432–33.
241. *On Royal and Papal Power* XXI (p. 227).

lished their domination by force, then others would be justified in throwing off Roman lordship by force as well. After all, their submission to Roman rule had been imposed on them.[242] But John went beyond representing the Roman Empire as perishable, that is, just as transient as the empires that had existed before the Romans created theirs. He declared empire itself as undesirable. It is true that he showed a sympathetic understanding for imperial power when he reflected on the "defence of the people against infidels and pagans" in cases "when there seemed no possibility of any other defender presenting himself."[243] This amounted to saying that imperial rule was preferable to infidel rule. But in normal circumstances, there seemed to be nothing to say in defense of empire. And when it came to imagining an ideal world order and to formulating principles, John of Paris wrote a famous, path-breaking[244] sentence: "it is better that many should rule in many kingdoms than one alone should rule the whole world."[245]

THE NAME *KING* IS MORE DIGNIFIED THAN THE NAME *EMPEROR: THE SONGE DU VERGIER*

In the year 1382, Pope Urban IV complained to Emperor Wenceslas that the "French nation has always aspired to the empire," not to speak of the papacy's sufferings at the hands of the French. "It is not only the papacy, not only the empire, that the French would be prepared to usurp if only their means matched their ambitions, but the monarchy of the whole world."[246] In their common decline, the two universal powers seem to have found some mutual understanding. But the universalist idea did not diminish along with them. It only became dissociated from its traditional bearers.

The development of French universalism was based on the growing power of the king. It blossomed first under Philip IV and flourished again under the rule of another king who had a vivid sense of princely grandeur, Charles V (1364–80). Charles was reputed to be wise, and his rule was described as intelligent and responsible. His court attracted a

242. Ibid., 227–28.
243. Ibid., XV (p. 173).
244. Cf. Zeller 1934, 296: "C'est la première atteinte portée à la conception unitaire du monde, dont la pensée du Moyen Age avait fait un dogme. Le monisme politique cesse d'être hors de discussion."
245. "[M]ellius est tamen plures in pluribus regnis dominari quam unum dominari toti mundo." *Über königl. u. päpstl. Gewalt* XXI (p. 190). Cf. *On Royal and Papal Power*, 227.
246. Quoted in Zeller 1934, 307–8.

number of able intellectuals.[247] In the political literature of Charles V's period, however, there was hardly anything new. Historians have argued that everything had been said in Philip IV's time, and the remainder was said by the close of the contest between Pope John XXII and Emperor Lewis of Bavaria (Marsiglio's *Defensor pacis* is a good example).[248] With regard to political ideas, especially those concerned with the relation between temporal and secular powers, the conflict between Philip IV and Boniface VIII held central place—at least from the time when early Gallican and Protestant authors began their search for sources that could buttress their arguments.[249]

A tract that has often been singled out among the literary productions of Charles V's court is a fictitious dialogue between a priest and a knight, the *Somnium viridarii,* probably written in 1376 or 1377. It also circulated in a vernacular translation as the *Songe du vergier.* This piece is said to merit the attention of historians of political ideas in particular.[250] The dialogue it contains is a "vast compilation of material on relations between Church and State and on royal rights in general." Apparently, it was commissioned by the king to be used as a dossier of arguments for royal power, "perhaps in view of his drive against clerical privileges and jurisdiction."[251] It drew heavily on French royalist polemics from the turn of the thirteenth and fourteenth centuries—so much that it has been characterized as an expansion of the *Dispute between a Priest and a Knight.*[252] The unidentified author also incorporated parts of the *Defensor pacis.*[253] In sum, the work is a "clumsy blend of extracts from many sources" and a "strange mosaic."[254] While all this is true, I argue that the *Songe du vergier*'s author not only added new emphases to the old themes[255] but, within a fairly conventional framework of discussion, also accomplished an important shift in the articulation of royal power.

The relation between temporal and spiritual powers was the *Songe du vergier*'s leading theme.[256] The priest unsuccessfully argued that

247. Cf. ibid., 305 f.; Willard 1984, 20 ff., 126 f.
248. McIlwain 1932, 314; Zeller 1934, 305. Cf. Beaune 1991, 177.
249. Lewis 1954, 1: 130; Lagarde 1956, 210.
250. Cf. McIlwain 1932, 315.
251. Smalley 1965, 38.
252. Lewis 1954, 1: 130.
253. *Defensor pacis* II,viii,9-II,ix,2; II,xxiii,3-II,xxiv,7.
254. Coopland 1949, 33–34.
255. Zeller 1934, 305.
256. For a comprehensive treatment of the political philosophy of the *Songe,* see Quillet 1977.

monarchical lordship over the world in spiritual and temporal affairs—
la monarchie du monde en espiritualité & temporalité—belonged to the
pope.[257] The priest's invocation of the pontiff's dignity and the ensuing
claim that the pope had the right to "lordship over the whole world"
were refuted by the knight as nonsensical. Such a claim was as absurd
as if France had wished to rule over Spain just because France was more
noble, dignified, and perfect than the *royaulme d'Espaigne*.[258] This argument is interesting for more than one reason. It reiterates the view that
the pope could not claim power in the temporal sphere as a self-evident
truth. It was simply "not true" that the pope was *souverain du maistre
de la loy seculiere*.[259] It followed from this "truth," moreover, that the
French Church was in temporal affairs subject to the king.[260] And finally
the argument displays a very clear sense of the rightful independence of
territorial powers and represents them as morally and politically self-
sufficient.[261] The king is responsible for seeing that men refrain from doing evil and for inducing them to good. Kingly power is limited, it is
true,[262] but in governing their kingdoms, kings recognize no power above
themselves: *ne recognoissent souverain en terre*.[263] They were "most sovereign" princes and lords[264] and considered themselves emperors in their
own realms.[265]

The juristic tag of king as emperor in his own kingdom was of course
not new. The novelty here was that the author of the *Songe du vergier*
overcame a feeling of royal inferiority vis-à-vis the emperor, which had
been inherent in the *rex imperator* formula. The priest in this dialogue
(whose literary role was to lose one argument after another) had to vindicate not only the pope but also the emperor. He defended the position
that the emperor was "the lord of the world," that to the emperor belonged "monarchy over the whole world," and that all nations of the
world were subject to the emperor.[266] The knight responded first with an
argument familiar from John of Paris's *On Royal and Papal Power*: there

257. *Le songe du vergier* I,55.
258. Ibid., I,50.
259. Ibid., I,96
260. E.g., ibid., I,98.
261. Ibid.
262. This aspect is of special interest to Carlyle and Carlyle 1903–36, 6: 37–39.
263. *Songe du vergier* I,136.
264. Cf. the addresses of the king in the *Songe*'s opening and closing exhortation. See
Babbitt 1985, 32, 43 (warning against considering such addresses and statements a "sovereignty in the sense given by Bodin").
265. *Songe du vergier* II,15. For *Imperator vel Rex,* cf. II,33.
266. Ibid., I,35.

was no law, either divine or human, on which the imperial monarchy and lordship (*monarchie & seigneurie de l'empire*) could be founded.[267] The emperor's lordship over the whole world and over kings and princes of the earth was, first of all, contrary to the "ordinance of God who had divided the lordships of the world among kings, dukes, and other earthly lords."[268] It could not be derived from either the Old or the New Testament. Nor could the justification of the imperial monarchy be deduced from any other species of law: natural, civil, ecclesiastical, or the law of nations. The empire had no legal basis.

After combining juridical with theological and historical arguments, the knight became more specific. He proffered evidence that France had never been subject to the empire or to a part of it[269] and that the king of France, neither de facto nor de jure, had recognized any superior.[270] The emperor had as much right to dictate laws to France as the French king had to dictate them to the empire.[271] In making these points, the knight drew on a stock of conventional ideas, but he used them to propound an unprecedented view that was, "from the Roman point of view, quasi-sacrilegious."[272] The priest insinuated that by representing the king as a prince who recognized no power superior to his own, the knight aimed at creating a "new emperor";[273] the knight responded that the king of France well might call himself emperor and his realm an empire.[274] But it was a much greater honor to him to be called *roy de France*. "The name of *king*," the royal apologist argued, "is namely older and more dignified: for the Old and New Testament evidence that the name *emperor* is of a newer date." Moreover, the knight continued, in the Scriptures the Creator of the world had been called the king of kings and not the emperor of emperors. The conclusion was emphatic: "I know," said the knight, that the king of France is "emperor in his realm and that he could call himself emperor, yet he cannot call himself by a more dignified name than King of France."[275]

---

267. Ibid., I,36.
268. Ibid.
269. Ibid., I,88.
270. Ibid., I,36. Cf. I,88 ("le roy de France peut estre dit empereur en son royaulme, car il ne recongnoist souverain en terre"); I,110 ("sur le roy de France n'a aucune seigneurie en la temporalité").
271. Ibid., I,8, 36.
272. Zeller 1934, 306.
273. *Songe du vergier* I,37.
274. Ibid., I,36.
275. Ibid., I,39.

The *Songe du vergier* was generally not as rhetorically efficient as this. Its author took almost a hundred chapters to arrive at the point that "all jurisdiction in any people or community is dependent on him who is the head and principal of that community." [276] An important element of that power was the right to wage war, which belonged exclusively to the prince who recognized no superior on earth. No other person could justly make war unless authorized by his sovereign prince.[277] The king was the *prins en guerre*.[278] This view of royal authority would have considerable material consequences. The right to make war, in the first place, would license "the kings who do not recognize a superior power in this world, such as the king of France," to levy extraordinary taxes if "the king wishes to go [to war] against the heretics, Saracens and other enemies of the faith." [279]

Extraordinary jurisdiction of the king had been discussed before, and the polemical literature from the confrontation between Philip IV and Boniface VIII, in which this issue had figured prominently, was not forgotten in Charles V's France. But the writer of the *Songe du vergier* took the debate on the authority to make war to a new conclusion. He denied the pope—whom he called somewhat inaccurately, given the pope's residence in Avignon, the "Roman Holy Father" [280]—the right to make war. The pope was not entitled to "give permission to Christians to wage war against the Saracens or against those who held in their hands and occupied the Church's patrimony." Nor was he allowed to grant remission of sins to "those who go beyond the sea to make war on the infidels or to those who go against the rebels against the Church without permission of their sovereign lord secular prince." [281] As a subsidiary argument, the author of the *Songe du vergier* reminded the reader of the old interdict barring clerics from bearing arms. But the author's main argument was that it was unlawful for the pope to make war because the right to make war, and to give his subjects permission to go to war, belonged solely to

276. Ibid., II,146.
277. Ibid., I,154.
278. Ibid., I,136.
279. Ibid.
280. A whole chapter was dedicated to demonstrating "que le saint pere doit mieulx demourer en France que à Romme" because France was the holiest place in Christendom. Ibid., I,156. An anonymous writer, probably Oresme, argued that Christ's vicar should dwell in the midst of Christendom, which was Marseille, but that, in any case, "ubi papa, ibi Roma." See Hay 1968, 75.
281. *Songe du vergier* I,154.

the secular ruler. The author insisted on the secular prince's exclusive right to war-making, even concluding (forgetting for a moment the canonical ban on the clerical participation in warfare) that the secular prince could give license to make war to the pope himself.[282] From papal monarchism's point of view, this was indeed the world turned upside down. However, not even the *souverain* was permitted to go to war against the Saracens if they "wished to live in peace," for if God had let them live in peace, Christians should as well.[283]

How radical this argument was may be better appreciated after comparison with Bonet's popular *Tree of Battles,* written a decade later. As did the author of the *Songe du vergier,* Bonet cited Matthew 5.45—that the heavenly Father "makes his sun rise on good and bad alike"—when discussing arguments against waging war on the unbelievers.[284] But Bonet's position was that "war can be made against the Saracens" on a number of grounds. First, God has power over both the faithful and the infidel. His vicar and provost-general on earth, the pope, therefore can punish the Saracens and Jews for their sins if they act against the law of nature. Second, the pope can give indulgences to those fighting against the unbelievers to "recover the holy land of Jerusalem which was gained by lawful conquest for Christians by the passion of Jesus Christ our Lord." Third, the pope can grant the right to conquest over those infidels who oppress the Christians living under their rule. A fourth reason was probably not found in canon law: If the emperor or Christian kings wished to undertake an expedition beyond the sea, the pope should not forbid it, "for he should confirm the devotion of Christian princes and aid them with all his power; but only if it appeared to him, on good counsel, that the war was expedient." [285] Moreover, for Bonet, the common weal of Christendom overrode the jurisdiction of a Christian prince within his own territory. Discussing, for example, the question of "whether a Christian king can give safe-conduct to a Saracen king," Bonet argued that, as a rule, such a treaty or agreement should be honored by neither Christian princes nor the Christian people.[286] In the *Songe du vergier,* on the other hand, jurisdiction of the territorial kingdom was

---

282. "[P]ar especial il n'appartient pas au pape faire guerre sans la licence du prince seculier." Ibid.

283. Ibid.

284. *Le songe du vergier* refers, among others, to Innocent IV.

285. *The Tree of Battles* IV,ii.

286. Ibid., IV,cvi.

rendered supreme. One proof that the pope was not *seigneur de tout le monde* was that he did not have power over the pagans.[287]

With the pope denied power over Christian kings and the infidels, one might expect that the crusade would be done away with. Actually, it was not. But holy war had to undergo a "structural adjustment." As I showed earlier, it began to pass from the hands of the universal powers into the hands of the territorial ruler. In the *Songe du vergier,* the king of France still wages war against the heretics, Saracens, and other "enemies of the faith,"[288] but no longer "at the bidding of the priest and at the command of the emperor."[289] Moreover, the king's first responsibility was to his own peace and the peace of his subjects, the "people."[290] But the enemies of the faith and the Church could not be forgotten, even though war against them could not be undertaken under just any circumstances or fought in just any manner.[291]

The discussion of war in the *Songe du vergier* relies heavily on the doctrine of just war. It deviates from that doctrine, however, on one important point. The author argues that the authority to make war descended from God.[292] Because the authority to make war belonged exclusively to the "sovereign prince," the author implies that that authority descended from God directly to the king. In the context of the *Songe du vergier's* main argument, this is just another assertion of the independence of the territorial *souverain* from the universal powers, in particular, the elimination of any mediator between the prince and God. (The author even made the *souverain* mediator between God and the pope.)[293] But bringing the prince's action closer to God has tricky consequences. It divinifies the princely business. In contrast to the traditional Christian doctrine of just war, in which the edict as a necessary requirement for just war is issued by a legitimate worldly authority,[294] the writer of the *Songe du vergier* argues that just war is dependent on God's will and command.[295] But war willed by God is holy. If just war as willed by God can only be waged by the "sovereign prince," then the secular ruler's war becomes

---

287. *Songe du vergier* II,35.
288. Cf. n. 279.
289. Cf. chap. 3 n. 341.
290. *Songe du vergier* I,154.
291. Cf. n. 283; *Songe du vergier* I,158.
292. *Songe du vergier* I,154.
293. See n. 282.
294. Cf. chap. 2 n. 22.
295. *Songe du vergier* I,154.

holy. Thus, I would maintain, the just war argument used in the *Songe du vergier* was directed against the pope, not against holy war.

TO PUT A STOP TO THE PROCESS
OF UNIFICATION: NICOLE ORESME

Nicole Oresme's view of power was so similar to that of the *Songe du vergier* that that text has been attributed to him. But only Oresme's influence on the author of the *Songe du vergier* seems to be certain.[296] Oresme is reputed to have been "the theoretician of kingly power" and "the advocate of the strictest particularism."[297] Arguing against universal rule, he introduced the notion of universal monarchy, marking, in my opinion, a decisive break with the belief in the legitimacy of the medieval universal powers; this notion was to become of great significance in the political literature of the early modern period.

Oresme was an adviser to King Charles V who translated into French a number of Aristotle's works so the king and his counselors could read them.[298] Oresme's argument against universal lordship is concentrated in a lengthy gloss to his translation of Aristotle's *Politics*. Oresme first summarized and then refuted one by one the arguments in favor of *monarchie sus tous, empire universel et total*. His refutation is based on the Aristotelian notion of perfect community—*communitas perfecta* (or, in Moerbeke's Latin translation, *communitas perfecta civitas*)—as a respectable alternative to the empire.[299] Oresme granted fullness of power to the pope. This, however, did not undermine Oresme's negative assessment of universal power in the temporal sphere, since different laws applied to the government of civil communities (*policies humaines*)[300] on

296. See Quillet 1977, pt. 3. Meunier, who compiled an annotated list of Oresme's work, had disputed Oresme's authorship of the *Somnium viridarii;* a more likely author, to his mind, was de Mézières, who had read Oresme's translation of *Politics.* Meunier 1857, 134 f., 85.

297. Quillet 1977, 130. Cf. Babbitt 1985.

298. Cf. Babbit 1985, 8–9; Guenée 1991, 109 f. These translations are listed in Meunier 1857, 85 ff.

299. Cf. Babbitt 1985, 46.

300. Oresme explained the French terms he used in the "Table des expositions des fors mos de *Politiques*." "*Policie* est l'ordenance du gouvernement de toute la communité ou multitude civile. Et policie est l'ordre des princeys ou offices publiques. Et est dit de *polis* en grec, qu'est multitude ou cité." And: "*Princey* est la puissance et auctorité ou domination et seigneurie du prince. Et est ce qui est en latin appellé *principatus*. Et en ceste science cest mot est pris assés largement. Car si comme il appert ou quart livre par le .xxi.e chapitre [of *Politics*], tous offices sunt diz *princeys* qui ont povoir de conseillier des choses publiques ou de faire jugemens ou de commander." *Le Livre de Politiques,* 373. A dictionary of Oresme's French terms was also compiled by Meunier 1857, 161 ff.

the one hand, and to the exercise of papal power on the other. Whereas the Holy Father was given power by divine miracle through the special grace of the Holy Spirit, political life was ruled by "practical reason," the science taught by the Philosopher.[301] According to that science, to be effectively and justly governed, a political community should be neither too small nor too big, but just big enough to be self-sufficient. A kingdom was such a moderate and measured political community. "Temporal universal monarchy," on the other hand, was "neither just nor expedient."[302] Belief in the possibility of just and effective universal monarchy was so removed from practical reason—*trop loing de raison pratique*—that, following Aristotle, it should be called a political sophism, deserving ridicule rather than serious debate.[303] This comment, however, did not stop Oresme from seriously discussing and refuting universal monarchy. (He even claimed credit for being the first to do so.)[304] It was unacceptable, he argued, mainly because it was ungovernable. The world in its entirety was ruled by divine knowledge and power. "But there is no human knowledge and power sufficient for ordering [*ordener*] all the men in the world."[305]

A similar argument, also referring to Aristotle's teaching, had been made by Dante's critic Guido Vernani. Because "the king must surpass and excel in virtue the entire multitude of his subjects, the monarch of the whole human race must surpass the whole human race in the moral virtues and in prudence." But since it was "impossible ever to find such a faultless human, . . . Jesus Christ alone and none other was the true monarch."[306] Guido admitted that Dante's argument for the need of temporal monarchy "has some truth." He agreed that "it is a good thing for the world to have a single monarch." Yet, Dante's "foolish mind" had been darkened by the "spirit of faction," and he had been "unable to discover the true monarch." For Guido, that true monarch was the pope. "God alone must principally possess and does possess the rank and power of a monarch." Through the Petrine commission, the monarchi-

---

301. *Le Livre,* 292–93 (250d, 251a).
302. Ibid., 292 (250d). The expediency argument was repeated by Bonet, but within a limited political horizon: it was not "expedient for the Holy Church, or for Christendom, that the King of France should be subject to the Emperor." *The Tree of Battles* IV,lxxxiii.
303. *Le Livre,* 293 (251c, 252a).
304. Ibid., 289–90 (247c-d).
305. Ibid., 288 (246a).
306. *De reprobatione Monarchiae* (Caesar 1989, 112).

cal power was given to His vicar on earth. Therefore "the monarch of the world is the supreme pontiff of the Christians."[307]

Although their premises were similar, Guido and Oresme came to diametrically opposite conclusions. Oresme parted ways with the very logic of universal power—which had been shared, for example, by both Dante and his critic Guido. For Oresme, there was no "true monarch." The world needed to be governed, but it could not be governed by any single person. "Practical reason" demonstrated that in too extensive a realm, no prince, even with the help of his plenipotentiaries, could know all the facts and all the persons of distinction and so would be unable "to either judge well or to distribute honors and offices."[308] He would have to rule foreign peoples, but this was both "against nature that a man rules a people whose mother tongue he does not know,"[309] and against the divine commandment that "you are not permitted to put a foreigner over you."[310] In such a situation, *communication civile* would be impossible, and as a consequence, political community would decline.[311] Because too big a polity could not be well ordered, "such big kingdoms were not true kingdoms but violent and tyrannical usurpations."[312] Oresme resolutely rejected the view that such huge monarchies created benefits for all. They were, rather, tyrannies in which only the princes grew rich while their subjects lived in misery and poverty.[313] Moreover, once kingdoms became excessively big, they inevitably declined and were destroyed.[314] Nature itself, with its variety of climates, dictated the existence of many separate kingdoms (*divisio regnorum*). Seas, large rivers, and deserts divided peoples from each other, and peoples divided in this way had different temperaments and customs. Human laws had to accommodate to

307. Ibid., 112–13. Cf. Lewis 1954, 1: 237; Wilks 1964, 417.

308. *Le Livre*, 291 (249c).

309. Marsiglio used this argument against the priests. It was scandalous that "the Roman bishops, using their plenary power . . . , appoint persons who are ignorant of divine letters, uneducated and incapable, and very often men of corrupt morals and notorious criminals, who cannot even speak the language of the people over whom they are placed." *Defensor pacis* II,xxiv,2; cf. II,xxiv,3.

310. "L'en ne doit pas avoir roy d'estrange nation." *Le Livre*, 291 (250a); referring to Deut 17.15. Claude de Seyssel repeated this argument in the early sixteenth century in his *La Monarchie de France* I,8, but applied it only to France itself, not to the countries conquered by France. For Seyssel, language was the most efficient and reliable instrument of imperial rule, and with this in view he lauded his king "[que] vous travaillez à enrichir et magnifier la langue française." *Exorde*, 65–7. The idea was to become a "humanistic commonplace." Pagden 1990, 55–56.

311. *Le Livre*, 291 (249d–250a).

312. Ibid., 289 (247c); 293 (252b).

313. Ibid., 293 (252b).

314. Ibid., 292 (250b-d).

these diversities. Both Oresme and the *Songe du vergier* argued against the universal validity of Roman law, and Oresme asserted that different peoples had to have different "positive laws."[315] Universal monarchy, contradicting this imperative, would be a monster: it would cease to be a *cité* and would become *une chose confuse.*[316] This was why "God and nature do not will such a monarchy." *Divisio regnorum* was not only a fact of nature, it was God's will: God "ordered things in such a way that there are many sovereign princes in the world."[317] It was right for different peoples to have different human laws and different governments.

Oresme not only rejected the idea of universal unity that had been central to medieval political thought (and survived well beyond the Middle Ages); he also did not spare the principle of *ordinatio ad unum* of the Philosopher he so admired. Because this Aristotelian principle played such a prominent role in Dante's imperial political vision, Oresme has been called the antipole of Dante's universalist aspirations.[318] Oresme's rejection of universal monarchy was indeed consistent and radical. While universal rule embodied the ideal of unity, its opposite, separatism, was a bête noire of medieval political thought. Oresme overthrew the value system in which the idea of universal unity was highly praised and separatism was disallowed. In response to the critique of separatism *(que multitude de princeys ou de royalmes est une separation),* he made the previously unheard of assertion that separatism was prudent and expedient, and drew out the logical conclusion of his argument: One should put a stop to the process of unification, *met[tre] arrest ou procés de la uniement.*[319]

Universal lordship had ceased to be self-evidently legitimate, natural, and accepted as a given. True enough, it had been questioned before. But never had the rejection of universal worldly rule been as clear as with Oresme. (John of Paris's advocacy of the pluralism of powers, for example, was, in at least one instance, fuzzy.)[320] Oresme founded the rejec-

---

315. Ibid., 291 (249d); 293 (251d).
316. Ibid., 291 (249b); 289 (247a).
317. Ibid., 291 (249d).
318. Quillet 1977, 158.
319. *Le Livre,* 294 (252c-d). Oresme's reference here was Augustine *De civitate Dei* XIX,7.
320. "[E]ach king is head in his own kingdom, and the emperor, if there is one, is monarch and head of the world [*et imperator monarcha si fuerit est caput mundi*]." *On Royal and Papal Power* XVIII (p. 193); *Über königl. u. päpstl. Gewalt,* 165. For Carlyle and Carlyle 1903–36, 5: 147, it was "not very easy to say what John means." In addition, John accepted empire as a shield against the infidels. Cf. n. 243.

tion of universal rule on firm theoretical principles and a positive vision of an alternative to empire. He considered universal temporal power an excessive augmentation of kingdom; it tended to *accrestre un royaulme excedenment,* and he rejected precisely this tendency to disproportionate growth.[321] Conventionally, the territorial kingdom had been seen as pathological and a pathogen—as a departure from the norm of unity and as eating away at empire. Oresme turned this picture upside down: empire became a deformation of kingdom, a deformed kingdom. Royal propagandists at the turn of the thirteenth and fourteenth centuries had striven to substitute the kingdom for empire and/or papacy as the new bearer of political universalism. Oresme rejected political universalism as such. He posited the territorially limited kingdom as the normal and ideal perfect political community. Others, inspired by the rediscovery of Aristole's political philosophy, had attempted to construct transitions from *polis* to kingdom and then to universal forms of power unknown to the Greek philosopher but dominating the medieval world.[322] Oresme, in contrast, assimilated the Aristotelian polity to the idea of kingdom, thus establishing a standard for judging worldly power.

For Oresme, kingdom was a well-ordered and legitimate territorial monarchy.[323] If a monarchy were to be the government of a perfect political community and not degenerate either in tyranny or "confusion," it had to be territorial—that is, limited in size. From this insight Oresme introduced the concept of universal monarchy (*universele monarchie* or *monarchie universele*), meaning a political monstrosity, a deformed political community (*cité*). At first glance, it seems odd to argue that the concept of universal monarchy was introduced only at this late stage of medieval political thought. The term *universal monarchy* is often used in histories of political thought as a description for a variety of claims to universal power. It is most frequently associated with Dante's *Monarchia*.[324] A closer scrutiny of the *Monarchia* shows, however, that what Dante argued for was empire. He used the term *universal monarchy* only once, in a descriptive, explanatory clause: "undivided universal

321. *Le Livre,* 292 (250d).
322. Cf. Woolf 1913, 266 ff.
323. "*Monarche* est cellui qu'un seul tient le souverain princey sus une cité ou sus un païz. . . ." "*Monarchie* est la policie ou le princey que tient un seul. Et sunt .ii. especes generals de monarchie; une est royaulme et l'autre est tyrannie." "Table des expositions," *Le Livre,* 372.
324. Cf. Mastnak 1993. For Dante (in this context), see especially Burns 1992, chap. 5. Cf. Jordan 1921.

monarchy [is] the essence of the Empire."[325] But elsewhere he asserted that the notion of empire did not need descriptive explanations.[326]

Universal monarchy, in Oresme's gloss to Aristotle's *Politics,* was not identical with empire. Oresme divested empire of its glamour by reducing the concept to its etymological meaning: *imperium* became a term merely denoting the exercise of power, a trait belonging to any form of princely power or authority.[327] By rejecting universal temporal power as such, Oresme extricated himself from his contemporaries' habit of playing one universal power against the other.[328] But what really distinguishes Oresme is that he saw universal monarchy not as a form of government but as a territorial power, albeit one that had lost its bearings. On the other hand, because by definition empire was without borders, it could not be a territorial power. It meant instead the lordship of the world, *monarchia mundi.*[329] For Oresme, universal monarchy was characterized by the excessive growth of princely power and territory beyond its due. With Oresme, the universalization of power had ceased to be legitimate. If not an outright usurpation, universal monarchy was bound to end up in usurpation. It was a tendency that had to be arrested.

Universal monarchy is an early modern concept.[330] It was a "new ideology" that finally emerged in the sixteenth century on the ruins of the *respublica christiana.*[331] It signified claims to power and domination

---

325. "[C]onsistente Imperio in unitate Monarchie universalis." *Monarchia* III,x,9. For another use of universal monarchy to describe the empire, cf. Marsiglio's *De translatione* I: "the term 'Roman Empire' signifies a universal or general monarchy over the whole world."

326. Having defined universal rule as the supreme office of command, "universale e inrepugnabile officio di commandare," Dante added: "E questo officio per eccellenza Imperio è chiamato, senza nulla addizione." *Convivio* IV,iv,6–7.

327. See "Table des expositions" (cf. n. 300), the entry *Princey:* "les souverains princes sunt appellés *empereurs.* Car *imperare,* ce est commander." *Le Livre,* 373.

328. A typical case in point was Guido Vernani's critique of Dante. See n. 307. Around 1400, another adversary of Dante, William of Cremona, similarly accepted world monarchy, but argued that the universal monarch was Christ: "Christus, verus deus, totius humani generis fuit et est universalis monarcha verus." *Tractatus de iure Monarchie;* quoted in Nardi 1944, 187.

329. For this reason I find Robertson's explanation of the introduction of the concept *monarchia universalis* questionable: "The development of the concept of empire in particular was complicated by the existence of the—Holy Roman—Empire, an association which encouraged the elaboration of a synonym, 'universal monarchy,' to convey the more general idea of rule over extensive territory." Robertson 1995, 5. In support of his explanation, Robertson refers to Bosbach 1988, whom I do not understand as saying precisely this.

330. Bosbach 1988.

331. Saitta 1948, 23; Brezzi 1954, 77.

beyond a ruler's own proper—legitimate—sphere of authority.[332] I see in Oresme's conceptualization of the universal monarchy two centuries earlier a decisive shift toward such an early-modern understanding. The time when the papacy would be portrayed as "no other, than the *Ghost* of the deceased *Romane Empire,* sitting crowned upon the grave thereof," [333] or when the European powers would be pictured as hounds on the chase of the "exorbitant power," [334] was still far away. There would be a revival of universalist ideology in the fifteenth century.[335] However, Oresme's refutation of the process of unification and his affirmation of separation marked the beginning of the end of an era.

THE CRUSADE SPIRIT: STILL "THE WILL OF GOD"

During the mid to late fourteenth century the papal monarchy and the empire were being challenged and Christendom was disintegrating, but the crusading movement did not share the fate of the world it had helped to create and whose expression it was. While the crusading movement remained relevant and popular, its character changed slightly. Three factors were important in determining the character of crusading in this period. One of these was the plague. The widespread economic and social dislocation it caused in Latin Christendom is well known. The destructiveness of the *bella intestina* (the wars among Christians, especially the Hundred Years' War) and the violence of the *routiers,* or "free companies" (unemployed mercenary soldiers who harassed the civilian population), were more acutely felt because of the devastating effects of the Black Death.[336] The perception of the horrors of warfare became sharper and the attitude toward war more critical.[337] John Gower in England deplored the "dedly werre" by which Christendom was being destroyed. In his desire to put an end to the wars between Christian nations, he sometimes "revived the arguments of Urban II that the crusade against the infidel provided an honourable outlet for the aggressive spirit of the

---

332. Bosbach 1988, 46.
333. Hobbes *Leviathan* 47 (p. 480).
334. "THE CHASE is *Exorbitant Power;* all the Powers of *Europe* are the Hounds." Defoe, *Review* VI,7 (19 April 1709). For the contemporary English debate on universal monarchy, see Pincus 1995.
335. See Eckermann 1933; Folz 1969; Burns 1992, 97–98, 100.
336. Cf. Setton 1976, 173; Housley 1986, 222 f.
337. Barnie 1974, 129; Housley 1992, 264.

second estate." [338] But the cumulative effect of these different "plagues" crippled practical crusade efforts.

A second factor was the weakness of the papacy and the related growing strengthening of territorial powers, which led to problems with the "political leadership" of the crusade.[339] But despite its increasing weakness, the papacy continued to play a central role in the crusading movement.[340]

A third factor was the rising power of the Ottoman Turks, because of which the anti-Turkish crusade emerged and grew in importance. In the second half of the fourteenth century the "Turk" became the most dangerous enemy of Christianity and Christendom.[341] Yet though the figure of the "Saracen" was fading, it had not yet disappeared. When Pope Urban V appealed in 1363 to mercenary companies in the Midi, hoping to recruit them for the crusade, the old and the new enemy figures made a joint appearance in his address. The *routiers* were reminded that "both the perfidious Saracens and those cruel pagans commonly called Turks, who live in the East close to Christian peoples . . . have invaded the lands of the faithful with such force and audacity that none or few can resist them." [342]

While specific crusading projects written at the turn of the thirteenth and fourteenth centuries may indeed have been gathering dust by the 1340s and thereafter,[343] the crusade idea itself lived on. The two authors considered in the remainder of this chapter, Philippe de Mézières and Catherine of Siena, both confronted the specific problems of their day. At the same time, they seem to have been inspired by and to have revived some distinctive features of the "pristine," "original" crusade idea. Their writings make it clear that far from becoming obsolete, the crusade idea was actually rejuvenated in this period.

THE CHRISTIAN SPARTA: PHILIPPE DE MÉZIÈRES

Philippe de Mézières was a leading crusade propagandist of the late fourteenth century. An "extraordinary, eccentric and extravagantly verbose

338. Barnie 1974, 124, 130.
339. Housley 1986, 239.
340. Cf. Setton 1976.
341. Cf. Housley 1992, chap. 3.
342. Quoted in Setton 1976, 248. "In all and any of the crusade plans in the 1360s, the companies were necessarily a vital element." Keen 1987, 103.
343. Housley 1986, 239.

figure," he was a "self-appointed herald to all Christendom of the crusading cause"—in a word, a "crusading fanatic." [344] From his youth, when he fed on chronicles relating to the Holy Land,[345] till his death, de Mézières had a single goal in his life: "to recommence the crusades and restore the Kingdom of Jerusalem." [346] He was a man of action. For about forty years of his life he worked on creating his own military order, the Militia Passionis Jhesu Christi.[347] He traveled throughout Latin Christendom as the chancellor of King Peter I of Cyprus on diplomatic and peacemaking missions and was a moving spirit behind, and a leading participant in, the crusading expedition that sacked and destroyed Alexandria in 1365.[348] He kept referring to that pillage as a *prise glorieuse,*[349] even though his feelings were not universally shared. Because the rich booty had cooled the crusading zeal, the expedition actually caused quite a bit of resentment and anger among the Latin Christians back home.[350] After Peter I's assassination, de Mézières became adviser to King Charles V of France and tutor to the young Charles VI. The king and the adviser dreamt together about the deliverance of Jerusalem,[351] and it was possibly de Mézières who organized a dramatic staging of the fall of Jerusalem during the First Crusade at Charles V's court in 1378 in honor of Emperor Charles IV's visit.[352] When King Charles V died, de Mézières retired to a convent of the Celestines in Paris, where he liked to call himself "the old pilgrim" or "the old solitary"—even while cultivating his connections with the world of power. He also wrote extensively and dedicated even the remainder of his life to the crusade.

In his younger years, de Mézières was a close collaborator with Pierre Thomas, the papal legate in the Levant. Pierre was "one of the most distinguished churchmen and devout crusaders of the fourteenth century," and a "personification of the crusade." [353] De Mézières was his loyal

344. Keen 1987, 106; Housley 1992, 39.
345. Setton 1976, 241.
346. Iorga 1896, 512.
347. Cf. Iorga 1896, 453 ff., 490f., 502f.; Atiya 1938, 140 ff.; Coopland 1975, xxxiii–xxxiv; and de Mézières's own works: *Le songe du vieil pèlerin; Letter to King Richard II,* 103 f.; *Epistre lamentable.*
348. See Iorga 1896. For the broader context in which de Mézières operated, see especially Setton 1976, chap. 11–12; Edbury 1991, chap. 7; Guenée 1991, 114–15. Cf. *Le songe,* 2: 434 ff.; *Epistre lamentable,* 489 f.
349. Iorga 1896, 473.
350. Thibault 1986, 39–40.
351. Rousset 1983, 132–33. Cf. Coopland 1975, xii–xiii. But Setton 1976, 249, remarked that "Charles lacked a crusading mentality."
352. Housley 1992, 393.
353. Setton 1976, 258–59.

friend and companion. His love for Thomas rested on their common hatred of the enemies of the cross. In his biography of Thomas, Philippe
described the legate as a man who almost wore himself out by his exertions: "By such works, that is by preaching, teaching, fighting, baptizing
infidels, bringing schismatics back into the fold, and extending God's
church, the lord legate was unremitting in his service, now at Smyrna,
now off to Rhodes, Constantinople, Cyprus, the island of Crete, and Turkey, now with many galleys, now with a few, and sometimes with only
one. He did not spare himself, putting to sea and making war, oppor-
tunely and otherwise, in winter as in summer, amid the perils of the
sea." [354] These two men, "by their dominating personality and influence,
contributed more to the promotion of crusades than probably any other
of their contemporaries." [355]

De Mézières was at the center of politics in his times, and his crusading ideas faithfully reflected the concerns of the day. They can be best
seen in his *Le songe du vieil pèlerin* (1388),[356] the *Epistre au Roi Richart*
(*Letter to King Richard II,* a letter commissioned by Charles VI and
addressed to the English king in 1395), and the *Epistre lamentable,* written after the crushing defeat of the Christian army by the Turks at Nicopolis in 1396.[357] Prominent among de Mézières's concerns were inter-
Christian violence and, in response to that violence, efforts to establish
peace in Christendom. Without peace, it would be impossible to get a
new crusade under way. De Mézières was instrumental in negotiating a
peace settlement between the papacy and Bernabò Visconti of Milan,[358]
but the conflict dominating his thoughts was the war between England
and France. Weighing heavily on him also was the Church schism, which
he desired to heal. Compared to the Anglo-French war and the Great
Schism, the *routiers* appeared as a minor problem—although a problem
serious enough to engage the curia and princes alike.[359] When Urban V
proclaimed the crusade in 1363, he especially addressed the *routiers*
as men in the most dreadful need of absolution who should respond
promptly to his call to arms "in a spirit of devotion and union." Skilled
in the exercise of arms, they should seek forgiveness for the crimes they

---

354. *Life of St. Peter Thomas;* quoted in Setton 1976, 237.
355. Atiya 1938, 129. Edbury 1991, 167, calls them "the two most ardent exponents
of the crusade ideal."
356. A résumé, published before Coopland's edition, is Bell 1955.
357. On the Nicopolis crusade, see Setton 1976, chap. 14; Housley 1992, 75 ff.
358. See Setton 1976, 246–47.
359. See Housley 1986, 223–27; 1992, 264.

had committed against God, ecclesiastics, and the innocent in a service acceptable to God. They could take possession of the Holy Land, and so "in this life they might seize the wealth of the enemies of Christendom, and by mending their ways also earn eternal wealth in the life to come." [360] De Mézières, seeing the crusade as an outlet for *routiers*' violence, was in line with this papal policy, and the *routiers* were with him in the sack of Alexandria.[361]

De Mézières's grand idea of peace and unity within Christendom coupled with the crusade for the recovery of the Holy Land was first clearly formulated in the *Le songe du vieil pèlerin*. The "old pilgrim" addresses the young King Charles VI and confides to him that his royal father, Charles V, had thought out a plan for reuniting and reforming Christendom. The ghost of the father and de Mézières himself now expected Charles VI to make their dreams come true. He was chosen by destiny to realize the ideal: to deliver the Holy Land. It is *la royne Verite*, Queen Truth, who explains to the young prince: "[B]ecause you have received more grace of the sweet Jesus, my Father, than other Christian kings, you have to work harder and be the first to commence what is the will of God; that is, to bring about peace and unity among the Christians. And, reasonably, the other kings will not refuse this holy request that you will present to them, that is, to bring about charity and amity, peace and calm." [362] This plan for peace and unity included the convocation of a general council (*grant conseil et parlement general*) in which the envoys of all the kingdoms and other dominions of Catholic Christians would meet to accomplish two things: first, to reach an agreement on the reform of Christendom and establish charity and unity among the kingdoms, principalities, and communes; and second, to heal the schism of the Church by electing a single pope.[363] After this had been achieved, a golden age would come. All the Christian princes would work for the spread of the Catholic faith and for the common good of Christendom. They would bring the schismatics, infidels, Tartars, Turks, Jews,[364] and

360. Setton 1976, 248; cf. 238.
361. Keen 1987, 104.
362. *Le Songe*, 2: 292.
363. Ibid., 2: 293–95.
364. What was, for Philippe, most disturbing about the Jews not living in the ghettos was that he could not discern them from the Christians: "alant parmy les rues de Paris, on ne pourroit cognoistre qui est Juif ou Crestien." Ibid., 2: 285. But de Mézières was far from being the first in the Latin Christian West to depict this as a problem. Canon 68 of the Fourth Lateran Council, for example, ordered that the Jews should wear distinctive clothes to prevent confusion, which could result in "mixed" marriages. See Hefele 1912–13, 5.2: 1386–87.

Saracens into the true faith by preaching, good example, and admonition, or—with the obstinate and rebellious ones—by the "holy sword." In this way the holy city of Jerusalem and the Holy Land would be delivered and the whole world would submit in holy obedience to the true cross.[365]

Besides this general plan, de Mézières worked out a more concrete and politically practicable project, outlined in the Songe[366] and elaborated in the Letter to King Richard. He invested his hopes in Charles VI and Richard II, newly ascended kings of France and England, and called on them to make peace between their two countries. The project was not mere wishful thinking, and its timing was good. Since 1384, when a truce was concluded, a reconciliatory mood had begun to predominate at the French and English courts. Peace had become a "matter of overriding concern to the governments of both kingdoms,"[367] and Richard II surrounded himself with advisers who sought a settlement with France rather than the escalation of hostilities.[368] But auspicious circumstances aside, Philippe was also on principle strongly opposed to war among Christians. The opening tones of his Letter to King Richard, his descriptions of the horrors and evils of war (reminiscent of later, Erasmian pacifist rhetoric), are a typical expression of the new awareness of and sensitivity to atrocities of warfare.[369] This new sensibility, however, continued to be buttressed with doctrinal and political underpinnings.

Philippe grieved over hostilities between Christian princes and condemned them because God, he said, abhors the spilling of "baptized Christians' blood."[370] Shedding the "human blood of Christians" should be held in abomination[371] as a great and inadmissible cruelty. By "shedding the blood of our brothers, English and French alike, once more we have killed sweet Jesus Christ."[372] War among Christians was therefore an offence against God, moreover, "war against Him."[373] De Mézières implied that there could be no just war between Christians,[374] and prayed to Lord God to "scatter and destroy all those who seek war against their

365. Le Songe, 2: 296.
366. Ibid., 2: 373 ff.
367. Barnie 1974, 31.
368. Tyerman 1988, 334. Cf. Barnie 1974, 24.
369. See n. 337.
370. Letter, 12/85. (The first page number refers to Coopland's translation, the second to his edition of the original.)
371. Ibid., 43/116.
372. Ibid., 44/117.
373. Ibid., 46/119.
374. Ibid., 52–53/126.

Christian brothers." For they are His enemies "who strive to prevent the descent of the peace of Heaven on our Kings." No mercy should be shown to them: "Let them be crushed and let them flee before the face of God."[375]

De Mézières also protested against war among Christians because it had led to the loss of the Holy Land. He admitted that the king of Jerusalem had ruled with "lack of justice and neglect of knightly discipline," and so his kingdom had been lost. But that did not excuse the westerners: "This failing was evident to the Emperor, the Roman Pope, and all the kings of the Christian world, who, for the sake of the Faith of Jesus Christ, were responsible for remedying these failings, in what was the common concern of all Christians." On account of their negligence, they were "parties to the loss of the Holy Land." To make things worse, they had "so long delayed the recovery of the Holy Land" because they were "occupied in shedding the blood of one another."[376] On top of these troubles, the schism in the Holy Church was an open wound in Christendom.[377] With all this in mind, Philippe's peace formula was obvious, simple, and clear: peace within Christendom, the union of the Church, and the crusade, *le saint passage d'oultremer.*[378]

Obsessed with the "holy passage" and aware that the political geography of the Latin West was being increasingly shaped by the rising territorial powers,[379] de Mézières entrusted his project to two of those powers. He hoped to advance his aims by bestowing on England a share in France's title of the elect Christian nation,[380] and he beseeched the two greatest kings of Christendom to end their protracted war and to make peace between their countries. But his objective was even more ambitious. It was no less than "the perpetual union [*confederacion*] and alliance, under God, true peace and comely, brotherly love between the

375. Ibid., 50/124.

376. Ibid., 27/100. Cf. Iorga 1896, 464, summarizing the argument of the Armenian king Leo IV, who in 1386, with French consent, visited the English court: "[I]l exposa l'état déplorable de l'Orient, qui souffrait depuis soixante ans les cruautés et les dévastations des Sarrasins. . . . La guerre entre chrétiens, cette guerre honteuse et inutile, puisques toutes les conquêtes avaient été perdues, devait cesser pour la confusion des ennemis de la croix. C'est ainsi qu'on pourrait reprendre aux Infidèles Bethléem et Sion."

377. *Letter*, 21 ff./93 ff.

378. Ibid., 115/42; cf. 50/123, 65/139; 119/45: "Il a este revele a vous ii. roys que par vous sera faitte la paix, et de vous et de la crestiente, l'eglise raunie, et conquise Surie."

379. "Lombardie demoura aus Lombars, Espaigne aus Espaigneux, France aus Francois, et Engleterre aus Anglois." Ibid., 14/87.

380. For a more conventional (and exclusivist) view on the *roy très-crestien*, see *Epistre lamentable*, 457.

two sons of St. Louis, King of France, that is, between Charles and Richard, by the grace of God, worthy kings of France and England, and among all their subjects, and, hence, the peace and unity of the Church and within the whole of Christendom." [381]

As de Mézières imagined things, Charles VI and Richard II, at peace with each other and united in brotherly love, would kindle the light, "and by their light all Catholic peoples [*toutes les generacions des crestiens catholiques*], who until now through war and division have wandered in darkness, will see clearly the straight way leading to Jerusalem." [382] A contemporary epistle to the kings of France and England by Deschamps made the same point: the two kings should choose the love of God, stop fighting each other, and henceforth direct their war against the Saracens so that their subjects may live in peace. [383] But similar ideas had also been a subject of diplomatic negotiations. Already Pope Gregory XI, at the time of peace talks between France and England in 1375, had conceived a "grand design for an Anglo-French peace to be sealed symbolically by the co-operation of the two powers in a crusade." [384] And in May 1395, when de Mézières's *Letter to King Richard* was probably composed,[385] Charles VI had sent a letter to Richard II expressing very same ideas. If the two kings made peace, "our mother, Holy Church, crushed and divided this long time by the accursed Schism, shall be revived in all her glory," wrote Charles. "Then, fair brother, it will be a fit moment," he continued, "that you and I, for the propitiation of the sins of our ancestors, should undertake a crusade to succour our fellow Christians and to liberate the Holy Land. . . . And so through the power of the Cross we shall spread the Holy Catholic Faith throughout all parts of the East, demonstrating the gallantry of the chivalry of England and France and of our other Christian brothers." [386]

De Mézières may have assisted in composing this letter. But be that as it may, this letter shows that he was not writing in a vacuum, an isolated figure spinning strange thoughts. Many of his peace-loving contemporaries wanted to kindle the crusading light. Philippe, for example, pictured those walking in the circle of that light as striving "toward the

---

381. *Letter,* 43/116.
382. Ibid., 18/91.
383. "Soit l'amour de Dieu prise, / Ne guerriez l'un l'autre desormais, / Sur Sarrazins soit votre guerre remise, / A voz subgez soit donné bonne paiz." Iorga 1896, 489.
384. Housley 1986, 227. See Thibault 1986, 174–75.
385. Coopland 1975, ix.
386. Quoted in Housley 1992, 74.

goal of peace in the service of God." He cursed those who might work
to extinguish the rays of that light and hinder the crusade: "It were better for them had they never been born." [387] And he reminded Charles
and Richard that Jesus had made them leaders of "His people of Israel,
that is, of western Christendom" to take them to the Promised Land.[388]
The "old solitary" had a glorious vision: God's temple in Jerusalem,
presently "befouled every day by the false followers of Mahommet, condemned in the sight of God," [389] "will once again shine with light, and
the holy sepulchre of Jesus and Mount Calvary will be restored to the
glory of the Catholic Faith." [390]

For Philippe de Mézières, Jerusalem was "the capital city of all Christendom" and "the foundation stone of the Catholic Faith." The Holy
Land was the "public land of Christendom" (terre publique de la crestiente) that belonged on grounds of faith and honor "not only to Christian peoples but also to all the kings and princes of Christendom." [391]
The conquest of Turkey, Egypt, and Syria would thus be a work done
for the Christian respublica, for la chose publique de la cresteinte.[392] The
fact that the Levantine countries were "overflowing with all manner of
riches and delights" while the western kingdoms were "cold and fro-
zen" [393] appears to have been merely circumstantial. What really mattered for de Mézières was that "the glory of the venerable Lady Holy
Faith should be from now on better guarded than it has been in our lamentable days." [394]

It was as a Catholic republican that de Mézières preached and organized the crusade. His austere republicanism took shape in the Militia
Passionis Jhesu Christi, his military order that never grew strong enough
to accomplish the historic mission for which it was intended, but which
is of interest as a semi-embodied idea. The order was to be summa per-
fectio, the model as well as the agent of spiritual and moral reform.[395]
Especially after the defeat of the crusaders at Nicopolis, de Mézières
gave vent to his critique of Christian knights who impeded their own
efforts by avarice, vainglory, incompetence, and lack of discipline and

387. Letter, 18/91.
388. Ibid., 45/118.
389. Ibid., 28/101.
390. Ibid., 18/90–91.
391. Ibid., 26/99.
392. Ibid., 30/103.
393. Ibid., 71/145.
394. Epistre lamentable, 523.
395. Tyerman 1985a, 109.

order and, as such, were easy prey for the Ottoman army. The defeat at Nicopolis was the divine chastisement of unworthy Christian knights.[396] The "Turks and enemies of faith" would never be defeated by an undisciplined armed multitude, Philippe wrote. Only a well-ordered and strictly disciplined Christian chivalry, unreservedly dedicated to holy war for the love of God and ready to die for the holy cause without hesitation,[397] stood a chance of overcoming the Turks. Philippe de Mézières's Militia Passionis Jhesu Christi was a model for this new type of Christian army. Its mission was to recommence the holy war. Here Philippe the peacemaker really let his warmonger self take wing. With great passion he urged the Christians to wage war against the infidels. He claimed that the destruction of the enemies of the cross[398] was the teaching of St. Paul: "one has to make every effort and use violence according to the teaching of Saint Paul the Apostle."[399] Such a war would undoubtedly be "God's own war," fought with God's assistance: God Himself would assail the Saracens.[400] As a military strategist, de Mézières proposed attacking Sultan "Baxhet" (Bayezid I), for to kill a serpent one has to crush its head.[401] But de Mézières was a prophet of holy war rather than a military strategist. To make a *bonne et forte guerre* against the Turks, "ferocious and dishonourable enemies of faith," and to either convert or wreak havoc on and destroy "the false sect of Mahomet" and "all idolatry," Philippe declared, was the will of God: the *chose Dieu nous veuille ottroier!*[402]

Three hundred years after Clermont, the cry of *Deus le volt!* could still be heard, voiced not by a robber, an incendiary, or a homicide,[403] but by a man who rubbed shoulders with eminent figures, like Pierre d'Ailly, for example.[404] This was a cry for holy war.[405] But the aim of the Militia Passionis Jhesu Christi was not only to engage in *la bataille de Dieu*

396. Cf. Setton 1976, 241.
397. *Epistre lamentable*, 473–74.
398. Cf. Setton 1976, 238, 241 (quoting the *Life of St. Peter Thomas*).
399. *Epistre lamentable*, 499.
400. Setton 1976, 261, 168 (quoting the *Life of St. Peter Thomas*).
401. *Epistre lamentable*, 494.
402. Ibid., 489, 467, 498. Cf. *Le Songe*, 2: 223.
403. Cf. chap. 1 n. 310.
404. D'Ailly dedicated an early work of his to de Mézières. Guenée 1991, 116. A founding father of radical conciliarist thought, d'Ailly has a share in the praise some historians of political thought lavish on conciliarism as a moment in the development of "modern theory of popular sovereignty in a secular state." Cf. Skinner 1978, 1: 65. For d'Ailly's linking the fight against the infidels with the reform of the Church, see his *De reformatione ecclesiae*, 75.
405. De Mézières's vocabulary belonged "à l'ancienne école." Rousset 1983, 133.

that would open the gates of the heavenly kingdom;[406] these "valiant combatants and God's elect" appeared almost as a church, a "holy congregation," no less so than God's "new people of Israel."[407] They were more than the new model army: they were the model settlers. These knights were to settle in the Holy Land and establish the City of God in the conquered territories, for "the time has come to build the City of God, according to Saint Augustine."[408] Their military order was to be the model settlement as well. The Militia Passionis Jhesu Christi was itself *la cité de Dieu*.[409] Occupied Palestine was to be ruled by military force. The new order in the Holy Land was to be a *monarchie militaire*[410] or—as de Mézières's biographer pointedly described it—a Christian Sparta.[411]

THE BLOOD OF CHRIST: ST. CATHERINE OF SIENA

Catherine of Siena was a mystic and a saint, a Dominican tertiary who lived a deeply religious life and stopped taking food and died when still a young woman. It was her intense piety that led her to take part in public life (*vivere civile*). She believed she had a mission, and in the 1370s she campaigned energetically for the return of the pope to Rome; for *dolce pace,* that is, peace among Christians; and for the crusade, *santo passagio*.[412] She traveled and sent epistles to whomever she thought might be instrumental in achieving those goals. Her three aims were closely interdependent. The return of the pope from his Avignon "Egyptian captivity" to the "Promised Land" of Rome was expected to lead to the spiritually reformed Church's victorious march to Jerusalem.[413] The causal link between the "sweet peace" and the crusade was expressed, among others, by Pope Gregory XI himself: "The crusade is particularly conducive to peace, and peace itself leads to the crusade."[414] In this, the pope—who was in Catherine's view the Archimedean point for getting the crusade under way—was a continuator of "the very old tradition of

406. *Epistre lamentable,* 490, 499.
407. Ibid., 490, 473.
408. Ibid., 500; cf. 503.
409. Ibid., 475; cf. 499: "Cette chevalerie sera la Cité portative de Dieu."
410. Ibid., 458.
411. See Iorga 1896, 455.
412. Cardini 1993c, 428, sees the reform of the Church, instead of peace, as one of the three goals of Catherine's public activity. For a sympathetic account of Catherine's notion of peace, see Petrocchi 1975.
413. Cf. Cardini 1993c, 426.
414. Quoted in Housley 1986, 223. On Gregory XI's crusade, see Thibault 1986, 49 ff.

regarding peace within Christendom."[415] The same may be said of Catherine of Siena. Her gift to her contemporaries was not only a "mystical version of the traditional theology"[416] but also a mystical version of the traditional crusade idea.

A strong mystical fervor colored Catherine's understanding of the crusade. Her letters drip with blood: the blood that Christ had shed to redeem humankind. She wrote "in his precious blood."[417] The crusade was a "mystery,"[418] and the mystical formula for the crusade was blood for blood. Just as Christ had shed his blood for the salvation of men, so Christians now had to shed their blood for Christ to free his patrimony from impious hands. "Fire up your desire to pay blood for blood," Catherine called on to Christian believers.[419] A martyr's death was high on the agenda again. To die for Christ and for the holy faith (*morire per la sante fede*) was to gain eternal life. The crusade was reunion with the Redeemer. Gregory XI's crusading bull was, for Catherine, "sweet good news." The "holy crusade" it proclaimed was "the fragrance of the flower that is just beginning to open." And when she urged her fellow Christians to join the crusade, she was inviting them "to the wedding feast of everlasting life." The crusade was "this sweet glorious wedding feast . . . full of joy, sweetness, and every delight."[420]

Her passionate mysticism aside, Catherine of Siena's crusading language was firmly conventional. A continuity of intention and argument can be traced from Urban II and the chroniclers of the First Crusade up to Catherine's writings.[421] It is as if the crusade idea had been filtered through the centuries to leave its pure essence in Catherine's letters: Peace among Christians and war against the infidels! This was the leading theme of Catherine's crusading propaganda, expressed time and again, sometimes strengthened by mention of the illegitimate possession of the Holy Land by the Muslims. To a legally minded person this point

415. Housley 1986, 223. A "deeply ingrained traditionalism" regarding the crusade blinded Gregory XI to the "realities of his age" and doomed his crusading efforts to fail. Thibault 1986, 37.

416. Knowles and Obolensky 1991, 326.

417. Catherine to Pope Gregory XI, 31 March 1376, *The Letters of St. Catherine of Siena*, 203.

418. Catherine to King Charles V of France, A.D. 1376, ibid., 239. For a more detailed (and sympathetic) discussion of Catherine's crusade idea, see Castellini 1938; Cardini 1993c.

419. Catherine to Nicolò Soderini, A.D. 1375, *The Letters*, 116–17.

420. Catherine to Giovanna d'Angiò, Queen of Naples, July 1375; to Nicolò Soderini, A.D. 1375; to Monna Paola, after 1 July 1375; to Bartolomeo della Pace Smeducci da Sanseverino, A.D. 1375 or 1376, ibid., 114, 116, 119, 161.

421. Rousset 1983, 122. Cf. Castellini 1938, 325; Cardini 1993c, 433.

could offer a justification for the crusade. But for Catherine the crusade did not need to be justified.

In the world of Catherine's political mysticism, the only thing needing justification, though in fact unjustifiable, was resisting or impeding the crusade. I let Catherine speak for herself: "What a shame and disgrace it is for Christians to allow the base unbelievers to possess what is rightfully ours. Yet we act like punyhearted fools, waging wars and campaigns only against one another! We are divided from one another in hatred and bitterness when we ought to be bound by ties of blazing divine charity—a bond so strong that it held the God-Man nailed fast to the wood of the most holy cross." [422] Catherine begged Cardinal Orsini to encourage the pope to press on with the crusade "so that the war Christians are waging against each other may be waged against them," the unbelievers. [423] The pope and Catherine differed in this regard. When Gregory XI gave audience to Catherine, he explained that he wanted first to make peace among Christians, and then he would command the crusade. Catherine replied that there was no better way to pacify Christians then to issue that command. [424] But this seems to be a difference in accentuation rather than substance. Though she believed in an apparently instant peace through the crusade, Catherine still saw inter-Christian peace as a necessary condition for the holy journey.

Catherine was aware of the problem of mercenary military companies that were either employed in wars against their fellow Christians or, when idle, harassed the civilians. She wrote about the issue to John Hawkwood, an English *condottiere* working for Italian employers. She considered him in "the devil's service and pay" and urged him to change his course and enlist himself and all his followers and companies instead in the service of Christ crucified:

> Then you would be one of Christ's companies, going to fight the unbelieving dogs who have possession of our holy place, where gentle First Truth lived and endured sufferings and death for us. You find so much satisfaction in fighting and waging war, so now I am begging you tenderly in Christ Jesus not to wage war any longer against Christians (for that offends God), but to go instead to fight the unbelievers, as God and our holy father have decreed.

422. Catherine to Bernabò Visconti, between 3 Nov. 1373 and 9 Jan. 1374, *The Letters*, 71.

423. Catherine to Cardinal Iacopo Orsini, A.D. 1374, ibid., 91.

424. Raymond of Capua *De Sancta Catherina Senensi Vita;* quoted in Castellini 1938, 340; Cardini 1993c, 443. But Gregory XI seems to have said different things at different times. Cf. n. 414.

> How cruel it is that we who are Christians, members bound together in the body of holy Church, should be persecuting one another![425]

This letter was written soon after Gregory XI's crusading bull was published on July 1, 1375, but the formulation that "God and our holy father" had decreed the crusade was dogmatic rather than just circumstantial. Catherine appears to have firmly believed that the crusade was "God's will."[426] "God wants it," she wrote.[427]

When the antipapal rebellion led by the Florentines had broken out, Catherine, in January 1376, exhorted the pope not to postpone the crusade, "for it is with the fragrance of the cross that you will gain peace. I beg you to invite those who have rebelled against you to a holy peace, so that all this fighting can be diverted toward the unbelievers."[428] And again, in a subsequent letter: "Ah—*God sweet love!*—do raise the standard of the most holy cross soon, *babbo,* and you will see the wolves become lambs. Peace! Peace! Peace!—so that war may not delay this sweet time!"[429] But she also addressed the *signori* of Florence: "So we must not go against our head [the pope], no matter what injustice may have been done to us. Nor must one Christian go against another. No, we should be going together against the unbelievers who are doing us injustice because they are holding what is not theirs but ours."[430]

In the same year Catherine reproached Charles V of France for obstructing the crusade by being at war with England. "No more, for love of Christ crucified!" For Catherine, Christians fighting Christians alone was war; the crusade she did not call war but "this sweet time." She was well aware of the immense physical and spiritual destruction that fighting between Christians caused. She referred to all the religious persons and women and children who were abused and displaced by soldiery. But all this became as if nothing before "the mystery of the holy crusade." When the violence was for the sake of the holy, it lost all its terrifying features and ceased to be violence. When it came to holy war, the agent of evil was he who did not promote it. She threatened the king with divine judgment should he continue to be "the obstacle to such a good as the recovery of the Holy Land." On this point, Catherine was less than

425. 27 June 1375, *The Letters,* 106.
426. Catherine to Pope Gregory XI, 31 March 1376, ibid., 205.
427. Catherine to Pope Gregory XI, Sept. 1376, ibid., 243.
428. Catherine to Pope Gregory XI, Jan. 1376, ibid., 169.
429. Catherine to Pope Gregory XI, 31 March 1376, ibid., 205.
430. Catherine to the Signori of Florence, near Easter 1376, ibid., 215.

gracious to the monarch. "What a scandal, humanly speaking, and what an abomination before God, that you should be making war against your brother and leaving your enemy alone, and that you should be seizing what belongs to another and not get back what is yours! Enough of this stupid blindness! I am telling you in the name of Christ crucified to wait no longer to make this peace. Make peace! Make peace! Make peace, and turn the whole war against the unbelievers. Help promote and raise the standard of the most holy cross."[431]

But in this letter Catherine also voiced concern for "all those poor souls who have no share in the blood of God's Son." This concern reappeared in Catherine's letters more than once. She wrote to the pope that by the crusade "we shall be freed—we from war and the divisions and many sins, and the unbelievers from their unbelief."[432] Thus the crusade became a war of liberation, delivering "our gentle Saviour's holy place from the unbelievers' hands, and their souls from the devil's hands so that they may share in the blood of God's Son as we do."[433] She even considered the unbelievers "our brothers and sisters, ransomed as we are by Christ's blood."[434]

I do not wish to question Catherine's sincerity in this regard. The fact is, however, that these tender feelings modified neither her view of the Muslims as "the wicked unbelieving dogs who have possession of what is ours,"[435] nor her determination "to rescue what has been stolen from us" so that "the holy place will no longer be held by these evil unbelievers."[436] Some historians have warned against being misled by the contemptuous terms Catherine used for the infidels, like *cani, cani infedeli, cani malvagi*. They argue that Catherine regarded the infidels as having the right to be loved, since they were called to conversion, and that the contradiction lay not in Catherine's "intention" but in the "customary and unreflected" vocabulary she employed.[437] But it seems to me

---

431. Catherine to King Charles V, July 1376, ibid., 239.
432. Catherine to Pope Gregory XI, 21 March 1376, ibid., 202. Cf. *De Sancta Catherina Senensi Vita* (quoted in Cardini 1993c, 443), that one of the three good things brought about by the crusade was "salus multorum sarracenorum."
433. Catherine to Giovanna d'Angiò, Queen of Naples, July 1375, *The Letters*, 114. Cf. Catherine to Bartolomeo della Pace Smeducci da Sanseverino, A.D. 1375 or 1376, ibid., 161.
434. Catherine to Bartolomeo della Pace Smeducci da Sanseverino, A.D. 1375 or 1376, ibid., 161.
435. Catherine to the Queen Mother, Elisabeth of Hungary, Summer 1375, ibid., 132.
436. Catherine to the Queen Mother, Elisabeth of Hungary, Summer 1375; to Giovanna d'Angiò, Queen of Naples, 4 Aug. 1375, ibid., 133, 129.
437. Rousset 1983, 124; Cardini 1993c, 452–53.

that such an argument comes close to taking the intention too lightly or to playing down the power of language. Moreover, considering the crusade an "act of love" was nothing new.[438] And Catherine's sisterly feelings for the unbelievers did not cool her crusading zeal or undermine her "holy resolve to make this sweet holy crusade." [439] To the contrary, they made the crusade appear even more urgent, for it was to save "all those poor souls" as well. But how anyone except Christ could save souls by shedding blood, especially the blood of others, remained a mystery embedded in the context of the crusade, itself seen as mystery—so much more so because Catherine did not specify any scheme for converting the infidels. Her thoughts were beyond the duality of the crusade and mission. Conversion was a result of the crusade.[440] Crusade was itself the mission.

Catherine of Siena has been praised for her keen intelligence, which could master even the most difficult problems. She has been described as "doubtlessly the most representative woman and saint of her own time." [441] But her intellectual brilliance never led to rejection of the crusade. When it came to the crusade, Catherine did not escape the common, "thoughtless" language of her age;[442] rather she expressed "the thought of the multitude," became "the echo of the voice of the public." [443] This is precisely what asks us to take Catherine's crusading propaganda seriously. She said what the public desired to hear and was used to hearing. And the public hears best when its own voice returns to it as an echo.

In her dealing with the conflict between Christendom and the Muslims, Catherine was no exception among intellectuals of the Latin Middle Ages. The greatest minds of the medieval Western world—the most profound, distinguished, subtle, sublime, illuminated, and angelic thinkers, as they used to be called by their contemporaries and by the admiring subsequent generations—as well as mystics and visionaries, all bent their heads and their knees before the spirit of the crusade. They all subscribed—rarely with silence, often with admirable eloquence—to the

438. See Riley-Smith 1980.
439. Catherine to the Queen Mother, Elisabeth of Hungary, Summer 1375, *The Letters*, 132.
440. Cf. Cardini 1993c, 452.
441. Knowles and Obolensky 1991, 398.
442. Cf. n. 437.
443. Rousset 1983, 120.

declaration that it was necessary to eliminate those who had been named
infidels and declared enemies. This made the greatest minds at one with
the mindless, those capable of the subtlest reasoning at one with those
considered reasonable only because God had endowed all humans with
reason. The most sublime idea and the most brutal force dwelt in a common house that they built together. This is not to say that the Crusades
cast a shadow on western Christian intellectual and spiritual achievements. To the contrary, these achievements blind us to the crusades as
an important force that shaped the Western world,[444] as a factor without which the creativity of the big names of the Christian West would
not have been what it was.

Intimately connected with the highest ideals and values of Christian
society—the ideals of unity and peace, in particular—and seen as a
prominent vehicle for achieving them, the Crusades were unchallenged
throughout the Middle Ages. They enjoyed continuing popularity and
the passionate support of all ranks of society all over Christendom.[445]
But their impress is not limited to the Middle Ages. As an ideal and as a
movement, the Crusades had a deep, crucial influence on the formation
of Western civilization, shaping culture, ideas, and institutions.[446] The
Crusades set a model for "expansionist campaigns by European Christians against non-Europeans and non-Christians in all parts of the
world."[447] The ideas, iconography, and discourse associated with the
Crusades made a profound imprint on "all Christian thinking about sacred violence" and exercised influence long after the end of actual crusading.[448] They continued to play a prominent role in European politics and political imagination. In fact, the crusading spirit has survived
through Modernity well into our own postmodern age.[449]

Manifestations of that survival can seem absurd. When a great histo-

444. The Crusades have played a far greater role in Western history than in the history of the Muslim world. For this asymmetry, see Sivan 1985.

445. See, for example, Munz 1969, 371 n. 2; Hillgarth 1971, 73; Siberry 1985, 21,
220; Schein 1991, 264, 266; Housley 1992, 11, 392; Riley-Smith 1992, 173. What Medieval Latin Christians criticized, if they criticized anything at all, were "abuses" of the
crusade, most prominent of which were "crusades against Christians." Villey 1942, 36;
Housley 1985; 1992, 11–12, 377 ff.; Siberry 1985, 217.

446. Cowdrey 1976, 11, 27; Brundage 1997, 251.

447. Brundage 1976, 124; 1997, 260.

448. Housley 1992, 456. When the "actual crusading" ended, remains an open question. The last of the crusading bulls granted by the popes to the kings of Spain expired
in 1940—when there was "no longer a Spanish king to receive another." Mayer 1993,
287–88.

449. Cf. Djuvara 1914; Boehm 1957; Cardini 1993b; Mastnak 1998a; 1998b,
chap. 4–5; Tyerman 1998.

rian describes the spillover of World War I into the Near East as a direct replay of the Crusades and calls Marshal Allenby's soldiers the descendants of King Richard I (possibly the best of all crusade commanders), it is easy to laugh.[450] We can laugh because it is clearly such an inaccurate assessment of the historical facts to interpret that episode of World War I as the fulfillment of the "epopee of Crusades."[451] But this is not a laughing matter. Such interpretations need to be taken seriously. Their inaccuracy only underscores the strength of the Crusades as a force shaping our thinking; their absurdity is a fact of the life we live today. The persistence of the crusading spirit was certainly clear to both the perpetrators and victims of the war on Bosnia as the twentieth century drew to a close. Both perpetrators and victims found in the language of the crusade a way to describe their goals and their predicaments. Those who stood by and watched the crimes unfold often found little to call absurd or reprehensible in that postmodern crusade. Their talk of peace only helped the crusade succeed. That success is still all too much with us today. If the story I have told in these pages has an end, then that end does not yet appear to be in sight.

450. In 1914, the "Franks" set foot in Syria again in order to, four years later, "deliver Tripoli, Beirut, and Tyre, the city of Raymond of Saint-Gilles, the city of John of Ibelin, the city of Philip de Montfort. As to Jerusalem, it was to be 'reoccupied' on December 9, 1917, by the descendants of King Richard under the command of Marshal Allenby." Grousset 1939, 384–85. For the characterization of Richard I, see Riley-Smith 1992, 113.

451. Mayer 1993, 288, is of course right to point out that "when the French army in 1914 established its first camp in the Levant where the Templars had left their last base in 1303, i.e. on the island of Ruad off Tortosa, it did so not as a distant reminder of the crusades but simply as a matter of military tactics."

Works Cited

ABBREVIATIONS

ANF   *Ante-Nicene Fathers*. Ed. A. Roberts, and J. Donald-
son. 10 vols. Reprint. Grand Rapids, Mich.: Eerdmans,
1993–96.

CCSL   *Corpus christianorum. Series latina*. Turnholt: Brepols,
1953–.

Mansi   J. D. Mansi, ed. *Sacrorum conciliorum nova, et amplis-
sima collectio*. Venice, 1759–98.

MGH   *Monumenta Germaniae Historica:*
    BfdtKz   *Briefe der deutschen Kaiserzeit*
    Conc.   *Concilia*
    Epp.   *Epistolae* (in quarto)
    Ldl   *Libelli de lite imperatorum et pontificum*
    SS   *Scriptores* (in folio)
    SS rer. Merov.   *Scriptores rerum Merovingicarum*

NPNF, 1st ser.   *Nicene and Post-Nicene Fathers of the Christian Church*.
1st ser. Ed. Ph. Schaff. 14 vols. Reprint. Grand Rapids,
Mich.: Eerdmans, 1989–96.

NPNF, 2d ser.   *Nicene and Post-Nicene Fathers of the Christian Church*.
2d ser. Ed. Ph. Schaff and H. Wace. 14 vols. Reprint.
Grand Rapids, Mich.: Eerdmans, 1989–97.

PL   *Patrologiae cursus completus*. Series latina. Ed. J.-P.
                            Migne. Paris 1844–64.

RHC Occ   *Recueil des historiens des croisades: historiens occiden-*
                            taux. Paris 1844–95.

RS   *Rerum Britannicarum Medii Aevi Scriptores* (Rolls Se-
                            ries). London 1858–1911.

PRIMARY SOURCES

(Selections of sources in English translation are listed under Secondary Sources)

Adalbero of Laon. *Poème au roi Robert*. Ed. C. Carozzi. Paris: Les Belles Let-
    tres, 1979.
Alain of Lille. *Textes inédits*. Ed. M.-Th. d'Alverny. Paris: Vrin, 1965.
Alcuin. *Alcuin of York: His Life and Letters*. Ed. and trans. S. Allott. York: Wil-
    liam Session, 1987.
———. *Epistolae*. Ed. E. Dümmler. MGH Epp 4 (Karolini aevi 2).
Ambrose of Milan. *The Letters*. Trans. H. de Romestin. In *The Principal Works
    of St. Ambrose*. Vol. 10 of NPNF, 2d ser.
———. *Of the Christian Faith*. Trans. H. de Romestin. In *The Principal Works
    of St. Ambrose*. Vol. 10 of NPNF, 2d ser.
Anna Comnena. *The Alexiad of Anna Comnena*. Trans. E. Sewer. Harmonds-
    worth: Penguin Books, 1969.
Annales Alamannici. MGH SS 1.
Annales Laubacenses. MGH SS 1.
Annales Laureshamenses. MGH SS 1.
Annales Mettenses. MGH SS 1.
Annales Mosellani. MGH SS 16.
Annales Nazariani. MGH SS 1.
Annales Petaviani. MGH SS 1.
Annales Sancti Amandi. MGH SS 1.
Annales Sangallenses maiores. MGH SS 1.
Annales Tiliani. MGH SS 1.
Anselm of Canterbury. *Cur deus homo*. Vol. 3 of *L'oeuvre d'Anselme de Cantor-
    béry*, ed. M. Corbin. Paris: Les Éditions du CERF, 1988.
Anselm of Lucca. *Liber contra Wibertum*. MGH Ldl 1.
———. *Sermo de caritate*. Ed. E. Pásztor. In Motivi dell'ecclesiologia di Anselmo
    di Lucca: In margine a un sermone inedito, by E. Pásztor. *Bullettino dell' Isti-
    tuto storico italiano per il medio evo e Archivio muratoriano* 77 (1965): 96–
    104.
Aquinas. *Contra errores Graecorum*. Vol. 40, pt. A of *Sancti Thomae de Aquino
    Opera omnia*, ed. Fratrum praedicatorum. Rome: Ad Sanctae Sabinae, 1967.
———. *De rationibus fidei*. Vol. 40, pt. B-C of *Sancti Thomae de Aquino Opera
    omnia*, ed. Fratrum praedicatorum. Rome: Ad Sanctae Sabinae, 1968.
———. *Država*. Ed. T. Vereš. Zagreb: Globus, 1990.
———. *Liber de Veritate Catholicae Fidei contra errores Infidelium seu Summa*

contra Gentiles. Ed. C. Pera. Textus Leoninus. Turin and Rome: Marietti, 1961.

———. *O razlozima vjere [De rationibus fidei].* In *Razgovor s pravoslavnima i muslimanima,* by Toma Akvinski, ed. and trans. A. Pavlović. Zagreb: Globus, 1992.

———. *Protiv zabluda Grkâ [Contra errores Graecorum].* In *Razgovor s pravoslavnima i muslimanima,* by Toma Akvinski, ed. and trans. A. Pavlović. Zagreb: Globus, 1992.

———. *Summa theologica.* Vols. 1–3 of *Opera omnia,* by Aquinas, ed. S. E. Fretté and P. Maré. Paris: L. Vivés, 1882.

———. *Summa theologica.* Trans. Fathers of the English Dominican Province. 5 vols. Westminster, Md.: Christian Classics, 1981.

Aristotle. *Nikomahova etika.* Trans. K. Gantar. Ljubljana: Cankarjeva založba, 1964.

———. *The Politics of Aristotle.* Trans. and ed. E. Barker. Oxford: Oxford University Press, 1958.

Augustine. *The City of God.* Trans. G. E. McCracken et al. The Loeb Classical Library. Cambridge, Mass.: Harvard University Press; London: William Heinemann, 1960.

———. *The City of God against the Pagans.* Ed. and trans. R. W. Dyson. Cambridge: Cambridge University Press, 1998.

———. *On Christian Doctrine.* Trans. D. W. Robertson, Jr. New York and London: Macmillan, 1958.

———. *The Letters.* Trans. J. G. Cunningham. In vol. 1 of NPNF, 1st ser.

———. *Select Letters.* Trans. J. H. Baxter. The Loeb Classical Library. Cambridge, Mass.: Harvard University Press; London: William Heinemann, 1980.

Bacon, Roger. *Compendium of the Study of Theology.* Ed. T. Maloney. Studien und Texte zur Geistesgeschichte des Mittelalters 20. Leiden: E. J. Brill, 1988.

———. *Compendium studii philosophiae.* In vol. 1 of *Opera quaedam hactenus inedita,* by Bacon, ed. J. S. Brewer. RS 15. London: Longman, Green, Longman, and Roberts, 1859.

———. *De speculis comburentibus.* In *Roger Bacon's Philosophy of Nature,* ed. D. C. Lindberg. Oxford: Clarendon Press, 1983.

———. *Epistola Fratris Rogerii Baconis de Secretis Operibus Artis et Naturae, et de Nullitate Magiae.* In vol. 1 of *Opera quaedam hactenus inedita,* by Bacon, ed. J. S. Brewer. RS 15. London: Longman, Green, Longman, and Roberts, 1859.

———. *The Opus Majus.* Trans. R. B. Burke. 2 vols. New York: Russell & Russell, 1962.

———. *Opus minus.* In vol. 1 of *Opera quaedam hactenus inedita,* by Bacon, ed. J. S. Brewer. RS 15. London: Longman, Green, Longman, and Roberts, 1859.

———. *Opus tertium.* In vol. 1 of *Opera quaedam hactenus inedita,* by Bacon, ed. J. S. Brewer. RS 15. London: Longman, Green, Longman, and Roberts, 1859.

———. *Part of the Opus tertium of Roger Bacon, Including a Fragment Now Printed for the First Time.* Ed. A. G. Little. British Society of Franciscan Studies 4. Aberdeen: The University Press, 1912.

Baldric of Dol [Bourgueil]. *Historia Jerosolimitana.* RHC Occ 4.

Bedae chronologia continuata. In vol. 3 of *The Complete Works of Venerable Bede,* ed. J. A. Giles. London: Whittaker, 1843.

Bede. *Chronicon, sive de sex hujus seculi aetatibus.* In *Bedae opera historica minora,* ed. J. Stevenson. London: Sumptibus societatis, 1841.

———. *De locis sanctis.* In vol. 4 of *The Complete Works of Venerable Bede,* ed. J. A. Giles. London: Whittaker, 1843.

———. *The Ecclesiastical History of the English People.* Trans. B. Colgrave. In *The Ecclesiastical History of the English People. The Greater Chronicle. Bede's Letter to Egbert,* ed. J. McClure and R. Collins. Oxford and New York: Oxford University Press, 1994.

———. *Expositio actuum apostolorum.* Ed. M. L. W. Laistner. In pt. 2, vol. 4 of *Bedae Venerabilis opera.* CCSL 121.

———. *The Greater Chronicle.* Trans. J. McClure and R. Collins. In *The Ecclesiastical History of the English People. The Greater Chronicle. Bede's Letter to Egbert,* ed. J. McClure and R. Collins. Oxford and New York: Oxford University Press, 1994.

———. *In primam partem Samuhelis libri IIII.* Ed. D. Hurst. In pt. 2, vol. 2 of *Bedae Venerabilis opera.* CCSL 119.

———. *Libri quatuor in principium Genesis usque ad nativitatem Isaac at eiectionem Ismahelis adnotationum.* Ed. Ch. W. Jones. In pt. 2, vol. 1 of *Bedae Venerabilis opera.* CCSL 118A.

———. *Nomina regionum atque locorum de actibus apostolorum.* Ed. M. L. W. Laistner. In pt. 2, vol. 4 of *Bedae Venerabilis opera.* CCSL 121.

———. *Opera historica (Historical Writings).* Trans. J. E. King. The Loeb Classical Library. London: William Heinemann; New York: G. P. Putnam's Sons, 1930.

Bernard of Clairvaux. *Briefe.* Vols. 2–3 of *Sämtliche Werke,* ed. G. B. Winkler. Innsbruck: Tyrolia, 1992.

———. *Éloge de la nouvelle chevalerie (De laude novae militiae).* Ed. P.-Y. Emery. Vol. 31 of *Oeuvres complètes.* Sources chrétiennes 367. Paris: Les éditions du CERF, 1990.

———. *Five Books on Consideration: Advice to a Pope.* Trans. J. D. Anderson and E. T. Kennan. Kalamazoo, Mich.: Cistercian Publications, 1976.

Biblia sacra iuxta vulgatam versionem. Ed. R. Gryson. 4th ed. Stuttgart: Deutsche Bibelgesellschaft, 1994.

Bonaventure. *Collationes in Hexaëmeron siue illumationes Ecclesia (Collazioni sull'Exameron ovvero le illuminazioni della Chiesa).* Vol. 6.1 of *Opere di San Bonaventura.* Rome: Città Nuova, 1994.

———. *Legenda S. Francisci.* In *Legendae duae de vita S. Francisci Seraphici,* by Bonaventure, ed. Collegium S. Bonaventurae. Clara Aqua, 1923.

———. *The Life of St. Francis (Legenda maior).* Trans. E. Cousins. In *The Soul's Journey into God. The Tree of Life. The Life of St. Francis,* by Bonaventure. Trans. E. Cousins. Mahwah, N.J.: Paulist Press, 1978.

———. *The Soul's Journey into God.* Trans. E. Cousins. In *The Soul's Journey into God. The Tree of Life. The Life of St. Francis,* by Bonaventure. Trans. E. Cousins. Mahwah, N.J.: Paulist Press, 1978.

Bonet, Honoré. *The Tree of Battles*. Ed. G. W. Coopland. Liverpool: At the University Press, 1949.

Boniface. *The Letters of Saint Boniface*. Ed. and trans. E. Emerton. New York: W. W. Norton, 1976.

Bonizo of Sutri. *Liber ad amicum*. MGH Ldl 1.

———. *Liber de vita christiana*. Ed. E. Perels. Texte zur Geschichte des römischen und kanonischen Rechts im Mittelalter 1. Berlin: Weidmannsche Buchhandlung, 1930.

The Book of Sainte Foy. Ed. and trans. P. Sheingorn. Philadelphia: University of Pennsylvania Press, 1995.

Carmen in victoriam Pisanorum. In Giuseppe Scalia, "Il Carme pisano sull'impresa contro i Saraceni del 1087," *Studi di filologia romanza offerti a Silvio Pellegrini* (Padua: Liviana editrice, 1971); and H. E. J. Cowdrey, "The Mahdia campaign of 1087," *English Historical Review* 92, no. 362 (1977).

Catherine of Siena. *The Letters of St. Catherine of Siena*. Ed. and trans. Suzanne Noffke. Vol. 1. Binghamton, N.Y.: Medieval & Renaissance Texts & Studies, 1988.

Chronicon moissiacense. MGH SS 1.

Cicero. *Država/De re publica*. Vol. 1 of Cicero *Libri politici,* ed. and trans. Daniel N. Hraste. Zagreb: Demetra, 1995.

Comenius, John Amos. *The Angel of Peace sent to the Peace Ambassadors of England and the Netherlands in Breda, Whence it is intended for transmission to all the Christians in Europe and thereafter to all the nations throughout the world, that they should call a halt, cease to wage war, And make way for the Prince of Peace, Christ, who now desireth to announce peace to the nations*. Ed. M. Safranek. New York: Pantheon Books, [1944].

Constitutum Constantini, Das Konstantinische Schenkung. Ed. H. Fuhrmann. Fontes iuris Germanici antiqui 10. Hannover: Hahnsche Buchhandlung, 1968.

Dante Alighieri. *Monarchy*. Ed. and trans. D. Nicholl. In *Monarchy and Three Political Letters*. New York: The Noonday Press, 1954.

———. *Opere*. Ed. F. Chiappelli. Milan: Ugo Mursia editore, 1967.

———. *Three Political Letters*. Trans. C. Hardie. In *Monarchy and Three Political Letters*. New York: The Noonday Press, 1954.

Defoe, Daniel. *Defoe's Review*. Ed. A. Secord. Facsimile Text Society. New York: Columbia University Press, 1938.

de Lorris, Guillaume, and Jean de Meun. *The Romance of the Rose*. Trans. Ch. Dahlberg. 3d ed. Princeton, N.J.: Princeton University Press, 1995.

de Mézières, Philippe, see Philippe de Mézières.

De unitate ecclesiae conservanda. In *Schriften über den Streit zwischen Regnum und Sacerdotium*, ed. I. Schmale-Ott. Vol. 2 of *Quellen zum Investiturstreit*. Darmstadt: Wissenschaftliche Buchgesellschaft, 1984.

A Dispute between a Priest and a Knight. Ed. and trans. N. N. Erickson. *Proceedings of the American Philosophical Society*, 111, no. 5 (1967).

Dubois, Pierre, see Pierre Dubois.

Early Christian Lives. Ed. and trans. C. White. Harmondsworth: Penguin Books, 1998.

Einhard. *The Life of Charlemagne*. Trans. S. E. Turner. Ann Arbor: University of Michigan Press, 1960.

Engelbert of Admont. *Engelberti Abbatis Admontensis, qui sub Rudolpho Habspurgio floruit, de Ortu & fine Romani Imperij Liber*. Basle, 1553.

Francis of Assisi. *Spisi svetega Frančiška*. In *Spisi sv. Frančiška Asiškega in sv. Klare*. Celje: Mohorjeva družba, 1982.

———. *St. Francis of Assisi: Writings and Early Biographies. English Omnibus of the Sources for the Life of St. Francis*. Ed. M. A. Habig. 2d ed. London: The Society for Promoting Christian Knowledge, 1979.

Fredegar. *Chronicarum quae dicuntur Fredegarii Scholastici libri IV cum continuationibus*. Ed. B. Krusch. MGH SS rer. Merov. 2.

———. *Fredegarii Chronicorum Liber Quartus cum Continuationibus (The Fourth Book of the Chronicle of Fredegar with Its Continuations)*. Ed. and trans. J. M. Wallace-Hadrill. London: Thomas Nelson and Sons, 1960.

Fulcher of Chartres. *Historia Iherosolymitana. Gesta Francorum Iherusalem peregrinatium, ab anno Domini MXCV usque ad annum MCXXVII*. RHC Occ 3.

———. *A History of the Expedition to Jerusalem 1095–1127*. Trans. F. R. Ryan, ed. H. S. Fink. Knoxville: University of Tennessee Press, 1969.

Gesta Francorum et aliorum Hierosolimitanorum (The Deeds of the Franks and the other Pilgrims to Jerusalem). Ed. R. Hill. London: Thomas Nelson and Sons, 1962.

Gibbon, Edward. *The English Essays of Edward Gibbon*. Ed. P. B. Craddock. Oxford: Clarendon Press, 1972.

———. *The History of the Decline and Fall of the Roman Empire*. Ed. D. Womersley. London: Penguin Books, 1995.

Giles of Rome. *On Ecclesiastical Power*. Trans. and ed. R. W. Dyson. Woodbridge: The Boydell Press, 1986.

Gratian. *Decretum magistri Gratiani*. Vol. 1 of *Corpus iuris canonici*, ed. E. Friedberg. Graz: Akademische Druck- u. Verlagsanstalt, 1959.

Gregory VII, Pope. *The Correspondence of Gregory VII: Selected Letters from the Registrum*. Ed. and trans. E. Emerton. Columbia Records of Civilization 14. New York: Columbia University Press, 1990.

———. *The Epistolae vagantes of Pope Gregory VII*. Ed. and trans. H. E. J. Cowdrey. Oxford: Clarendon Press, 1972.

———. *Das Register Gregors VII*. Ed. E. Caspar. Vol. 2 of MGH Epistolae selectae. 2 parts. Berlin: Weidmannsche Buchhandlung, 1920–23.

Gregory of Tours. *The History of the Franks*. Trans. L. Thorpe. Harmondsworth: Penguin Books, 1974.

Guibert of Nogent. *The Deeds of God through the Franks*. Trans. R. Levine. Woodbridge: The Boydell Press, 1997.

———. *Historia quae dicitur Gesta Dei per Francos*. RHC Occ 4.

Hagenmeyer, Heinrich, ed. *Die Kreuzzugsbriefe aus den Jahren 1088–1100*. Reprint. Hildesheim and New York: Georg Olms, 1973.

Henry IV, Emperor. *Die Briefe Heinrichs IV*. Ed. C. Erdmann. Deutsches Mittelalter 1. Leipzig: Karl W. Hiersmann, 1937.

Historia de expeditione Friderici imperatoris. In *Quellen zur Geschichte des*

Kreuzzuges Kaiser Friedrichs I., ed. A. Chroust. MGH Scriptores rerum Germanicarum, n. s., 5.

Hobbes, Thomas. *Leviathan*. Ed. R. Tuck. Cambridge: Cambridge University Press, 1991.

Humbert of Romans. *Treatise on the Formation of Preachers*. In *Early Dominicans: Selected Writings,* ed. and trans. S. Tugwell. Ramsey, N.J.: Paulist Press, 1982.

Humbert of Silva Candida. *Adversus simoniacos libri tres*. PL 143.

Isidore of Seville. *Etymologiarvm sive originvm libri XX*. Ed. W. M. Lindsay. Oxford Classical Texts. Oxford: Oxford University Press, 1911.

Jacopone da Todi. *The Lauds*. Trans. S. Hughes and E. Hughes. Ramsey, N.J.: Paulist Press, 1982.

Jaffé, Phillippus. *Regesta pontificum Romanorum ab condita ecclesia ad annum post Christum natum MCXCVIII*. Leipzig: Veit et. Comp., 1888.

James of Viterbo. *On Christian Government (De regimine christiano)*. Trans. and ed. R. W. Dyson. Woodbridge: The Boydell Press, 1995.

Jerome, St. *Commentariorum in Ezechielem prophetam*. PL 25.

———. *The Principal Works of St. Jerome*. Trans. W. H. Fremantle. Vol. 6 of NPNF, 2d ser.

John VIII, Pope. *Joannis Papae VIII Epistolae et decreta*. PL 126.

John of Paris. *On Royal and Papal Power*. Trans. and ed. J. A. Watt. Toronto: The Pontifical Institute of Medieval Studies, 1971.

———. *Über königliche und päpstliche Gewalt: Textkritische Edition mit deutscher Übersetzung*. Ed. F. Bleienstein. Stuttgart: Ernst Klett, 1969.

John of Salisbury. *Policraticus*. Ed. and trans. C. J. Nederman. Cambridge: Cambridge University Press, 1990.

Jonas of Orleans. *Le métier de roi (De institutione regia)*. Ed. A. Dubreucq. Sources chrétiens 407. Paris: Les Éditions du CERF, 1995.

Josephus. *Jewish Antiquities*. Trans. H. St. J. Thackeray. The Loeb Classical Library. London: William Heinemann; New York: G. P. Putnam's Sons, 1930.

Kant, Immanuel. *Zum ewigen Frieden*. In vol. 11 of *Werkausgabe,* ed. W. Weischedel. Frankfurt am Main: Suhrkamp, 1977.

King Horn: A Middle-English Romance. Ed. J. Hall. Oxford: Clarendon Press, 1901.

Leibniz, Gottfried Wilhelm. *Political Writings*. Ed. and trans. P. Riley. 2d ed. Cambridge: Cambridge University Press, 1988.

Liber miraculorum sancte Fidis. Ed. L. Robertini. Spoleto: Centro italiano di studi sull'alto medioevo, 1994.

Liudprand of Cremona. *A Chronicle of Otto's Reign (Liber de rebus gestis Ottonis)*. In *The Embassy to Constantinople and Other Writings,* trans. F. A. Wright, ed. J. J. Norwich. London: J. M. Dent; Rutland, Vt.: Charles E. Tuttle, 1993.

Loewenfeld, Samuel, ed. *Epistolae pontificum romanorum ineditae*. Leipzig: Veit et. Comp., 1885.

Lull, Ramon. *Blanquerna: A Thirteenth Century Romance*. Trans. E. Allison Peers. London: Jarrolds, [1926].

———. *The Book of the Gentile and the Three Wise Men*. In vol. 1 of *Selected*

Works of Ramon Llull (1232–1316), ed. and trans. A. Bonner. Princeton, N.J.: Princeton University Press, 1985.

————. *Contemporary Life (Vita coaetanea).* Trans. (with interpolations) A. Bonner. In "Historical Background and Life of Ramon Llull." *Selected Works of Ramon Llull (1232–1316),* ed. and trans. A. Bonner. Vol. 1. Princeton, N.J.: Princeton University Press.

————. *De participatione Christianorum et Saracenorum.* In *Politics and Culture in Medieval Spain and Italy,* by H. Wieruszowski. Rome: Storia e letteratura, 1971.

————. *Felix, or the Book of Wonders.* In vol. 2 of *Selected Works of Ramon Llull (1232–1316),* ed. and trans. A. Bonner. Princeton, N.J.: Princeton University Press, 1985.

————. *Liber de fine.* In *Ramon Lulls Kreuzzugsideen,* by A. Gottron. Berlin: Walther Rothschild, 1912.

————. *Libre de Blanquerna.* Ed. A. M. Alcover. Vol. 9 of *Obres Originals del Illuminat Doctor Mestre Ramon Lull.* Palma de Mallorca: Comissió editora Lulliana, 1914.

————. *Petitio Raymundi in concilio generali ad acquirendam terram sanctam.* In *Politics and Culture in Medieval Spain and Italy,* by H. Wieruszowski. Rome: Storia e letteratura, 1971.

————. *Selected Works of Ramon Llull (1232–1316).* Ed. and trans. A. Bonner. 2 vols. Princeton, N.J.: Princeton University Press, 1985.

Manegold of Lautenbach. *Ad Geberhardum liber.* MGH Ldl 1.

Marsiglio of Padua. *Defensor minor.* Trans. C. J. Nederman. In *Writings on the Empire,* by Marsiglio of Padua, ed. C. J. Nederman. Cambridge: Cambridge University Press, 1993.

————. *Defensor Pacis.* Trans. and ed. A. Gewirth. Toronto: University of Toronto Press, in association with the Medieval Academy of America, 1980.

————. *Defensor Pacis.* Ed. R. Scholz. Fontes iuris Germanici antiqui. Hanover: Hahnsche Buchhandlung, 1932–33.

————. *De translatione Imperii.* Trans. F. Watson and C. J. Nederman. In *Writings on the Empire,* by Marsiglio of Padua, ed. C. J. Nederman. Cambridge: Cambridge University Press, 1993.

Mirbt, Carl, and Kurt Aland. *Quellen zur Geschichte des Papsttums und des römischen Katholizismus.* Vol. 1. 6th ed. Tübingen: J. C. B. Mohr (Paul Siebeck), 1967.

The New Oxford Annotated Bible. New Revised Standard Version. New York: Oxford University Press, 1994.

Nithard. *Histories.* In *Carolingian Chronicles,* ed. and trans. B. W. Scholz. Ann Arbor: University of Michigan Press, 1972.

Odo of Deuil. *De profectione Ludovici VII in orientem (The Journey of Louis VII to the East).* Ed. and trans. V. G. Berry. New York: W. W. Norton, 1948.

Oresme, Nicole. *Le Livre de Politiques d'Aristote.* Ed. A. D. Menut. Transactions of the American Philosophical Society 60, no. 6 (1970), Philadelphia.

Otto of Freising [and his continuator, Rahewin]. *The Deeds of Friderick Barbarossa.* Trans. Ch. Ch. Mierow. Toronto: University of Toronto Press, in association with the Medieval Academy of America, 1994.

Peter the Venerable. *Epistola Petri Cluniacensis ad Bernardum Claraevallis.* In *Peter the Venerable and Islam,* by J. Kritzeck. Princeton, N.J.: Princeton University Press, 1964.

———. *The Letters of Peter the Venerable.* Ed. G. Constable. Cambridge, Mass.: Harvard University Press, 1967.

———. *Liber contra sectam sive haeresim Saracenorum.* In *Peter the Venerable and Islam,* by J. Kritzeck. Princeton, N.J.: Princeton University Press, 1964.

———. *Schriften zum Islam.* Ed. R. Glei. Corpus islamo-christanum. Series latina 1. Altenberge: CIS-Verlag, 1985.

———. *Sermo domni Petri abbatis cluniacensis de laude Domini sepulchri.* In G. Constable, "Petri Venerabilis sermones tres," *Révue bénédictine* 64 (1954), nos. 3–4.

———. *Summa totius haeresis Saracenorum.* In *Peter the Venerable and Islam,* by J. Kritzeck. Princeton, N.J.: Princeton University Press, 1964.

Petrus Crassus. *Defensio Heinrici IV. regis.* In *Schriften über den Streit zwischen Regnum und Sacerdotium,* ed. I. Schmale-Ott. Vol. 2 of *Quellen zum Investiturstreit.* Darmstadt: Wissenschaftliche Buchgesellschaft, 1984.

Philippe de Beaumanoir. *The* Coutumes de Beauvaisis *of Philippe de Beaumanoir.* Trans. and ed. F. R. P. Akehurst. Philadelphia: University of Pennsylvania Press, 1992.

Philippe de Mézières. *Epistre lamentable et consolatoire sur le fait de la desconfiture lacrimable du noble et vaillant roy de Honguerie par les Turcs devant la ville de Nicopoli* etc. In vol. 16 of *Oeuvres de Froissart,* ed. Kervyn de Lettenhove. Brussels: Imprimerie et librairie Victor Devaux, 1872.

———. *Letter to King Richard II: A plea made in 1395 for peace between England and France.* Ed. and trans. G. W. Coopland. Liverpool: Liverpool University Press, 1975.

———. *Le songe du vieil pèlerin.* Ed. G. W. Coopland. 2 vols. Cambridge: At the University Press, 1969.

Pierre d'Ailly. *De reformatione ecclesiae.* In *De concilio tractatus varii.* Paris, 1671.

Pierre Dubois. *De recuperatione terre sancte: Traité de politique générale par Pierre Dubois, avocat des causes ecclésiastiques au bailliage de Coutances sous Philippe le Bel.* Ed. Ch.-V. Langlois. Paris: Alphonse Picard, 1891.

———. *Oppinio cujusdam suadentis regi Francie ut regnum Jerosolimitanum et Cipri acquireret pro altero filiorum suorum, ac de invasione regni Egipti.* In Dubois, *De recuperatione terre sancte,* ed. Ch.-V. Langlois (Paris: Alphonse Picard, 1891); trans. in Dubois, *The Recovery of the Holy Land,* trans. and ed. W. I. Brandt (New York: Columbia University Press, 1956).

———. *The Recovery of the Holy Land.* Trans. and ed. W. I. Brandt. New York: Columbia University Press, 1956.

———. *Summaria brevis et compendiosa doctrina felicis expedicionis et abbrevacionis guerrarum ac litium regni Francorum.* Ed. H. Kämpf. Leipzig and Berlin: B. G. Teubner, 1936.

Potthast, August. *Regesta pontificum romanorum inde ab a. post Christum natum MCXCVIII ad a. MCCCIV.* Berlin: Decker, 1874–75.

Raymond of Aguilers. *Le "Liber" de Raymond d'Aguilers.* Ed. J. H. Hill and

L. L. Hill. *Documents relatifs à l'histoire des croisades publiés par l'Académie des inscriptions et belles-lettres* 9. Paris: Librairie orientaliste Paul Geuthner, 1969.

Robert the Monk. *Roberti Monachi historia Iherosolimitana.* RHC Occ 3.

Rodulfus Glaber. *Historiarvm libri quinqve (The Five Books of the Histories).* Ed. and trans. J. France. Oxford: Clarendon Press, 1989.

Sandys, Edwin. *Europae speculum, or a View or Survey of the State of Religion in the western parts of the world, wherein The Roman Religion, and the Pregnant Policies of the Church of Rome to support the same, are notably displayed, with some other memorable Discoveries and Commemorations.* London, 1673.

Sermo cum rex Franciae est processurus ad bellum. In Dom Jean Leclercq, "Un sermon prononcé pendant la guerre de Flandre sous Philippe le Bel," *Revue du moyen âge latin* 1(1945), no. 2.

Seyssel, Claude de. *Exorde en la translation de l'Histoire de Justin.* In *La Monarchie de France et deux autres fragments politiques,* ed. J. Poujol. Paris: Librairie d'Argences, 1961.

———. *La Monarchie de France.* In *La Monarchie de France et deux autres fragments politiques,* ed. J. Poujol. Paris: Librairie d'Argences, 1961.

The Song of Roland. Trans. Glyn Burgess. London: Penguin Books, 1990.

Le songe du vergier, qui parle de la disputacion du clerc et du chevalier. Pts. 1 and 2. Ed. F. Chatillon. *Revue du Moyen Age Latin* 13 (1957); 14 (1958).

Sozomen. *The Ecclesiastical History.* Revised trans. Ch. D. Hartranft. In vol. 2 of NPNF, 2d ser.

Thiel, Andreas, ed. *Epistolae Romanorum pontificum genuinae et quae ad eos scriptae sunt a S. Hilaro usque ad Pelagium II.* Vol. 1. Braunsberg: Eduard Peter, 1868.

Thomas of Celano. *The First Life of St. Francis.* In *St. Francis of Assisi: Writings and Early Biographies. English Omnibus of the Sources for the Life of St. Francis,* ed. M. A. Habig. 2d ed. London: The Society for Promoting Christian Knowledge, 1979.

———. *The Second Life of St. Francis.* In *St. Francis of Assisi: Writings and Early Biographies. English Omnibus of the Sources for the Life of St. Francis,* ed. M. A. Habig. 2d ed. London: The Society for Promoting Christian Knowledge, 1979.

Vita beati fratris Egidii. In *Scripta Leonis, Rufini et Angeli Sociorum S. Francisci (The Writings of Leo, Rufino and Angelo, Companions of St. Francis),* ed. and trans. R. M. Brooke. Oxford: Clarendon Press, 1990.

Voltaire. *Oeuvres complètes de Voltaire.* Paris: Garnier Frères, 1877–85.

Wenrich of Trier. *Wenrici scolastici Treuirensis Epistola sub Theoderici episcopi Virdunensis nomine composita.* In *Schriften über den Streit zwischen Regnum und Sacerdotium,* ed. I. Schmale-Ott. Vol. 2 of *Quellen zum Investiturstreit.* Darmstadt: Wissenschaftliche Buchgesellschaft, 1984.

Wido of Osnabrück. *De controversia inter Hildebrandum et Heinricum imperatorem.* In *Schriften über den Streit zwischen Regnum und Sacerdotium,* ed. I. Schmale-Ott. Vol. 2 of *Quellen zum Investiturstreit.* Darmstadt: Wissenschaftliche Buchgesellschaft, 1984.

William of Tyre. *A History of Deeds Done beyond the Sea*. Trans. E. A. Babcock and A. C. Krey. 2 vols. New York: Columbia University Press, 1943.

SECONDARY SOURCES

Abulafia, Anna Sapir. 1995. *Christians and Jews in the Twelfth-Century Renaissance*. London and New York: Routledge.

Abulafia, David. 1977. Kantorowicz and Frederick II. *History* 62.

———. 1992. *Frederick II: A Medieval Emperor*. New York and Oxford: Oxford University Press.

———. 1997. *The Western Mediterranean Kingdoms, 1200–1500: The Struggle for Dominion*. London and New York: Longman.

Allen, J. W. 1923. Marsilio of Padua and Mediaeval Secularism. In *The Social and Political Ideas of Some Great Mediaeval Thinkers*, ed. F. J. C. Hearnshaw. London: George G. Harrap.

Alphandéry, Paul. 1954. *La Chrétienté et l'idée de croisade*. Ed. A. Dupront. Vol. 1. Paris: Albin Michel.

———. 1959. *La Chrétienté et l'idée de croisade*. Ed. A. Dupront. Vol. 2. Paris: Albin Michel.

Anton, Hans Hubert. 1968. *Fürstenspiegel und Herrscherethos in der Karolingerzeit*. Bonn: Ludwig Röhrschied.

———. 1987. Frühe Stufen der Kirchenreform. In *Sant'Anselmo, Mantova e la lotta per le investiture: Atti del Convegno Internazionale di Studi (Mantova, 23–24–25 maggio 1986)*, ed. P. Golinelli. Bologna: Pàtron.

Appelt, Heinrich. 1983. Christianitas und Imperium in der Stauferzeit. In *La cristianità dei secoli XI e XII in Occidente: Coscienza e strutture di una società*. Miscellanea del Centro di Studi Medioevali 10. Milan: Vita e pensiero.

Armstrong, Karen. 1992. *Holy War: The Crusades and Their Impact on Today's World*. New York: Anchor Books.

Arquillière, H.-X. 1934. *Saint Grégoire VII: Essai sur sa conception du pouvoir pontifical*. Paris: Vrin.

———. 1939. *L'église au moyen âge*. Paris: Bloud & Gay.

———. 1947. Origines de la théorie des deux glaives. *Studi gregoriani* 1.

Atiya, Aziz Suryal. 1938. *The Crusade in the Later Middle Ages*. London: Methuen.

———. 1962. *Crusade, Commerce, and Culture*. Bloomington: Indiana University Press.

Aziz, Mohammed A. 1996. La croisade de l'empereur Frédéric II et l'Orient Latin. In *Autour de la première croisade: Actes du Colloque de la Society for the Study of the Crusades and the Latin East (Clermont-Ferrand, 22–25 juin 1995)*, ed. M. Balard. Paris: Publications de la Sorbonne.

Babbitt, Susan M. 1985. Oresme's *Livre de Politiques and the France of Charles V*. Transactions of the American Philosophical Society 75, pt. 1. Philadelphia: American Philosophical Society.

Baethgen, Friedrich. 1964. Zur Geschichte der Weltherrschatsidee im späteren Mittelalter. In *Festschrift Percy Ernst Schramm zu seinem siebzigsten Ge-*

burtstag von Schülern und Freunden zugeeignet. Vol. 1. Wiesbaden: Franz Steiner.

Bainton, Roland H. 1960. *Christian Attitudes toward War and Peace.* Nashville and New York: Abingdon Press.

Balan, Pietro. [1890?]. Il pontificato di Giovanni VIII libri tre. In *Il papato di Giovanni VIII dal 872 al 882, ed Il processo di Bonifazio VIII.* [Rome?].

Balard, Michel. 1997. L'image de l'autre: Génois et Sarrasins. In *Itinéraire de cultures croisées: de Toulouse à Tripoli.* Tripoli: Publications de l'Université de Balamand.

Barber, Malcolm. 1982. The world picture of Philip the Fair. *Journal of Medieval History* 8, no. 1.

———. 1993. *The Trial of the Templars.* Cambridge: Cambridge University Press.

———. 1995. *The New Knighthood: A History of the Order of the Templars.* Cambridge: Cambridge University Press.

Barber, Richard. 1982. *The Knight and Chivalry.* New York: Harper Colophon Books.

Barnes, Jonathan. 1988. The just war. In *The Cambridge History of Later Medieval Philosophy,* ed. N. Kretzmann, A. Kenny, and J. Pinborg. Cambridge: Cambridge University Press.

Barnie, John. 1974. *War in Medieval English Society: Social Values in the Hundred Years War, 1337–99.* Ithaca, N.Y.: Cornell University Press.

Bartlett, Robert. 1993. *The Making of Europe: Conquest, Colonization, and Cultural Change, 950–1350.* Princeton, N.J.: Princeton University Press.

Basetti-Sani, Giulio. 1959. *Mohammed et Saint François.* Ottawa: Commisariat de Terre-Sainte.

Beaune, Colette. 1991. *The Birth of an Ideology: Myths and Symbols of Nation in Late-Medieval France.* Trans. S. Ross Huston, ed. F. L. Cheyette. Berkeley and Los Angeles: University of California Press.

Beazley, Charles Raymond. 1897–1906. *The Dawn of Modern Geography.* 3 vols. London: J. Murray.

Becker, Alfons. 1964. *Herkunft und kirchliche Laufbahn: Der Papst und die lateinische Christenheit.* Vol. 1 of *Papst Urban II. (1088–1099).* Stuttgart: Anton Hiersemann.

———. 1988. *Der Papst, die griechische Christenheit und der Kreuzzug.* Vol. 2 of *Papst Urban II. (1088–1099).* Stuttgart: Anton Hiersemann.

Beckingham, C. F. 1976. Misconceptions of Islam: Medieval and Modern. *Journal of the Royal Society of Arts* 124.

Bell, Dora M. 1955. *Étude sur Le songe du vieil pèlerin de Philippe de Mézières (1327–1405) d'après le manuscrit français B.N. 22542: Document historique et moral du règne de Charles VI.* Geneva: Droz.

Bennett, Matthew. 1986. First Crusaders' Images of Muslims: The Influence of Vernacular Poetry? *Forum for Modern Language Studies* 22, no. 2.

Benson, Robert L. 1982. The Gelasian Doctrine: Uses and Transformations. In *La notion d'autorité au Moyen Age: Islam, Byzance, Occident,* ed. G. Makdisi, D. Sourdel, and J. Sourdel-Thomine. Paris: Presses Universitaires de France.

Berg, Dieter. 1985. Gesellschaftspolitische Implikationen der vita minorum, insbesondere des franziskanischen Friedensgedankens, im 13. Jahrhundert. In *Renovatio et Reformatio: Wider das Bild vom "finsteren" Mittelalter. Festschrift für Ludwig Hödl*, ed. M. Gerwing and G. Ruppert. Münster: Aschendorff.

Berger, Élie. 1893. *Saint Louis et Innocent IV.: Étude sur les rapports de la France et du Saint-Siège.* Paris: Thorin & Fils.

Berry, Virginia. 1956. Peter the Venerable and the Crusades. In *Petrus Venerabilis, 1156–1956: Studies and Texts Commemorating the Eighth Centenary of His Death*, ed. G. Constable and J. Kritzeck. Rome: Herder.

Berschin, Walter. 1972. *Bonizo von Sutri: Leben und Werk.* Beiträge zur Geschichte und Quellenkunde des Mittelalters 2. Berlin and New York: Walter de Gruyter.

———. 1987. Bonizone da Sutri e lo stato di vita laicale: Il Codice Mantova 439. In *Sant'Anselmo, Mantova e la lotta per le investiture: Atti del Convegno Internazionale di Studi (Mantova, 23–24–25 maggio 1986)*, ed. P. Golinelli. Bologna: Pàtron.

Beumann, Helmut. 1981. Unitas ecclesiae—unitas imperii—unitas regni: Von der imperialen Reichseinheitsidee zur Einheit der regna. In *Nascita dell'Europa ed Europa carolingia: Un'equazione da verificare.* Settimane di studio del Centro italiano di studi sull'alto medioevo 27. Spoleto: Presso la Sede del Centro.

Bisson, Thomas N. 1977. The Organized Peace in Southern France and Catalonia, ca. 1140—ca. 1233. *American Historical Review* 82, no. 2.

Black, Antony. 1992. *Political Thought in Europe, 1250–1450.* Cambridge: Cambridge University Press.

Blake, E. O. 1970. The Formation of the "Crusade Idea." *Journal of Ecclesiastical History* 21, no. 1.

Bleienstein, Fritz. 1969. Introduction to *Über königliche und päpstliche Gewalt*, by John of Paris. Stuttgart: Ernst Klett.

Bloch, Marc. 1983. *La société féodale.* Paris: Albin Michel.

Bloch, R. Howard. 1977. *Medieval French Literature and Law.* Berkeley and Los Angeles: University of California Press.

Blumenthal, Uta-Renate. 1988. *The Investiture Controversy: Church and Monarchy from the Ninth to the Twelfth Century.* Philadelphia: University of Pennsylvania Press.

———. 1991. Papal and Local Councils: The Evidence of the *Pax* and *Treuga Dei. Studi gregoriani* 14.

Boehm, Laetitia. 1957. "Gesta Dei per Francos"—oder "Gesta Francorum"? Die Kreuzzüge als historiographisches Problem. *Saeculum* 8, no. 1.

Bonnaud Delamare, Roger. 1939. *L'idée de paix à l'époque carolingienne.* Paris: Domat-Montchrestien.

Bonner, Anthony. 1985a. Historical Background and Life of Ramon Llull. In *Selected Works of Ramon Llull (1232–1316)*, ed. and trans. A. Bonner. Vol. 1. Princeton, N.J.: Princeton University Press.

———. 1985b. Llull's Thought. In *Selected Works of Ramon Llull (1232–1316)*, ed. and trans. A. Bonner. Vol. 1. Princeton, N.J.: Princeton University Press.

————. 1985c. Llull's Influence: The History of Llullism. In *Selected Works of Ramon Llull (1232–1316)*, ed. and trans. A. Bonner. Vol. 1. Princeton, N.J.: Princeton University Press.

Borgolte, Michael. 1976. *Der Gesandtenaustausch der Karolinger mit den Abbasiden und mit den Patriarchen von Jerusalem*. Münchener Beiträge zur Mediävistik und Renaissance-Forschung 25. Munich: Arbeo Gesellschaft.

Bosbach, Franz. 1988. *Monarchia universalis: Ein politischer Leitbegriff der frühen Neuzeit*. Göttingen: Vandenhoeck & Ruprecht.

Brandt, W. I. 1956. Introduction to *The Recovery of the Holy Land*, by Pierre Dubois. New York: Columbia University Press.

Bredero, Adriaan H. 1994. *Christendom and Christianity in the Middle Ages: The Relation between Religion, Church, and Society*. Trans. R. Bruinsma. Grand Rapids, Mich.: W. B. Eerdmans.

————. 1996. *Bernard of Clairvaux: Between Cult and History*. Grand Rapids, Mich.: W. B. Eerdmans.

Brezzi, Paolo. 1954. *Realtà e mito dell'Europa dall'antichità al giorni nostri*. Rome: Studium.

Brown, Elizabeth A. R. 1974. The Tyranny of a Construct: Feudalism and Historians of Medieval Europe. *American Historical Review* 79, no. 4.

Brown, P. R. L. 1967. *Augustine of Hippo: Biography*. Berkeley and Los Angeles: University of California Press.

————. 1972. St. Augustine's Attitude to Religious Coercion. In id. *Religion and Society in the Age of Saint Augustine*. London: Faber and Faber.

————. 1996. *The Rise of Western Christendom: Triumph and Diversity, AD 200–1000*. Cambridge, Mass., and Oxford: Blackwell.

Brundage, James A. 1969. *Medieval Canon Law and the Crusader*. Madison: University of Wisconsin Press.

————. 1976. Holy War and the Medieval Lawyers. In *The Holy War*, ed. T. P. Murphy. Columbus: Ohio State University Press.

————. 1991. St. Anselm, Ivo of Chartres, and the Ideology of the First Crusade. In id. *The Crusades, Holy War and Canon Law*. Aldershot: Variorum.

————. 1992. St. Bernard and the Jurists. In *The Second Crusade and the Cistercians*, ed. M. Gervers. New York: St. Martin's Press.

————. 1997. Immortalizing the Crusades: Law and Institutions. In *Montjoie: Studies in Crusade History in Honour of Hans Eberhard Mayer*, ed. B. Z. Kedar, J. Riley-Smith, and R. Hiestand. Aldershot: Variorum.

————, ed. 1964. *The Crusades: Motives and Achievements*. Boston: D. C. Heath.

Bryce, James. 1889. *The Holy Roman Empire*. London and New York: Macmillan.

Buckler, F. W. 1931. *Harunu'l-Rashid and Charles the Great*. Cambridge, Mass.: The Medieval Academy of America.

Bull, Marcus. 1993. *Knightly Piety and the Lay Response to the First Crusade: The Limousin and Gascony, c. 970–c. 1130*. Oxford: Clarendon Press.

Bulst-Thiele, Marie Luise. 1992. The Influence of St. Bernard of Clairvaux on the Formation of the Order of the Knights Templar. In *The Second Crusade and the Cistercians*, ed. M. Gervers. New York: St. Martin's Press.

Burns, C. Delisle. 1947. *The First Europe: A Study of the Establishment of Medieval Christendom, A.D. 400–800.* London: George Allen & Unwin.

Burns, J. H. 1992. *Lordship, Kingship and Empire: The Idea of Monarchy, 1400–1525.* Oxford: Clarendon Press.

———, ed. 1988. *The Cambridge History of Medieval Political Thought, c. 350–c. 1450.* Cambridge: Cambridge University Press.

Burns, Robert I. 1971. Christian-Islamic Confrontation in the West: The Thirteenth-Century Dream of Conversion. *American Historical Review* 76, no. 5.

Caesar, Michael, ed. 1989. *Dante: The Critical Heritage, 1314(?)-1870.* London and New York: Routledge.

Callahan, Daniel F. 1992. The Peace of God and the Cult of the Saints in Aquitaine in the Tenth and Eleventh Centuries. In *The Peace of God,* ed. Th. Head and R. Landes. Ithaca, N.Y.: Cornell University Press.

Canning, J. P. 1988. Introduction: Politics, Institutions and Ideas. In *The Cambridge History of Medieval Political Thought, c. 350–c. 1450,* ed. J. H. Burns. Cambridge: Cambridge University Press.

———. 1989. *The Political Thought of Baldus de Ubaldis.* Cambridge: Cambridge University Press.

———. 1996. *A History of Medieval Political Thought, 300–1450.* London and New York: Routledge.

Cantor, Norman F. 1991. *Inventing the Middle Ages: The Lives, Works, and Ideas of the Great Medievalists of the Twentieth Century.* New York: William Morrow.

———, ed. 1963. *The Medieval World, 300–1300.* Ideas and Institutions in Western Civilization 2. New York and London: Macmillan.

Capitani, O. 1992. Sondaggio sulla terminologia militare in Urbano II. In *"Militia Christi" e Crociata nei secoli XI-XIII.* Miscellanea del Centro di studi medioevali. Milan: Vita e pensiero.

Cardini, Franco. 1974. "Nella presenza del soldan superba": Bernardo, Francesco, Bonaventura e il superamento spirituale dell'idea di crociata. *Studi francescani* 71.

———. 1981. *Alle radici della cavalleria medievale.* Florence: La Nuova Italia.

———. 1992a. *Guerre di primavera: Studi sulla cavalleria e la tradizione cavalleresca.* Florence: Le Lettere.

———. 1992b. La guerra santa nella cristianità. In *"Militia Christi" e Crociata nei secoli XI-XIII.* Miscellanea del Centro di studi medioevali. Milan: Vita e pensiero.

———. 1993a. Bernardo e la crociata. In id. *Studi sulla storia e sull'idea di crociata.* Rome: Jouvence.

———. 1993b. Le crociate tra Illuminismo ed età napoleonica. In id. *Studi sulla storia e sull'idea di crociata.* Rome: Jouvence.

———. 1993c. L'idea di crociata in santa Caterina da Siena. In id. *Studi sulla storia e sull'idea di crociata.* Rome: Jouvence.

Carlyle, R. W., and A. J. Carlyle. 1903–1936. *A History of Mediaeval Political Theory in the West.* 6 vols. Edinburgh and London: William Blackwood & Sons.

Carozzi, Claude. 1979. Introduction to *Poème au roi Robert,* by Adalbero of Laon. Paris: Les Belles Lettres.

————. 1983. D'Adalbéron de Laon à Humbert de Moyenmoutier: La désacralisation de la royauté. In *La cristianità dei secoli XI e XII in Occidente: Coscienza e strutture di una società.* Miscellanea del Centro di Studi Medioevali 10. Milan: Vita e pensiero.

Carton, Raoul. 1924. *La synthèse doctrinale de Roger Bacon.* Paris: Vrin.

Cassirer, Ernst, Paul Oskar Kristeller, and John Herman Randall, Jr., eds. 1948. *The Renaissance Philosophy of Man.* Chicago and London: University of Chicago Press.

Castellini, A. 1938. I due grandi animatori della crociata: Santa Caterina da Siena e Pio II. *Bulettino senese di storia patria,* n.s., 9.

Chabod, Federico. 1991. *Storia dell'idea d'Europa.* Ed. E. Sestan and A. Saitta. 10th ed. Bari: Laterza.

Cheira, M. A. 1947. *La lutte entre Arabes et Byzantins: La conquête et l'organisation des frontières aux VII*ᵉ* et VIII*ᵉ* siècles.* Alexandria: Société de publications égyptiennes.

Chew, Samuel C. 1965. *The Crescent and the Rose: Islam and England during the Renaissance.* New York: Octagon Books.

Christiansen, Eric. 1980. *The Northern Crusades: The Baltic and the Catholic Frontier, 1100–1525.* Minneapolis: University of Minnesota Press.

Cohn, Norman. 1993. *The Pursuit of Millenium: Revolutionary Millenarians and Mystical Anarchists of the Middle Ages.* 3d ed. London: Pimlico.

Colbert, Edward. 1962. *The Martyrs of Córdoba (850–859): A Study of Sources.* Washington, D.C.: Catholic University of America Press.

Cole, Penny J. 1991. *The Preaching of the Crusades to the Holy Land, 1095–1270.* Cambridge, Mass.: The Medieval Academy of America.

————. 1993. "O God, the heathen have come into your inheritance" (Ps. 78.1): The Theme of Religious Pollution in Crusade Documents, 1095–1188. In *Crusaders and Muslims in twelfth-century Syria,* ed. M. Shatzmiller. Leiden: E. J. Brill.

Collins, Roger. 1996. *Fredegar.* Authors of the Middle Ages 13. In Authors of the Middle Ages. Vol. IV, 12–13. Aldershot: Variorum.

Compagnon, Antoine, and Jacques Seebacher. 1993. *L'Esprit de l'Europe.* Paris: Flammarion.

Conrad, Hermann. 1941. Gottesfrieden und Heeresverfassung in der Zeit der Kreuzzüge: Ein Beitrag zur Geschichte des Heeresstrafrechts im Mittelalter. *Zeitschrift der Savigny-Stiftung für Rechtsgeschichte, Germanistische Abteilung 61.*

Constable, Giles. 1953. The Second Crusade as Seen by Contemporaries. *Traditio 9.*

————. 1954. Petri Venerabilis sermones tres. *Révue bénédictine 64,* nos. 3–4.

————. 1995. *Three Studies in Medieval Religious and Social Thought.* Cambridge: Cambridge University Press.

————. 1997. The Crusading Project of 1150. In *Montjoie: Studies in Crusade History in Honour of Hans Eberhard Mayer,* ed. B. Z. Kedar, J. Riley-Smith, and R. Hiestand. Aldershot: Variorum.

Constantinescu-Bagdat, Elise. 1924. *La "Qerella pacis" d'Érasme (1517)*. Vol. 1 of *Études d'histoire pacifiste*. Paris: Presses Universitaires de France.

Contamine, Philippe. 1986. *La guerre au Moyen Age*. Paris: Presses Universitaires de France.

Coopland, G. W. 1949. Introduction to *The Tree of Battles*, by Honoré Bonet. Liverpool: At the University Press.

———. 1969. Introduction to *Le songe du vieil pèlerin*, by Philippe de Mézières. Cambridge: At the University Press.

———. 1975. Introduction to *Letter to King Richard II*, by Philippe de Mézières. Liverpool: Liverpool University Press.

Cottrell, Alan. 1993. *Auctoritas* and *potestas*: A Reevaluation of the Correspondence of Gelasius I on Papal-Imperial Relations. *Medieval Studies* 55.

Courtois, Christian. 1945. Grégoire VII et l'Afrique du Nord: Remarques sur les communautés chrétiennes d'Afrique au XIe siècle. *Revue historique* 195.

Cousin, Dom Patrice. 1953. Les débuts de l'Ordre des Templiers et Saint Bernard. In *Mélanges Saint Bernard. XXIVe Congrès de l'Association bourguignonne des sociétés savantes*. Dijon: Marilier.

Cowdrey, H. E. J. 1970a. The Peace and the Truce of God in the Eleventh Century. *Past & Present*, no. 46.

———. 1970b. Pope Urban II's Preaching of the First Crusade. *History* 55.

———. 1973. Cluny and the First Crusade. *Revue bénédictine* 83.

———. 1976. The Genesis of the Crusades: The Springs of Western Ideas of Holy War. In *The Holy War*, ed. T. P. Murphy. Columbus: Ohio State University Press.

———. 1977. The Mahdia campaign of 1087. *English Historical Review* 92, no. 362.

———. 1982. Pope Gregory VII's "Crusading" Plans of 1074. In *Outremer: Studies in the History of the Crusading Kingdom of Jerusalem, Presented to Joshua Prawer*, ed. B. Z. Kedar, H. E. Mayer, and R. C. Smail. Jerusalem: Yad Izhak Ben-Zvi Institute.

———. 1983. *The Age of Abbot Desiderius: Montecassino, the Papacy, and the Normans in the Eleventh and Early Twelfth Centuries*. Oxford: Clarendon Press.

———. 1985. Martyrdom and the First Crusade. In *Crusade and Settlement*, ed. P. W. Edbury. Cardiff: University College Cardiff Press.

———. 1995. Pope Urban II and the Idea of Crusade. *Studi medievali*, 3d ser., 36.

———. 1997. Pope Gregory VII and the Bearing of Arms. In *Montjoie: Studies in Crusade History in Honour of Hans Eberhard Mayer*, ed. B. Z. Kedar, J. Riley-Smith, and R. Hiestand. Aldershot: Variorum.

———. 1998. *Pope Gregory VII, 1073–1085*. Oxford: Clarendon Press.

Cushing, Kathleen G. 1998. *Papacy and Law in the Gregorian Revolution: The Canonistic Work of Anselm of Lucca*. Oxford: Clarendon Press.

d'Alverny, Marie Thérèse. 1965a. La connaissance de l'Islam en Occident du IXe au milieu du XIIe siècle. In *L'Occidente e l'Islam nell'alto medioevo*. Settimane di studio del Centro italiano di studi sull'alto medioevo 12. Spoleto: Presso la sede del Centro.

———. 1965b. Introduction to *Textes inédits*, by Alain of Lille. Paris: Vrin.

Daniel, N. 1975. *The Arabs and Mediaeval Europe*. London: Longman; Beirut: Librairie du Liban.

———. 1989a. The Legal and Political Theory of the Crusade. In *The Impact of the Crusades on Europe*, ed. H. W. Hazard and N. M. Zacour. Vol. 6 of *A History of the Crusades*, ed. K. M. Setton. Madison: University of Wisconsin Press.

———. 1989b. Crusade Propaganda. In *The Impact of the Crusades on Europe*, ed. H. W. Hazard and N. M. Zacour. Vol. 6 of *A History of the Crusades*, ed. K. M. Setton. Madison: University of Wisconsin Press.

———. 1993. *Islam and the West: The Making of an Image*. 2d ed. Oxford: Oneworld.

Davis, Charles Till. 1959. Remigo de' Girolami and Dante: A Comparison of Their Conceptions of Peace. *Studi danteschi* 36.

———. 1993. Dante and Empire. In *The Cambridge Companion to Dante*, ed. R. Jacoff. Cambridge: Cambridge University Press.

———, ed. 1967. *Western Awakening: Sources of Medieval History 2 (c. 1000–1500)*. New York: Appelton-Century-Crofts.

Davis, R. H. C. 1973. William of Tyre. In *Relations between East and West in the Middle Ages*, ed. D. Baker. Edinburgh: At the University Press.

Dawson, Christopher. 1954. *Medieval Essays*. New York: Sheed and Ward.

Deanesly, Margaret. 1991. *Medieval Church, 590–1500*. London and New York: Routledge.

Debord, André. 1992. The Castellan Revolution and the Peace of God in Aquitaine. In *The Peace of God*, ed. Th. Head and R. Landes. Ithaca, N.Y.: Cornell University Press.

Dedouvres, Louis. 1894. *De Patris Josephi Turciados libris quinque*. Angers: Germain et G. Grassin.

———. 1932. *Le Père Joseph de Paris, capucin, l'éminence grise*. 2 vols. Paris: Gabriel Beauchesne; Angers: S^te A^me des Éditions de l'Ouest.

Delanty, Gerard. 1995. *Inventing Europe: Idea, Identity, Reality*. New York: St. Martin's Press.

Delaruelle, Étienne. 1953. L'idée de croisade chez saint Bernard. In *Mélanges Saint Bernard. XXIVe Congrès de l'Association bourguignonne des sociétés savantes*. Dijon: Marilier.

———. 1969. Paix de Dieu et croisade dans la chrétienté du XIIe siècle. In *Paix de Dieu et guerre sainte en Languedoc au XIIIe siècle*. Cahiers de Fanjeaux 4. Toulouse: Édouard Privat.

———. 1980. Essai sur la formation de l'idée de Croisade. In id. *L'idée de croisade au moyen âge*. Turin: Bottega d'Erasmo.

Delaville le Roulx, J. 1886. *La France en Orient au XIVe siècle*. Paris: Ernest Thorin.

delle Piane, Mario. 1959. *Vecchio e nuovo nelle idee politiche di Pietro Dubois*. Florence: Felice le Mounier.

d'Entrèves, A. Passerin. 1952. *Dante as a Political Thinker*. Oxford: Clarendon Press.

———. 1967. *The Notion of the State: An Introduction to Political Theory*. Oxford: Clarendon Press.

Dérumaux, Pierre. 1953. Saint Bernard et les infidèles. In *Mélanges Saint Bernard. XXIVe Congrès de l'Association bourguignonne des sociétés savantes.* Dijon: Marilier.

Djuvara, T. G. 1914. *Cent projets de partage de la Turquie (1281–1913).* Paris: F. Alcan.

Dondaine, H.-F. 1968. Foreword to *De rationibus fidei,* by Aquinas. Rome: Ad Sanctae Sabinae.

Douglas, David C. 1969. *The Norman Achievement, 1050–1100.* Berkeley and Los Angeles: University of California Press.

Dreitzel, Horst. 1992. *Monarchiebegriffe in der Fürstengesellschaft: Semiotik und Theorie der Einherrschaft in Deutschland von der Reformation bis zum Vormärz.* 2 vols. Cologne: Böhlau.

Dubreucq, Alain. 1995. Introduction to *Le métier de roi,* by Jonas of Orleans. Paris: Les Éditions du CERF.

Duby, Georges. 1968a. Les laïcs et la paix de Dieu. In *I laici nella "societas christiana" dei secoli XI e XII.* Miscellanea del Centro di studi medioevali. Milan: Vita e pensiero.

———. 1968b. Les origines de la chevalerie. In *Ordinamenti militari in Occidente nell'alto medioevo.* Settimane del studio del Centro italiano di studi sull'alto medioevo 15. Spoleto: Centro italiano di studi sull'alto medioevo.

———. 1974. *The Early Growth of the European Economy: Warriors and Peasants from the Seventh to the Twelfth Century.* Trans. H. B. Clarke. Ithaca, N.Y.: Cornell University Press.

———. 1985. *Trije redi ali imaginarij fevdalizma.* Trans. G. Moder. Ljubljana: Studia humanitatis.

Dümmler, E. 1876. Gedichte aus dem elften Jahrhundert. *Neues Archiv der Gesellschaft für ältere deutsche Geschichtskunde* 1.

Dupront, A. 1959. La croisade après les croisades. In *La Chrétienté et l'idée de croisade,* by Paul Alphandéry, ed. A. Dupront. Vol. 2. Paris: Albin Michel.

———. 1969. Guerre sainte et chrétienté. In *Paix de Dieu et guerre sainte en Languedoc au XIIIe siècle.* Cahiers de Fanjeaux 4. Toulouse: Édouard Privat.

Dyson, R. W. 1986. Introduction to *On Ecclesiastical Power,* by Giles of Rome. Woodbridge: The Boydell Press.

———. 1995. Introduction to *On Christian Government,* by James of Viterbo. Woodbridge: The Boydell Press.

Eckermann, Karla. 1933. *Studien zur Geschichte des monarchischen Gedankens im 15. Jahrhundert.* Berlin: W. Rotschild.

Edbury, Peter W. 1991. *The Kingdom of Cyprus and the Crusades, 1191–1374.* Cambridge: Cambridge University Press.

Edbury, Peter W., and John G. Rowe. 1990. *William of Tyre: Historian of the Latin East.* Cambridge: Cambridge University Press.

el-Khodeiry, Zeynab. 1988. St Thomas d'Aquin entre Avicenne et Averroes. In *Thomas von Aquin: Werk und Wirkung im Licht neuerer Forschungen,* ed. A. Zimmermann. Miscellanea mediaevalia 19. Berlin and New York: Walter de Gruyter.

Emery, Pierre-Yves. 1990. Introduction to *Éloge de la nouvelle chevalerie,* by Bernard of Clairvaux. Paris: Les éditions du CERF.

Engelberger, Johann. 1996. *Gregor VII. und die Investiturfrage: Quellenkritische Studien zum angeblichen Investiturverbot von 1075.* Cologne: Böhlau.

Engreen, Fred E. 1945. Pope John the Eighth and the Arabs. *Speculum* 20, no. 3.

Erdmann, Carl. 1930. Der Kreuzzugsgedanke in Portugal. *Historische Zeitscrift* 141.

———. 1932. Endkaiserglaube und Kreuzzugsgedanke im 11. Jahrhundert. *Zeitschrift für Kirchengeschichte,* 3d ser., 51.

———. 1935. *Die Entstehung des Kreuzzugsgedankens.* Stuttgart: W. Kohlhammer.

———. 1936. Die Anfänge der staatlichen Propaganda im Investiturstreit. *Historische Zeitschrift* 154.

Erickson, Norma N. 1967. Introduction to "A Dispute between a Priest and a Knight." *Proceedings of the American Philosophical Society* 111, no. 5.

Evans, G. R. 1983. *Alan of Lille: The Frontiers of Theology in the Later Twelfth Century.* Cambridge: Cambridge University Press.

Ewald, Paul. 1880. Die Papstbriefe der Britischen Sammlung. *Neues Archiv der Gesellschaft für ältere deutsche Geschichtskunde* 5.

Fasoli, Gina. 1968. Pace e guerra nell'alto medioevo. In *Ordinamenti militari in Occidente nell'alto medioevo.* Settimane del studio del Centro italiano di studi sull'alto medioevo 15. Spoleto: Centro italiano di studi sull'alto medioevo.

Fasolt, Constantin. 1991. *Council and Hierarchy: The Political Thought of William Durant the Younger.* Cambridge: Cambridge University Press.

Fawtier, Robert. 1960. *The Capetian Kings of France: Monarchy and Nation, 987–1328.* Trans. L. Butler and R. J. Adam. Houndmills and London: Macmillan.

Fell, A. London. 1991. *Medieval or Renaissance Origins? Historiographical Debates and Deconstructions.* Vol. 4 of *Origins of Legislative Sovereignty and the Legislative State.* New York: Praeger.

Fernández-Santamaria, J. A. 1983. *Reason of State and Statecraft in Spanish Political Thought, 1595–1640.* Lanham, Md.: University Press of America.

Ferreiro, Alberto. 1983. The Siege of Barbastro, 1064–65: A Reassessment. *Journal of Medieval History* 9, no. 2.

Fichtenau, Heinrich. 1978. *The Carolingian Empire.* Trans. P. Munz. Toronto: University of Toronto Press, in association with the Medieval Academy of America.

Figgis, John Neville. 1922. *The Divine Right of Kings.* 2d ed. Cambridge: At the University Press.

Finucane, Ronald C. 1983. *Soldiers of Faith: Crusaders amd Moslems at War.* New York: St. Martin's Press.

Fita, Fidel. 1890. Cortes y usajes de Barcelona en 1064: Textos inéditos. *Boletín de la Real Academia de la Historia* 17.

Fleckenstein, Joseph. 1964. Rex canonicus: Über Entstehung und Bedeutung des mittelalterlichen Königskanonikates. In *Festschrift Percy Ernst Schramm zu seinem siebzigsten Geburtstag von Schülern und Freunden zugeeignet.* Vol. 1. Wiesbaden: Franz Steiner.

Fliche, Augustine. 1929. *La chrétienté médiévale (395–1254)*. Vol. VII² of *Histoire de monde*, ed. M. Cavignac. Paris: Boccard.

———. 1924–37. *La réforme grégorienne*. 3 vols. Louvain: Spicilegium sacrum lovaniense; Paris: Librairie Ancienne Honoré Champon.

———. 1920. *Saint Grégoire VII*. Paris: V. Lecoffre.

Flori, Jean. 1983. *L'idéologie du glaive: Préhistoire de la chevalerie*. Geneva: Droz.

———. 1986. *L'essor de la chevalerie, XIᵉ–XIIᵉ siècles*. Geneva: Droz.

———. 1992. *La première croisade: L'Occident chrétien contre l'Islam*. Brussels: Éditions Complexe.

Folz, Robert. 1969. *The Concept of Empire in Western Europe from the Fifth to the Fourteenth Century*. Trans. Sh. A. Ogilvie. London: Edward Arnold.

Forey, Alan J. 1985. The Emergence of the Military Order in the Twelfth Century. *Journal of Ecclesiastical History* 36, no. 2.

———. 1992. *The Military Orders: From the Twelfth to the Early Fourteenth Century*. Toronto and Buffalo: University of Toronto Press.

Fowden, Garth. 1993. *Empire to Commonwealth: Consequences of Monotheism in Late Antiquity*. Princeton, N.J.: Princeton University Press.

Fowler, George Bingham. 1947. *Intellectual Interests of Engelbert of Admont*. New York: Columbia University Press.

France, John. 1988. War and Christendom in the Thought of Rodulfus Glaber. *Studia monastica* 30.

———. 1996. Les origines de la première croisade: Un nouvel examen. In *Autour de la première croisade: Actes du Colloque de la Society for the Study of the Crusades and the Latin East (Clermont-Ferrand, 22–25 juin 1995)*, ed. M. Balard. Paris: Publications de la Sorbonne.

Freedman, Paul, and Gabrielle Spiegel. 1999. Srednjeveško, moderno in postmoderno. In *Gestrinov zbornik*, ed. D. Mihelič. Ljubljana: ZRC.

Friedman, John B. 1994. Cultural conflicts in medieval world maps. In *Implicit Understandings: Observing, Reporting, and Reflecting on the Encounters between Europeans and Other Peoples in the Early Modern Era*, ed. S. B. Schwartz. Cambridge: Cambridge University. Press.

Gantar, Kajetan. 1965. Herman de Carinthia. *Jezik in slovstvo* 10, no. 8.

Gatto, Ludovico. 1959. *Il pontificato di Gregorio X (1271–1276)*. Rome: Istituto Storico Italiano per il Medio Evo.

Gauss, Julia. 1967. *Ost und West in der Kirchen- und Papstgeschichte des 11. Jahrhunderts*, Zürich: EVZ-Verlag.

Gewirth, Alan. 1956. *Marsilius of Padua and Medieval Political Philosophy*. Vol. 1 of *Marsilius of Padua: The Defender of Peace*. New York: Columbia University Press.

———. 1980. Introduction to *Defensor pacis*, by Marsilius of Padua. Toronto: University of Toronto Press, in association with the Medieval Academy of America.

Gibert, Rafael. 1962. Lulio y Vives sobre la paz. In *La Paix*. Recueils de la Société Jean Bodin 15. Brussels: Éditions de la librairie encyclopédique.

Gierke, Otto. 1913. *Political Theories of the Middle Ages*. Trans. F. W. Maitland. Cambridge: At the University Press.

Gieysztor, Alexander. 1948–50. The Genesis of the Crusades: The Encyclical of Sergius IV (1009–1012). *Medievalia et Humanistica* 5, 6.

Gilchrist, John. 1985. The Erdmann Thesis and the Canon Law, 1083–1141. In *Crusade and Settlement,* ed. P. W. Edbury. Cardiff: University College Cardiff Press.

———. 1988. The Papacy and War against the "Saracens," 795–1216. *The International History Review* 10, no. 2.

———. 1993. The Lord's War as the Proving Ground of Faith: Pope Innocent III and the Propagation of Violence (1198–1216). In *Crusaders and Muslims in twelfth-century Syria,* ed. M. Shatzmiller. Leiden: E. J. Brill.

Gilson, Etienne. 1952. *Les métamorphoses de la Cité de Dieu.* Louvain: Publications Universitaires de Louvain; Paris: Vrin.

———. 1963. *Dante and Philosophy.* Trans. D. Moore. New York: Harper & Row.

———. 1989. *History of Christian Philosophy in the Middle Ages.* London: Sheed and Ward.

Gmür, Harry. 1933. *Thomas von Aquino und der Krieg.* Beiträge zur Kulturgeschichte des Mittelalters und der Renaissance 51. Leipzig and Berlin: B. G. Teubner.

Goetz, Hans-Werner. 1992. Protection of the Church, Defense of the Law, and Reform: On the Purposes and Character of the Peace of God, 989–1038. In *The Peace of God,* ed. Th. Head and R. Landes. Ithaca, N.Y.: Cornell University Press.

Gottron, Adam. 1912. *Ramon Lulls Kreuzzugsideen.* Berlin: Walther Rothschild.

Graboïs, Aryeh. 1992. *Militia* and *Malitia:* The Bernardine Vision of Chivalry. In *The Second Crusade and the Cistercians,* ed. M. Gervers. New York: St. Martin's Press.

Grousset, René. 1939. *L'épopée des Croisades.* Paris: Plon.

Grundmann, Herbert. 1977. Bonifaz VIII. und Dante. In id. *Ausgewählte Aufsätze, Teil 2: Joachim von Fiore.* MGH Schriften 25.2. Stuttgart: Anton Hiersemann.

Guenée, Bernard. 1991. *Between Church and State: The Lives of Four French Prelates in the Late Middle Ages.* Trans. A. Goldhammer. Chicago: University of Chicago Press.

Gutas, Dimitri. 1998. *Greek Thought, Arabic Culture: The Graeco-Roman Translation Movement in Baghdad and Early 'Abbasid Society (2nd–4th/ 8th–10th centuries).* London and New York: Routledge.

Hagemann, Ludwig. 1988. Missionstheoretische Ansätze bei Thomas von Aquin in seiner Schrift De rationibus fidei. In *Thomas von Aquin: Werk und Wirkung im Licht neuerer Forschungen,* ed. A. Zimmermann. Miscellanea mediævalia 19. Berlin and New York: Walter de Gruyter.

Haines, Roy M. 1983. An English Archbishop and the Cerberus of War. In *The Church and War,* ed. W. J. Sheils. Studies in Church History 20. Oxford: Basil Blackwell.

Haskins, Charles Homer. 1967. *The Renaissance of the Twelfth Century.* Cleveland and New York: Meridian Books.

Hauck, Albert. 1904. *Der Gedanke der päpstlichen Weltherrschaft bis auf Bonifaz VIII.* Leipzig: Alexander Edelmann.

Hay, Denys. 1953. *From Roman Empire to Renaissance Europe.* London: Methuen.

————. 1968. *Europe: The Emergence of an Idea.* 2d ed. Edinburgh: Edinburgh University Press.

————. 1977. *The Italian Renaissance in its Historical Background.* 2d ed. Cambridge: Cambridge University Press.

Hazard, H. W., and N. M. Zacour, eds. 1989. *The Impact of the Crusades on Europe.* Vol. 6 of *A History of the Crusades,* ed. K. M. Setton. Madison: University of Wisconsin Press.

Head, Thomas. 1992. The Judgement of God: Andrew of Fleury's Account of the Peace League of Bourges. In *The Peace of God,* ed. Th. Head and R. Landes. Ithaca, N.Y.: Cornell University Press.

Head, Thomas, and Richard Landes. 1992a. Introduction to *The Peace of God,* ed. Thomas Head and Richard Landes. Ithaca, N.Y.: Cornell University Press.

————, eds. 1992b. *The Peace of God: Social Violence and Religious Response in France around the Year 1000.* Ithaca, N.Y.: Cornell University Press.

Heater, Derek. 1992. *The Idea of European Unity.* Leicester and London: Leicester University Press.

Heck, Erich. 1957. *Roger Bacon: Ein mittelalterlicher Versuch einer historischen und systematischen Religionswissenschaft.* Bonn: H. Bouvier.

Hefele, Charles-Joseph. 1912–13. *Histoire des conciles d'après les documents originaux.* Trans. and ed. H. Leclercq. Vol. 5. Paris: Letouzey et Ané.

Hehl, Ernst-Dieter. 1980. *Kirche und Krieg im 12. Jahrhundert: Studien zu kanonischem Recht und politischer Wirklichkeit.* Stuttgart: Anton Hiersemann.

Heidelberger, Franz. 1911. *Kreuzzugsversuche um die Wende des 13. Jahrhunderts.* Abhandlungen zur Mittleren und Neueren Geschichte 31. Berlin: W. Rothschild.

Hemleben, Sylvester John. 1943. *Plans for World Peace through Six Centuries.* Chicago: University of Chicago Press.

Hentsch, Thierry. 1992. *Imagining the Middle East.* Montreal and New York: Black Rose.

Herrin, Judith. 1987. *The Formation of Christendom.* Oxford: Basil Blackwell.

Hettinger, Anette. 1993. *Die Beziehungen des Papsttums zu Afrika von der Mitte des 11. bis zum Ende des 12. Jahrhunderts.* Cologne: Böhlau.

Hiestand, Rudolf. 1986. Kreuzzug und höfisches Leben. In *Höfische Literatur, Hofgesellschaft, Höfische Lebensformen um 1200,* ed. G. Kaiser and J.-D. Müller. Düsseldorf: Droste.

Hillgarth, J. N. 1971. *Ramon Lull and Lullism in Fourteenth-Century France.* Oxford: Clarendon Press.

Hodgen, Margaret T. 1964. *Early Anthropology in the Sixteenth and Seventeenth Centuries.* Philadelphia: University of Pennsylvania Press.

Hoffmann, Hartmut. 1964. *Gottesfriede und Treuga Dei,* MGH Schriften 20. Stuttgart: Anton Hiersemann.

Höffner, Joseph. 1972. *Kolonialismus und Evangelium: Spanische Koloniale-thik im Goldenen Zeitalter.* 3d ed. Trier: Paulinus.

Holmes, George. 1988. *Dante.* Oxford: Oxford University Press.

Holtzmann, Robert. 1939. Der Weltherrschaftsgedanke der mittelalterlichen Kaisertums und die Souveränität der europäischen Staaten. *Historische Zeit-schrift* 159.

Housley, Norman. 1985. Crusades against Christians: Their Origins and Early Development, *c.* 1000–1216. In *Crusade and Settlement,* ed. P. W. Edbury. Cardiff: University College Cardiff Press.

———. 1986. *The Avignon Papacy and the Crusades, 1305–1378.* Oxford: Clarendon Press.

———. 1992. *The Later Crusades, 1274–1580: From Lyons to Alcazar.* Oxford: Oxford University Press.

Hoye, William J. 1988. Die Unerkennbarkeit Gottes als die letzte Erkenntnis nach Thomas von Aquin. In *Thomas von Aquin: Werk und Wirkung im Licht neuerer Forschungen,* ed. A. Zimmermann. Miscellanea mediaevalia 19. Berlin and New York: Walter de Gruyter.

Iorga, N. 1896. *Philippe de Mézières, 1327–1405, et la croisade au XIVᵉ siècle.* Paris: Librairie Émile Bouillon.

Izbicki, Thomas K. 1989. *Clericis laicos* and the canonists. In *Popes, Teachers, and Canon Law in the Middle Ages,* ed. J. R. Sweeney and S. Chodrow. Ithaca, N.Y.: Cornell University Press.

Jenkins, Helen. 1933. *Papal Efforts for Peace under Benedict XII, 1334–1342.* Philadelphia: University of Pennsylvania.

Jensen, Kurt Villads. 1996. War against Muslims according to Benedict of Alignano, OFM. *Archivum franciscanum historicum* 89, fasc. 1–2.

Johnson, James Turner. 1981. *Just War Tradition and the Restraint of War.* Princeton, N.J.: Princeton University Press.

———. 1997. *The Holy War Idea in Western and Islamic Traditions.* University Park, Pa.: Pennsylvania State University Press.

Johrendt, Johann. 1971. *"Milites" und "Militia" im 11. Jahrhundert: Untersuchung zur Frühgeschichte des Rittertums in Frankreich und Deutschland.* Inaugural-Dissertation. Erlangen and Nürnberg: Friedrich-Alexander-Universität.

Jordan, E. 1921. Le gibelinisme de Dante: la doctrine de la Monarchie universelle. In *Dante: Mélanges de critique et d'érudition françaises publiés à l'occasion du VIᵉ centenaire de la mort du Poète.* Paris: Librairie française.

Jordan, William Chester. 1979. *Louis IX and the Challenge of the Crusade: A Study in Rulership.* Princeton, N.J.: Princeton University Press.

Kahl, Hans-Dietrich. 1992. Crusade Eschatology as Seen by St. Bernard in the Years 1146 to 1148. In *The Second Crusade and the Cistercians,* ed. M. Gervers. New York: St. Martin's Press.

Kämpf, Hellmut. 1935. *Pierre Dubois und die geistigen Grundlagen des franzözischen Nationalbewusstseins um 1300.* Leipzig and Berlin: B. G. Teubner.

Kantorowicz, Ernst K. 1951. *Pro Patria Mori* in Medieval Political Thought. *American Historical Review* 56, no. 3.

———. 1957. *The King's Two Bodies: A Study in Medieval Political Theology*. Princeton, N.J.: Princeton University Press.

———. 1993. *Kaiser Friedrich der Zweite*. Stuttgart: Klett-Cotta.

Katzir, Yael. 1992. The Second Crusade and the Redefinition of *Ecclesia, Christianitas,* and Papal Coercive Power. In *The Second Crusade and the Cistercians,* ed. M. Gervers. New York: St. Martin's Press.

Kaufman, Peter Iver. 1990. *Redeeming Politics*. Princeton, N.J.: Princeton University Press.

Kedar, Benjamin Z. 1984. *Crusade and Mission: European Approaches toward the Muslims*. Princeton, N.J.: Princeton University Press.

———. 1996. Croisade et *jihad* vus par l'enemi: une étude des perceptions mutuelles des motivations. In *Autour de la première croisade: Actes du Colloque de la Society for the Study of the Crusades and the Latin East (Clermont-Ferrand, 22–25 juin 1995),* ed. M. Balard. Paris: Publications de la Sorbonne.

Keen, Maurice. 1984. *Chivalry*. New Haven and London: Yale University Press.

———. 1987. War, Peace and Chivalry. In *War and Peace in the Middle Ages,* ed. B. P. McGuire. Copenhagen: C. A. Reitzels.

Kempf, Friedrich. 1960. Das Problem der Christianitas im 12. und 13. Jahrhundert. *Historisches Jahrbuch* 79.

Kern, Fritz. 1910. *Die Anfänge der französischen Ausdehnungspolitik bis zum Jahr 1308*. Tübingen: J. C. B. Mohr (Paul Siebeck).

———. 1968. *Kingship and Law in the Middle Ages*. Trans. and ed. S. B. Chrimes. Oxford: Basil Blackwell.

Knabe, Lotte. 1936. *Die gelasianische Zweigewaltentheorie bis zum Ende des Investiturstreits*. Historische Studien 292. Berlin: Emil Ebering.

Knowles, M. D., and D. Obolensky. 1991. *Srednji vek (600–1500)*. Vol. 2 of *Zgodovina cerkve*. Prev. J. Dolenc. Ljubljana: Družina.

Koebner, Richard. 1961. *Empire*. Cambridge: At the University Press.

Kritzeck, James. 1964. *Peter the Venerable and Islam*. Princeton, N.J.: Princeton University Press.

Laarhoven, Jan van. 1959–61. "Christianitas" et réforme Grégorienne. *Studi Gregoriani* 6.

Lacroix, Benoît. 1974. Deus le volt!: la théologie d'un cri. In *Études de civilisation médiévale (IXe–XIIe siècles): Mélanges offerts à Edmond-René Labande*. Poitiers: C.É.S.C.M.

Ladner, Gerhart B. 1983. *Images and Ideas in the Middle Ages: Selected Studies in History and Art*. Vol. 2. Rome: Storia e letteratura.

Lagarde, Georges de. 1932. Marsile de Padoue et Guillaume de Nogaret. *Revue historique de droit français et étranger* 11.

———. 1956. *Bilan du XIIIème siècle*. 2d ed. Vol. 1 of *La naissance de l'esprit laïque au déclin de moyen âge*. Louvain: Éditions Nauwelaerts; Paris: Béatrice Nauwelaerts.

Landes, Richard. 1992. Between Aristocracy and Heresy: Popular Participation in the Limousin Peace of God, 994–1033. In *The Peace of God,* ed. Th. Head and R. Landes. Ithaca, N.Y.: Cornell University Press.

————. 1995. *Relics, Apocalypse, and the Deceits of History: Ademar of Chabannes, 989—1034.* Cambridge, Mass.: Harvard University Press.

Landry, Bernard. 1929. *L'idée de chrétienté chez les scolastiques du XIIIe siècle.* Paris: Félix Alcan.

Lange, Chr. 1927. *Histoire de la doctrine pacifique et de son influence sur le développement du droit international.* Académie de droit international. Recueil de cours 1926. Paris: Hachette.

Lauranson-Rosaz, Christian. 1992. Peace from the Mountains: The Auvergnant Origins of the Peace of God. In *The Peace of God,* ed. Th. Head and R. Landes. Ithaca, N.Y.: Cornell University Press.

Lecler, Joseph. 1931. L'argument des deux glaives (*Luc* xxii, 38) dans les controverses politiques du Moyen Age: ses origines et son développement. *Recherches de science religieuse* 21, no. 3.

Leclercq, Dom Jean. 1945. Un sermon prononcé pendant la guerre de Flandre sous Philippe le Bel. *Revue du moyen âge latin* 1, no. 2.

————. 1974. Pour l'histoire de l'encyclique de saint Bernard sur la croisade. In *Études de civilisation médiévale (IXe–XIIe siècles): Mélanges offerts à Edmond-René Labande.* Poitiers: C.É.S.C.M.

Lefort, Claude. 1981. *L'invention démocratique.* Paris: Fayard.

————. 1986. *Essais sur la politique, XIXe–XXe siècles.* Paris: Seuil.

Le Goff, Jacques. 1985. Zapis o tridelni družbi, monarhični ideologiji in gospodarski obnovi v krščanskem svetu od IX. do XII. stoletja. In id. *Za drugačen srednji vek.* Trans. B. Rotar. Ljubljana: Studia Humanitatis.

————. 1990. *Medieval Civilization, 400–1500.* Trans. J. Barrow. Oxford: Basil Blackwell.

Lewis, Ewart. 1954. *Medieval Political Ideas.* 2 vols. New York: Alfred A. Knopf.

Leyser, Karl. 1965. The Polemics of the Papal Revolution. In *Trends in Medieval Political Thought,* ed. B. Smalley. Oxford: Basil Blackwell.

————. 1989. *Rule and Conflict in an Early Medieval Society: Ottonian Saxony.* Oxford: Basil Blackwell.

————. 1994. Warfare in the Western European Middle Ages: The Moral Debate. In id. *Communications and Power in Medieval Europe: The Gregorian Revolution and Beyond,* ed. T. Reuter. London and Rio Grande, Ohio: Hambledon Press.

Libertini, Christopher G. 1996. Practical Crusading: The Transformation of Crusading Practice, 1095–1221. In *Autour de la première croisade: Actes du Colloque de la Society for the Study of the Crusades and the Latin East (Clermont-Ferrand, 22–25 juin 1995),* ed. M. Balard. Paris: Publications de la Sorbonne.

Lobrichon, Guy. 1992. The Chiaroscuro of Heresy: Early Eleventh-Century Aquitaine as seen from Auxerre. In *The Peace of God,* ed. Th. Head and R. Landes. Ithaca, N.Y.: Cornell University Press.

Loutchitskaja, S. 1996. *Barbarae nationes:* les peuples musulmans dans les chroniques de la Première Croisade. In *Autour de la première croisade: Actes du Colloque de la Society for the Study of the Crusades and the Latin East (Clermont-Ferrand, 22–25 juin 1995),* ed. M. Balard. Paris: Publications de la Sorbonne.

Lupprian, Karl-Ernst. 1981. *Die Beziehungen der Päpste zu islamischen und mongolischen Herrschern im 13. Jahrhundert anhand ihres Briefwechsels.* Città del Vaticano: Biblioteca Apostolica Vaticana.

Luscombe, D. E. 1988. Introduction: the formation of political thought in the west. In *The Cambridge History of Medieval Political Thought, c. 350– c. 1450,* ed. J. H. Burns. Cambridge: Cambridge University Press.

Luttrell, Anthony. 1965. The Crusade in the Fourteenth Century. In *Europe in the Late Middle Ages,* ed. J. Hale, R. Highfield, and B. Smalley. London: Faber and Faber.

Lynch, Joseph H. 1992. *The Medieval Church: A Brief History.* London and New York: Longman.

Maccarrone, Michele. 1974. La teologia del primato Romano del secolo XI. In *Le istituzioni ecclesiastiche della "societas christiana" dei secoli XI-XII.* Miscellanea del Centro di studi medioevali 7. Milan: Vita e pensiero.

MacKinney, Loren C. 1930. The People and the Public Opinion in the Eleventh-Century Peace Movement. *Speculum* 5.

Magnou-Nortier, Elisabeth. 1984. Les évêques et la paix dans l'espace franc (VIe–XIe siècles). In *L'évêque dans l'histoire de l'église: Actes de la Septième rencontre d'Histoire Religieuse tenue à Fontevraud les 14 et 15 octobre 1983.* Angers: Presses de l'Université d'Angers.

———. 1992. The Enemies of Peace: Reflections on a Vocabulary, 500–1100. In *The Peace of God,* ed. Th. Head and R. Landes. Ithaca, N.Y.: Cornell University Press.

Maloney, T. 1988. Introduction to *Compendium of the Study of Theology,* by Roger Bacon. Leiden: E. J. Brill.

Manselli, Raoul. 1965. La res publica cristiana e l'Islam. In *L'Occidente e l'Islam nell'alto medioevo.* Settimane di studio del Centro italiano di studi sull'alto medioevo 12. Spoleto: Presso la sede del centro.

Markowski, Michael. 1984. *Crucesignatus:* Its Origin and Early Usage. *Journal of Medieval History* 10, no. 3.

Markus, R. A. 1983. Saint Augustine's Views on the "Just War." In *The Church and War,* ed. W. J. Sheils. Studies in Church History 20. Oxford: Basil Blackwell.

———. 1997. *Gregory the Great and His World.* Cambridge: Cambridge University Press.

Mastnak, Tomaž. 1993. Notica o univerzalni monarhiji. *Filozofski vestnik /Acta philosophica* 14, no. 1.

———. 1998a. Abbé de Saint-Pierre: European Union and the Turk. *History of Political Thought* 19, no. 4.

———. 1998b. *Evropa: med evolucijo in evtanazijo.* Ljubljana: Studia humanitatis.

Mayer, Hans Eberhard. 1993. *The Crusades.* Trans. J. Gillingham. 2d ed. Oxford: Oxford University Press.

Mazzotta, Guiseppe. 1993. Life of Dante. In *The Cambridge Companion to Dante,* ed. R. Jacoff. Cambridge: Cambridge University Press.

McCready, William D. 1973. Papal *plenitudo potestatis* and the Source of Temporal Authority in Late Medieval Papal Hierocratic Theory. *Speculum* 48.

McGinn, Bernard. 1978. *Iter Sancti Sepulchri:* The Piety of the First Crusaders. In *Essays on Medieval Civilization,* ed. B. K. Lackner and K. R. Philp. The Walter Prescott Webb Memorial Lectures 12. Austin: University of Texas Press.

McIlwain, Charles Howard. 1932. *The Growth of Political Thought in the West: From the Greeks to the End of the Middle Ages.* New York: Macmillan.

McKitterick, Rosamond. 1983. *The Frankish Kingdoms under the Carolingians, 751–987.* London and New York: Longman.

McLynn, Neil B. 1994. *Ambrose of Milan: Church and Court in a Christian Capital.* Berkeley and Los Angeles: University of California Press.

McNamara, Jo Ann. 1973. *Gilles Aycelin: The Servant of Two Masters.* New York: Syracuse University Press.

Menache, Sophia. 1982. Contemporary Attitudes Concerning the Templars' Affair: Propaganda's Fiasco. *Journal of Medieval History* 8, no. 2.

———. 1990. *The Vox Dei: Communication in the Middle Ages.* Oxford: Oxford University Press.

Menzel, Ottokar. 1941. Bemerkungen zur Staatslehre Engelbert von Admont und ihrer Wirkung. In *Corona quernea: Festgabe Karl Strecker zum 80. Geburtstage dargebracht.* MGH Schriften 6. Leipzig: Karl W. Hiersemann.

Metlitzki, Dorothee. 1977. *The Matter of Araby in Medieval England.* New Haven and London: Yale University Press.

Meunier, Francis. 1857. *Essai sur la vie et les ouvrages de Nicole Oresme.* Paris: Ch. Lahure.

Michaud, M. 1838. *Histoire des croisades.* 5th ed. Paris: A.-J. Ducollet.

Michel, Anton. 1947. Die folgenschweren Ideen des Kardinals Humbert und ihr Einfluss auf Gregor VII. *Studi gregoriani* 1.

Moore, R. I. 1987. *The Formation of a Persecuting Society: Power and Deviance in Western Europe, 950–1250.* Oxford: Basil Blackwell.

———. 1992. Postscript: The Peace of God and the Social Revolution. In *The Peace of God,* ed. Th. Head and R. Landes. Ithaca, N.Y.: Cornell University Press.

Morghen, Raffaello. 1975. *Bonifacio VIII e il Giubileo del 1300 nella storiografia moderna.* Rome: Edizioni dell'elefante.

Morisi, Anna. 1963. *La guerra nel pensiero cristiano dalle origini alle crociate.* Florence: Sansoni.

Morrall, John B. 1971. *Political Thought in Medieval Times.* 3d ed. London: Hutchinson University Library.

Morris, Christopher. 1967. *Western Political Thought.* Vol. 1, *Plato to Augustine.* New York: Basic Books.

Morris, Colin. 1983. Propaganda for War: The Dissemination of the Crusading Ideal in the Twelfth Century. In *The Church and War,* ed. W. J. Sheils. Studies in Church History 20. Oxford: Basil Blackwell.

———. 1984. Policy and Visions: The Case of the Holy Lance at Antioch. In *War and Government in the Middle Ages: Essays in Honour of J. O. Prestwich,* ed. J. Gillingham and J. C. Holt. Woodbridge: The Boydell Press; Totowa, N.J.: Barnes & Noble.

————. 1991. *The Papal Monarchy: The Western Church from 1050 to 1250.* Oxford: Clarendon Press.

Morrison, Karl F. 1964. *The Two Kingdoms: Ecclesiology in Carolingian Political Thought.* Princeton, N.J.: Princeton University Press.

————. 1969. *Tradition and Authority in the Western Church, 300–1140.* Princeton, N.J.: Princeton University Press.

Muldoon, James. 1979. *Popes, Lawyers, and Infidels: The Church and the Non-Christian World, 1250–1550.* Liverpool: Liverpool University Press.

Munro, D. C. 1905. The Speech of Pope Urban II at Clermont, 1095. *The American Historical Review* 9.

————. 1931. The Western Attitude toward Islam during the Period of the Crusades. *Speculum* 6.

Munz, Peter. 1969. *Frederick Barbarossa: A Study in Medieval Politics.* London: Eyre & Spottiswood.

Nader, Albert N. 1988. Éléments de la philosophie musulmane médiévale dans la pensée de St. Thomas d'Aquin. In *Thomas von Aquin: Werk und Wirkung im Licht neuerer Forschungen,* ed. A. Zimmermann. Miscellanea mediaevalia 19. Berlin and New York: Walter de Gruyter.

Nardi, Bruno. 1944. *Nel mondo di Dante.* Rome: Storia e letteratura.

Nederman, Cary J. 1993. Introduction to *Writings on the Empire,* by Marsiglio of Padua. Cambridge: Cambridge University Press.

Nelson, Janet. 1983. The Church's Military Service in the Ninth Century: A Contemporary Comparative View? In *The Church and War,* ed. W. J. Sheils. Studies in Church History 20. Oxford: Basil Blackwell.

————. 1988. Kingship and Empire. In *The Cambridge History of Medieval Political Thought, c. 350–c. 1450,* ed. J. H. Burns. Cambridge: Cambridge University Press.

Nicholson, Helen. 1995. *Templars, Hospitallers and Teutonic Knights: Images of the Military Orders, 1128–1291.* Leicester: Leicester University Press.

Nirenberg, David. 1996. *Communities of Violence: Persecution of Minorities in the Middle Ages.* Princeton, N.J.: Princeton University Press.

Noth, Albrecht. 1966. *Heiliger Krieg und Heiliger Kampf in Islam und Christentum: Beiträge zur Vorgeschichte und Geschichte der Kreuzzüge.* Bonn: Ludwig Röhrscheid.

Nys, Ernest. 1894. *Les origines du droit international.* Brussels: Alfred Castaigne; Paris: Thorin & fils.

Oakley, Francis. 1979. *The Crucial Centuries: The Medieval Experience.* London: Terra Nova Editions.

————. 1981. Natural Law, the Corpus Mysticum, and Consent in Conciliar Thought from John of Paris to Matthias Ugonius. *Speculum* 56, no. 4.

————. 1991. *The Western Church in the Later Middle Ages.* Ithaca, N.Y.: Cornell University Press.

Olschki, Leonardo. 1943. *Marco Polo's Precursors.* Baltimore: The Johns Hopkins University Press.

Ozment, Steven. 1980. *The Age of Reform, 1250–1550: An Intellectual and Religious History of Late Medieval and Reformation Europe.* New Haven and London: Yale University Press.

Pacaut, Marcel. 1953. L'opposition des canonistes aux doctrines politiques de Saint Bernard. In *Mélanges Saint Bernard. XXIVe Congrès de l'Association bourguignonne des sociétés savantes*. Dijon: Marilier.

Paciocco, Roberto. 1992. "Sub iugo servitutis": Francesco, i francescani e la "militia Christi". In *"Militia Christi" e Crociata nei secoli XI-XIII*. Miscellanea del Centro di studi medioevali. Milan: Vita e pensiero.

Pagden, Anthony. 1990. *Spanish Imperialism and the Political Imagination: Studies in European and Spanish-American Social and Political Theory, 1513–1830*. New Haven and London: Yale University Press.

———, ed. 1987. *The Languages of Political Theory in Early-Modern Europe*. Cambridge: Cambridge University Press.

La Paix. 1961–62. Receuils de la Société Jean Bodin 14–15. Brussels: Éditions de la librairie encyclopédique.

Paravicini-Bagliani, Agostino. 2000. *The Pope's Body*. Trans. D. S. Peterson. Chicago: Chicago University Press.

Partner, Peter. 1972. *The Lands of St Peter: The Papal State in the Middle Ages and the Early Renaissance*. London: Eyre Methuen.

———. 1996. Holy War, Crusade and *jihad*: an attempt to define some problems. In *Autour de la première croisade: Actes du Colloque de la Society for the Study of the Crusades and the Latin East (Clermont-Ferrand, 22–25 juin 1995)*, ed. M. Balard. Paris: Publications de la Sorbonne.

———. 1997. *God of Battles: Holy Wars in Christianity and Islam*. Princeton, N.J.: Princeton University Press.

Pásztor, Edith. 1965. Motivi dell'ecclesiologia di Anselmo di Lucca: In margine a un sermone inedito. *Bullettino dell' Istituto storico italiano per il medio evo e Archivio muratoriano 77*.

———. 1987. Lotta per le investiture e "ius belli": la posizione di Anselmo di Lucca. In *Sant'Anselmo, Mantova e la lotta per le investiture: Atti del Convegno Internazionale di Studi (Mantova, 23–24–25 maggio 1986)*, ed. P. Golinelli. Bologna: Pàtron Editore.

Patzelt, Erna. 1978. *Die fränkische Kultur und der Islam mit besonderer Berücksichtigung der nordischen Entwicklung: Eine universalhistorische Studie*. 2d ed. Aalen: Scientia.

Pavlović, Augustin. 1992. Introduction to *Razgovor s pravoslavnima i muslimanima. Protiv zabluda Grkâ. O razlozima vjere (protiv Saracena)*, by Aquinas. Zagreb: Globus.

Paxton, Frederick S. 1992. History, Historians, and the Peace of God. In *The Peace of God*, ed. Th. Head and R. Landes. Ithaca, N.Y.: Cornell University Press.

Pelikan, Jaroslav. 1985. *Jesus through the Centuries: His Place in the History of Culture*. New York: Harper & Row.

Pennington, Kenneth. 1993a. Pope Innocent III's Views on Church and State: A Gloss to *Per Venerabilem*. In id. *Popes, Canonists and Texts, 1150–1550*. Aldershot: Variorum.

———. 1993b. *The Prince and the Law, 1200–1600: Sovereignty and Rights in the Western Legal Tradition*. Berkeley and Los Angeles: University of California Press.

Peters, Edward, ed. 1989. *The First Crusade: The Chronicle of Fulcher of Char-*

tres and Other Source Materials. Philadelphia: University of Pennsylvania Press.

———, ed. 1991. *Christian Society and the Crusades, 1198–1229*. Philadelphia: University of Pennsylvania Press.

Peters, Francis E. 1985. *Jerusalem: The Holy City in the Eyes of Chroniclers, Visitors, Pilgrims, and Prophets from the Days of Abraham to the Beginnings of Modern Times*. Princeton, N.J.: Princeton University Press.

Petrocchi, Girogio. 1975. La "pace" in S. Caterina da Siena. In *La pace nel pensiero, nella politica, negli ideali del trecento*. Convegni del Centro di studi sulla spiritualità medievale 15. Todi: Presso L'Academia tudertina.

Phillips, J. R. S. 1988. *The Medieval Expansion of Europe*. Oxford: Oxford University Press.

Phillips, Seymour. 1994. The outer world of the European Middle Ages. In *Implicit Understandings: Observing, Reporting, and Reflecting on the Encounters Between Europeans and Other Peoples in the Early Modern Era*, ed. S. B. Schwartz. Cambridge: Cambridge University Press.

Pincus, Steven. 1995. The English Debate over Universal Monarchy. In *A Union for Empire: Political Thought and the British Union of 1707*, ed. J. Robertson. Cambridge: Cambridge University Press.

Pindl, Theodor. 1996. Ramon Lull, Protagonist des interkulturellen Dialogs. *Concordia*, no. 30.

Pirenne, Henri. 1937. *Mahomet et Charlemagne*. 3d ed. Paris: Félix Alcan; Brussels: Nouvelle Société d'éditions.

———. 1939. *Histoire de l'Europe des invasions au XVIe siècle*. 14th ed. Paris: Félix Alcan; Brussels: Nouvelle Société d'éditions.

Pocock, J. G. A. 1987. *The Ancient Constitution and the Feudal Law: A Study of English Historical Thought in the Seventeenth Century. A Reissue with a Retrospect*. Cambridge: Cambridge University Press.

Poggiaspalla, Fermino. 1959. La Chiesa e la partecipazione dei chierici alla guerra nella legislazione conciliare fino alla Decretali di Gregorio IX. *Ephemerides iuris canonici* 15, nos. 1–4.

Posch, Andreas. 1920. *Die staats- und kirchenpolitische Stellung Engelbert von Admont*. Paderborn: Ferdinand Schöning.

Post, Gaines. 1964. *Studies in Medieval Legal Thought: Public Law and the State, 1100–1322*. Princeton, N.J.: Princeton University Press.

Powell, James M. 1986. *Anatomy of a Crusade, 1213–1221*. Philadelphia: University of Pennsylvania Press.

———. 1990. The Papacy and the Muslim Frontier. In *Muslims under Latin Rule, 1100–1300*, ed. J. M. Powell. Princeton, N.J.: Princeton University Press.

———. 1996. Myth, Legend, Propaganda, History: The First Crusade, 1140– ca. 1300. In *Autour de la première croisade: Actes du Colloque de la Society for the Study of the Crusades and the Latin East (Clermont-Ferrand, 22–25 juin 1995)*, ed. M. Balard. Paris: Publications de la Sorbonne.

Power, Eileen. 1923. Pierre Du Bois and the Domination of France. In *The Social and Political Ideas of Some Great Mediaeval Thinkers*, ed. F. J. C. Hearnshaw. London: George G. Harrap.

Prawer, J. 1986. The Roots of Medieval Colonialism. In *The Meeting of Two Worlds,* ed. V. P. Goss and Ch. Verzár Bornstein. Medieval Institute Publications. Kalamazoo: Western Michigan University.

Prinz, Friedrich. 1971. *Klerus und Krieg im frühen Mittelalter: Untersuchungen zur Rolle der Kirche beim Aufbau der Königsherrschaft.* Stuttgart: Anton Hiersemann.

———. 1979. King, Clergy, and War at the Time of the Carolingians. In *Saints, Scholars, and Heroes: Studies in Medieval Culture in Honour of Charles W. Jones,* ed. M. H. King and W. M. Stevens. Vol. 2. Saint John's Abbey: Hill Monastic Library; Collegeville, Minn.: University Press.

Prodi, Paolo. 1982. *Il sovrano pontefice. Un corpo e due anime: la monarchia papale nella prima età moderna.* Bologna: Il Mulino.

Purcell, Maureen. 1975. *Papal Crusading Policy: The Chief Instruments of Papal Crusading Policy and Crusade to the Holy Land from the final loss of Jerusalem to the fall of Acre, 1244–1291.* Leiden: E. J. Brill.

Quaritsch, Helmut. 1970. *Staat und Souveränität.* Vol. 1, *Grundlagen.* Frankfurt am Main: Athenäum.

Quillet, Jeannine. 1977. *La philosophie politique du Songe du vergier (1378): Sources doctrinales.* Paris: Vrin.

———. 1989. Saint Bernard et le pouvoir. In *Mediaevalia christiana, XIᵉ–XIIIᵉ siècle: Hommage à Raymonde Foreville de ses amis, ses collègues et ses anciens élèves,* ed. C. É. Viola. Tournai: Editions Universitaires.

Regout, R. H. W. 1934. *La doctrine de la guerre juste de Saint Augustine à nos jours d'après les théologiens et les canonistes chatoliques.* Paris: A. Pedone.

Reilly, Bernard F. 1993. *The Medieval Spains.* Cambridge: Cambridge University Press.

Remensnyder, Amy G. 1992. Pollution, Purity, and Peace: An Aspect of Social Reform between the Late Tenth Century and 1076. In *The Peace of God,* ed. Th. Head and R. Landes. Ithaca, N.Y.: Cornell University Press.

Renna, Thomas J. 1973. Kingship in the *Disputatio inter clericum et militem. Speculum* 48.

———. 1978. Aristotle and the French Monarchy, 1260–1303. *Viator* 9.

Reynolds, Susan. 1986. *Kingdoms and Communities in Western Europe, 900–1300.* Oxford: Clarendon Press.

Riché, Pierre. 1993. *The Carolingians: A Family Who Forged Europe.* Trans. M. I. Allen. Philadelphia: University of Pennsylvania Press.

Riezler, Sigmund. 1874. *Die literarischen Widersacher der Päpste zur Zeit Ludwig des Baiers: Ein Beitrag zur Geschichte der Kämpfe zwischen Staat und Kirche.* Leipzig: Duncker & Humblot.

Riley-Smith, Jonathan. 1977. *What were the Crusades?* London and Basingstoke: Macmillan.

———. 1980. Crusading as an Act of Love. *History* 65.

———. 1992. *The Crusades: A Short History.* London: The Athlone Press.

———. 1993a. *The First Crusade and the Idea of Crusading.* London: The Athlone Press.

———. 1993b. History, the Crusades and the Latin East, 1095–1204: A Personal

View. In *Crusaders and Muslims in twelfth-century Syria,* ed. M. Shatzmiller. Leiden: E. J. Brill.

———. 1997. *The First Crusaders, 1095–1131.* Cambridge: Cambridge University Press.

Riley-Smith, Louise, and Jonathan Riley-Smith. 1981. *The Crusades: Idea and Reality, 1095–1274.* Documents of Medieval History 4. London: Edward Arnold.

Rivière, Jean. 1926. *Le problème de l'église et de l'état au temps de Philippe le Bel: Étude de théologie positive.* Louvain: Spicilegium sacrum lovaniense; Paris: Librairie Ancienne Honoré Champion.

Robertson, John. 1995. Empire and Union: Two Concepts of the Early Modern European Political Order. In *A Union for Empire: Political Thought and the British Union of 1707,* ed. J. Robertson. Cambridge: Cambridge University Press.

Robinson, I. S. 1973. Gregory VII and the Soldiers of Christ. *History* 58.

———. 1978. *Authority and Resistance in the Investiture Contest: The Polemical Literature of the Late Eleventh Century.* Manchester: Manchester University Press; New York: Holmes & Meier.

———. 1985. Pope Gregory VII (1073–1085). *Journal of Ecclesiastical Studies* 36, no. 3.

———. 1988. Church and Papacy. In *The Cambridge History of Medieval Political Thought, c. 350-c. 1450,* ed. J. H. Burns. Cambridge: Cambridge University Press.

———. 1990. *The Papacy, 1073–1198: Continuity and Innovation.* Cambridge: Cambridge University Press.

Rodinson, Maxime. 1991. *Europe and the Mystique of Islam.* Trans. R. Veinus. Seattle: University of Washington Press.

Roscher, Helmut. 1969. *Papst Innocenz III. und die Kreuzzüge.* Göttingen: Vandenhoeck & Ruprecht.

Rosenwein, Barbara H. 1982. *Rhinoceros Bound: Cluny in the Tenth Century.* Philadelphia: University of Pennsylvania Press.

Rotter, Ekkehart. 1979. *Die Darstellung der Araber in den lateinischen Quellen des frühen Mittelalters von ausgehenden sechsten bis zur Mitte des achten Jahrhunderts.* Inauguraldissertation. Frankfurt am Main: Johann Wolfgang Goethe Universität.

———. 1986. *Abendland und Sarazenen: Das okzidentale Araberbild und seine Entstehung im Frühmittelalter.* Studien zur Sprache, Geschichte und Kultur des islamischen Orients 11. Berlin and New York: Walter de Gruyter.

Rousset, P. 1945. *Les origines et les charactères de la première croisade.* Neuchâtel: Baconnière.

———. 1963. La notion de Chrétienté aux XIe et XIIe siècles. *Le moyen âge* 69.

———. 1983. *Histoire d'une idéologie: La croisade.* Lousanne: L'Age d'homme.

Rousset de Pina, Jean. 1952. L'Entrevue de Pape Alexandre III et d'un prince sarrasin à Montpellier le 11 avril 1162: Notes sur les relations islamo-chrétiennes à la fin du XIIe siècle. In *Études médiévales offertes à M. le Doyen Augustin Fliche.* Montpellier: Faculté des Lettres.

Rowe, John G. 1993. Alexander III and the Jerusalem Crusade: An Overview of Problems and Failures. In *Crusaders and Muslims in twelfth-century Syria,* ed. M. Shatzmiller. Leiden: E. J. Brill.

Roy, Jean-Henri, and Jean Deviosse. 1966. *La Bataille de Poitiers.* Paris: Gallimard.

Rubinstein, Nicolai. 1965. Marsilius of Padua and Italian Political Thought of His Time. In *Europe in the Late Middle Ages,* ed. J. Hale, R. Highfield, and B. Smalley. London: Faber and Faber.

Runciman, Steven. 1986. Byzantium and the Crusades. In *The Meeting of Two Worlds: Cultural Exchange between East and West during the Period of the Crusades,* ed. V. P. Goss and Ch. Verzár Bornstein. Medieval Institute Publications. Kalamazoo: Western Michigan University.

———. 1991. *A History of the Crusades.* 3 vols. Harmondsworth: Penguin.

Rupp, Jean. 1939. *L'idée de chrétienté dans la pensée pontificale des origines à Innocent III.* Paris: Les presses modernes.

Russell, Frederick H. 1975. *The Just War in the Middle Ages.* Cambridge: Cambridge University Press.

Saenger, Paul. 1981. John of Paris, Principal Author of the *Quaestio de potestate papae (Rex pacificus). Speculum* 56, no. 1.

Saitta, Armando. 1948. *Dalla* Res Publica Christiana *agli Stati uniti di Europa: Sviluppo dell'idea pacifista in Francia nei secoli XVII–XIX.* Rome: Storia e letteratura.

Sayers, Jane. 1994. *Innocent III: Leader of Europe, 1198–1216.* London and New York: Longman.

Scalia, Giuseppe. 1971. Il Carme pisano sull'impresa contro i Saraceni del 1087. In *Studi di filologia romanza offerti a Silvio Pellegrini.* Padua: Liviana.

Schein, Sylvia. 1973. *Gesta Dei per Mongolos* 1300: The Genesis of a Non-Event. *English Historical Review* 94, no. 373.

———. 1985. Philip IV and the Crusade: A Reconsideration. In *Crusade and Settlement,* ed. P. W. Edbury. Cardiff: University College Cardiff Press.

———. 1991. *Fideles Crucis: The Papacy, the West, and the Recovery of the Holy Land, 1274–1314.* Oxford: Clarendon Press.

———. 1996. Jérusalem: Objectif originel de la première croisade? In *Autour de la première croisade: Actes du Colloque de la Society for the Study of the Crusades and the Latin East (Clermont-Ferrand, 22–25 juin 1995),* ed. M. Balard. Paris Publications de la Sorbonne.

Schieffer, Rudolf. 1981. *Die Entstehung des päpstlichen Investiturverbots für den deutschen König.* MGH Schriften 28. Stuttgart: Anton Hiersemann.

Schmid, Karl. 1938. *Idee und Ideologie des Abendlandes an der Wende von Mittelalter und Neuzeit.* Berlin: Die Runde.

Scholz, Richard. 1903. *Die Publizistik zur Zeit Philipps des Schönen und Bonifaz VIII.: Ein Beitrag zur Geschichte der politischen Anschauungen des Mittelalters.* Stuttgart: Ferdinand Enke.

———. 1932. Introduction to *Defensor Pacis,* by Marsiglio of Padua. Hanover: Hahnsche Buchhandlung.

Schramm, Percy Ernst. 1970. *Kaiser, Könige und Päpste: Gesammelte Aufsätze zur Geschichte des Mittelalters.* Vol. 4, pt. 1. Stuttgart: Anton Hiersemann.

———. 1992. *Kaiser, Rom und Renovatio: Studien zur Geschichte des römischen Erneuerungsgedankens vom Ende des Karolingischen Reiches bis zum Investiturstreit.* Darmstadt: Wissenschaftliche Buchgesellschaft.

Schwerin, Ursula. 1937. *Die Aufrufe der Päpste zur Befreiung des Heiligen Landes von den Anfängen bis zum Ausgang Innozenz IV.: Ein Beitrag zur Geschichte der kurialen Kreuzzugspropaganda und der päpstlichen Epistolographie.* Historische Studien 301. Berlin: Emil Ebering.

Schwinges, Rainer Ch. 1977. *Kreuzzugsideologie und Toleranz: Studien zu Wilhelm von Tyrus.* Stuttgart: Anton Hiersemann.

Segall, Hermann. 1959. *Der "Defensor Pacis" des Marsilius von Padua: Grundfragen der Interpretation.* Wiesbaden: Franz Steiner.

Selwood, Dominic. 1996. *Quidam autem dubitaverunt:* The Saint, the Sinner, the Temple and a Possible Chronology. In *Autour de la première croisade: Actes du Colloque de la Society for the Study of the Crusades and the Latin East (Clermont-Ferrand, 22–25 juin 1995),* ed. M. Balard. Paris: Publications de la Sorbonne.

Sénac, Philippe. 1983. *L'image de l'autre: L'Occident médiéval face à l'Islam.* Paris: Flammarion.

Setton, Kenneth M. 1976. *The Papacy and the Levant (1204–1571).* Vol. 1, *The Thirteenth and Fourteenth Centuries.* Philadelphia: The American Philosophical Society.

———. 1992. *Western Hostility to Islam and Prophecies of Turkish Doom.* Memoirs of the American Philosophical Society 201. Philadelphia: American Philosophical Society.

———, ed. 1969–89. *A History of the Crusades.* 6 vols. Madison: University of Wisconsin Press.

Shennan, J. H. 1974. *The Origins of the Modern European State, 1450–1725.* London: Hutchinson University Library.

Sherwood, Merriam. 1955. Pierre Dubois on the Arbitration of International Disputes. In *Essays in Medieval Life and Thought,* ed. J. H. Mundy, R. W. Emery, and B. N. Nelson. New York: Columbia University Press.

Siberry, Elizabeth. 1983. Missionaries and Crusaders, 1095–1274: Opponents or Allies? In *The Church and War,* ed. W. J. Sheils. Studies in Church History 20. Oxford: Basil Blackwell.

———. 1985. *Criticism of Crusading, 1095–1274.* Oxford: Clarendon Press.

Sicard, G. 1969. Paix et guerre dans le droit canon du XIIe siècle. In *Paix de Dieu et guerre sainte en Languedoc au XIIIe siècle.* Cahiers de Fanjeaux 4. Toulouse: Édouard Privat.

Sivan, Emmanuel. 1985. Modern Arab Historiography of the Crusades. In id. *Interpretations of Islam: Past and Present.* Princeton, N.J.: The Darwin Press.

Skinner, Quentin. 1978. *The Foundations of Modern Political Thought.* 2 vols. Cambridge: Cambridge University Press.

———. 1986. Ambrogio Lorenzetti: The Artist as Political Philosopher. *Proceedings of the British Academy* 72.

———. 1989. The State. In *Political Innovation and Conceptual Change,* ed. T. Ball, J. Farr, and R. L. Hanson. Cambridge: Cambridge University Press.

Smalley, Beryl. 1965. Church and State, 1300–1377: Theory and Fact. In *Eu-*

rope in the Late Middle Ages, ed. J. Hale, R. Highfield, and B. Smalley. London: Faber and Faber.

Smith, Colin. 1988–89. *Christians and Moors in Spain.* 2 vols. Warminster: Aris & Phillips.

Sommerville, Robert. 1972. *Decreta Claromontensia.* Vol. 1 of *The Councils of Urban II.* Amsterdam: Adolf M. Hakkert.

Souleyman, Elizabeth V. 1972. *The Vision of World Peace in Seventeenth- and Eighteenth-Century France.* Port Washington, N.Y.: Kennikat Press.

Southern, R. W. 1962. *Western Views of Islam in the Middle Ages.* Cambridge, Mass.: Harvard University Press.

———. 1967. *The Making of the Middle Ages.* London: Hutchinson University Library.

———. 1970. *Western Society and the Church in the Middle Ages.* Harmondsworth: Penguin.

———. 1973. Dante and Islam. In *Relations between East and West in the Middle Ages,* ed. D. Baker. Edinburgh: At the University Press.

———. 1990. *Saint Anselm: A Portrait in a Landscape.* Cambridge: Cambridge University Press.

Speed, Diane. 1990. The Saracens of *King Horn. Speculum* 65, no. 3.

Spiegel, Gabrielle. 1978. *The Chronicle Tradition of Saint-Denis: A Survey.* Brookline, Mass., and Leyden: Classical Folia Editions.

———. 1997. *The Past as Text: The Theory and Practice of Medieval Historiography.* Baltimore: The Johns Hopkins University Press.

Sprandel, Rolf. 1962. *Ivo von Chartres und seine Stellung in der Kirchengeschichte.* Stuttgart: Anton Hiersemann.

Stevenson, W. B. 1968. *The Crusaders in the East: A Brief History of the Wars of Islam with the Latins in Syria during the Twelfth and Thirteenth Centuries.* Beirut: Librairie du Liban.

Stickel, Erwin. 1975. *Der Fall von Akkon: Untersuchungen zum Abklingen des Kreuzzugsgedankens am Ende des 13. Jahrhunderts.* Bern: Herbert Lang; Frankfurt am Main: Peter Lang.

Stickler, Alfonso. 1947. Il potere coattivo materiale della Chiesa nella Riforma Gregoriana secondo Anselmo di Lucca. *Studi gregoriani* 2.

———. 1948. Il "gladius" nel Registro di Gregorio VII. *Studi gregoriani* 3.

Strayer, Joseph R. 1970. *On the Medieval Origins of the Modern State.* Princeton, N.J.: Princeton University Press.

———. 1971. *Medieval Statecraft and the Perspectives of History.* Princeton, N.J.: Princeton University Press.

———. 1992. *The Albigensian Crusades.* Ann Arbor: University of Michigan Press.

Stürner, Wolfgang. 1991. Gregors VII. Sicht vom Ursprung der herrscherlichen Gewalt. *Studi gregoriani* 14.

Sugranyes de Franch, Ramón. 1986. Raymond Lulle: philosophe et missionnaire. In *Raymond Lulle: Christianisme, Judaïsme, Islam. Les Actes du Colloque sur R. Lulle. Université de Fribourg, 1984,* ed. R. Imbach and R. Sugranyes de Franch. Fribourg: Éditions Universitaires Fribourg.

Tellenbach, Gerd. 1947. Die Bedeutung der Reformpapsttums für die Einigung des Abendlandes. *Studi Gregoriani* 2.

———. 1991. *Church, State and the Christian Society at the Time of the Investiture Contest.* Trans. R. F. Bennett. Toronto: University of Toronto Press, in association with the Medieval Academy of America.

———. 1993. *The Church in Western Europe from the Tenth to the Early Twelfth Century.* Trans. T. Reuter. Cambridge: Cambridge University Press.

ter Meulen, Jacob. 1917. *Der Gedanke der internationalen Organisation in seiner Entwicklung 1300–1800.* The Hague: Martinus Nijhoff.

Thibault, Paul R. 1986. *Pope Gregory XI: The Failure of Tradition.* Lanham, Md.: University Press of America.

Throop, Palmer A. 1940. *Criticism of the Crusade: A Study of Public Opinion and Crusade Propaganda.* Amsterdam: N. V. Swets & Zeitlinger.

Tierney, Brian. 1988. *The Crisis of Church and State, 1050–1300.* Toronto: University of Toronto Press, in association with the Medieval Academy of America.

Tooley, Marian J. 1953. Bodin and the Mediaeval Theory of Climate. *Speculum* 28.

Töpfer, Brenhard. 1992. The Cult of Relics and Pilgrimage in Burgundy and Aquitaine at the Time of the Monastic Reform. In *The Peace of God,* ed. Th. Head and R. Landes. Ithaca, N.Y.: Cornell University Press.

Tyerman, C. J. 1984. Sed nihil fecit? The Last Capetians and the Recovery of the Holy Land. In *War and Government in the Middle Ages: Essays in Honour of J. O. Prestwich,* ed. J. Gillingham and J. C. Holt. Woodbridge: The Boydell Press; Totowa, N.J.: Barnes & Noble.

———. 1985a. The Holy Land and the Crusades of the Thirteenth and Fourteenth Centuries. In *Crusade and Settlement,* ed. P. W. Edbury. Cardiff: University College Cardiff Press.

———. 1985b. Philip VI and the Recovery of the Holy Land. *English Historical Review* 100, no. 394.

———. 1988. *England and the Crusades, 1095–1588.* Chicago: University of Chicago Press.

———. 1998. *The Invention of the Crusades.* Toronto: University of Toronto Press.

Ullmann, Walter. 1961. *Principles of Government and Politics in the Middle Ages.* London: Methuen.

———. 1965. *A History of Political Thought: The Middle Ages.* Harmondsworth: Penguin.

———. 1973. Von Canossa nach Pavia: Zum Strukturwandel der Herrschaftsgrundlagen im salischen und staufischen Zeitalter. *Historisches Jahrbuch* 93.

———. 1975. St. Bernard and the Nascent International Law. In id. *The Church and the Law in the Earlier Middle Ages: Selected Essays.* London: Variorum.

———. 1977. *Medieval Origins of Renaissance Humanism.* London: Paul Elek.

———. 1981. *Gelasius I. (492–496): Das Papsttum an der Wende der Spätantike zum Mittelalter.* Stuttgart: Anton Hiersemann.

Valous, Guy de. 1953. Quelques observations sur la toute primitive observance des templiers et la *Regula pauperum commilitonum Christi templi Salomo-nici*, rédigée par saint Bernard au concile de Troyes (1128). In *Mélanges Saint Bernard. XXIVᵉ Congrès de l'Association bourguignonne des sociétés savan-tes*. Dijon: Marilier.

van Caenegem, R. 1988. Government, Law and Society. In *The Cambridge History of Medieval Political Thought, c. 350–c. 1450,* ed. J. H. Burns. Cambridge: Cambridge University Press.

Vandecasteele, Maurits. 1996. A Remarkable Account of the Origin and Spread of Islam Contained in a Fifteenth-Century Redaction of the Gregorian Report. *Medieval Studies* 58.

Vanderpol, A. 1911. *La droit de guerre d'après les théologiens et les canonistes du moyen-âge*. Paris: A. Tralin; Brussels: Goemaere.

———. 1919. *La doctrine scolastique du droit de Guerre*. Paris: A. Pedone.

Van Engen, John. 1986. The Christian Middle Ages as an Historiographical Problem. *American Historical Review* 91, no. 3.

Vasoli, Cesare. 1975. La pace nel pensiero filosofico e teologico-politico da Dante a Ockham. In *La pace nel pensiero, nella politica, negli ideali del trecento*. Convegni del Centro di studi sulla spiritualità medievale 15. Todi: Presso L'Academia tudertina.

Vereker, Charles. 1964. *The Development of Political Theory*. 2d ed. London: Hutchinson University Library.

Villey, Michel. 1942. *La croisade: Essai sur la formation d'une théorie juridique*. Paris: Vrin.

Viroli, Maurizio. 1992. *From Politics to Reason of State: The Acquisition and Transformation of the Language of Politics, 1250–1600*. Cambridge: Cambridge University Press.

Vismara, Giulio. 1968. Problemi storici e istituti giuridici della guerra alto-medievale. In *Ordinamenti militari in Occidente nell'alto medioevo*. Spoleto: Centro italiano di studi sull'alto medioevo.

———. 1974. *Impium fœdus: Le origini della "respublica christiana"*. Milan: A. Giuffrè.

Waley, Daniel. 1985. *Later Medieval Europe: From St Louis to Luther*. 2d ed. London and New York: Longman.

Wallace-Hadrill, J. M. 1960. Introduction to *Fredegarii Chronicorum Liber Quartus cum Continuationibus (The Fourth Book of the Chronicle of Fredegar with Its Continuations)*, ed. and trans. J. M. Wallace-Hadrill. London: Thomas Nelson and Sons.

———. 1962. *The Barbarian West: The Early Middle Ages, A.D. 400–1000*. New York: Harper & Row.

———. 1975. *Early Medieval History*. Oxford: Basil Blackwell.

———. 1983. *The Frankish Church*. Oxford: Clarendon Press.

Watt, John A. 1965. *The Theory of Papal Monarchy in the Thirteenth Century: The Contribution of the Canonist*. New York: Fordham University Press.

———. 1971. Introduction to *On Royal and Papal Power,* by John of Paris. Toronto: The Pontifical Institute of Medieval Studies.

———. 1988. Spiritual and temporal powers. In *The Cambridge History of Me-*

dieval Political Thought, c. 350–c. 1450, ed. J. H. Burns. Cambridge: Cambridge University Press.

Watt, W. Montgomery. 1972. *The Influence of Islam on Medieval Europe.* Edinburgh: At the University Press.

———. 1976. Islamic Conceptions of the Holy War. In *The Holy War,* ed. T. P. Murphy. Columbus: Ohio State University Press.

Wenskus, Reinhard. 1956. *Studien zur historisch-politischen Gedankenwelt Bruns von Querfurt.* Münster and Cologne: Böhlau.

Wieruszowski, Helene. 1933. *Vom Imperium zum nationalen Königtum: Vergleichende Studien über die publizistischen Kämpfe Kaiser Friedrichs II. und König Philipps des Schönen mit der Kurie.* Munich and Berlin: R. Oldenbourg.

———. 1971. *Politics and Culture in Medieval Spain and Italy.* Rome: Storia e letteratura.

Wilken, Robert L. 1992. *The Land Called Holy: Palestine in Christian History and Thought.* New Haven: Yale University Press.

Wilks, Michael. 1964. *The Problem of Sovereignty in the Later Middle Ages: The Papal Monarchy with Augustinus Triumphus and the Publicists.* Cambridge: At the University Press.

Willard, Charity Cannon. 1984. *Christine de Pizan: Her Life and Works.* New York: Persea Books.

Wolf, Kenneth Baxter. 1988. *Christian Martyrs in Muslim Spain.* Cambridge: Cambridge University Press.

Wood, Charles T., ed. 1976. *Philip the Fair and Boniface VIII: State vs. Papacy,* 2d ed. Huntington, N.Y.: Robert E. Krieger.

Woolf, Cecil N. Sidney. 1913. *Bartolus of Sassoferrato: His Position in the History of Medieval Political Thought.* Cambridge: At The University Press.

Wright, John Kirtland. 1925. *The Geographical Lore of the Time of the Crusades: A Study in the History of Medieval Science and Tradition in Western Europe.* New York: American Geographical Society.

Wynner, Edith, and Georgia Lloyd. 1944. *Searchlight on Peace Plans: Choose Your Road to World Government.* New York: E. P. Dutton.

Zeck, Ernst. 1911. *Der Publizist Pierre Dubois, seine Bedeutung im Rahmen der Politik Philipps IV. des Schönen und seine literarische Denk- und Arbeitsweise im Traktat "De recuperatione Terre Sancte."* Berlin: Weidmannsche Buchhandlung.

Zeller, Gaston. 1934. Les rois de France candidats à l'Empire. Essai sur l'idéologie impériale en France. *Revue historique* 173.

Zerbi, Pietro. 1948. Il termine "fidelitas" nelle lettere di Gregorio VII. *Studi gregoriani* 3.

———. 1955. *Papato, Imperio e "respublica christiana" dal 1187 al 1198.* Milan: Vita e pensiero.

———. 1992. La "militia Christi" per i Cisterciensi. In *"Militia Christi" e Crociata nei secoli XI–XIII.* Miscellanea del Centro di studi medioevali. Milan: Vita e pensiero.

Index

Text: 10/13 Sabon
Display: Sabon
Compositor: G&S Typesetters, Inc.
Printer: Sheridan Books, Inc.